C. CARTER

WEBSTER'S NEW POCKET SPANISH DICTIONARY

D0027682

Wiley Publishing, Inc.

Webster's New Pocket Spanish Dictionary
Harrap's Little Spanish-English Dictionary © CHP 2004; © Larousse 2010.
All rights reserved

Published by Wiley Publishing, Inc., Hoboken, New Jersey
Published simultaneously in Canada

For general information on our other products and services or to obtain technical support please contact our Customer Care Department within the U.S.
at (877) 762-2974, outside the U.S. at (317) 572-3993 or fax (317) 572-4002.

Wiley also publishes its books in a variety of electronic formats. Some content that appears in print may not be available in electronic books. For more
information about Wiley products, please visit our web site at
www.wiley.com.

ISBN 978-0-470-48872-0

Designed and typeset by Chambers Harrap Publishers Ltd., Edinburgh

Printed in the United States of America

10 9 8 7 6 5 4 3

Contents

Preface

This handy dictionary is an accurate, reliable tool for learners of Spanish. With more than 25,000 words and expressions and with around 1,500 new words and phrases added to this edition, it provides a wide-ranging selection of the most useful and up-to-date vocabulary of both Spanish (in its different regional varieties) and English.

The dictionary is designed to be easily read and used, with bold headwords and a compact, time-saving format.

Phrasal verbs are indicated by a bullet point and are listed after the verb on which they are based (e.g., see entry for **get**).

Numbers are used to divide grammatical categories of headwords with a solid block ▪ denoting meaning categories with longer entries (e.g., see entry for **do**).

A number code (1–65) against a Spanish verb means that the verb is irregular. Model verbs for these irregular forms are displayed on pages (5) to (12) of the central supplement.

An asterisk against an English verb denotes that it is irregular. Forms for these verbs are located on pages (13) to (17) of the supplement. A double asterisk against a Spanish noun, however, means that the feminine noun takes the masculine definite article **el** (e.g., **el agua**). The plural form is **las**.

The new system for Spanish alphabetical order has been adopted. In this system, **ch** and **ll** are no longer considered as separate letters of the alphabet, but each is incorporated at its respective position under **c** and **l**.

Finally, the syllabification of all English headwords has been included in this edition, providing the user with extra help.

Guide to the pronunciation of Spanish

Table of phonetic symbols

Letter	Phonetic symbol	Examples	Approximate English equivalent
Vowels:			
a	[a]	gato, amar, mesa	as in father, but shorter
e	[e]	estrella, vez, firme	as in labor
i	[i]	inicio, iris	as in see, but shorter
o	[o]	bolo, cómodo, oso	between lot and taught
u	[u]	turista, puro, tribu	as in food, but shorter, but u in -que- or -qui- and -gue- or -gui- is silent (unless -güe- or -güi-)
Diphthongs:			
ai, ay	[ai]	baile, hay	as in life, aisle
au	[au]	fauna	as in fowl, house
ei, ey	[ei]	peine, ley	as in hate, feign
eu	[eu]	feudo	pronounce each vowel separately
oi, oy	[oi]	boina, hoy	as in boy
Semi-consonants:			
u	[w]	buey, cuando, fuiste	as in wait
i	[j]	viernes, vicio, ciudad, fiarse	as in yes
Consonants:			
b	[b]	boda, burro, ambos	as in be
	[β]	haba, trabar	a very light b
c	[k]	cabeza, cucu, acoso, frac	as in car, keep
	[s]	cocer, cielo	as s in silly, but in parts of Spain as in thing
ch	[tʃ]	chepa, ocho	as in chamber

Guide to the pronunciation of Spanish

d	[d]	de**d**o, an**d**ar	as in **d**ay
	[ð]	de**d**o, aca**d**emia, aba**d**	as in **th**is (often omitted in spoken Spanish when at the end of a word)
f	[f]	**f**iesta, a**f**ición	as in **f**or
g	[g]	**g**as, ran**g**o, **g**ula	as in **g**et
	[ɣ]	a**g**ua, a**g**osto, la**g**arto	a very light g
g	[χ]	**g**enio, le**g**ión	similar to Scottish [χ] in lo**ch**
h		**h**ambre, a**h**ínco	Spanish h is silent
j	[χ]	**j**abón, a**j**o, relo**j**	similar to Scottish [χ] in lo**ch**
k	[k]	**k**ilo, **k**imono	as in **c**ar, **k**eep
l	[l]	**l**abio, háb**l**, e**l**egante	as in **l**aw
ll	[j]	**ll**uvia, ca**ll**e	similar to the sound in **y**ellow
m	[m]	**m**ano, a**m**igo, ha**m**bre	as in **m**an
n	[n]	**n**ata, rató**n**, a**n**tes, e**n**emigo	as in **n**ight
ñ	[ɲ]	a**ñ**o, **ñ**o**ñ**o	similar to the sound in o**ni**on
p	[p]	**p**i**p**a, **p**elo	as in **p**oint
q	[k]	**q**uiosco, **q**uerer, tabi**q**ue	as in **c**ar
r(r̄)	[r]	pe**r**o, co**rr**er, pad**r**e	always pronounced, rolled as in Scots
	[rr]	re**í**r, hon**r**ado, pe**rr**o	rr is a lengthened r sound
s	[s]	**s**auna, a**s**ado, corté**s**	similar to the s in hi**ss**ing
t	[t]	**t**eja, es**t**én, a**t**raco	as in **t**ime
v	[b]	**v**erbena, **v**ena	as in **b**e
	[β]	a**v**e, vi**v**o	a very light b
x	[ks]	é**x**ito, e**x**amen	as in e**x**ercise
	[s]	e**x**tensión	as in e**s**tate
y	[j]	**y**erno, a**y**er, re**y**	as in **y**es
	[i]	**y**	as in s**ee**, but shorter
z	[s]	**z**orro, a**z**ul, ca**z**a, soe**z**	as in si**ll**y, but in parts of Spain as in **th**ing

Stress rules

If a word ends in a vowel, **-n** or **-s**, the stress falls on the second last syllable: ma**no**, e**xa**men, boca**di**llos

If a word has any other ending, the stress falls on the last syllable: ha**bla**, Ma**drid**, a**yer**

Exceptions to these rules carry a written accent on the stressed syllable: **có**modo, le**gión**, **há**bil

Abbreviations

Abbreviations   Abreviaturas

abbreviation	*abbr, abr*	abreviatura
adjective	*adj*	adjetivo
adverb	*adv*	adverbio
somebody, someone	*algn*	alguien
Latin America	*Am*	Hispanoamérica
Argentina	*Arg*	Argentina
article	*art*	artículo
Bolivia	*Bol*	Bolivia
Central America	*CAm*	Centroamérica
Caribe	*Carib*	Caribe
Colombia	*Col*	Colombia
conjunction	*conj*	conjunción
Southern Cone region (Argentina, Uruguay, Paraguay, Chile)	*CSur*	Cono Sur (Argentina, Uruguay, Paraguay, Chile)
definite	*def*	definido
demonstrative	*dem*	demostrativo
Ecuador	*Ecuad*	Ecuador
Spain	*Esp*	España
feminine	*f*	femenino
familiar	*fam*	familiar
figurative use	*fig*	uso figurado
feminine plural	*fpl*	femenino plural
future	*fut*	futuro
impersonal	*impers*	impersonal
indefinite	*indef*	indefinido
indeterminate	*indet*	indeterminado
indicative	*indic*	indicativo
interjection	*interj*	interjección
interrogative	*interr*	interrogativo
invariable	*inv*	invariable
irregular	*irreg*	irregular
masculine	*m*	masculino
Mexico	*Méx*	México
masculine plural	*mpl*	masculino plural
noun	*n*	nombre
Panama	*Pan*	Panamá
personal	*pers*	personal
plural	*pl*	plural
possessive	*poss, pos*	posesivo
past participle	*pp*	participio pasado
preposition	*prep*	preposición
present	*pres*	presente
preterite	*pret*	pretérito
pronoun	*pron*	pronombre
past tense	*pt*	pretérito
relative	*rel*	relativo
somebody, someone	*sb*	alguien
singular	*sing*	singular
something	*sth*	algo
subjunctive	*subj*	subjuntivo

Abbreviations   ## Abreviaturas

auxiliary verb	*v aux*	verbo auxiliar
Venezuela	*Ven*	Venezuela
intransitive verb	*vi*	verbo intransitivo
impersonal verb	*v impers*	verbo impersonal
reflexive verb	*vr*	verbo reflexivo
transitive verb	*vt*	verbo transitivo
cultural equivalent	≃	equivalente cultural

Spanish–English
Español–Inglés

A

a *prep (dirección)* to; **llegar a Valencia** to arrive in Valencia; **subir al tren** to get on the train. ▪ *(lugar)* at, on; **a la derecha** on the right; **a lo lejos** in the distance; **a mi lado** next to me; **al sol** in the sun. ▪ *(tiempo)* at; **a las doce** at twelve o'clock; **a los tres meses/la media hora** three months/half an hour later; **al final** in the end; **al principio** at first. ▪ *(distancia)* **a cien kilómetros de aquí** a hundred kilometers from here. ▪ *(manera)* **a mano** by hand. ▪ *(proporción)* **a 90 kilómetros por hora** at 90 kilometers an hour; **a 30 pesos el kilo** thirty pesos a kilo; **tres veces a la semana** three times a week. ▪ **ganar cuatro a dos** to win four (to) two. ▪ *(complemento)* to; *(procedencia)* from; **díselo a Javier** tell Javier; **te lo di a ti** I gave it to you; **comprarle algo a algn** to buy sth from sb; *(para algn)* to buy sth for sb; **saludé a tu tía** I said hello to your aunt. ▪ *fam* **ir a por algn/algo** to go and get sb/sth. ▪ *(verbo + a + infinitivo)* to; **aprender a nadar** to learn (how) to swim. ▪ **a decir verdad** to tell (you) the truth; **a no ser que** unless; **¡a ver!** let's see; **¡a comer!** food's ready!; **¡a dormir!** bedtime!; **¿a que no lo haces?** *(desafío)* I bet you don't do it!

abajeño, -a *mf Am* lowlander.

abajo 1 *adv (en una casa)* downstairs; *(dirección)* down; **el piso de a.** the apartment downstairs; **ahí/aquí a.** down there/here; **la parte de a.** the bottom (part); **más a.** further down; **hacia a.** down; **venirse a.** *(edificio)* to fall down. **2** *interj* **¡a. la censura!** down with censorship!

abalanzarse [40] *vr* **a. sobre/contra** to rush towards.

abalear *vt Andes, CAm, Ven* to shoot at.

abandonar *vt (lugar)* to leave; *(persona, cosa)* to abandon; *(proyecto, plan)* to give up.

abanico *m* fan; *(gama)* range.

abarcar [44] *vt* to include.

abarrotado, -a *adj* crammed (**de** with).

abarrote *m Andes, CAm, Méx* grocer's shop, grocery store; **abarrotes** groceries; **tienda de abarrotes** grocer's (shop), grocery store.

abastecer [33] **1** *vt* to supply. **2 abastecerse** *vr* to stock up (**de** o **con** with).

abatible *adj* folding; **asiento a.** folding seat.

abatido, -a *adj* downcast.

abatir 1 *vt (derribar)* to knock down; *(desanimar)* to depress. **2 abatirse** *vr (desanimarse)* to become depressed.

abdicar [44] *vt/i* to abdicate.

abdominales *mpl* sit-ups.

abecedario *m* alphabet.

abedul *m* birch.

abeja *f* bee; **a. reina** queen bee.

abejorro *m* bumblebee.

abertura *f (hueco)* opening; *(grieta)* crack.

abeto *m* fir (tree).

abierto, -a *adj* open; *(grifo)* (turned) on; *(persona)* open-minded.

abismo *m* abyss.

ablandar 1 *vt* to soften. **2 ablandarse** *vr* to go soft; *fig (persona)* to mellow.

abnegado, -a *adj* selfless.

abogado, -a *mf* lawyer; *(en tribunal supremo)* attorney; **a. defensor** counsel for the defense.

abolir *vt defectivo* to abolish.

abollar *vt* to dent.

abonado, -a *mf* subscriber.

abonar 1 *vt (tierra)* to fertilize; *(pagar)* to pay (for); *(subscribir)* to subscribe. **2 abonarse** *vr* to subscribe (**a** to).

abono *m* *(producto)* fertilizer; *(estiércol)* manure; *(pago)* payment; *(billete)* season ticket; *(a revista etc)* subscription.

abordar *vt* *(persona)* to approach; *(barco)* to board; **a. un asunto** to tackle a subject.

aborrecer [33] *vt* to detest.

abortar 1 *vi* *(involuntariamente)* to miscarry, to have a miscarriage; *(intencionadamente)* to abort, to have an abortion. **2** *vt* to abort.

aborto *m* miscarriage; *(provocado)* abortion.

abrasar 1 *vti* to scorch. **2 abrasarse** *vr* to burn.

abrazadera *f* clamp.

abrazar [40] **1** *vt* to embrace. **2 abrazarse** *vr* **abrazarse a algn** to embrace sb; **se abrazaron** they embraced each other.

abrazo *m* hug.

abrelatas *m inv* can opener.

abreviar [43] **1** *vt* to shorten; *(texto)* to abridge; *(palabra)* to abbreviate. **2** *vi* to be quick o brief; **para a.** to cut a long story short.

abreviatura *f* abbreviation.

abridor *m* *(de latas, botellas)* opener.

abrigado, -a *adj* wrapped up.

abrigar [42] **1** *vt* to keep warm; *(esperanza)* to cherish; *(duda)* to harbor. **2** *vi* **esta chaqueta abriga mucho** this cardigan is very warm.

abrigo *m* *(prenda)* coat; **ropa de a.** warm clothes *pl*.

abril *m* April.

abrir[1] *m* **en un a. y cerrar de ojos** in the twinkling of an eye.

abrir[2] *(pp abierto)* **1** *vi* to open. **2** *vt* to open; *(cremallera)* to undo; *(gas, grifo)* to turn on. **3 abrirse** *vr* to open; **abrirse paso** to make one's way.

abrochar *vt*, **abrocharse** *vr* *(botones)* to do up; *(camisa)* to button (up); *(cinturón)* to fasten; *(zapatos)* to tie up; *(cremallera)* to do up.

abrumar *vt* to overwhelm.

abrupto, -a *adj* *(terreno)* steep.

absceso *m* abscess.

absolutamente *adv* absolutely.

absoluto, -a *adj* absolute; **en a.** not at all.

absolver [4] *(pp absuelto)* *vt* to acquit.

absorbente *adj* *(papel)* absorbent; *(fascinante)* engrossing.

absorber *vt* to absorb.

absorto, -a *adj* engrossed (**en** in).

abstenerse [24] *vr* to abstain (**de** from); *(privarse)* to refrain (**de** from).

abstracto, -a *adj* abstract.

abstraído, -a *adj* *(ensimismado)* engrossed (**en** in).

absuelto, -a *adj pp* **de absolver.**

absurdo, -a *adj* absurd.

abuchear *vt* to boo.

abuela *f* grandmother; *fam* grandma, granny.

abuelo *m* grandfather; *fam* grandad, grandpa; **abuelos** grandparents.

abultado, -a *adj* bulky.

abundancia *f* abundance; **... en a.** plenty of ...

abundante *adj* abundant.

aburrido, -a *adj* **ser a.** to be boring; **estar a.** to be bored; *(harto)* to be tired (**de** of).

aburrimiento *m* boredom; **¡qué a.!** what a bore!

aburrir 1 *vt* to bore. **2 aburrirse** *vr* to get bored.

abusar *vi* *(propasarse)* to go too far; **a. de** *(situación, persona)* to take (unfair) advantage of; *(poder, amabilidad)* to abuse; **a. de la bebida/del tabaco** to drink/smoke too much o to excess.

abuso *m* abuse.

a. C. *abr de* **antes de Cristo** before Christ, BC.

acá *adv* *(lugar)* over here; **más a.** nearer; **¡ven a.!** come here!

acabar 1 *vt* to finish (off); *(completar)* to complete. **2** *vi* to finish; **a. de ...** to have just ...; **acaba de entrar** he has just come in; **acabaron**

casándose *o* **por casarse** they ended up getting married. **3 acabarse** *vr* to finish; **se nos acabó la gasolina** we ran out of gas.

acacia *f* acacia.

academia *f* academy; **a. de idiomas** language school.

académico, -a *adj & mf* academic.

acalorado, -a *adj* hot; *(debate etc)* heated.

acampar *vi* to camp.

acantilado *m* cliff.

acaparar *vt* *(productos)* to hoard; *(mercado)* to corner.

acápite *m Am* *(párrafo)* paragraph.

acariciar [43] *vt* to caress; *(pelo, animal)* to stroke.

acarrear *vt* *(transportar)* to transport; *(conllevar)* to entail.

acaso *adv* perhaps, maybe; **por si a.** just in case; **si a. viene ...** if he should come ....

acatar *vt* to comply with.

acatarrado, -a *adj* **estar a.** to have a cold.

acatarrarse *vr* to catch a cold.

acceder *vi* **a. a** *(consentir)* to consent to.

accesible *adj* accessible; *(persona)* approachable.

acceso *m* *(entrada)* access; *(en carretera)* approach; **a. a Internet** Internet access.

accesorio, -a *adj* *(terreno)* uneven; *(viaje, vida)* eventful. **2** *mf* casualty.

accidental *adj* accidental; **un encuentro a.** a chance meeting.

accidente *m* accident; **a. laboral** industrial accident.

acción *f* action; *(acto)* act; *(en la bolsa)* share; **poner en a.** to put into action; **película de a.** adventure film.

accionar *vt* to drive.

accionista *mf* shareholder.

acechar *vt* to lie in wait for.

aceite *m* oil; **a. de girasol/maíz/oliva** sunflower/corn/olive oil.

aceituna *f* olive; **a. rellena** stuffed olive.

acelerador *m* accelerator.

acelerar *vti* to accelerate.

acento *m* accent; *(énfasis)* stress.

acentuar [30] **1** *vt* to stress. **2 acentuarse** *vr* to become more pronounced.

aceptar *vt* to accept.

acequia *f* irrigation ditch *o* channel.

acera *f* sidewalk.

acerca *adv* **a. de** about.

acercar [44] **1** *vt* to bring (over). **2 acercarse** *vr* to approach (**a** -); *(ir)* to go; *(venir)* to come.

acero *m* steel; **a. inoxidable** stainless steel.

acérrimo, -a *adj* *(partidario)* staunch; *(enemigo)* bitter.

acertado, -a *adj* *(solución)* correct; *(decisión)* wise.

acertar [1] **1** *vt* *(pregunta)* to get right; *(adivinar)* to guess correctly. **2** *vti* to be right.

acertijo *m* riddle.

achacar [44] *vt* *(atribuir)* to attribute.

achaque *m* ailment.

achicharrar *vt* to burn to a crisp.

acholado, -a *adj Andes* mixed.

achuchar *vt* *(empujar)* to shove.

aciago, -a *adj* ill-fated.

acicalarse *vr* to dress up.

acidez *f* *(de sabor)* sharpness; **a. de estómago** heartburn.

ácido, -a 1 *adj* *(sabor)* sharp. **2** *m* acid.

acierto *m* *(buena decisión)* good choice.

aclamar *vt* to acclaim.

aclaración *f* explanation.

aclarado *m* rinse.

aclarar 1 *vt* *(explicar)* to explain; *(color)* to make lighter; *(enjuagar)* to rinse. **2** *v impers (tiempo)* to clear (up). **3 aclararse** *vr* **aclararse la voz** to clear one's throat.

aclimatarse *vr* **a. algo** to get used to sth.

acné *m* acne.

acobardarse *vr* to get frightened.

acogedor, -a *adj (habitación)* cozy.

acoger [53] **1** *vt (recibir)* to receive; *(persona desvalida)* to take in. **2 acogerse** *vr* **acogerse a** to take refuge in; **acogerse a la ley** to have recourse to the law.

acogida *f* reception, welcome.

acometer *vt (emprender)* to undertake; *(atacar)* to attack.

acomodado, -a *adj* well-off.

acomodador, -a *mf* usher.

acomodar 1 *vt (alojar)* to accommodate; *(en cine etc)* to find a place for. **2 acomodarse** *vr (instalarse)* to make oneself comfortable; *(adaptarse)* to adapt.

acompañanta 1 *mf* companion. **2** *adj* accompanying.

acompañar *vt* to accompany; **¿te acompaño a casa?** can I walk you home?; *(en funeral)* **le acompaño en el sentimiento** my condolences.

acomplejado, -a *adj* **estar a.** to have a complex (**por** about).

acomplejar 1 *vt* to give a complex. **2 acomplejarse** *vr* **acomplejarse por** to develop a complex about.

acondicionado, -a *adj* **aire a.** air conditioning.

acondicionador *m* conditioner.

acondicionar *vt* to prepare, to set up; *(mejorar)* to improve; *(cabello)* to condition.

aconsejable *adj* advisable.

aconsejar *vt* to advise.

acontecimiento *m* event.

acopio *m* **hacer a. de** to store.

acordar [2] **1** *vt* to agree; *(decidir)* to decide. **2 acordarse** *vr* to remember.

acordeón *m* accordion.

acordonar *vt (zona)* to cordon off.

acorralar *vt* to corner.

acortar *vt* to shorten.

acosar *vt* to harass; *fig* **a. a algn a preguntas** to bombard sb with questions.

acoso *m* harassment; **a. sexual** sexual harassment.

acostar [2] **1** *vt* to put to bed. **2 acos-**

tarse *vr* to go to bed.

acostumbrado, -a *adj* usual; **es lo a.** it is the custom; **a. al frío/calor** used to the cold/heat.

acostumbrar 1 *vi* **a. a** *(soler)* to be in the habit of. **2** *vt* **a. a algn a algo** *(habituar)* to get sb used to sth. **3 acostumbrarse** *vr* to get used (**a** to).

acotamiento *m Méx (de autopista)* shoulder.

acre *m (medida)* acre.

acreditar *vt* to be a credit to; *(probar)* to prove.

acreedor, -a *mf* creditor.

acrílico, -a *adj* acrylic.

acriollarse *vr Am* to adopt native ways.

acrobacia *f* acrobatics *sing.*

acta *f (de reunión)* minutes *pl*; *(certificado)* certificate.

actitud *f* attitude.

activar *vt* to activate; *(avivar)* to liven up.

actividad *f* activity.

activo, -a *adj* active.

acto *m* act; *(ceremonia)* ceremony; *(de teatro)* act; **en el a.** at once; **a. seguido** immediately afterwards.

actor *m* actor.

actriz *f* actress.

actuación *f* performance; *(intervención)* intervention.

actual *adj* current, present.

actualidad *f* present time; *(hechos)* current affairs *pl*; **en la a.** at present.

actualizar [40] *vt (software, hardware)* to upgrade.

actualmente *adv (hoy en día)* nowadays.

actuar [30] *vi* to act.

acuarela *f* watercolor.

acuario *m* aquarium.

aculanta *adj* urgent.

acudir *vi (ir)* to go; *(venir)* to come.

acuerdo *m* agreement; **¡de a.!** all right!, OK!; **de a. con** in accordance with; **ponerse de a.** to agree.

acumular *vt*, **acumularse** *vr* to accumulate.

acuñar vt (moneda) to mint; (frase) to coin.

acurrucarse [44] vr to curl up.

acusación f accusation; (en juicio) charge.

acusado, -a 1 mf accused. **2** adj (marcado) marked.

acusar 1 vt to accuse (**de** of); (en juicio) to charge (**de** with). **2 acusarse** vr (acentuarse) to become more pronounced.

acústica f acoustics sing.

acústico, -a adj acoustic.

adaptador m adapter.

adaptar 1 vt to adapt; (ajustar) to adjust. **2 adaptarse** vr to adapt (oneself) (**a** to).

adecuado, -a adj appropriate.

a. de J. C. abr de antes de Jesucristo before Christ, BC.

adelantado, -a adj advanced; (desarrollado) developed; (reloj) fast; **pagar por a.** to pay in advance.

adelantamiento m overtaking.

adelantar 1 vt to move forward; (reloj) to put forward; (en carretera) to overtake; (fecha) to move forward. **2** vi to advance; (progresar) to make progress; (reloj) to be fast. **3 adelantarse** vr (ir delante) to go ahead; (reloj) to be fast.

adelante 1 adv forward; **más a.** (lugar) further on; (tiempo) later. **2** interj ¡a.! (pase) come in!

adelanto m advance; (progreso) progress; **el reloj lleva diez minutos de a.** the watch is ten minutes fast.

adelgazar [40] vi to slim.

ademán m gesture.

además adv moreover, furthermore; **a. de él** besides him.

adentro 1 adv (dentro) inside; **mar a.** out to sea; **tierra a.** inland. **2** mpl **decir algo para sus adentros** to say sth to oneself.

adherir [5] **1** vt to stick on. **2 adherirse** vr **adherirse a** to adhere to.

adhesión f adhesion.

adhesivo, -a adj & m adhesive.

adicción f addiction.

adicto, -a 1 mf addict. **2** adj addicted (**a** to).

adiestrar vt to train.

adinerado, -a adj wealthy.

adiós (pl **adioses**) interj goodbye; fam bye-bye; (al cruzarse) hello.

aditivo, -a adj & m additive.

adivinanza f riddle.

adivinar vt to guess.

adjetivo m adjective.

adjudicar [44] **1** vt (premio, contrato) to award; (en subasta) to sell. **2 adjudicarse** vr to appropriate.

adjuntar vt to enclose.

adjunto, -a 1 adj enclosed, attached. **2** mf (profesor) assistant teacher.

administración f (gobierno) authorities pl; (de empresa) management; (oficina) (branch) office; **a. central** (gobierno) central government; **a. pública** civil service.

administrador, -a 1 mf administrator. **2** adj administrating.

administrar vt to administer; (dirigir) to run.

administrativo, -a 1 adj administrative. **2** mf (funcionario) official.

admiración f admiration; (ortográfica) exclamation mark.

admirar 1 vt to admire; (sorprender) to amaze. **2 admirarse** vr to be amazed.

admisión f admission.

admitir vt to let in; (aceptar) to accept; (permitir) to allow; (reconocer) to acknowledge.

ADN m abr de **ácido desoxirribonucleico** deoxyribonucleic acid, DNA.

adobe m adobe.

adobo m marinade.

adolescencia f adolescence.

adolescente adj & mf adolescent.

adónde adv where (to)?

adonde adv where.

adondequiera adv where.

adopción f adoption.

adoptar vt to adopt.

adoptivo, -a adj (hijo) adopted; (padres) adoptive.

adorar vt to worship.

adormecer [33] **1** vt to make sleepy. **2 adormecerse** vr (dormirse) to doze off; (brazo etc) to go numb.

adormilarse vr to doze, to drowse.

adornar vt to adorn.

adorno m decoration; **de a.** decorative.

adosado, -a adj adjacent; (casa) semidetached.

adquirir [31] vt to acquire; (comprar) to purchase.

adquisición f acquisition; (compra) purchase.

adrede adv deliberately, on purpose.

aduana f customs pl.

aduanero, -a mf customs officer.

aducir [10] vt to adduce.

adueñarse vr a. de to take over.

aduje pt indef de **aducir**.

adular vt to adulate.

adulterar vt to adulterate.

adulterio m adultery.

adulto, -a adj & mf adult.

aduzco indic pres de aducir.

adverbio m adverb.

adversario, -a 1 mf opponent. **2** adj opposing.

adversidad f adversity; (revés) setback.

adverso, -a adj adverse.

advertencia f warning.

advertir [5] vt to warn; (informar) to advise; (notar) to notice.

adviento m Advent.

adyacente adj adjacent.

aéreo, -a adj aerial; (correo, transporte) air; **por vía aerea** by air.

aerodinámico, -a adj aerodynamic; **de línea aerodinámica** streamlined.

aeromoza f Am flight attendant.

aeronáutico, -a adj **la industria aeronáutica** the aeronautics industry.

aeroplano m light airplane.

aeropuerto m airport.

aerosol m aerosol.

afable adj affable.

afán m (pl **afanes**) (esfuerzo) effort; (celo) zeal.

afanarse vr a. por conseguir algo to do one's best to achieve sth.

afección f disease.

afectar vt a. a to affect; **le afectó mucho** she was deeply affected.

afecto m affection; **tomarle a. a algn** to become fond of sb.

afectuoso, -a adj affectionate.

afeitar vt, **afeitarse** vr to shave.

afeminado, -a adj effeminate.

aferrarse vr to cling (a to).

afianzar [40] vt to strengthen.

afiche m Am poster.

afición f liking; **tiene a. por la música** he is fond of music; (de deporte) **la a.** the fans pl.

aficionado, -a 1 mf enthusiast; (no profesional) amateur. **2** adj keen; (no profesional) amateur; **ser a. a algo** to be fond of sth.

aficionarse vr to take a liking (a to).

afilado, -a adj sharp.

afiliarse [43] vr a. a to join, to become a member of.

afinar vt (puntería) to sharpen; (instrumento) to tune.

afinidad f affinity.

afirmación f statement.

afirmar vt (aseverar) to state; (afianzar) to strengthen.

afligir [57] **1** vt to afflict. **2 afligirse** vr to be distressed.

aflojar 1 vt to loosen. **2 aflojarse** vr (rueda) to work loose.

afluencia f influx; **gran a. de público** great numbers of people.

afluente m tributary.

afónico, -a adj estar a. to have lost one's voice.

afortunado, -a adj lucky, fortunate.

afrontar vt to confront; **a. las consecuencias** to face the consequences.

afuera 1 adv outside; **la parte de a.** the outside; **más a.** further out. **2 afueras** fpl outskirts.

agachar 1 vt to lower. **2 agacharse** vr to duck.

agarrado, -a adj fam (tacaño) stingy, tight; **baile a.** cheek-to-cheek dancing.

agarrar 1 vt to grasp; Am (tomar) to take; **agárralo fuerte** hold it tight; **a. un taxi** to take a taxi. **2 agarrarse** vr to hold on.

agasajar vt to smother with attentions.

agazaparse vr to crouch (down).

agencia f agency; (sucursal) branch; **a. de viajes** travel agency; **a. de seguros** insurance agency; **a. inmobiliaria** estate agency.

agenda f diary.

agente mf agent; **a. de policía** (hombre) policeman; (mujer) policewoman; **a. de seguros** insurance broker.

ágil adj agile.

agilidad f agility.

agilizar [40] vt (trámites) to speed up.

agitación f agitation; (inquietud) restlessness.

agitado, -a adj agitated; (persona) anxious; (mar) rough.

agitar 1 vt (botella) to shake. **2 agitarse** vr (persona) to become agitated.

aglomeración f (de gente) crowd.

agobiado, -a adj **a. de problemas** snowed under with problems; **a. de trabajo** up to one's eyes in work.

agobiante adj (trabajo) overwhelming; (lugar) claustrophobic; (calor) oppressive; (persona) tiresome.

agobiar [43] **1** vt to overwhelm. **2 agobiarse** vr (angustiarse) to worry too much.

agobio m (angustia) anxiety; (sofoco) suffocation.

agolparse vr to crowd.

agonía f agony, last days.

agonizar [40] vi to be dying.

agosto m August.

agotado, -a adj (cansado) exhausted; (existencias) sold out; (provisiones) exhausted; (libro) out of print.

agotador, -a adj exhausting.

agotamiento m exhaustion.

agotar 1 vt (cansar) to exhaust; (acabar) to use up (completely). **2 agotarse** vr (acabarse) to run out; (producto) to be sold out; (persona) to become exhausted o tired out.

agradable adj pleasant.

agradar vti to please; **no me agrada** I don't like it.

agradecer [33] vt (dar las gracias) to thank for; (estar agradecido) to be grateful to; **te lo agradezco mucho** thank you very much.

agradecido, -a adj grateful; **le estoy muy a.** I am very grateful to you.

agradecimiento m gratitude.

agrado m pleasure; **no es de su a.** it isn't to his liking.

agrandar 1 vt to enlarge. **2 agrandarse** vr to become larger.

agrario, -a adj agrarian.

agravar 1 vt to aggravate. **2 agravarse** vr to get worse.

agredir vt defectivo to assault.

agregado, -a adj **profesor a.** (de escuela) secondary school teacher; (de universidad) teaching assistant.

agregar [42] vt (añadir) to add.

agresión f aggression.

agresivo, -a adj aggressive.

agrícola adj agricultural.

agricultor, -a mf farmer.

agricultura f agriculture.

agridulce adj bittersweet.

agrietar 1 vt to crack; (piel, labios) to chap. **2 agrietarse** vr to crack; (piel) to get chapped.

agringarse [42] vr Am to behave like a gringo.

agrio, -a adj sour.

agropecuario, -a adj agricultural.

agrupación f association.

agua** *f* water; **a. potable** drinking water; **a. corriente/del grifo** running/tap water; **a. dulce/salada** fresh/salt water; **a. mineral sin/con gas** still/fizzy mineral water.

aguacate *m (fruto)* avocado (pear).

aguacero *m* downpour.

aguafiestas *mf inv* spoilsport, wet blanket.

aguafuerte *m* etching.

aguanieve *f* sleet.

aguantar 1 *vt (soportar)* to tolerate; *(sostener)* to support; **no lo aguanto más** I can't stand it any longer; **aguanta la respiración** hold your breath. **2 aguantarse** *vr (contenerse)* to keep back; *(resignarse)* to resign oneself; **no pude aguantarme la risa** I couldn't help laughing.

aguardar 1 *vt* to await. **2** *vi* to wait.

aguardiente *m* brandy.

aguarrás *m* turpentine.

aguatero, -a *mf Am* water-carrier *o* seller.

agudizar [40] *vt*, **agudizarse** *vr* to intensify.

agudo, -a *adj (dolor)* acute; *(voz)* high-pitched; *(sonido)* high.

aguijón *m* sting.

águila** *f* eagle.

aguja *f* needle; *(de reloj)* hand; *(de tocadiscos)* stylus.

agujerear *vt* to make holes in.

agujero *m* hole; **a. negro** black hole.

agujetas *fpl* **tener a.** to be stiff.

aguzar [40] *vt* **a. el oído** to prick up one's ears; **a. la vista** to look attentively.

ahí *adv* there; **a. está** there he/she/it is; **por a.** *(en esa dirección)* that way; *(aproximadamente)* over there.

ahijado, -a *mf* godchild; *(niño)* godson; *(niña)* goddaughter; **ahijados** godchildren.

ahínco *m* **con a.** eagerly.

ahogado, -a 1 *adj (en líquido)* drowned; *(asfixiado)* suffocated;

morir **a.** to drown. **2** *mf* drowned person.

ahogar [42] *vt*, **ahogarse** *vr (en líquido)* to drown; *(asfixiar)* to suffocate; *(motor)* to flood.

ahondar 1 *vt* to deepen. **2** *vi* to go deep; *fig* **a. en un problema** to go into a problem in depth.

ahora 1 *adv* now; **a. mismo** right now; **de a. en adelante** from now on; **por a.** for the time being; **a. voy** I'm coming; **hasta a.** *(hasta el momento)* until now, so far; *(hasta luego)* see you later. **2** *conj* **a. bien** *(sin embargo)* however.

ahorcar [44] **1** *vt* to hang. **2 ahorcarse** *vr* to hang oneself.

ahorita, ahoritica *adv Andes, CAm, Carib, Méx fam (en el presente)* (right) now; **a. voy** I'm just coming; *(pronto)* in a second; *(hace poco)* just now, a few minutes ago.

ahorrar *vt* to save.

ahorrativo, -a *adj* thrifty.

ahorros *mpl* savings; **caja de a.** savings bank.

ahuevado, -a *adj Andes, CAm fam* stupid.

ahumado, -a *adj* smoked; *(bacon)* smoky.

ahuyentar *vt* to scare away.

aindiado, -a *adj Am* Indian-like.

airado, -a *adj* angry.

aire *m* air; *(de automóvil)* choke; *(viento)* wind; *(aspecto)* appearance; **a. acondicionado** air conditioning; **al a.** *(al descubierto)* uncovered; **al a. libre** in the open air; **en el a.** *(pendiente)* in the air; **tomar el a.** to get some fresh air; **cambiar de aires** to change one's surroundings; **darse aires** to put on airs.

aislado, -a *adj* isolated; *(cable)* insulated.

aislante 1 *adj* **cinta a.** insulating tape. **2** *m* insulator.

aislar *vt* to isolate; *(cable)* to insulate.

ajedrez *m (juego)* chess; *(piezas y tablero)* chess set.

ajeno, -a adj belonging to other people; **por causas ajenas a nuestra voluntad** for reasons beyond our control.

ajetreado, -a adj hectic.

ajetreo m activity, hard work, bustle.

ajo m garlic; **cabeza/diente de a.** head/clove of garlic.

ajustado, -a adj tight.

ajustar vt to adjust; (apretar) to tighten.

ajuste m adjustment; (de precio) fixing; (de cuenta) settlement; **a. de cuentas** settling of scores.

ajusticiar [43] vt to execute.

al (contracción de **a** & **el**) ver **a**; (al + infinitivo) **al salir** on leaving.

ala f wing; (de sombrero) brim.

alabar vt to praise.

alabastro m alabaster.

alacena f (food) cupboard.

alambrada f, **alambrado** m barbed wire fence.

alambre m wire; **a. de púas** barbed wire.

alameda f poplar grove; (paseo) avenue, boulevard.

álamo m poplar.

alarde m (ostentación) bragging; **hacer a. de** to show off.

alardear vi to brag.

alargadera f (cable) extension.

alargado, -a adj elongated.

alargar [42] **1** vt to lengthen; (estirar) to stretch; (prolongar) to prolong; (dar) to pass. **2 alargarse** vr to get longer; (prolongarse) to go on.

alarido m shriek; **dar un a.** to howl.

alarma f alarm; **falsa a.** false alarm; **señal de a.** alarm (signal).

alarmante adj alarming.

alarmar 1 vt to alarm. **2 alarmarse** vr to be alarmed.

alba** f dawn.

albañil m bricklayer; (obrero) building worker.

albaricoque m (fruta) apricot; (árbol) apricot tree.

alberca f (depósito) water tank; Méx (para nadar) swimming pool.

albergar [42] **1** vt (alojar) to house. **2 albergarse** vr to stay.

albergue m (lugar) hostel; (refugio) refuge; **a. juvenil** youth hostel.

albino, -a adj & mf albino.

albóndiga f meatball.

albornoz m bathrobe.

alborotar 1 vt (desordenar) to turn upside down. **2** vi to make a racket. **3 alborotarse** vr to get excited; (mar) to get rough.

alboroto m (jaleo) din, racket; (desorden) disturbance, uproar.

albufera f lagoon.

álbum m album.

alcachofa f artichoke.

alcalde m mayor.

alcaldesa f mayoress.

alcaldía f (cargo) mayorship; (oficina) mayor's office.

alcance m reach; **dar a. a** to catch up with; **fuera del a. de los niños** out of the reach of children.

alcantarilla f sewer; (boca) drain.

alcanzar [40] **1** vt to reach; (persona) to catch up with; (conseguir) to achieve. **2** vi (ser suficiente) to be sufficient.

alcaparra f (fruto) caper.

alcayata f hook.

alcazaba f citadel.

alcázar m (fortaleza) fortress; (castillo) castle.

alcoba f bedroom.

alcohol m alcohol.

alcoholemia f **prueba de a.** breath test.

alcohólico, -a adj & mf alcoholic.

alcoholímetro m Breathalyzer®.

alcornoque m cork oak.

alcurnia f ancestry.

aldea f village.

aleccionador, -a adj (ejemplar) exemplary.

alegar [42] vt (aducir) to claim.

alegrar 1 vt (complacer) to make glad; **me alegra que se lo hayas**

dicho I am glad you told her. **2 alegrarse** vr to be glad; **me alegro de verte** I am pleased to see you.

alegre adj (contento) glad; (color) bright; (música) lively.

alegría f happiness.

alejado, -a adj remote.

alejar 1 vt to move further away. **2 alejarse** vr to go away.

alemán, -ana adj & mf German. **2** m (idioma) German.

alentar [1] vt to encourage.

alergia f allergy.

alérgico, -a adj allergic.

alerta f & adj alert.

aleta f (de pez) fin; (de foca, de nadador) flipper.

aletargar [42] **1** vt to make lethargic. **2 aletargarse** vr to become lethargic.

aletear vi to flutter o flap its wings.

alfabetización f campaña de a. literacy campaign.

alfabeto m alphabet.

alfalfa f alfalfa grass.

alfarería f pottery.

alféizar m windowsill.

alférez m second lieutenant.

alfil m (en ajedrez) bishop.

alfiler m pin; Andes, RP, Ven a. de gancho (imperdible) safety pin.

alfombra f rug; (moqueta) carpet.

alga f (marina) seaweed.

álgebra** f algebra.

álgido, -a adj el punto a. the climax.

algo 1 pron indef (afirmativo) something; (interrogativo) anything; (cantidad indeterminada) some; **a. así** something like that; **¿a. más?** anything else?; **¿queda a. de pastel?** is there any cake left? **2** adv (un poco) somewhat; **está a. mejor** she's feeling a bit better.

algodón m cotton.

alguacil m bailiff.

alguien pron indef (afirmativo) somebody, someone; (interrogativo) anybody, anyone.

algún adj (delante de nombres masculinos en singular) ver **alguno**.

alguno, -a 1 adj (delante de nombre) (afirmativo) some; (interrogativo) any; **alguna que otra vez** now and then; **¿le has visto alguna vez?** have you ever seen him?; **no vino persona alguna** nobody came. **2** pron indef (afirmativo) someone, somebody; (interrogativo) anyone, anybody; **algunos, -as** some (people).

alhaja f jewel.

alhelí m (pl alhelíes) wallflower.

aliado, -a adj allied.

alianza f (pacto) alliance; (anillo) wedding ring.

aliarse [29] vr to ally, to become allies.

alicates mpl pliers pl.

aliciente m (atractivo) charm; (incentivo) incentive.

aliento m breath; **sin a.** breathless.

aligerar 1 vt (carga) to lighten; (acelerar) to speed up; **a. el paso** to quicken one's pace. **2** vi fam **¡aligera!** hurry up!

alijo m haul; **un a. de drogas** a consignment of drugs.

alimaña f vermin.

alimentación f (comida) food; (acción) feeding.

alimentar 1 vt (dar alimento) to feed; (ser nutritivo para) to be nutritious for. **2 alimentarse** vr **alimentarse con** o **de** to live on.

alimenticio, -a adj nutritious; **valor a.** nutritional value.

alimento m food.

alinear 1 vt to align. **2 alinearse** vr to line up.

aliñar vt (ensalada) to dress.

aliño m (de ensalada) dressing.

alistar 1 vt (en el ejército) to enlist. **2 alistarse** vr (en el ejército) to enlist; Am (prepararse) to get ready.

aliviar [43] **1** vt (dolor) to relieve; (carga) to lighten. **2 aliviarse** vr (dolor) to diminish.

alivio *m* relief.

allá *adv (lugar alejado)* over there; **a. abajo/arriba** down/up there; **más a.** further on; **más a. de** beyond; **a. tú** that's your problem.

allí *adv* there; **a. abajo/arriba** down/up there; **por a.** *(movimiento)* that way; *(posición)* over there.

alma** *f* soul.

almacén *m (local)* warehouse; **grandes almacenes** department store.

almacenar *vt* to store.

almanaque *m* calendar.

almeja *f* clam.

almendra *f* almond.

almendro *m* almond tree.

almíbar *m* syrup.

almirante *m* admiral.

almizcle *m* musk.

almohada *f* pillow.

almohadilla *f* (small) cushion.

almohadón *m* large pillow.

almorrana *f* fam pile.

almorzar [2] **1** *vi* to have lunch. **2** *vt* to have for lunch.

almuerzo *m* lunch.

aló *interj Andes, Carib (al teléfono)* hello.

alojamiento *m* accommodations; **dar a.** to accommodate.

alojar 1 *vt* to accommodate. **2 alojarse** *vr* to stay.

alondra *f* lark.

alpargata *f* canvas sandal.

alpinismo *m* mountaineering.

alpinista *mf* mountaineer.

alquilar *vt* to hire; *(pisos, casas)* to rent; **'se alquila'** 'to let', 'for rent'.

alquiler *m (acción)* hiring; *(de pisos, casas)* letting; *(precio)* rental; *(de pisos, casas)* rent; **a. de coches** car rental; **de a.** *(pisos, casas)* to let; *(coche)* for hire; **en una casa de a.** in a rented house.

alquitrán *m* tar.

alrededor 1 *adv (lugar)* round. **2** *prep* **a. de** round; **a. de quince** about fifteen. **3 alrededores** *mpl*

surrounding area *sing*.

alta *f* **dar de o el a.** *(a un enfermo)* to discharge from hospital.

altamente *adv* extremely.

altanero, -a *adj* arrogant.

altar *m* altar.

altavoz *m* loudspeaker.

alteración *f (cambio)* alteration; *(alboroto)* quarrel; *(excitación)* agitation.

alterar 1 *vt* to alter. **2 alterarse** *vr (inquietarse)* to be upset.

altercado *m* argument.

alternar 1 *vt* to alternate. **2** *vi (relacionarse)* to socialize. **3 alternarse** *vr* to alternate.

alternativa *f* alternative.

alterno, -a *adj* alternate.

altibajos *mpl* ups and downs.

altiplano *m* high plateau.

altitud *f* altitude.

altivez *f* arrogance.

alto¹ *m (interrupción)* stop; **dar el a. a algn** to tell sb to stop; **un a. el fuego** a cease-fire.

alto, -a² *adj (persona, árbol, edificio)* tall; *(montaña, techo, presión)* high; *(sonido)* loud; *(precio, tecnología)* high; *(agudo)* high; **en lo a.** at the top; **clase alta** upper class; **en voz alta** aloud; **a altas horas de la noche** late at night. **2** *adv* high; *(fuerte)* loud; **¡habla más a.!** speak up. **3** *m (altura)* height; **¿cuánto tiene de a.?** how tall/high is it?

altoparlante *m Am* loudspeaker.

altura *f* height; *(nivel)* level; **de diez metros de a.** ten meters high; **estar a la a. de las circunstancias** to meet the challenge; *fig* **a estas alturas** by now.

alubia *f* bean.

alucinar 1 *vt* to hallucinate; *fig (encantar)* to fascinate. **2** *vi* fam to be amazed.

alud *m* avalanche.

aludir *vi* to allude.

alumbrar *vt (iluminar)* to illuminate; *(parir)* to give birth to.

aluminio m aluminum.

alumno, -a mf (de colegio) pupil; (de Universidad) student.

alusión f allusion.

alverja, alverjana f Am pea.

alza** f rise; **en a.** rising.

alzamiento m (rebelión) uprising.

alzar [40] 1 vt to raise; **a. la vista** to look up. 2 **alzarse** vr (levantarse) to rise; (rebelarse) to rebel.

ama f (dueña) owner; **a. de casa** housewife.

amabilidad f kindness; **tenga la a. de esperar** would you be so kind as to wait.

amable adj kind, nice.

amaestrar vt (animal) to train; (domar) to tame.

amainar vi (viento etc) to die down.

amamantar vt to breast-feed; (entre animales) to suckle.

amanecer [33] 1 v impers **¿a qué hora amanece?** when does it get light?; **amaneció lluvioso** it was rainy at daybreak. 2 vi **amanecimos en Finlandia** we were in Finland at daybreak; **amaneció muy enfermo** he woke up feeling very ill. 3 m dawn; **al a.** at dawn.

amanerado, -a adj affected.

amante mf lover.

amapola f poppy.

amar 1 vt to love. 2 **amarse** vr to love each other.

amargar [42] 1 vt to make bitter; (relación) to embitter. 2 **amargarse** vr to become embittered.

amargo, -a adj bitter.

amargor m, **amargura** f bitterness.

amarillento, -a adj yellowish.

amarillo, -a adj & m yellow.

amarilloso, -a adj Ven yellowish.

amarrar vt (atar) to tie (up).

amasar vt to knead.

amateur adj & mf amateur.

ámbar m amber.

ambición f ambition.

ambicionar vt to have an ambi-

tion; **ambiciona ser presidente** his ambition is to become president.

ambicioso, -a 1 adj ambitious. 2 mf ambitious person.

ambientador m air freshener.

ambiental adj environmental.

ambiente 1 m environment; Andes, RP (habitación) room. 2 adj environmental; **temperatura a.** room temperature.

ambiguo, -a adj ambiguous.

ámbito m field.

ambos, -as adj & pron pl both.

ambulancia f ambulance.

ambulatorio m surgery.

amedrentar vt to frighten.

amenaza f threat.

amenazador, -a, amenazante adj threatening.

amenazar [40] vt to threaten.

ameno, -a adj entertaining.

americana f (prenda) jacket.

americano, -a adj & mf American.

ametralladora f machine gun.

amigable adj friendly.

amígdala f tonsil.

amigdalitis f tonsillitis.

amigo, -a mf friend; **hacerse amigos** to become friends; **son muy amigos** they are very good friends.

aminorar vt to reduce; **a. el paso** to slow down.

amistad f friendship; **amistades** friends.

amistoso, -a adj friendly.

amnistía f amnesty.

amo m (dueño) owner.

amodorrarse vr to become sleepy.

amoldar vt, **amoldarse** vr to adapt.

amonestación f reprimand.

amontonar 1 vt to pile up. 2 **amontonarse** vr to pile up; (gente) to crowd together.

amor m love; **hacer el a.** to make love; **a. proprio** self-esteem.

amoratado, -a adj (frío) blue with cold; (de un golpe) black and blue.

amordazar [40] vt (a una persona) to gag.

amoroso, -a *adj* loving.

amortiguador *m (de vehículo)* shock absorber.

amortiguar [45] *vt (golpe)* to cushion; *(ruido)* to muffle.

amortizar [40] *vt* to pay off.

amotinar 1 *vt* to incite to riot. **2 amotinarse** *vr* to rise up.

amparar 1 *vt* to protect. **2 ampararse** *vr* to seek refuge.

ampliación *f* enlargement; *(de plazo, casa)* extension.

ampliar [29] *vt* to enlarge; *(casa, plazo)* to extend.

amplificador *m* amplifier.

amplio, -a *adj* large; *(ancho)* broad.

ampolla *f (vejiga)* blister; *(de medicina)* ampule.

amputar *vt* to amputate.

amueblar *vt* to furnish.

amuleto *m* amulet.

anaconda *f* anaconda.

anacronismo *m* anachronism.

anales *mpl* annals.

analfabeto, -a *mf* illiterate.

analgésico, -a *adj & m* analgesic.

análisis *m inv* analysis; **a. de sangre** blood test.

analizar [40] *vt* to analyze.

analogía *f* analogy.

análogo, -a *adj* analogous.

ananá *m (pl ananaes)*, **ananás** *m (pl ananases) Am* pineapple.

anarquista *adj & mf* anarchist.

anatomía *f* anatomy.

ancho, -a 1 *adj* wide, broad; **a lo a.** breadthwise; **te está muy a.** it's too big for you. **2** *m (anchura)* width, breadth; **dos metros de a.** two meters wide; **¿qué a. tiene?** how wide is it?

anchoa *f* anchovy.

anchura *f* width, breadth.

anciano, -a 1 *adj* very old. **2** *mf* old person.

ancla** *f* anchor.

ándale *interj CAm, Méx fam* come on!

andaluz, -a *adj & mf* Andalusian.

andamiaje *m* scaffolding.

andamio *m* scaffold.

andar¹ *m*, **andares** *mpl* gait *sing.*

andar² [8] **1** *vi* to walk; *(coche etc)* to move; *(funcionar)* to work; *fam* **anda por los cuarenta** he's about forty; **¿cómo andamos de tiempo?** how are we on time?; **tu bolso debe de a. por ahí** your bag must be over there somewhere. **2** *vt (recorrer)* to walk.

andariego, -a *adj* fond of walking.

andén *m (en estación)* platform; *Andes, CAm (acera)* sidewalk.

andinismo *m Am* mountaineering.

andino, -a *adj & mf* Andean.

andrajo *m* rag.

anécdota *f* anecdote.

anegar *vt*, **anegarse** *vr* to flood.

anejo, -a *adj* attached (**a** to).

anemia *f* anemia.

anestesia *f* anesthesia.

anexión *f* annexation.

anexionar *vt* to annex.

anexo, -a 1 *adj* attached (**a** to). **2** *m* appendix.

anfitrión, -ona *mf (hombre)* host; *(mujer)* hostess.

ángel *m* angel; *Am (micrófono)* hand microphone.

angina *f* **tener anginas** to have tonsillitis; **a. de pecho** angina pectoris.

anglosajón, -ona *adj & mf* Anglo-Saxon.

angosto, -a *adj* narrow.

anguila *f* eel.

angula *f* elver.

ángulo *m* angle.

angustia *f* anguish.

anhelar *vt* to long for, to yearn for.

anhídrido *m* **a. carbónico** carbon dioxide.

anilla *f* ring.

anillo *m* ring.

animado, -a *adj (fiesta etc)* lively.

animadversión *f* animosity.

animal 1 *m* animal; *fig (basto)* brute. **2** *adj* animal.

animar 1 *vt (alentar)* to encourage;

(alegrar) (persona) to cheer up; *(fiesta, bar)* to liven up. **2 animarse** *vr (persona)* to cheer up; *(fiesta, reunión)* to brighten up.

ánimo *m (valor, coraje)* courage; **estado de á.** state of mind; **con á. de** with the intention of; **¡á.!** cheer up!

aniñado, -a *adj (gesto)* childlike; *(comportamiento)* childish.

aniquilar *vt* to annihilate.

anís *m (bebida)* anisette.

aniversario *m* anniversary.

anoche *adv* last night; *(por la tarde)* yesterday evening; **antes de a.** the night before last.

anochecer [33] **1** *v impers* to get dark. **2** *m* nightfall.

anodino, -a *adj (insustancial)* insubstantial; *(soso)* insipid.

anómalo, -a *adj* anomalous.

anonadado, -a *adj* **me quedé/me dejó a.** I was astonished.

anónimo, -a 1 *adj (desconocido)* anonymous; **sociedad anónima** corporation. **2** *m (carta)* anonymous letter.

anorak *m (pl anoraks)* anorak.

anormal *adj* abnormal; *(inusual)* unusual.

anotar *vt (apuntar)* to note.

anquilosarse *vr* to stagnate.

ansiar [29] *vt* to long for.

ansiedad *f* anxiety; **con a.** anxiously.

ansioso, -a *adj (deseoso)* eager (**por** for); *(avaricioso)* greedy.

antagonismo *m* antagonism.

antaño *adv* in the past.

antártico, -a 1 *adj* Antarctic. **2** *m* **el A.** the Antarctic.

ante¹ *m (piel)* suede.

ante² *prep (delante de)* in the presence of; *(en vista de)* faced with; **a. todo** most of all.

anteanoche *adv* the night before last.

anteayer *adv* the day before yesterday.

antecedente 1 *adj* previous. **2 an-** **tecedentes** *mpl (historial)* record *sing*; **antecedentes penales** criminal record *sing*.

antecesor, -a *mf (en un cargo)* predecessor.

antelación *f* **con un mes de a.** a month beforehand.

antemano *adv* **de a.** beforehand, in advance.

antena *f (de radio, televisión, animal)* antenna; **a. parabólica** satellite dish; **en a.** on the air.

anteojos *mpl (binoculares)* binoculars; *Am (gafas)* glasses, spectacles.

antepecho *m (de ventana)* sill.

antepenúltimo, -a *adj* **el capítulo a.** the last chapter but two.

anteproyecto *m* draft; **a. de ley** draft bill.

antepuesto, -a *pp de* **anteponer**.

antepuse *pt indef de* **anteponer**.

anterior *adj* previous; *(delantero)* front.

anteriormente *adv* previously.

antes 1 *adv* before; *(antaño)* in the past; **mucho a.** long before; **cuanto a.** as soon as possible; **a. prefiero hacerlo yo** I'd rather do it myself; **a. (bien)** on the contrary. **2** *prep* **a. de** before.

antiadherente *adj* nonstick.

antibiótico, -a *adj & m* antibiotic.

anticaspa *adj* anti-dandruff.

anticipar 1 *vt (acontecimiento)* to bring forward; *(dinero)* to pay in advance. **2 anticiparse** *vr (llegar pronto)* to arrive early; **él se me anticipó** he beat me to it.

anticonceptivo, -a *adj & m* contraceptive.

anticongelante *adj & m (de radiador)* antifreeze; *(de parabrisas)* deicer.

anticonstitucional *adj* unconstitutional.

anticuado, -a *adj* antiquated.

anticuario, -a *mf* antique dealer.

anticuerpo *m* antibody.

antídoto *m* antidote.

antier adv Am fam the day before yesterday.

antifaz m mask.

antigüedad f (período histórico) antiquity; (en cargo) seniority; **tienda de antigüedades** antique shop.

antiguo, -a adj old; (pasado de moda) old-fashioned; (anterior) former.

antihistamínico m antihistamine.

antiniebla adj inv **luces a.** foglights.

antipático, -a adj unpleasant.

antirrobo 1 adj inv **alarma a.** burglar alarm; (para coche) car alarm. **2** m burglar alarm; (para coche) car alarm.

antiséptico, -a adj & m antiseptic.

antivirus m inv antivirus system.

antojarse vr **cuando se me antoja** when I feel like it; **se le antojó un helado** he wanted an ice-cream.

antojo m (capricho) whim; (de embarazada) craving.

antorcha f torch.

antropología f anthropology.

anual adj annual.

anudar vt (atar) to knot.

anular vt (matrimonio) to annul; (ley) to repeal.

anunciar [43] vt (producto etc) to advertise; (avisar) to announce.

anuncio m (comercial) advertisement; (aviso) announcement; (cartel) notice.

anzuelo m (fish)hook.

añadir vt to add (a to).

añejo, -a adj (vino, queso) mature.

añicos mpl smithereens; **hacer a.** to smash to smithereens.

año m year; **el a. pasado** last year; **el a. que viene** next year; **hace años** a long time ago; **los años noventa** the nineties; **todo el a.** all the year (round); **¿cuántos años tienes?** how old are you?; **tiene seis años** he's six years old.

añorar vt to long for.

apacible adj mild.

apagado, -a adj (luz, cigarro) out; (color) dull; (voz) sad; (mirada) expressionless, lifeless; (carácter, persona) spiritless.

apagar [42] vt (fuego) to put out; (luz, tele etc) to switch off.

apagón m power cut.

apaisado, -a adj (papel) landscape.

aparador m (mueble) sideboard.

aparato m (dispositivo) device; (instrumento) instrument; **a. de radio/televisión** radio/television set; **a. digestivo** digestive system.

aparatoso, -a adj (pomposo) ostentatious, showy; (espectacular) spectacular; (grande) bulky.

aparcamiento m (en la calle) parking place; (parking) parking lot.

aparcar [44] vti to park.

aparecer [33] **1** vi to appear; **no aparece en mi lista** he is not on my list; (en un sitio) to turn up; **¿apareció el dinero?** did the money turn up?; **no apareció nadie** nobody turned up. **2 aparecerse** vr to appear.

aparejador, -a mf quantity surveyor.

aparejo m (equipo) equipment.

aparentar 1 vt (simular) to affect; (tener aspecto) **no aparenta esa edad** she doesn't look that age. **2** vi to show off.

apariencia f appearance; **en a.** apparently; **guardar las apariencias** to keep up appearances.

apartamento m apartment.

apartar 1 vt (alejar) to remove; (guardar) to put aside. **2** vi **¡aparta!** move out of the way! **3 apartarse** vr (alejarse) to move away.

aparte 1 adv aside; **modestia/bromas a.** modesty/joking apart; **eso hay que pagarlo a.** (separadamente) you have to pay for that separately; **punto y a.** full stop, new paragraph. **2** prep **a. de eso** (además) besides that; (excepto) apart from that.

apasionado, -a *adj* passionate.

apasionante *adj* exciting.

apasionar *vt* to excite.

apático, -a 1 *adj* apathetic. **2** *mf* apathetic person.

apearse *vi* (de un autobús, tren) to get off; (de un coche) to get out.

apedrear *vt* to throw stones at.

apelar *vi* (sentencia) to appeal; (recurrir) to resort (**a** to).

apellidarse *vr* to have as a surname, to be called.

apellido *m* surname; **a. de soltera** maiden name.

apenar 1 *vt* to grieve. **2 apenarse** *vr* to be grieved; *Andes, CAm, Carib, Méx (avergonzarse)* to be ashamed.

apenas *adv* (casi no) hardly, scarcely; **a. (si) hay nieve** there is hardly any snow; **a. llegó, sonó el teléfono** he hardly had arrived when the phone rang.

apéndice *m* appendix.

apendicitis *f* appendicitis.

aperitivo *m* (bebida) apéritif; (comida) appetizer.

apertura *f* (comienzo) opening.

apestar *vi* to stink (**a** of).

apetecer [33] *vi* **¿qué te apetece para cenar?** what would you like for supper?; **¿te apetece ir al cine?** do you want to go to the movie theater?

apetito *m* appetite; **tengo mucho apetito** I'm really hungry.

apetitoso, -a *adj* appetizing, tempting; (comida) delicious, tasty.

apiadarse *vr* to take pity (**de** on).

apilar *vt*, **apilarse** *vr* to pile up.

apiñarse *vr* to crowd together.

apio *m* celery.

apisonadora *f* steamroller.

aplacar [44] *vt*, **aplacarse** *vr* to calm down.

aplanar *vt* to level.

aplastar *vt* to squash.

aplaudir *vt* to applaud.

aplauso *m* applause.

aplazamiento *m* postponement.

aplazar [40] *vt* to postpone.

aplicado, -a *adj* hard-working.

aplicar [44] **1** *vt* to apply. **2 aplicarse** *vr* (esforzarse) to apply oneself; (usar) to apply.

aplique *m* wall lamp.

aplomo *m* aplomb.

apocado, -a *adj* shy, timid.

apoderado, -a *mf* representative.

apoderarse *vr* **a. de** to take possession of.

apodo *m* nickname.

apogeo *m* **estar en pleno a.** (fama etc) to be at its height.

apoplejía *f* apoplexy.

aporrear *vt* to beat; (puerta) to bang.

aportar *vt* to contribute.

aposento *m* (cuarto) room.

aposta *adv* on purpose.

apostar [2] *vti*, **apostarse** *vr* to bet (**por** on).

apoyacabezas *m* headrest.

apoyar 1 *vt* to lean; (causa) to support. **2 apoyarse** *vr* **apoyarse en** to lean on; (basarse) to be based on.

apoyo *m* support.

apreciar [43] **1** *vt* to appreciate; (percibir) to see. **2 apreciarse** *vr* (notarse) to be noticeable.

aprecio *m* regard; **tener a. a algn** to be fond of sb.

aprender *vt* to learn.

aprendiz, -a *mf* apprentice.

aprensivo, -a 1 *adj* apprehensive. **2** *mf* apprehensive person.

apresar *vt* to capture.

apresurar 1 *vt* (paso etc) to speed up. **2 apresurarse** *vr* to hurry up.

apretado, -a *adj* (ropa, cordón) tight; **íbamos todos apretados en el coche** we were all squashed together in the car.

apretar [1] **1** *vt* (botón) to press; (nudo, tornillo) to tighten; **me aprietan las botas** these boots are too tight for me. **2 apretarse** *vr* to squeeze together.

apretón *m* squeeze; **a. de manos** handshake.

apretujar 1 *vt* to squeeze, to crush. **2 apretujarse** *vr* to squeeze together, to cram together.

aprieto *m* tight spot; **poner a algn en un a.** to put sb in an awkward position.

aprisa *adv* quickly.

aprisionar *vt* to trap.

aprobación *f* approval.

aprobado *m* (*nota*) pass.

aprobar [2] *vt* (*autorizar*) to approve; (*estar de acuerdo con*) to approve of; (*examen*) to pass; (*ley*) to pass.

apropiado, -a *adj* suitable.

apropiarse [43] *vr* **a. de** to appropriate.

aprovechado, -a *adj* (*egoísta*) self-seeking; (*espacio*) well-planned; **bien a.** put to good use; **mal a.** (*recurso, tiempo*) wasted.

aprovechamiento *m* use.

aprovechar 1 *vt* to make good use of; (*recursos etc*) to take advantage of. **2** *vi* **¡que aproveche!** enjoy your meal! **3 aprovecharse** *vr* **aprovecharse de algo/algn** to take advantage of sth/sb.

aproximadamente *adv* approximately.

aproximado, -a *adj* approximate.

aproximar 1 *vt* to bring nearer. **2 aproximarse** *vr* to approach (**a -**).

aptitud *f* aptitude; **prueba de a.** aptitude test.

apto, -a *adj* (*apropiado*) suitable; (*capacitado*) capable; (*examen*) passed.

apuesta *f* bet.

apuesto, -a *adj* handsome.

apuntador, -a *mf* (*en el teatro*) prompter.

apuntalar *vt* to prop up.

apuntar 1 *vt* (*con arma*) to aim; (*anotar*) to note; (*indicar*) to suggest. **2 apuntarse** *vr* (*en una lista*) to put one's name down; *fam* to take part (**a** in).

apuntes *mpl* notes; **tomar apuntes** to take notes

apuñalar *vt* to stab.

apurar 1 *vt* (*terminar*) to finish off; (*preocupar*) to worry. **2 apurarse** *vr* (*preocuparse*) to worry; (*darse prisa*) to hurry.

apuro *m* (*situación difícil*) tight spot; (*escasez de dinero*) hardship; (*vergüenza*) embarrassment; **pasar apuros** to be hard up; **¡qué a.!** how embarrassing!

aquel, -ella *adj dem* that; **a. niño** that boy; **aquellos, -as** those; **aquellas niñas** those girls.

aquél, -élla *pron dem mf* that one; (*el anterior*) the former; **todo a. que** anyone who; **aquéllos, -as** those; (*los anteriores*) the former.

aquella *adj dem f ver* **aquel**.

aquélla *pron dem f ver* **aquél**.

aquello *pron dem neutro* that, it.

aquellos, -as *adj dem pl ver* **aquel**.

aquéllos, -as *pron dem mfpl ver* **aquél**.

aquí *adv* (*lugar*) here; **a. arriba/fuera** up/out here; **a. mismo** right here; **de a. para allá** up and down, to and fro; **hasta a.** this far; **por a., por favor** this way please; **está por a.** it's around here somewhere; (*tiempo*) **de a. en adelante** from now on.

árabe 1 *adj & mf* Arab. **2** *m* (*idioma*) Arabic.

arado *m* plow.

aragonés, -esa *adj & mf* Aragonese.

arancel *m* customs duty.

arandela *f* washer.

araña *f* spider.

arañar *vt* to scratch.

arañazo *m* scratch.

arar *vti* to plow.

arbitrario, -a *adj* arbitrary.

árbitro, -a *mf* referee; (*de tenis*) umpire; (*mediador*) arbitrator.

árbol *m* tree; **á. genealógico** family tree.

arbusto *m* bush.

arcada *f* (*de puente*) arch; (*náusea*) retching.

arcén *m* verge; *(de autopista)* hard shoulder.

archipiélago *m* archipelago.

archivador *m* filing cabinet.

archivar *vt (documento etc)* to file (away); *(caso, asunto)* to shelve.

archivo *m* file; *(archivador)* filing cabinet; **archivos** archives; **a. adjunto** *(en email)* attachment.

arcilla *f* clay.

arco *m (de edificio etc)* arch; *(de violín, para flechas)* bow; **a. iris** rainbow.

arder *vi* to burn.

ardiente *adj (encendido)* burning; *fig (fervoroso)* eager; **capilla a.** chapel of rest.

ardilla *f* squirrel.

ardor *m* fervor; **a. de estómago** heartburn.

área *f* area; *(medida)* are (100 square meters).

arena *f* sand; *(en plaza de toros)* bullring; **playa de a.** sandy beach.

arenisca *f* sandstone.

arenque *m* herring.

arete *m Andes, Méx* earring.

argelino, -a *adj & mf* Algerian.

argentino, -a *adj & mf* Argentinian, Argentine.

argolla *f (aro)* (large) ring; *Andes, Méx (alianza)* wedding ring.

argot *m (popular)* slang; *(técnico)* jargon.

argüir [62] *vt* to argue.

argumentar *vt* to argue.

argumento *m (trama)* plot; *(razonamiento)* argument.

árido, -a *adj* arid.

arisco, -a *adj (persona)* unfriendly; *(áspero)* gruff; *(animal)* unfriendly.

aristócrata *mf* aristocrat.

aritmética *f* arithmetic.

arma *f* weapon; **a. de fuego** firearm; **a. nuclear** nuclear weapon.

armada *f* navy.

armado, -a *adj* armed; **ir a.** to be armed; **lucha armada** armed struggle.

armador, -a *mf* shipowner.

armadura *f (armazón)* frame.

armamento *m (armas)* armaments; **a. nuclear** nuclear weapons.

armar 1 *vt (tropa, soldado)* to arm; *(montar)* to assemble. **2 armarse** *vr* to arm oneself; **armarse de paciencia** to summon up one's patience; **armarse de valor** to pluck up courage.

armario *m (para ropa)* wardrobe; *(de cocina)* cupboard; **a. empotrado** built-in wardrobe/cupboard.

armazón *m* frame; *(de madera)* timberwork.

armisticio *m* armistice.

armonioso, -a *adj* harmonious.

aro *m* hoop; *(servilletero)* napkin ring.

aroma *m* aroma; *(de vino)* bouquet.

arpa** *f* harp.

arpón *m* harpoon.

arqueología *f* archaeology.

arquitectura *f* architecture.

arrabales *mpl* slums.

arraigado, -a *adj* deeply rooted.

arrancar [44] **1** *vt (planta)* to uproot; *(diente, pelo)* to pull out; *(coche, motor)* to start; **a. de raíz** to uproot. **2** *vi (coche, motor)* to start; *(empezar)* to begin.

arrasar *vt* to devastate.

arrastrar 1 *vt* to drag (along); **lo arrastró la corriente** he was swept away by the current. **2 arrastrarse** *vr* to drag oneself.

arrebatar 1 *vt (coger)* to seize. **2 arrebatarse** *vr (enfurecerse)* to become furious; *(exaltarse)* to get carried away.

arrebato *m* outburst.

arreciar [43] *vi (viento, tormenta)* to get worse.

arrecife *m* reef.

arreglado, -a *adj (reparado)* repaired; *(solucionado)* settled; *(habitación)* tidy; *(persona)* smart.

arreglar *vt* to arrange; *(problema)* to sort out; *(habitación)* to tidy; *(papeles)* to put in order; *(reparar)* to repair. **2 arreglarse** *vr (vestirse)* to get ready; *fam* **arreglárselas** to manage.

arreglo *m* arrangement; *(acuerdo)* compromise; *(reparación)* repair; **no tiene a.** it is beyond repair; **con a.** in accordance with.

arremangarse [42] *vr* to roll one's sleeves/trousers up.

arremeterse [5] *vr* **a. de** to regret; *(en confesión)* to repent.

arrendar [1] *vt (piso)* to rent; *(dar en arriendo)* to lease; *(tomar en arriendo)* to take on a lease.

arrepentido, -a *adj* regretful.

arrepentirse [5] *vr* **a. de** to regret; *(en confesión)* to repent.

arrestar *vt* to arrest; *(encarcelar)* to put in prison.

arriba 1 *adv* up; *(encima)* on the top; *(en casa)* upstairs; **ahí a.** up there; **de a. abajo** from top to bottom; **mirar a algn de a. abajo** to look sb up and down; **desde a.** from above; **hacia a.** upwards; **más a.** further up; **la parte de a.** the top (part); **vive a.** he lives upstairs; **véase más a.** see above. **2** *interj* up you go!; **¡a. la República!** long live the Republic!; **¡a. las manos!** hands up! **3** *prep Am* **a. (de)** on top of.

arribeño, -a *Am* **1** *adj* highland. **2** *mf* highlander.

arriendo *m* lease.

arriesgado, -a *adj (peligroso)* risky; *(persona)* daring.

arriesgar [42] *vt*, **arriesgarse** *vr* to risk.

arrimar 1 *vt* to move closer; *fam* **a. el hombro** to lend a hand. **2 arrimarse** *vr* to move nearer.

arrinconar *vt (poner en un rincón)* to put in a corner; *(acorralar)* to corner.

arrodillarse *vr* to kneel down.

arrogante *adj* arrogant.

arrojar 1 *vt (tirar)* to throw. **2 arrojarse** *vr* to throw oneself.

arrollador, -a *adj* overwhelming; *(éxito)* resounding; *(personalidad)* captivating.

arrollar 1 *vt (atropellar)* to run over, to knock down. **2** *vi* to win easily.

arropar 1 *vt* to wrap up; *(en cama)* to tuck in. **2 arroparse** *vr* to wrap oneself up.

arroyo *m* stream.

arroz *m* rice; **a. con leche** rice pudding.

arruga *f (en piel)* wrinkle; *(en ropa)* crease.

arrugar [42] **1** *vt (piel)* to wrinkle; *(ropa)* to crease; *(papel)* to crumple (up). **2 arrugarse** *vr (piel)* to wrinkle; *(ropa)* to crease.

arruinar 1 *vt* to ruin. **2 arruinarse** *vr* to be ruined.

arsenal *m* arsenal.

arte *m o f* art; *(habilidad)* skill; **bellas artes** fine arts.

artefacto *m* device.

arteria *f* artery.

artesanal *adj* handmade.

artesanía *f* craftsmanship; *(objetos)* crafts *pl.*

ártico, -a **1** *adj* arctic; **el océano a.** the Arctic Ocean. **2 el A.** the Arctic.

articulación *f (de huesos)* joint.

artículo *m* article.

artificial *adj* artificial; *(sintético)* man-made, synthetic.

artillería *f* artillery.

artista *mf* artist; **a. de cine** film star.

artritis *f* arthritis.

arveja *f Am* pea.

as *m* ace.

asa** *f* handle.

asado, -a 1 *adj* roast; **pollo a.** roast chicken. **2** *m* roast.

asaltar *vt* to assault, to attack; *(banco)* to rob; *fig* to assail.

asamblea *f* meeting; **a. general** general meeting.

asar 1 *vt* to roast. **2 asarse** *vr fig* to be roasting.

ascender [3] **1** *vt (en un cargo)* to promote. **2** *vi* move upward; *(temperatura etc)* to rise; **a. de categoría** to be promoted; **la factura asciende a ...** the bill adds up to ....

ascenso *m* promotion; *(subida)* rise.

ascensor *m* elevator.

asco *m* disgust; **me da a.** it makes me (feel) sick; **¡qué a.!** how disgusting!

ascua** *f* live coal, ember.

aseado, -a *adj* tidy, neat.

asear 1 *vt* to tidy up. **2 asearse** *vr* to wash.

asedio *m* siege.

asegurador, -a 1 *adj* insurance. **2** *mf* insurer.

asegurar 1 *vt* to insure; *(garantizar)* to assure; *(cuerda)* to fasten. **2 asegurarse** *vr* to insure oneself; **asegurarse de que ...** to make sure that ....

asemejarse *vr* **a. a** to look like.

asentamiento *m* settlement.

asentir [5] *vi* to agree; **a. con la cabeza** to nod.

aseo *m* *(limpieza)* tidiness; *(cuarto de baño)* toilet.

asequible *adj* affordable; *(alcanzable)* attainable.

aserrín *m* sawdust.

asesinar *vt* to murder; *(rey, ministro)* to assassinate.

asesinato *m* murder; *(de rey, ministro)* assassination.

asesino, -a 1 *adj* murderous. **2** *mf* *(hombre)* murderer; *(mujer)* murderess; *(de político)* assassin.

asesor, -a 1 *mf* advisor; **a. fiscal** tax advisor. **2** *adj* advisory.

asesorar *vt* to advise.

asesoría *f* consultancy.

asfalto *m* asphalt.

asfixiar [43] *vt*, **asfixiarse** *vr* to asphyxiate.

así 1 *adv* *(de esta manera)* like this *o* that, this way; **ponlo a.** put it this way; **a. de grande/alto** this big/tall; **algo a.** something like this *o* that; **¿no es a.?** isn't that so *o* right?; *Am* **a. no más** *o* **nomás** just like that; **a las seis o a.** around six o'clock; **a. como** as well as; **aun a.** and despite that. **2** *conj* **a. pues ...** so ...; **a. que ... so ....**

asiático, -a *adj* & *mf* Asian.

asiduo, -a 1 *adj* assiduous. **2** *mf* regular customer.

asiento *m* seat; **a. trasero/delantero** back/front seat; **tome a.** take a seat.

asignar *vt* to allocate; *(nombrar)* to appoint.

asignatura *f* subject.

asilo *m* asylum; **a. de ancianos** old people's home.

asimismo *adv* also, as well.

asir [46] *vt* to grasp, to seize.

asistencia *f* *(presencia)* attendance; *(público)* audience; **falta de a.** absence; **a. médica/técnica** medical/technical assistance.

asistenta *f* cleaning lady.

asistente 1 *adj* **el público a.** the audience; *(en estadio)* the spectators *pl*. **2** *mf* *(ayudante)* assistant; **a. social** social worker; **los asistentes** the audience; *(en estadio)* the spectators.

asistir 1 *vt* to assist. **2** *vi* to attend (a -).

asma *f* asthma.

asno *m* donkey.

asociación *f* association.

asociar [43] **1** *vt* to associate. **2 asociarse** *vr* to be associated.

asomar 1 *vt* to stick out; **asomó la cabeza por la ventana** he put his head out the window. **2** *vi* to appear. **3 asomarse** *vr* to lean out; **asomarse a la ventana** to lean out of the window.

asombrar 1 *vt* to astonish. **2 asombrarse** *vr* to be astonished; **asombrarse de algo** to be amazed at sth.

asombro *m* astonishment.

asombroso, -a *adj* astonishing.

asorocharse *vr* *Andes* to suffer from altitude sickness.

aspa *f* *(de molino)* arm; *(de ventilador)* blade; *(cruz)* cross.

aspecto *m* look; *(de un asunto)* aspect.

áspero, -a *adj* rough; *(carácter)* surly.

aspersor *m* sprinkler.

aspiradora *f* vacuum cleaner.

aspirante *mf* candidate.

aspirar *vt (respirar)* to inhale.

aspirina *f* aspirin.

asquerosidad *f* filthy o revolting thing; **¡que a.!** how revolting!

asqueroso, -a 1 *adj (sucio)* filthy; *(desagradable)* disgusting. **2** *mf* filthy o revolting person.

asterisco *m* asterisk.

astilla *f* splinter.

astillero *m* shipyard.

astringente *adj & m* astringent.

astro *m* star.

astrología *f* astrology.

astronauta *mf* astronaut.

astronave *f* spaceship.

astronomía *f* astronomy.

asturiano, -a *adj & mf* Asturian.

astuto, -a *adj* astute.

asumir *vt* to assume.

asunto *m* subject; **no es a. tuyo** it's none of your business.

asustar 1 *vt* to frighten. **2 asustarse** *vr* to be frightened.

atacar [44] *vt* to attack.

atajar *vi* to take a shortcut (**por** across o through).

atajo *m* shortcut.

atañer *vi* to concern.

ataque *m* attack; *(nervios, tos)* fit; **a. cardíaco** o **al corazón** heart attack.

atar 1 *vt (ligar)* to tie; **a. cabos** to put two and two together; *fam* **loco de a.** as mad as a hatter. **2 atarse** *vr fig* to get tied up; **átate los zapatos** do your shoes up.

atardecer [33] **1** *v impers* to get dark. **2** *m* evening.

atareado, -a *adj* busy.

atascar [44] **1** *vt (bloquear)* to block. **2 atascarse** *vr (bloquearse)* to become blocked.

atasco *m* traffic jam.

ataúd *m* coffin.

atemorizar [40] *vt* to frighten.

atención 1 *f* attention; **llamar la a.** to attract attention; **prestar/poner**

a. to pay attention (**a** to). **2** *interj* attention!; *(cuidado)* watch out!

atender [3] **1** *vt* to attend to. **2** *vi (alumno)* to pay attention (**a** to).

atenerse [24] *vr* **a. a** *(reglas)* to abide by; **a. a las consecuencias** to bear the consequences; **me atengo a sus palabras** I'm going by what he said; **no saber a qué a.** not to know what to expect.

atentado *m* attack.

atentamente *adv (con atención)* attentively; **le saluda a.** *(en carta)* yours sincerely.

atentar *vi* **a. a** o **contra** to commit a crime against; **a. contra la vida de algn** to make an attempt on sb's life.

atento, -a *adj* attentive; *(amable)* thoughtful; **estar a. a** to be attentive.

ateo, -a 1 *adj* atheistic. **2** *mf* atheist.

aterrador, -a *adj* terrifying.

aterrar *vt* to terrify. **2 aterrarse** *vr* to be terrified.

aterrizaje *m* landing.

aterrizar [40] *vi* to land.

aterrorizar [40] **1** *vt* to terrify. **2 aterrorizarse** *vr* to be terrified.

ático *m* attic; *(vivienda)* attic apartment.

atingencia *f Am* connection.

atizar [40] *vt (fuego)* to poke.

atlas *m inv* atlas.

atleta *mf* athlete.

atletismo *m* athletics *sing.*

atmósfera *f* atmosphere.

atolondrado, -a *adj* stunned; *(atontado)* stupid.

atómico, -a *adj* atomic.

átomo *m* atom.

atónito, -a *adj* astonished.

atontado, -a *adj (tonto)* silly; *(aturdido)* bewildered.

atorarse *vr* to get stuck.

atormentar 1 *vt* to torment. **2 atormentarse** *vr* to torment oneself.

atornillar *vt* to screw on.

atracar [44] **1** *vt* to hold up; *(persona)* to rob. **2** *vi (barco)* to come alongside. **3 atracarse** *vr (de comida)* to

atracción f attraction; **parque de atracciones** amusement park.

atraco m hold-up; **a. a mano armada** armed robbery.

atracón m fam binge.

atractivo, -a 1 adj attractive. **2** m attraction.

atraer [25] vt to attract.

atragantarse vr to choke (**con** on).

atraigo indic pres de **atraer**.

atraje pt indef de **atraer**.

atrancar [44] **1** vt (puerta) to bolt. **2 atrancarse** vr to get stuck.

atrapar vt to catch.

atrás adv (lugar) at the back, behind; **hacia/para a.** backwards; **puerta de a.** back o rear door; **echarse a.** to back out; **venir de muy a.** to go back a long time.

atrasado, -a adj late; (pago) overdue; (reloj) slow; (país) backward.

atrasar 1 vt to put back. **2** vi (reloj) to be slow. **3 atrasarse** vr to lag behind; (tren) to be late.

atraso m delay; (de país) backwardness; **atrasos** (en pago) arrears.

atravesado, -a adj (cruzado) lying crosswise; (persona) difficult; **lo tengo a.** I can't stand him.

atravesar [1] **1** vt (cruzar) to cross; (traspasar) to go through; (poner a través) to put across. **2 atravesarse** vr to get in the way.

atreverse vr to dare; **a. a hacer algo** to dare to do sth.

atrevido, -a adj (osado) daring; (insolente) insolent; (ropa etc) daring.

atributo m attribute.

atrochar vi to take a short cut.

atropellar vt to knock down.

atroz adj (bárbaro) atrocious; fam (hambre, frío) tremendous.

ATS mf abr de **ayudante técnico sanitario** nurse.

atuendo m attire.

atún m tuna.

aturdido, -a adj stunned.

aturdir vt (con un golpe) to stun;

(confundir) to bewilder.

audaz adj audacious.

audición f hearing; (en el teatro) audition.

audiencia f (público) audience; (entrevista) audience; (tribunal) high court.

audiovisual adj audio-visual.

auditor, -a mf auditor.

auge m peak; (económico) boom; **estar en a.** to be booming.

aula** f (en colegio) classroom; (en universidad) lecture room.

aulaga f gorse.

aullido m howl.

aumentar 1 vt to increase; (precios) to put up; (producción) to step up; (imagen) to magnify. **2** vi (precios) to go up; (valor) to appreciate.

aumento m increase; (de imagen) magnification; **ir en a.** to be on the increase.

aun adv even; **a. así** even so.

aún adv still; (en negativas) yet; **a. está aquí** he's still here; **ella no ha venido a.** she hasn't come yet; **a. más** even more.

aunque conj although, though; (enfático) even if, even though.

aureola f halo.

auricular m (del teléfono) receiver; **auriculares** headphones.

aurora f dawn.

auscultar vt to sound (with a stethoscope).

ausencia f absence.

ausentarse vr (irse) to go away.

ausente 1 adj absent. **2** mf absentee.

austero, -a adj austere.

australiano, -a adj & mf Australian.

austríaco, -a adj & mf Austrian.

auténtico, -a adj authentic.

autista 1 adj autistic. **2** mf autistic person.

auto¹ m RP car.

auto² m (sentencia) writ; **autos** (pleito) documents.

autoadhesivo, -a *adj* self-adhesive.

autobiografía *f* autobiography.

autobiográfico, -a *adj* autobiographical.

autobús *m* bus.

autocar *m* coach.

autóctono, -a *adj* indigenous.

autodefensa *f* self-defense.

autoescuela *f* driving school.

autogobierno *m* self-government.

autógrafo *m* autograph.

automático, -a *adj* automatic.

automotor *m* diesel train.

automóvil *m* car.

automovilista *mf* motorist.

automovilístico, -a *adj* car.

autonomía *f* autonomy; *(región)* autonomous region.

autonómico, -a *adj* autonomous.

autopista *f* highway; **autopista(s) de la información** information superhighway.

autopsia *f* autopsy.

autor, -a *mf* author; *(de crimen)* perpetrator.

autoridad *f* authority.

autoritario, -a *adj* authoritarian.

autorizar [40] *vt* to authorize.

autoservicio *m* self-service; *(tienda)* supermarket.

autostop *m* hitch-hiking; **hacer a.** to hitch-hike.

autostopista *mf* hitch-hiker.

autosuficiencia *f* self-sufficiency.

auxiliar [14] **1** *adj & mf* auxiliary. **2** *vt* to assist.

auxilio *m* assistance; **primeros auxilios** first aid *sing*.

avalancha *f* avalanche.

avalar *vt* to guarantee, to endorse.

avance *m* advance.

avanzado, -a *adj* advanced; **de avanzada edad** advanced in years.

avanzar [40] *vt* to advance.

avaricia *f* avarice.

avaricioso, -a *adj* greedy.

avaro, -a 1 *adj* miserly. **2** *mf* miser.

avasallar *vt* to subdue.

ave** *f* bird.

avellana *f* hazelnut.

avellano *m* hazelnut tree.

avena *f* oats *pl*.

avenida *f* avenue.

avenido, -a *adj* **bien/mal avenidos** on good/bad terms.

aventajar *vt* (*ir por delante de*) to be ahead, be in front (**a** of); (*superar*) to outdo.

aventar [1] **1** *vt Andes, CAm, Méx* (*tirar*) to throw; *CAm, Méx, Perú* (*empujar*) to push, to shove. **2 aventarse** *vr Méx* (*tirarse*) to throw oneself; (*atreverse*) **aventarse a hacer algo** to dare to do sthg.

aventura *f* adventure; (*amorosa*) (love) affair.

aventurarse *vr* to venture.

aventurero, -a 1 *adj* adventurous. **2** *mf* adventurous person.

avergonzado, -a *adj* ashamed.

avergonzar [63] **1** *vt* to shame. **2 avergonzarse** *vr* to be ashamed (**de** of).

avería *f* breakdown.

averiar [29] **1** *vt* to break. **2 averiarse** *vr* (*estropearse*) to malfunction; (*coche*) to break down.

averiguar [45] *vt* to find out.

aversión *f* aversion.

avestruz *m* ostrich.

aviación *f* aviation; (*militar*) air force; **accidente de a.** plane crash.

aviador, -a *mf* aviator; (*piloto militar*) air force pilot.

ávido, -a *adj* avid; **a. de** eager for.

avión *m* airplane; **por a.** (*en carta*) airmail.

avioneta *f* light aircraft.

avisar *vt* (*informar*) to inform; (*advertir*) to warn; (*llamar*) to call for.

aviso *m* notice; (*advertencia*) warning; (*nota*) note; *Am* (*anuncio*) advertisement; **sin previo a.** without notice.

avispa *f* wasp.

avivar *vt* (*fuego*) to stoke (up); (*paso*) to quicken.

axila f armpit.
ay interj (dolor) ouch!
ayer adv yesterday; **a. por la maña-na/por la tarde** yesterday morning/afternoon; **a. por la noche** last night; **antes de a.** the day before yesterday.
ayuda f help.
ayudante mf assistant.
ayudar 1 vt to help. **2 ayudarse** vr (unos a otros) to help; **ayudarse de** to make use of.
ayunas en a. without having eaten breakfast.
ayuntamiento m (institución) town council; (edificio) town hall.
azafata f (de avión) flight attendant; (de congresos) stewardess; (de concurso) hostess.
azafrán m saffron.
azahar m (del naranjo) orange blossom.
azar m chance; **al a.** at random.
azorado, -a adj embarrassed.
azorar 1 vt to embarrass. **2 azorarse** vr to be embarrassed.
azotar vt to beat; (lluvia) to beat down on; (con látigo) to whip.
azotea f flat roof.
azteca adj & mf Aztec.
azúcar m o f sugar; **a. blanco** refined sugar; **a. moreno** brown sugar.
azucarado, -a adj sweetened.
azucarero, -a 1 m sugar bowl. **2** adj sugar.
azucena f lily.
azul adj & m blue; **a. celeste** sky blue; **a. marino** navy blue.
azulejo m (glazed) tile.

B

baba f dribble.
babero m bib.
babor m port.

babosa f slug.
baboso, -a adj fam slimy; Am (tonto) stupid.
babucha f slipper.
baca f roof rack.
bacalao m cod.
bache m (en carretera) pot hole; (mal momento) bad patch.
bachillerato m high school diploma.
bacon m bacon.
bacteriológico, -a adj bacteriological; **guerra bacteriológica** germ warfare.
baden m (en carretera) bump.
bádminton m badminton.
bafle m loudspeaker.
bahía f bay.
bailar vti to dance.
bailarín, -ina mf dancer.
baile m (danza) dance; (formal) ball.
baja f (disminución) drop; (en batalla) loss; **dar de b. a algn** (despedir) to lay sb off; **darse de b.** (por enfermedad) to take sick leave.
bajada f (descenso) descent; (señal) way down; (cuesta) slope.
bajar 1 vt to come/go down; (descender) to get down; (volumen) to turn down; (voz, telón) to lower; (precios etc) to cut; (cabeza) to lower; **b. la escalera** to come/go downstairs. **2** vi to come/go down; (apearse) to get off; (de un coche) to get out (**de** of); (disminuir) to fall. **3 bajarse** vr to come/go down; (apearse) to get off; (de un coche) to get out (**de** of).
bajinis: por lo bajinis adv fam on the sly.
bajío m Am lowland.
bajo, -a 1 adj low; (persona) short; (sonido) faint; **en voz baja** in a low voice; **planta baja** ground floor; **de baja calidad** of poor quality. **2** adv low; **hablar b.** to speak quietly. **3** prep (lugar) under, underneath; **b. tierra** underground; **b. cero** below zero; **b. juramento** under oath; **b. fianza** on bail.

bajón *m (bajada)* sharp fall.

bala *f* bullet; **como una b.** like a shot.

balance *m* balance; *(declaración)* balance sheet.

balanza *f* scales *pl*; **b. comercial** balance of trade; **b. de pagos** balance of payments.

balazo *m (disparo)* shot; *(herida)* bullet wound; **matar a algn de un b.** to shoot sb dead.

balbucear, balbucir *vi (adulto)* to stutter, stammer; *(niño)* to babble.

balcón *m* balcony.

balde *m* **de b.** free; **en b.** in vain.

baldosa *f* (ceramic) floor tile.

balear *vt Am* to shoot.

baleo *m Am* shootout.

baliza *f (boya)* buoy; *(en aviación)* beacon.

ballena *f* whale.

ballet *m* ballet.

balneario *m* health resort.

balón *m* ball.

baloncesto *m* basketball.

balonmano *m* handball.

balonvolea *m* volleyball.

balsa *f* raft.

bálsamo *m* balm.

balsero, -a *mf (de Cuba)* = refugee fleeing Cuba on a raft.

bambú *m (pl* bambúes*)* bamboo.

banana *f* banana.

banano *m (árbol)* banana tree; *Col (fruto)* banana.

banca *f (asiento)* bench; **la b.** (the) banks; **b. electrónica** electronic banking.

bancarrota *f* bankruptcy.

banco *m* bank; *(asiento)* bench.

banda *f (de música)* band; *(cinta)* sash; **b. sonora** sound track; **(línea de) b.** touchline; **saque de b.** throw-in.

bandada *f* flock.

bandeja *f* tray.

bandera *f* flag.

bandido *m* bandit.

bando *m* side.

bandolero *m* bandit.

banquero, -a *mf* banker.

banqueta *f* stool.

banquete *m* banquet; **b. de bodas** wedding reception.

bañador *m (de mujer)* swimming suit; *(de hombre)* swimming trunks *pl.*

bañar 1 *vt* to bath. **2 bañarse** *vr (en baño)* to have a bath; *(en mar, piscina)* to go for a swim; *Am (ducharse)* to have a shower.

bañera *f* bath.

bañista *mf* swimmer.

baño *m* bath; *(de chocolate etc)* coating; *(cuarto de baño)* bathroom; *(lavabo)* toilet; **tomar un b.** to take a bath.

bar *m* bar, pub.

baraja *f* pack, deck.

barajar *vt (cartas)* to shuffle; *fig (nombres, cifras)* to juggle with.

baranda, barandilla *f (de escalera)* banister; *(de balcón)* handrail.

baratija *f* knick-knack.

barato, -a 1 *adj* cheap. **2** *adv* cheaply.

barba *f (pelo)* beard.

barbacoa *f* barbecue.

barbaridad *f* atrocity; *(disparate)* piece of nonsense; **una b.** a lot.

bárbaro, -a 1 *adj (germano)* barbarian; *(cruel)* barbaric, barbarous; *fam (enorme)* massive; *RP fam (estupendo)* tremendous, terrific. **2** *mf* barbarian.

barbería *f* barber's (shop).

barbero *m* barber.

barbilla *f* chin.

barbo *m* barbel.

barbudo, -a *adj* with a heavy beard.

barca *f* small boat.

barcaza *f* lighter.

barco *m* ship; **b. de vapor** steamer.

barlovento *m* windward.

barman *m* barman.

barniz *m (en madera)* varnish; *(en cerámica)* glaze.

barómetro *m* barometer.

barquillo m wafer.

barra f bar; **b. de pan** French loaf; **b. de labios** lipstick; *Andes, RP fam (grupo de amigos)* gang, group of friends; **b. brava** = group of violent soccer fans.

barraca f *(caseta)* hut; *(en Valencia y Murcia)* thatched farmhouse.

barranco m *(despeñadero)* cliff; *(torrentera)* ravine.

barrendero, -a mf (street) sweeper.

barreno m *(taladro)* large drill; *(explosivo)* charge.

barreño m tub.

barrer vt to sweep.

barrera f barrier.

barriada f Am *(de chabolas)* shanty town.

barricada f barricade.

barriga f belly, *fam* tummy.

barril m barrel; **cerveza de b.** draft beer.

barrio m district; **del b.** local; **b. chino** red-light district; **barrios bajos** slums.

barro m *(lodo)* mud; *(arcilla)* clay; **objetos de b.** earthenware *sing*.

bártulos mpl *fam* bits and pieces.

barullo m *(alboroto)* row; *(confusión)* confusion.

basar 1 vt to base (**en** on). **2 basarse** vr *(teoría, película)* to be based (**en** on).

báscula f scales pl.

base f base; *(de argumento, teoría)* basis; *(de partido)* grass roots; **sueldo b.** minimum wage; **b. de datos** database; **a b. de estudiar** by studying; **a b. de productos naturales** using natural products.

básico, -a adj basic.

básquet m basketball.

bastante 1 adj *(suficiente)* enough; **b. tiempo/comida** enough time/food; *(abundante)* quite a lot of; **hace b. calor/frío** it's quite hot/cold; **bastantes amigos** quite a lot of friends. **2** adv *(suficiente)* enough; *(considera-*

blemente) fairly, quite; **con esto hay b.** that is enough; **no soy lo b. rico (como) para …** I am not rich enough to …; **me gusta b.** I quite like it; **vamos b. al cine** we go to the cinema quite often.

bastar vi to be sufficient o enough; **basta con tres** three will be enough; **¡basta (ya)!** that's enough!

bastardo, -a adj & mf bastard.

basto, -a adj *(cosa)* rough; *(persona)* coarse.

bastón m stick.

bastos mpl *(in Spanish pack of cards)* ≃ clubs.

basura f trash.

basurero m *(persona)* garbage collector; *(lugar)* garbage dump.

bata f *(para casa)* dressing gown; *(de médico etc)* white coat.

batalla f battle.

batata f sweet potato.

bate m *(de béisbol)* bat.

batería 1 f battery; *(percusión)* drums pl; **b. de cocina** set of pans. **2** mf drummer.

batida f *(de la policía)* raid.

batido, -a 1 adj *(huevo, crema)* whipped. **2** m milk shake.

batidora f mixer.

batir vt to beat; *(huevo)* to beat; *(nata)* to whip; *(récord)* to break.

baudio m baud.

baúl m *(caja)* trunk; *Am (de vehículo)* trunk.

bautizar [40] vt to baptize, christen.

bautizo m baptism.

baya f berry.

bayeta f floorcloth.

bazar m bazaar.

bazo m spleen.

bazofia f *fam* garbage.

be f *(letra)* b; Am **be baja** o **corta** v *(to distinguish from "b")*; Am **be alta** o **grande** o **larga** b *(to distinguish from "v")*.

beato, -a adj *peyorativo* sanctimonious.

bebé m baby.

beber *vt* to drink.

bebida *f* drink.

bebido, -a *adj* drunk.

beca *f* grant.

becario, -a *mf* grant holder.

becerro *m* calf.

bechamel *f* bechamel; **salsa b.** white sauce.

bedel *m* janitor.

beige *adj & m inv* beige.

béisbol *m* baseball.

belga *adj & mf* Belgian.

bélico, -a *adj* warlike; *(preparativos etc)* war.

belleza *f* beauty.

bello, -a *adj* beautiful.

bellota *f* acorn.

bencina *f Chile* gas.

bencinera *f Chile* gas station.

bendición *f* blessing.

bendito, -a *adj* blessed.

beneficencia *f* charity.

beneficiar [43] **1** *vt* to benefit. **2 beneficiarse** *vr* **beneficiarse de** *o* **con algo** to profit from sth.

beneficio *m* profit; *(bien)* benefit; **en b. propio** in one's own interest; **un concierto a b. de ...** a concert in aid of ....

beneficioso, -a *adj* beneficial.

benevolencia *f* benevolence.

bengala *f* flare.

benigno, -a *adj (persona)* gentle.

benjamín, -ina *mf* youngest child.

berberecho *m* (common) cockle.

berbiquí *m* drill.

berenjena *f* eggplant.

Bermudas 1 *fpl* **las (Islas) B.** Bermuda *sing.* **2** *mpl* o *fpl* **bermudas** *(prenda)* Bermuda shorts.

berrear *vi* to bellow.

berrinche *m fam* tantrum.

berro *m* watercress.

berza *f* cabbage.

besar *vt,* **besarse** *vr* to kiss.

beso *m* kiss.

bestia 1 *f* beast. **2** *mf fam* brute. **3** *adj fig* brutish.

besugo *m (pez)* sea bream.

betún *m (para el calzado)* shoe polish.

biberón *m* baby's bottle.

Biblia *f* Bible.

bibliografía *f* bibliography.

biblioteca *f (edificio)* library; *(estantería)* bookcase.

bicarbonato *m* bicarbonate; **b. sódico** bicarbonate of soda.

bíceps *m inv* biceps.

bicho *m* bug.

bici *f fam* bike.

bicicleta *f* bicycle; **montar en b.** to ride a bicycle.

bidé *m* bidet.

bidón *m* drum.

bien¹ *adv (correctamente)* well; **responder b.** to answer correctly; **hiciste b. en decírmelo** you were right to tell me; **las cosas le van b.** things are going well for him; **¡b.!** good!, great!; **¡muy b.!** excellent!; **¡qué b.!** great!; **vivir b.** to live comfortably; **¡está b.! (¿de acuerdo?)** fine!, all right!; **¡ya está b.!** that's (quite) enough!; **esta falda te está b.** this skirt suits you; **ese libro está muy b.** that book is very good. ■ *(intensificador)* very; **b. temprano** nice and early; **b. caliente** pretty hot; **más b.** rather. **2** *conj* **o b.** or else; **b. ... o b. ...** either ... or ...; **no b. llegó ...** no sooner had she arrived than ...; **si b.** although.

bien² *m (bondad)* good; **el b. y el mal** good and evil; **por el b. de** for the good of; **lo hace por tu b.** he does it for your sake; **bienes** goods; **bienes inmuebles** real estate; **bienes de consumo** consumer goods.

bienestar *m* well-being.

bienvenida *f* welcome; **dar la b. a algn** to welcome sb.

bienvenido, -a *adj* welcome.

bifurcación *f (de la carretera)* fork.

bigote *m (de persona)* mustache; **bigotes** *(de animal)* whiskers *pl.*

bilateral *adj* bilateral.

bilingüe *adj* bilingual.

bilis *f* bile.

billar *m* (*juego*) billiards *sing*; (*mesa*) billiard table; **b. americano** pool; **b. ruso** snooker.

billete *m* ticket; (*de banco*) bill; **b. de ida y vuelta** round-trip ticket; **b. sencillo** *o* **de ida** one-way (ticket); **un b. de mil pesos** a thousand peso note.

billetera *f*, **billetero** *m* wallet.

billón *m* thousand billion.

bingo *m* (*juego*) bingo; (*sala*) bingo hall.

biografía *f* biography.

biología *f* biology.

biombo *m* (folding) screen.

biopsia *f* biopsy.

bioquímica *f* biochemistry.

bióxido *m* **b. de carbono** carbon dioxide.

biquini *m* bikini.

birria *f* *fam* garbage.

bisabuela *f* great-grandmother.

bisabuelo *m* great-grandfather; **bisabuelos** great-grandparents.

bisagra *f* hinge.

bisiesto *adj* año b. leap year.

bisnieto, -a *mf* (*niño*) great-grandson; (*niña*) great-granddaughter; **mis bisnietos** my great-grandchildren.

bisonte *m* bison.

bisté, bistec *m* steak.

bisturí *m* scalpel.

bisutería *f* imitation jewelry.

bizco, -a 1 *adj* cross-eyed. **2** *mf* cross-eyed person.

bizcocho *m* sponge cake.

biznieto, -a *mf* = **bisnieto.**

blanco, -a¹ *adj* white; (*tez*) fair. **2** *mf* (*hombre*) white man; (*mujer*) white woman; **los blancos** whites.

blanco² *m* (*color*) white; (*hueco*) blank; (*diana*) target; **pasar la noche en b.** to have a sleepless night; **me quedé en b.** my mind went blank; **ser el b. de todas las miradas** to be the center of attention.

blancura *f* whiteness.

blando, -a *adj* soft.

blanquear *vt* (*encalar*) to whitewash.

blasfemar *vi* to blaspheme (**contra** against).

blindado, -a *adj* (*carro*) armoured; (*antibalas*) bullet-proof; **coche b.** bullet-proof car; **puerta blindada** reinforced door.

bloc *m* pad; **b. de notas** notepad.

bloque *m* block; **b. de pisos** block (of apartments).

bloquear *vt* to block; (*sitiar*) to blockade.

blusa *f* blouse.

blusón *m* loose blouse.

bobada *f* nonsense; **decir bobadas** to talk nonsense.

bobina *f* reel.

bobo, -a 1 *adj* (*tonto*) stupid, silly; (*ingenu*) naïve. **2** *mf* fool.

boca *f* mouth; **b. abajo** face downward; **b. arriba** face upward; *fam* **¡cierra la b.!** shut up!; **con la b. abierta** open-mouthed; **se le hizo la b. agua** his mouth watered; **la b. del metro** the entrance to the subway station.

bocacalle *f* entrance to a street.

bocadillo *m* sandwich; **un b. de jamón/tortilla** a ham/omelette sandwich.

bocado *m* bite.

bocanada *f* (*de humo*) puff; **una b. de viento** a gust of wind.

bocata *m* *fam* sandwich.

bocazas *mf inv fam* bigmouth.

boceto *m* (*de cuadro etc*) sketch; (*esquema*) outline.

bochinche *m* *fam* uproar; **armar un b.** to kick up a row.

bochorno *m* (*tiempo*) sultry weather; (*calor sofocante*) stifling heat; (*vergüenza*) embarrassment.

bochornoso, -a *adj* (*tiempo*) sultry, close, muggy; (*calor*) stifling; *fig* (*vergonzoso*) shameful, embarrassing.

bocina f horn; **tocar la b.** to sound one's horn.

boda f marriage; **bodas de plata** silver wedding sing.

bodega f (en casa) wine cellar; (tienda) wine shop; Am grocery store, grocer's.

body m bodystocking.

bofetada f, **bofetón** m slap on the face; **dar una b./un b. a algn** to slap sb's face.

bohío m Am hut.

boicotear vt to boycott.

boina f beret.

bol m bowl.

bola f ball; (canica) marble; **b. de nieve** snowball; **no dar pie con b.** to be unable to do anything right.

bolera f bowling alley.

boletería f Am (de estadio, estación) ticket office; (de teatro) box office.

boletero, -a mf Am box office attendant.

boletín m bulletin.

boleto m Am ticket.

boli m biro®.

boliche m (juego) bowling; (bola) jack; (lugar) bowling alley; CSur fam (bar) small bar.

bólido m (coche) racing car.

bolígrafo m ballpoint (pen).

boliviano, -a adj & mf Bolivian.

bollo m (de pan) roll; (abolladura) dent.

bolo m skittle; **bolos** (juego) skittles.

bolsa¹ f bag; **b. de deportes** sports bag; **b. de la compra** shopping bag; **b. de viaje** travel bag.

bolsa² f (de valores) Stock Exchange.

bolsillo m (prenda) pocket; **de b.** pocket; **libro de b.** paperback.

bolso m purse.

boludo, -a mf RP fam (estúpido) idiot, twit.

bomba¹ f pump; **b. de incendios** fire engine; Andes, Ven **b. (de gasolina)** (surtidor) gas pump.

bomba² f (explosivo) bomb; **b. atómica/de hidrógeno/de neutrones**

atom/hydrogen/neutron bomb; **b. de relojería** time bomb; fam **pasarlo b.** to have a great time.

bombardear vt to bomb.

bombazo m bomb blast.

bombero, -a mf (hombre) fireman; (mujer) firewoman; (ambos sexos) firefighter; **cuerpo de bomberos** fire brigade; **parque de bomberos** fire station.

bombilla f (light) bulb.

bombillo m CAm, Carib, Col, Méx light bulb.

bombín m bowler hat.

bombo m (de percusión) bass drum; (de sorteo) lottery drum; (de lavadora) drum.

bombón m chocolate.

bombona f cylinder.

bonachón, -ona adj good-natured.

bonanza f (tiempo) fair weather; (prosperidad) prosperity.

bondadoso, -a adj good-natured.

boniato m sweet potato.

bonificación f bonus.

bonito, -a¹ adj pretty, nice.

bonito² m tuna.

bono m (vale) voucher; (título) bond.

bono-bus m bus pass.

boquerón m anchovy.

boquete m hole.

boquiabierto, -a adj open-mouthed; **se quedó b.** he was flabbergasted.

boquilla f (de cigarro) tip; (de pipa) mouthpiece.

borda f gunwale; **arrojar** o **echar por la b.** to throw overboard; **un fuera b.** (motor) an outboard motor.

bordado, -a 1 adj embroidered. **2** m embroidery.

bordar vt to embroider.

borde m (de mesa, camino) edge; (de prenda) hem; (de vasija) rim; **al b. del mar** at the seaside.

bordear vt to skirt.

bordillo m curb.

bordo *m* a b. on board; **subir a b.** to go on board.

borrachera *f (embriaguez)* drunkenness; *(curda)* binge; **coger o pillar una b.** to get drunk.

borracho, -a 1 *adj (bebido)* drunk; *(bizcocho)* with rum; **estar b.** to be drunk. **2** *mf* drunk.

borrador *m (escrito)* rough copy; *(de pizarra)* duster.

borrar *vt (con goma)* to rub out; *(pizarra)* to clean; *(en pantalla)* to delete.

borrasca *f* area of low pressure.

borrego, -a *mf (animal)* yearling lamb; *(persona)* sheep.

borrico *m* ass, donkey; *fam fig* ass, dimwit.

borroso, -a *adj* blurred; **veo b.** I can't see clearly.

bosque *m* wood.

bosquejo *m (de dibujo)* sketch; *(de plan)* draft.

bostezar [40] *vi* to yawn.

bostezo *m* yawn.

bota *f* boot; *(de vino)* wineskin.

botana *f Méx* snack.

botánico, -a *adj* botanic; **jardín b.** botanic gardens *pl.*

botar 1 *vi (saltar)* to jump; *(pelota)* to bounce. **2** *vt (barco)* to launch; *(pelota)* to bounce; *Am (arrojar)* to throw out.

bote¹ *m* jump; *(de pelota)* bounce.

bote² *m (lata)* can, tin; *(para propinas)* jar o box for tips.

bote³ *m (lancha)* boat; **b. salvavidas** lifeboat.

botella *f* bottle.

botellín *m* small bottle.

botijo *m* earthenware pitcher (with spout and handle).

botín *m (de un robo)* loot.

botiquín *m* medicine cabinet; *(portátil)* first aid kit; *(enfermería)* first aid post.

botón *m* button.

botones *m inv (en hotel)* bellboy, bellhop; *(recadero)* errand boy.

boutique *f* boutique.

boxeador *m* boxer.

boxeo *m* boxing.

boya *f (baliza)* buoy; *(corcho)* float.

boy-scout *m* boy scout.

bozal *m* muzzle.

bracear *vi (nadar)* to swim.

bragas *fpl* panties *pl*, knickers *pl.*

bragueta *f (de pantalón)* fly, flies *pl.*

braille *m* Braille.

bramido *m* bellowing.

brandy *m* brandy.

brasa *f* ember; **chuletas a la b.** barbecued chops.

brasero *m* brazier.

brasileño, -a, *RP* **brasilero, -a** *adj & mf* Brazilian.

bravo, -a 1 *adj (valiente)* brave; **un toro b.** a fighting bull. **2** *interj* ¡b.! well done!

braza *f* breast stroke; **nadar a b.** to do the breast stroke.

brazada *f* stroke.

brazalete *m (pulsera)* bracelet; *(insignia)* armband.

brazo *m* arm; **en brazos** in one's arms; **ir del b.** to walk arm in arm; **con los brazos abiertos** with open arms.

brecha *f (en muro)* gap; *(herida)* wound.

brécol *m* broccoli.

breva *f (higo)* early fig; *fam* ¡**no caerá esa b.!** no such luck!

breve *adj* brief; **en b., en breves momentos** shortly, soon.

brezo *m* heather.

bribón, -ona 1 *adj* roguish. **2** *mf* rogue.

bricolaje *m* do-it-yourself, DIY.

bridge *m* bridge.

brigada *f* brigade; *(de policías)* squad.

brillante 1 *adj* brilliant. **2** *m* diamond.

brillantina *f* brilliantine.

brillar *vi (resplandecer)* to shine; *(ojos, joyas)* to sparkle; *(lentejuelas etc)* to glitter.

brillo m (resplandor) shine; (del sol, de la luna) brightness; (de lentejuelas etc) glittering; (del cabello, de tela) sheen; (de zapatos) shine; **sacar b.** a to polish.

brincar [44] vi to skip.

brindar 1 vi to drink a toast; **b. por algn/algo** drink to sb/sth. **2 brindarse** vr to volunteer (**a** to).

brindis m toast.

brío m energy.

brisa f breeze; **b. marina** sea breeze.

británico, -a 1 adj British; **las Islas Británicas** the British Isles. **2** mf Briton; **los británicos** the British.

brocha f (para pintar) paintbrush; (de afeitar) shaving brush.

broche m (joya) brooch; (de vestido) fastener.

bróculi m broccoli.

broma f (chiste) joke; **en b.** as a joke; **¡ni en b.!** not on your life!; **b. pesada** practical joke; **gastar una b.** to play a joke.

bromear vi to joke.

bromista 1 adj fond of joking o playing jokes. **2** mf joker, prankster.

bronca f (riña) row; **echar una b.** a **algn** to bawl sb out.

bronce m bronze.

bronceado, -a 1 adj (sun) tanned. **2** m (sun) tan.

bronceador, -a 1 adj **leche bronceadora** suntan lotion. **2** m suntan lotion.

broncearse vr to get a tan o a suntan.

bronquitis f inv bronchitis.

brotar vi (planta) to sprout; (agua) to gush; (epidemia) to break out.

bruces: de bruces adv face downwards; **se cayó de b.** he fell flat on his face.

bruja f witch.

brújula f compass.

bruma f mist.

brusco, -a adj (persona) brusque; (repentino) sudden.

bruto, -a 1 adj (necio) stupid; (grosero) coarse; (no neto) gross; **un diamante en b.** an uncut diamond. **2** mf blockhead.

bucear vi to swim under water.

bucle m curl.

budín m pudding.

budista adj Buddhist.

buen adj (delante de un nombre masculino singular) good; **¡b. viaje!** have a good trip!; ver **bueno**.

buenamente adv **haz lo que b. puedas** just do what you can; **si b. puedes** if you possibly can.

bueno, -a 1 adj good; (amable) (con ser) good, kind; (sano) (con estar) well, in good health; **un alumno muy b.** a very good pupil; **lo b.** the good thing; **hoy hace buen tiempo** it's fine today; **un buen número de** a good number of; **una buena cantidad** a considerable amount; **un buen trozo de pastel** a nice o good big piece of cake; **¡en buen lío te has metido!** that's a fine mess you've got yourself into!; **¡buenas!** (saludos) hello!; **buenas tardes** (desde mediodía hasta las cinco) good afternoon; (desde las cinco) good evening; **buenas noches** (al llegar) good evening; (al irse) good night; **buenos días** good morning; **de buenas a primeras** all at once; **por las buenas** willingly; **por las buenas o por las malas** willy-nilly; **¡buena la has hecho!** that's done it!; **¡estaría b.!** I should hope not!; **librarse de una buena** to get off scot free. **2 interj ¡b.!** (de acuerdo) all right, OK; Col, Méx (al teléfono) hello.

buey m ox.

búfalo, -a mf buffalo.

bufanda f scarf.

bufete m (despacho de abogado) lawyer's office.

buhardilla f attic.

búho m owl.

buitre m vulture.

bujía f (de coche) spark plug.

bulbo m bulb.

bulla f (ruido) noise; **armar b.** to make a lot of noise.

bullicio m noise.

bulto m (cosa indistinta) shape; (maleta, caja) piece of luggage; (hinchazón) lump; **hacer mucho b.** to be very bulky.

búnker m bunker.

buñuelo m doughnut.

buque m ship; **b. de guerra** warship; **b. de pasajeros** passenger ship.

burbuja f bubble.

burdel m brothel.

burguesía f bourgeoisie.

burla f gibe, jeer; **hacer b. de algo** o **algn** to make fun of sth o sb; **hacer b. a algn** to stick one's tongue out at sb.

burladero m refuge in bullring.

burlarse vr to make fun (**de** of).

burlón, -ona adj mocking.

burocracia f bureaucracy.

burocrático, -a adj bureaucratic.

burro, -a 1 mf donkey; fam (estúpido) blockhead. **2** adj fam (necio) stupid; (obstinado) stubborn.

bursátil adj stock market.

busca f search; **ir en b. de** to go in search of.

buscar [44] **1** vt to look o search for; **ir a b. algo** to go and get sth; **fue a buscarme a la estación** she picked me up at the station. **2** buscarse vr fam **buscarse la vida** to try and earn one's living; **se busca** wanted.

búsqueda f search.

busto m bust.

butaca f (sillón) armchair; (de teatro, cine) seat; **b. de platea** o **patio** seat in the stalls.

butano m (gas) **b.** butane gas.

buzo m diver.

buzón m mailbox; **echar una carta al b.** to mail a letter.

C

cabalgar [42] vti to ride.

caballa f mackerel.

caballería f (cuerpo) cavalry; (cabalgadura) mount, steed.

caballero m gentleman; **ropa de c.** menswear; **caballeros** (en letrero) gents.

caballeroso, -a adj gentlemanly.

caballo m horse; (de ajedrez) knight; (de naipes) queen; **a c.** on horseback; **montar a c.** to ride; fig **a c. entre …** halfway between ….

cabaña f (choza) cabin.

cabaret m (pl cabarets) cabaret.

cabecera f top, head.

cabecilla mf leader.

cabello m hair

caber [9] vi to fit; **cabe en el maletero** it fits in the boot; **en este coche/jarro caben …** this car/jug holds …; **no cabe duda** there is no doubt; **cabe la posibilidad de que …** there is a possibility that …; **no está mal dentro de lo que cabe** it isn't bad, under the circumstances.

cabestrillo m sling.

cabeza 1 f head; **en c.** in the lead; **por c.** a head, per person; **a la c. de** at the head of; **estar mal de la c.** to be a mental case. **2** mf el o la c. de familia** the head of the family.

cabezota fam **1** adj pigheaded. **2** mf pigheaded person.

cabida f capacity.

cabina f cabin; **c. telefónica** telephone booth.

cable m cable.

cabo m (extremo) end; (rango) corporal; (policía) sergeant; (de barco) rope, cable; (geográfico) cape; **al c. de** after; **atar cabos** to put two and two together.

cabra f goat.

cabré *indic fut de* **caber**.

cabriola *f* skip.

cacahuete *m* peanut.

cacao *m* cacao; *(polvo, bebida)* cocoa.

cacatúa *f* cockatoo.

cacería *f* *(actividad)* hunting; *(partida)* hunt.

cacerola *f* saucepan.

cacharro *m* earthenware pot *o* jar; *fam (cosa)* thing, piece of junk; **cacharros** *(de cocina)* pots and pans.

cachear *vt* to frisk, search.

cachetada *f Am* slap.

cachete *m* *(bofetada)* slap; *Am (mejilla)* cheek.

cachimba *f* pipe.

cachivache *m* *fam* thing, knick-knack.

cacho¹ *m* *fam (pedazo)* bit, piece.

cacho² *m* *Andes, Ven (cuerno)* horn.

cachondeo *m* *fam* laugh; **tomar algo a c.** to take sth as a joke.

cachorro, -a *mf* *(de perro)* pup, puppy; *(de gato)* kitten; *(de otros animales)* cub, baby.

cacique *m* *(jefe)* local boss.

caco *m* *fam* thief.

cacto *m*, **catus** *m inv* cactus.

cada *adj* *(de dos)* each; *(de varios)* each, every; **c. día** every day; **c. dos días** every second day; **c. vez más** more and more; **¿c. cuánto?** how often?; **cuatro de c. diez** four out of (every) ten.

cadáver *m* *(de persona)* corpse, body; *(de animal)* body, carcass.

cadena *f* chain; *(correa de perro)* lead, leash; *(canal)* channel; *(de montañas)* range; **trabajo en c.** assembly line work; **c. perpetua** life imprisonment; *(para ruedas)* **cadenas** tire chains.

cadera *f* hip.

caducar [44] *vi* to expire.

caducidad *f* expiration; **fecha de c.** *(en alimentos)* ≃ sell-by date; *(en medicinas)* to be used before.

caer [39] **1** *vi* to fall; *(entender)* to understand, to see; *(hallarse)* to be; **dejar c.** to drop; **ya caigo** I get it; **cae por Granada** it is somewhere near Granada; **me cae bien/mal** I like/don't like her. **2 caerse** *vr* to fall (down); **me caí de la moto** I fell off the motorbike; **se le cayó el pañuelo** she dropped her handkerchief.

café *m* coffee; *(cafetería)* café; **c. solo/con leche** black/white coffee.

cafeína *f* caffeine.

cafetera *f* *(para hacerlo)* coffee-maker; *(para servirlo)* coffeepot.

cafetería *f* snack bar, coffee bar; *(en tren)* buffet car.

caída *f* fall; *(de pelo, diente)* loss; *(de gobierno)* downfall, collapse.

caigo *indic pres de* **caer**.

caimán *m* cayman, alligator.

caja *f* box; *(de embalaje)* crate, case; *(en tienda)* cash desk; *(en banco)* cashier's desk; *(féretro)* coffin, casket; **c. fuerte** safe; **c. de cerveza** case of beer; **c. de cambios** gearbox; **c. de ahorros** *o* **de pensiones** savings bank.

cajero, -a *mf* cashier; **c. automático** automatic teller machine (ATM).

cajetilla *f* packet, pack.

cajón *m* *(en un mueble)* drawer; *(caja grande)* crate, chest.

cal *f* lime; **a c. y canto** hermetically.

calabacín *m* *(pequeño)* zucchini; *(grande)* squash.

calabaza *f* pumpkin, gourd.

calabozo *m* *(prisión)* jail, prison; *(celda)* cell.

calado, -a *adj* *(mojado)* soaked.

calamar *m* squid *inv*; **calamares a la romana** squid fried in batter.

calambre *m* *(descarga)* electric shock; *(en músculo)* cramp; **ese cable da c.** that wire is live.

calamidad *f* calamity.

calar 1 *vt* *(mojar)* to soak, to drench. **2** *vi* *(prenda)* to let in water. **3 calarse** *vr* *(prenda, techo)* to let in water; *(mojarse)* to get soaked; *(coche)* to stall; **calarse el sombrero** to pull one's hat down.

calavera f skull.

calcar [44] vt (dibujo) to trace; (imitar) to copy, to imitate.

calcetín m sock.

calcio m calcium.

calco m tracing; **papel de c.** carbon paper.

calculadora f calculator.

calcular vt to calculate; (evaluar) to (make an) estimate; (suponer) to guess.

cálculo m calculation; (matemático) calculus.

caldera f boiler.

caldo m stock, broth; **c. de cultivo** breeding ground.

calefacción f heating; **c. central** central heating.

calendario m calendar.

calentador m heater.

calentar [1] **1** vt (agua, horno) to heat; (comida, habitación) to warm up. **2 calentarse** vr to get hot, heat up.

calentura f fever, temperature.

calidad f quality; **de primera c.** first-class; **vino de c.** good-quality wine.

cálido, -a adj warm.

caliente adj hot; (debate) heated.

calificar [44] vt to describe (**de** as); (examen) to mark, grade.

caligrafía f calligraphy; (modo de escribir) handwriting.

caliza f limestone.

callado, -a adj quiet; **te lo tenías muy c.** you were keeping that quiet.

callar 1 vi (dejar de hablar) to stop talking; (no hablar) to keep quiet, to say nothing; **¡calla!** be quiet!, shut up! **2** vt (noticia) not to mention, to keep to oneself. **3 callarse** vr to be quiet, to shut up; **¡cállate!** shut up!

calle f street, road; (de piscina, pista) lane; **c. de dirección única** one-way street.

callejón m back alley, back street; **c. sin salida** cul-de-sac, dead end.

callejuela f narrow street, lane.

callista mf chiropodist.

callo m callus, corn; **callos** tripe sing.

calma f calm; **¡c.!** calm down!; **en c.** calm; **tómatelo con c.** take it easy.

calmante m painkiller; (relajante) tranquillizer.

calmar 1 vt (persona) to calm (down); (dolor) to soothe, to relieve. **2 calmarse** vr (persona) to calm down; (dolor, viento) to ease off.

calor m heat; (entusiasmo) warmth; **hace c.** it's hot; **tengo c.** I'm hot; **entrar en c.** to warm up.

caloría f calorie.

calumnia f slander.

caluroso, -a adj hot; (acogida etc) warm.

calvicie f baldness.

calvo, -a 1 adj bald. **2** m bald man.

calzada f road.

calzado m shoes pl.

calzador m shoehorn.

calzar [40] **1** vt (poner calzado) to put shoes on; (mueble) to wedge; **¿qué número calzas?** what size shoe do you wear? **2 calzarse** vr **calzarse los zapatos** to put on one's shoes.

calzoncillos mpl briefs, underpants.

calzones mpl trousers.

cama f bed; **estar en o guardar c.** to be confined to bed; **hacer la c.** to make the bed; **irse a la c.** to go to bed; **c. doble/sencilla** double/single bed.

cámara 1 f (aparato) camera; (de rueda) inner tube; **a c. lenta** in slow motion; **c. frigorífica** cold-storage room. **2** mf (hombre) cameraman; (mujer) camerawoman.

camarada mf comrade.

camarera f (de hotel) (chamber)-maid.

camarero, -a mf (de restaurante) (hombre) waiter; (mujer) waitress; (tras la barra) bartender.

camarón m prawn.

camarote m cabin.

cambiar [43] **1** vt to change; (intercambiar) to swap, to exchange; **c. algo de sitio** to move sth. **2** vi to change; **c. de casa** to move (house); **c. de idea** to change one's mind. **3 cambiarse** vr (de ropa) to change (clothes); (de casa) to move (house).

cambio m change; (de impresiones) exchange; (de divisas) exchange; **c. de marcha** gear change; **a c. de** in exchange for; **en c.** on the other hand; **¿tienes c. de mil pesos?** have you got change for a thousand pesos?

camello, -a mf camel.

camilla f stretcher.

caminar 1 vi to walk. **2** vt to walk; **caminaron diez kilómetros** they walked (for) ten kilometers.

camino m (ruta) route, way; (vía) path, track; **ponerse en c.** to set off; **abrirse c.** to break through; **a medio c.** half-way; **estar en c.** to be on the way; **nos coge** o **pilla de c.** it is on the way.

camión m truck; CAm, Méx (autobús) bus; **c. cisterna** tanker; **c. de la basura** garbage truck; **c. frigorífico** refrigerated truck.

camionero, -a mf truck driver.

camioneta f van.

camisa f shirt; **en mangas de c.** in one's shirtsleeves; **c. de fuerza** straightjacket.

camiseta f (de uso interior) undershirt; (de uso exterior) T-shirt; (de deporte) shirt.

camisón m nightgown.

camote m Andes, CAm, Méx sweet potato.

campamento m camp.

campana f bell.

campanada f peal of a bell.

campanario m belfry, bell tower.

campanilla f small bell.

campaña f campaign; **c. electoral** election campaign; **c. publicitaria** advertising campaign.

campeón, -ona mf champion; **c.**

mundial world champion.

campeonato m championship.

campesino, -a mf (hombre) countryman; (mujer) countrywoman.

camping m campsite; **hacer** o **ir de c.** to go camping.

campiña f open country.

campista mf camper.

campo m country, countryside; (de fútbol) pitch; (de tenis) court; (de golf) course; (parcela, ámbito) field; **a c. traviesa** o **través** cross-country; **c. de batalla** battlefield; **c. de concentración** concentration camp; **c. de trabajo** work camp.

camposanto m cemetery.

cana f (gris) gray hair; (blanco) white hair; **tener canas** to have gray hair.

canal m (artificial) canal; (natural, de televisión) channel; **C. de la Mancha** English Channel.

canalla mf swine, rotter.

canalón m gutter.

canapé m canapé; (sofá) couch, sofa.

canario, -a 1 adj & mf Canarian; **Islas Canarias** Canary Islands, Canaries. **2** m (pájaro) canary.

canasta f basket.

cancela f wrought-iron gate.

cancelar vt to cancel; (deuda) to pay off; Chile, Ven (compra) to pay for.

cáncer m cancer; **c. de pulmón/mama** lung/breast cancer.

cancerígeno, -a adj carcinogenic.

canceroso, -a adj cancerous.

cancha f ground; (de tenis, baloncesto) court.

canciller mf chancellor.

cancillería f Am foreign ministry.

canción f song.

candado m padlock.

candela f Carib fire.

candelabro m candelabra.

candidato, -a mf candidate; (a un puesto) applicant.

candidatura f (lista) list of candidates.

cándido, -a adj candid.

candoroso, -a *adj* innocent, pure.

canela *f* cinnamon.

canelones *mpl (pasta)* cannelloni.

cangrejo *m (de mar)* crab; *(de río)* freshwater crayfish.

canguro 1 *m* kangaroo. **2** *mf fam* baby-sitter.

caníbal *adj & mf* cannibal.

canica *f* marble.

caniche *m* poodle.

canícula *f* dog days, midsummer heat.

canillera *f Am (cobardía)* cowardice; *(miedo)* fear.

canillita *m Andes, RP* newspaper boy.

canino, -a 1 *adj* canine. **2** *m (colmillo)* canine.

canoa *f* canoe.

canoso, -a *adj (de pelo blanco)* white-haired; *(de pelo gris)* gray-haired; *(pelo)* white; gray.

cansado, -a *adj (agotado)* tired, weary.

cansancio *m* tiredness, weariness.

cansar 1 *vt* to tire. **2** *vi* to be tiring. **3 cansarse** *vr* to get tired; **se cansó de esperar** he got tired of waiting, he got fed up (with) waiting.

cantaleta *f Am* **la misma c.** the same old story.

cantante 1 *mf* singer. **2** *adj* singing.

cantaor, -a *mf* flamenco singer.

cantar *vti* to sing.

cántaro *m* pitcher; **llover a cántaros** to rain cats and dogs.

cante *m (canto)* singing; **c. hondo, c. jondo** flamenco.

cantera *f (de piedra)* quarry; *(de equipo)* young players *pl.*

cantidad *f* quantity; *(de dinero)* sum; *fam* **c. de gente** thousands of people.

cantina *f* canteen.

cantinero, -a *mf* bar attendant.

canto[1] *m (arte)* singing; *(canción)* song.

canto[2] *m (borde)* edge; **de c.** on its side.

canturrear *vi* to hum, croon.

caña *f (de cerveza)* draft beer; *(tallo)* cane, stem; *(de pescar)* rod; *Andes, Cuba, RP (aguardiente)* cane spirit, cheap rum; **c. de azúcar** sugar cane.

cañada *f (barranco)* gully, ravine.

cañería *f* (piece of) piping; **cañerías** plumbing *sing.*

caño *m (tubería)* pipe; *(tubo)* tube; *(chorro)* spout.

cañón *m* cannon; *(de fusil)* barrel; *(garganta)* canyon.

cañonazo *m* gunshot.

caoba *f* mahogany.

caos *m* chaos.

caótico, -a *adj* chaotic.

capa *f (prenda)* cloak, cape; *(de pintura)* layer, coat.

capacidad *f* capacity.

caparazón *m* shell.

capataz *mf (hombre)* foreman; *(mujer)* forewoman.

capaz *adj* capable, able; **ser c. de hacer algo** *(tener la habilidad de)* to be able to do sth; *(atreverse a)* to dare to do sth; *Am* **es c. que** it is likely that.

capicúa *adj* **número c.** reversible number; **palabra c.** palindrome.

capilla *f* chapel.

capital 1 *f* capital. **2** *m (dinero)* capital. **3** *adj* capital, main; **pena c.** capital punishment.

capitalismo *m* capitalism.

capitalista *adj & mf* capitalist.

capitán, -ana *mf* captain.

capitulación *f* agreement; *(pacto)* capitulation.

capítulo *m (de libro)* chapter; *(tema)* subject.

capó *m (de coche)* hood.

capota *f (de coche)* convertible top.

capote *m (de torero)* cape.

capricho *m (antojo)* whim, caprice.

caprichoso, -a *adj* whimsical.

cápsula *f* capsule.

captar *vt (ondas)* to receive, to pick up; *(comprender)* to understand, to grasp; *(interés etc)* to attract.

captura *f* capture.

capturar vt (criminal) to capture; (cazar, pescar) to catch.

capucha f hood.

capullo m (de insecto) cocoon; (de flor) bud.

caqui 1 adj (color) khaki. **2** m (fruto) persimmon.

cara 1 f face; (lado) side; (de moneda) right side; fam (desfachatez) cheek, nerve; **c. a c.** face to face; **tener buena/mala c.** to look good/bad; **(de) c. a** with a view to; **echarle a algn algo en c.** to reproach sb for sth; **¿c. o cruz?** heads or tails?; **echar algo a c. o cruz** to flip (a coin) for sth; **¡qué c. (más dura) tienes!** you've got a lot of nerve! **2** m fam (desvergonzado) bold person.

caracol m (animal) snail; (cubierta) shell.

caracola f conch.

carácter m (pl caracteres) character; (índole) nature; **tener buen/mal c.** to be good-natured/bad-tempered.

característica f characteristic.

característico, -a adj characteristic.

caradura mf fam cheeky devil; **¡qué c. eres!** you're so cheeky!

caramba interj (sorpresa) good grief!; (enfado) damn it!

carámbano m icicle.

caramelo m (dulce) candy; (azúcar quemado) caramel.

caravana f caravan; (cola) hatchback.

carbón m coal; **c. vegetal** charcoal; **c. mineral** coal.

carbonizar [40] vt, **carbonizarse** vr to char.

carbono m carbon.

carburador m carburetor.

carburante m fuel.

carcajada f guffaw.

cárcel f prison, jail.

carcelero, -a mf warden.

cardenal m cardinal; (en la piel) bruise.

cardiaco, -a, cardíaco, -a adj cardiac, heart; **ataque c.** heart attack.

cardinal adj cardinal; **punto/número c.** cardinal point/number.

cardiólogo, -a mf cardiologist.

cardo m (con espinas) thistle.

carecer [33] vi **c. de** to lack.

carencia f lack (de of).

careta f mask; **c. antigás** gas mask.

carezco indic pres de carecer.

carga f (acción) loading; (cosa cargada) load; (de avión, barco) cargo, freight; (explosiva, eléctrica) charge; (obligación) burden.

cargado, -a adj loaded; (bebida) strong; **un café c.** a strong coffee; **atmósfera cargada** stuffy atmosphere; **c. de deudas** full of debt.

cargamento m (carga) load; (mercancías) cargo, freight.

cargar [42] **1** vt to load; (mechero, pluma) to fill; (batería) to charge; **cárguelo a mi cuenta** charge it to my account. **2** vi **c. con** (llevar) to carry; **c. con las consecuencias** to suffer the consequences. **3** cargarse vr to load oneself with; fam (estropear) to smash, to ruin; fam (matar) to kill, to bump off.

cargo m (puesto) post, position; (persona) top person; (débito) charge, debit; (acusación) charge, accusation; **alto c.** (puesto) top job; **estar al c. de** to be in charge of; **correr a c. de** (gastos) to be met by; **hacerse c. de** to take charge of; **hazte c. de mi situación** please try to understand my situation; **con c. a mi cuenta** charged to my account.

cargoso, -a adj CSur annoying.

caricatura f caricature.

caricia f caress, stroke.

caridad f charity.

caries f inv decay, caries.

cariño m (amor) affection; (querido) darling; **coger/tener c. a algo/algn** to grow/to be fond of sth/sb; **con c.** (en carta) love.

cariñoso, -a *adj* loving, affectionate.

caritativo, -a *adj* charitable.

cariz *m* look.

carmín *m* (de color) c. carmine; c. (de labios) lipstick.

carnaval *m* carnival.

carne *f* flesh; *(alimento)* meat; **ser de c. y hueso** to be only flesh and blood; **c. de gallina** goose pimples; **c. de cerdo/cordero/ternera/vaca** pork/lamb/veal/beef.

carné, carnet *m* card; **c. de conducir** driver's license; **c. de identidad** identity card.

carnero *m* ram; *(carne)* mutton.

carnicería *f* butcher's (shop).

caro, -a 1 *adj (precios)* expensive; *(querido)* dear. **2** *adv* **salir c.** to cost a lot; **te costará c.** *(amenaza)* you'll pay dearly for this.

carpa *f (pez)* carp; *(de circo)* big top, marquee; *Am (de camping)* tent.

carpeta *f* folder.

carpintería *f (oficio)* carpentry; *(taller)* carpenter's (shop).

carpintero, -a *mf* carpenter.

carraspear *vi* to clear one's throat.

carrera *f* run; *(de media)* run, ladder; *(competición)* race; *(estudios)* degree; *(profesión)* career, profession; **c. de coches** rally, meeting; **echar una c. a algn** to race sb.

carrerilla *f* **tomar c.** to take a run; **de c.** parrot fashion.

carreta *f* cart.

carrete *m (de hilo)* reel; *(de película)* spool.

carretera *f* road; **c. de circunvalación** bypass; **c. de acceso** access road; *Méx* **c. de cuota** toll road.

carretilla *f* wheelbarrow.

carril *m (de trenes)* rail; *(de carretera)* lane.

carrillo *m* cheek.

carriola *f* *Méx (de bebé)* baby carriage.

carro *m (carreta)* cart; *(de máquina de escribir)* carriage; *Andes, CAm,*

Carib, Méx car; **c. de combate** tank.

carrocería *f* bodywork.

carta *f* letter; *(menú)* menu; *(de baraja)* card; **c. certificada/urgente** registered/express letter; **a la c.** à la carte; **c. de vinos** wine list; **tomar cartas en un asunto** to take part in an affair.

cartel *m* poster.

cartera *f (de bolsillo)* wallet; *(para documentos)* briefcase; *(de colegial)* satchel, schoolbag; *Andes, RP (de mujer)* purse.

cartero, -a *mf (hombre)* postman; *(mujer)* postwoman.

cartilla *f (libreta)* book; *(para leer)* first reader; **c. de ahorros** savings book.

cartón *m (material)* card, cardboard; *(de cigarrillos)* carton.

cartucho *m* cartridge; *(de papel)* cone.

cartulina *f* card.

casa *f (edificio)* house; *(hogar)* home; *(empresa)* company, firm; **c. de huéspedes** boarding house; **c. de socorro** first aid post.

casado, -a 1 *adj* married. **2** *mf* married person; **los recién casados** the newlyweds.

casamiento *m* marriage; *(boda)* wedding.

casar 1 *vt* to marry. **2 casarse** *vr* to marry, to get married.

cascabel *m* bell.

cascada *f* waterfall, cascade.

cascanueces *m inv* nutcracker.

cascar [44] *vt*, **cascarse** *vr* to crack.

cáscara *f* shell; *(de fruta)* skin, peel; *(de grano)* husk.

cascarón *m* eggshell.

casco *m* helmet; *(de caballo)* hoof; *(envase)* empty bottle; *(de barco)* hull; **c. urbano** city center; **cascos** *(auriculares)* headphones.

casero, -a 1 *adj (hecho en casa)* home-made; *(persona)* home-loving. **2** *mf (dueño) (hombre)* landlord; *(mujer)* landlady.

caseta f hut, booth; *(de feria, exposición)* stand, stall.

casete 1 m *(magnetófono)* cassette player o recorder. **2** f *(cinta)* cassette (tape).

casi adv almost, nearly; **c. nunca** hardly ever; **c. nadie** hardly anyone; **c. me caigo** I almost fell.

casino m casino.

caso m case; **el c. es que ...** the thing is that ...; **el c. Mattei** the Mattei affair; **(en) c. contrario** otherwise; **en c. de necesidad** if need be; **en cualquier c.** in any case; **en el mejor/peor de los casos** at best/worst; **en ese c.** in such a case; **en todo c.** in any case; **hacer c. a** o **de algn** to pay attention to sb; **no venir al c.** to be beside the point; **pongamos por c.** let's say.

caspa f dandruff.

cassette m o f = **casete**.

castaña f chestnut.

castaño, -a 1 adj chestnut-brown; *(pelo, ojos)* brown, dark. **2** m *(árbol)* chestnut.

castellano, -a 1 adj Castilian. **2** mf *(persona)* Castilian. **3** m *(idioma)* Spanish, Castilian.

castigar [42] vt to punish; *(penalizar)* to penalize.

castigo m punishment; *(pena)* penalty.

castillo m castle.

casual adj accidental, chance.

casualidad f chance, coincidence; **de** o **por c.** by chance; **dio la c. de que ...** it so happened that ...; **¿tienes un lápiz, por c.?** do you happen to have a pencil?; **¡que c.!** what a coincidence!

casualmente adv by chance.

cataclismo m cataclysm.

catalejo m telescope.

catalogar [42] vt to catalog; *(clasificar)* to classify.

catálogo m catalog.

catapulta f catapult.

catarata f waterfall; *(enfermedad)* cataract.

catarro m (common) cold.

catástrofe f catastrophe.

catecismo m catechism.

cátedra f *(universidad)* chair.

catedral f cathedral.

catedrático, -a mf *(de universidad)* professor; *(de instituto)* head of department.

categoría f category; **de c.** *(persona)* important.

cateto, -a mf *(paleto)* yokel, bumpkin.

católico, -a adj & mf Catholic.

catorce adj & m inv fourteen.

cauce m *(de un río)* bed; *fig* channel.

caucho m rubber; Am *(cubierta)* tire.

caudal m *(de un río)* flow; *(riqueza)* wealth.

caudillo m leader, head.

causa f cause; **a** o **por c. de** because of.

causante 1 adj causal. **2** mf **el c. del incendio** the person who caused the fire.

causar vt to cause; **c. buena/mala impresión** to make a good/bad impression.

cautela f caution.

cautivar vt to capture, to take prisoner.

cautiverio m, **cautividad** f captivity.

cautivo, -a adj & mf captive.

cava 1 f *(bodega)* wine cellar. **2** m *(vino espumoso)* champagne.

cavar vt to dig.

caverna f cave.

caviar m caviar.

cavidad f cavity.

cavilar vt to ponder.

cayado m *(de pastor)* crook.

caza f hunting; *(animales)* game; *(persecución)* hunt; **ir de c.** to go hunting; **c. furtiva** poaching; **c. mayor/menor** big/small game.

cazador, -a mf hunter.

cazadora f (waist-length) jacket.

cazar [40] vt to hunt.

cazo m *(cacerola)* saucepan; *(cucharón)* ladle.

cazuela f saucepan; *(guiso)* casserole, stew; **a la c.** stewed.

cebada f barley.

cebo m bait.

cebolla f onion.

cebolleta f spring onion.

cebra f zebra; **paso de c.** crosswalk.

cecear vi to lisp.

ceder 1 vt to give, to hand over; **c. el paso** to give way. **2** vi *(cuerda, cable)* to give way; *(consentir)* to give in.

cédula f document, certificate; **c. de identidad** identity card.

cegar [1] vt to blind; *(puerta, ventana)* to wall up.

ceguera f blindness.

ceja f eyebrow.

celador, -a mf attendant; *(de cárcel)* warder.

celda f cell.

celebración f *(festejo)* celebration; *(de juicio etc)* holding.

celebrar 1 vt to celebrate; *(reunión, juicio, elecciones)* to hold. **2 celebrarse** vr to take place, be held.

célebre adj famous, well-known.

celeste 1 adj *(de cielo)* celestial; *(color)* sky-blue. **2** m sky blue.

celibato m celibacy.

celo m zeal; **en c.** *(macho)* in rut; *(hembra)* in heat; **celos** jealousy sing; **tener celos (de algn)** to be jealous (of sb).

celo® m Scotch tape®.

celofán m cellophane.

celoso, -a adj jealous.

célula f cell.

celular 1 adj cellular; **coche c.** police van; Am **teléfono c.** cellphone, mobile phone. **2** m Am cellphone, mobile.

celulitis f inv cellulite.

cementerio m cemetery.

cemento m cement; *(hormigón)* concrete.

cena f dinner.

cenar 1 vi to have dinner. **2** vt to have for dinner.

cenicero m ashtray.

cenit m zenith.

ceniza f ash.

censo m census; **c. electoral** electoral roll.

censura f censorship; **moción de c.** vote of no confidence.

censurar vt *(libro, película)* to censor.

centavo m Am cent.

centellear vi to flash, sparkle.

centena f, **centenar** m hundred.

centenario m centenary.

centeno m rye.

centésimo, -a adj & mf hundredth.

centígrado, -a adj centigrade.

centilitro m centiliter.

centímetro m centimeter.

céntimo m cent.

centinela m sentry.

centollo m spider crab.

central 1 adj central. **2** f *(oficina principal)* head office; **c. nuclear/térmica** nuclear/coal-fired power station.

centralismo m centralism.

centralita f switchboard.

centralizar [40] vt to centralize.

centrar 1 vt to center; *(esfuerzos, atención)* to concentrate, to center *(en* on). **2 centrarse** vr to be centered o based; *(concentrarse)* to concentrate *(en* on).

céntrico, -a adj centrally situated.

centrifugar [42] vt *(ropa)* to spin-dry.

centro m center; **c. de la ciudad** city center; **c. comercial** shopping center, mall.

ceñido, -a adj tight-fitting, clinging.

ceñirse [6] vr *(prenda)* to cling *(a* to); *(atenerse, limitarse)* to limit oneself *(a* to); **c. al tema** to keep to the subject.

cepillar vt, **cepillarse** vr to brush.

cepillo m brush; *(en carpintería)* plane; **c. de dientes** toothbrush;

c. del pelo hairbrush.

cera f wax; *(de abeja)* beeswax.

cerámica f ceramics *sing.*

cerca[1] **1** *adv* near, close; **de c.** closely. **2** *prep* **c. de** *(al lado de)* near, close to; *(casi)* nearby, around; **el colegio está c. de mi casa** the school is near my house; **c. de cien personas** about one hundred people.

cerca[2] f enclosure.

cercanía f proximity, nearness; **cercanías** outskirts, suburbs; **(tren de) c.** suburban train.

cercano, -a *adj* nearby; **el C. Oriente** the Near East.

cercar [44] *vt (tapiar)* to fence, enclose; *(rodear)* to surround.

cerdo m pig; *(carne)* pork.

cereal m cereal.

cerebro m brain; *(inteligencia)* brains *pl.*

ceremonia f ceremony.

cereza f cherry.

cerezo m cherry tree.

cerilla f match.

cero m zero; *(en resultado)* nil; **ser un c. a la izquierda** to be useless.

cerrado, -a *adj* closed, shut; *(intransigente)* uncompromising; *(acento)* broad; *(curva)* sharp.

cerradura f lock.

cerrar [1] **1** *vt* to shut, to close; *(grifo, gas)* to turn off; *(cremallera)* to do up; *(negocio)* to close down; *(cuenta)* to close; *(sobre)* to seal; **c. con llave** to lock; **c. el paso a algn** to block sb's way. **2** *vi* to close, to shut. **3 cerrarse** *vr* to close, to shut.

cerril *adj (obstinado)* pig-headed, headstrong.

cerro m hill.

cerrojo m bolt; **echar el c. (de una puerta)** to bolt (a door).

certamen m competition, contest.

certeza, certidumbre f certainty; **tener la c. de que ...** to be certain that ....

certificado, -a 1 *adj* certified; *(correo)* registered. **2** m certificate; **c.**

médico medical certificate.

cervecería f *(bar)* pub, bar; *(fábrica)* brewery.

cerveza f beer; **c. de barril** draft beer; **c. negra** stout.

cesar 1 *vi* to stop, cease (**de -**); **sin c.** incessantly. **2** *vt (empleado)* to dismiss.

cese m cessation, suspension; *(despido)* dismissal.

césped m lawn, grass.

cesta f basket.

cesto m basket.

ceviche m = raw fish marinated in lemon and garlic.

chabola f shack.

chacal m jackal.

chacinería f pork butcher's shop.

chacra f *Andes, RP* small farm.

chafar *vt fam (plan etc)* to ruin; *(aplastar)* to squash.

chal m shawl.

chalado, -a *adj fam* crazy, nuts (**por** about).

chalé m *(pl* chalés*)* villa.

chaleco m vest; *(de punto)* sleeveless pullover; **c. salvavidas** life jacket.

chalet m villa.

chalupa f *(embarcación)* boat, launch; *Méx (torta)* = small tortilla with a raised rim to contain a filling.

chamaco, -a *mf Méx fam* kid.

champán, champaña m champagne.

champiñón m mushroom.

champú m shampoo.

chamuscar [44] *vt* to singe, scorch.

chancaca f *CAm* syrup cake.

chance m *Am* opportunity.

chancear *vi* to joke, horse around.

chanchada f *Am fam* dirty trick.

chancho, -a *mf Am* pig.

chancla f flipflop.

chándal m track suit, jogging suit.

chantaje m blackmail; **hacer c. a algn** to blackmail sb.

chantajear *vt* to blackmail

chantajista *mf* blackmailer.

chapa f (de metal) sheet; (tapón) bottle top, cap; (de adorno) badge; Col (cerradura) lock.

chapado, -a adj (metal) plated; **c. en oro** gold-plated.

chaparrón m downpour, heavy shower.

chapotear vi to splash about, to paddle.

chapucero, -a adj fam (trabajo) slapdash, shoddy; (persona) bungling.

chapurrear vt (idioma) to speak badly.

chapuza f fam (trabajo mal hecho) shoddy piece of work; (trabajo ocasional) odd job.

chapuzón m (baño corto) dip; **darse un c.** to have a dip.

chaqueta f jacket.

charca f pond, pool.

charco m puddle.

charcutería f delicatessen.

charla f (conversación) talk, chat; (conferencia) informal lecture.

charlar vi to talk, to chat.

charlatán, -ana 1 adj (parlanchín) talkative. **2** mf (parlanchín) chatterbox; (embaucador) charlatan.

charol m patent leather.

chárter adj inv **vuelo c.** charter flight.

chasca f Andes (cabellera) mop of hair, tangled hair.

chasco m fam (decepción) disappointment; **llevarse un c.** to be disappointed.

chasis m inv chassis.

chasqui m Am messenger, courier.

chasquido m (de la lengua) click; (de los dedos) snap; (de látigo, madera) crack.

chatarra f scrap (metal), scrap iron; (cosa inservible) junk.

chato, -a adj (nariz) snub; (persona) snub-nosed.

chauvinista adj & mf chauvinist.

chaval, -a mf (chico) boy, lad; (chica) girl, lass.

chavo, -a fam.**1** mf Méx (chico) guy; (chica) girl. **2** m (dinero) **no tener un c.** to be broke.

chepa f hump.

cheque m check; **c. de viaje** traveler's check.

chequeo m checkup.

chévere adj Andes, CAm, Carib, Méx fam great, fantastic.

chicano, -a adj & mf chicano.

chicha f Andes maize liquor.

chícharo m CAm, Méx pea.

chicharra f cicada.

chichón m bump, lump.

chicle m chewing gum.

chico, -a 1 mf (muchacho) boy, lad; (muchacha) girl, lass. **2** adj (pequeño) small, little.

chicote m Am whip.

chiflado, -a adj fam mad, crazy (por about).

chiflar vt (silbar) to hiss (at), to boo (at); fam **le chiflan las motos** he's really into motorbikes.

chiflido m whistle, whistling.

chillar vi (persona) to scream, to shriek; (ratón) to squeak.

chillido m (de persona) scream, shriek; (de ratón) squeak.

chillón, -ona adj (voz) shrill, highpitched; (sonido) harsh; (color) loud.

chimenea f fireplace, hearth; (conducto) chimney.

chincheta f thumbtack.

chinchín interj ¡c.! cheers!, (to) your (good) health!

chingana f Perú fam bar.

chip m (pl chips) chip.

chipirón m baby squid.

chiquillo, -a mf kid, youngster.

chirimoya f custard apple.

chiringuito m (en playa etc) refreshment stall; (en carretera) roadside snack bar.

chirriar [29] vi (puerta) to creak; (frenos) to screech.

chirrido m (de puerta) creak, creaking; (de frenos) screech.

chisme m (habladuría) piece of

gossip; *fam (trasto)* knick-knack; *(cosa)* thing.

chismear *vi* to gossip.

chismoso, -a 1 *adj (murmurador)* gossipy. **2** *mf* gossip.

chispa *f* spark.

chispear *vi* to spark; *(lloviznar)* to spit.

chiste *m* joke; **contar un c.** to tell a joke.

chistoso, -a *adj (persona)* funny, witty; *(anécdota)* funny, amusing.

chivatazo *m fam (soplo)* tip-off; **dar el c.** to squeal.

chivato, -a *mf fam (acusica)* telltale; *(delator)* grass.

chivo, -a *mf (animal)* kid, young goat; *fig* **c. expiatorio** scapegoat.

chocante *adj (sorprendente)* surprising; *(raro)* strange.

chocar [44] **1** *vi (topar)* to crash, to collide; *(pelota)* to hit, to strike; **c. con o contra** to run into, to collide with. **2** *vt* to knock; *(sorprender)* to surprise.

chochear *vi (viejo)* to be senile.

chocolate *m* chocolate.

chocolatina *f* bar of chocolate, chocolate bar.

chófer *m (pl* chóferes*)*, *Am* **chofer** *m (pl* choferes*)* driver; *(particular)* chauffeur.

chollo *m fam* bargain, snip.

chomba *f Arg* jumper, pullover.

chonta *f Am* palm tree.

chopo *m* poplar.

choque *m* impact; *(de coches etc)* crash, collision.

chorizo *m* highly-seasoned pork sausage.

choro *m Andes* mussel.

chorrear *vi* to gush, to spurt; *(gotear)* to drip, to trickle; *fam* **estoy chorreando** I am soaking wet.

chorro *m (de agua etc)* spurt; *(muy fino)* trickle; **salir a chorros** to gush forth.

chovinista 1 *adj* chauvinistic. **2** *mf* chauvinist.

choza *f* hut, shack.

chubasco *m* heavy shower, downpour.

chubasquero *m* raincoat.

chuchería *f fam* candy.

chuleta *f* chop, cutlet; **c. de cerdo** pork chop.

chulo, -a *fam* **1** *mf* show-off. **2** *adj (bonito)* smashing.

chupachup® *m* lollipop.

chupar 1 *vt* to suck; *(lamer)* to lick; *(absorber)* to soak up, to absorb. **2** *vi* to suck. **3 chuparse** *vr* **está para chuparse los dedos** it's really mouthwatering.

chupete *m* pacifier.

churrasco *m* barbecued meat.

churrete *m* dirty mark, grease spot.

churro *m* cruller.

chutar *vi (a gol)* to shoot.

cicatriz *f* scar.

cicatrizar [40] *vti* to heal.

ciclismo *m* cycling.

ciclista 1 *adj* cycling. **2** *mf* cyclist.

ciclo *m* cycle; *(de conferencias etc)* series.

ciclomotor *m* moped.

ciclón *m* cyclone.

ciego, -a 1 *adj* blind; **a ciegas** blindly. **2** *mf* blind person; **los ciegos** the blind *pl*.

cielo *m* sky; *(gloria)* heaven; *(de la boca)* roof.

ciempiés *m inv* centipede.

cien *adj & m inv* hundred; **c. libras** a o one hundred pounds; **c. por c.** one hundred per cent.

ciencia *f* science; **saber algo a c. cierta** to know something for certain; **c. ficción** science fiction.

ciento *adj* hundred; **c. tres** one hundred and three; **por c.** per cent.

científico, -a 1 *adj* scientific. **2** *mf* scientist.

cierre *m (acción)* closing, shutting; *(de fábrica)* shutdown; *(de emisión)* close-down; *(de bolso)* clasp; *(de puerta)* catch; *Am* **c. relámpago** zipper.

cierto, -a 1 *adj* certain; *(verdadero)* true; **lo c. es que ...** the fact is that ...; **por c.** by the way. **2** *adv* certainly.

ciervo, -a *mf* deer; *(macho)* stag; *(hembra)* doe, hind.

cifra *f (número)* figure, number; *(suma)* amount.

cigala *f* Norway lobster.

cigarra *f* cicada.

cigarrillo *m* cigarette.

cigarro *m (cigarrillo)* cigarette; *(puro)* cigar.

cigüeña *f* stork.

cilindro *m* cylinder.

cima *f* summit.

cimientos *mpl* foundations.

cinco *adj & m inv* five.

cincuenta *adj & m inv* fifty.

cine *m* movie theater; *(arte)* cinema.

cinematográfico, -a *adj* cinematographic; **la industria cinematográfica** the movie industry.

cínico, -a 1 *adj* shameless. **2** *mf* shameless person.

cinismo *m* shamelessness.

cinta *f (tira)* band, strip; *(para adornar)* ribbon; *(película)* film; **c. adhesiva/aislante** adhesive/insulating tape; **c. de vídeo** video tape; **c. transportadora** conveyor belt.

cintura *f* waist.

cinturón *m* belt; **c. de seguridad** safety belt.

ciprés *m* cypress.

circo *m* circus.

circuito *m* circuit.

circulación *f* circulation; *(tráfico)* traffic.

circular 1 *adj & f* circular. **2** *vi (moverse)* to circulate; *(líquido)* to flow; *(tren, autobús)* to run; *(rumor)* to go round.

círculo *m* circle.

circuncisión *f* circumcision.

circundante *adj* surrounding.

circunferencia *f* circumference.

circunscripción *f* district.

circunstancia *f* circumstance.

cirio *m* wax candle.

ciruela *f* plum; **c. claudia** greengage; **c. pasa** prune.

ciruelo *m* plum tree.

cirugía *f* surgery; **c. estética** *o* **plástica** plastic surgery.

cirujano, -a *mf* surgeon.

cisne *m* swan.

cisterna *f* cistern, tank.

cita *f* appointment; *(amorosa)* date; *(mención)* quotation.

citar *vt (mencionar)* to quote; **me ha citado el dentista** I have an appointment with the dentist.

cítrico, -a 1 *adj* citric, citrus. **2 cítricos** *mpl* citrus fruits.

ciudad *f* town; *(grande)* city.

ciudadano, -a 1 *mf* citizen. **2** *adj* civic.

cívico, -a *adj* civic.

civil *adj* civil; *(no militar)* civilian; **matrimonio c.** civil marriage.

civilización *f* civilization.

civilizado, -a *adj* civilized.

civismo *m* civility.

clamoroso, -a *adj* resounding.

clan *m* clan.

clandestino, -a *adj* clandestine.

clara *f (de huevo)* white.

claraboya *f* skylight.

clarear *vi (amanecer)* to dawn; *(despejar)* to clear up.

clarete *adj & m* claret.

claridad *f (luz)* brightness; *(inteligibilidad)* clarity; **con c.** clearly.

clarificar [44] *vt* to clarify.

clarinete *m* clarinet.

claro, -a 1 *adj* clear; *(líquido, salsa)* thin; *(color)* light. **2** *interj* of course!; **¡c. que no!** of course not!; **¡c. que sí!** certainly! **3** *m (en un bosque)* clearing; *(tiempo despejado)* bright spell. **4** *adv* clearly.

clase *f* class; *(tipo)* kind, sort; *(curso)* class; *(aula)* classroom; **c. alta/media** upper/middle class; **primera/segunda c.** first/second class; **toda c. de ...** all kinds of ....

clásico, -a 1 *adj* classical; *(típico, en el vestir)* classic. **2** *m* classic.

clasificación *f* classification; *(para campeonato, concurso)* qualification.

clasificar [44] **1** *vt* to classify, to class. **2 clasificarse** *vr* to qualify.

claustrofobia *f* claustrophobia.

cláusula *f* clause.

clausura *f (cierre)* closure.

clausurar *vt* to close.

clavar 1 *vt* to nail; *(clavo)* to hammer in; *(estaca)* to drive in. **2 clavarse** *vr* **clavarse una astilla** to get a splinter.

clave *f* key; **la palabra c.** the key word.

clavel *m* carnation.

clavícula *f* collarbone.

clavo *m* nail; *fig* **dar en el c.** to hit the nail on the head; *(especia)* clove.

claxon *m (pl* **cláxones)** horn; **tocar el c.** to sound the horn.

clemencia *f* mercy, clemency.

clementina *f* clementine.

clérigo *m* priest.

clero *m* clergy.

cliché *m (tópico)* cliché; *(negativo)* negative.

cliente *mf* customer, client.

clima *m* climate.

climatizado, -a *adj* air-conditioned.

climatizar [40] *vt* to air-condition.

clínica *f* clinic.

clip *m (para papel)* clip.

cloaca *f* sewer, drain.

cloro *m* chlorine.

cloroformo *m* chloroform.

club *m (pl* **clubs** *o* **clubes)** club; **c. náutico** yacht club.

coacción *f* coercion.

coalición *f* coalition.

coartada *f* alibi.

cobarde 1 *adj* cowardly. **2** *mf* coward.

cobaya *f* guinea pig.

cobertizo *m* shed, shack.

cobertor *m* bedspread.

cobija *f Am* blanket.

cobijar *vt*, **cobijarse** *vr* to shelter.

cobra *f* cobra.

cobrador, -a *mf (de autobús) (hombre)* conductor; *(mujer)* conductress; *(de luz, agua etc)* collector.

cobrar *vt (dinero)* to charge; *(cheque)* to cash; *(salario)* to earn; **c. importancia** to become important.

cobre *m (metal)* copper; *Am (moneda)* copper cent.

cobro *m (pago)* collecting; *(de cheque)* cashing; **llamada a c. revertido** collect call.

coca *f* coca.

cocaína *f* cocaine.

cocción *f* cooking; *(en agua)* boiling; *(en horno)* baking.

cocer [41] *vt*, **cocerse** *vr (comida)* to cook; *(hervir)* to boil; *(en horno)* to bake.

cochambroso, -a *adj* squalid.

coche *m* car; **en c.** by car; **c. de bomberos** fire engine; *(vagón)* carriage, coach; **c. cama** sleeper.

cochecito *m (de niño)* baby carriage.

cochera *f* garage; *(de autobuses)* depot.

cochino, -a 1 *mf (macho)* pig; *(hembra)* sow; *fig (persona)* pig. **2** *adj (sucio)* filthy.

cocido *m* stew.

cocina *f* kitchen; *(aparato)* cooker; *(arte)* cooking; **c. eléctrica/de gas** electric/gas cooker; **c. casera** home cooking.

cocinar *vt/i* to cook.

cocinero, -a *mf* cook.

coco *m* coconut.

cocodrilo *m* crocodile.

cocotero *m* coconut palm.

cóctel *m* cocktail.

codazo *m (señal)* nudge with one's elbow; *(golpe)* blow with one's elbow.

codicia *f* greed.

codicioso, -a 1 *adj* covetous. **2** *mf* greedy person.

código *m* code.

codo *m* elbow; *fam* **hablar por los codos** to talk nonstop.

coeficiente *m* **c. intelectual** IQ.

coetáneo, -a *adj & mf* contemporary.

coexistir *vi* to coexist.

cofre *m* trunk, chest.

coger [53] **1** *vt* to take; *(del suelo)* to pick (up); *(fruta, flores)* to pick; *(asir)* to seize, to take hold of; *(coche, bus)* to take, to catch; *(pelota, ladrón, resfriado)* to catch; *(atropellar)* to run over. **2 cogerse** *vr (agarrarse)* to hold on.

cogote *m* back of the neck.

cohabitar *vi* to live together, to cohabit.

coherente *adj* coherent.

cohete *m* rocket.

cohibido, -a *adj* inhibited.

cohibir 1 *vt* to inhibit. **2 cohibirse** *vr* to feel inhibited.

coincidencia *f* coincidence.

coincidir *vi* to coincide; *(concordar)* to agree; *(encontrarse)* to meet by chance.

cojear *vi (persona)* to limp; *(mesa etc)* to wobble.

cojín *m* cushion.

cojinete *m* bearing.

cojo, -a 1 *adj (persona)* lame; *(mueble)* rickety. **2** *mf* lame person.

col *f* cabbage; **c. de Bruselas** Brussels sprout.

cola¹ *f* tail; *(de vestido)* train; *(de pelo)* ponytail; *(fila)* line; **a la c.** at the back; **hacer c.** stand in line.

cola² *f* glue.

colaboración *f* collaboration.

colaborador, -a 1 *mf* collaborator. **2** *adj* collaborating.

colaborar *vi* to collaborate.

colada *f* wash, laundry; **hacer la c.** to do the washing.

colador *m* colander, sieve; *(de té, café)* strainer.

colapso *m* collapse; **c. circulatorio** traffic jam.

colar [2] **1** *vt (líquido)* to strain. **2 colarse** *vr* to slip in; *(a fiesta)* to gatecrash; *(en una cola)* to cut in line.

colcha *f* bedspread.

colchón *m* mattress.

colchoneta *f* air bed.

colección *f* collection.

coleccionar *vt* to collect.

colecta *f* collection.

colectivo, -a 1 *adj* collective. **2** *m (asociación)* association; *Andes (taxi)* long-distance taxi; *Arg (autobús)* bus.

colega *mf* colleague.

colegial, -a 1 *adj (escolar)* school. **2** *mf (alumno)* schoolboy; *(alumna)* schoolgirl; **los colegiales** the schoolchildren.

colegio *m (escuela)* school; **c. mayor** *o* **universitario** *(residencia)* residence hall.

cólera¹ *f* anger, rage.

cólera² *m (enfermedad)* cholera.

colesterol *m* cholesterol.

colgante 1 *m (joya)* pendant. **2** *adj* hanging.

colgar [2] **1** *vt* to hang (up); *(colada)* to hang (out); *(ahorcar)* to hang. **2** *vi* to hang *(de* from); *(teléfono)* to hang up. **3 colgarse** *vr (ahorcarse)* to hang oneself.

cólico *m* colic.

coliflor *f* cauliflower.

colilla *f* cigarette end.

colina *f* hill.

colindante *adj* adjoining, adjacent.

colirio *m* eyedrops.

colisión *f* collision, crash.

collar *m (adorno)* necklace; *(de perro)* collar.

colmado, -a *adj* full, filled; *(cucharada)* heaped.

colmena *f* beehive.

colmillo *m* eye tooth; *(de carnívoro)* fang; *(de jabalí, elefante)* tusk.

colmo *m* ¡eso es el c.! that's the last straw!; **para c.** to top it all off.

colocación *f (acto)* positioning; *(situación)* situation; *(empleo)* job.

colocar [44] **1** *vt* to place, to put; *(emplear)* to give work to. **2 colocarse** *vr (situarse)* to put oneself; *(emplearse)* to take a job *(de* as).

Colón *n* Columbus.

colonia¹ *f* colony; *(campamento)* summer camp; *Méx (barrio)* district.

colonia² *f (agua de colonia)* cologne.

colonial *adj* colonial.

colonizar [40] *vt* to colonize.

coloquio *m* discussion.

color *m* color; **de colores** multi-colored.

colorado, -a 1 *adj* red; **ponerse c.** to blush. **2** *m* red.

colorante *m* coloring.

colorear *vt* to color.

colorete *m* rouge.

colorido *m* color.

columna *f* column; **c. vertebral** spinal column.

columpio *m* swing.

coma¹ *f (ortográfica)* comma.

coma² *m (estado)* coma.

comadrona *f* midwife.

comandante *m* commander, commanding officer; *(de avión)* captain.

comarca *f* region.

combate *m* combat; *(de boxeo)* fight; *(batalla)* battle; **fuera de c.** out for the count.

combatir *vti* to fight.

combinación *f* combination; *(prenda)* slip.

combinar *vt*, **combinarse** *vr* to combine.

combustible 1 *m* fuel. **2** *adj* combustible.

comedia *f* comedy.

comedido, -a *adj* self-restrained, reserved.

comedor *m* dining room.

comentar *vt (escribir)* to comment on; *(discutir)* to discuss.

comentario *m* comment; **sin c.** no comment.

comentarista *mf* commentator.

comenzar [51] *vti* to begin, to start; **comenzó a llover** it started raining *o* to rain; **comenzó diciendo que …** he started by saying that ….

comer 1 *vti* to eat; **dar de c. a algn** to

feed sb. **2 comerse** *vr* to eat.

comercial *adj* commercial.

comercializar [40] *vt* to market.

comerciante *mf* merchant.

comerciar [43] *vi* to trade; **comercia con oro** he trades in gold.

comercio *m* commerce, trade; *(tienda)* shop.

comestible 1 *adj* edible. **2** *mpl* **comestibles** food *sing.*

cometa 1 *m* comet. **2** *f (juguete)* kite.

cometer *vt (error, falta)* to make; *(delito, crimen)* to commit.

cometido *m (tarea)* task, assignment; *(deber)* duty; **cumplir su c.** to do one's duty.

comezón *m* itch.

comicios *mpl* elections.

cómico, -a 1 *adj (divertido)* comical, funny; **actor c.** comedian. **2** *mf* comic; *(hombre)* comedian; *(mujer)* comedienne.

comida *f (alimento)* food; *(almuerzo, cena)* meal.

comienzo *m* beginning, start; **dar c. (a algo)** to start (sth).

comillas *fpl* inverted commas; **entre c.** in inverted commas.

comilón, -ona 1 *adj* greedy. **2** *mf* big eater.

comilona *f fam* big meal, feast.

comisaría *f* police station.

comisión *f (retribución)* commission; *(comité)* committee.

como 1 *adv (manera)* as; **hazlo c. quieras** do it however you like. ▪ *(comparación)* as; **blanco c. la nieve** as white as snow; **habla c. su padre** he talks like his father. ▪ *(según)* as; **c. decíamos ayer** as we were saying yesterday. ▪ *(en calidad de)* as; **lo compré c. recuerdo** I bought it as a souvenir. ▪ *(aproximadamente)* about; **c. unos diez** about ten. **2** *conj* **c. + subj** *(si)* if; **c. no estudies vas a suspender** if you don't study hard, you'll fail. ▪ *(porque)* as, since; **c. no venías me marché** as you didn't come I left. ▪ **c. si** as if; **c. si nada** o **tal cosa** as if nothing had happened.

cómo adv ¿**c.?** (¿perdón?) what? ▪ (interrogativo) how; ¿**c. estás?** how are you?; ¿**a c. están los tomates?** (a cuánto) how much are the tomatoes?; (por qué) ¿**es eso?** how come?; ¿**c. fue que no viniste a la fiesta?** how come you didn't come to the party? ▪ (exclamativo) how; ¡**c. has crecido!** you've really grown a lot!; ¡**c. no!** but of course!

cómoda f chest of drawers.

comodidad f comfort; (conveniencia) convenience.

comodín m joker.

cómodo, -a adj comfortable; (útil) handy, convenient.

compacto, -a adj compact; **disco c.** compact disc.

compadecer [33] **1** vt to feel sorry for, to pity. **2 compadecerse** vr to take pity (**de** on).

compadre m (padrino) godfather; Am fam (amigo) friend, mate.

compañero, -a mf companion; **c. de piso** roommate.

compañía f company; **hacer c. a algn** to keep sb company.

comparación f comparison; **en c.** comparatively; **en c. con** compared to; **sin c.** beyond compare.

comparar vt to compare (**con** with).

compartimento, compartimiento m compartment.

compartir vt to share.

compás m (pair of) compasses; (brújula) compass; (ritmo) rhythm; **al c. de** in time to.

compasión f compassion, pity; **tener c. de algn** to feel sorry for sb.

compasivo, -a adj compassionate.

compatible adj compatible.

compatriota mf compatriot; (hombre) fellow countryman; (mujer) fellow countrywoman.

compensar 1 vt (pérdida, error) to make up for; (indemnizar) to compensate (for). **2** vi to be worthwhile.

competencia f (rivalidad, empresas rivales) competition; (capacidad) competence; (incumbencia) field.

competente adj competent.

competición f competition.

competir [6] vi to compete.

competitivo, -a adj competitive.

compinche mf (cómplice) accomplice.

complacer [60] vt to please.

complejo, -a adj & m complex.

complemento m complement; (objeto) object.

completamente adv completely.

completar vt to complete.

completo, -a adj (terminado) complete; (lleno) full; **por c.** completely.

complicado, -a adj (complejo) complicated; (implicado) involved.

complicar [44] **1** vt to complicate; (involucrar) to involve (**en** in). **2 complicarse** vr to get complicated.

cómplice mf accomplice.

complot m (pl complots) conspiracy, plot.

componer [19] (pp compuesto) **1** vt to compose; (reparar) to mend, repair. **2 componerse** vr (consistir) to be made up (**de** of), consist (**de** of).

comportamiento m behavior.

composición f composition.

compota f compote.

compra f (acción) buying; (cosa comprada) purchase, buy; **ir de compras** to go shopping.

comprar vt to buy.

comprender vt (entender) to understand; (contener) to comprise, to include.

comprensión f understanding.

comprensivo, -a adj understanding.

compresa f (para mujer) sanitary napkin.

comprimido, -a 1 m tablet. **2** adj compressed.

comprobante m (de compra) voucher, receipt.

comprobar [2] *vt* to check.

comprometer 1 *vt (arriesgar)* to compromise; *(obligar)* to compel. **2 comprometerse** *vr (involucrarse)* to involve oneself; *(novios)* to become engaged; **comprometerse a hacer algo** to undertake to do sth.

compromiso *m (obligación)* obligation, commitment; *(acuerdo)* agreement; **por c.** out of a sense of duty; **poner a algn en un c.** to put sb in a difficult situation.

compuesto, -a 1 *adj* compound; **c. de** composed of. **2** *m* compound.

compuse *pt indef de* **componer**.

computadora *f* computer.

comulgar [42] *vi* to receive Holy Communion; *fig* **no comulgo con sus ideas** I don't share his ideas.

común *adj* common; *(compartido)* shared; **poco c.** unusual; **por lo c.** generally.

comuna *f Am (municipalidad)* municipality.

comunicación *f* communication; *(oficial)* communiqué; *(telefónica)* connection; *(unión)* link, connection.

comunicar [44] **1** *vt* to communicate; **comuníquenoslo lo antes posible** let us know as soon as possible. **2** *vi* to communicate; *(teléfono)* to be engaged. **3 comunicarse** *vr* to communicate.

comunidad *f* community; **C. Europea** European Community.

comunión *f* communion.

con *prep* with; **c. ese frío/niebla** in that cold/fog; **estar c. (la) gripe** to have the flu; **una bolsa c. dinero** a bag (full) of money; **habló c. todos** he spoke to everybody. ▪ *(con infinitivo)* **c. llamar será suficiente** it will be enough just to phone. ▪ *(con que + subj)* **bastará c. que lo esboces** a general idea will do; **c. tal (de) que ...** provided that ....

concebir [6] **1** *vt (plan, hijo)* to conceive; *(entender)* to understand.

2 *vi (mujer)* to conceive.

conceder *vt* to grant; *(premio)* to award; *(admitir)* to concede.

concejal, -a *mf* town councilor.

concentración *f* concentration; *(de manifestantes)* gathering.

concentrado *m* concentrate.

concentrar *vt*, **concentrarse** *vr* to concentrate (**en** on).

concepción *f* conception.

concepto *m* concept; **bajo/por ningún c.** under no circumstances.

concerniente *adj* concerning, regarding (**a** -); *fml* **en lo c. a** with regard to.

concernir [54] *v impers (afectar)* to concern; *(corresponder)* to be up to; **en lo que a mí concierne** as far as I am concerned; **en lo que concierne a** with regard/respect to.

concesión *f* concession; *(de premio, contrato)* awarding.

concha *f (caparazón)* shell; *(carey)* tortoiseshell.

conciencia *f* conscience; *(conocimiento)* consciousness, awareness; **a c.** conscientiously.

concienzudo, -a *adj* conscientious.

concierto *m* concert; *(composición)* concierto; *(acuerdo)* agreement.

conciso, -a *adj* concise.

concluir [37] *vt* to conclude.

conclusión *f* conclusion; **sacar una c.** to draw a conclusion.

concretamente *adv* specifically.

concretar *vt (precisar)* to specify, to state explicitly; *(fecha, hora)* to fix.

concreto, -a 1 *adj (preciso, real)* concrete; *(particular)* specific; **en c.** specifically. **2** *m Am* concrete.

concurrido, -a *adj* crowded, busy.

concursante *mf* contestant, competitor.

concursar *vi* to compete, to take part.

concurso *m (competición)* competition; *(de belleza etc)* contest; *(televisivo)* quiz show.

condecorar *vt* to decorate.

condena *f* sentence; *(desaprobación)* condemnation, disapproval.

condenado, -a 1 *adj* convicted; **c. a muerte** condemned to death. **2** *mf* convicted person; *(a muerte)* condemned person.

condenar *vt* to convict, find guilty; *(desaprobar)* to condemn.

condensado, -a *adj* condensed; **leche condensada** condensed milk.

condensar *vt*, **condensarse** *vr* to condense.

condición *f* condition; **en buenas/ malas condiciones** in good/bad condition; **con la c. de que ...** on condition that ....

condimentar *vt* to season, to flavor.

condimento *m* seasoning, flavoring.

condominio *m* *Am* *(edificio)* condominium.

condón *m* condom.

conducir [10] **1** *vt* *(coche)* to drive; *(electricidad)* to conduct. **2** *vi* to drive; *(llevar)* to lead; **permiso de c.** driver's license.

conducta *f* behavior, conduct.

conducto *m* *(tubería)* pipe.

conductor, -a *mf* driver.

conectar *vt* to connect up; *(enchufar)* to plug in, to switch on.

conejillo *m* **c. de Indias** guinea pig.

conejo *m* rabbit.

conexión *f* connection.

confección *f* dressmaking; *(de ropa masculina)* tailoring; *(de plan)* making.

conferencia *f* lecture; *(telefónica)* long-distance call.

confesar [1] **1** *vti* to confess. **2 confesarse** *vr* to confess; *(de pecados)* to go to confession; **confesarse culpable** to admit one's guilt.

confiado, -a *adj (seguro)* self-confident; *(crédulo)* gullible, unsuspecting.

confianza *f (seguridad)* confidence;

tener c. en uno mismo to be self-confident; **de c.** reliable; **tener c. con algn** to be on intimate terms with sb.

confiar [29] **1** *vt (entregar)* to entrust; *(información, secreto)* to confide. **2** *vi* **c. en** to trust; **no confíes en su ayuda** don't count on his help. **3 confiarse** *vr* to confide (en, a in).

confidencia *f* confidence.

confidencial *adj* confidential.

confidente, -a *mf (hombre)* confidant; *(mujer)* confidante; *(de la policía)* informer.

confirmar *vt* to confirm.

confiscar [44] *vt* to confiscate.

confitería *f* candy store; *CSur* café.

confitura *f* preserve, jam.

conflicto *m* conflict.

conformarse *vr* **tendrás que conformarte (con esto)** you will have to be content with that.

conforme 1 *adj (satisfecho)* satisfied; **no estoy c.** I don't agree. **2** *conj* as. **3** *prep* **c. a** in accordance with.

confort *m (pl* **conforts)** comfort.

confortable *adj* comfortable.

confrontación *f* confrontation.

confrontar *vt* to confront; *(comparar)* to compare, to collate.

confundir 1 *vt* to confuse (con with); *(engañar)* to mislead; **c. a una persona con otra** to mistake somebody for somebody else. **2 confundirse** *vr (equivocarse)* to be mistaken; *(mezclarse)* to mingle; *(colores, formas)* to blend.

confusión *f* confusion.

confuso, -a *adj* confused; *(formas, recuerdo)* vague.

congelado, -a 1 *adj* frozen. **2** *mpl* **congelados** frozen food *sing*.

congelador *m* freezer.

congelar 1 *vt* to freeze. **2 congelarse** *vr* to freeze.

congoja *f* sorrow, grief.

congreso *m* congress, conference; **c. de los Diputados** ≃ Congress.

congrio *m* conger eel.

conjugación *f* conjugation.

conjunción *f* conjunction.

conjunto, -a 1 *m (grupo)* collection, group; *(todo)* whole; *(pop)* group, band; *(prenda)* outfit; **de c.** overall; **en c.** on the whole. **2** *adj* joint.

conllevar *vt* to entail.

conmemoración *f* commemoration.

conmigo *pron pers* with me; **él habló c.** he talked to me.

conmoción *f* commotion, shock; **c. cerebral** concussion.

conmovedor, -a *adj* touching.

conmover [4] *vt* to touch, to move.

conmutador *m* switch; *Am* switchboard.

cono *m* cone.

conocedor, -a *adj & mf* expert; *(de vino, arte etc)* connoisseur.

conocer [34] **1** *vt* to know; *(por primera vez)* to meet; *(reconocer)* to recognize; **dar (algo/algn) a c.** to make (sth/sb) known. **2 conocerse** *vr (dos personas)* to know each other; *(por primera vez)* to meet.

conocido, -a 1 *adj* known; *(famoso)* well-known. **2** *mf* acquaintance.

conocimiento *m* knowledge; *(conciencia)* consciousness; **perder/ recobrar el c.** to lose/regain consciousness; **conocimientos** knowledge.

conquista *f* conquest.

conquistador, -a *mf* conqueror.

conquistar *vt (país, ciudad)* to conquer; **c. a algn** to make a conquest of sb.

consabido, -a *adj (bien conocido)* well-known; *(usual)* familiar, usual.

consagrar 1 *vt (artista)* to establish; *(vida, tiempo)* to devote. **2 consagrarse** *vr (dedicarse)* to devote oneself (a to); *(lograr fama)* to establish oneself.

consciente *adj* conscious.

consecuencia *f* consequence; *(coherencia)* consistency; **a o como c. de** as a consequence of; **en c.** therefore.

consecuente *adj* consistent.

consecutivo, -a *adj* consecutive; **tres días consecutivos** three days in a row.

conseguir [6] *vt* to get, to obtain; *(objetivo)* to achieve; *(lograr)* to manage.

consejero, -a *mf (asesor)* adviser; *(ministro)* regional minister.

consejo *m (recomendación)* advice; *(junta)* council; *(reunión)* cabinet meeting; **un c.** a piece of advice; **c. de ministros** cabinet; **c. de administración** board of directors.

consentido, -a *adj* spoiled.

consentimiento *m* consent.

consentir [5] **1** *vt (tolerar)* to allow, to permit; *(mimar)* to spoil; **no consientas que haga eso** don't allow him to do that. **2** *vi* to consent; **c. en** to agree to.

conserje *m (bedel)* janitor.

conserva *f* tinned o canned food.

conservador, -a *adj & mf* conservative; *(derechista)* Conservative.

conservante *m* preservative.

conservar 1 *vt* to conserve, to preserve; *(mantener)* to keep up; *(alimentos)* to preserve. **2 conservarse** *vr (tradición etc)* to survive.

conservatorio *m* conservatory.

considerado, -a *adj (atento)* considerate, thoughtful.

considerar *vt* to consider; **lo considero imposible** I think it's impossible.

consigna *f (para maletas)* checkroom.

consigo[1] *pron pers (tercera persona) (hombre)* with him; *(mujer)* with her; *(cosa, animal)* with it; *(plural)* with them; *(usted)* with you; **hablar c. mismo** to speak to oneself.

consigo[2] *indic pres de* **conseguir**.

consiguiente *adj* consequent; **por c.** therefore, consequently.

consistente adj (firme) firm, solid.

consistir vi to consist (en of).

consola f console.

consolar [2] **1** vt to console, to comfort. **2 consolarse** vr to console oneself.

consomé m clear soup, consommé.

consonante adj & f consonant.

consorte mf (cónyuge) partner, spouse.

conspiración f conspiracy, plot.

conspirar vi to conspire, to plot.

constancia f perseverance; (testimonio) proof, evidence.

constante 1 adj constant; (persona) steadfast. **2** f constant feature.

constantemente adv constantly.

constar vi (figurar) to figure in, be included (in); **me consta que ...** I am absolutely certain that ...; **c. de** (consistir) to consist of.

constatar vt to state; (comprobar) to check.

constipado, -a 1 adj **estar c.** to have a cold. **2** m cold.

constiparse vr to catch a cold.

constitución f constitution.

constituir [37] **1** vt (formar) to constitute; (suponer) to represent; (fundar) to constitute, to set up; **estar constituido por** to consist of. **2 constituirse** vr to set oneself up (en as).

construcción f construction; (sector) building industry.

constructor, -a 1 mf builder. **2** adj **empresa constructora** builders pl, construction company.

construir [37] vt to construct, to build.

consuelo m consolation.

cónsul mf consul.

consulado m consulate.

consulta f consultation; (médica) surgery; (despacho) consulting room; **horas de c.** surgery hours.

consultar vt to consult.

consultivo, -a adj consultative, advisory.

consultorio m (médico) medical center.

consumidor, -a 1 mf consumer. **2** adj consuming.

consumir 1 vt to consume. **2 consumirse** vr (agua, jugo) to boil away.

consumo m consumption; **bienes de c.** consumer goods; **sociedad de c.** consumer society.

contabilidad f (profesión) accountancy; (de empresa, sociedad) accounting.

contabilizar [40] vt (en contabilidad) to enter in the books; (en partido) to score.

contable mf accountant.

contactar vi **c. con** to contact.

contacto m contact; (en coche) ignition; **ponerse en c.** to get in touch.

contado, -a 1 adj (pocos) few and far between; **contadas veces** very seldom. **2** m **pagar al c.** to pay cash.

contador m meter.

contagiar [43] **1** vt (enfermedad) to pass on. **2 contagiarse** vr (enfermar) to get infected; (transmitirse) to be contagious.

contagio m contagion.

contagioso, -a adj contagious; (risa) infectious.

contaminación f contamination; (del aire) pollution.

contar [2] **1** vt (sumar) to count; (narrar) to tell. **2** vi to count; **c. con** (confiar en) to count on; (tener) to have.

contemplar vt to contemplate; (considerar) to consider.

contemporáneo, -a adj & mf contemporary.

contenedor m container.

contener [24] **1** vt to contain; (reprimir) to restrain, to hold back. **2 contenerse** vr to control oneself, to hold (oneself) back.

contenido m content, contents pl.

contentar 1 vt (satisfacer) to please; (alegrar) to cheer up. **2 contentarse**

contento, -a adj happy, pleased (con with).

contestación f answer.

contestador m c. **automático** answering machine.

contestar vt to answer.

contienda f struggle.

contigo pron pers with you.

contiguo, -a adj adjoining.

continente m continent.

continuación f continuation; **a c.** next.

continuamente adv continuously.

continuar [30] vti to continue.

continuo, -a adj continuous; (reiterado) continual, constant.

contra 1 prep against; **en c. de** against. **2** mpl **los pros y los contras** the pros and cons.

contrabajo m double bass.

contrabandista mf smuggler; **c. de armas** gunrunner.

contrabando m smuggling; **pasar algo de c.** to smuggle sth in.

contracción f contraction.

contracepción f contraception.

contracorriente 1 f crosscurrent. **2** adv **ir (a) c.** to go against the tide.

contradecir [12] (pp **contradicho**) vt to contradict.

contradicción f contradiction.

contraer [25] **1** vt to contract; **c. matrimonio** to get married. **2 contraerse** vr to contract.

contraigo indic pres de **contraer**.

contraje pt indef de **contraer**.

contramano: a contramano adv in the wrong direction, the wrong way.

contrapeso m counterweight.

contraproducente adj counterproductive.

contrariamente adv **c. a** ... contrary to ....

contrariar [29] vt (oponerse a) to oppose, to go against; (disgustar) to upset.

contrariedad f (contratiempo) obstacle, setback; (decepción) annoyance.

contrario, -a 1 adj opposite; **en el lado/sentido c.** on the other side/in the other direction; **al c., por el c.** on the contrary; **de lo c.** otherwise; **todo lo c.** quite the opposite. **2** mf opponent, rival. **3** f **llevar la contraria** to be contrary.

contrarrestar vt to offset, to counteract.

contraseña f password.

contrastar vt to contrast (con with).

contraste m contrast.

contratar vt (empleado) to hire, to engage.

contratiempo m setback, hitch.

contratista mf contractor.

contrato m contract.

contraventana f shutter.

contribución f contribution; (impuesto) tax.

contribuir [37] vti to contribute (a to).

contribuyente mf taxpayer.

contrincante mf rival, opponent.

control m control; (inspección) check; (de policía etc) checkpoint; **c. remoto** remote control.

controlador, -a mf **c. (aéreo)** air traffic controller.

controlar 1 vt to control. **2 controlarse** vr to control oneself.

controversia f controversy.

contundente adj (arma) blunt; (argumento) forceful, convincing.

contusión f contusion, bruise.

convalecencia f convalescence.

convalidar vt to validate; (documento) to ratify.

convencer [49] vt to convince; **c. a algn de algo** to convince sb about sth.

convencional adj conventional.

conveniencia f (provecho) convenience; **conveniencias sociales** social proprieties.

conveniente *adj (oportuno)* convenient; *(aconsejable)* advisable; *(precio)* good, fair.

convenio *m* agreement.

convenir [27] *vti (acordar)* to agree; *(ser oportuno)* to suit, to be good for; **c. en** to agree on; **conviene recordar que** it's as well to remember that.

convento *m (de monjas)* convent.

conversación *f* conversation.

conversar *vi* to converse, to talk.

conversión *f* conversion.

convertir [54] **1** *vt* to change, to convert. **2 convertirse** *vr* convertirse en to turn into, to become.

convicción *f* conviction.

convidado, -a *adj* & *mf* guest.

convidar *vt* to invite.

convivencia *f* life together.

convivir *vi* to live together.

convocar [44] *vt* to summon; *(reunión, elecciones)* to call.

convocatoria *f (a huelga etc)* call.

convulsión *f* convulsion.

conyugal *adj* conjugal; **vida c.** married life.

cónyuge *mf* spouse; **cónyuges** married couple *sing*, husband and wife.

coñac *m* brandy, cognac.

cooperación *f* co-operation.

cooperar *vi* to co-operate (**a, en** in; **con** with).

cooperativa *f* co-operative.

coordenada *f* co-ordinate.

coordinar *vt* to co-ordinate.

copa *f* glass; *(de árbol)* top; *(premio)* cup; **tomar una c.** to have a drink.

copia *f* copy; **c. de seguridad** *(archivo)* backup; **hacer una c. de seguridad de algo** to back up sth.

copiar [43] *vt* to copy.

copla *f* verse, couplet.

copo *m* flake; **c. de nieve** snowflake; **copos de maíz** cornflakes.

coquetear *vi* to flirt.

coqueto, -a *adj* coquettish.

coraje *m (valor)* courage; *(ira)* anger, annoyance.

coral¹ *m* coral.

coral² *f (composición)* choral, chorale.

Corán *m* Koran.

coraza *f* armor.

corazón *m* heart; *(de fruta)* core; **tener buen c.** to be kind-hearted.

corazonada *f* hunch, feeling.

corbata *f* necktie.

corcho *m* cork; *(de pesca)* float.

cordel *m* rope, cord.

cordero, -a *mf* lamb.

cordial *adj* cordial, warm.

cordillera *f* mountain range.

cordón *m* string; *(de zapatos)* shoelace.

cordura *f* common sense.

cornada *f (de toro)* goring.

córner *m* corner (kick).

corneta *f* bugle.

cornisa *f* cornice.

coro *m (musical)* choir; *(en tragedia)* chorus; **a c.** all together.

corona *f* crown; *(de flores etc)* wreath, garland.

coronación *f* coronation.

coronel *m* colonel.

coronilla *f* crown of the head; *fam* **estar hasta la c.** to be fed up (**de** with).

corporación *f* corporation.

corporal *adj* corporal; **olor c.** body odor, BO.

corpulento, -a *adj* corpulent, stout.

corral *m* corral.

correa *f (tira)* strap; *(de pantalón)* belt; *(de perro)* lead, leash; *(de motor)* belt.

corrección *f (rectificación)* correction; *(educación)* courtesy, politeness.

correcto, -a *adj (sin errores)* correct; *(educado)* polite, courteous (**con** to); *(conducta)* proper.

corredizo, -a *adj (puerta etc)* sliding; **nudo c.** slipknot.

corredor, -a *mf (deportista)* runner; *(balconada)* gallery.

corregir [58] **1** vt to correct. **2 corregirse** vr (persona) to mend one's ways.

correo m post, mail; **echar al c.** to post; **por c.** by post; **correos** (edificio) post office sing; **c. aéreo** airmail; **c. certificado** registered post; **c. electrónico** electronic mail, e-mail; **me envió un c. (electrónico)** (un mensaje) she e-mailed me, she sent me an e-mail.

correr 1 vi to run; (coche) to go fast; (conductor) to drive fast; (viento) to blow; **c. prisa** to be urgent. **2** vt (cortina) to draw; (cerrojo) to close; (mover) to pull up, to draw up; **c. el riesgo** to run the risk. **2 correrse** vr (moverse) to move over.

correspondencia f correspondence.

corresponder 1 vi to correspond (a to; **con** with); (ajustarse) to go (**con** with); (incumbir) to concern; (pertenecer) to be one's due; **me dieron lo que me correspondía** they gave me my share. **2 corresponderse** vr (ajustarse) to correspond; (dos cosas) to tally; **no se corresponde con la descripción** it does not match the description.

correspondiente adj corresponding (**a** to).

corresponsal mf correspondent.

corrida f **c. (de toros)** bullfight.

corriente 1 adj (común) common; (agua) running; (mes, año) current, present; (cuenta) current; **estar al c.** to be up to date. **2** f current, stream; (de aire) draft; (tendencia) trend, current; fam **seguirle** o **llevarle la c. a algn** to humor sb; **c. (eléctrica)** (electric) current.

corrijo indic pres de **corregir**.

corro m circle, ring; (juego) ring-a-ring-a-roses.

corroborar vt to corroborate.

corromper 1 vt to rot. **2 corromperse** vr to go bad, to rot.

corrosivo, -a adj (sustancia) corrosive; fig (comentario) caustic.

corrupción f corruption.

corrupto, -a adj corrupt.

cortacésped m o f lawnmower.

cortado, -a 1 adj cut (up); (leche) sour; (labios) chapped; fam (tímido) shy. **2** m small coffee with a dash of milk.

cortar 1 vt to cut; (carne) to carve; (árbol) to cut down; (piel) to chap, to crack; (luz, teléfono) to cut off; (paso, carretera) to block. **2 cortarse** vr (herirse) to cut oneself; (leche etc) to curdle; **cortarse el pelo** to have one's hair cut; **se cortó la comunicación** we were cut off.

corte m cut; (sección) section; **c. de pelo** haircut.

cortés adj courteous, polite.

cortesía f courtesy, politeness.

corteza f (de árbol) bark; (de queso) rind; (de pan) crust.

cortijo m Andalusian farmhouse.

cortina f curtain.

corto, -a adj (distancia, tiempo) short; **c. de vista** short-sighted; **luz corta** dipped headlights pl; **quedarse c.** (calcular mal) to underestimate.

cortocircuito m short circuit.

cosa f thing; (asunto) matter, business; **eso es c. tuya** that's your business; **eso es otra c.** that's different; **hace c. de una hora** about an hour ago.

coscorrón m knock on the head.

cosecha f harvest, crop; (año del vino) vintage.

coser vt to sew.

cosmético, -a adj & m cosmetic.

cosmonauta mf cosmonaut.

coso m (taurino) bullring; CSur fam (objeto) whatnot, thing.

cosquillas fpl **hacer c. a algn** to tickle sb; **tener c.** to be ticklish.

costa f coast; (litoral) coastline; (playa) beach, seaside.

costado m (lado) side; **de c.** sideways.

costar [2] vi to cost; **¿cuánto cuesta?** how much is it?; **c. barato/caro**

to be cheap/expensive; **c. trabajo** o **mucho** to be hard; **me cuesta hablar francés** I find it hard to speak French.

coste m cost; **c. de la vida** cost of living.

costear 1 vt to afford, to pay for. **2 costearse** vr to pay for.

costilla f (hueso) rib; (chuleta) cutlet.

costo m cost.

costoso, -a adj costly, expensive.

costra f crust; (de herida) scab.

costumbre f (hábito) habit; (tradición) custom; **como de c.** as usual; **tengo la c. de levantarme temprano** I usually get up early; **tenía la c. de ...** he used to ....

costura f sewing; (confección) dressmaking; (línea de puntadas) seam; **alta c.** haute couture.

costurero m sewing basket.

cotidiano, -a adj daily.

cotilla mf fam busybody, gossip.

cotillear vi fam to gossip (de about).

cotilleo m fam gossip.

cotización f (market) price, quotation.

coto m enclosure; **c. de caza** game reserve.

cotorra f parrot; (persona) chatterbox.

coz f kick.

cráneo m cranium, skull.

cráter m crater.

creación f creation.

crear vt to create.

creativo, -a adj creative.

crecer [33] vi to grow.

crecimiento m growth.

credencial adj credential; **cartas credenciales** credentials.

crédito m credit; **dar c. a** to believe.

creencia f belief.

creer [36] **1** vt to believe; (pensar) to think; **creo que no** I don't think so; **creo que sí** I think so; **ya lo creo** I should think so. **2** vi to believe. **3 creerse** vr **se cree guapo** he thinks he's good-looking.

creíble adj credible, believable.

crema f cream.

cremallera f zipper.

crematorio m crematory.

cremoso, -a adj creamy.

crepe f pancake.

crepúsculo m twilight.

cresta f crest; (de gallo) comb.

cretino, -a 1 adj stupid, cretinous. **2** mf cretin.

creyente mf believer.

crezco indic pres de **crecer**.

cría f (cachorro) young; (crianza) breeding.

criada f maid.

criado, -a 1 adj **mal c.** spoiled. **2** mf servant.

criar [29] vt (animales) to breed; (niños) to bring up.

criatura f (living) creature; (crío) baby, child.

criba f sieve.

crimen m (pl crímenes) crime.

criminal adj & mf criminal.

crin f, **crines** fpl mane sing.

crío, -a mf kid.

criollo, -a adj & mf Creole.

crisis f inv crisis; **c. nerviosa** nervous breakdown.

crispar vt to make tense; **me crispa los nervios** it makes me nervous.

cristal m crystal; (vidrio) glass; (de gafas) lens; (de ventana) (window) pane.

cristiano, -a adj & mf Christian.

Cristo m Christ.

criterio m (pauta) criterion; (opinión) opinion.

crítica f criticism; (reseña) review.

criticar [44] **1** vt to criticize. **2** vi (murmurar) to gossip.

crítico, -a 1 adj critical. **2** mf critic.

croissant m croissant.

crol m (en natación) crawl.

cromo m (metal) chromium, chrome; (estampa) picture card.

cromosoma m chromosome.

crónica f feature.

crónico, -a adj chronic.

cronológico, -a *adj* chronological.

cronometrar *vt* to time.

cronómetro *m* stopwatch.

croqueta *f* croquette.

croquis *m inv* sketch.

cruce *m* crossing; *(de carreteras)* crossroads.

crucero *m (viaje)* cruise; *(barco)* cruiser.

crucifijo *m* crucifix.

crucigrama *m* crossword (puzzle).

crudo, -a 1 *adj (natural)* raw; *(comida)* underdone; *(color)* cream. **2** *m (petróleo)* crude.

cruel *adj* cruel.

crueldad *f* cruelty.

crujiente *adj* crunchy.

crujir *vi (madera)* to creak; *(comida)* to crunch; *(hueso)* to crack.

cruz *f* cross; **C. Roja** Red Cross; **¿cara o c.?** ≃ heads or tails?

cruzado, -a *adj* crossed; *(atravesado)* lying across; **con los brazos cruzados** arms folded.

cruzar [40] **1** *vt* to cross; *(palabra, mirada)* to exchange. **2** *vi (atravesar)* to cross. **2 cruzarse** *vr* to cross; **cruzarse con algn** to pass sb.

cuaderno *m* notebook.

cuadra *f (establo)* stable; *Am* block (of houses).

cuadrado, -a *adj & m* square; **elevar (un número) al c.** to square (a number).

cuadriculado, -a *adj* **papel c.** squared paper.

cuadro *m* square; *(gráfico)* chart, graph; *(pintura)* painting, picture; **tela a cuadros** checked cloth; **c. de mandos** control panel.

cual *pron rel* **el/la c.** *(persona)* who; *(cosa)* which; **con el/la c.** with whom/which; **lo c.** which.

cuál 1 *pron interr* which (one)?; **¿c. quieres?** which one do you want? **2** *adj interr* which.

cualidad *f* quality.

cualquier *adj indef* any; **c. cosa**

anything; **en c. momento** at any moment.

cualquiera *(pl* cualesquiera*)* **1** *adj indef (indefinido)* any; *(corriente)* ordinary. **2** *pron indef (persona)* anybody, anyone; *(cosa, animal)* any one; **c. que sea** whatever it is.

cuando *adv & conj* when; **de c. en c., de vez en c.** from time to time; **c. quieras** whenever you want; **c. vengas** when you come; **(aun)** c. even if.

cuándo *adv interr* when; **¿desde c.?** since when; **¿para c. lo quieres?** when do you want it for?

cuanto, -a 1 *adj* **toma cuantos caramelos quieras** take all the sweets you want; **unas cuantas niñas** a few girls. **2** *pron rel* as much as; **coma (todo) c. quiera** eat as much as you want. **3** *pron indef pl* **unos cuantos** a few. **4** *adv (tiempo)* **c. antes** as soon as possible; **en c.** as soon as; **c. más … más** the more … the more; **en c. a** with respect to, regarding.

cuánto, -a 1 *adj & pron interr* how much; **¿cuántas veces?** how many times; **¿c. es?** how much is it? **2** *adv* how, how much; **¡cuánta gente hay!** what a lot of people there are!

cuarenta *adj & m inv* forty.

cuaresma *f* Lent.

cuartel *m (militar)* barracks *pl*; **c. general** headquarters.

cuartilla *f* sheet of paper.

cuarto, -a 1 *m (habitación)* room; *(cuarta parte)* quarter; **c. de baño** bathroom; **c. de estar** living room; **c. de hora** quarter of an hour. **2** *adj & m* fourth.

cuate *mf Méx fam* pal, buddy.

cuatro *adj & m inv* four.

cuatrocientos, -as *adj & mf* four hundred.

cubalibre *m* rum o gin and coke.

cubano, -a *adj & mf* Cuban.

cubata *m fam* cubalibre.

cubierta *f* cover; *(de rueda)* tire; *(de barco)* deck.

cubierto, -a 1 *adj* covered; *(piscina*

etc) indoor; *(cielo)* overcast. **2** *mpl* **cubiertos** cutlery *sing.*

cubo *m* bucket; *(en matemática)* cube; **c. de la basura** trash bin.

cubrecama *m* bedspread.

cubrir *(pp* **cubierto)** **1** *vt* to cover. **2 cubrirse** *vr (cielo)* to become overcast.

cucaracha *f* cockroach.

cuchara *f* spoon.

cucharada *f* spoonful.

cucharilla *f* teaspoon; **c. de café** coffee spoon.

cucharón *m* ladle.

cuchichear *vi* to whisper.

cuchilla *f* blade; **c. de afeitar** razor blade.

cuchillo *m* knife.

cuchitril *m fam* hovel, hole.

cuco *m* cuckoo.

cucurucho *m (de helado)* cornet; *(envoltorio)* paper cone.

cuello *m* neck; *(de camisa etc)* collar.

cuenco *m* bowl.

cuenta *f (factura)* check; *(de banco)* account; *(cálculo)* count; *(de collar)* bead; **caer en la c., darse c.** to realize; **tener en c.** to take into account; **traer c.** to be worthwhile; **en resumidas cuentas** in short; **trabajar por c. propia** to be self-employed.

cuentakilómetros *m inv (distancia)* ≃ milometer; *(velocidad)* speedometer.

cuento *m* story; **contar un c.** to tell a story; **c. de hadas** fairy story.

cuerda *f (cordel)* rope; *(de instrumento)* string; *(del reloj)* spring; **dar c. al reloj** to wind up a watch.

cuerdo, -a *adj* sane.

cuerno *m* horn; *(de ciervo)* antler; *fam* **¡vete al c.!** get lost!

cuero *m* leather; **chaqueta de c.** leather jacket; **c. cabelludo** scalp.

cuerpo *m* body; *(cadáver)* corpse; **c. de bomberos** fire brigade; **c. diplomático** diplomatic corps; **c. de policía** police force.

cuervo *m* raven.

cuesta *f* slope; **c. abajo** downhill; **c. arriba** uphill. **2 a cuestas** *adv* on one's back.

cuestión *f (asunto)* matter, question; *(pregunta)* question; **en c. de unas horas** in just a few hours.

cuestionario *m* questionnaire.

cueva *f* cave.

cuezo *indic pres de* **cocer.**

cuidado, -a **1** *adj* careful. **2 m** care; **con c.** carefully; **tener c.** to be careful; **estar al c. de** to be in charge of; *(persona)* to look after; **me trae sin c.** I couldn't care less; **cuidados intensivos** intensive care *sing.* **3** *interj* **¡c.!** look out!

cuidadoso, -a *adj* careful.

cuidar 1 *vt* to care for, to look after. **2 cuidarse** *vr* **cuídate** take care of yourself.

culebra *f* snake.

culebrón *m* soap opera.

culo *m fam (trasero)* backside; *(de recipiente)* bottom.

culpa *f* blame; *(culpabilidad)* guilt; **echar la c. a algn** to put the blame on sb; **fue c. mía** it was my fault; **por tu c.** because of you.

culpable **1** *adj* guilty; **declararse c.** to plead guilty. **2** *mf* offender, culprit.

culpar *vt* to blame; **c. a algn de un delito** to accuse sb of an offence.

cultivar *vt* to cultivate.

culto, -a **1** *adj* educated; *(palabra)* learned. **2 m** *(devoción)* worship; *(religión)* cult.

cultura *f* culture.

culturismo *m* body building.

cumbre *f (de montaña)* summit, top; **(conferencia) c.** summit conference.

cumpleaños *m inv* birthday; **¡feliz c.!** happy birthday!

cumplir 1 *vt* to carry out; *(deseo)* to fulfil; *(promesa)* to keep; **ayer cumplí veinte años** I was twenty (years old) yesterday. **2** *vi (plazo)* to expire, end; **c. con el deber** to do one's duty.

3 cumplirse vr (deseo) to come true; (plazo) to expire.

cuna f cot.

cundir vi (extenderse) to spread; **cundió el pánico** panic spread; **cundió la voz de que ...** rumor had it that ...; **me cunde mucho el trabajo o el tiempo** I seem to get a lot done.

cuneta f (de la carretera) gutter.

cuñado, -a mf (hombre) brother-in-law; (mujer) sister-in-law.

cuota f (de club etc) membership fees pl; (porción) quota, share; Méx **carretera de c.** toll road.

cupe pt indef de **caber**.

cupiera subj imperfecto de **caber**.

cupón m coupon, voucher.

cura 1 m (religioso) priest. **2** f (de enfermedad) cure.

curación f cure, treatment.

curandero, -a mf quack.

curar 1 vt to cure; (herida) to dress; (enfermedad) to treat. **2** vi, **curarse** vr (sanar) to recover, to get well; (herida) to heal up.

curiosidad f curiosity.

curioso, -a 1 adj (extraño) strange, odd; (indiscreto) curious, inquisitive. **2** mf (mirón) onlooker.

currículum m c. vitae curriculum vitae.

cursi adj posh.

cursillo m short course; **c. de reciclaje** refresher course.

curso m (año académico) year; (clase) class; (de acontecimientos, río) course; **en el c. de** in the course of; **moneda de c. legal** legal tender.

cursor m cursor.

curtir vt (cuero) to tan; (endurecer) to harden.

curva f curve; (en carretera) bend; **c. cerrada** sharp bend.

cutis m complexion.

cuyo, -a pron rel & pos (persona) whose; (de cosa) of which; **en c. caso** in which case.

D

D. abr de **don** Mister, Mr.

D.ª abr de **doña** Mrs; (señorita) Miss.

dactilar adj **huellas dactilares** fingerprints.

dado m dice.

dálmata mf Dalmatian.

dama f (señora) lady; **damas** (juego) checkers.

danés, -esa 1 adj Danish. **2** mf (persona) Dane. **3** m (idiom) Danish; **gran d.** (perro) Great Dane.

danza f dancing; (baile) dance.

dañar vt (cosa) to damage; (persona) to hurt, to harm.

dañino, -a adj harmful, damaging (**para** to).

daño m (a cosa) damage; (a persona) (físico) hurt; (perjuicio) harm.

dar [11] **1** vt to give; (noticia) to tell; (mano de pintura, cera) to apply; (fruto, flores) to bear; (beneficio, interés) to yield; (hora) to strike; **dale a la luz** switch the light on; **d. la mano a algn** (saludo) to shake hands with sb; **d. los buenos días/las buenas noches a algn** to say good morning/good evening to sb; **me da lo mismo** or **me da igual** it's all the same to me; **¿qué más da?** what difference does it make?; **d. de comer** to feed; **d. a conocer** (noticia) to release; **d. a entender que ...** to imply that ...; **d. por** (considerar) to consider; **d. por descontado/sabido** to take for granted. **2** vi **me dio un ataque de tos/risa** I had a coughing fit/an attack of the giggles; **d. a** (ventana, habitación) to overlook; (puerta) to open onto; **d. con la solución** to hit upon the solution; **d. de sí** (ropa) to stretch; **el presupuesto no da para más** the budget will not stretch any further; **d. que hablar** to get people talking. **3 darse** *vr* **se dio la circunstancia de que** it happened that; **se dio a la bebida** he started drinking; **darse con** *o* **contra** to bump into; **darse por satisfecho** to feel satisfied; **darse por vencido** to give in; **se le da bien/mal el francés** she's good/bad at French.

dardo *m* dart.

dársena *f* dock.

dátil *m* date.

dato *m* piece of information; **datos** *(de ordenador)* data.

d.C. *abr de* **después de Cristo** Anno Domini, AD.

dcha. *abr de* **derecha** right.

de *prep (pertenencia)* of; **el título de la novela** the title of the novel; **el coche/hermano de Sofía** Sofia's car/brother. ▪ *(procedencia)* from; **vino de Madrid** he came from Madrid. ▪ *(descripción)* **el niño de ojos azules** the boy with blue eyes; **una avenida de quince kilómetros** an avenue fifteen kilometres long; **una botella de litro** a liter bottle; **el señor de la chaqueta** the man in the jacket; **un reloj de oro** a gold watch. ▪ *(contenido)* of; **un saco de patatas** a sack of potatoes. ▪ *(oficio)* by, as; **trabaja de secretaria** she's working as a secretary. ▪ *(acerca de)* about; **curso de informática** computer course. ▪ *(tiempo)* **a las tres de la tarde** at three in the afternoon; **de día** by day; **de noche** at night; **de lunes a jueves** from Monday to Thursday; **de pequeño** as a child. ▪ *(con superlativo)* in; **el más largo de España** the longest in Spain. ▪ *(causa)* with, because of; **llorar de alegría** to cry with joy; **morir de hambre** to die of hunger. ▪ **de cuatro en cuatro** four at a time; **de semana en semana** every week.

debajo 1 *adv* underneath, below. **2** *prep* **d. de** under(neath); **por d. de lo normal** below normal.

debate *m* debate.

debatir 1 *vt* to debate. **2 debatirse** *vr* to struggle.

deber¹ *m* duty; *(en el colegio)* **deberes** homework *sing*.

deber² **1** *vt (dinero, explicación)* to owe. **2** *vi* **debe irse ahora** she has to leave now; **la factura debe pagarse mañana** the bill must be paid tomorrow; **deberías vistar a tus padres** you ought to visit your parents; **debería haber ido ayer** I should have gone yesterday; **no debiste hacerlo** you shouldn't have done it; **deben de estar fuera** they must be out. **3 deberse** *vr* **deberse a** to be due to.

debidamente *adv* duly.

debido, -a *adj* **d. a** due to.

débil *adj* weak; *(luz)* dim; **punto d.** weak spot.

debilitar 1 *vt* to weaken. **2 debilitarse** *vr* to weaken, to grow weak.

debutar *vi* to make one's debut.

década *f* **en la d. de los noventa** during the nineties.

decadencia *f* decadence.

decaer [39] *vi* to deteriorate.

decano, -a *mf* dean.

decena *f (about)* ten; **una d. de veces** (about) ten times; **por decenas** in tens.

decenio *m* decade.

decente *adj* decent; *(decoroso)* modest.

decepción *f* disappointment.

decepcionante *adj* disappointing.

decepcionar *vt* to disappoint.

decidido, -a *adj* determined.

decidir 1 *vti* to decide. **2 decidirse** *vr* **decidirse (a hacer algo)** to make up one's mind (to do sth); **decidirse por algo** to decide on sth.

décima *f* tenth.

decimal *adj & m* decimal.

décimo, -a 1 *adj & mf* tenth. **2** *m (parte)* tenth.

decir [12] *(pp* **dicho) 1** *vt* to say; **d. una mentira/la verdad** to tell a lie/the truth; **dígame** *(al teléfono)* hello; **esta película no me dice nada** this film doesn't appeal to me; **querer d.** to mean; *(locuciones)* **es d.** that is (to say); **por así decirlo** so to speak; **digamos** let's say; **digo yo** in my opinion; **ni que d. tiene** needless to say; **¡no me digas!** really! **2 decirse** *vr* **¿cómo se dice 'mesa' en inglés?** how do you say 'mesa' in English?; **se dice que ...** they say that ....

decisión *f* decision; *(resolución)* determination; **tomar una d.** to make a decision; **con d.** decisively.

decisivo, -a *adj* decisive.

declaración *f* declaration; **d. de (la) renta** tax return; *(afirmación)* statement; **hacer declaraciones** to comment.

declarar 1 *vt* to declare; *(afirmar)* to state; **d. la guerra a** to declare war on. **2** *vi (en juicio)* to testify. **3 declararse** *vr (guerra, incendio)* to break out; **declararse a favor/en contra de** to declare oneself in favor of/against; **declararse en huelga** to go on strike; **declararse a algn** to declare one's love for sb.

decoración *f* decoration.

decorador, -a *mf* decorator; *(en teatro)* set designer.

decorar *vt* to decorate.

decorativo, -a *adj* decorative.

decretar *vt* to decree.

decreto *m* decree.

decreto-ley *m* decree.

dedal *m* thimble.

dedicar [44] **1** *vt* to dedicate; *(tiempo, esfuerzos)* to devote (a to). **2 dedicarse** *vr* **¿a qué se dedica Vd.?** what do you do for a living?; **los fines de semana ella se dedica a pescar** on weekends she spends her time fishing.

dedicatoria *f* dedication.

dedo *m (de la mano)* finger; *(del pie)* toe; **d. anular/corazón/índice/meñique** ring/middle/index/little finger; **d. pulgar, d. gordo** thumb.

deducir [10] **1** *vt* to deduce. **2 deducirse** *vr* **de aquí se deduce que ...**

from this it follows that ....

defecar [44] *vi* to defecate.

defecto *m* defect.

defectuoso, -a *adj* defective.

defender [3] **1** *vt* to defend (**contra** against; **de** from). **2 defenderse** *vr* to defend oneself.

defensa 1 *f* defense; **en d. propia, en legítima d.** in self-defense. **2** *m (en equipo)* defender.

defensor, -a *mf* defender; **abogado d.** counsel for the defense; **el defensor del pueblo** the ombudsman.

deficiente 1 *adj* deficient. **2** *m (nota)* fail.

definición *f* definition.

definir *vt* to define.

definitivamente *adv (para siempre)* for good, once and for all; *(con toda seguridad)* definitely.

definitivo, -a *adj* definitive; **en definitiva** in short.

deformar 1 *vt* to deform; *(cara)* to disfigure; *(la verdad, una imagen)* to distort. **2 deformarse** *vr* to become distorted.

deforme *adj* deformed; *(objeto)* misshapen.

defraudar *vt* to disappoint; **d. a Hacienda** to evade taxes.

defunción *f* demise.

degenerado, -a *adj & mf* degenerate.

degenerar *vi* to degenerate.

degollar [2] *vt* to behead.

degradante *adj* degrading.

degradar *vt* to degrade.

degustación *f* tasting.

dejar 1 *vt* to leave; *(prestar)* to lend; *(abandonar)* to give up; *(permitir)* to let, to allow; **déjame en paz** leave me alone; **dejé el tabaco y la bebida** I gave up smoking and drinking; **d. caer** to drop; **d. entrar/salir** to let in/out; **d. triste** to make sad; **d. preocupado/sorprendido** to worry/surprise. **2** *v aux* **d. de + inf** to stop; *(renunciar)* to give up; **no deja de llamarme** she's always calling me. **3**

dejarse *vr* me he dejado las llaves **dentro** I've left the keys inside; **dejarse barba** to grow a beard; **dejarse llevar por** to be influenced by.

del *(contracción de* **de** + **el)** *ver* **de**.

delantal *m* apron.

delante 1 *adv* in front; **la entrada de d.** the front entrance; **por d.** in front; **se lo lleva todo por d.** he destroys everything in his path; **tiene toda la vida por d.** he has his whole life ahead of him. **2** *prep* **d. de** in front of; *(en serie)* ahead of.

delantero, -a 1 *adj* front. **2** *m (en fútbol)* forward; **d. centro** center forward.

delatar *vt* to inform against.

delegación *f (acto, delegados)* delegation; *(oficina)* local office.

delegado, -a *mf* delegate.

delegar [42] *vt* to delegate (**en** to).

deletrear *vt* to spell (out).

delfín *m* dolphin.

delgado, -a *adj* slim; *(capa)* fine.

deliberado, -a *adj* deliberate.

deliberar *vi* to deliberate (on).

delicadeza *f (finura)* daintiness; *(tacto)* tactfulness; **falta de d.** tactlessness.

delicado, -a *adj* delicate.

delicioso, -a *adj (comida)* delicious; *(agradable)* delightful.

delimitar *vt* to delimit.

delincuencia *f* crime.

delincuente *mf* criminal.

delineante *mf (hombre)* draftsman; *(mujer)* draftswoman.

delinquir [48] *vi* to break the law, to commit an offense.

delirar *vi* to be delirious.

delirio *m* delirium.

delito *m* crime.

delta *m* delta.

demacrado, -a *adj* emaciated.

demanda *f (judicial)* lawsuit.

demandar *vt* to sue.

demás 1 *adj* **los/las d.** the rest of. **2** *pron* **lo/los/las d.** the rest; **por lo d.** otherwise, apart from that.

demasiado, -a 1 *adj (singular)* too much; *(plural)* too many. **2** *adv* too (much); **es d. grande/caro** it is too big/dear; **fumas/trabajas d.** you smoke/work too much.

demencia *f* insanity.

democracia *f* democracy.

demócrata 1 *adj* democratic. **2** *mf* democrat.

democrático, -a *adj* democratic.

demográfico, -a *adj* demographic; **crecimiento d.** population growth.

demoledor, -a *adj* devastating.

demonio *m* devil.

demora *f* delay.

demorar 1 *vt* to delay, to hold up. **2 demorarse** *vr (retrasarse)* to be delayed, to be held up.

demostrar [2] *vt (mostrar)* to show; *(evidenciar)* to prove.

denegar [1] *vt* to refuse.

denigrante *adj* humiliating.

denominación *f* denomination.

denominar *vt* to name.

denotar *vt* to denote.

densidad *f* density.

denso, -a *adj* dense.

dentadura *f* teeth; **d. postiza** false teeth *pl*, dentures *pl*.

dental *adj* dental.

dentera *f* me da d. it sets my teeth on edge.

dentífrico, -a 1 *adj* pasta/crema **dentífrica** toothpaste. **2** *m* toothpaste.

dentista *mf* dentist.

dentro 1 *adv (en el interior)* inside; **aquí d.** in here; **por d.** (on the) inside. **2** *prep* **d. de** *(lugar)* inside; **d. de poco** shortly, soon; **d. de un mes** in a month's time.

denuncia *f (a la policía)* report; *(crítica)* denunciation.

denunciar [43] *vt (delito)* to report (**a** to).

departamento *m* department; *(territorial)* province; *Am (piso)* apartment.

depender *vi* to depend (**de** on); *(económicamente)* to be dependent (**de** on).

dependienta *f* shop assistant.

dependiente 1 *adj* dependent (**de** on). **2** *m* shop assistant.

depilación *f* depilation.

depilar *vt* to remove the hair from; *(cejas)* to pluck.

depilatorio, -a *adj & m* depilatory; **crema depilatoria** hair-remover.

deportar *vt* to deport.

deporte *m* sport; **hacer d.** to go out for sports.

deportista 1 *mf (hombre)* sportsman; *(mujer)* sportswoman. **2** *adj* sporty.

deportivo, -a 1 *adj* sports; **club d./ chaqueta deportiva** sports club/ jacket. **2** *m (coche)* sports car.

depositar 1 *vt (colocar)* to put. **2 depositarse** *vr* to settle.

depósito *m (dinero)* deposit; *(de agua, gasolina)* tank.

depresión *f* depression.

deprimente *adj* depressing.

deprimir 1 *vt* to depress. **2 deprimirse** *vr* to get depressed.

deprisa *adv* quickly.

depuradora *f* purifier.

derecha *f (mano)* right hand; *(lugar)* right, right-hand side; **a la d.** on the right, on the right-hand side; *(en política)* **la d.** the right.

derecho, -a 1 *adj (de la derecha)* right; *(recto)* straight. **2** *m (privilegio)* right; *(carrera)* law; **derechos civiles/humanos** civil/human rights; **tener d. a** to be entitled to; **no hay d.** it's not fair. **3** *adv* **siga todo d.** go straight ahead.

derivar 1 *vi* to drift; **d. de** to derive from. **2 derivarse** *vr* to stem (**de** from).

dermatólogo, -a *mf* dermatologist.

derramar 1 *vt* to spill; *(lágrimas)* to shed. **2 derramarse** *vr* to spill.

derrapar *vi* to skid.

derretir [6] *vt*, **derretirse** *vr* to melt; *(hielo, nieve)* to thaw.

derribar *vt (demoler)* to knock down; *(gobierno)* to bring down.

derrochar *vt* to waste.

derroche *m* waste.

derrota *f* defeat.

derrotar *vt* to defeat.

derruir [37] *vt* to demolish.

derrumbar 1 *vt (edificio)* to knock down. **2 derrumbarse** *vr* to collapse; *(techo)* to fall in.

desabrido, -a *adj (tono)* harsh; *(persona)* irritable.

desabrochar 1 *vt* to undo. **2 desabrocharse** *vr* to come undone; **desabróchate la camisa** undo your shirt.

desacertado, -a *adj* unwise.

desaconsejar *vt* to advise against.

desacreditar *vt (desprestigiar)* to discredit; *(criticar)* to disparage.

desactivar *vt (bomba)* to defuse.

desacuerdo *m* disagreement.

desafiante *adj* defiant.

desafiar [29] *vt* to challenge.

desafinado, -a *adj* out of tune.

desafinar 1 *vi* to sing out of tune; *(instrumento)* to play out of tune. **2 desafinarse** *vr* to go out of tune.

desafío *m* challenge.

desafortunado, -a *adj* unfortunate.

desagradable *adj* unpleasant.

desagradar *vt* to displease.

desagradecido, -a 1 *adj* ungrateful. **2** *mf* ungrateful person.

desagrado *m* displeasure.

desagüe *m (cañería)* drainpipe; *(vaciado)* drain.

desaguisado *m* mess.

desahogado, -a *adj (acomodado)* well-off; *(espacioso)* spacious.

desahogarse [42] *vr* to let off steam.

desahuciar [43] *vt (desalojar)* to evict; *(enfermo)* to deprive of all hope.

desairar *vt* to slight.

desajuste *m* disorder, imbalance.

desalentar [1] **1** *vt* to dishearten. **2 desalentarse** *vr* to get discouraged.

desaliento *m* discouragement.

desaliñado, -a *adj* untidy.

desalmado, -a *adj* heartless.

desalojar *vt* (*inquilino*) to evict; (*público*) to move on; (*lugar*) to evacuate; (*abandonar*) to abandon.

desamparado, -a *adj* (*persona*) helpless.

desangrarse *vr* to lose (a lot of) blood.

desanimado, -a *adj* (*persona*) downhearted; (*fiesta etc*) dull.

desanimar **1** *vt* to dishearten. **2 desanimarse** *vr* to lose heart.

desánimo *m* dejection.

desapacible *adj* unpleasant.

desaparecer [33] *vi* to disappear.

desaparición *f* disappearance.

desapercibido, -a *adj* pasar d. to go unnoticed.

desaprovechar *vt* (*dinero, tiempo*) to waste.

desarmar *vt* (*desmontar*) to dismantle; (*ejército*) to disarm.

desarme *m* disarmament; **d. nuclear** nuclear disarmament.

desarraigado, -a *adj* rootless.

desarreglar *vt* to mess up.

desarrollado, -a *adj* developed.

desarrollar **1** *vt* to develop. **2 desarrollarse** *vr* (*persona, enfermedad*) to develop; (*tener lugar*) to take place.

desarrollo *m* development; **países en vías de d.** developing countries.

desarticular *vt* to dismantle.

desasir [46] **1** *vt* to release. **2 desasirse** *vr* to get loose; **desasirse de** to free oneself from.

desasosiego *m* uneasiness.

desastrado, -a *adj* scruffy.

desastre *m* disaster.

desastroso, -a *adj* disastrous.

desatar **1** *vt* to untie, undo. **2 desatarse** *vr* (*zapato, cordón*) to come undone.

desatascar [44] *vt* to clear.

desatornillar *vt* to unscrew.

desatrancar [44] *vt* to unblock; (*puerta*) to unbolt.

desautorizar [40] *vt* to disallow; (*huelga etc*) to ban.

desavenencia *f* disagreement.

desayunar **1** *vi* to have breakfast. **2** *vt* to have for breakfast.

desayuno *m* breakfast.

desbarajuste *m* confusion.

desbaratar *vt* to ruin.

desbordar **1** *vt* to overflow. **2** *vi* to overflow (**de** with). **3 desbordarse** *vr* to overflow.

descabellado, -a *adj* crazy.

descafeinado, -a *adj* decaffeinated.

descalabro *m* misfortune.

descalificar [44] *vt* to disqualify.

descalzarse [40] *vr* to take one's shoes off.

descalzo, -a *adj* barefoot.

descaminado, -a *adj* fig **ir d.** to be on the wrong track.

descampado *m* garbage dump.

descansado, -a *adj* (*persona*) rested; (*vida, trabajo*) restful.

descansar *vi* to rest, to have a rest; (*poco tiempo*) to take a break.

descansillo *m* landing.

descanso *m* rest; (*en teatro, cine*) interval; (*en deporte*) half-time; **un día de d.** a day off.

descapotable *adj & m* convertible.

descarado, -a **1** *adj* (*insolente*) rude; (*desvergonzado*) shameless. **2** *mf* rude person.

descarga *f* unloading; (*eléctrica, explosiva*) discharge.

descargar [42] **1** *vt* to unload; (*golpe*) to deal. **2** *vi* (*tormenta*) to burst. **3 descargarse** *vr* to go flat.

descaro *m* cheek.

descarrilar *vi* to be derailed.

descartar *vt* to rule out.

descato *m* lack of respect (**a** for).

descender [3] **1** *vi* (*temperatura, nivel*) to fall; **d. de** to descend from. **2** *vt* to lower.

descendiente *mf* descendant.

descenso *m* descent; *(de temperatura)* fall.

descifrar *vt* to decipher; *(mensaje)* to decode; *(misterio)* to solve.

descolgar [2] *vt (el teléfono)* to pick up; *(cuadro, cortinas)* to take down.

descolorido, -a *adj* faded.

descomponer [19] *(pp descompuesto)* **1** *vt* to break down; *(corromper)* to decompose. **2 descomponerse** *vr (corromperse)* to decompose; *(ponerse nervioso)* to lose one's cool.

descomposición *f (de carne)* decomposition.

descompuse *pt indef de* **descomponer**.

descomunal *adj* massive.

desconcertar [1] **1** *vt* to disconcert. **2 desconcertarse** *vr* to be bewildered.

desconcierto *m* chaos, confusion.

desconectar *vt* to disconnect.

desconfiado, -a *adj* distrustful.

desconfiar [29] *vi* to distrust (**de** -).

descongelar *vt* to defrost.

desconocer [34] *vt* not to know.

desconocido, -a 1 *adj* unknown; *(irreconocible)* unrecognizable. **2** *m* **lo d.** the unknown. **3** *mf* stranger.

desconsiderado, -a 1 *adj* inconsiderate, thoughtless. **2** *mf* inconsiderate *o* thoughtless person.

desconsolado, -a *adj* disconsolate.

descontado, -a *adj fam* **dar por d.** to take for granted; **por d.** needless to say, of course.

descontar [2] *vt* to deduct.

descontento, -a 1 *adj* unhappy. **2** *m* dissatisfaction.

descontrolarse *vr* to lose control.

desconvocar *vt* to call off.

descorchar *vt* to uncork.

descorrer *vt* to draw back.

descortés *adj* impolite, discourteous.

descoser *vt* to unpick.

descoyuntar *vt* to dislocate.

descrédito *m* disrepute.

descremado, -a *adj* skimmed.

describir *(pp descrito)* *vt* to describe.

descripción *f* description.

descuartizar [40] *vt* to cut into pieces.

descubierto, -a 1 *adj* open. **2** *m* **al d.** in the open; **poner al d.** to bring out into the open.

descubrimiento *m* discovery.

descubrir *(pp descubierto)* *vt* to discover; *(conspiración)* to uncover; *(placa)* to unveil.

descuento *m* discount.

descuidado, -a *adj (negligente)* careless; *(desaseado)* untidy; *(desprevenido)* off one's guard.

descuidar 1 *vt* to neglect, to overlook. **2** *vi* **descuida, voy yo** don't worry, I'll go. **3 descuidarse** *vr (despistarse)* to be careless; **como te descuides, llegarás tarde** if you don't watch out, you'll be late.

descuido *m* oversight; *(negligencia)* carelessness; **por d.** inadvertently.

desde *adv (tiempo)* since; *(lugar)* from; **no lo he visto d. hace un año** I haven't seen him for a year; **d. siempre** always; **d. luego** of course; **d. que** ever since.

desdén *m* disdain.

desdeñar *vt* to disdain.

desdichado, -a 1 *adj* unfortunate. **2** *mf* poor devil.

desdoblar *vt* to unfold.

desear *vt* to desire; *(querer)* to want; **¿qué desea?** can I help you?; **estoy deseando que vengas** I'm looking forward to your coming; **te deseo buena suerte/feliz Navidad** I wish you good luck/a Merry Christmas.

desechable *adj* disposable.

desechar *vt (tirar)* to discard; *(idea, proyecto)* to drop.

desembalar *vt* to unpack.

desembarcar [44] **1** vt (mercancías) to unload; (personas) to disembark. **2** vi to disembark.

desembarco, desembarque m (de mercancías) unloading; (de personas) disembarkation.

desembocadura f mouth.

desembocar [44] vi (río) to flow (en into); (calle, situación) to lead (en to).

desembolsar vt to pay out.

desembolso m expenditure.

desembrollar vt fam (aclarar) to clear up; (desenredar) to disentangle.

desempaquetar vt to unpack.

desempatar vi to break the deadlock.

desempate m play-off.

desempeñar vt (cargo) to hold; (función) to fulfill; (papel) to play.

desempleado, -a 1 adj unemployed, out of work. **2** mf unemployed person; **los desempleados** the unemployed.

desempleo m unemployment; **cobrar el d.** to be on welfare.

desencadenar 1 vt (provocar) to unleash. **2 desencadenarse** vr (viento, pasión) to rage; (conflicto) to break out.

desencaminado, -a adj = **descaminado.**

desencanto m disillusion.

desenchufar vt to unplug.

desenfadado, -a adj free and easy.

desenfocado, -a adj out of focus.

desenfrenado, -a adj frantic, uncontrolled; (vicio, pasión) unbridled.

desenganchar vt to unhook; (vagón) to uncouple.

desengañar 1 vt **d. a algn** to open sb's eyes. **2 desengañarse** vr to be disappointed; fam **¡desengáñate!** get real!

desengaño m disappointment.

desengrasar vt to remove the grease from.

desenlace m outcome; (de historia) ending.

desenmascarar vt to unmask.

desenredar vt to disentangle.

desenrollar vt to unroll; (cable) to unwind.

desenroscar [44] vt to unscrew.

desentenderse [3] vr **se desentendió de mi problema** he didn't want to have anything to do with my problem.

desentonar vi to be out of tune; (colores etc) not to match; (persona, comentario) to be out of place.

desentrañar vt to unravel.

desentrenado, -a adj out of training.

desenvolver [4] (pp desenvuelto) **1** vt to unwrap. **2 desenvolverse** vr (persona) to manage.

desenvuelto, -a adj relaxed.

deseo m wish; (sexual) desire.

deseoso, -a adj eager; **estar d. de** be eager to.

desequilibrado, -a 1 adj unbalanced. **2** mf unbalanced person.

desértico, -a adj desert.

desertor, -a mf deserter.

desesperado, -a adj (sin esperanza) desperate; (exasperado) exasperated.

desesperante adj exasperating.

desesperar 1 vt to drive to despair; (exasperar) to exasperate. **2 desesperarse** vr to despair.

desestabilizar [40] vt to destabilize.

desestimar vt to reject.

desfachatez f cheek.

desfallecer [33] vi (debilitarse) to feel faint; (desmayarse) to faint.

desfasado, -a adj outdated; (persona) old-fashioned, behind the times.

desfavorable adj unfavorable.

desfigurar vt (cara) to disfigure.

desfiladero m narrow pass.

desfilar vi to march in single file; (soldados) to march past.

desfile m (militar) parade; **d. de modas** fashion show.

desganado, -a adj (apático) apathetic; **estar d.** (inapetente) to have no appetite.

desgarbado, -a adj ungraceful, ungainly.

desgarrador, -a adj bloodcurdling.

desgarrar vt to tear.

desgastar vt, **desgastarse** vr to wear away.

desgaste m wear.

desgracia f misfortune; **por d.** unfortunately.

desgraciadamente adv unfortunately.

desgraciado, -a 1 adj unfortunate; (infeliz) unhappy. **2** mf unfortunate person.

desgravación f deduction; **d. fiscal** tax deduction.

desgravar vt to deduct.

deshabitado, -a adj uninhabited.

deshacer [15] (pp deshecho) **1** vt (paquete) to undo; (maleta) to unpack; (destruir) to destroy; (disolver) to dissolve; (derretir) to melt. **2 deshacerse** vr to come undone; **deshacerse de algn/algo** to get rid of sb/sth; (disolverse) to dissolve; (derretirse) to melt.

deshidratar vt to dehydrate.

deshielo m thaw.

deshonesto, -a adj dishonest; (indecente) indecent.

deshonrar vt to dishonor; (a la familia etc) to bring disgrace on.

deshora a d. adv at an inconvenient time; **comer a d.** to eat at odd times.

deshuesar vt (carne) to bone; (fruta) to stone.

desierto, -a 1 m desert. **2** adj (deshabitado) uninhabited; (vacío) deserted.

designar vt to designate; (fecha, lugar) to fix.

desigual adj uneven.

desigualdad f inequality; (del terreno) unevenness.

desilusión f disappointment.

desilusionar vt to disappoint.

desinfectante adj & m disinfectant.

desinfectar vt to disinfect.

desinflar 1 vt to deflate; (rueda) to let down. **2 desinflarse** vr to go flat.

desintegrar vt, **desintegrarse** vr to disintegrate.

desinterés m (indiferencia) lack of interest, apathy; (generosidad) unselfishness.

desinteresado, -a adj selfless.

desintoxicar [44] **1** vt to detoxicate; (de alcohol) to dry out. **2 desintoxicarse** vr to detoxicate oneself; (de alcohol) to dry out.

desistir vi to desist.

deslenguado, -a adj (insolente) insolent.

desliz m slip.

deslizar [40] **1** vi to slide. **2 deslizarse** vr (patinar) to slide; (bajar) to slide down.

deslumbrador, -a, deslumbrante adj dazzling; fig stunning.

deslumbrar vt to dazzle.

desmadrarse vr fam to go wild.

desmandarse vr to get out of hand.

desmano: a desmano adv out of the way; **me coge a d.** it is out of my way.

desmantelar vt to dismantle.

desmaquillador, -a 1 m make-up remover. **2** adj **leche desmaquilladora** cleansing cream.

desmaquillarse vr to remove one's make-up.

desmayarse vr to faint.

desmayo m fainting fit; **tener un d.** to faint.

desmedido, -a adj out of proportion.

desmejorar(se) vi & vr to deteriorate.

desmemoriado, -a adj forgetful.

desmentir [5] vt to deny.

desmenuzar [40] vt to crumble.

desmesurado, -a adj excessive.

desmontable adj that can be taken apart.

desmontar vt to dismantle.

desmoralizar [40] vt to demoralize.

desmoronarse vr to crumble.

desnatado, -a adj (leche) skim milk.

desnivel m drop.

desnudar vt, **desnudarse** vr to undress.

desnudista adj & mf nudist.

desnudo, -a adj naked.

desnutrido, -a adj undernourished.

desobedecer [33] vt to disobey.

desobediente 1 adj disobedient. **2** mf disobedient person.

desocupado, -a adj (vacío) empty; (ocioso) free.

desocupar vt to empty, to vacate.

desodorante adj & m deodorant.

desolar vt to devastate.

desollar [2] **1** vt to skin. **2 desollarse** vr to scrape; **me desollé el brazo** I scraped my arm.

desorbitado, -a adj (precio) exorbitant.

desorden m mess; **d. público** civil disorder.

desordenado, -a adj untidy.

desordenar vt to make untidy, to mess up.

desorganizar [40] vt to disorganize, to disrupt.

desorientar 1 vt to disorientate. **2 desorientarse** vr to lose one's bearings.

despabilado, -a adj (sin sueño) wide awake; (listo) quick.

despachar vt (asunto) to get through; (en tienda) to serve.

despacho m (oficina) office; (en casa) study.

despacio adv (lentamente) slowly.

desparramar vt, **desparramarse** vr to scatter; (líquido) to spill.

despavorido, -a adj terrified.

despectivo, -a adj derogatory.

despedida f goodbye.

despedir [6] **1** vt (empleado) to sack; (decir adiós a) to say goodbye to; (olor, humo etc) to give off. **2 despedirse** vr (decir adiós) to say goodbye (**de** to).

despegado, -a adj unstuck; (persona) couldn't-care-less.

despegar [42] **1** vt to detach. **2** vi (avión) to take off. **3 despegarse** vr to come unstuck.

despegue m takeoff.

despeinado, -a adj dishevelled.

despejado, -a adj clear; (cielo) cloudless.

despejar 1 vt to clear. **2 despejarse** vr (cielo) to clear; (persona) to clear one's head.

despeje m (de balón) clearance.

despensa f pantry.

despeñarse vr to go over a cliff.

desperdiciar [43] vt to waste; (oportunidad) to throw away.

desperdicio m waste; **desperdicios** (basura) trash sing; (desechos) leftovers.

desperdigar [42] vt, **desperdigarse** vr to scatter.

desperezarse [40] vr to stretch (oneself).

desperfecto m (defecto) flaw; (daño) damage.

despertador m alarm clock.

despertar [1] vt, **despertarse** vr to wake (up).

despiadado, -a adj merciless.

despido m dismissal.

despierto, -a adj (desvelado) awake; (listo) quick.

despilfarrar vt to squander.

despilfarro m squandering.

despistado, -a 1 adj scatterbrained. **2** mf scatterbrain.

despistar 1 vt (hacer perder la pista a) to lose. **2 despistarse** vr (perderse) to get lost; (distraerse) to switch off.

desplazamiento m (viaje) journey.

desplazar [40] **1** vt to displace. **2 desplazarse** vr to travel.

despojar vt to strip (**de** of); fig to deprive (**de** of).

desposar vt to marry.

déspota mf despot, tyrant.

despreciar [43] vt (desdeñar) to scorn; (rechazar) to reject.

desprecio m (desdén) scorn, disdain; (desaire) slight, snub.

desprender 1 vt (separar) to remove; (olor, humo etc) to give off. **2 desprenderse** vr (soltarse) to come off; **desprenderse de** to rid oneself (**de** of).

despreocupado, -a adj (tranquilo) unconcerned; (descuidado) careless; (estilo) casual.

despreocuparse vr (tranquilizarse) to stop worrying; (desentenderse) to be unconcerned, to be indifferent (**de** to).

desprestigiar [43] vt to discredit.

desprestigio m discredit, loss of reputation; **campaña de d.** smear campaign.

desprevenido, -a adj unprepared; **coger** o **pillar a algn d.** to catch sb unawares.

desproporcionado, -a adj disproportionate.

desprovisto, -a adj lacking (**de** of).

después 1 adv afterwards, later; (entonces) then; (seguidamente, lugar) next; **poco d.** soon after. **2** prep **d. de** after. **3** conj **d. de que** after.

destacar [44] **1** vt to stress. **2 destacar(se)** vi & vr to stand out.

destapador m Am bottle opener.

destapar 1 vt to take the lid off; (botella) to open. **2 destaparse** vr to get uncovered.

destartalado, -a adj rambling; (desvencijado) ramshackle.

destello m sparkle.

desteñir [6] **1** vti to discolor. **2 desteñirse** vr to fade.

desternillarse vi **d. (de risa)** to split one's sides laughing.

desterrar [1] vt to exile.

destiempo: a destiempo adv at the wrong time o moment.

destierro m exile.

destilería f distillery.

destinar vt (dinero etc) to assign; (empleado) to appoint.

destino m (rumbo) destination; (sino) fate; (de empleo) post; **el avión con d. a Bilbao** the plane to Bilbao.

destituir [37] vt to remove from office.

destornillador m screwdriver.

destreza f skill.

destrozar [40] vt (destruir) to destroy; (abatir) to shatter.

destrozo m destruction; **destrozos** damage.

destrucción f destruction.

destructivo, -a adj destructive.

destruir [37] vt to destroy.

desuso m disuse; **caer en d.** to fall into disuse.

desvalijar vt (robar) to rob; (casa, tienda) to burgle.

desván m loft.

desvanecerse [33] vr (disiparse) to vanish; (desmayarse) to faint.

desvariar [29] vi to talk nonsense.

desvelar 1 vt to keep awake. **2 desvelarse** vr to make every effort.

desvencijarse vr to fall apart.

desventaja f disadvantage; (inconveniente) drawback; **estar en d.** to be at a disadvantage.

desvergonzado, -a 1 adj (indecente) shameless; (descarado) insolent. **2** mf (sinvergüenza) shameless person; (fresco) insolent person.

desvergüenza f (indecencia) shamelessness; (atrevimiento) insolence; (acto impertinente) insolent o rude remark; **tuvo la d. de negarlo** he had the cheek to deny it.

desvestir [6] vt, **desvestirse** vr to undress.

desviar [29] **1** vt (río, carretera) to divert; (golpe, conversación) to deflect. **2 desviarse** vr to go off course; *(coche)* to turn off.

desvío *m* diversion.

detallado, -a *adj* detailed.

detallar *vt* to give the details of.

detalle *m* detail; *(delicadeza)* nice thought.

detallista *adj* perfectionist.

detectar *vt* to detect.

detective *mf* detective. **d. privado** private detective.

detener [24] **1** *vt* to stop; *(arrestar)* to arrest. **2 detenerse** *vr* to stop.

detenidamente *adv* carefully.

detenido, -a 1 *adj (parado)* stopped; *(arrestado)* detained; *(minucioso)* thorough. **2** *mf* detainee.

detenimiento *m* **con d.** carefully, thoroughly.

detergente *adj & m* detergent.

deteriorar 1 *vt* to spoil. **2 deteriorarse** *vr (estropearse)* to get damaged.

determinado, -a *adj (preciso)* definite; *(resuelto)* resolute.

determinar 1 *vt (fecha etc)* to set; *(decidir)* to decide on. **2 determinarse** *vr* **determinarse a** to make up one's mind to.

detestar *vt* to hate.

detrás 1 *adv* behind. **2** *prep* **d. de** behind.

detuve *pt indef de* **detener**.

deuda *f* debt; **d. pública** national debt.

deudor, -a *mf* debtor.

devaluar [30] *vt* to devalue.

devastador, -a *adj* devastating.

devastar *vt* to devastate, to ravage.

devoción *f* devoutness; *(al trabajo etc)* devotion.

devolución *f* return; *(de dinero)* refund.

devolver [4] *(pp* **devuelto)** **1** *vt* to give back; *(dinero)* to refund. **2** *vi (vomitar)* to vomit. **3 devolverse** *vr Am* to go/come back.

devorar *vt* to devour.

devoto, -a 1 *adj* devout. **2** *mf* pious person; *(seguidor)* devotee.

devuelto, -a *pp de* **devolver**.

DF *m abr de* **Distrito Federal** *(en México)* Mexico City.

di *pt indef de* **dar**; *imperativo de* **decir**.

día *m* day; **¿qué d. es hoy?** what's the date today?; **d. a d.** day by day; **de d.** by day; **durante el d.** during the daytime; **un d. sí y otro no** every other day; **pan del d.** fresh bread; **hoy (en) d.** nowadays; **el d. de mañana** in the future; **d. festivo** holiday; **d. laborable** working day; **d. libre** day off; **es de d.** it is daylight; **hace buen/mal d.** it's a nice/rotten day.

diabético, -a *adj & mf* diabetic.

diablo *m* devil.

diadema *f* tiara.

diagnosticar [44] *vt* to diagnose.

diagnóstico *m* diagnosis.

diagonal *adj & f* diagonal; **en d.** diagonally.

dial *m* dial.

dialogar [42] *vi* to have a conversation; *(para negociar)* to talk.

diálogo *m* dialog.

diamante *m* diamond.

diámetro *m* diameter.

diana *f (blanco)* bull's eye.

diapositiva *f* slide.

diariamente *adv* daily.

diario, -a 1 *adj* daily; **a d.** daily. **2** *m (diario)* newspaper; *(memorias)* diary.

diarrea *f* diarrhea.

dibujante *mf* drawer; *(de cómic)* cartoonist; *(delineante)* *(hombre)* draftsman; *(mujer)* draftswoman.

dibujar *vt* to draw.

dibujo *m* drawing; **dibujos animados** cartoons.

diccionario *m* dictionary.

dicho, -a *adj* said; **mejor d.** or rather; **d. y hecho** no sooner said than done; **dicha persona** the abovementioned person.

dichoso, -a *adj (feliz)* happy; *fam (maldito)* damned.

diciembre *m* December.

dictado *m* dictation.

dictadura *f* dictatorship.

dictáfono® *m* Dictaphone®.

dictar *vt* to dictate; *(ley)* to enact.

didáctico, -a *adj* didactic.

diecinueve *adj & m inv* nineteen.

dieciocho *adj & m inv* eighteen.

dieciséis *adj & m inv* sixteen.

diecisiete *adj & m inv* seventeen.

diente *m* tooth; **d. de ajo** clove of garlic; **d. de leche** milk tooth; **dientes postizos** false teeth.

diera *subj imperfecto de* **dar**.

diesel *adj & m* diesel.

diestro, -a 1 *adj (hábil)* skillful. **2** *m* bullfighter.

dieta *f (paga)* diet; **estar a d.** to be on a diet; **dietas** expenses.

diez *adj & m inv* ten.

diferencia *f* difference; **a d. de** unlike.

diferenciar [43] **1** *vt* to differentiate (**entre** between). **2 diferenciarse** *vr* to differ (**de** from).

diferente 1 *adj* different (**de** than). **2** *adv* differently.

diferido, -a *adj* **en d.** recorded.

difícil *adj* difficult; **d. de creer/hacer** difficult to believe/do; **es d. que venga** it is unlikely that she'll come.

dificultad *f* difficulty; *(aprieto)* problem.

dificultar *vt* to make difficult.

dificultoso, -a *adj* difficult, hard.

difundir *vt*, **difundirse** *vr* to spread.

difunto, -a *mf* deceased.

digerir [5] *vt* to digest; *fig* to assimilate.

digestión *f* digestion.

digestivo, -a *adj* easy to digest.

digital *adj* digital; **huellas digitales** fingerprints.

dígito *m* digit.

dignarse *vr* to deign (**a** to), to condescend (**a** to).

dignidad *f* dignity.

digno, -a *adj (merecedor)* worthy; *(decoroso)* decent.

digo *indic pres de* **decir**.

dije *pt indef de* **decir**.

dilatar *vt*, **dilatarse** *vr* to expand.

dilema *m* dilemma.

diluir [37] *vt*, **diluirse** *vr* to dilute.

diluyo *indic pres de* **diluir**.

dimensión *m* dimension; **de grandes dimensiones** very large.

dimisión *f* resignation; **presentar la d.** to hand in one's resignation.

dimitir *vi* to resign (**de** from).

dinámico, -a *adj* dynamic.

dinamita *f* dynamite.

dinamo *f*, **dínamo** *f* dynamo.

dinastía *f* dynasty.

dinero *m* money; **d. efectivo** *o* **en metálico** cash.

dinosaurio *m* dinosaur.

dios *m* god; **¡D. mío!** my God!; **¡por D.!** for goodness sake!

diploma *m* diploma.

diplomacia *f* diplomacy.

diplomarse *vr* to graduate.

diplomático, -a 1 *adj* diplomatic. **2** *mf* diplomat.

diptongo *m* diphthong.

diputación *f* **d. provincial** ≃ county council.

diputado, -a *mf & (hombre)* Congressman; *(mujer)* Congresswoman; **Congreso de los Diputados** ≃ Congress.

dique *m* dike.

diré *fut de* **decir**.

dirección *f* direction; *(señas)* address; *(destino)* destination; *(de vehículo)* steering; *(dirigentes)* management; *(cargo)* directorship; *(de un partido)* leadership; **d. prohibida** no entry; **calle de d. única** one-way street.

directa *f (marcha)* top gear.

directamente *adv* directly.

directiva *f* board of directors.

directo, -a *adj* direct; **en d.** live.

director, -a *mf* director; *(de colegio) (hombre)* headmaster; *(mujer)* headmistress; *(de periódico)* editor; **d. de cine** (film) director; **d. de orquesta**

conductor; **d. gerente** managing director.

dirigir [57] **1** *vt* to direct; *(empresa)* to manage; *(negocio, colegio)* to run; *(orquesta)* to conduct; *(partido)* to lead; *(periódico)* to edit; **d. la palabra a algn** to speak to sb. **2 dirigirse** *vr* **dirigirse a** o **hacia** *(ir)* to make one's way towards; *(hablar)* to speak to.

discapacidad *f* disability.

discernir [54] *vt* to discern.

disciplina *f* discipline.

discípulo, -a *mf* disciple.

disco *m* disk; *(de música)* record; **d. compacto** compact disk; **d. duro** hard disk; **d. óptico** optical disk.

discontinuo, -a *adj* discontinuous; **línea discontinua** *(en carretera)* broken line.

discoteca *f* discotheque.

discrepar *vi* *(disentir)* to disagree (**de** with; **en** on).

discreto, -a *adj* discreet.

discriminación *f* discrimination.

disculpa *f* excuse; **dar disculpas** to make excuses; **pedir disculpas a algn** to apologize to sb (**por** for).

discurrir *vi* to think.

discurso *m* speech; **dar** o **pronunciar un d.** to make a speech.

discusión *f* argument.

discutir **1** *vi* to argue (**de** about). **2** *vt* to discuss.

diseñar *vt* to design.

diseño *m* design.

disfrazar [40] **1** *vt* to disguise. **2 disfrazarse** *vr* to disguise oneself.

disfrutar **1** *vi* *(gozar)* to enjoy oneself; *(poseer)* to enjoy (**de** -). **2** *vt* to enjoy.

disgustado, -a *adj* upset, displeased.

disgustar **1** *vt* to upset. **2 disgustarse** *vr* *(molestarse)* to get upset; *(dos amigos)* to quarrel.

disgusto *m* *(preocupación)* upset; *(desgracia)* trouble; **llevarse un d.** to get upset; **dar un d. a algn** to

upset sb; **a d.** unwillingly.

disimular *vt* to conceal.

disimulo *m* pretense.

disipar **1** *vt* *(niebla)* to drive away; *(temor, duda)* to dispel. **2 disiparse** *vr* *(niebla, temor etc)* to disappear.

disketera *f* disk drive.

dislocar [44] *vt* to dislocate.

disminuir [37] **1** *vt* to reduce. **2** *vi* to diminish.

disolvente *adj & m* solvent.

disolver [4] *(pp* **disuelto***) vt* to dissolve.

disparar **1** *vt* *(pistola etc)* to fire; *(flecha, balón)* to shoot. **2 dispararse** *vr* *(arma)* to go off; *(precios)* to rocket.

disparate *m* *(dicho)* nonsense; **decir disparates** to talk nonsense; *(acto)* foolish act.

disparo *m* shot.

dispersar *vt*, **dispersarse** *vr* to disperse.

disponer [19] *(pp* **dispuesto***)* **1** *vt* *(arreglar)* to arrange; *(ordenar)* to order. **2** *vi* **d. de** to have at one's disposal. **3 disponerse** *vr* to get ready.

disponible *adj* available.

disposición *f* *(colocación)* layout; *(orden)* law; **a su d.** at your service.

dispositivo *m* device.

disputa *f* *(discusión)* argument; *(contienda)* contest.

disputar **1** *vt* *(premio)* to compete for; *(partido)* to play. **2 disputarse** *vr* *(premio)* to compete for.

disquete *m* diskette, floppy disk.

disquetera *f* disk drive.

distancia *f* distance.

distante *adj* distant.

distinguir [59] **1** *vt* *(diferenciar)* to distinguish; *(reconocer)* to recognize. **2** *vi* *(diferenciar)* to discriminate. **3 distinguirse** *vr* to distinguish oneself.

distintivo, -a 1 *adj* distinctive. **2** *m* distinctive mark.

distinto, -a *adj* different.

distracción *f* entertainment; *(pasatiempo)* pastime; *(descuido)* absentmindedness.

distraer [25] **1** vt (atención) to distract; (divertir) to entertain. **2 distraerse** vr (divertirse) to amuse oneself; (abstraerse) to let one's mind wander.

distraído, -a adj entertaining; (abstraído) absent-minded.

distribuidor, -a 1 adj distributing. **2** mf distributor.

distribuir [37] vt to distribute; (trabajo) to share out.

distrito m district; **d. postal** postal district.

disturbio m riot.

disuadir vt to dissuade.

disuelto, -a pp de **disolver**.

divagar [42] vi to digress, to wander.

diván m couch.

diversión f fun.

diverso, -a adj different; **diversos** various.

divertido, -a adj funny.

divertir [54] vt **1** vt to amuse. **2 divertirse** vr to enjoy oneself.

dividir vt, **dividirse** vr to divide (**en** into).

divino, -a adj divine.

divisa f foreign currency.

división f division.

divorciado, -a 1 adj divorced. **2** mf (hombre) divorcé; (mujer) divorcée.

divorciarse [43] vr to get divorced.

divorcio m divorce.

divulgación f (de ciencia) popularization.

divulgar [42] vt (noticia) to spread; (ciencia) to popularize.

DNI m abr de **Documento Nacional de Identidad** Identity Card, ID card.

dóberman m Doberman (pinscher).

dobladillo m hem.

doblar 1 vt to double; (plegar) to fold up; (torcer) to bend; (la esquina) to go round. **2** vi (girar) to turn. **3 doblarse** vr (plegarse) to fold; (torcerse) to bend.

doble 1 adj double. **2** m double; **gana el d. que tú** she earns twice as much as you do.

doce adj & m inv twelve.

docena f dozen.

docente adj teaching; **centro d.** educational center.

dócil adj docile.

doctor, -a mf doctor.

doctorado m doctorate, PhD.

documentación f documentation; (DNI, de conducir etc) papers pl.

documental adj & m documentary.

documento m document; **d. nacional de identidad** identity card.

dogo m bulldog.

dólar m dollar.

doler [4] vi to ache; **me duele la cabeza** I've got a headache.

dolor m pain; (pena) grief; **d. de cabeza** headache; **d. de muelas** toothache.

domar vt to tame; (caballo) to break in.

doméstico, -a adj domestic; **animal d.** pet.

domicilio m residence; (señas) address.

dominante adj dominant; (déspota) domineering.

dominar 1 vt to dominate; (situación) to control; (idioma) to speak very well. **2** vi to dominate; (resaltar) to stand out. **3 dominarse** vr to control oneself.

domingo m Sunday; **D. de Resurrección** o **Pascua** Easter Sunday.

dominical 1 adj Sunday. **2** m (suplemento) Sunday supplement.

dominicano, -a adj & mf Dominican; **República Dominicana** Dominican Republic.

dominio m (poder) control; (de un idioma) command; (territorio) dominion.

dominó, dómino m dominoes pl.

don¹ m (habilidad) gift; **tener el d. de** to have a knack for.

don² m Señor D. José García Mr José García; **D. Fulano de Tal** Mr So-and-So.

donante *mf* donor; **d. de sangre** blood donor.

donar *vt (sangre etc)* to donate.

donativo *m* donation.

dónde *adv* where *(in questions)*; **¿por d. se va a la playa?** which way is it to the beach?

donde *adv rel* where; **a** *o* **en d.** where; **de** *o* **desde d.** from where.

doña *f* Señora D. Leonor Benítez Mrs Leonor Benítez.

dorada *f (pez)* gilthead bream.

dorado, -a *adj* golden.

dormido, -a *adj* asleep; **quedarse d.** to fall asleep; *(no despertarse)* to oversleep.

dormilón, -ona *fam* **1** *adj* sleepy-headed. **2** *mf* sleepyhead.

dormir [7] **1** *vi* to sleep. **2** *vt* **d. la siesta** to have an afternoon nap. **3** **dormirse** *vr* to fall asleep; **se me ha dormido el brazo** my arm has gone to sleep.

dormitorio *m (de una casa)* bedroom; *(de colegio, residencia)* dormitory.

dorsal **1** *adj* espina d. spine. **2** *m (de camiseta)* number.

dorso *m* back; **instrucciones al d.** instructions over; **véase al d.** see overleaf.

dos **1** *adj* two. **2** *m inv* two; **los d.** both; **nosotros/vosotros d.** both of us/you.

doscientos, -as *adj & mf* two hundred.

dosis *f inv* dose.

dotar *vt* **d. de** to provide with.

doy *indic pres de* **dar**.

Dr. *abr de* **doctor** doctor, Dr.

Dra. *abr de* **doctora** doctor, Dr.

dragón *m* dragon.

drama *m* drama.

dramático, -a *adj* dramatic.

drástico, -a *adj* drastic.

droga *f* drug; **d. blanda/dura** soft/hard drug.

drogadicto, -a *mf* drug addict.

drogar [42] **1** *vt* to drug. **2** **drogarse** *vr* to take drugs.

droguería *f* hardware and household goods shop.

ducha *f* shower; **darse/tomar una d.** to take/have a shower.

ducharse *vr* to take a shower.

duda *f* doubt; **sin d.** without a doubt; **no cabe d.** (there is) no doubt.

dudar **1** *vi* to doubt; *(vacilar)* to hesitate **(en** to). **2** *vt* to doubt.

dudoso, -a *adj (poco honrado)* dubious; **ser d.** *(incierto)* to be uncertain *o* doubtful; **estar d.** *(indeciso)* to be undecided.

dueña *f* owner; *(de pensión)* landlady.

dueño *m* owner; *(de casa etc)* landlord.

dulce **1** *adj (sabor)* sweet; *(carácter, voz)* gentle; *(agua)* fresh. **2** *m (pastel)* cake; *(caramelo)* candy.

duna *f* dune.

duodécimo, -a *adj & mf* twelfth.

duplicar [44] **1** *vt* to duplicate; *(cifras)* to double. **2** **duplicarse** *vr* to double.

duración *f* duration.

duradero, -a *adj* durable, lasting.

durante *prep* during.

durar *vi* to last.

durazno *m Am (fruto)* peach; *(árbol)* peach tree.

dureza *f* hardness; *(severidad)* severity; *(callosidad)* corn.

duro, -a **1** *adj* hard; *(resistente)* tough. **2** *adv* hard.

E

e *conj (before words beginning with i or hi)* and.

ébano *m* ebony.

echar **1** *vt* to throw; *(carta)* to post; *(vino, agua)* to pour; *(expulsar)* to throw out; *(despedir)* to sack; *(humo,* *olor etc)* to give off; **e. una mano** to give a hand; **e. una mirada/una ojeada** to have a look/a quick look; **e. gasolina al coche** to put gas in the car; **e. de menos** *o* **en falta** to miss. **2** *vi* (+ **a** + *infinitivo*) *(empezar)* to begin to; **echó a correr** he ran off. **3 echarse** *vr (tumbarse)* to lie down; *(lanzarse)* to throw oneself; (+ **a** + *infinitivo*) *(empezar)* to begin to; *fig* **echarse atrás** to get cold feet; **echarse a llorar** to burst into tears; **echarse a perder** *(comida)* to go bad.

eclesiástico, -a 1 *adj* ecclesiastical. **2** *m* clergyman.

eclipse *m* eclipse.

eco *m* echo.

ecológico, -a *adj* ecological.

ecologista 1 *adj* ecological. **2** *mf* ecologist.

economía *f* economy; *(ciencia)* economics *sing*.

económico, -a *adj* economic; *(barato)* economical.

economizar [40] *vti* to economize.

ecuación *f* equation.

ecuador *m* equator.

ecuánime *adj (temperamento)* even-tempered; *(juicio)* impartial.

ecuatoriano, -a *adj & mf* Ecuadorian.

ecuestre *adj* equestrian.

edad *f* age; **¿qué e. tienes?** how old are you?; **E. Media** Middle Ages *pl.*

edición *f (publicación)* publication; *(conjunto de ejemplares)* edition.

edicto *m* edict.

edificar [44] *vt* to build.

edificio *m* building.

edil, -a *mf* town councilor.

editar *vt (libro, periódico)* to publish; *(disco)* to release; *(en ordenador)* to edit.

editor, -a 1 *adj* publishing. **2** *mf* publisher. **3** *m* **e. de textos** text editor.

editorial 1 *adj* publishing. **2** *f* publishing house. **3** *m* editorial.

edredón *m* duvet, eiderdown.

educación *f* education; *(formación)* upbringing; **buena/mala e.** *(modales)* good/bad manners; **falta de e.** bad manners.

educado, -a *adj* polite.

educar [44] *vt (hijos)* to raise.

educativo, -a *adj* educational.

edulcorante *m* sweetener.

efectivamente *adv* yes indeed!

efectivo, -a 1 *adj* effective; **hacer e. un cheque** to cash a check. **2** *m* **en e.** in cash.

efecto *m (resultado)* effect; *(impresión)* impression; **efectos personales** personal belongings; **en e.** yes indeed!

efectuar [30] *vt* to carry out; *(viaje)* to make; *(pedido)* to place.

efervescente *adj* effervescent; **aspirina e.** soluble aspirin.

eficacia *f (de persona)* efficiency; *(de remedio, medida)* effectiveness.

eficaz *adj (persona)* efficient; *(remedio, medida)* effective.

eficiencia *f* efficiency.

eficiente *adj* efficient.

efusivo, -a *adj* effusive.

egipcio, -a *adj & mf* Egyptian.

egoísmo *m* egoism.

egoísta 1 *adj* selfish. **2** *mf* ego(t)ist.

egresar *vi Am* to leave school; to graduate.

ej. *abr de* **ejemplo** example.

eje *m (de rueda)* axle; *(de máquina)* shaft.

ejecutar *vt (ajusticiar)* to execute; *(sinfonía)* to perform.

ejecutiva *f (gobierno)* executive.

ejecutivo, -a 1 *adj* executive; **el poder e.** the government. **2** *mf* executive.

ejemplar 1 *m (de libro)* copy; *(de revista, periódico)* issue; *(especimen)* specimen. **2** *adj* exemplary.

ejemplo *m* example; **por e.** for example; **dar e.** to set an example.

ejercer [49] *vt (profesión etc)* to practice; *(influencia)* to exert.

ejercicio *m* exercise; *(de profesión)*

practice; **hacer e.** to take exercise.
ejercitar *vt* to practice.
ejército *m* army.
el 1 *art def m* the; **el Sr. García** Mr. García. ▪ *(no se traduce)* **el hambre/destino** hunger/fate. ▪ *(con partes del cuerpo, prendas de vestir)* **me he cortado el dedo** I've cut my finger; **métetelo en el bolsillo** put it in your pocket. ▪ *(con días de la semana)* **el lunes** on Monday. **2** *pron* the one; **el de las once** the eleven o'clock one; **el que tienes en la mano** the one you've got in your hand; **el que quieras** whichever one you want; **el de tu amigo** your friend's.
él *pron pers (sujeto) (persona)* he; *(animal, cosa)* it; *(complemento) (persona)* him; *(animal, cosa)* it.
elaboración *f (de un producto)* production.
elaborar *vt (producto)* to produce.
elasticidad *f* elasticity; *fig* flexibility.
elástico, -a *adj & m* elastic.
elección *f* choice; *(votación)* election.
electorado *m* electorate *pl.*
electoral *adj* electoral; **campaña e.** election campaign; **colegio e.** polling station.
electricidad *f* electricity.
electricista *mf* electrician.
eléctrico, -a *adj* electric.
electrocutar *vt* to electrocute.
electrodoméstico *m* (domestic) electrical appliance.
electrónico, -a *adj* electronic.
elefante *m* elephant.
elegancia *f* elegance.
elegante *adj* elegant.
elegir [58] *vt* to choose; *(en votación)* to elect.
elemental *adj (fundamental)* basic; *(simple)* elementary.
elemento *m* element; *(componente)* component.
elepé *m* LP (record).

elevación *f* elevation; *(de precios)* rise.
elevado, -a *adj* high; *(edificio)* tall.
elevalunas *m inv* **e. eléctrico** electric windows *pl.*
elevar 1 *vt* to raise. **2 elevarse** *vr (subir)* to rise; **elevarse a** *(cantidad)* to come to.
elijo *indic pres de* **elegir**.
eliminar *vt* to eliminate.
eliminatoria *f* heat, qualifying round.
eliminatorio, -a *adj* qualifying.
ella *pron pers f (sujeto)* she; *(animal, cosa)* it, she; *(complemento)* her; *(animal, cosa)* it, her.
ellas *pron pers fpl (sujeto)* they; *(complemento)* them.
ello *pron pers neutro* it; **por e.** for that reason.
ellos *pron pers mpl (sujeto)* they; *(complemento)* them.
elocuente *adj* eloquent.
elogiar [43] *vt* to praise.
elote *m CAm, Méx* tender corncob.
eludir *vt* to avoid.
embajada *f* embassy.
embajador, -a *mf* ambassador.
embalaje *m* packing.
embalse *m* reservoir; *(presa)* dam.
embarazada 1 *adj* pregnant. **2** *f* pregnant woman.
embarazo *m (preñez)* pregnancy; *(turbación)* embarrassment.
embarazoso, -a *adj* embarrassing.
embarcación *f* boat.
embarcadero *m* quay.
embarcar [44] **1** *vt* to ship. **2** *vi* to go on board. **3 embarcarse** *vr* to go on board (**en** -); *(en avión)* to board (**en** -).
embargar [42] *vt (bienes)* to seize, to impound; *fig* **le embarga la emoción** he's overwhelmed with joy.
embarque *m (de persona)* boarding; *(de mercancías)* loading; **tarjeta de e.** boarding card.
embellecer [33] *vt* to embellish.

embestida f onslaught; (de toro) charge.

embestir [6] vt (a torero) to charge; (atacar) to attack.

emblema m emblem.

embobado, -a adj fascinated.

embobarse vr to be fascinated o besotted (con, de by).

émbolo m piston.

embolsar vt, **embolsarse** vr to pocket.

emborrachar vt, **emborracharse** vr to get drunk.

emboscada f ambush.

embotellamiento m traffic jam.

embotellar vt to bottle; (tráfico) to block.

embrague m clutch.

embriagar [42] 1 vt to intoxicate. 2 **embriagarse** vr to get drunk.

embriaguez f intoxication.

embrollar 1 vt to confuse. 2 **embrollarse** vr to get confused.

embrujado, -a adj (sitio) haunted.

embudo m funnel.

embuste m lie.

embustero, -a mf cheat.

embutido m sausage.

emergencia f emergency; **salida de e.** emergency exit; **en caso de e.** in an emergency.

emigración f emigration.

emigrante adj & mf emigrant.

emigrar vi to emigrate.

emisión f emission; (de radio, TV) broadcasting.

emisora f (de radio) radio station; (de televisión) television station.

emitir vt to emit; (luz, calor) to give off; (opinión, juicio) to express; (programa) to transmit.

emoción f emotion; (excitación) excitement; **¡qué e.!** how exciting!

emocionado, -a adj deeply moved o touched.

emocionante adj (conmovedor) moving; (excitante) exciting.

emocionar 1 vt (conmover) to move; (excitar) to thrill. 2 **emocionarse** vr

(conmoverse) to be moved; (excitarse) to get excited.

emotivo, -a adj emotional.

empacar [44] vt Am (mercancías) to pack.

empacho m (de comida) indigestion.

empalagoso, -a adj (dulce) sickly sweet.

empalizada f fence.

empalmar 1 vt (unir) to join; (cuerdas, cables) to splice. 2 vi to converge; (trenes) to connect.

empanada f pie.

empanadilla f pastry.

empañar vt, **empañarse** vr (cristales) to steam up.

empapar 1 vt (mojar) to soak; (absorber) to soak up. 2 **empaparse** vr (persona) to get soaked; fam fig to take in (de -).

empapelar vt to wallpaper.

empaquetar vt to pack.

emparedado m sandwich.

empastar vt (diente) to fill.

empaste m (de diente) filling.

empatar vi to draw; Am (unir) to join.

empate m draw.

empedrado, -a 1 adj cobbled. 2 m (adoquines) cobblestones pl.

empeine m (de pie, de zapato) instep.

empellón m shove.

empeñar 1 vt to pawn. 2 **empeñarse** vr (insistir) to insist (en on); (endeudarse) to get into debt.

empeño m (insistencia) insistence; (deuda) pledge.

empeoramiento m deterioration, worsening.

empeorar 1 vi to deteriorate. 2 vt to make worse. 3 **empeorarse** vr to deteriorate.

emperador m emperor.

empezar [51] vti to begin, start (a hacer algo to do sth).

empinado, -a adj (cuesta) steep.

empinar 1 vt to raise. 2 **empinarse**

vr (persona) to stand on tiptoe.

emplazamiento *m (colocación)* location.

empleado, -a *mf* employee; *(de oficina, banco)* clerk.

emplear *vt (usar)* to use; *(contratar)* to employ; *(dinero, tiempo)* to spend.

empleo *m* employment; *(oficio)* job; *(uso)* use; **modo de e.** instructions for use.

emplomar *vt Am (diente)* to fill.

empobrecer [33] **1** *vt* to impoverish. **2 empobrecerse** *vr* to become impoverished.

empobrecimiento *m* impoverishment.

empollón, -ona *mf fam* grind.

emporio *m Am* department store.

empotrado, -a *adj* fitted.

emprendedor, -a *adj* enterprising.

emprender *vt* to undertake; *fam* **emprenderla con algn** to pick on sb.

empresa *f* firm; *(tarea)* undertaking.

empresarial *adj (de empresa)* business; *(espíritu)* entrepreneurial; **(ciencias) empresariales** business studies.

empresario, -a *mf (hombre)* businessman; *(mujer)* businesswoman; *(patrón)* employer.

empujar *vt* to push, to shove.

empujón *m* push, shove.

emulsión *f* emulsion.

en *prep (posición)* in; at; *(sobre)* on; **en Madrid/Bolivia** in Madrid/Bolivia; **en casa/el trabajo** at home/ work; **en la mesa** on the table. ▪ *(movimiento)* into; **entrar en la casa** to go into the house. ▪ *(tiempo)* in; on; at; **en 1940** in 1940; *Am* **en la mañana** in the morning; **cae en martes** it falls on a Tuesday; **en ese momento** at that moment. ▪ *(transporte)* by; **en coche/tren** by car/train. ▪ *(modo)* **en español** in Spanish; **en broma** jokingly; **en serio** seriously. ▪ *(reducción, aumento)* by; **los precios**

aumentaron en un diez por ciento the prices went up by ten percent. ▪ *(tema, materia)* at, in; **bueno en deportes** good at sports; **experto en política** expert in politics. ▪ *(división, separación)* in; **lo dividió en tres partes** he divided it in three. ▪ *(con infinitivo)* **fue rápido en responder** he was quick to answer.

enaguas *fpl* petticoat *sing.*

enamorado, -a 1 *adj* in love. **2** *mf* person in love.

enamorar 1 *vt* to win the heart of. **2 enamorarse** *vr* to fall in love (**de** with).

enano, -a *adj & mf* dwarf.

encabezamiento *m (de carta)* heading; *(de periódico)* headline.

encabezar [40] *vt (carta, lista)* to head; *(periódico)* to lead; *(rebelión, carrera, movimiento)* to lead.

encajar 1 *vt (ajustar)* to insert; **e. un golpe a algn** to land sb a blow. **2** *vi (ajustarse)* to fit; **e. con** to fit (in) with.

encaje *m* lace.

encallar *vi* to run aground.

encantado, -a *adj (contento)* delighted; *(embrujado)* enchanted; **e. de conocerle** pleased to meet you.

encantador, -a *adj* charming.

encantar *vt (hechizar)* to cast a spell on; **me encanta nadar** I love swimming.

encanto *m* charm; **ser un e.** to be charming.

encapricharse *vr* to set one's mind (**con** on).

encaramarse *vr* to climb up.

encarar 1 *vt* to face. **2 encararse** *vr* **encararse con** to face up to.

encarcelar *vt* to imprison.

encarecer [33] **1** *vt* to put up the price of. **2 encarecerse** *vr* to go up (in price).

encarecidamente *adv* earnestly, insistently.

encargado, -a 1 *mf* manager; *(responsable)* person in charge. **2** *adj* in charge.

encargar [42] **1** *vt* to entrust with; *(mercancías)* to order. **2 encargarse** *vr* **encargarse de** to see to.

encargo *m* order; *(recado)* errand; *(tarea)* job.

encariñarse *vr* to become fond (con of).

encarnado, -a *adj (rojo)* red.

encarnizado, -a *adj* fierce.

encauzar [40] *vt* to channel.

encendedor *m* lighter.

encender [3] **1** *vt (luz, radio, tele)* to switch on, to put on; *(cigarro, vela, fuego)* to light; *(cerilla)* to strike. **2 encenderse** *vr (fuego)* to catch; *(lámpara etc)* to go o come on.

encendido *m* ignition.

encerado *m (pizarra)* blackboard.

encerrar [1] **1** *vt* to shut in; *(con llave)* to lock in. **2 encerrarse** *vr* to shut oneself in; *(con llave)* to lock oneself in.

enchaquetado, -a *adj* smartly dressed.

encharcar [44] *vt*, **encharcarse** *vr* to flood.

enchufado, -a 1 *adj* fig fam **estar e.** to have good connections. **2** *mf (favorito)* pet.

enchufar *vt* to plug in; *(unir)* to join.

enchufe *m (hembra)* socket; *(macho)* plug; *fam* contact.

encía *f* gum.

enciclopedia *f* encyclopedia.

encima 1 *adv* on top; *(arriba)* above; *(en el aire)* overhead; *(además)* besides. **2** *prep* **e. de** *(sobre)* on; *(además)* besides; **ahí e.** up there; **por e.** above; **leer un libro por e.** to skim through a book.

encina *f* holm oak.

encinta *adj* pregnant.

enclenque *adj (débil)* puny; *(enfermizo)* sickly.

encoger [53] **1** *vti* to contract; *(prenda)* to shrink. **2 encogerse** *vr (contraerse)* to contract; *(prenda)* to shrink; **encogerse de hombros** to shrug (one's shoulders).

encolar *vt (papel)* to paste; *(madera)* to glue.

encolerizar [40] **1** *vt* to infuriate. **2 encolerizarse** *vr* to become furious.

encono *m* spitefulness.

encontrar [2] **1** *vt (hallar)* to find; *(a persona)* to meet; *(problema)* to come up against. **2 encontrarse** *vr (sentirse)* to feel, to be; *(estar)* to be; **encontrarse a gusto** to feel comfortable; **encontrarse con algn** to meet sb.

encontronazo *m (choque)* clash.

encorvarse *vr* to bend (over).

encrucijada *f* crossroads.

encuadernar *vt* to bind.

encubrir *vt* to conceal.

encuentro *m* meeting; *(deportivo)* match.

encuesta *f (sondeo)* (opinion) poll; *(investigación)* investigation.

encuestar *vt* to poll.

endeble *adj* weak.

endémico, -a *adj* endemic.

enderezar [40] **1** *vt (poner derecho)* to straighten out; *(poner vertical)* to set upright. **2 enderezarse** *vr* to straighten up.

endeudarse *vr* to get into debt.

endiablado, -a *adj* mischievous.

endibia *f* endive.

endosar *vt (cheque)* to endorse; *fam (tarea)* to lumber with.

endulzar [40] *vt* to sweeten.

endurecer [33] *vt*, **endurecerse** *vr* to harden.

enemigo, -a *adj & mf* enemy.

enemistad *f* hostility, enmity.

enemistar 1 *vt* to set at odds. **2 enemistarse** *vr* to become enemies; **enemistarse con algn** to fall out with sb.

energético, -a *adj* energy.

energía *f* energy; **e. nuclear** nuclear power; **e. vital** vitality.

enérgico, -a *adj* energetic; *(tono)* emphatic.

enero *m* January.

enfadado, -a *adj* angry.

enfadar 1 *vt* to make angry. **2 enfadarse** *vr* to get angry (con with); *(dos personas)* to fall out.

enfado *m* anger.

énfasis *m inv* emphasis.

enfático, -a *adj* emphatic.

enfatizar [40] *vt* to emphasize, to stress.

enfermar *vi*, **enfermarse** *vr Am* to fall ill.

enfermedad *f* illness; *(contagiosa)* disease.

enfermería *f* infirmary.

enfermero, -a *mf (mujer)* nurse; *(hombre)* male nurse.

enfermizo, -a *adj* unhealthy.

enfermo, -a 1 *adj* ill. **2** *mf* ill person; *(paciente)* patient.

enfocar [44] *vt (imagen)* to focus; *(tema)* to approach; *(con linterna)* to shine a light on.

enfrentamiento *m* clash.

enfrentar 1 *vt (situación, peligro)* to confront; *(enemistar)* to set at odds. **2 enfrentarse** *vr* enfrentarse con *o* a *(encararse)* to confront.

enfrente 1 *adv* opposite; **la casa de e.** the house opposite. **2** *prep* **e. de** opposite.

enfriamiento *m (proceso)* cooling; *(catarro)* chill.

enfriar [29] **1** *vt* to cool (down). **2 enfriarse** *vr* to get cold; *(resfriarse)* to catch a cold.

enfurecer [33] **1** *vt* to enrage. **2 enfurecerse** *vr* to get furious.

engalanar 1 *vt* to deck out, to adorn. **2 engalanarse** *vr* to dress up, to get dressed up.

enganchar 1 *vt* to hook. **2 engancharse** *vr (ropa)* to get caught; *(persona)* to get hooked.

engañar 1 *vt* to deceive; *(estafar)* to cheat; *(mentir a)* to lie to; *(al marido, mujer)* to be unfaithful to. **2 engañarse** *vr* to deceive oneself.

engaño *m* deceit; *(estafa)* fraud; *(mentira)* lie.

engañoso, -a *adj (palabras)* deceitful; *(apariencias)* deceptive.

engarzar [40] *vt (unir)* to link; *(engastar)* to mount.

engatusar *vt fam* to coax; **e. a algn para que haga algo** to coax sb into doing sth.

engendrar *vt fig* to engender.

englobar *vt* to include.

engordar 1 *vt* to make fat. **2** *vi* to put on weight; *(comida, bebida)* to be fattening.

engorro *m* nuisance.

engranaje *m* gearing.

engrasar *vt (lubricar)* to lubricate; *(manchar)* to make greasy.

engreído, -a *adj* conceited.

engrudo *m* paste.

engullir *vt* to gobble up.

enharinar *vt* to cover with flour.

enhebrar *vt* to thread.

enhorabuena *f* congratulations *pl*; **dar la e. a algn** to congratulate sb.

enigma *m* enigma.

enjabonar *vt* to soap.

enjambre *m* swarm.

enjaular *vt (animal)* to cage.

enjuagar [42] *vt* to rinse.

enjugar [42] *vt*, **enjugarse** *vr (secar)* to mop up; *(lágrimas)* to wipe away.

enjuiciar [43] *vt (criminal)* to prosecute.

enjuto, -a *adj* lean, skinny.

enlace *m* connection; *(casamiento)* marriage.

enlatado, -a *adj* canned.

enlatar *vt* to can.

enlazar [40] *vti* to connect (con with).

enloquecedor, -a *adj* maddening.

enloquecer [33] **1** *vi* to go mad. **2** *vt* to drive mad. **3 enloquecerse** *vr* to go mad.

enmarañar 1 *vt (pelo)* to tangle; *(complicar)* to complicate. **2 enmarañarse** *vr (pelo)* to get tangled.

enmarcar [44] *vt* to frame.

enmascarar *vt (problema, la verdad)* to disguise.

enmendar [1] **1** *vt (corregir)* to put right. **2 enmendarse** *vr (persona)* to mend one's ways.

enmienda *f* correction; *(de ley)* amendment.

enmohecerse [33] *vr (metal)* to rust; *(comida)* to get moldy.

enmoquetar *vt* to carpet.

enmudecer [33] *vi* to fall silent; *(por sorpresa etc)* to be dumbstruck.

ennegrecer [33] *vt*, **ennegrecerse** *vr* to turn black.

enojado, -a *adj* angry.

enojar 1 *vt* to anger. **2 enojarse** *vr* to get angry.

enojo *m* anger, annoyance.

enorgullecer [33] **1** *vt* to fill with pride. **2 enorgullecerse** *vr* to be proud (**de** of).

enorme *adj* enormous.

enraizado, -a *adj* rooted.

enraizar [40] *vi*, **enraizarse** *vr (planta, costumbre)* to take root.

enrarecerse [33] *vr (aire)* to become rarefied.

enredadera *f* climbing plant.

enredar 1 *vt (enmarañar)* to entangle; *fig (implicar)* to involve (**en** in). **2 enredarse** *vr (enmarañarse)* to get tangled up; *fig (involucrarse)* to get involved, to get entangled (**con** with).

enredo *m (maraña)* tangle; *fig (lío)* muddle, mess.

enrejado *m (de ventana)* lattice.

enrevesado, -a *adj* complicated, difficult.

enriquecer [33] **1** *vt* to make rich; *fig* to enrich. **2 enriquecerse** *vr* to become rich; *fig* to become enriched.

enrojecer [33] **1** *vt* to redden, to turn red. **2** *vi (ruborizarse)* to blush.

enrollado, -a *adj* rolled up.

enrollar 1 *vt* to roll up; *(cable)* to coil; *(hilo)* to wind up. **2 enrollarse** *vr fam (hablar)* to go on and on.

enroscar [44] **1** *vt* to coil (round); *(tornillo)* to screw in; *(tapón)* to screw on. **2 enroscarse** *vr* to coil.

ensaimada *f* kind of spiral pastry from Majorca.

ensalada *f* salad.

ensaladera *f* salad bowl.

ensaladilla rusa *f* Russian salad.

ensamblaje *m* assembly.

ensamblar *vt* to assemble.

ensanchar 1 *vt* to widen; *(ropa)* to let out. **2 ensancharse** *vr* to widen.

ensangrentado, -a *adj* bloodstained.

ensañarse *vr* to be brutal (**con** with); *(cebarse)* to delight in tormenting (**con** -).

ensayar *vt* to try out; *(obra, canción)* to rehearse.

ensayo *m* trial; *(de obra)* rehearsal; **e. general** dress rehearsal.

enseguida, en seguida *adv (inmediatamente)* at once, straight away; *(poco después)* in a minute, soon.

ensenada *f* inlet.

enseñanza *f (educación)* education; *(de idioma etc)* teaching.

enseñar *vt* to teach; *(mostrar)* to show; *(señalar)* to point out; **e. a algn a hacer algo** to teach sb how to do sth.

ensimismado, -a *adj (absorbido)* engrossed; *(abstraído)* lost in thought.

ensimismarse *vr (absorberse)* to become engrossed; *(abstraerse)* to be lost in thought.

ensombrecer [33] **1** *vt* to cast a shadow over. **2 ensombrecerse** *vr* to darken.

ensopar *vt Am* to soak.

ensordecedor, -a *adj* deafening.

ensuciar [43] *vt*, **ensuciarse** *vr* to get dirty.

ensueño *m* dream.

entablar *vt (conversación)* to begin; *(amistad)* to strike up.

entallado, -a *adj (vestido)* close-fitting; *(camisa)* fitted.

entender [3] **1** vt (comprender) to understand; **dar a algn a e. que ...** to give sb to understand that .... **2** vi (comprender) to understand; **e. de** (saber) to know about. **3 entenderse** vr (comprenderse) to be understood.

entendimiento m understanding.

enteramente adv entirely.

enterarse vr to find out; **me he enterado de que ...** I understand ...; **ni me enteré** I didn't even realize it.

entereza f strength of character.

enternecedor, -a adj moving.

enternecer [33] **1** vt to move. **2 enternecerse** vr to be moved.

entero, -a adj (completo) entire, whole.

enterrador nm gravedigger.

enterrar [1] vt to bury.

entidad f organization, entity.

entierro m burial; (ceremonia) funeral.

entonar vt (canción) to intone, to sing.

entonces adv then; **por aquel e.** at that time.

entornar vt (ojos etc) to half-close; (puerta) to leave ajar.

entorno m environment.

entorpecer [33] vt (obstaculizar) to hinder.

entrada f entrance; (billete) ticket; (recaudación) takings pl; (plato) starter; **entradas** (en la frente) receding hairline.

entrañable adj (lugar) intimate, close; (persona) affectionate, warmhearted.

entrar 1 vi to enter; (venir dentro) to come in; (ir dentro) to go in; (encajar) to fit; **me entró dolor de cabeza** I got a headache; **me entraron ganas de reír** I felt like laughing. **2** vt (datos) to enter.

entre prep (dos) between; (más de dos) among(st).

entreabierto, -a adj (ojos etc) half-open; (puerta) ajar.

entreacto m interval.

entrecejo m space between the eyebrows.

entrecortado, -a adj (voz) faltering.

entrecot m fillet steak.

entredicho m **estar en e.** to be suspect; **poner algo en e.** to bring sth into question.

entrega f (de productos) delivery; (de premios) presentation; (devoción) selflessness.

entregar [42] **1** vt (dar) to hand over; (deberes etc) to hand in; (mercancía) to deliver. **2 entregarse** vr (rendirse) to give in; **entregarse a** to devote oneself to.

entrelazar [40] vt, **entrelazarse** vr to entwine.

entremedias adv in between.

entremés m hors d'oeuvres.

entremeterse vr = **entremeterse**.

entremezclarse vr to mix, to mingle.

entrenador, -a mf trainer.

entrenamiento m training.

entrenar vi, **entrenarse** vr to train.

entresuelo m mezzanine.

entretanto adv meanwhile.

entretención f Am entertainment.

entretener [24] **1** vt (divertir) to entertain; (retrasar) to delay; (detener) to detain. **2 entretenerse** vr (distraerse) to amuse oneself; (retrasarse) to be held up.

entretenido, -a adj entertaining.

entretenimiento m entertainment.

entretiempo adj **ropa de e.** lightweight clothing.

entrever [28] vt to glimpse, to catch sight of; fig **dejó e. que ...** she hinted that ...

entrevista f interview.

entrevistador, -a mf interviewer.

entrevistar 1 vt to interview. **2 entrevistarse** vr **entrevistarse con algn** to have an interview with sb.

entristecer [33] **1** vt to sadden. **2**

entristecerse *vr* to be sad (**por** about).

entrometerse *vr* to meddle (**en** in, with).

entumecerse [33] *vr* to go numb.

enturbiar [43] **1** *vt* to make cloudy. **2** enturbiarse *vr* to become cloudy.

entusiasmar **1** *vt* to fill with enthusiasm. **2** entusiasmarse *vr* to get enthusiastic (**con** about).

entusiasmo *m* enthusiasm; **con e.** enthusiastically.

enumerar *vt* to enumerate.

envasar *vt* (embotellar) to bottle; (empaquetar) to pack; (enlatar) to can, to tin.

envase *m* (recipiente) container; (botella vacía) empty.

envejecer [33] *vti* to age.

envejecimiento *m* aging.

envenenar *vt* to poison.

envergadura *f* de gran e. large-scale.

enviar [29] *vt* to send.

envidia *f* envy; **tener e. de algn** to envy sb.

envidiable *adj* enviable.

envidiar [43] *vt* to envy.

envidioso, -a *adj* envious.

envío *m* sending; (remesa) consignment; (paquete) parcel; **gastos de e.** postage and packing.

enviudar *vi* (hombre) to become a widower; (mujer) to become a widow.

envoltorio *m*, **envoltura** *f* wrapping.

envolver [4] (pp envuelto) **1** *vt* (con papel) to wrap; (en complot etc) to involve (**en** in). **2** envolverse *vr* to wrap oneself up (**en** in).

enyesar *vt* to put in plaster.

epidemia *f* epidemic.

episodio *m* episode.

época *f* time; (periodo) period.

equilibrar *vt* to balance.

equilibrio *m* balance.

equilibrista *mf* tightrope walker; *Am* opportunist.

equipaje *m* luggage; **hacer el e.** to pack.

equipar *vt* to equip (**con, de** with).

equiparar *vt* to compare (**con** with).

equipo *m* (de expertos, jugadores) team; (aparatos) equipment; (ropas) outfit; **e. de alta fidelidad** hi-fi stereo system.

equitación *f* horseriding.

equitativo, -a *adj* equitable.

equivalente *adj* equivalent.

equivaler [26] *vi* to be equivalent (**a** to).

equivocación *f* error.

equivocado, -a *adj* mistaken.

equivocar [44] **1** *vt* to mix up. **2** equivocarse *vr* to make a mistake.

equívoco, -a *adj* misleading.

era *pt imperfecto de* **ser**.

eras *pt imperfecto de* **ser**.

eres *indic pres de* **ser**.

erguir [55] *vt* to erect.

erizarse [40] *vr* to stand on end.

erizo *m* hedgehog; **e. de mar, e. marino** sea urchin.

ermita *f* shrine.

erosión *f* erosion.

erosionar *vt* to erode.

erótico, -a *adj* erotic.

erradicar [44] *vt* to eradicate.

errante *adj* wandering.

errar [50] *vt* to miss, to get wrong. **2** *vi* (vagar) to wander, to roam; (fallar) to err.

errata *f* misprint.

erróneo, -a *adj* erroneous.

error *m* mistake.

eructar *vi* to belch.

eructo *m* belch, burp.

erudito, -a **1** *adj* erudite. **2** *mf* scholar.

erupción *f* (de volcán) eruption; (en la piel) rash.

es *indic pres de* **ser**.

esa *adj dem* that.

ésa *pron dem ver* **ése**.

esbelto, -a *adj* slender.

esbozar [40] *vt* to sketch, to outline.

escabeche *m* brine.

escabullirse *vr* to scurry off.

escala *f* scale; *(parada) (de barco)* port of call; *(escalera)* ladder; **a gran e.** on a large scale; **hacer e. en** to stop over in.

escalada *f* climb.

escalador, -a *mf* climber.

escalar *vt* to climb.

escaldar *vt* to scald.

escalera *f* stair; *(escala)* ladder; **e. de incendios** fire escape; **e. mecánica** escalator.

escalerilla *f* steps *pl.*

escalfar *vt* to poach.

escalinata *f* stoop.

escalofriante *adj* hair-raising, bloodcurdling.

escalofrío *m* shiver.

escalón *m* step; **e. lateral** *(en letrero)* ramp.

escalonar *vt* to space out.

escama *f* *(de animal)* scale; *(de jabón)* flake.

escamotear *vt* to cheat out of.

escampar *vi* to clear up.

escandalizar [40] **1** *vt* to scandalize. **2 escandalizarse** *vr* to be shocked (**de** at, by).

escándalo *m* *(alboroto)* racket; *(desvergüenza)* scandal; **armar un e.** to kick up a fuss.

escandaloso, -a *adj* *(ruidoso)* noisy, rowdy; *(ofensivo)* scandalous.

escanear *vt* to scan.

escáner *m* scanner.

escaño *m* *(parlamentario)* seat.

escapada *f* *(de prisión)* escape.

escapar **1** *vi* to escape. **2 escaparse** *vr* to escape; *(gas etc)* to leak.

escaparate *m* shop window.

escapatoria *f* escape; **no tener e.** to have no way out.

escape *m* *(huida)* escape; *(de gas etc)* leak; **tubo de e.** exhaust (pipe).

escarabajo *m* beetle.

escarbar *vt* *(suelo)* to scratch.

escarcha *f* frost.

escarlata *adj* scarlet.

escarlatina *f* scarlet fever.

escarmentar [1] *vi* to learn one's lesson.

escarmiento *m* lesson.

escarola *f* escarole.

escarpado, -a *adj* *(paisaje)* craggy.

escasear *vi* to be scarce.

escasez *f* scarcity.

escaso, -a *adj* scarce; *(dinero)* tight; *(conocimientos)* scant.

escatimar *vt* to skimp on; **no escatimó esfuerzos para ...** he spared no efforts to ...

escayola *f* plaster of Paris; *(para brazo etc)* plaster.

escayolar *vt* *(brazo etc)* to put in plaster.

escena *f* scene; *(escenario)* stage.

escenario *m* *(en teatro)* stage; *(de película)* setting.

escéptico, -a *adj & mf* sceptic.

esclarecer [33] *vt* to shed light on.

esclavo, -a *adj & mf* slave.

esclusa *f* lock.

escoba *f* brush.

escocer [41] *vi* to sting.

escocés, -a **1** *adj* Scottish, Scots; **falda escocesa** kilt. **2** *mf* Scot.

escoger [53] *vt* to choose.

escolar **1** *adj* *(curso, año)* school. **2** *mf* *(niño)* schoolboy; *(niña)* schoolgirl.

escollo *m* reef; *(obstáculo)* pitfall.

escolta *f* escort.

escoltar *vt* to escort.

escombros *mpl* debris *sing.*

esconder *vt*, **esconderse** *vr* to hide (**de** from).

escondidas: a escondidas *adv* secretly.

escondite *m* *(lugar)* hiding place; *(juego)* hide-and-seek.

escondrijo *m* hiding place.

escopeta *f* shotgun; **e. de aire comprimido** air gun.

escorpión *m* scorpion.

escotado, -a *adj* low-cut.

escote *m* low neckline.

escotilla *f* hatch.

escozor *m* stinging.

escribir (*pp* **escrito**) **1** *vt* to write; **e. a máquina** to type. **2 escribirse** *vr* (*dos personas*) to write to each other.

escrito, -a *adj* written; **por e.** in writing. **2** *m* (*documento*) document.

escritor, -a *mf* writer.

escritorio *m* (*mueble*) writing desk; (*en computadora*) desktop.

escritura *f* (*documento*) document.

escrúpulo *m* (*recelo*) scruple; **una persona sin escrúpulos** an unscrupulous person.

escrupuloso, -a *adj* squeamish; (*honesto*) scrupulous; (*meticuloso*) painstaking.

escrutinio *m* (*de votos*) count.

escuadra *f* (*instrumento*) square; (*militar*) squad; (*de barcos*) squadron.

escuálido, -a *adj* emaciated.

escuchar 1 *vt* to listen to; (*oír*) to hear. **2** *vi* to listen.

escudarse *vr fig* **e. en algo** to hide behind sth.

escudo *m* (*arma defensiva*) shield; (*blasón*) coat of arms.

escuela *f* school; **e. de idiomas** language school.

escueto, -a *adj* plain.

escuezo *indic pres de* **escocer**.

esculcar [44] *vt Am* (*registrar*) to search.

escultor, -a *mf* (*hombre*) sculptor; (*mujer*) sculptress; (*de madera*) woodcarver.

escultura *f* sculpture.

escupidera *f* (*recipiente*) spittoon, cuspidor; (*orinal*) chamberpot.

escupir 1 *vi* to spit. **2** *vt* to spit out.

escurreplatos *m inv* dish rack.

escurridizo, -a *adj* slippery.

escurridor *m* colander; (*escurreplatos*) dish rack.

escurrir 1 *vt* (*plato, vaso*) to drain; (*ropa*) to wring out; **e. el bulto** to wriggle out. **2 escurrirse** *vr* (*resbalarse*) to slip.

ese, -a *adj dem* that; **esos, -as** those.

ése, -a *pron dem mf* that one; **ésos, -as** those (ones); *fam* **¡ni por ésas!** no way!

esencia *f* essence.

esencial *adj* essential; **lo e.** the main thing.

esencialmente *adv* essentially.

esfera *f* sphere; (*de reloj de pulsera*) dial; (*de reloj de pared*) face.

esforzarse [2] *vr* to endeavor (**por** to).

esfuerzo *m* effort.

esfumarse *vr fam* to beat it.

esgrima *f* fencing.

esgrimir *vt* to wield.

esguince *m* sprain.

eslabón *m* link.

eslogan *m* (*pl* **eslóganes**) slogan.

esmalte *m* enamel; (*de uñas*) nail polish.

esmeralda *f* emerald.

esmerarse *vr* to be careful; (*esforzarse*) to go to great lengths.

esmero *m* great care.

esmoquin *m* (*pl* **esmóquines**) tuxedo.

esnob (*pl* **esnobs**) **1** *adj* (*persona*) snobbish; (*restaurante etc*) posh. **2** *mf* snob.

eso *pron dem neutro* that; **¡e. es!** that's it!; **por e.** that's why; **a e. de las diez** around ten.

esos, -as *adj dem pl* those.

ésos, -as *pron dem mfpl* those.

espabilado, -a *adj* (*despierto*) wide awake; (*listo*) clever.

espabilar *vt*, **espabilarse** *vr* to wake up.

espacial *adj* spatial; **nave e.** spaceship.

espacio *m* space; (*de tiempo*) length; (*programa*) program.

espacioso, -a *adj* spacious.

espada *f* sword; **pez e.** swordfish.

espaguetis *mpl* spaghetti *sing*.

espalda *f* back; (*en natación*) backstroke; **espaldas** back *sing*; **a espaldas de algn** behind sb's back; **por la e.** from behind; **volver la e. a algn**

to turn one's back on sb.
espantajo *m (muñeco)* scarecrow.
espantapájaros *m inv* scarecrow.
espantar 1 *vt (asustar)* to frighten; *(ahuyentar)* to frighten away. **2 espantarse** *vr* to become frightened (de of).
espantoso, -a *adj* dreadful.
español, -a 1 *adj* Spanish. **2** *mf* Spaniard; **los españoles** the Spanish. **3** *m (idioma)* Spanish.
esparadrapo *m* sticking plaster.
esparcir [52] **1** *vt (papeles, semillas)* to scatter; *(rumor)* to spread. **2 esparcirse** *vr* to be scattered.
espárrago *m* asparagus.
espátula *f* spatula.
especia *f* spice.
especial *adj* special; **en e.** especially.
especialidad *f* specialty.
especialista *mf* specialist.
especializarse [40] *vr* to specialize (en in).
especialmente *adv (exclusivamente)* specially; *(muy)* especially.
especie *f* species *inv*; *(clase)* kind.
específicamente *adv* specifically.
especificar [44] *vt* to specify.
específico, -a *adj* specific.
espectacular *adj* spectacular.
espectáculo *m* show.
espectador, -a *mf* spectator; *(en teatro, cine)* member of the audience; **los espectadores** the audience *sing; (de televisión)* viewers.
especulación *f* speculation.
espejismo *m* mirage.
espejo *m* mirror; **e. retrovisor** rearview mirror.
espeluznante *adj* horrifying.
espera *f* wait; **en e. de** waiting for; **a la e. de** expecting; **sala de e.** waiting room.
esperanza *f* hope; **e. de vida** life expectancy.
esperanzador, -a *adj* encouraging.
esperar 1 *vi (aguardar)* to wait;

(tener esperanza) to hope. **2** *vt (aguardar)* to wait for; *(tener esperanza)* to hope for; *(estar a la espera de, bebé)* to expect; **espero que sí** I hope so; **espero que vengas** I hope you'll come.
esperma *m* sperm; *Am (vela)* candle.
espesar *vt*, **espesarse** *vr* to thicken.
espeso, -a *adj . (bosque, niebla)* dense; *(líquido)* thick; *(masa)* stiff.
espesor *m* thickness; **tres metros de e.** three meters thick.
espía *mf* spy.
espiar [29] **1** *vi* to spy. **2** *vt* to spy on.
espiga *f (de trigo)* ear.
espigado, -a *adj* slender.
espina *f (de planta)* thorn; *(de pescado)* bone; **e. dorsal** spine.
espinaca *f* spinach.
espinazo *m* spine.
espinilla *f* shin; *(en la piel)* spot.
espionaje *m* spying.
espiral *adj & f* spiral.
espirar *vi* to breathe out.
espíritu *m* spirit; *(alma)* soul.
espiritual *adj* spiritual.
espléndido, -a *adj (magnífico)* splendid; *(generoso)* lavish.
esplendor *m* splendor.
espliego *m* lavender.
esponja *f* sponge.
espontáneo, -a *adj* spontaneous.
esposado, -a *adj (con esposas)* handcuffed.
esposas *fpl* handcuffs.
esposo, -a *mf* spouse; *(hombre)* husband; *(mujer)* wife.
esprint *m* sprint.
espuela *f* spur.
espuma *f* foam; *(de cerveza)* head; *(de jabón)* lather; **e. de afeitar** shaving foam.
espumoso, -a *adj* frothy; *(vino)* sparkling.
esqueleto *m* skeleton.
esquema *m* diagram.
esquemático, -a *adj (escueto)*

schematic; *(con diagramas)* diagrammatic.

esquí *m (objeto)* ski; *(deporte)* skiing; **e. acuático** water-skiing.

esquiador, -a *m* skier.

esquiar [29] *vi* to ski.

esquimal *adj & mf* Eskimo.

esquina *f* corner.

esquivar *vt (a una persona)* to avoid; *(un golpe)* to dodge.

esta *adj dem* this.

está *indic pres de* estar.

ésta *pron dem f* this (one).

estabilidad *f* stability.

estable *adj* stable.

establecer [33] **1** *vt* to establish; *(récord)* to set. **2 establecerse** *vr (instalarse)* to settle.

establecimiento *m* establishment.

establo *m* cow shed.

estaca *f* stake; *(de tienda de campaña)* peg.

estación *f* station; *(del año)* season; **e. de servicio** service station; **e. de esquí** ski resort; **e. de trabajo** work station.

estacionamiento *m (acción)* parking.

estacionar *vt*, **estacionarse** *vr* to park.

estacionario, -a *adj* stationary.

estada *f*, **estadía** *f Am* stay.

estadio *m (deportivo)* stadium; *(fase)* stage.

estadística *f* statistics *sing*; **una e.** a statistic.

estado *m* state; **e. civil** marital status; **e. de cuentas** statement of account.

estadounidense 1 *adj* United States, American. **2** *mf* United States citizen.

estafa *f* swindle.

estafar *vt* to swindle.

estafeta *f* **e. de Correos** sub post office.

estallar *vi* to burst; *(bomba)* to explode; *(guerra)* to break out.

estallido *m* explosion; *(de guerra)* outbreak.

estampa *f* illustration.

estampado, -a 1 *adj (tela)* printed. **2** *m (de tela)* print.

estampilla *f Am (postage)* stamp.

estancar [44] **1** *vt (agua)* to hold back; *(paralizar)* to block; *(negociaciones)* to bring to a standstill. **2 estancarse** *vr* to stagnate.

estancia *f (permanencia)* stay; *(habitación)* room; *Am (hacienda)* ranch.

estanco *m* tobacconist's.

estándar *(pl estándares)* *adj & m* standard.

estanque *m* pond.

estante *m* shelf; *(para libros)* bookcase.

estantería *f* shelves.

estaño *m* tin.

estar [13] **1** *vi* to be; **¿está tu madre?** is your mother in?; **¿cómo estás?** how are you?; **está escribiendo** she is writing; **es a 2 de noviembre** it is the 2nd of November; **están a 20 pesos el kilo** they're 20 pesos a kilo; **¿estamos?** OK?; **e. de más** not to be needed. ■ *(+ para)* **estará para las seis** it will be finished by six; **hoy no estoy para bromas** I'm in no mood for jokes today; **el tren está para salir** the train is just about to leave. ■ *(+ por)* **está por hacer** it has still to be done; **eso está por ver** it remains to be seen. ■ *(+ con)* to have; **e. con la gripe** to have the flu. ■ *(+ sin)* to have no. **2 estarse** *vr* **¡estáte quieto!** keep still!

estatal *adj* state.

estatua *f* statue.

estatura *f* height.

estatuto *m* statute; *(de empresa etc)* rules *pl*.

este 1 *adj* eastern; *(dirección)* easterly. **2** *m* east; **al e. de** to the east of.

esté *subj pres de* estar.

este, -a *adj dem* this; **estos, -as** these.

éste, -a *pron dem mf* this one; **aquél**

... é. the former ... the latter; **éstos, -as** these (ones); **aquéllos ... éstos** the former ... the latter.

estela f (de barco) wake; (de avión) vapor trail.

estepa f steppe.

estera f rush mat.

estercolero m dunghill.

estéreo adj & m stereo.

estereofónico, -a adj stereophonic.

estereotipo m stereotype.

estéril adj sterile.

esterilla f small mat.

esterlina adj libra e. pound (sterling).

esternón m breastbone.

estero m Am marsh.

esteticienne, esteticista f beautician.

estético, -a adj aesthetic; **cirugía estética** plastic surgery.

estiércol m manure.

estilarse vr to be in vogue.

estilo m style; (modo) manner; (en natación) stroke.

estilográfica f (pluma) e. fountain pen.

estima f esteem.

estimación f (estima) esteem; (valoración) evaluation; (cálculo aproximado) estimate.

estimado, -a adj respected; **E. Señor** (en carta) Dear Sir.

estimar vt (apreciar) to esteem; (considerar) to think; (valuar) to value.

estimativo, -a adj approximate, estimated.

estimulante 1 adj stimulating. **2** m stimulant.

estimular vt to stimulate.

estímulo m stimulus.

estirar vt, **estirarse** vr to stretch.

estival adj summer.

esto pron dem (esta cosa) this, this thing; (este asunto) this matter.

estocada f stab.

estofado m stew.

estómago m stomach; **dolor de e.** stomach ache.

estoque m sword.

estorbar 1 vt (dificultar) to hinder. **2** vi to be in the way.

estorbo m (obstáculo) obstacle.

estornudar vi to sneeze.

estornudo m sneeze.

estos, -as adj dem pl these.

éstos, -as pron dem mfpl these.

estoy indic pres de **estar**.

estragos mpl **hacer e. en** to wreak havoc with o on.

estrangular vt to strangle.

estraperlo m black market.

estratagema f ruse.

estratégico, -a adj strategic.

estrechamente adv (íntimamente) closely.

estrechamiento m narrowing; **'e. de calzada'** (en letrero) 'road narrows'.

estrechar 1 vt to make narrow; **e. la mano a algn** to shake sb's hand; (lazos de amistad) to tighten. **2 estrecharse** vr to narrow.

estrechez f narrowness; **pasar estrecheces** to be hard up.

estrecho, -a 1 adj narrow; (ropa, zapato) tight; (amistad, relación) close. **2** m strait.

estrella f star; **e. de cine** film star; **e. de mar** starfish; **e. fugaz** shooting star.

estrellado, -a adj (en forma de estrella) star-shaped; (cielo) starry; (huevos) scrambled.

estrellar 1 vt fam to smash. **2 estrellarse** vr (chocar) to crash (**contra** into).

estremecedor, -a adj bloodcurdling.

estremecer [33] vt, **estremecerse** vr to shake.

estrenar vt to use for the first time; (ropa) to wear for the first time; (obra, película) to premiere. -

estreno m (teatral) first performance; (de película) premiere.

estreñido, -a adj constipated.

estreñimiento m constipation.

estrépito m din.

estrepitoso, -a adj (fracaso) spectacular.

estrés m stress.

estresante adj stressful.

estribillo m (en canción) chorus; (en poema) refrain.

estribo m stirrup; fig perder los estribos to fly off the handle.

estribor m starboard.

estricto, -a adj strict.

estropajo m scourer.

estropear 1 vt (máquina, cosecha) to damage; (fiesta, plan) to spoil; (pelo, manos) to ruin. **2 estropearse** vr to be ruined; (máquina) to break down.

estropicio m fam (destrozo) damage; (ruido) crash, clatter.

estructura f structure; (armazón) framework.

estruendo m roar.

estrujar vt (limón etc) to squeeze; (apretar) to crush.

estuche m case.

estudiante mf student.

estudiantil adj student.

estudiar [43] vti to study.

estudio m study; (encuesta) survey; (sala) studio; (apartamento) studio (apartment).

estudioso, -a 1 adj studious. **2** mf specialist.

estufa f heater.

estupefaciente m drug.

estupefacto, -a adj astounded.

estupendamente adv marvelously.

estupendo, -a adj marvelous; ¡e.! great!

estupidez f stupidity.

estúpido, -a 1 adj stupid. **2** mf idiot.

estuve pt indef de **estar**.

ETA f abr de **Euzkadi Ta Askatasuna** (Patria Vasca y Libertad) ETA.

etapa f stage.

etcétera adv etcetera.

eterno, -a adj eternal.

ético, -a adj ethical.

etílico, -a adj alcohol e. ethyl alcohol.

etiqueta f (de producto) label; (ceremonia) etiquette; **de e.** formal.

étnico, -a adj ethnic.

EU f abr de **Unión Europea** European Union, EU.

eucalipto m eucalyptus.

eufórico, -a adj euphoric.

euro m euro.

europeo, -a adj & mf European.

euskera m Basque.

eutanasia f euthanasia.

evacuación f evacuation.

evacuar [47] vt to evacuate.

evadir 1 vt (respuesta, peligro, impuestos) to avoid; (responsabilidad) to shirk. **2 evadirse** vr to escape.

evaluación f evaluation; (en colegio) assessment.

evaluar [30] vt to evaluate, to assess.

evangelio m gospel.

evaporación f evaporation.

evaporar vt, **evaporarse** vr to evaporate.

evasión f (fuga) escape; (escapismo) escapism; **e. de capitales** flight of capital.

evasiva f evasive answer.

evasivo, -a adj evasive.

evento m (acontecimiento) event; (incidente) unforeseen event.

eventual adj (posible) possible; (trabajo, obrero) casual.

evidencia f obviousness; **poner a algn en e.** to show sb up.

evidenciar [43] vt to show, to demonstrate.

evidente adj obvious.

evidentemente adv obviously.

evitar vt to avoid; (problema futuro) to prevent; (desastre) to avert.

evocar [44] vt (traer a la memoria) to evoke.

evolución f evolution; (desarrollo) development.

evolucionar *vi* to develop; *(especies)* to evolve.

ex *prefijo* former, ex-; **ex alumno** former pupil; **ex marido** ex-husband; *fam* **mi ex** my ex.

exabrupto *m* sharp comment.

exacerbar 1 *vt (agravar)* to exacerbate. **2 exacerbarse** *vr (irritarse)* to feel exasperated.

exactamente *adv* exactly.

exactitud *f* accuracy; **con e.** precisely.

exacto, -a *adj* exact; ¡**e.!** precisely!

exageración *f* exaggeration.

exagerado, -a *adj* exaggerated; *(excesivo)* excessive.

exagerar *vti* to exaggerate.

exaltarse *vr (acalorarse)* to get carried away.

examen *m* examination, exam; **e. de conducir** driving test.

examinador, -a *mf* examiner.

examinar 1 *vt* to examine. **2 examinarse** *vr* to sit for an examination.

exasperante *adj* exasperating.

exasperar 1 *vt* to exasperate. **2 exasperarse** *vr* to become exasperated.

excavación *f* excavation; *(en arqueología)* dig.

excavadora *f* digger.

excavar *vt* to excavate, to dig.

excedencia *f (de empleado)* leave (of absence); *(de profesor)* sabbatical.

excedente *adj & m* surplus.

exceder 1 *vt* to exceed. **2 excederse** *vr* to go too far.

excelencia *f* excellence.

excelente *adj* excellent.

excéntrico, -a *adj* eccentric.

excepción *f* exception; **a e.** except for.

excepcional *adj* exceptional.

excepto *adv* except (for).

exceptuar [30] *vt* to except.

excesivo, -a *adj* excessive.

exceso *m* excess; **e. de velocidad** speeding.

excitación *f (sentimiento)* excitement; *(acción)* excitation.

excitante *adj* exciting.

excitar 1 *vt* to excite. **2 excitarse** *vr* to get excited.

exclamación *f* exclamation.

exclamar *vti* to exclaim.

excluir [37] *vt* to exclude.

exclusive *adv (en fechas)* exclusive.

exclusivo, -a *adj* exclusive.

excremento *m* excrement.

exculpar *vt* to exonerate.

excursión *f* excursion.

excursionista *mf* tripper; *(a pie)* hiker.

excusa *f (pretexto)* excuse; *(disculpa)* apology.

excusado *m (retrete)* toilet.

excusar 1 *vt (justificar)* to excuse; *(eximir)* to exempt (**de** from). **2 excusarse** *vr (disculparse)* to apologize.

exención *f* exemption.

exento, -a *adj* exempt (**de** from).

exhalar *vt* to breathe out.

exhaustivo, -a *adj* exhaustive.

exhausto, -a *adj* exhausted.

exhibición *f* exhibition.

exhibir 1 *vt (mostrar)* to exhibit; *(lucir)* to show off. **2 exhibirse** *vr* to show off.

exigencia *f* demand; *(requisito)* requirement.

exigente *adj* demanding.

exigir [57] *vt* to demand.

exilado, -a 1 *adj* exiled. **2** *mf* exile.

exilar 1 *vt* to exile. **2 exilarse** *vr* to go into exile.

exiliado, -a *adj & mf* = **exilado**.

exiliar [43] *vt* = **exilar**.

exilio *m* exile.

existencia *f (vida)* existence; **existencias** stocks.

existente *adj* existing.

existir *vi* to exist.

éxito *m* success; **con é.** successfully; **tener é.** to be successful.

exitoso, -a *adj* successful.

éxodo *m* exodus.

exorbitante *adj* exorbitant.

exótico, -a *adj* exotic.

expandir *vt*, **expandirse** *vr* to expand.

expansión *f* expansion; *(de noticia)* spreading; *(diversión)* relaxation.

expatriar [29] **1** *vt* to exile, to banish. **2 expatriarse** *vr* to leave one's country.

expectación *f (interés)* excitement.

expectativa *f* expectancy.

expedición *f* expedition.

expediente *m (informe)* record; *(ficha)* file; **e. académico** student's record.

expedir [6] *vt (pasaporte etc)* to issue.

expendeduría *f* tobacconist's.

expensas *fpl* **a e. de** at the expense of.

experiencia *f* experience; *(experimento)* experiment.

experimentado, -a *adj* experienced.

experimental *adj* experimental.

experimentar 1 *vi* to experiment. **2** *vt* to undergo; *(aumento)* to show; *(pérdida)* to suffer; *(sensación)* to experience.

experimento *m* experiment.

experto, -a *adj* & *mf* expert.

expirar *vi* to expire.

explanada *f* esplanade.

explicación *f* explanation.

explicar [44] **1** *vt* to explain. **2 explicarse** *vr (persona)* to explain (oneself); **no me lo explico** I can't understand it.

exploración *f* exploration.

explorador, -a *mf* explorer.

explorar *vt* to explore.

explosión *f* explosion; **hacer e.** to explode.

explosionar *vti* to explode, to blow up.

explosivo, -a *adj* & *m* explosive.

explotación *f* exploitation.

explotar 1 *vi (bomba)* to explode, to go off. **2** *vt* to exploit.

exponer [19] *(pp* **expuesto) 1** *vt* *(mostrar)* to exhibit; *(presentar)* to put forward; *(arriesgar)* to expose. **2 exponerse** *vr* to expose oneself **(a** to).

exportación *f* export.

exportar *vt* to export.

exposición *f* exhibition.

exprés *adj* express; **olla e.** pressure cooker; **café e.** espresso (coffee).

expresamente *adv* expressly.

expresar 1 *vt* to express; *(manifestar)* to state. **2 expresarse** *vr* to express oneself.

expresión *f* expression.

expresivo, -a *adj* expressive.

expreso, -a 1 *adj* express. **2** *m* express (train). **3** *adv* on purpose.

exprimidor *m* juicer.

exprimir *vt (limón)* to squeeze; *(zumo)* to squeeze out.

expulsar *vt* to expel; *(jugador)* to send off.

expuse *pt indef de* **exponer**.

exquisito, -a *adj* exquisite; *(comida)* delicious; *(gusto)* refined.

extender [3] **1** *vt* to extend; *(agrandar)* to enlarge; *(mantel, mapa)* to spread (out); *(mano, brazo)* to stretch (out); *(crema, mantequilla)* to spread. **2 extenderse** *vr (en el tiempo)* to last; *(en el espacio)* to stretch; *(rumor, noticia)* to spread.

extendido, -a *adj* extended; *(mapa, plano)* open; *(mano, brazo)* outstretched; *(costumbre, rumor)* widespread.

extensión *f (de libro etc)* length; *(de terreno)* expanse.

extenso, -a *adj (terreno)* extensive; *(libro, película)* long.

extenuar [30] **1** *vt* to exhaust. **2 extenuarse** *vr* to exhaust oneself.

exterior 1 *adj (de fuera)* outer; *(puerta)* outside; *(política, deuda)* foreign; **Ministerio de Asuntos Exteriores** State Department. **2** *m (parte de fuera)* outside; *(extranjero)* abroad.

exteriormente *adv* outwardly.

exterminar *vt* to exterminate.

externo, -a *adj* external.

extinguir [59] **1** *vt (fuego)* to extinguish; *(raza)* to wipe out. **2 extinguirse** *vr (fuego)* to go out; *(especie)* to become extinct.

extintor *m* fire extinguisher.

extirpar *vt (tumor)* to remove; *fig* to eradicate, to stamp out.

extorsión *f* extortion.

extorsionar *vt* to extort.

extra 1 *adj* extra; *(superior)* top quality; **horas e.** overtime; **paga e.** bonus. **2** *mf* extra.

extracto *m* extract; **e. de cuenta** statement of account.

extraer [25] *vt* to extract.

extranjero, -a 1 *adj* foreign. **2** *mf* foreigner. **3** *m* abroad; **en el e.** abroad.

extrañar 1 *vt (sorprender)* to surprise; *Am (echar de menos)* to miss. **2 extrañarse** *vr* **extrañarse de** *(sorprenderse)* to be surprised at.

extrañeza *f (sorpresa)* surprise; *(singularidad)* strangeness.

extraño, -a 1 *adj* strange. **2** *mf* stranger.

extraoficial *adj* unofficial.

extraordinario, -a *adj* extraordinary.

extrarradio *m* suburbs *pl.*

extraterrestre *mf* alien.

extravagante *adj* outlandish.

extravertido, -a *adj & mf* = **extrovertido**.

extraviar [29] **1** *vt* to mislay. **2 extraviarse** *vr* to be missing.

extremeño, -a *adj & mf* Estremaduran.

extremidad *f (extremo)* tip; *(miembro)* limb.

extremo, -a 1 *m (de calle, cable)* end; *(máximo)* extreme; **en último e.** as a last resort; *f* **e. derecha/izquierda** outside-right/-left. **2** *adj* extreme; **E. Oriente** Far East.

extrovertido, -a *adj & mf* extrovert.

exuberante *adj* exuberant; *(vegetación)* lush.

F

fabada *f* stew of beans, pork sausage and bacon.

fábrica *f* factory.

fabricación *f* manufacture.

fabricante *mf* manufacturer.

fabricar [44] *vt* to manufacture.

fabuloso, -a *adj* fabulous.

facción *f* faction; **facciones** *(rasgos)* features.

facha *f fam* look.

fachada *f* façade.

facial *adj* facial.

fácil *adj* easy; **es f. que ...** it's (quite) likely that ...

facilidad *f (sencillez)* easiness; *(soltura)* ease; **facilidades de pago** easy terms.

facilitar *vt (simplificar)* to make easy *o* easier; **f. algo a algn** to provide sb with sth.

fácilmente *adv* easily.

facsímil, facsímile *m* facsimile.

factible *adj* feasible.

factor *m* factor.

factoría *f* factory.

factura *f* invoice.

facturación *f (en aeropuerto)* check-in; *(en estación)* registration.

facturar *vt (en aeropuerto)* to check in; *(en estación)* to register.

facultad *f* faculty.

faena *f (tarea)* task; *(en corrida)* performance.

faisán *m* pheasant.

faja *f (corsé)* corset.

fajo *m (de billetes)* wad.

falda *f (prenda)* skirt; *(de montaña)* slope; **f. pantalón** culottes *pl.*

falla *f Am (defecto)* fault.

fallar 1 *vi* to fail; **le falló la puntería** he missed his target. **2** *vt* to miss.

fallecer [33] *vi* to pass away, die.

fallecimiento *m* demise.

fallo *m* (error) mistake; (del corazón, de los frenos) failure.

falsear *vt* (hechos, la verdad) to distort.

falsificar [44] *vt* to falsify; (cuadro, firma, moneda) to forge.

falso, -a *adj* false; (persona) insincere.

falta *f* (carencia) lack; (escasez) shortage; (ausencia) absence; (error) mistake; (defecto) fault, defect; (fútbol) foul; (tenis) fault; **sin f.** without fail; **echar algo/a algn en f.** to miss sth/sb; **f. de ortografía** spelling mistake; **hacer f.** to be necessary; **(nos) hace f. una escalera** we need a ladder; **harán f. dos personas para mover el piano** it'll take two people to move the piano; **no hace f. que ...** there is no need for ....

faltar *vi* (no estar) to be missing; (escasear) to be lacking o needed; (quedar) to be left; **¿quién falta?** who is missing?; **le falta confianza en sí mismo** he lacks confidence in himself; **¡lo que me faltaba!** that's all I needed!; **¡no faltaría o faltaba más!** (por supuesto) (but) of course!; **¿cuántos kilómetros faltan para Managua?** how many kilometres is it to Managua?; **ya falta poco para las vacaciones** it won't be long now until the holidays; **f. a la verdad** not to tell the truth.

fama *f* fame; (reputación) reputation.

familia *f* family.

familiar 1 *adj* (de la familia) family; (conocido) familiar. **2** *mf* relation, relative.

familiarizarse [40] *vr* to familiarize oneself (con with).

famoso, -a *adj* famous.

fan *mf* fan.

fanático, -a 1 *adj* fanatical. **2** *mf* fanatic.

fanfarrón, -ona 1 *adj* boastful. **2** *mf* show-off.

fango *m* (barro) mud.

fantasía *f* fantasy.

fantasma *m* ghost.

fantástico, -a *adj* fantastic.

fardo *m* bundle.

farmacéutico, -a 1 *adj* pharmaceutical. **2** *mf* pharmacist.

farmacia *f* pharmacy.

fármaco *m* medicine, medication.

faro *m* (torre) lighthouse; (de coche) headlight.

farol *m* (luz) lantern; (en la calle) streetlight, streetlamp.

farola *f* streetlight, streetlamp.

farsante *mf* fake, impostor.

fascículo *m* installment.

fascinar *vt* to fascinate.

fascista *adj & mf* fascist.

fase *f* phase, stage.

fastidiar [43] **1** *vt* (molestar) to annoy, to bother. **2 fastidiarse** *vr* (aguantarse) to put up with it; **que se fastidie** that's his tough luck; **fastidiarse el brazo** to hurt one's arm.

fastidio *m* nuisance.

fastuoso, -a *adj* (acto) splendid, lavish.

fatal 1 *adj* (muy malo) awful; (mortal) fatal. **2** *adv* awfully; **lo pasó f.** he had a rotten time.

fatiga *f* (cansancio) fatigue.

fatigar [42] *vt*, **fatigarse** *vr* to tire.

fauna *f* fauna.

favor *m* favor; **¿puedes hacerme un f.?** can you do me a favor?; **estar a f. de** to be in favor of; **por f.** please; **haga el f. de sentarse** please sit down.

favorable *adj* favorable.

favorecedor, -a *adj* flattering.

favorecer [33] *vt* to favor; (sentar bien) to flatter.

favorito, -a *adj & mf* favorite.

fe *f* faith; **fe de bautismo/matrimonio** baptism/marriage certificate.

fealdad *f* ugliness.

febrero *m* February.

fecha *f* date; **f. de caducidad** sell-by

date; **hasta la f.** so far.

fechar *vt* to date.

fecundación *f* fertilization.

federación *f* federation.

felicidad *f* happiness; **(muchas) felicidades** *(en cumpleaños)* many happy returns.

felicitación *f* **tarjeta de f.** greeting card.

felicitar *vt* to congratulate (**por** on); **¡te felicito!** congratulations!

feligrés, -a *mf* parishioner.

feliz *adj* (contento) happy; **¡felices Navidades!** Merry Christmas!

felpa *f* (tela) plush; **oso** *o* **osito de f.** teddy bear.

felpudo *m* mat.

femenino, -a *adj* feminine; *(equipo, ropa)* women's; **sexo f.** female sex.

feminista *adj & mf* feminist.

fémur *m* femur.

fenomenal 1 *adj* phenomenal; *fam (fantástico)* great. **2** *adv fam* wonderfully.

fenómeno *m* phenomenon; *(prodigio)* genius; *(monstruo)* freak.

feo, -a *adj* ugly.

féretro *m* coffin.

feria *f* fair; **f. de muestras/del libro** trade/book fair.

feriado, -a *Am* **1** *adj* **día f.** (public) holiday. **2** *m* (public) holiday.

fermentar *vi* to ferment.

feroz *adj* fierce, ferocious.

ferretería *f* hardware store.

ferrocarril *m* railroad.

ferroviario, -a *adj* railway, rail.

ferry *m* ferry.

fértil *adj* fertile.

fertilizante *m* fertilizer.

fertilizar [40] *vt* to fertilize.

fervor *m* fervor.

festejar *vt* to celebrate.

festín *m* feast.

festival *m* festival.

festividad *f* festivity.

festivo, -a 1 *adj* (ambiente etc) festive; **día f.** holiday. **2** *m* holiday.

feto *m* fetus.

fiable *adj* reliable, trustworthy.

fiador, -a *mf* guarantor.

fiambre *m* cold meat.

fiambrera *f* lunch box.

fianza *f* (depósito) deposit; *(jurídica)* bail.

fiarse [29] *vr* to trust (**de** -).

fibra *f* fibre.

ficción *f* fiction.

ficha *f* (de archivo) filing card; *(en juegos)* counter; *(de ajedrez)* piece.

fichaje *m* signing.

fichar 1 *vt* to put on file; *(deportista)* to sign up. **2** *vi* (en el trabajo) (al entrar) to clock in; *(al salir)* to clock out; *(deportista)* to sign.

fichero *m* card index; *(de ordenador)* file.

ficticio, -a *adj* fictitious.

fidelidad *f* faithfulness; **alta f.** high fidelity, hi-fi.

fideo *m* noodle.

fiebre *f* fever; **tener f.** to have a temperature.

fiel 1 *adj* (leal) faithful, loyal. **2** *mpl* **los fieles** the congregation.

fieltro *m* felt.

fiera *f* wild animal.

fierro *m* *Am* (hierro) iron; *(navaja)* knife.

fiesta *f* (entre amigos) party; *(vacaciones)* holiday; *(festividad)* celebration.

figura *f* figure.

figurar 1 *vi* (aparecer) to figure. **2** **figurarse** *vr* to imagine; **ya me lo figuraba** I thought as much; **¡figúrate, figúrese!** just imagine!

fijador *m* (gomina) gel.

fijamente *adv* **mirar f.** to stare.

fijar 1 *vt* to fix. **2** **fijarse** *vr* (darse cuenta) to notice; *(poner atención)* to pay attention, to watch.

fijo, -a *adj* fixed; *(trabajo)* steady.

fila *f* file; *(de cine, teatro)* row; **en f. india** in single file.

filántropo, -a *mf* philanthropist.

filarmónico, -a *adj* philharmonic.

filatelia *f* stamp collecting, philately.

filete *m* fillet.

filial 1 *adj (de hijos)* filial. **2** *f (empresa)* subsidiary.

filmar *vt* to film.

film(e) *m* film.

filo *m* edge.

filosofía *f* philosophy.

filosófico, -a *adj* philosophical.

filósofo, -a *mf* philosopher.

filtración *f* filtration; *(de noticia)* leak(ing).

filtrar 1 *vt* to filter; *(noticia)* to leak. **2 filtrarse** *vr (líquido)* to seep; *(noticia)* to leak out.

filtro *m* filter.

fin *m (final)* end; *(objetivo)* purpose, aim; **dar** *o* **poner f. a** to put an end to; **en f.** anyway; **¡por** *o* **al f.!** at last!; **f. de semana** weekend; **al f. y al cabo** when all's said and done; **a f. de** in order to, so as to.

final 1 *adj* final. **2** *m* end; **al f.** in the end; **a finales de octubre** at the end of October. **3** *f (de campeonato)* final.

finalizar [40] *vti* to end, to finish.

finalmente *adv* finally.

financiación *f* financing.

financiar [43] *vt* to finance.

financiero, -a *adj* financial.

financista *mf Am* financier.

finanzas *fpl* finances.

finca *f (de campo)* country house.

fingir [57] **1** *vt* to feign. **2** *vi* to pretend.

fino, -a 1 *adj (hilo, capa)* fine; *(flaco)* thin; *(educado)* refined, polite; *(oído)* sharp, acute. **2** *m (vino)* type of dry sherry.

firma *f* signature; *(empresa)* firm.

firmar *vt* to sign.

firme 1 *adj* firm; **tierra f.** terra firma. **2** *adv* hard.

firmemente *adv* firmly.

fiscal 1 *adj* fiscal, tax. **2** *mf* district attorney.

fisco *m* treasury.

fisgar [42] *vi fam* to snoop, to pry.

fisgón, -ona *mf* snooper.

física *f* physics *sing.*

físico, -a *adj* physical.

fisioterapia *f* physiotherapy.

flaco, -a *adj (delgado)* skinny.

flamante *adj (nuevo)* brand-new; *(vistoso)* splendid, brilliant.

flamenco, -a 1 *adj (música)* flamenco; *(de Flandes)* Flemish. **2** *m (música)* flamenco.

flan *m* caramel custard.

flanco *m* flank, side.

flaquear *vi (fuerzas, piernas)* to weaken, to give way.

flaqueza *f* weakness.

flash *m* flash.

flauta *f* flute.

flecha *f* arrow.

flechazo *m (enamoramiento)* love at first sight.

fleco *m* fringe.

flema *f* phlegm.

flemático, -a *adj* phlegmatic.

flemón *m* gumboil.

flequillo *m* bangs *pl.*

fletar *vt* to charter.

flexible *adj* flexible.

flexión *f* flexion.

flexionar *vt* to bend; *(músculo)* to flex.

flexo *m* reading lamp.

flirtear *vi* to flirt.

flojear *vi (ventas etc)* to fall off, to go down; *(piernas)* to weaken, to grow weak; *(memoria)* to fail; *Andes fam (holgazanear)* to laze around *o* about.

flojera *f fam* weakness, faintness.

flojo, -a *adj (tornillo, cuerda etc)* loose, slack; *(perezoso)* lazy, idle.

flor *f* flower.

flora *f* flora.

floreado, -a *adj* flowery.

florecer [33] *vi (plantas)* to flower; *(negocio)* to flourish, to thrive.

floreciente *adj* flourishing, prosperous.

florero *m* vase.

floristería f florist's (shop).

flota f fleet.

flotador m *(para nadar)* rubber ring.

flotar vi to float.

flote m a f. afloat.

flotilla f flotilla.

fluctuar [30] vi to fluctuate.

fluidez f fluency.

fluido, -a 1 adj fluid; *(estilo etc)* fluent. **2** m liquid.

fluir [37] vi to flow.

flujo m flow; *(de la marea)* rising tide.

flúor m fluorine.

fluorescente adj fluorescent.

fluvial adj river.

FMI m abr de **Fondo Monetario Internacional** International Monetary Fund, IMF.

fobia f phobia (**a** of).

foca f seal.

foco m *(lámpara)* spotlight, floodlight; *Andes, Méx (bombilla)* (electric light) bulb; *Am (de coche)* (car) headlight; *Am (farola)* street light.

fofo, -a adj soft; *(persona)* flabby.

fogata f bonfire.

fogón m *(de cocina)* ring.

folio m sheet of paper.

folklórico, -a adj música folklórica folk music.

follaje m foliage.

folletín m *(relato)* newspaper serial.

folleto m leaflet; *(turístico)* brochure.

follón m fam *(alboroto)* ruckus; *(enredo, confusión)* mess.

fomentar vt to promote.

fomento m promotion.

fonda f inn.

fondear vi to anchor.

fondista mf *(corredor)* long-distance runner.

fondo[1] m *(parte más baja)* bottom; *(de habitación)* back; *(de pasillo)* end; *(segundo término)* background; **a f.** thoroughly; **al f. de la calle** at the end of the street; **en el f. es bueno** deep down he's kind; **música de f.** background music.

fondo[2] m *(dinero)* fund; **cheque sin fondos** bad check.

fonético, -a adj phonetic.

fontanero, -a mf plumber.

footing m jogging; **hacer f.** to go jogging.

forastero, -a mf outsider.

forcejear vi to wrestle.

forense 1 adj forensic. **2** mf **(médico) f.** forensic surgeon.

forestal adj forest; **repoblación f.** re-afforestation.

forjar vt to forge.

forma f form, shape; *(manera)* way; **¿qué f. tiene?** what shape is it?; **de esta f.** in this way; **de f. que** so that; **de todas formas** anyway, in any case; **estar en f.** to be in shape; **estar en baja f.** to be out of shape.

formación f formation; *(enseñanza)* training; **f. profesional** vocational training.

formal adj formal; *(serio)* serious; *(fiable)* reliable.

formalizar [40] vt *(hacer formal)* to formalize; *(contrato)* to legalize.

formar 1 vt to form; **f. parte de algo** to be a part of sth; *(enseñar)* to educate, to train. **2 formarse** vr to be formed, to form.

formatear vt to format.

formato m format; *(del papel)* size.

formidable adj *(estupendo)* terrific.

fórmula f formula.

formular vt *(quejas, peticiones)* to make; *(deseo)* to express; *(pregunta)* to ask; *(una teoría)* to formulate.

formulario m form.

forrar vt *(por dentro)* to line; *(por fuera)* to cover.

forro m *(por dentro)* lining; *(por fuera)* cover.

fortalecer [33] vt to fortify, to strengthen.

fortificar [44] vt to fortify.

fortísimo, -a adj very strong.

fortuito, -a adj fortuitous.

fortuna f (suerte) luck; (capital) fortune; **por f.** fortunately.

forzado, -a adj forced; **trabajos forzados** hard labor.

forzar [2] vt to force.

forzosamente adv necessarily.

forzoso, -a adj obligatory, compulsory.

fosa f (sepultura) grave; (hoyo) pit.

fósforo m (cerilla) match.

fósil adj & m fossil.

foso m (hoyo) pit.

foto f photo.

fotocopia f photocopy.

fotocopiadora f photocopier.

fotocopiar [43] vt to photocopy.

fotografía f photograph; **hacer fotografías** to take photographs.

fotografiar [29] vt to photograph, to take a photograph of.

fotógrafo, -a mf photographer.

FP f abr de **Formación Profesional** vocational training.

frac m (pl **fracs** o **fraques**) dress coat, tails pl.

fracasar vi to fail.

fracaso m failure.

fraccionar vt, **fraccionarse** vr to break up.

fractura f fracture.

fragancia f fragrance.

frágil adj (quebradizo) fragile; (débil) frail.

fragmento m fragment; (de novela etc) passage.

fraile m friar, monk.

frambuesa f raspberry.

francamente adv frankly.

francés, -esa 1 adj French. **2** mf (hombre) Frenchman; (mujer) Frenchwoman. **3** m (idioma) French.

franco, -a[1] adj (persona) frank; **puerto f.** free port.

franco[2] m (moneda) franc.

franela f flannel.

franja f (de terreno) strip; (de bandera) stripe.

franqueo m postage.

frasco m small bottle, flask.

frase f (oración) sentence; (expresión) phrase.

fraterno, -a adj fraternal, brotherly.

fraude m fraud.

frazada f Am blanket.

frecuencia f frequency; **con f.** frequently.

frecuentar vt to frequent.

frecuente adj frequent.

frecuentemente adv frequently, often.

fregadero m (kitchen) sink.

fregar [1] vt (lavar) to wash; (suelo) to mop; Am to annoy.

fregón, -ona adj Am annoying.

fregona f mop.

freidora f (deep) fryer.

freír [56] (pp **frito**) vt to fry.

frenar vti to brake.

frenazo m sudden braking.

frenético, -a adj frantic.

freno m brake; **pisar/soltar el f.** to press/release the brake; **f. de mano** handbrake.

frente 1 m front; **chocar de f.** to crash head on; **hacer f. a algo** to face up to sth. **2** f (de la cara) forehead; **f. a f.** face to face. **3** prep **f. a** opposite.

fresa f strawberry.

fresco, -a 1 adj (frío) cool; (comida, fruta) fresh; (descarado) rude. **2** m (frescor) fresh air; (caradura) cheek; **hace f.** it's chilly.

frescor m freshness.

frescura f freshness; (desvergüenza) nerve.

fresón m (large) strawberry.

fríamente adv coolly.

fricción f friction.

friegaplatos mf inv (persona) dishwasher.

frígido, -a adj frigid.

frigorífico m refrigerator, fridge.

frijol, fríjol m kidney bean.

frío, -a 1 adj cold; (indiferente) cold, cool. **2** m cold; **hace f.** it's cold.

friolento, -a adj Am sensitive to the cold.

friolero, -a *adj* sensitive to the cold, chilly.

frívolo, -a *adj* frivolous.

frontera *f* frontier.

fronterizo, -a *adj* frontier, border; **países fronterizos** neighboring countries.

frontón *m* pelota.

frotar 1 *vt* to rub. **2 frotarse** *vr* **f. las manos** to rub one's hands together.

fruncir [52] *vt* **f. el ceño** to frown.

frustrar 1 *vt* to frustrate. **2 frustrarse** *vr* (esperanza) to fail; (persona) to be frustrated o disappointed.

fruta *f* fruit; **f. del tiempo** fresh fruit.

frutería *f* fruit shop.

frutero *m* fruit dish o bowl.

frutilla *f* Bol, CSur, Ecuad strawberry.

fruto *m* fruit; **frutos secos** nuts.

fucsia *f* fuchsia.

fuego *m* fire; (lumbre) light; **fuegos artificiales** fireworks; **¿me da f., por favor?** have you got a light, please?

fuel, fuel-oil *m* diesel.

fuente *f* (artificial) fountain; (recipiente) dish; (origen) source; (de caracteres) font.

fuera¹ 1 *adv* outside; **desde f.** from (the) outside; **por f.** on the outside; **la puerta de f.** the outer door. **2** *prep* **f. de** out of; **f. de serie** extraordinary.

fuera² 1 *subj imperfecto de* **ir**. **2** *subj imperfecto de* **ser**.

fuerte 1 *adj* strong; (dolor) severe; (sonido) loud; (comida) heavy. **2** *m* (fortaleza) fort. **3** *adv* **¡abrázame f.!** hold me tight!; **¡habla más f.!** speak up!; **¡pégale f.!** hit him hard!

fuerza *f* (fortaleza) strength; (cuerpo) force; **a la f.** (por obligación) of necessity; (con violencia) by force; **por f.** of necessity; **Fuerzas Armadas** Armed Forces.

fuese 1 *subj imperfecto de* **ir**. **2** *subj imperfecto de* **ser**.

fuete *m* Am whip.

fuga *f* (huida) escape; (de gas etc) leak.

fugarse [42] *vr* to escape.

fui 1 *pt indef de* **ir**. **2** *pt indef de* **ser**.

fulano, -a *mf* so-and-so; (hombre) what's his name; (mujer) what's her name; **Doña Fulana de tal** Mrs So-and-so.

fullería *f* cheating; **hacer fullerías** to cheat.

fullero, -a 1 *adj* cheating. **2** *mf* cheat.

fulminante *adj* (muerte, enfermedad) sudden; (mirada) withering.

fumador, -a *mf* smoker; **los no fumadores** non-smokers.

fumar 1 *vti* to smoke; **no f.** (en letrero) no smoking. **2 fumarse** *vr* **f. un cigarro** to smoke a cigarette.

función *f* function; (cargo) duties *pl*; (de teatro, cine) performance.

funcionamiento *m* operation; **poner/entrar en f.** to put/come into operation.

funcionar *vi* to work; **no funciona** (en letrero) out of order.

funcionario, -a *mf* civil servant.

funda *f* cover; (de gafas etc) case; **f. de almohada** pillowcase.

fundación *f* foundation.

fundamental *adj* fundamental.

fundamento *m* basis, grounds *pl*; **sin f.** unfounded.

fundar 1 *vt* (crear) to found. **2 fundarse** *vr* (empresa) to be founded; (teoría, afirmación) to be based.

fundir *vt*, **fundirse** *vr* (derretirse) to melt; (bombilla, plomos) to blow; (unirse) to merge.

fúnebre *adj* (mortuorio) funeral; **coche f.** hearse.

funeral *m* funeral.

funeraria *f* funeral parlor.

fungir *vi* Am to act (**de** as).

funicular *m* funicular (railway).

furgoneta *f* van.

furia *f* fury.

furioso, -a *adj* furious.

furor *m* fury.

furtivo, -a *adj* furtive; **cazador/**

pescador f. poacher.

furúnculo *m* boil.

fusible *m* fuse.

fusil *m* gun, rifle.

fusilar *vt* to shoot, to execute.

fusión *f (de metales)* fusion; *(del hielo)* thawing, melting; *(de empresas)* merger.

fusionar *vt*, **fusionarse** *vr (metales)* to fuse; *(empresas)* to merge.

fútbol *m* soccer; **f. americano** football.

futbolín *m* table football.

futbolista *mf* football/soccer player.

futuro, -a 1 *adj* future. **2** *m* future.

G

gabardina *f (prenda)* raincoat.

gabinete *m (despacho)* study; *(de gobierno)* cabinet.

gacho, -a *adj* con la cabeza gacha hanging one's head.

gafas *fpl* glasses, spectacles; **g. de sol** sunglasses.

gafe *m* ser (un) g. to be a jinx.

gaita *f* bagpipes *pl*.

gajes *mpl fam* irón g. del oficio occupational hazards.

gajo *m (de naranja, pomelo etc)* segment.

gala *f (espectáculo)* gala; **de g.** dressed up; *(ciudad)* decked out.

galán *m* handsome young man; *(personaje)* leading man.

galante *adj* gallant.

galápago *m* turtle.

galardón *m* prize.

galardonar *vt* to award a prize to.

galería *f (corredor)* covered balcony; *(museo)* art gallery.

Gales *m (el país de)* G. Wales.

galés, -esa 1 *adj* Welsh. **2** *mf*

(hombre) Welshman; *(mujer)* Welshwoman; **los galeses** the Welsh. **3** *m (idioma)* Welsh.

galgo *m* greyhound.

Galicia *f* Galicia.

galimatías *m inv* gibberish.

gallego, -a 1 *adj* Galician; *Am* Spanish. **2** *mf* Galician; *Am* Spaniard. **3** *m (idioma)* Galician.

galleta *f* cracker.

gallina *f* hen.

gallinero *m* henhouse.

gallo *m* cock.

galopante *adj (inflación etc)* galloping.

galopar *vi* to gallop.

galope *m* gallop; **a g. tendido** flat out.

gama *f* range.

gamba *f* prawn.

gamberro, -a 1 *mf* hooligan. **2** *adj* uncouth.

gamo *m* fallow deer.

gamuza *f (trapo)* chamois o shammy leather.

gana *f (deseo)* wish (**de** for); *(apetito)* appetite; **de buena g.** willingly; **de mala g.** reluctantly; **tener ganas de (hacer) algo** to feel like (doing) sth.

ganadero, -a *mf* livestock farmer.

ganado *m* livestock.

ganador, -a 1 *adj* winning. **2** *mf* winner.

ganancia *f* profit.

ganar 1 *vt (sueldo)* to earn; *(premio)* to win; *(aventajar)* to beat. **2 ganarse** *vr* to earn.

ganchillo *m* crochet work.

gancho *m* hook; *Am (para el pelo)* hairpin; *Andes, CAm, Méx, Ven (para la ropa)* hanger.

ganga *f* bargain.

ganso, -a *m* goose; *(macho)* gander; *fam* dolt.

garabato *m* scrawl.

garaje *m* garage.

garantía *f* guarantee.

garantizar [40] *vt (cosa)* to guarantee; *(a persona)* to assure.

garbanzo m chickpea.

garfio m hook.

garganta f throat; (desfiladero) narrow pass.

gargantilla f short necklace.

gárgara f Am (elixir) gargling solution; **gárgaras** gargling sing; **hacer gárgaras** to gargle.

garra f claw; (de ave) talon; fig **tener g.** to be compelling.

garrafa f carafe.

garrafal adj monumental.

garrapata f tick.

garrote m (porra) club.

gas m gas; (en bebida) fizz; **g. ciudad** town gas; **gases (nocivos)** fumes; **g. de escape** exhaust fumes; **agua con g.** fizzy water.

gasa f gauze.

gaseosa f lemonade.

gasoducto m gas pipeline.

gasoil, gasóleo m diesel oil.

gasolina f gasoline.

gasolinera f gas station.

gastar 1 vt (consumir) (dinero, tiempo) to spend; (gasolina, electricidad) to consume; (malgastar) to waste; (ropa) to wear; **g. una broma a algn** to play a practical joke on sb. **2 gastarse** vr (zapatos etc) to wear out.

gasto m expenditure; **gastos** expenses.

gatas: a gatas adv on all fours.

gatear vi to crawl.

gatillo m (de armas) trigger.

gato m cat; (de coche) jack.

gauchada f CSur favor.

gaucho, -a 1 adj RP fam (servicial) helpful, obliging. **2** mf gaucho.

gaveta f (cajón) drawer; Am (guantera) glove compartment.

gaviota f seagull.

gay adj inv & m (pl gays) gay.

gazpacho m gazpacho.

gel m gel; **g. (de ducha)** shower gel.

gelatina f (ingrediente) gelatin; (para postre) jelly.

gema f gem.

gemelo, -a 1 adj & mf (identical)

twin. **2** mpl **gemelos** (de camisa) cufflinks; (anteojos) binoculars.

gemido m groan.

gemir [6] vi to groan.

generación f generation.

general adj general; **por lo o en g.** in general.

generalizar [40] **1** vt to generalize. **2 generalizarse** vr to become widespread o common.

generalmente adv generally.

generar vt to generate.

género m (clase) kind, sort; (mercancía) article; (gramatical) gender.

generoso, -a adj generous (con, para to).

genético, -a adj genetic.

genial adj brilliant.

genio mf inv genius; (mal carácter) temper; **estar de mal g.** to be in a bad mood.

genocidio m genocide.

gente f people pl; Am respectable people.

gentuza f riffraff.

genuino, -a adj (puro) genuine; (verdadero) authentic.

geografía f geography.

geología f geology.

geometría f geometry.

geranio m geranium.

gerente mf manager.

gérmen m germ.

gerundio m gerund.

gestación f gestation.

gesticular vi to gesticulate.

gestión f (administración) management; **gestiones** (negociaciones) negotiations; (trámites) formalities.

gestionar vt to take steps to acquire o obtain; (negociar) to negotiate.

gesto m (mueca) face; (con las manos) gesture.

gestor, -a mf ≃ solicitor.

gigante adj & m giant.

gigantesco, -a adj gigantic.

gil, -ila mf CSur fam twit, idiot.

gimnasia f gymnastics pl.

gimnasio *m* gym, gymnasium.

gimotear *vi* to whine.

ginebra *f (bebida)* gin.

ginecólogo, -a *mf* gynecologist.

gira *f (musical, teatral)* tour.

girar *vi (dar vueltas)* to spin; **g. a la derecha/izquierda** to turn right/left.

girasol *m* sunflower.

giratorio, -a *adj* revolving.

giro *m (vuelta)* turn; *(frase)* turn of phrase; *(libranza)* draft; **g. telegráfico** giro o money order; **g. postal** postal o money order.

gitano, -a *adj & mf* gypsy.

glaciar *m* glacier.

glándula *f* gland.

global *adj* comprehensive.

globo *m* balloon; *(esfera)* globe.

gloria *f (fama)* glory; *(cielo)* heaven.

glorieta *f (plazoleta)* small square; *(encrucijada de calles)* roundabout, traffic circle.

glosario *m* glossary.

glotón, -ona 1 *adj* greedy. **2** *mf* glutton.

glucosa *f* glucose.

gobernación *f* government; **Ministerio de la Gobernación** ≃ Department of the Interior.

gobernador, -a *mf* governor.

gobernante 1 *adj* ruling. **2** *mpl* **los gobernantes** the rulers.

gobernar [1] *vt* to govern; *(un país)* to rule.

gobierno *m* government; *(mando)* running.

gofio *m (en América y Canarias)* roasted maize meal.

gol *m* goal.

golf *m* golf; **palo de g.** golf club.

golfo, -a[1] *mf* good for nothing.

golfo[2] *m* gulf.

golondrina *f* swallow.

golosina *f* candy.

goloso, -a *adj* sweet-toothed.

golpe *m* blow; *(llamada)* knock; *(puñetazo)* punch; *(choque)* bump; *(desgracia)* blow; **de g.** all of a sudden;

g. de estado coup d'état.

golpear *vt* to hit; *(con el puño)* to punch; *(puerta, cabeza)* to bang.

goma *f* rubber; *(elástico)* rubber band; *Cuba, CSur (para ruedas)* tire; **g. de borrar** eraser.

gomal *m Am* rubber plantation.

gomero *m Am* gum tree; *(recolector)* rubber collector.

gordo, -a 1 *adj (carnoso)* fat; *(grueso)* thick. **2** *mf* fat person, *fam* fatty; *Am fam (como apelativo)* **¿cómo estás, gorda?** hey, how are you doing? **3** *m* **el g.** *(de lotería)* first prize.

gorila *m* gorilla.

gorra *f* cap.

gorrión *m* sparrow.

gorro *m* cap.

gota *f* drop; **g. a g.** drop by drop; **ni g.** not a bit.

gotear *v impers* to drip; **el techo gotea** there's a leak in the ceiling.

gotera *f* leak.

gozar [40] **1** *vt* to enjoy. **2** *vi (disfrutar)* to enjoy (**de** -).

gozne *m* hinge.

grabación *f* recording.

grabado *m (arte)* engraving; *(dibujo)* drawing.

grabadora *f* tape recorder.

grabar *vt (sonidos, imágenes)* to record; *(en ordenador)* to save.

gracia *f (chiste)* joke; *(indulto)* pardon; **hacer** o **tener g.** to be funny.

gracias *fpl* thanks; **muchas** o **muchísimas g.** thank you very much.

gracioso, -a 1 *adj (divertido)* funny. **2** *mf (personaje)* comic character.

grada *f (peldaño)* step; **gradas** *(estadio)* terracing.

grado *m* degree; **de buen g.** willingly.

gradual *adj* gradual.

gradualmente *adv* gradually.

graduar [30] **1** *vt (regular)* to regulate. **2 graduarse** *vr (soldado, alumno)* to graduate; **g. la vista** to have one's eyes tested.

gráfico, -a 1 *adj* graphic. **2** *mf*

graph; **gráficos** *(de ordenador)* graphics.

gragea *f* pill.

gral. *abr de* **General** Gen.

gramática *f* grammar.

gramo *m* gram.

gran *adj ver* **grande**.

granada *f (fruto)* pomegranate; *(explosivo)* grenade.

granate 1 *adj inv* maroon. **2** *m* maroon.

grande *adj (before singular noun* **gran** *is used) (tamaño)* big, large; *fig (persona)* great; *(cantidad)* large; **pasarlo en g.** to have a great time.

granel: a granel *adv* loose.

granero *m* granary.

granito *m* granite.

granizada *f,* **granizado** *m* iced drink.

granizo *m* hail.

granja *f* farm.

granjear(se) *vt & vr* to gain.

granjero, -a *mf* farmer.

grano *m* grain; *(de café)* bean; *(espinilla)* spot.

granuja *m* **1** *(pilluelo)* rascal. **2** *(estafador)* con-man.

grapa *f* staple.

grapadora *f* stapler.

grasa *f* grease.

grasiento, -a *adj* greasy.

graso, -a *adj (pelo)* greasy; *(materia)* fatty.

gratis *adv* free.

gratitud *f* gratitude.

gratuito, -a *adj (de balde)* free (of charge); *(arbitrario)* gratuitous.

grava *f (guijas)* gravel; *(en carretera)* gravel *pl.*

gravar *vt (impuestos)* to tax.

grave *adj (importante)* serious; *(muy enfermo)* seriously ill; *(voz, nota)* low.

gravedad *f* seriousness; *(fuerza)* gravity.

gravilla *f (en carretera)* gravel *pl.*

griego, -a 1 *adj & mf* Greek. **2** *m (idioma)* Greek.

grieta *f* crack; *(en la piel)* chap.

grifo *m* faucet.

grillo *m* cricket.

gringo, -a *adj & mf* gringo, yankee.

gripe *f* flu.

gris *adj & m* gray.

grisáceo, -a *adj* grayish.

gritar *vti* to shout.

grito *m* shout.

grosella *f (fruto)* redcurrant; **g. negra** blackcurrant; **g. silvestre** gooseberry.

grosería *f (ordinariez)* rude word *o* expression.

grosero, -a *adj (tosco)* coarse; *(maleducado)* rude.

grosor *m* thickness.

grotesco, -a *adj* grotesque.

grúa *f (en construcción)* crane; *(para coches)* tow truck.

grueso, -a 1 *adj* thick; *(persona)* stout. **2** *m (parte principal)* bulk.

grumo *m* lump.

gruñido *m* grunt.

gruñir *vi* to grunt.

gruñón, -ona *adj* grumpy.

grupo *m* group.

gruta *f* cave.

guacamol, guacamole *m Am* avocado sauce.

guachafita *f Am* uproar.

guacho, -a *adj & mf Am* orphan.

guagua[1] *f (en Canarias y Cuba)* bus.

guagua[2] *f Am* baby.

guajiro, -a *mf Cuba fam (campesino)* peasant.

guante *m* glove.

guantera *f (en coche)* glove compartment.

guapo, -a 1 *adj* good-looking; *(mujer)* beautiful, pretty; *(hombre)* handsome. **2** *m Am (matón)* bully.

guaraca *f Am* sling.

guarango, -a *adj Am* rude.

guarda *mf* guard; **g. jurado** security guard.

guardacoches *mf inv* parking attendant.

guardacostas *m inv (persona)*

coastguard; (embarcación) coast-guard vessel.

guardaespaldas mf inv body-guard.

guardameta mf goalkeeper.

guardar vt (conservar, reservar) to keep; (un secreto) to keep; (poner en un sitio) to put away; (en ordenador) to save.

guardarropa m (cuarto) cloak-room; (armario) wardrobe.

guardería infantil f nursery (school).

guardia 1 f (vigilancia) watch; (turno de servicio) duty; **la g. civil** the civil guard. **2** mf (hombre) police-man; (mujer) policewoman.

guardián, -ana mf (hombre) watchman; (mujer) watchwoman.

guarecerse [33] vr to take shelter o refuge (**de** from).

guarro, -a 1 adj filthy. **2** mf pig.

guaso, -a adj Am peasant.

guasón, -ona 1 adj humorous. **2** mf joker.

guata f (relleno) padding; Am (barriga) paunch.

guayabera f CAm, Carib, Col short jacket.

guayabo, -a mf Am (chica bonita) pretty young girl; (chico guapo) good-looking boy.

güero, -a adj Méx fam blond, blonde.

guerra f war; **g. civil/fría/mundial/ nuclear** civil/cold/world/nuclear war.

guerrilla f (partida armada) guerril-la force o band; (lucha) guerrilla warfare.

guía 1 mf (persona) guide. **2** f (libro) guide; **la g. de teléfonos** the tele-phone directory.

guiar [29] **1** vt (indicar el camino) to guide; (automóvil) to drive. **2** guiarse vr to be guided (**por** by).

guijarro m pebble.

guindilla f chili.

guiñapo m (andrajo) rag.

guiñar vt i to wink.

guiño m wink.

guión m (de cine, televisión) script; (ortográfico) hyphen; (esquema) sketch.

guirnalda f garland.

guisante m pea.

guisar vt to cook.

guiso m dish; (guisado) stew.

guita f rope.

guitarra 1 f guitar. **2** mf guitarist.

gula f gluttony.

gusano m worm; (oruga) caterpillar.

gustar 1 vt me gusta el vino I like wine; me gustaban los caramelos I used to like sweets; me gusta nadar I like swimming; me gustaría ir I would like to go. **2** vi g. de to enjoy.

gusto m taste; **con (mucho) g.** with (great) pleasure; **tanto g.** pleased to meet you; **estar a g.** to feel comfort-able o at ease; **ser de buen/mal g.** to be in good/bad taste; **tener buen/ mal g.** to have good/bad taste.

H

ha indic pres de **haber**.

haba f broad bean.

habano m Havana (cigar).

haber [14] **1** v aux (en tiempos com-puestos) to have; **lo he visto** I have seen it; **ya lo había hecho** he had al-ready done it. ▪ **h. de** + infinitivo (obligación) to have to; **has de ser bueno** you must be good. **2** v impers (special form of present tense: **hay**) (existir, estar) (singular used also with plural nouns) **hay** there is o are; **había** there was o were; **habrá una fiesta** there will be a party; **había una vez ...** once upon a time ...; **no hay de qué** you're welcome; **¿qué hay?** how are things? ▪ **hay que** +

infinitivo it is necessary to.

habichuela *f* kidney bean.

hábil *adj (diestro)* skillful; **días hábiles** working days.

habitación *f (cuarto)* room; *(dormitorio)* bedroom; **h. individual/doble** single/double room.

habitante *mf* inhabitant.

hábito *m (costumbre)* habit; *(de monje)* habit.

habitual *adj* usual, habitual.

habituar [30] **1** *vt* to accustom (a to). **2 habituarse** *vr* to get used (a to), to become accustomed (a to).

hablador, -a *adj (parlanchín)* talkative.

hablar 1 *vi* to speak, to talk; **h. con algn** to speak to sb; **¡ni h.!** no way!; *fam* **¡quién fue a h.!** look who's talking! **2** *vt (idioma)* to speak. **3 hablarse** *vr* to speak o talk to one another; **'se habla español'** 'Spanish spoken'.

habré *indic fut de* **haber**.

hacer [15] **1** *vt* to do; *(crear, fabricar)* to make; **hazme un favor** do me a favor; **¿qué haces?** *(en este momento)* what are you doing?; *(para vivir)* what do you do (for a living)?; **tengo mucho que h.** I have a lot to do; **lo hizo con sus propias manos** he made it with his own hands; **h. la cama** to make the bed; **h. la cena** to make dinner; **el negro le hace más delgado** black makes him look slimmer; **ya no puedo leer como solía hacerlo** I can't read as well as I used to; **¡bien hecho!** well done! **2** *vi (actuar)* to play; **hizo de Desdémona** she played Desdemona. **h. por o para + infinitivo** to try to; **haz por venir** try and come. **3** *v impers* **hace calor/frío** it's hot/cold; **hace mucho (tiempo)** a long time ago; **hace dos días que no lo veo** I haven't seen him for two days; **hace dos años que vivo en Chicago** I've been living in Chicago for two years. **4 hacerse** *vr (volverse)* to become, to grow; *(simular)*

to pretend; **hacerse el dormido** to pretend to be sleeping; **hacerse con** *(apropiarse)* to get hold of; **hacerse a** *(habituarse)* to get used to.

hacha *f (herramienta)* ax.

hachís *m* hashish.

hacia *prep (dirección)* towards, to; *(aproximadamente)* at about, at around; **h. abajo** down, downwards; **h. adelante** forwards; **h. arriba** up, upwards; **h. atrás** back, backwards.

hacienda *f* ranch.

hada *f* fairy; **cuento de hadas** fairy tale.

hago *indic pres de* **hacer**.

halagar [42] *vt* to flatter.

halago *m* flattery.

halcón *m* falcon.

hallar 1 *vt (encontrar)* to find; *(descubrir)* to discover. **2 hallarse** *vr (estar)* to be, to find oneself; *(estar situado)* to be situated.

hallazgo *m (descubrimiento)* discovery; *(cosa encontrada)* find.

hamaca *f* hammock.

hambre *f (apetito)* hunger; *(inanición)* starvation; *(catástrofe)* famine; **tener h.** to be hungry.

hambriento, -a *adj* starving.

hamburguesa *f* hamburger.

han *indic pres de* **haber**.

haré *indic fut de* **hacer**.

harina *f* flour.

hartar 1 *vt (cansar, fastidiar)* to annoy; *(atiborrar)* to satiate. **2 hartarse** *vr (saciar el apetito)* to eat one's fill; *(cansarse)* to get fed up (**de** with).

harto, -a *adj (lleno)* full; *(cansado)* fed up; **estoy h. de trabajar** I'm fed up with working.

has *indic pres de* **haber**.

hasta 1 *prep (lugar)* up to, as far as; *(tiempo)* until, up to; *(con cantidad)* up to, as many as; *(incluso)* even; **h. la fecha** up to now; **h. luego** see you later. **2 conj h. que** until.

hay *indic pres de* **haber**.

haya *subj pres de* **haber**.

haz *imperativo de* **hacer**.

hazmerreír *m* laughing stock.

he *indic pres de* **haber**.

hebilla *f* buckle.

hebra *f* thread.

hebreo, -a 1 *adj* Hebrew. **2** *mf* Hebrew.

hechizo *m* (*embrujo*) spell.

hecho, -a 1 *adj* made, done; (*carne*) done; (*ropa*) ready-made. **2** *m* (*realidad*) fact; (*acto*) act, deed; (*suceso*) event, incident; **de h.** in fact.

hectárea *f* hectare.

heder [3] *vi* to stink, to smell foul.

hedor *m* stink, stench.

helada *f* frost.

heladería *f* ice-cream parlor.

helado, -a 1 *m* ice cream. **2** *adj* (*muy frío*) freezing cold; *fig* **quedarse h.** (*atónito*) to be flabbergasted.

helar [1] **1** *vt* (*congelar*) to freeze. **2** *v impers* to freeze; **anoche heló** there was a frost last night. **3 helarse** *vr* (*congelarse*) to freeze.

helecho *m* fern.

hélice *f* (*de avión, barco*) propeller.

helicóptero *m* helicopter.

hembra *f* (*animal, planta*) female; (*mujer*) woman.

hemorragia *f* hemorrhage.

hemos *indic pres de* **haber**.

hendidura *f* crack.

heno *m* hay.

herbolario *m* (*tienda*) herbalist's (shop).

heredar *vt* to inherit.

heredero, -a *mf* (*hombre*) heir; (*mujer*) heiress.

herencia *f* inheritance, legacy; (*biológica*) heredity.

herida *f* (*lesión*) injury; (*corte*) wound.

herido, -a 1 *adj* injured, hurt. **2** *m* injured person.

herir [5] **1** *vt* (*físicamente*) (*lesionar*) to injure; (*cortar*) to wound. **2 herirse** *vr* to injure o hurt oneself.

hermana *f* sister.

hermanastro, -a *mf* (*hombre*) stepbrother; (*mujer*) stepsister.

hermano *m* brother; **primo h.** first cousin; **hermanos** brothers and sisters.

herméticamente *adv* **h. cerrado** hermetically sealed.

hermético, -a *adj* (*cierre*) hermetic, airtight; *fig* (*grupo*) secretive.

hermoso, -a *adj* beautiful, lovely; (*grandioso*) fine.

hermosura *f* beauty.

héroe *m* hero.

heroína *f* (*mujer*) heroine; (*droga*) heroin.

herradura *f* horseshoe.

herramienta *f* tool.

hervir [5] **1** *vt* (*hacer bullir*) to boil. **2** *vi* (*bullir*) to boil.

heterogéneo, -a *adj* heterogeneous.

hice *pt indef de* **hacer**.

hiciste *pt indef de* **hacer**.

hidratante *adj* moisturizing; **crema/leche h.** moisturizing cream/lotion.

hidráulico, -a *adj* hydraulic.

hidroavión *m* hydroplane.

hiedra *f* ivy.

hielo *m* ice.

hiena *f* hyena.

hierba *f* grass; **mala h.** weed.

hierbabuena *f* mint.

hierro *m* iron.

hígado *m* liver.

higiene *f* hygiene.

higiénico, -a *adj* hygienic; **papel h.** toilet paper.

higo *m* fig; *fam fig* **hecho un h.** wizened, crumpled.

hija *f* daughter.

hijastro, -a *mf* (*hombre*) stepson; (*mujer*) stepdaughter.

hijo *m* son; **hijos** children.

hilera *f* line, row.

hilo *m* thread; (*grueso*) yarn; (*fibra*) linen; **perder el h.** to lose the thread; **h. musical** background music.

himno *m* hymn; **h. nacional** national anthem.

hincapié *m* **hacer h. en** *(insistir)* to insist on; *(subrayar)* to emphasize.

hincar [44] **1** *vt (clavar)* to drive (in). **2 hincarse** *vr* **hincarse de rodillas** to kneel (down).

hincha **1** *mf (de equipo)* fan, supporter. **2** *f (antipatía)* grudge, dislike.

hinchado, -a *adj* swollen.

hinchar **1** *vt (inflar)* to inflate, to blow up. **2 hincharse** *vr* to swell (up); *fam (hartarse)* to stuff oneself.

hindú *adj & mf* Hindu.

hipermercado *m* hypermarket.

hípico, -a *adj* horse.

hipnotizar [40] *vt* to hypnotize.

hipo *m* **tener h.** to have the hiccups.

hipócrita **1** *adj* hypocritical. **2** *mf* hypocrite.

hipopótamo *m* hippopotamus.

hipoteca *f* mortgage.

hipótesis *f inv* hypothesis.

hispánico, -a *adj* Hispanic.

hispano, -a **1** *adj* Hispanic. **2** *mf* Spanish American, Hispanic.

hispanohablante **1** *adj* Spanish-speaking. **2** *mf* Spanish speaker.

histérico, -a *adj* hysterical.

historia *f (estudio del pasado)* history; *(narración)* story.

historial *m* record; *(antecedentes)* background.

histórico, -a *adj* historical; *(de gran importancia)* historic, memorable.

historieta *f (tira cómica)* comic strip.

hizo *indic indef de* **hacer**.

hocico *m (de animal)* snout.

hogar *m (casa)* home; *(de la chimenea)* hearth.

hoguera *f* bonfire.

hoja *f* leaf; *(de papel)* sheet; *(de cuchillo, espada)* blade; *(impreso)* hand-out.

hojalata *f* tin.

hojaldre *m* puff pastry.

hojear *vt (libro)* to leaf through.

hola *interj* hello!

holgado, -a *adj (ropa)* loose, baggy; *(económicamente)* comfortable; *(espacio)* roomy.

holgazán, -ana **1** *adj* lazy. **2** *mf* lazybones *inv*.

hollín *m* soot.

hombre **1** *m* man; **h. de negocios** businessman. **2** *interj (saludo)* hey!; **¡sí h.!, ¡h. claro!** *(enfático)* sure!, you bet!

hombrera *f* shoulder pad.

hombro *m* shoulder; **a hombros** on one's shoulders; **encogerse de hombros** to shrug one's shoulders; **mirar a algn por encima del h.** to look down one's nose at sb.

homenaje *m* homage, tribute.

homicida **1** *mf (hombre)* murderer; *(mujer)* murderess. **2** *adj* homicidal.

homicidio *m* homicide.

homogéneo, -a *adj* homogeneous, uniform.

homosexual *adj & mf* homosexual.

hondo, -a *adj* deep; **plato h.** soup dish.

honesto, -a *adj (honrado)* honest; *(recatado)* modest.

hongo *m* fungus; *(sombrero)* derby (hat); **h. venenoso** toadstool.

honor *m* honor; **palabra de h.** word of honor.

honorario, -a **1** *adj* honorary. **2** *mpl* **honorarios** fees.

honra *f (dignidad)* dignity; *(honor)* honor; **¡a mucha h.!** and proud of it!

honradez *f* honesty.

honrado, -a *adj (de fiar)* honest.

honrar *vt (respetar)* to honor; *(enaltecer)* to be a credit to.

honroso, -a *adj (loable)* honorable.

hora *f* hour; *(cita)* appointment; **media h.** half an hour; **h. punta** rush hour; **horas extra** overtime (hours); **¿qué h. es?** what time is it?; **a última h.** at the last moment; **pedir h.** *(al médico etc)* to ask for an appointment.

horario *m* schedule.

horca *f* gallows *pl*.

horchata f sweet milky drink made from chufa nuts.

horizonte m horizon.

hormiga f ant.

hormigón m concrete.

hormigueo m pins and needles pl, tingling o itching sensation.

hormiguero m anthill.

hormona f hormone.

horno m (de cocina) oven; (para metales) furnace; (para cerámica etc) kiln; **pescado al h.** baked fish.

horóscopo m horoscope.

horquilla f (del pelo) hair-grip.

horrendo, -a adj horrifying, horrible.

horrible adj horrible.

horror m horror; **¡qué h.!** how awful!; fam **tengo h. a las motos** I hate motorbikes.

horrorizar [40] vt to horrify; (dar miedo) to terrify.

horroroso, -a adj horrifying; (que da miedo) terrifying; fam (muy feo) hideous; fam (malísimo) awful.

hortaliza f vegetable.

hortera adj fam (persona) flashy; (cosa) tacky.

hospedaje m lodgings pl, accommodations.

hospedar 1 vt to put up. **2 hospedarse** vr to stay (en at).

hospicio m (para huérfanos) orphanage.

hospital m hospital.

hospitalizar [40] vt to send into hospital, to hospitalize.

hostal m guest house.

hostelería f (negocio) catering business; (estudios) hotel management.

hostería f Am hostel, inn.

hostil adj hostile.

hotel m hotel.

hoy adv (día) today; **h. (en) día** nowadays.

hoyo m hole.

hube pt indef de **haber**.

hubiera subj imperfecto de **haber**.

hucha f piggy bank.

hueco, -a 1 adj (vacío) empty, hollow; (sonido) resonant. **2** m (cavidad) hollow, hole; (sitio no ocupado) empty space.

huele indic pres de **oler**.

huelga f strike; **estar en** o **de h.** to be on strike; **hacer h.** to go on strike.

huella f (del pie) footprint; (coche) track; **h. dactilar** fingerprint; fig (vestigio) trace.

huérfano, -a adj & mf orphan.

huerta f (parcela) truck garden; (región) irrigated area used for cultivation.

huerto m (de verduras) vegetable garden; (de frutales) orchard.

hueso m (del cuerpo) bone; (de fruto) pit; Am (enchufe) contact.

huésped, -a mf guest; **casa de huéspedes** guesthouse.

huevo m egg; **h. duro** hard-boiled egg; **h. frito** fried egg; **h. pasado por agua,** Am **h. tibio** soft-boiled egg; **huevos revueltos** scrambled eggs.

huevón, -ona muy fam mf Andes, Arg, Ven dork.

huida f flight, escape.

huir [37] vi (escaparse) to run away (de from); (evadirse) to escape (de from).

hule m (tela impermeable) oilcloth; (de mesa) tablecloth; Am rubber.

humanitario, -a adj humanitarian.

humano, -a 1 adj (relativo al hombre) human; (compasivo) humane; **ser h.** human being. **2** m human (being).

humeante adj (chimenea) smoky, smoking.

humedad f (atmosférica) humidity; (de lugar) dampness.

humedecer [33] **1** vt to moisten, to dampen. **2 humedecerse** vr to become damp o moist.

húmedo, -a adj (casa, ropa) damp; (clima) humid, damp.

humildad f (de persona) humility;

(de cosa) humbleness.

humilde *adj* humble; *(familia)* poor.

humillante *adj* humiliating.

humillar 1 *vt* to humiliate. **2 humillarse** *vr* **humillarse ante algn** to humble oneself before sb.

humo *m* smoke; *(gas)* fumes *pl*; *(vapor)* vapor, steam.

humor *m (genio)* mood; *(gracia)* humor; **estar de buen** *o* **mal h.** to be in a good *o* bad mood; **sentido del h.** sense of humor.

hundimiento *m (de edificio)* collapse; *(de barco)* sinking; *(de tierra)* subsidence; *(ruina)* downfall.

hundir 1 *vt (barco)* to sink; *(derrumbar)* to bring *o* knock down. **2 hundirse** *vr (barco)* to sink; *(edificio, empresa)* to collapse.

huracán *m* hurricane.

huraño, -a *adj* unsociable.

hurgar [42] **1** *vi (fisgar)* to poke one's nose (**en** in). **2** *vt (fuego etc)* to poke.

hurto *m* petty theft.

huyo *indic pres de* **huir.**

I

ibérico, -a *adj* Iberian.

iberoamericano, -a *adj & mf* Latin American.

iceberg *m (pl* **icebergs)** iceberg.

icono *m* icon.

ida *f* **billete de i. y vuelta** round trip ticket.

idea *f* idea; **hacerse a la i. de** to get used to the idea of; **ni i.** no idea; **cambiar de i.** to change one's mind.

ideal *adj & m* ideal.

idear *vt (inventar)* to devise; *(concebir)* to think up.

idéntico, -a *adj* identical.

identidad *f* identity; **carnet de i.** identity card.

identificación *f* identification.

identificar [44] **1** *vt* to identify. **2 identificarse** *vr* to identify oneself; *(simpatizar)* to identify (**con** with).

idilio *m (romance)* romance.

idioma *m* language.

idiota 1 *adj* stupid. **2** *mf* idiot.

idiotez *f* **decir/hacer una i.** to say/ to do something stupid.

ídolo *m* idol.

idóneo, -a *adj* suitable.

iglesia *f (edificio)* church; **la I.** the Church.

ignorante 1 *adj (sin instrucción)* ignorant; *(no informado)* unaware (**de** of). **2** *mf* ignoramus.

ignorar 1 *vt (algo)* not to know; *(algn)* to ignore. **2 ignorarse** *vr* to be unknown.

igual 1 *adj (lo mismo)* the same; *(equivalente)* equal; **i. que** the same as; **a partes iguales** fifty-fifty; **al i. que** just like; **por i.** equally; **6 más 7 i. a 13** 6 plus 7 equals 13. **2** *m* equal. **3** *adv* **lo haces i. que yo** you do it the same way I do; **es i.** it doesn't matter.

igualar *vt* to make equal; *(nivelar)* to level.

igualdad *f* equality; *(identidad)* sameness; **en i. de condiciones** on equal terms.

igualmente *adv* equally; *(también)* also, likewise; **¡gracias! — ¡i.!** thank you! — the same to you!

ilegal *adj* illegal.

ilegalmente *adv* illegally.

ilegible *adj* illegible, unreadable.

ilegítimo, -a *adj* illegitimate.

ileso, -a *adj* unharmed.

ilícito, -a *adj* unlawful.

ilimitado, -a *adj* unlimited.

iluminación *f (alumbrado)* illumination.

iluminar *vt* to illuminate.

ilusión *f (esperanza)* hope; *(esperanza vana)* illusion; *(emoción)* excitement; **hacerse ilusiones** to build up one's hopes; **me hace i. verla** I'm looking forward to seeing her;

¡qué i.! how exciting!

ilusionar 1 vt (esperanzar) **i. a algn** to build up sb's hopes; (entusiasmar) to excite. **2 ilusionarse** vr (esperanzarse) to build up one's hopes; (entusiasmarse) to be excited (**con** about).

ilustración f (grabado) illustration; (erudición) learning.

ilustrar vt to illustrate.

ilustre adj distinguished.

imagen f image; (de televisión) picture.

imaginación f imagination.

imaginar 1 vt to imagine. **2 imaginarse** vr to imagine; **me imagino que sí** I suppose so.

imaginario, -a adj imaginary.

imán m magnet.

imbatible adj unbeatable.

imbécil 1 adj stupid. **2** mf imbecile.

imitar vt to imitate; (gestos) to mimic.

impacientar 1 vt **i. a algn** to exasperate sb. **2 impacientarse** vr to get impatient (**por** at).

impaciente adj (deseoso) impatient; (intranquilo) anxious.

impactar vt to shock, to stun.

impactante adj **una noticia i.** a sensational piece of news.

impacto m impact.

impar adj odd.

imparable adj unstoppable.

imparcial adj impartial.

impartir vt (clases) to give.

impasible adj impassive.

impecable adj impeccable.

impedimento m impediment; (obstáculo) hindrance.

impedir [6] vt (obstaculizar) to impede; (imposibilitar) to prevent, to stop.

impenetrable adj impenetrable.

impensable adj unthinkable.

imperante adj (gobernante) ruling; (predominante) prevailing.

imperativo, -a 1 adj imperative. **2** m imperative.

imperdible m safety pin.

imperdonable adj unforgivable, inexcusable.

imperfecto, -a adj imperfect; (defectuoso) defective; (tiempo verbal) imperfect.

imperio m empire.

impermeable 1 adj impervious; (ropa) waterproof. **2** m raincoat.

impertinente adj (insolente) impertinent; (inoportuno) irrelevant.

impetuoso, -a adj (violento) violent; (fogoso) impetuous.

implacable adj implacable.

implicar [44] vt (involucrar) to involve (**en** in); (conllevar) to imply.

implícito, -a adj implicit.

implorar vt to implore.

imponente adj (impresionante) imposing; (sobrecogedor) stunning.

imponer [19] (pp impuesto) **1** vt to impose; (impresionar) to be impressive; **i. respeto** to inspire respect. **2 imponerse** vr (prevalecer) to prevail; (ser necesario) to be necessary.

importación f (mercancía) import; (acción) importing; **artículos de i.** imported goods.

importancia f importance; (tamaño) size.

importante adj important; (grande) significant.

importar¹ 1 vi (tener importancia) to be important; **no importa** it doesn't matter; **eso no te importa a ti** that doesn't concern you; **¿te importa si fumo?** do you mind if I smoke? **2** vt (valer) to amount to.

importar² vt to import.

importe m amount.

importunar vt to bother, to pester.

imposibilitar vt (impedir) to make impossible; (incapacitar) to disable.

imposible adj impossible; **me es i. hacerlo** I can't (possibly) do it.

impostor, -a mf impostor.

impotencia f powerlessness.

imprenta f (taller) printer's; (aparato) printing press.

imprescindible adj essential.

impresentable *adj* unpresent-able.

impresión *f (efecto, opinión)* impression; *(acto, de revista etc)* printing; *(edición)* edition.

impresionante *adj* impressive.

impresionar *vt (causar admiración)* to impress; *(sorprender)* to stun.

impresionismo *m* impressionism.

impreso, -a 1 *adj* printed. **2** *m (papel, folleto)* printed matter; *(formulario)* form; **i. de solicitud** application form.

impresora *f* printer; **i. de chorro de tinta** ink-jet (printer); **i. láser** laser (printer); **i. matrical** dot matrix (printer).

imprevisible *adj* unforeseeable.

imprevisto, -a 1 *adj* unforeseen. **2** *m* unforeseen event.

imprimir *(pp* impreso*)* *vt* to print.

impropio, -a *adj (inadecuado)* inappropriate.

improvisado, -a *adj (espontáneo)* improvised; *(provisional)* makeshift.

improvisar *vt* to improvise.

imprudencia *f* rashness; *(indiscreción)* indiscretion.

imprudente *adj* imprudent, unwise; *(indiscreto)* indiscreet.

impuesto *m* tax; **i. sobre la renta** income tax; **libre de impuestos** tax-free.

impulsar *vt* to drive.

impulso *m* impulse.

impunemente *adv* with impunity.

impureza *f* impurity.

impuse *pt indef de* imponer.

inacabable *adj* endless.

inaccesible *adj* inaccessible.

inaceptable *adj* unacceptable.

inadaptado, -a 1 *adj* maladjusted. **2** *mf* misfit.

inadecuado, -a *adj* unsuitable.

inadmisible *adj* inadmissible.

inadvertido, -a *adj* unnoticed; **pasar i.** to escape notice, to pass unnoticed.

inagotable *adj (recursos etc)* inexhaustible; *(persona)* tireless.

inaguantable *adj* unbearable.

inalcanzable *adj* unattainable, unachievable.

inapreciable *adj (valioso)* invaluable; *(insignificante)* insignificant.

inasequible *adj (producto)* unaffordable; *(meta)* unattainable; *(persona)* unapproachable.

inaudito, -a *adj* unprecedented.

inauguración *f* inauguration.

inaugurar *vt* to inaugurate.

inca *adj & mf* Inca.

incalculable *adj* incalculable.

incandescente *adj* white hot.

incansable *adj* tireless.

incapacidad *f* inability; *(incompetencia)* incompetence.

incapacitar *vt* to incapacitate; *(inhabilitar)* to disqualify.

incapaz *adj* incapable (**de** of).

incendiar [43] **1** *vt* to set fire to. **2 incendiarse** *vr* to catch fire.

incendio *m* fire; **i. forestal** forest fire.

incentivo *m* incentive.

incertidumbre *f* uncertainty.

incidente *m* incident.

incierto, -a *adj* uncertain.

incinerar *vt (basura)* to incinerate; *(cadáveres)* to cremate.

incipiente *adj* incipient.

incitar *vt* to incite.

inclinación *f (de terreno)* slope; *(del cuerpo)* stoop; *(reverencia)* bow.

inclinar 1 *vt* to incline; *(cabeza)* to nod. **2 inclinarse** *vr* to lean; *(al saludar)* to bow; *(optar)* **inclinarse a** to be inclined to.

incluir [37] *vt* to include; *(contener)* to contain; *(adjuntar)* to enclose.

inclusive *adv (incluido)* inclusive; *(incluso)* even; **hasta la lección ocho i.** up to and including lesson eight.

incluso *adv* even.

incógnita *f (misterio)* mystery.

incoherente *adj* incoherent.

incoloro, -a adj colorless.

incombustible adj incombustible.

incomodar 1 vt (causar molestia) to inconvenience, to put out; (fastidiar) to bother, to annoy. **2 incomodarse** vr (tomarse molestias) to put oneself out, to go out of one's way; (disgustarse) to get annoyed o angry.

incomodidad f discomfort; (molestia) inconvenience.

incómodo, -a adj uncomfortable.

incompatible adj incompatible.

incompetencia f incompetence.

incompetente 1 adj incompetent. **2** mf incompetent person.

incompleto, -a adj incomplete; (inacabado) unfinished.

incomprensible adj incomprehensible.

incomunicado, -a adj (aislado) isolated; (en la cárcel) in solitary confinement; **el pueblo se quedó i.** the town was cut off.

inconcebible adj inconceivable.

incondicional adj unconditional; (apoyo) wholehearted; (amigo) faithful; (partidario) staunch.

inconexo, -a adj (incoherente) incoherent, confused.

inconfundible adj unmistakable.

incongruente adj incongruous.

inconsciencia f unconsciousness; (irresponsabilidad) irresponsibility.

inconsciente 1 adj (con estar) (desmayado) unconscious; (con ser) (despreocupado) unaware (**de** of); (irreflexivo) thoughtless.

inconsistente adj (argumento) weak.

inconstante adj fickle.

incontrolable adj uncontrollable.

inconveniencia f inconvenience; (impropiedad) unsuitability.

inconveniente 1 adj inconvenient; (inapropiado) unsuitable. **2** m (objeción) objection; (desventaja) disadvantage; (problema) difficulty.

incordiar [43] vt fam to bother, to pester.

incordio m fam nuisance, pain.

incorporación f incorporation.

incorporar 1 vt to incorporate (**en** into); (levantar) to help to sit up. **2 incorporarse** vr (en la cama) to sit up; **incorporarse a** (sociedad) to join; (trabajo) to start.

incorrecto, -a adj (equivocado) incorrect.

incorregible adj incorrigible.

incrédulo, -a 1 adj incredulous. **2** mf disbeliever.

increíble adj incredible.

incrementar 1 vt to increase. **2 incrementarse** vr to increase.

inculto, -a 1 adj uneducated. **2** mf ignoramus.

incultura f ignorance, lack of culture.

incumplimiento m (de un deber) non-fulfillment; (de una orden) failure to execute.

incumplir vt not to fulfill; (deber) to fail to fulfill; (promesa, contrato) to break; (orden) to fail to carry out.

incurrir vi to fall (**en** into).

indagar [42] vt to investigate.

indebido, -a adj (desconsiderado) undue; (ilegal) unlawful.

indecente adj indecent.

indeciso, -a 1 adj hesitant. **2** m (en encuesta) don't know.

indefenso, -a adj defenseless.

indefinidamente adv indefinitely.

indefinido, -a adj (indeterminado) indefinite; (impreciso) vague; (tiempo verbal) indefinite.

indemnización f (acto) indemnification; (compensación) compensation.

indemnizar [40] vt to compensate (**por** for).

independencia f independence.

independiente adj (libre) independent; (individualista) self-reliant.

independientemente adv independently (**de** of); (aparte de) irrespective (**de** of).

indescriptible *adj* indescribable.

indeseable *adj & mf* undesirable.

indeterminado, -a *adj* indefinite; *(impreciso)* vague; *(artículo)* indefinite.

indicación *f (señal)* indication; *(instrucción)* instruction.

indicador *m* indicator.

indicar [44] *vt* to indicate.

indicativo, -a *adj* indicative (**de** of); **(modo) i.** indicative (mode).

índice *m (de libro)* index; *(relación)* rate; **í. de natalidad/mortalidad** birth/death rate; **(dedo) í.** index finger.

indicio *m* indication (**de** of).

índico, -a *adj* Indian; **Océano I.** Indian Ocean.

indiferente *adj* indifferent; **me es i.** it makes no difference to me.

indígena 1 *adj* indigenous (**de** to). **2** *mf* native (**de** of).

indigestión *f* indigestion.

indignación *f* indignation.

indignar 1 *vt* to infuriate. **2 indignarse** *vr* to be indignant (**por** at, about).

indigno, -a *adj* unworthy (**de** of); *(despreciable)* wretched, dreadful.

indio, -a *adj & mf* Indian.

indirecta *f fam* insinuation.

indirecto, -a *adj* indirect.

indiscreto, -a *adj* indiscreet.

indiscutible *adj* indisputable.

indispensable *adj* indispensable.

indisponer [19] *(pp* **indispuesto) 1** *vt* to make ill. **2 indisponerse** *vr* to become ill.

indispuse *pt indef de* **indisponer**.

indistintamente *adv* **pueden escribir en inglés o en español i.** you can write in English or Spanish, it doesn't matter which.

individual *adj* individual; **habitación i.** single room.

individuo *m* individual.

índole *f (carácter)* character; *(clase, tipo)* kind.

inducir [10] *vt* to lead.

indudable *adj* indubitable; **es i. que** there is no doubt that.

induje *pt indef de* **inducir**.

indultar *vt* to pardon.

indumentaria *f* clothing.

industria *f* industry.

industrial 1 *adj* industrial. **2** *mf* manufacturer.

industrialización *f* industrialization.

induzco *indic pres de* **inducir**.

ineficacia *f (ineptitud)* inefficiency; *(inutilidad)* ineffectiveness.

ineficaz *adj (inepto)* inefficient; *(inefectivo)* ineffective.

ineludible *adj* inescapable, unavoidable.

ineptitud *f* ineptitude, incompetence.

inepto, -a 1 *adj* inept. **2** *mf* incompetent person.

inequívoco, -a *adj* unmistakable, unequivocal.

inerte *adj (inanimado)* inert; *(inmóvil)* motionless.

inesperado, -a *adj (fortuito)* unexpected; *(imprevisto)* sudden.

inestabilidad *f* instability.

inevitable *adj* inevitable.

inexistente *adj* non-existent.

inexperiencia *f* lack of experience.

inexplicable *adj* inexplicable.

infalible *adj* infallible.

infame *adj (vil)* infamous, vile; *(despreciable)* dreadful, awful.

infancia *f* childhood.

infantería *f* infantry.

infantil *adj* **literatura i.** *(para niños)* children's literature. **2** *(aniñado)* childlike; *(peyorativo)* childish.

infarto *m* **i. (de miocardio)** heart attack.

infección *f* infection.

infectar 1 *vt* to infect. **2 infectarse** *vr* to become infected (**de** with).

infeliz 1 *adj* unhappy; *(desdichado)* unfortunate. **2** *mf fam* simpleton.

inferior 1 *adj (más bajo)* lower;

(calidad) inferior; *(cantidad)* lower. **2**
mf (persona) subordinate.

infestado, -a *adj* **i. de** infested
with; **i. de turistas** swarming with
tourists.

infidelidad *f* unfaithfulness.

infierno *m* hell; *(horno)* inferno;
fam **¡vete al i.!** go to hell!

infinidad *f* infinity; *(sinfín)* great
number; **en i. de ocasiones** on
countless occasions.

infinitivo, -a *adj & m* infinitive.

infinito, -a 1 *adj* infinite. **2** *m*
infinity.

inflable *adj* inflatable.

inflación *f* inflation.

inflamable *adj* flammable.

inflamación *f* inflammation.

inflamar 1 *vt* to inflame; *(encender)*
to set on fire. **2 inflamarse** *vr* to become inflamed; *(incendiarse)* to
catch fire.

inflar 1 *vt* to inflate. **2 inflarse** *vr* to
inflate.

inflexible *adj* inflexible.

influencia *f* influence; **ejercer o tener i. sobre algn** to have an influence on sb.

influir [37] **1** *vt* to influence. **2** *vi* to
have influence; **i. en o sobre** to
influence.

información *f* information; *(servicio telefónico)* directory enquiries *pl.*

informal *adj (reunión, cena)* informal; *(comportamiento)* casual; *(persona)* unreliable.

informar 1 *vt (enterar)* to inform
(**de** of); *(dar informes)* to report. **2 informarse** *vr (procurarse noticias)* to
find out (**de** about); *(enterarse)* to inquire (**de** about).

informática *f* information technology, IT.

informático, -a 1 *adj* computer,
computing. **2** *mf* (computer) technician.

informe *m* report; **informes**
references.

infracción *f* infringement.

infraestructura *f* infrastructure.

infringir [57] *vt* **i. una ley** to break a
law.

infundir *vt* to infuse; *(idea etc)* to
instil.

infusión *f* infusion.

ingeniero, -a *mf* engineer; **i. de caminos** civil engineer; **i. técnico**
technician.

ingenio *m (talento)* talent; *(inventi-
va)* inventiveness; *(agudeza)* wit.

ingenioso, -a *adj* ingenious; *(vivaz)* witty.

ingenuo, -a 1 *adj* naïve. **2** *mf* naïve
person.

ingerir [5] *vt (comida)* to ingest, to
consume; *(líquidos, alcohol)* to
drink, to consume.

ingle *f* groin.

inglés, -esa 1 *adj* English. **2** *mf*
(hombre) Englishman; *(mujer)* Eng-
lishwoman; **los ingleses** the English.
3 *m (idioma)* English.

ingratitud *f* ingratitude.

ingrediente *m* ingredient.

ingresar 1 *vt (dinero)* to pay in; *(enfermo)* to admit; **la ingresaron en el
hospital** she was admitted to the
hospital. **2** *vi* to enter.

ingreso *m (dinero)* deposit; *(entrada)* entry (**en** into); *(admisión)* admission (**en** to); **ingresos** *(sueldo,
renta)* income *sing,* *(beneficios)* reve-
nue *sing.*

inhalador *m* inhaler.

inhalar *vt* to inhale.

inhumano, -a *adj* inhumane;
(cruel) inhuman.

inicial *adj & f* initial.

iniciar [43] **1** *vt (empezar)* to begin,
to start; *(discusión)* to initiate; *(una
cosa nueva)* to pioneer. **2 iniciarse**
vr to begin, to start.

iniciativa *f* initiative; **por i. propia**
on one's own initiative.

inicio *m* beginning, start.

ininterrumpido, -a *adj* unin-
terrupted.

injerirse *vr* to interfere (**en** in).

injuria *f* insult.

injusticia *f* injustice.

injustificado, -a *adj* unjustified.

injusto, -a *adj* unjust.

inmaduro, -a *adj* immature.

inmediaciones *fpl* neighborhood *sing.*

inmediatamente *adv* immediately, at once.

inmediato, -a *adj* (*en el tiempo*) immediate; (*en el espacio*) next (**a** to); **de i.** at once.

inmejorable *adj* (*trabajo*) excellent; (*precio*) unbeatable.

inmenso, -a *adj* immense.

inmigración *f* immigration.

inmigrante *adj* & *mf* immigrant.

inminente *adj* imminent.

inmiscuirse [37] *vr* to interfere (**en** in).

inmobiliaria *f* real estate company.

inmoral *adj* immoral.

inmortal *adj* & *mf* immortal.

inmóvil *adj* motionless.

inmovilizar [40] *vt* to immobilize.

inmueble *m* building.

inmune *adj* immune (**a** to).

inmunidad *f* immunity (**contra** to).

inmunizar [40] *vt* to immunize (**contra** against).

inmutarse *vr* ni **se inmutó** he didn't turn a hair.

innato, -a *adj* innate.

innecesario, -a *adj* unnecessary.

innegable *adj* undeniable.

innovación *f* innovation.

innumerable *adj* countless.

inocencia *f* innocence; (*ingenuidad*) naïvety.

inocentada *f* ≃ April Fools' joke.

inocente 1 *adj* innocent. **2** *mf* innocent (person).

inocuo, -a *adj* innocuous.

inofensivo, -a *adj* harmless.

inolvidable *adj* unforgettable.

inoportuno, -a *adj* inappropriate.

inoxidable *adj* **acero i.** stainless steel.

inquietante *adj* worrying.

inquietar 1 *vt* to worry. **2 inquietarse** *vr* to worry (**por** about).

inquieto, -a *adj* (*preocupado*) worried (**por** about); (*intranquilo*) restless.

inquietud *f* (*preocupación*) worry; (*agitación*) restlessness.

inquilino, -a *mf* tenant.

insaciable *adj* insatiable.

insatisfecho, -a *adj* dissatisfied.

inscribir (*pp* inscrito) **1** *vt* (*registrar*) to register; (*matricular*) to enroll; (*grabar*) to inscribe. **2 inscribirse** *vr* (*registrarse*) to register; (*hacerse miembro*) to join; (*matricularse*) to enroll; **inscribirse en un club** to join a club.

inscripción *f* (*matriculación*) enrollment; (*escrito etc*) inscription.

insecticida *m* insecticide.

insecto *m* insect.

inseguridad *f* (*falta de confianza*) insecurity; (*duda*) uncertainty; (*peligro*) lack of safety.

inseguro, -a *adj* (*poco confiado*) insecure; (*dubitativo*) uncertain; (*peligroso*) unsafe.

insensato, -a 1 *adj* foolish. **2** *mf* fool.

insensible *adj* (*indiferente*) unfeeling; (*imperceptible*) imperceptible; (*miembro*) numb.

inseparable *adj* inseparable.

insertar *vt* to insert.

inservible *adj* useless.

insignia *f* badge.

insignificante *adj* insignificant.

insinuar [30] *vt* to insinuate.

insistir *vi* to insist (**en** on).

insolación *f* sunstroke.

insolente *adj* insolent.

insólito, -a *adj* (*poco usual*) unusual; (*extraño*) strange, odd.

insomnio *m* insomnia.

insoportable *adj* unbearable.

insospechado, -a *adj* unsuspected.

insostenible *adj* untenable.

inspección *f* inspection.

inspeccionar *vt* to inspect.

inspector, -a *mf* inspector; **i. de Hacienda** tax inspector.

inspiración *f* inspiration; *(inhalación)* inhalation.

inspirar 1 *vt* to inspire; *(inhalar)* to inhale. **2 inspirarse** *vr* **inspirarse en** to be inspired by.

instalación *f* installation; **instalaciones deportivas** sports facilities.

instalar 1 *vt* to install; *(erigir)* to set up. **2 instalarse** *vr* to settle (down).

instancia *f (solicitud)* request; **a instancia(s) de** at the request of; **en última i.** as a last resort.

instantáneamente *adv* instantly.

instantáneo, -a *adj* instantaneous; **café i.** instant coffee.

instante *m* instant; **a cada i.** constantly; **al i.** immediately.

instaurar *vt* to found.

instigar [42] *vt* to instigate.

instintivo, -a *adj* instinctive.

instinto *m* instinct; **por i.** instinctively.

institución *f* institution.

instituto *m* institute; *(colegio)* high school.

institutriz *f* governess.

instrucción *f (educación)* education; **instrucciones para el** *o* **de uso** instructions *o* directions for use.

instructivo, -a *adj* instructive.

instruir [37] *vt* to instruct; *(enseñar)* to educate.

instrumento *m* instrument.

insubordinarse *vr* to rebel (**contra** against).

insuficiente 1 *adj* insufficient. **2** *m (nota)* fail.

insulso, -a *adj* insipid.

insultar *vt* to insult.

insulto *m* insult.

insuperable *adj (inmejorable)* unsurpassable; *(problema)* insurmountable.

insurrección *f* insurrection.

intacto, -a *adj* intact.

integral *adj* integral; **pan i.** wholewheat bread.

integrante 1 *adj* integral; **ser parte i. de** to be an integral part of. **2** *mf* member.

integrar 1 *vt* to integrate; *(formar)* to compose. **2 integrarse** *vr* to integrate (**en** with).

integridad *f* integrity.

integro, -a *adj (entero)* whole; *(honrado)* upright; **versión integra** unabridged version.

intelectual *adj & mf* intellectual.

inteligencia *f* intelligence.

inteligente *adj* intelligent.

inteligible *adj* intelligible.

intemperie *f* **a la i.** in the open (air).

intención *f* intention; **con i.** deliberately; **tener la i. de hacer algo** to intend to do sth.

intencionadamente *adv* on purpose.

intencionado, -a *adj* deliberate.

intensidad *f* intensity; *(del viento)* force.

intensificar [44] *vt*, **intensificarse** *vr* to intensify; *(relación)* to strengthen.

intenso, -a *adj* intense.

intentar *vt* to try.

intento *m* attempt; **i. de suicidio** attempted suicide.

intercambiar [43] *vt* to exchange.

interceder *vi* to intercede.

interceptar *vt (detener)* to intercept; *(carretera)* to block; *(tráfico)* to hold up.

interés *m* interest; *(provecho personal)* self-interest; **tener i. en** *o* **por** to be interested in; **tipos de i.** interest rates.

interesante *adj* interesting.

interesar 1 *vt (tener interés)* to interest; *(concernir)* to concern. **2** *vi (ser importante)* to be of interest. **2 interesarse** *vr* **interesarse por** *o* **en** to be interested in.

interferencia *f* interference; *(en radio, televisión)* jamming.

interfono *m* intercom.

interior 1 *adj* inner; *ropa* i. underwear; *(política, vuelo)* domestic; *(región)* inland. **2** *m* inside; *(de un país)* interior; **Ministerio del I.** Department of the Interior.

interjección *f* interjection.

interlocutor, -a *mf* speaker.

intermediario, -a *mf* intermediary, middleman.

intermedio, -a 1 *adj* intermediate. **2** *m (en televisión)* break.

interminable *adj* endless.

intermitente 1 *adj* intermittent. **2** *m (de automóvil)* indicator.

internacional *adj* international.

internado *m (colegio)* boarding school.

internauta *mf* Net user.

Internet *f* Internet; **está en I.** it's on the Internet.

interno, -a 1 *adj* internal; *(política)* domestic. **2** *mf (alumno)* boarder.

interpretación *f* interpretation.

interpretar *vt* to interpret; *(papel)* to play; *(obra)* to perform; *(concierto)* to perform; *(canción)* to sing.

intérprete *mf (traductor)* interpreter; *(actor, músico)* performer; *(cantante)* singer.

interrogación *f* interrogation; **(signo de) i.** question mark.

interrogante *f fig* question mark.

interrogar [42] *vt* to question; *(con amenazas)* to interrogate.

interrogatorio *m* interrogation.

interrumpir *vt* to interrupt; *(tráfico)* to block.

interruptor *m* switch.

interurbano, -a *adj* intercity; **conferencia interurbana** long-distance call.

intervalo *m* interval.

intervenir [27] **1** *vi (mediar)* to intervene (**en** in); *(participar)* take part (**en** in). **2** *vt (teléfono)* to tap.

interviú *m (pl interviús)* interview.

intestino *m* intestine.

intimidar *vt* to intimidate.

íntimo, -a *adj* intimate; *(vida)* private; *(amigo)* close.

intolerante 1 *adj* intolerant. **2** *mf* intolerant person.

intoxicación *f* poisoning; **i. alimenticia** food poisoning.

intranquilizarse *vr* to get worried.

intranquilo, -a *adj (preocupado)* worried; *(agitado)* restless.

intransigente *adj* intransigent.

intransitivo, -a *adj* intransitive.

intriga *f* intrigue; *(trama)* plot.

intrigar [42] **1** *vt (interesar)* to intrigue. **2** *vi (maquinar)* to plot.

intrínseco, -a *adj* intrinsic.

introducir [10] *vt* to introduce; *(meter)* to insert.

introvertido, -a 1 *adj* introverted. **2** *mf* introvert.

intruso, -a *mf* intruder.

intuición *f* intuition.

intuir [37] *vt* to know by intuition.

inundación *f* flood.

inusitado, -a *adj* unusual.

inútil 1 *adj* useless; *(esfuerzo, intento)* pointless. **2** *mf fam* good-for-nothing.

inutilizar [40] *vt* to make useless.

invadir *vt* to invade; **los estudiantes invadieron la calle** students poured out onto the street.

inválido, -a 1 *adj (nulo)* invalid; *(minusválido)* disabled. **2** *mf* disabled person.

invariable *adj* invariable.

invasión *f* invasion.

invencible *adj (enemigo)* invincible; *(obstáculo)* insurmountable.

invención *f (invento)* invention; *(mentira)* fabrication.

inventar *vt (crear)* to invent; *(excusa, mentira)* to concoct.

inventario *m* inventory.

invento *m* invention.

invernadero *m* greenhouse.

invernal *adj* winter.

inversión *f* inversion; *(de dinero)* investment.

inverso, -a *adj* **en sentido i.** in the

opposite direction; **en orden i.** in reverse order.

invertir [5] *vt (orden)* to invert; *(dinero)* to invest (**en** in); *(tiempo)* to
spend (**en** on).

investigación *f (policial etc)* investigation; *(científica)* research.

investigar [42] *vt (indagar)* to investigate; *(científicamente)* to research.

invierno *m* winter.

invisible *adj* invisible.

invitado, -a 1 *adj* invited. **2** *mf*
guest.

invitar *vt* to invite; **me invitó a una
copa** he treated me to a drink.

involucrarse *vr* to get involved (**en**
in).

involuntario, -a *adj* involuntary;
(impremeditado) unintentional.

inyección *f* injection; **poner una i.**
to give an injection.

inyectar *vt* to inject (**en** into); **i. algo
a algn** to inject sb with sth.

ir [16] **1** *vi* to go; **¡vamos!** let's go!; **¡ya
voy!** (I'm) coming!; **¿cómo le va el
nuevo trabajo?** how is he doing in
his new job?; **el negro no te va**
black doesn't suit you; **ir con falda**
to wear a skirt; **ir de blanco/de uniforme** to be dressed in white/in uniform; **va para abogado** he's studying
to be a lawyer; **ir por la derecha** to
keep (to the) right; **ve (a) por agua**
go and fetch some water; **voy por la
página noventa** I've got as far as
page ninety; **en lo que va de año** so
so far this year; **ir a parar** to end up;
¡qué va! of course not!; **va a lo suyo**
he looks after his own interests; **¡vamos a ver!** let's see!; **¡vaya!** fancy
that; **¡vaya moto!** what a bike! **2** *v
aux* **ir andando** to go on foot; **iba me-
jorando** she's improving; **ya van ro-
tos tres** three (of them) have already
been broken; **iba a decir que ...** I
was going to say that ...; **va a llover**
it's going to rain. **3** *irse vr (marcharse)* to go away; **me voy** I'm off; **¡vá-

monos!** let's go!; **¡vete!** go away!;
¡vete a casa! go home!; **¿por dónde
se va a ...?** which is the way to ...?

ira *f* rage.

iraní *adj & mf (pl iraníes)* Iranian.

iraquí *adj & mf (pl iraquíes)* Iraqi.

irascible *adj* irascible.

iris *m inv* arco i. rainbow.

irlandés, -esa 1 *adj* Irish. **2** *mf
(hombre)* Irishman; *(mujer)* Irishwo-
man; **los irlandeses** the Irish. **3** *m
(idioma)* Irish.

ironía *f* irony.

irónico, -a *adj* ironic.

irracional *adj* irrational.

irreal *adj* unreal.

irregular *adj* irregular.

irremediable *adj* incurable.

irresistible *adj (impulso, persona)*
irresistible; *(insoportable)* unbearable.

irresponsable *adj* irresponsible.

irrisorio, -a *adj* derisory, ridiculous.

irritación *f* irritation.

irritante *adj* irritating.

irritar 1 *vt* to irritate. **2 irritarse** *vr* to
become irritated.

irrompible *adj* unbreakable.

irrumpir *vi* to burst (**en** into).

isla *f* island.

islámico, -a *adj* Islamic.

israelí *adj & mf (pl israelíes)* Israeli.

italiano, -a 1 *adj* Italian. **2** *mf (persona)* Italian. **3** *m (idioma)* Italian.

itinerario *m* itinerary.

IVA *m abr de* impuesto sobre el valor añadido value-added tax, VAT.

izqda., izqd° *abr de* izquierda left.

izqdo., izqd° *abr de* izquierdo left.

izquierda *f* left; *(mano)* left hand; **a
la i.** on the left; **girar a la i.** to turn
left.

izquierdo, -a *adj* left.

J

jabalí *m (pl* jabalíes) wild boar.

jabalina *f* javelin.

jabón *m* soap; **j. de afeitar/tocador** shaving/toilet soap.

jabonera *f* soap dish.

jaca *f* gelding.

jacaré *m Am* caiman.

jacinto *m* hyacinth.

jactarse *vr* to boast (**de** about).

jadear *vi* to pant.

jalar 1 *vt Andes, CAm, Carib, Méx (tirar)* to pull; *fam (comer)* to wolf down. **2 jalarse** *vr fam (comerse)* to wolf down, to scoff.

jalea *f* jelly.

jaleo *m (alboroto)* ruckus; *(confusión)* muddle.

jalón *m Am* lift.

jamás *adv* never; **j. he estado allí** I have never been there; **el mejor libro que j. se ha escrito** the best book ever written; **nunca j.** never again.

jamón *m* ham; **j. de York/serrano** boiled/cured ham.

japonés, -esa *adj & mf* Japanese; **los japoneses** the Japanese.

jaque *m* check; **j. mate** checkmate; **j. al rey** check.

jaqueca *f* migraine.

jarabe *m* syrup; **j. para la tos** cough mixture.

jardín *m* garden; **j. botánico** botanical garden; **j. de infancia** nursery school.

jardinero, -a *mf* gardener.

jarra *f* pitcher.

jarro *m (recipiente)* jug; *(contenido)* jugful.

jarrón *m* vase.

jaula *f* cage.

jazmín *m* jasmine.

J.C. *abr de* **Jesucristo** Jesus Christ, J.C.

jeep *m* jeep.

jefa *f* manager.

jefatura *f (cargo, dirección)* leadership; *(sede)* central office.

jefe *m* head; *(de empresa)* manager; *(de partido)* leader; **J. de Estado** Head of State.

jengibre *m* ginger.

jerarquía *f* hierarchy; *(categoría)* rank.

jerez *m* sherry.

jerga *f (técnica)* jargon; *(vulgar)* slang.

jeringa *f* syringe.

jeringuilla *f* (hypodermic) syringe.

jeroglífico *m* hieroglyphic; *(juego)* rebus.

jersey *m (pl* jerseis) pullover.

Jesucristo *m* Jesus Christ.

Jesús 1 *m* Jesus. **2** *interj (al estornudar)* bless you!

jíbaro, -a *mf Am* peasant.

jícara *f Am* gourd.

jilguero *m* goldfinch.

jinete *m* horseman, rider.

jirafa *f* giraffe.

jirón *m (trozo desgarrado)* strip; *(pedazo suelto)* scrap; **hecho jirones** in tatters.

JJOO *mpl abr de* **Juegos Olímpicos** Olympic Games.

jornada *f* **j. (laboral)** *(día de trabajo)* working day; **trabajo de media j./j. completa** part-time/full-time work.

jornal *m* day's wage.

jornalero, -a *mf* day laborer.

joroba *f* hump.

jorobado, -a 1 *adj* hunchbacked. **2** *mf* hunchback.

joven 1 *adj* young; **de aspecto j.** young-looking. **2** *mf (hombre)* young man; *(mujer)* young woman; **de j.** as a young man/woman; **los jóvenes** young people.

joya *f* jewel; **ser una j.** *(persona)* to be a gem.

joyería *f (tienda)* jewelry shop.

joyero, -a 1 *mf* jeweler. **2** *m* jewel case.

jubilado, -a 1 *adj* retired. **2** *mf* retired person; **los jubilados** retired people.

judía *f* bean; **j. verde** green bean.

judío, -a 1 *adj* Jewish. **2** *mf* Jew.

judo *m* judo.

juego *m* game; *(conjunto de piezas)* set; *(apuestas)* gambling; **j. de azar** game of chance; **j. de cartas** card game; **Juegos Olímpicos** Olympic Games; **terreno de j.** field; **fuera de j.** offside; **j. de café/té** coffee/tea service; **ir a j. con** to match.

juerga *f fam* rave-up; **ir de j.** to go on a binge.

jueves *m inv* Thursday; **J. Santo** Holy Thursday.

juez, -a *mf* judge; **j. de línea** linesman.

jugada *f* move; *fam* dirty trick.

jugador, -a *mf* player; *(apostador)* gambler.

jugar [32] **1** *vi* to play; **j. a(l) fútbol** to play football; **j. sucio** to play dirty. **2** *vt* to play; *(apostar)* to bet. **3** **jugarse** *vr (arriesgar)* to risk; *(apostar)* to bet.

jugo *m* juice.

juguete *m* toy; **pistola de j.** toy gun.

juicio *m (facultad mental)* judgement; *(sensatez)* reason; *(opinión)* opinion; *(en tribunal)* trial; **j. de** in the opinion of; **a mi j.** in my opinion; **perder el j.** to go mad.

julio *m* July.

junco *m* rush.

jungla *f* jungle.

junio *m* June.

júnior *adj* junior.

junta *f (reunión)* meeting; *(dirección)* board; *(gobierno militar)* junta.

juntar 1 *vt (unir)* to join; *(piezas)* to assemble; *(dinero)* to raise. **2** **juntarse** *vr (unirse)* to join; *(ríos, caminos)* to meet; *(personas)* to gather.

junto, -a 1 *adj* together. **2** *adv* **j. con** together with; **j. a** next to.

jurado *m* jury.

juramento *m* oath; **bajo j.** under oath.

jurar 1 *vi* to swear. **2** *vt* to swear; **j. el cargo** to take the oath of office.

jurídico, -a *adj* legal.

justamente *adv* **¡j.!** precisely!; **j. detrás de** right behind.

justicia *f* justice; **tomarse la j. por su mano** to take the law into one's own hands.

justificado, -a *adj* justified.

justificante *m* written proof.

justificar [44] **1** *vt* to justify. **2** **justificarse** *vr* to justify oneself.

justo, -a 1 *adj* just; *(apretado) (ropa)* tight; *(exacto)* accurate; **un trato j.** a fair deal; **estamos justos de tiempo** we're pressed for time; **llegamos en el momento j. en que salían** we arrived just as they were leaving; **lo j.** just enough. **2** *adv (exactamente)* precisely; **j. al lado de** right beside.

juvenil *adj* young; **ropa j.** *(de joven)* young people's clothes; **delincuencia j.** juvenile delinquency.

juventud *f (edad)* youth; *(jóvenes)* young people.

juzgado *m* court.

juzgar [42] *vt* to judge; **a j. por ...** judging by ....

K

kárate *m* karate.

kilo *m (medida)* kilo.

kilogramo *m* kilogram.

kilometraje *m* ≃ mileage.

kilómetro *m* kilometer.

kiosco *m* kiosk.

kiwi *m (fruto)* kiwi (fruit).

kleenex® *m* tissue.

L

la¹ 1 *art def f* the. **2** *pron dem* the one; **la del vestido azul** the one in the blue dress.

la² *pron pers f (persona)* her; *(usted)* you; *(cosa)* it; **la invitaré** I'll invite her along; **ya la avisaremos, señora** we'll let you know, madam; **no la dejes abierta** don't leave it open.

labio *m* lip.

labor *f* job; *(de costura)* needlework.

laborable *adj* **día l.** working day.

laboral *adj* industrial; **accidente l.** industrial accident; **jornada l.** working day.

laboratorio *m* laboratory.

labrar 1 *vt (tierra)* to till; *(madera)* to carve; *(piedra)* to cut; *(metal)* to work. **2 labrarse** *vr fig* **labrarse un porvenir** to build a future for oneself.

laca *f* hairspray; **l. de uñas** nail polish.

ladear 1 *vt (inclinar)* to tilt; *(cabeza)* to lean. **2 ladearse** *vr (inclinarse)* to lean, to tilt; *(desviarse)* to go off to one side.

ladera *f* slope.

ladino, -a 1 *adj (astuto)* crafty; *CAm, Méx, Ven (no blanco)* non-white. **2** *mf CAm, Méx, Ven (no blanco)* = nonwhite Spanish-speaking person.

lado *m* side; **a un l.** aside; **al l.** close by, nearby; **al l. de** next to; **ponte de l.** stand sideways; **por todos lados** on all sides; **por otro l.** *(además)* moreover; **por un l. …, pro otro l. …** on the one hand …, on the other hand ….

ladrar *vi* to bark.

ladrillo *m* brick.

ladrón, -ona *mf* thief.

lagartija *f* small lizard.

lagarto *m* lizard.

lago *m* lake.

lágrima *f* tear.

laguna *f* small lake.

lamentar 1 *vt* to regret; **lo lamento** I'm sorry. **2 lamentarse** *vr* to complain.

lamer *vt* to lick.

lámina *f* sheet.

lámpara *f* lamp; *(bombilla)* bulb.

lana *f* wool; *Andes, Méx fam (dinero)* dough, cash.

lancha *f* motorboat; **l. motora** speedboat; **l. neumática** rubber dinghy; **l. salvavidas** lifeboat.

langosta *f* lobster; *(insecto)* locust.

langostino *m* king prawn.

lanza *f* spear.

lanzar [40] **1** *vt (arrojar)* to throw; *(grito)* to let out; *(ataque, producto)* to launch. **2 lanzarse** *vr* to throw oneself.

lapicera *f CSur* ballpoint (pen); **l. fuente** fountain pen.

lápiz *m* pencil; **l. de labios** lipstick; **l. de ojos** eyeliner.

largo, -a 1 *adj* long; **a lo l. de** *(espacio)* along; *(tiempo)* through; **a la larga** in the long run. **2** *m (longitud)* length; **¿cuánto tiene de l.?** *fam* how long is it?; *fam* **esto va para l.** this is going to last a long time. **3** *adv fam* **¡l. (de aquí)!** clear off!

largometraje *m* feature film.

las¹ 1 *art def fpl* the. **2** *pron dem* **l. que** *(personas)* those who; *(objetos)* those that; **toma l. que quieras** take whichever ones you want.

las² *pron pers fpl (ellas)* them; *(ustedes)* you; **no l. rompas** don't break them; **l. llamaré mañana** *(a ustedes)* I'll call you tomorrow.

láser *m inv* laser.

lástima *f* pity; **¡qué l.!** what a pity!; **es una l. que …** it's a pity (that) ….

lata¹ *f (envase)* tin, can; *(hojalata)* tin(plate); **en l.** tinned, canned.

lata² *f fam* drag; **dar la l.** to be a nuisance.

lateral *adj* side; **escalón l.** *(en letrero)* ramp.

latido *m* beat.

látigo *m* whip.

latín *m* Latin.

latinoamericano, -a *adj & mf* Latin American.

latir *vi* to beat.

latón *m* brass.

laucha *f Am* mouse.

laurel *m* bay leaf.

lava *f* lava.

lavable *adj* washable.

lavabo *m (pila)* washbasin; *(cuarto de aseo)* washroom; *(retrete)* toilet.

lavadero *m (de coches)* carwash.

lavado *m* washing; **l. en seco** dry-cleaning.

lavadora *f* washing machine.

lavanda *f* lavender.

lavandería *f* laundromat; *(atendida por personal)* laundry.

lavaplatos *m inv* dishwasher.

lavar *vt* to wash.

lavavajillas *m inv* dishwasher.

laxante *adj & m* laxative.

lazo *m (adorno)* bow; *(nudo)* knot; **lazos** *(vínculo)* links.

le 1 *pron pers mf (objeto indirecto) (a él)* (to/for) him; *(a ella)* (to/for) her; *(a cosa)* (to/for) it; *(a usted)* (to/for) you; **lávale la cara** wash his face; **le compraré uno** I'll buy one for her; **¿qué le pasa (a usted)?** what's the matter with you? **2** *pron pers m (objeto directo) (él)* him; *(usted)* you; **no le oigo** I can't hear him; **no quiero molestarle** I don't wish to disturb you.

leal *adj* faithful.

lección *f* lesson.

leche *f* milk; **dientes de l.** milk teeth; **l. descremada** *o* **desnatada** skim milk.

lechuga *f* lettuce.

lechuza *f* owl.

lector, -a *mf (persona)* reader; *(de colegio)* (language) assistant.

lectura *f* reading.

leer [36] *vt* to read.

legal *adj* legal.

legalizar [40] *vt* to legalize; *(documento)* to authenticate.

legislación *f* legislation.

legítimo, -a *adj* legitimate; *(auténtico)* real; **en legítima defensa** in self-defense; **oro l.** pure gold.

legumbres *fpl* pulses.

lejano, -a *adj* far-off.

lejía *f* bleach.

lejos *adv* far (away); **a lo l.** in the distance; **de l.** from a distance; *fig* **sin ir más l.** to take an obvious example.

lema *m* motto.

lencería *f (prendas)* lingerie; *(ropa blanca)* linen (goods *pl*).

lengua *f* tongue; *(idioma)* language; **l. materna** mother tongue.

lenguado *f* sole.

lenguaje *m* language; **l. corporal** body language.

lente 1 *f* lens; **lentes de contacto** contact lenses. **2** *mpl* **lentes** *Am* glasses, spectacles; **lentes de contacto** contact lenses.

lenteja *f* lentil.

lentejuela *f* sequin.

lentilla *f* contact lens.

lento, -a *adj* slow; **a fuego l.** on a low heat.

leña *f* firewood.

leño *m* log.

león *m* lion.

leopardo *m* leopard.

leotardos *mpl* thick tights.

les *pron pers mfpl (a ellos/ellas)* them; *(a ustedes)* you; **dales el dinero** give them the money; **l. he comprado un regalo** I've bought you/them a present; **l. esperaré** I shall wait for you/them; **no quiero molestarles** I don't wish to disturb you/them.

lesión *f (física)* injury.

lesionar *vt* to injure.

letal *adj* lethal.

letargo *m* lethargy.

letra *f* letter; *(escritura)* (hand)writing; *(de canción)* lyrics *pl*; **l. de imprenta** block capitals; **l. mayúscula**

capital letter; **l. minúscula** small letter; **l. (de cambio)** bill of exchange; *(carrera)* **letras** arts.

letrero *m (aviso)* notice; *(cartel)* poster.

levadura *f* yeast; **l. en polvo** baking powder.

levantamiento *m* lifting; *(insurrección)* uprising; **l. de pesos** weightlifting.

levantar 1 *vt* to lift; *(mano, voz)* to raise; *(edificio)* to erect; *(ánimos)* to raise. **2 levantarse** *vr* to get up; *(ponerse de pie)* to stand up.

levante *m* **(el) L.** Levante, the regions of Valencia and Murcia.

leve *adj (ligero)* light; *(de poca importancia)* slight.

levemente *adv* slightly.

ley *f* **aprobar una l.** to pass a bill; **oro de l.** pure gold; **plata de l.** sterling silver.

leyenda *f (relato)* legend; *(bajo ilustración)* caption.

liar [29] **1** *vt (envolver)* to wrap up; *(cigarrillo)* to roll; *(enredar)* to muddle up; *(confundir)* to confuse. **2 liarse** *vr (embarullarse)* to get muddled up.

liberal 1 *adj* liberal; *(generoso)* generous; *(carácter)* open-minded; **profesión l.** profession. **2** *mf* liberal.

liberalizar [40] *vt* to liberalize.

liberar *vt (país)* to liberate; *(prisionero)* to release.

libertad *f* freedom; **(en) l. bajo palabra/fianza** (on) parole/bail; **(en) l. condicional** (on) parole.

libio, -a *adj & mf* Libyan.

libra *f* pound; **l. esterlina** pound sterling.

librar 1 *vt* to free; *(preso)* to release. **2 librarse** *vr* to escape; **librarse de algn** to get rid of sb.

libre *adj* free; *(sin restricción)* open to the public; **entrada l.** admission free; **l. de impuestos** tax-free.

librería *f (tienda)* bookstore; *(estante)* bookcase.

libreta *f* notebook.

libro *m* book; **l. de texto** textbook.

licencia *f (permiso)* permission; *(documentos)* licence; *Am* driver's license.

licenciado, -a *mf* graduate; *Am* lawyer; **l. en Ciencias** Bachelor of Science.

licenciar [43] **1** *vt (soldado)* to discharge; *(estudiante)* to confer a degree on. **2 licenciarse** *vr (estudiante)* to graduate.

licenciatura *f (título)* (bachelor's) degree (course); *(carrera)* degree (course).

licor *m* liquor.

licuadora *f* liquidizer.

líder *mf* leader.

liderar *vt* to lead, to head.

liderato, liderazgo *m* leadership; *(en deportes)* top *o* first position.

lidia *f* bullfighting.

lidiar [43] *vt* to fight.

liebre *f* hare.

liga *f* league.

ligar [42] **1** *vt* to join. **2** *vi fam* **l. con una chica** to flirt with a girl.

ligeramente *adv (levemente)* lightly; *(un poco)* slightly.

ligereza *f* lightness; *(frivolidad)* flippancy; *(acto)* indiscretion; *(rapidez)* speed.

ligero, -a 1 *adj (peso)* light; *(veloz)* quick; *(leve)* slight; **l. de ropa** lightly clad; **brisa/comida ligera** light breeze/meal. **2** *adv* **ligero** *(rápido)* fast.

liguero *m* garter belt.

lija *f* sandpaper; **papel de l.** sandpaper.

lima *f (herramienta)* file; **l. de uñas** nailfile.

limar *vt* to file.

limitar 1 *vt* to restrict. **2** *vi* **l. con** to border on.

límite *m* limit; *(de país)* border; **fecha l.** deadline; **velocidad l.** maximum speed.

limón *m* lemon.

limonada f lemon squash.

limonero m lemon tree.

limosna f alms; **pedir l.** to beg.

limpiabotas m inv bootblack, shoeshine.

limpiaparabrisas m inv windshield wiper.

limpiar [43] vt to clean; (con un trapo) to wipe; (zapatos) to polish.

limpieza f (calidad) cleanliness; (acción) cleaning.

limpio, -a 1 adj (aseado) clean; (neto) net; **juego l.** fair play. **2** adv **limpio** fairly; **jugar l.** to play fair.

lindar vi **l. con** to border on.

lindo, -a 1 adj (bonito) pretty; **de lo l.** a great deal. **2** adv Am (bien) nicely.

línea f line; **l. aérea** airline; **en líneas generales** roughly speaking; **guardar la l.** to watch one's figure.

lino m (fibra) linen.

linterna f torch.

lío m (paquete) bundle; (embrollo) mess; **hacerse un l.** to get mixed up; **meterse en líos** to get into trouble.

lipotimia f fainting fit.

liquidación f (saldo) clearance sale; (de deuda, cuenta) settling.

liquidar 1 vt (deuda, cuenta) to settle; (mercancías) to sell off. **2** vr **liquidarse a algn** (matar) to bump sb off.

líquido, -a 1 adj liquid; (cantidad) net. **2** m liquid.

lirio m iris.

lisiado, -a 1 adj crippled. **2** mf cripple.

liso, -a adj (superficie) smooth; (pelo, falda) straight; (tela) self-colored; Am (desvergonzado) rude.

lista f (relación) list; (franja) stripe; **l. de espera** waiting list; (en avión) standby; **pasar l.** to call the register; **de/a listas** striped.

listín m **l. telefónico** telephone directory.

listo, -a adj **ser l.** to be clever; **estar l.** to be ready.

litera f (cama) bunk bed; (en tren) couchette.

literatura f literature.

litigio m lawsuit.

litoral 1 m coast. **2** adj coastal.

litro m liter.

llaga f sore; (herida) wound.

llama f flame; **en llamas** in flames.

llamada f call; **l. interurbana** long-distance call.

llamado, -a 1 adj so-called. **2** m Am (telefónico) call; (a la puerta) knock; (con timbre) ring; (llamamiento) appeal, call; **hacer un l.** to make a phone call.

llamamiento m appeal.

llamar 1 vt to call; **l. (por teléfono)** to call; **l. la atención** to attract attention. **2** vi (a la puerta) to knock. **3** llamarse vr to be called; **¿cómo te llamas?** what's your name?

llano, -a 1 adj (superficie) flat. **2** m plain.

llanta f (de rueda) wheel rim; Am tire.

llanto m crying.

llanura f plain.

llave f key; (interruptor) switch; (herramienta) spanner; **cerrar con l.** to lock; (de coche) **l. de contacto** ignition key; **l. inglesa** adjustable spanner; **l. de paso** stopcock.

llavero m key ring.

llegada f arrival; (meta) finish.

llegar [42] vi to arrive; **l. a Madrid** to arrive in Madrid; **¿llegas al techo?** can you reach the ceiling?; **l. a + infinitivo** to go so far as to; **l. a ser** to become.

llenar 1 vt to fill; (satisfacer) to satisfy. **2** vi (comida) to be filling. **3** llenarse vr to fill (up).

lleno, -a adj full (up).

llevar 1 vt to take; (hacia el oyente) to bring; (transportar) to carry; (prenda) to wear; (negocio) to be in charge of; **llevo dos años aquí** I've been here for two years; **esto lleva mucho tiempo** this takes a long time. **2** *v aux* **I.** + *gerundio* to have been + *present participle*; **llevo dos años estudiando español** I've been studying Spanish for two years. ▪ **I.** + *participio pasado* to have + *past participle*; **llevaba escritas seis cartas** I had written six letters. **3 llevarse** *vr* to take away; *(premio)* to win; *(estar de moda)* to be fashionable; **llevarse bien con algn** to get along well with sb.

llorar *vi* to cry.

lloriquear *vi* to whimper, to snivel.

llover [4] *v impers* to rain.

llovizna *f* drizzle.

lloviznar *v impers* to drizzle.

lluvia *f* rain.

lluvioso, -a *adj* rainy.

lo¹ *art def neutro* the; **lo mismo** the same thing; **lo mío** mine; **lo tuyo** yours.

lo² *pron pers m & neutro (cosa)* it; **debes hacerlo** you must do it; *(no se traduce)* **no se lo dije** I didn't tell her; **lo que ...** what ...; **lo cual ...** which ...; **lo de ...** the business of ...; **cuéntame lo del juicio** tell me about the trial.

lobo *m* wolf; **como boca de l.** pitch-dark.

local 1 *adj* local. **2** *m (recinto)* premises *pl*.

localidad *f (pueblo)* locality; *(asiento)* seat.

localizar [40] *vt (encontrar)* to find; *(fuego, dolor)* to localize.

loción *f* lotion.

loco, -a 1 *adj* mad; **a lo l.** crazily; **l. por** crazy about; **volverse l.** to go mad. **2** *mf (hombre)* madman; *(mujer)* madwoman.

locomotora *f* locomotive.

locura *f* madness.

locutor, -a *mf* presenter.

locutorio *m* telephone booth.

lodo *m* mud.

lógico, -a *adj* logical; **era l. que ocurriera** it was bound to happen.

lograr *vt* to get, to obtain; *(premio)*

to win; *(meta)* to achieve; **l. hacer algo** to manage to do something.

lombriz *f* earthworm.

lomo *m* back; *(para filete)* loin.

lona *f* canvas.

loncha *f* slice.

lonchería *f Méx* snack bar.

longaniza *f* spicy (pork) sausage.

longitud *f* length; **dos metros de l.** two meters long; **salto de l.** long jump.

lonja *f* market.

loquería *f Am* mental hospital.

lord *m (pl* **lores)** lord.

loro *m* parrot.

los¹ 1 *art def mpl* the. **2** *pron* **l. que** *(personas)* those who; *(cosas)* the ones (that); **toma l. que quieras** take whichever ones you want; **esos son l. míos/tuyos** these are mine/yours.

los² *pron pers mpl* them; **¿l. has visto?** have you seen them?

losa *f* slab.

lote *m (de productos)* lot; *Am (terreno)* plot (of land).

lotería *f* lottery; **tocarle la l. a algn** to win a prize in the lottery.

loza *f (material)* earthenware; *(vajilla)* crockery.

lubricante *m* lubricant.

lucha *f* fight; *(deporte)* wrestling; **l. libre** free-style *o* all-in wrestling.

luchar *vi* to fight; *(como deporte)* to wrestle.

lucir [35] **1** *vi (brillar)* to shine. **2** *vt (ropa)* to sport. **3 lucirse** *vr (hacer buen papel)* to do very well; *(pavonearse)* to show off.

luego 1 *adv (después)* then, next; *(más tarde)* later (on); **¡hasta l.!** so long!; *Am* **l. de** after; **desde l.** of course. **2** *conj* therefore.

lugar *m* place; **en primer l.** in the first place; **en l. de** instead of; **sin l. a dudas** without a doubt; **tener l.** to take place; **dar l. a** to give rise to.

lujo *m* luxury.

lujoso, -a *adj* luxurious.

lujuria *f* lust.

lumbre *f* fire.

luminoso, -a *adj* luminous; *fig* bright.

luna *f* moon; *(espejo)* mirror; *fig* **estar en la l.** to have one's head in the clouds; **l. llena** full moon; **l. de miel** honeymoon.

lunar *m (en la ropa)* dot; *(en la piel)* mole.

lunes *m inv* Monday.

lupa *f* magnifying glass.

lustre *m* shine.

luto *m* mourning.

luz *f* light; **apagar la l.** to put out the light; **dar a l.** *(parir)* to give birth to; **luces de cruce** dipped headlights; **luces de posición** sidelights; **luces largas** headlights; **traje de luces** bullfighter's costume.

luzco *indic pres de* **lucir**.

M

macabro, -a *adj* macabre.

macana *f Am (palo)* club; *(trasto)* rubbish.

macanear *vt Am* to make up.

macarrones *mpl* macaroni *sing*.

macedonia *f* fruit salad.

maceta *f* flowerpot.

machacar [44] *vt* to crush.

machista *adj & m* male chauvinist.

macho 1 *adj* male; *fam (viril)* manly. **2** *m* male; *fam (hombre viril)* macho.

machote *m Am* rough draft.

macizo, -a 1 *adj* solid. **2** *m* massif.

macuto *m* haversack.

madeja *f* hank.

madera *f* wood; *(de construcción)* lumber; **de m.** wooden.

madrastra *f* stepmother.

madre 1 *f* mother; **m. de familia** housewife; **m. política** mother-in-law; **m. soltera** unmarried mother. **2** *interj* **¡m. mía!** good heavens!

madrina *f (de bautizo)* godmother; *(de boda)* ≃ bridesmaid.

madrugada *f* small hours *pl*; **de m.** in the small hours; **las tres de la m.** three o'clock in the morning.

madrugador, -a 1 *adj* early rising. **2** *mf* early riser.

madrugar [42] *vi* to get up early.

madurar *vi (persona)* to mature; *(fruta)* to ripen.

madurez *f* maturity; *(de fruta)* ripeness.

maduro, -a *adj* mature; *(fruta)* ripe; **de edad madura** middle-aged.

maestro, -a 1 *mf* teacher; *(especialista)* master; *(músico)* maestro. **2** *adj* **obra maestra** masterpiece.

magdalena *f* bun.

magia *f* magic; **por arte de m.** as if by magic.

magnetofón, magnetófono *m* tape recorder.

magnífico, -a *adj* magnificent.

mago, -a *mf* wizard; **los (tres) Reyes Magos** the Three Wise Men, the Three Kings.

magro, -a 1 *m (de cerdo)* lean meat. **2** *adj (sin grasa)* lean.

magullar 1 *vt* to bruise. **2** **magullarse** *vr* to get bruised.

mahonesa *f* mayonnaise.

maíz *m* corn.

majestad *f* majesty.

majo, -a *adj (bonito)* pretty, nice; *fam (simpático)* nice.

mal 1 *m* evil; *(daño)* harm; *(enfermedad)* illness. **2** *adj* bad; **un m. año** a bad year; *ver* **malo**. **3** *adv* badly; **menos m. que ...** it's a good job (that) ...; **no está (nada) m.** it is not bad (at all); **te oigo/veo (muy) m.** I can hardly hear/see you.

malabarista *mf* juggler.

malcriado, -a *adj* spoiled.

malcriar [29] *vt* to spoil.

maldad *f* badness; *(acción perversa)* evil thing.

maldecir [12] *vti* to curse.

maldición 1 *f* curse. **2** *interj* damnation!

maldito, -a *adj fam (molesto)* damned; ¡**maldita sea!** damn it!

maleducado, -a 1 *adj* bad-mannered. **2** *mf* bad-mannered person.

malentendido *m* misunderstanding.

malestar *m (molestia)* discomfort; *(inquietud)* uneasiness.

maleta *f* suitcase; **hacer la m.** to pack one's case.

maletero *m (de coche)* trunk.

maletín *m* briefcase.

maleza *f (arbustos)* undergrowth; *(malas hierbas)* weeds *pl*.

malgastar *vt* to waste.

malhablado, -a 1 *adj* foul-mouthed. **2** *mf* foul-mouthed person.

malhechor, -a *mf* wrongdoer.

malhumor *m* bad mood; **de m.** in a bad mood.

malicia *f (mala intención)* malice; *(astucia)* cunning; *(maldad)* badness.

malintencionado, -a 1 *adj* ill-intentioned. **2** *mf* ill-intentioned person.

malla *f (red)* mesh; *Am (bañador)* swimsuit; *(mallas)* leotard.

malo, -a *adj* bad; *(persona) (malvado)* wicked; *(travieso)* naughty; *(enfermo)* ill; *(cosa)* bad; *(perjudicial)* harmful; **por las malas** by force; **lo m. es que …** the problem is that ….

maloliente *adj* foul-smelling.

malpensado, -a 1 *adj* nasty-minded. **2** *mf* nasty-minded person.

malta *f* malt.

maltratado, -a *adj* battered.

maltratar *vt* to ill-treat.

malvado, -a 1 *adj* evil, wicked. **2** *mf* villain, evil person.

malvender *vt* to sell at a loss.

malvivir *vi* to live badly.

mama *f (de mujer)* breast; *(de animal)* teat; *(mamá)* mum.

mamá *f fam* mum, mummy.

mamadera *f Am* feeding bottle.

mamar *vt* to suck.

mamífero, -a *mf* mammal.

mampara *f* screen.

manada *f (de vacas, elefantes)* herd; *(de ovejas)* flock; *(de lobos, perros)* pack; *(de leones)* pride.

manantial *m* spring.

mancha *f* stain.

manchar 1 *vt* to stain. **2 mancharse** *vr* to get dirty.

manco, -a 1 *adj (de un brazo)* one-armed; *(de una mano)* one-handed. **2** *mf (de un brazo)* one-armed person; *(de una mano)* one-handed person.

mancornas *fpl Am* cufflinks.

mandado *m (recado)* errand; **hacer un m.** to run an errand.

mandar *vt (ordenar)* to order; *(dirigir)* to be in charge of; *(ejército)* to command; *(enviar)* to send; **m. (a) por** to send for; **m. algo por correo** to send sth by post.

mandarina *f* mandarin.

mandíbula *f* jaw.

mando *m (autoridad)* command; *(control)* controls *pl*; **cuadro** o **tablero de mandos** dashboard; **m. a distancia** remote control.

manecilla *f (de reloj)* hand.

manejar 1 *vt (máquina, situación)* to handle; *(dirigir)* to manage; *Am (coche)* to drive. **2 manejarse** *vr* to manage.

manejo *m (uso)* handling, use; *(de un negocio)* management; *Am (de un coche)* driving; **de fácil m.** easy-to-use.

manera *f* way, manner; **de cualquier m.** *(mal)* carelessly; *(en cualquier caso)* in any case; **de esta m.** in this way; **de ninguna m.** certainly not; **de todas maneras** anyway; **de m. que** so; **de tal m. que** in such a way that; **maneras** manners; **con buenas maneras** politely.

manga *f* sleeve; *(de riego)* hose;

(vuelta) leg; *(en tenis)* set; **de m. corta/larga** short-/long-sleeved; **sin mangas** sleeveless; *fig* **sacarse algo de la m.** to pull sth out of one's hat.

mango *m* handle.

manguera *f* hose.

maní *m* *(pl* **manises)** *Am* peanut.

maniático, -a 1 *adj* fussy. **2** *mf* fusspot.

manicomio *m* mental hospital.

manifestación *f* demonstration; *(expresión)* expression.

manifestante *mf* demonstrator.

manifestar [1] **1** *vt (declarar)* to state; *(mostrar)* to show. **2 manifestarse** *vr (por la calle)* to demonstrate.

manilla *f (de reloj)* hand; *Am (palanca)* lever.

manillar *m* handlebar.

maniobra *f* maneuver.

manipular *vt* to manipulate; *(máquina)* to handle.

maniquí *m* dummy.

manivela *f* crank.

manjar *m* delicacy, dish.

mano *f* hand; **a m.** *(sin máquina)* by hand; *(asequible)* at hand; **escrito a m.** hand-written; **hecho a m.** handmade; **estrechar la m. a algn** to shake hands with sb; **de segunda m.** second-hand; **¡manos a la obra!** hands on the wheel!; **equipaje de m.** hand luggage; **a m. derecha/izquierda** on the right/left(-hand side); **m. de pintura** coat of paint; **m. de obra** labor (force).

manojo *m* bunch.

manopla *f* mitten.

manso, -a *adj (animal)* tame.

manta *f* blanket.

manteca *f* fat; **m. de cacao/cacahuete** cocoa/peanut butter.

mantecado *m* shortcake.

mantel *m* tablecloth.

mantener [24] **1** *vt (conservar)* to keep; *(entrevista, reunión)* to have; *(familia)* to support; *(sostener)* to hold up; **m. la línea** to keep in trim.

2 mantenerse *vr (sostenerse)* to stand; *(sustentarse)* to live (**de** on); **mantenerse firme** *(perseverar)* to hold one's ground.

mantenimiento *m (de máquina)* maintenance; *(alimento)* sustenance.

mantequilla *f* butter.

manto *m* cloak.

mantón *m* shawl.

mantuve *pt indef de* **mantener.**

manual 1 *adj* manual; **trabajos manuales** handicrafts. **2** *m (libro)* manual.

manufactura *f* manufacture.

manzana *f* apple; *(de edificios)* block.

manzanilla *f (infusión)* camomile tea; *(vino)* manzanilla.

maña *f (astucia)* cunning; *(habilidad)* skill.

mañana 1 *f (parte de día)* morning; **de m.** early in the morning; **por la m.** in the morning. **2** *m* **el m.** tomorrow. **3** *adv* tomorrow; **¡hasta m.!** see you tomorow!; **m. por la m.** tomorrow morning; **pasado m.** the day after tomorrow.

mañoso, -a *adj* skillful.

mapa *m* map.

maquillaje *m* make-up.

maquillar 1 *vt* to make up. **2 maquillarse** *vr (ponerse maquillaje)* to put one's make-up on; *(usar maquillaje)* to wear make-up.

máquina *f* machine; **escrito a m.** typewritten; **hecho a m.** machine-made; **m. de afeitar (eléctrica)** (electric) shaver; **m. de coser** sewing machine; **m. de escribir** typewriter; **m. fotográfica** *o* **de fotos** camera.

maquinaria *f* machinery; *(mecanismo)* mechanism.

maquinilla *f* **m. de afeitar** safety razor.

mar *m* *o f* sea; **en alta m.** on the high seas; *fam* **está la m. de guapa** she's looking really beautiful; **llover a mares** to rain cats and dogs.

maratón *m o f* marathon.

maravilla *f* marvel; **de m.** wonderfully; **¡qué m. de película!** what a wonderful film!

maravilloso, -a *adj* wonderful, marvellous.

marca *f* mark; *(de producto)* brand; *(récord)* record; **m. registrada** registered trademark.

marcador *m (tablero)* scoreboard; *(persona)* scorer; *Am (rotulador)* felt-tip pen; *Méx (fluorescente)* highlighter pen.

marcar [44] *vt* to mark; *(número)* to dial; *(indicar)* to indicate; *(gol, puntos)* to score; *(cabello)* to set.

marcha *f* march; *(de coche)* gear; **hacer algo sobre la m.** to do sth as one goes along; **estar en m.** *(vehículo)* to be in motion; *(máquina)* to be working; **poner en m.** to start; **m. atrás** reverse (gear).

marchar 1 *vi (ir)* to walk; *(aparato)* to be on; **m. bien** *(negocio)* to be going well. **2 marcharse** to leave, to go away.

marchitar *vt*, **marchitarse** *vr* to shrivel, to wither.

marco *m (de cuadro etc)* frame; *(moneda)* mark.

marea *f* tide; **m. alta/baja** high/low tide; **m. negra** oil slick.

marear *vt* to make sick; *(en el mar)* to make seasick; *(en un avión)* to make airsick; *(en un coche)* to make carsick; *(aturdir)* to make dizzy; *fam (fastidiar)* to annoy. **2 marearse** *vr* to get sick/seasick/airsick/carsick; *(quedar aturdido)* to get dizzy.

marejada *f* swell.

mareo *m (náusea)* sickness; *(en el mar)* seasickness; *(en un avión)* airsickness; *(en un coche)* carsickness; *(aturdimiento)* dizziness.

marfil *m* ivory.

margarina *f* margarine.

margarita *f* daisy.

margen *m* edge; *(de folio)* margin; *fig* **mantenerse al m.** not to get involved.

marginado, -a 1 *adj* excluded. **2** *mf* dropout.

marginar *vt (a una persona)* to exclude.

marido *m* husband.

marihuana, marijuana, mariguana *f* marijuana.

marinero *m* sailor.

marioneta *f* marionette.

mariposa *f* butterfly.

mariquita *f* ladybird.

marisco *m* shellfish; **mariscos** seafood.

marítimo, -a *adj* maritime; **paseo m.** promenade.

mármol *m* marble.

marqués *m* marquis.

marrano, -a 1 *adj (sucio)* filthy. **2** *mf (animal)* pig; *fam* slob.

marrón *adj & m* brown.

marroquí *adj & mf (pl* **marroquíes)** Moroccan.

Marte *m* Mars.

martes *m inv* Tuesday.

martillo *m* hammer.

mártir *mf* martyr.

marzo *m* March.

más 1 *adv* more; **m. gente de la que esperas** more people than you're expecting; **de** more than, over; **cada día o vez m.** more and more; **es m.** what's more, furthermore; **lo m. posible** as much as possible; **m. bien** rather; **m. o menos** more or less; **m. aún** even more; **¿qué m. da?** what's the difference? • *(comparativo)* **es m. alta/inteligente que yo** she's taller/more intelligent than me. • *(superlativo)* **el m. bonito/caro** the prettiest/most expensive. • *(exclamación)* **¡qué casa m. bonita!** what a lovely house!; **¡está m. guapa!** she looks so beautiful! • *(después de pron interr e indef)* else; **¿algo m.?** anything else?; **no, nada m.** no, nothing else; **¿quién m.?** who else?; **nadie/alguien m.** nobody/somebody else. • **por m. +** *(adj/adv +)* **que + subj** however (much); **por m.**

fuerte que sea however strong he may be. **2** *m inv* **los/las m.** most people. **3** *prep (en sumas)* plus.

masa *f* mass; *(de cosas)* bulk; *(de pan etc)* dough; **medios de comunicación de masas** mass media.

masaje *m* massage; **dar masaje(s) (a)** to massage.

mascar [44] *vt* to chew.

máscara *f* mask; **m. de gas** gas mask.

mascarilla *f* mask; **m. de oxígeno** oxygen mask; *(cosmética)* face pack.

mascota *f* mascot.

masculino, -a *male; (para hombre)* men's; *(género)* masculine.

máster *m* master's degree.

masticar [44] *vt* to chew.

mástil *m* mast.

mastín *m* mastiff.

mata *f (matorral)* shrub.

matador *m* matador, bullfighter.

matanza *f* slaughter.

matar *vt* to kill.

mate¹ *adj (sin brillo)* matt.

mate² *m* mate; **jaque m.** checkmate.

matemática *f*, **matemáticas** *fpl* mathematics *sing.*

materia *f* matter; *(tema)* question; *(asignatura)* subject; **m. prima** raw material; **índice de materias** table of contents.

material 1 *adj* material. **2** *m* material; **m. escolar/de construcción** teaching/building materials *pl*; **m. de oficina** office equipment.

materialmente *adv* physically.

maternal *adj* maternal.

maternidad *f* maternity, motherhood.

materno, -a *adj* maternal; **abuelo m.** maternal grandfather; **lengua materna** mother tongue.

matiz *m (de color)* shade.

matizar [40] *vt* to clarify, to explain.

matorral *m* thicket.

matrero, -a *mf Am (bandolero)* bandit.

matrícula *f* registration; *(de coche)*

(número) registration number; *(placa)* license plate.

matricular *vt*, **matricularse** *vr* to register.

matrimonio *m* marriage; *(pareja casada)* married couple; **m. civil/religioso** civil/church wedding; **contraer m.** to marry; **cama de m.** double bed.

matriz *f* matrix; *(útero)* womb.

matrona *f (comadrona)* midwife.

maullar *vi* to mew.

maxilar 1 *adj* maxillary. **2** *m* jaw.

máximo, -a 1 *adj* maximum. **2** *m* maximum; **al m.** to the utmost; **como m.** *(como mucho)* at the most; *(lo más tarde)* at the latest.

mayo *m* May.

mayonesa *f* mayonnaise.

mayor *adj (comparativo) (tamaño)* bigger (**que** than); *(edad)* older, elder; *(superlativo) (tamaño)* biggest; *(edad)* oldest, eldest; *(adulto)* grown-up; *(maduro)* mature; *(principal)* major; **la m. parte** the majority; **la m. parte de las veces** most often; **ser m. de edad** to be of age; **al por m.** wholesale.

mayoría *f* majority; **la m. de los niños** most children; **m. de edad** majority.

mayorista 1 *adj* wholesale. **2** *mf* wholesaler; **precios de m.** wholesale prices.

mayoritario, -a *adj* majority; **un gobierno m.** a majority government.

mayúscula *f* capital letter.

mazapán *m* marzipan.

me *pron pers (objeto directo)* me; **no me mires** don't look at me. ▪ *(objeto indirecto)* me, to me, for me; **¿me das un caramelo?** will you give me a sweet?; **me lo dio** he gave it to me. ▪ *(pron reflexivo)* myself; **me he cortado** I've cut myself; **me voy/muero** *(no se traduce)* I'm off/dying.

mecánico, -a 1 *adj* mechanical. **2** *mf* mechanic.

mecanismo *m* mechanism.

mecanografía f typing.

mecanografiar [29] vt to type.

mecanógrafo, -a mf typist.

mecedora f rocking chair.

mecer [49] **1** vt to rock. **2 mecerse** vr to rock.

mecha f (de vela) wick; (de pelo) streak.

mechero m (cigarette) lighter.

mechón m (de pelo) lock; (de lana) tuft.

medalla f medal.

media f stocking; Am (calcetín) sock; (promedio) average; **a medias** (incompleto) unfinished; (entre dos) half and half.

medialuna f Am (pasta) croissant.

mediano, -a adj (tamaña) medium-sized.

medianoche f midnight.

mediante prep by means of.

medicación f medication.

medicamento m medicine.

medicina f medicine; **estudiante de m.** medical student.

médico, -a 1 mf doctor; **m. de cabecera** family doctor. **2** adj medical.

medida f measure; (dimensión) measurement; **a (la) m.** (ropa) made-to-measure; **a m. que avanzaba** as he advanced; **adoptar o tomar medidas** to take steps.

medieval adj medieval.

medio, -a 1 adj half; (intermedio) middle; (normal) average; **una hora y media** an hour and a half; **a media mañana/tarde** in the middle of the morning/afternoon; **clase media** middle class; **salario m.** average wage. **2** adv half; **está m. muerta** she is half dead. **3** m (mitad) half; (centro) middle; **en m. (de)** (en el centro) in the middle (of); (entre dos) in between; **medios de transporte** means of transport; **por m. de** by means of; **medios de comunicación** (mass) media; **m. ambiente** environment.

medioambiental adj environmental.

mediocre adj mediocre.

mediodía m (hora exacta) midday; (período aproximado) early afternoon; (sur) south.

medir [6] **1** vt to measure. **2** vi to measure; **mide 2 metros** he is 2 meters tall; **mide dos metros de alto/ancho/largo** it is two meters high/wide/long.

médula f marrow; **m. ósea** bone marrow.

megafonía f public-address system.

mejicano, -a adj & mf Mexican.

mejilla f cheek.

mejillón m mussel.

mejor 1 adj (comparativo) better (que than); (superlativo) best; **tu m. amiga** your best friend; **lo m.** the best thing. **2** adv (comparativo) better (que than); (superlativo) best; **cada vez m.** better and better; **m. dicho** or rather; **es el que m. canta** he is the one who sings the best; **a lo m.** (quizás) perhaps; (ojalá) hopefully.

mejora f improvement.

mejorar 1 vti to improve. **2 mejorarse** vr to get better; **¡que te mejores!** get well soon!

melancolía f melancholy.

melancólico, -a adj melancholic.

melena f (head of) hair; (de león) mane.

mellado, -a adj (sin dientes) gap-toothed.

mellizo, -a adj & mf twin.

melocotón m peach.

melodía f tune.

melón m melon.

membrana f membrane.

membrillo m quince.

memoria f memory; (informe) report; **memorias** (biografía) memoirs; **aprender/saber algo de m.** to learn/know sth by heart.

memorizar [40] vt to memorize.

mencionar vt to mention.

mendigo, -a mf beggar.

mendrugo *m* crust (of stale bread).

menear 1 *vt* to shake; *(cola)* to wag. **2 menearse** *vr* to shake.

menestra *f* vegetable stew.

menguar [45] *vti* to diminish.

menopausia *f* menopause.

menor 1 *adj (comparativo) (de tamaño)* smaller (**que** than); *(de edad)* younger (**que** than); *(superlativo) (de tamaño)* smallest; *(de intensidad)* least, slightest; *(de edad)* youngest; **ser m. de edad** to be a minor, to be under age; **al por m.** retail. **2** *mf* minor.

menos 1 *adj (comparativo) (con singular)* less; *(con plural)* fewer; **m. dinero/leche/tiempo** less money/milk/time than; **m. libros que** fewer books than; **tiene m. años de lo que parece** he's younger than he looks; *(superlativo)* **fui el que perdí m. dinero** I lost the least money. **2** *adv* **m. de** *(con singular)* less than; *(con plural)* fewer than, less than. ▪ *(superlativo) (con singular)* least; **el m. inteligente de la clase** the least intelligent boy in the class. ▪ *(con plural)* the fewest; **ayer fue cuando vinieron m. personas** yesterday was when the fewest people came. ▪ *(locuciones)* **a m. que +** *subj* unless; **al** *o* **por lo m.** at least; **echar a algn de m.** to miss sb; **¡m. mal!** just as well!; **ni mucho m.** far from it. **3** *prep* except; *(en restas)* minus.

menosprecio *m* contempt.

mensaje *m* message.

mensajero, -a *mf* messenger.

mensual *adj (monthly)*.

mensualidad *f (pago)* monthly payment; *(sueldo)* monthly salary *o* wage.

menta *f* mint; *(licor)* crème de menthe.

mental *adj* mental.

mentalidad *f* mentality; **de m. abierta/cerrada** open-/narrow-minded.

mentalizar [40] **1** *vt (concienciar)* to make aware. **2 mentalizarse** *vr (concienciarse)* to become aware; *(hacerse a la idea)* to come to terms (**a** with).

mente *f* mind.

mentir [5] *vi* to lie.

mentira *f* lie.

mentón *m* chin.

menú *m* menu.

menudo, -a 1 *adj* minute; **¡m. lío/susto!** what a mess/fright! **2** *adv* **a m.** often.

meñique *adj* & *m* (**dedo**) **m.** little finger.

mercado *m* market; **M. Común** Common Market.

mercadotecnia *f* marketing.

mercancías *fpl* goods.

mercantil *adj* commercial.

merecer [33] *vt* **1** to deserve; *(uso impers)* **no merece la pena hacerlo** it's not worth while doing it. **2 merecerse** *vr* to deserve.

merecido, -a 1 *adj* deserved; **lo tiene m.** *(castigo)* it serves him right. **2** *m* just deserts *pl*.

merendar [1] **1** *vt* to have for tea. **2** *vi* to have tea.

merendero *m (en el campo)* picnic spot.

merezco *indic pres de* **merecer**.

meridional *adj* southern.

merienda *f* afternoon snack.

mérito *m* merit.

merluza *f* hake.

mermelada *f* jam; *(de agrios)* marmalade; **m. de fresa** strawberry jam; **m. de naranja** orange marmalade.

mes *m* month; **el m. pasado/que viene** last/next month.

mesa *f* table; *(de despacho etc)* desk; **poner/recoger la m.** to set/clear the table.

mesada *f Am (dinero)* monthly payment; *RP (para adolescentes)* (monthly) allowance.

mesero, -a *mf CAm, Col, Méx (hombre)* waiter; *(mujer)* waitress.

meseta f plateau.

mesilla f **m. de noche** bedside table.

mesón m old-style tavern.

meta f (objetivo, portería) goal; (de carrera) finishing line.

metal m metal.

metálico, -a 1 adj metallic. **2** m **pagar en m.** to pay (in) cash.

meteorológico, -a adj meteorological; **parte m.** weather report.

meter 1 vt (poner) to put (en in); (comprometer) to involve (en in). **2 meterse** vr (entrar) to go/come in; (entrometerse) to meddle; (estar) **¿dónde te habías metido?** where have you been (all this time)?; **meterse con algn** (en broma) to get at sb.

método m method.

metralleta f submachine-gun.

métrico, -a adj metric; **sistema m.** metric system.

metro m meter; (tren) subway.

mexicano, -a adj & mf Mexican.

mezcla f (producto) mixture; (acción) mixing.

mezclar 1 vt to mix; (involucrar) to involve. **2 mezclarse** vr (cosas) to get mixed up; (gente) to mingle.

mezquino, -a adj (tacaño) mean; (escaso) miserable.

mezquita f mosque.

mi adj my; **mis cosas/libros** my things/books.

mí pron pers me; **a mí me dio tres** he gave me three; **compra otro para mí** buy one for me too; **por mí mismo** by myself.

mía adj & pron pos f ver **mío**.

microbús m minibus.

micrófono m microphone.

microonda f **un (horno) microondas** a microwave (oven).

microprocesador m microprocessor.

miedo m (pavor) fear; (temor) apprehension; **una película de m.** a horror film; **tener m. de algo/algn** to be afraid of sth/sb.

miedoso, -a adj fearful.

miel f honey.

miembro m (socio) member; (de cuerpo) limb.

mientras 1 conj while; (cuanto) m. más/menos ... the more/less .... **2** adv m. (tanto) meanwhile, in the meantime.

miércoles m inv Wednesday; **M. de Ceniza** Ash Wednesday.

miga f (de pan etc) crumb.

mil adj & m thousand; **m. pesos** a o one thousand pesos.

milagro m miracle.

milagroso, -a adj miraculous.

milésimo, -a adj & mf thousandth.

mili f military service; **hacer la m.** to do one's military service.

milímetro m millimeter.

militar 1 adj military. **2** mf soldier.

milla f mile.

millar m thousand.

millón m million.

millonario, -a adj & mf millionaire.

mimar vt to spoil.

mimbre f wicker.

mina f (de lápiz) lead.

mineral 1 adj mineral. **2** m ore.

minero, -a 1 mf miner. **2** adj mining.

miniatura f miniature.

minifalda f miniskirt.

mínimo, -a 1 adj (muy pequeño) minute; (en matemáticas) minimum. **2** m minimum; **como m.** at least.

ministerio m department.

ministro, -a mf minister; **primer m.** Prime Minister.

minoría f minority; **m. de edad** minority.

minúsculo, -a adj minute; **letra minúscula** small letter.

minusválido, -a 1 adj disabled. **2** mf disabled person.

minuto m minute.

mío, -a 1 adj pos of mine; **un amigo m.** a friend of mine; **no es asunto m.** it is none of my business. **2** pron pos mine.

miope mf short-sighted person.

mirada f look; **lanzar** o **echar una m. a** to glance at.

mirar 1 vt to look at; (observar) to watch; (cuidar) **mira que no le pase nada** see that nothing happens to him. **2** vi **la casa mira al norte** the house faces north.

mirlo m blackbird.

misa f mass.

miserable adj (mezquino) (persona) despicable; (sueldo etc) miserable; (pobre) wretched.

miseria f (pobreza extrema) extreme poverty; (insignificancia) pittance; (tacañería) meanness.

misión f mission.

mismo, -a 1 adj same; (uso enfático) **yo m.** I myself; **por eso m.** that is why; **por uno** o **sí m.** by oneself; **aquí m.** right here. **2** pron same; **es el m. de ayer** it's the same one as yesterday; **lo m.** the same (thing); **dar** o **ser lo m.** to make no difference. **3** adv **así m.** likewise.

misterio m mystery.

mitad f half; (centro) middle; **a m. de camino** half-way there; **a m. de precio** half price; **en la m. del primer acto** half-way through the first act.

mitote m Am uproar.

mixto adj mixed.

mobiliario m furniture.

moca m mocha.

mochila f rucksack.

moco m snot; **sonarse los mocos** to blow one's nose.

mocoso, -a mf fam brat.

moda f fashion; **a la m., de m.** in fashion; **pasado de m.** old-fashioned.

modales mpl manners.

modelo 1 adj inv & m model. **2** mf (fashion) model; **desfile de modelos** fashion show.

módem m modem.

moderado, -a adj moderate.

modernizar [40] vt, **modernizarse** vr to modernize.

moderno, -a adj modern.

modesto, -a adj modest.

modificar [44] vt to modify.

modisto, -a mf fashion designer.

modo m (manera) way, manner; (en lingüística) mood; **m. de empleo** instructions for use; **modos** manners.

mofarse vr to laugh (**de** at).

moflete m chubby cheek.

mohoso, -a adj moldy; (oxidado) rusty.

mojar 1 vt to wet; (humedecer) to dampen. **2 mojarse** vr to get wet.

molde m mold.

moldeador m (de pelo) wave.

mole f mass.

moler [4] vt to grind.

molestar 1 vt (incomodar) to disturb; (causar malestar) to hurt; **¿le molestaría esperar fuera?** would you mind waiting outside? **2 molestarse** vr (tomarse la molestia) to bother; (ofenderse) to take offense.

molestia f bother; (dolor) slight pain.

molesto, -a adj (irritante) annoying; **estar m. con algn** (enfadado) to be annoyed with sb.

molino m mill; **m. de viento** windmill.

momentáneo, -a adj momentary.

momento m (instante) moment; (periodo) time; **al m.** at once; **de m.** for the time being; **en cualquier m.** at any time.

monasterio m monastery.

mondar 1 vt to peel. **2 mondarse** vr fam **mondarse (de risa)** to laugh one's head off.

moneda f (pieza) coin; (dinero) currency; **m. suelta** small change.

monedero m purse.

monetario, -a adj monetary.

monigote m (persona) wimp; (dibujo) rough sketch (of a person).

monitor, -a mf monitor; (profesor) instructor.

monja f nun.

monje m monk.

mono, -a 1 m monkey; (prenda) (de

trabajo) overalls *.pl; (de vestir)* cat-suit. **2** *adj fam (bonito)* pretty.

monopolio *m* monopoly.

monótono, -a *adj* monotonous.

monstruo *m* monster; *(genio)* genius.

montaje *m (instalación)* fitting; *(ensamblaje)* assembling.

montaña *f* mountain; **m. rusa** big dipper.

montañismo *m* mountaineering.

montañoso, -a *adj* mountainous.

montar 1 *vi (en bici, a caballo)* to ride; *(en coche, tren)* to travel; *(subirse)* to get in. **2** *vt (colocar)* to put on; *(máquina etc)* to assemble; *(negocio)* to set up. **3 montarse** *vr (subirse)* to get on; *(en coche)* to get in.

monte *m (montaña)* mountain; *(con nombre propio)* mount.

montón *m* heap; **un m. de** a load of.

montura *f (cabalgadura)* mount; *(de gafas)* frame.

monumento *m* monument.

moño *m* bun.

moqueta *f* fitted carpet.

mora *f (zarzamora)* blackberry.

morado, -a *adj & m* purple.

moral 1 *adj* moral. **2** *f (ética)* morals *pl; (ánimo)* morale.

morboso, -a *adj (malsano)* morbid.

morcilla *f* black pudding.

mordaz *adj* biting.

morder [4] *vt* to bite.

mordida *f Am (soborno)* bribe.

mordisco *m* bite.

moreno, -a 1 *adj (pelo)* dark-haired; *(piel)* dark-skinned; *(bronceado)* tanned; **ponerse m.** to get a suntan; **pan/azúcar m.** brown bread/sugar. **2** *mf (persona) (de pelo)* dark-haired person; *(mujer)* brunette; *(de piel)* dark-skinned person.

morgue *f Am* morgue.

moribundo, -a 1 *adj* moribund. **2** *mf* dying person.

morir [7] **1** *vi* to die; **m. de frío/hambre/cáncer** to die of cold/hunger/

cancer. **2 morirse** *vr* to die; **morirse de hambre** to starve to death; *fig* to be starving; **morirse de aburrimiento** to be bored to death; **morirse de risa** to die laughing.

moro, -a *adj & mf* Moor; *fam (musulmán)* Muslim; *(árabe)* Arab.

morocho, -a *adj Am (moreno)* swarthy.

morro *m (hocico)* snout.

mortadela *f* mortadella.

mortal *adj* mortal; *(mortífero)* fatal; **un accidente m.** a fatal accident.

mortalidad *f* mortality; **índice de m.** death rate.

mortandad *f* death toll.

mosca *f* fly; *fam* **estar m.** *(suspicaz)* to be suspicious; *fam* **por si las moscas** just in case.

moscardón *m* blowfly.

mosquitero *m (red)* mosquito net.

mosquito *m* mosquito.

mostaza *f* mustard.

mostrador *m (de tienda)* counter; *(de bar)* bar.

mostrar [4] **1** *vt* to show. **2 mostrarse** *vr* to be; **se mostró muy comprensiva** she was very understanding.

mota *f* speck.

mote¹ *m (apodo)* nickname.

mote² *m Am* boiled salted corn.

motín *m (amotinamiento)* mutiny; *(disturbio)* riot.

motivo *m (causa)* reason; **motivos** grounds; **con m. de** on the occasion of; **sin m.** for no reason at all.

moto *f* motorbike.

motocicleta *f* motorbike.

motociclista *mf* motorcyclist.

motoneta *f Am (motor)* scooter.

motor *m (grande)* engine; *(pequeño)* motor; **m. de reacción** jet engine.

motora *f* motorboat.

motorista *mf* motorcyclist.

mover [4] **1** *vt* to move; *(hacer funcionar)* to drive. **2 moverse** *vr* to move.

móvil 1 *adj* mobile; **teléfono m.** mobile phone; **unidad m.** *(de radio,*

TV) outside broadcast unit. **2** *m* (*de delito*) motive; (*teléfono*) mobile.

movimiento *m* movement; (*en física*) motion; (*actividad*) activity; (**poner algo**) **en m.** (to set sth) in motion.

moza *f* young girl.

mozo *m* boy; (*de estación*) porter; (*de hotel*) bellboy.

mucamo, -a *mf Am* servant.

muchacha *f* girl.

muchacho *m* boy.

muchedumbre *f* crowd.

mucho, -a 1 *adj sing* lots of; (*en frases negativas e interrogativas*) much; **hay m. tonto suelto** there are lots of idiots around; **no tengo m. dinero** I don't have much money; **¿bebes m. café?** do you drink a lot of coffee?; **m. tiempo** a long time; **tengo m. sueño/mucha sed** I am very sleepy/thirsty. ▪ **muchos, -as** lots of; (*en frases negativas e interrogativas*) many; **no hay muchas chicas** there aren't many girls; **¿tienes muchos amigos?** do you have many friends?; **tiene muchos años** he is very old. **2** *pron* lots; **¿cuánta leche queda?** — **mucha** how much milk is there left? — a lot; **muchos, -as** lots; **¿cuántos libros tienes?** — **muchos** how many books have you got? — lots; **muchos creemos que …** many of us believe that …. **3** *adv* a lot; **lo siento m.** I'm very sorry; **como m.** at the most; **con m.** by far; **m. antes/después** long before/after; **¡ni m. menos!** no way!; **por m. (que)** + *subj* however much; **hace m. que no viene por aquí** he has not been to see us for a long time.

mudanza *f* move; **estar de m.** to be moving; **camión de m.** removal van.

mudar 1 *vt* (*ropa*) to change; (*plumas, pelo*) to molt; (*de piel*) to shed. **2 mudarse** *vr* **mudarse de casa/ropa** to move house/to change one's clothes.

mudo, -a 1 *adj* (*que no habla*) dumb. **2** *mf* mute.

mueble *m* piece of furniture; **muebles** furniture *sing*; **con/sin muebles** furnished/unfurnished.

muela *f* molar; **dolor de muelas** toothache; **m. del juicio** wisdom tooth.

muelle¹ *m* spring.

muelle² *m* (*en puerto*) dock.

muerte *f* death; **dar m. a algn** to kill sb; **odiar a algn a m.** to loathe sb; **un susto de m.** the fright of one's life.

muerto, -a 1 *adj* dead; **m. de hambre** starving; **m. de frío** frozen to death; **m. de miedo** scared stiff; **m. de risa** laughing one's head off; (**en**) **punto m.** (in) neutral. **2** *mf* (*difunto*) dead person; **hacerse el m.** to pretend to be dead.

muestra *f* (*espécimen*) sample; (*modelo a copiar*) model; (*prueba, señal*) sign; **dar muestras de** to show signs of; **m. de cariño/respeto** token of affection/respect.

mugido *m* (*de vaca*) moo; (*de toro*) bellow.

mugre *f* filth.

mugriento, -a *adj* filthy.

mujer *f* woman; (*esposa*) wife; **m. de la limpieza** cleaning lady; **m. de su casa** houseproud woman.

muleta *f* (*prótesis*) crutch; (*de torero*) muleta.

mulo, -a *mf* mule.

multa *f* fine; (*de tráfico*) ticket.

multicopista *f* duplicator.

multinacional *adj & f* multinational.

múltiple *adj* multiple.

multiplicación *f* multiplication.

multiplicar [44] **1** *vti* to multiply (**por** by). **2 multiplicarse** *vr* to multiply.

multitud *f* (*de personas*) crowd; (*de cosas*) multitude.

mundial 1 *adj* worldwide; **campeón m.** world champion; **de fama m.**

world-famous. **2** *m* world championship.

mundialmente *adv* m. famoso world-famous.

mundo *m* world; **todo el m.** everyone.

munición *f* ammunition.

municipal *adj* municipal; *(policía)* local.

municipio *m* municipality; *(ayuntamiento)* town council.

muñeca *f* wrist; *(juguete, muchacha)* doll.

muñeco *m (juguete)* (little) boy doll; **m. de trapo** rag doll; **m. de nieve** snowman.

murciélago *m* bat.

murmullo *m* murmur.

murmurar *vi (criticar)* to gossip; *(susurrar)* to whisper; *(producir murmullo)* to murmur.

muro *m* wall.

músculo *m* muscle.

musculoso, -a *adj* muscular.

museo *m* museum.

musgo *m* moss.

música *f* music; **m. clásica** classical music.

musical *adj* musical.

músico, -a *mf* musician.

muslo *m* thigh.

musulmán, -ana *adj & mf* Muslim.

mutilado, -a *mf* disabled person.

mutuo, -a *adj* mutual.

muy *adv* very; **m. bueno/malo** very good/bad; **¡m. bien!** very good!; **M. señor mío** Dear Sir; **m. de mañana/ noche** very early/late.

N

n° *abr de* **número** number, n.

nabo *m* turnip.

nácar *m* mother-of-pearl.

nacer [60] *vi* to be born; *(pelo)* to begin to grow; *(río)* to rise; **nací en Montoro** I was born in Montoro.

nacimiento *m* birth; *(de río)* source; *(belén)* Nativity scene; **lugar de n.** place of birth.

nación *f* nation; **las Naciones Unidas** the United Nations.

nacional 1 *adj* national; *(producto, mercado, vuelo)* domestic. **2** *mf* national.

nacionalidad *f* nationality.

nada 1 *pron* nothing; *(con verbo)* not … anything, nothing; **no sé n.** I don't know anything; **yo no digo n.** I'm saying nothing, I'm not saying anything; **más que n.** more than anything; **sin decir n.** without saying anything; **casi n.** hardly anything; **gracias — de n.** thanks — don't mention it; **para n.** not at all; **como si n.** just like that; **n. de eso** nothing of the kind; **n. de n.** nothing at all; **n. más verla** as soon as he saw her. **2** *adv* not at all; **no me gusta n.** I don't like it at all.

nadar *vi* to swim; **n. a braza** to do the breaststroke.

nadador, -a *mf* swimmer.

nadie *pron* no one, nobody; *(con verbo)* not … anyone o anybody; **no conozco a n.** I don't know anyone o anybody; **más que n.** more than anyone; **sin decírselo a n.** without telling anyone; **casi n.** hardly anyone.

nafta *f Am (gasolina)* gasoline.

nailon *m* nylon; **medias de n.** nylons.

naipe *m* playing card.

nalga *f* buttock.

nana *f* lullaby.

naranja 1 *f* orange. **2** *adj & m (color)* orange.

naranjada *f* orangeade.

naranjo *m* orange tree.

narcotraficante *mf* drug trafficker.

narcotráfico *m* drug trafficking.

nariz *f* nose; **narices** nose *sing*; *fam* **meter las narices en algo** to poke one's nose into sth.

nata *f* cream; *(de leche hervida)* skin; **n. batida/montada** whipped cream.

natación *f* swimming.

natal *adj* **mi país n.** my native country; **su pueblo n.** his home town.

natillas *fpl* custard *sing*.

nativo, -a *adj & mf* native.

nato, -a *adj* born.

natural 1 *adj* natural; *(fruta, flor)* fresh; *(bebida)* at room temperature; **de tamaño n.** life-size. **2** *mf* native.

naturaleza *f* nature; **en plena n.** in unspoilt countryside.

naturalidad *f (sencillez)* naturalness; *(espontaneidad)* ease; **con n.** straightforwardly.

naturalizar [40] **1** *vt* to naturalize. **2 naturalizarse** *vr* to become naturalized.

naturalmente *adv* naturally; **¡n.!** of course!

naturismo *m* naturism.

naufragar [42] *vi (barco)* to be wrecked.

naufragio *m* shipwreck.

náusea *f* nausea; **me da n.** it makes me sick; **sentir náuseas** to feel sick.

náutico, -a *adj* nautical.

navaja *f (cuchillo)* penknife; **n. de afeitar** razor.

nave *f* ship; *(de iglesia)* nave; **n. (espacial)** spaceship; **n. industrial** plant.

navegable *adj* navigable.

navegar [42] *vi* to sail; *(en avión)* to navigate, to fly; **n. por Internet** to surf the Net.

Navidad(es) *f(pl)* Christmas; **árbol de Navidad** Christmas tree; **Feliz Navidad/Felices Navidades** Merry Christmas.

navideño, -a *adj* Christmas.

navío *m* ship.

neblina *f* mist.

necesario, -a *adj* necessary; **es n.**

hacerlo it has to be done; **es n. que vayas** you must go; **no es n. que vayas** it's not necessary for you to go; **si fuera n.** if need be.

neceser *m* make-up bag.

necesidad *f* need; **por n.** of necessity; **tener n. de** to need.

necesitado, -a 1 *adj (pobre)* needy, poor; **n. de** in need of. **2** *mpl* **los necesitados** the needy.

necesitar *vt* to need.

necio, -a 1 *adj* silly. **2** *mf* fool.

nectarina *f* nectarine.

neerlandés, -esa 1 *adj* Dutch. **2** *mf (hombre)* Dutchman; *(mujer)* Dutchwoman; **los neerlandeses** the Dutch. **3** *m (idioma)* Dutch.

nefasto, -a *adj (perjudicial)* harmful; *(funesto)* ill-fated.

negación *f* negation; *(negativa)* denial; *(gramatical)* negative.

negar [1] **1** *vt* to deny; *(rechazar)* to refuse; **negó haberlo robado** he denied stealing it; **le negaron la beca** they refused him the grant. **2 negarse** *vr* to refuse (**a** to).

negativo, -a *adj & m* negative.

negligencia *f* negligence.

negociación *f* negotiation.

negociante *mf* dealer; *(hombre)* businessman; *(mujer)* businesswoman.

negociar [43] **1** *vt* to negotiate. **2** *vi (comerciar)* to do business.

negocio *m* business; *(transacción)* deal; *(asunto)* affair; **hombre de negocios** businessman; **mujer de negocios** businesswoman.

negro, -a 1 *adj* black; **verlo todo n.** to be very pessimistic. **2** *mf (hombre)* black; *(mujer)* black (woman); *fam* **trabajar como un n.** to work like a dog. **3** *m (color)* black.

nene, -a *mf (niño)* baby boy; *(niña)* baby girl.

neocelandés, -esa 1 *adj* New Zealand. **2** *mf* New Zealander.

neoyorkino, -a 1 *adj* New York. **2** *mf* New Yorker.

neozelandés, -esa *adj & mf* = neocelandés.

nervio *m* nerve; *(de la carne)* sinew; **nervios** nerves; **ataque de nervios** a fit of hysterics; **ser un manojo de nervios** to be a bundle of nerves.

nervioso, -a *adj* nervous; **poner n. a algn** to get on sb's nerves.

neto, -a *adj (peso, cantidad)* net.

neumático, -a 1 *adj* pneumatic. **2** *m* tire; **n. de recambio** spare tire.

neumonía *f* pneumonia.

neurótico, -a *adj & mf* neurotic.

neutral *adj* neutral.

neutro, -a *adj (imparcial)* neutral; *(género)* neuter.

nevada *f* snowfall.

nevar [1] *v impers* to snow.

nevera *f (frigorífico)* fridge; *(portátil)* cool box.

ni *conj* no ... ni, ni ... ni neither ... nor, not ... or; **ni se te ocurra** don't even think about it.

nicaragüense, nicaragüeño, -a *adj & mf* Nicaraguan.

nido *m* nest.

niebla *f* fog; **hay mucha n.** it is very foggy.

nieto, -a *mf (niño)* grandson; *(niña)* granddaughter; **mis nietos** my grandchildren.

nieve *f* snow.

nigeriano, -a *adj & mf* Nigerian.

ningún *adj (delante de m sing)* ver **ninguno**.

ninguno, -a 1 *adj (con verbo)* not ... any; **en ninguna parte** nowhere; **de ningún modo** no way. **2** *pron (persona)* nobody, no one; **n. de los dos** neither of the two; **n. de ellos** none of them; *(cosa)* not ... any of them; *(enfático)* none of them; **n. me gusta** I don't like any of them; **no vi n.** I saw none of them.

niña *f* girl; *(pupila)* pupil.

niñera *f* nanny.

niñez *f* childhood.

niño, -a *mf* child; *(bebé)* baby; *(muchacho)* (small) boy; *(muchacha)* (little) girl; **de n.** as a child; **niños** children.

nitrógeno *m* nitrogen.

nivel *m (altura)* level; *(categoría)* standard; **a n. del mar** at sea level; **n. de vida** standard of living.

no *adv* not; *(como respuesta)* no; **no vi a nadie** I did not see anyone, I didn't see anyone; **aún no** not yet; **ya no** no longer; **¿por qué no?** why not?; **no fumar/aparcar** *(en letrero)* no smoking/parking; **no sea que +** *subj* in case; **es rubia, ¿no?** she's blonde, isn't she?; **llegaron anoche, ¿no?** they arrived yesterday, didn't they?

noble 1 *adj* noble. **2** *mf (hombre)* nobleman; *(mujer)* noblewoman; **los nobles** the nobility *sing*.

noche *f* evening; *(después de las diez)* night; **de n., por la n.** at night; **esta n.** tonight; **mañana por la n.** tomorrow night/evening; **buenas noches** *(saludo)* good evening; *(despedida)* good night.

nochebuena *f* Christmas Eve.

nochevieja *f* New Year's Eve.

nocturno, -a *adj* night; **clases nocturnas** evening classes.

nombrar *vt* to name.

nombre *m* name; *(sustantivo)* noun; **n. de pila** Christian name; **n. y apellidos** full name; **n. propio** proper noun.

nordeste *adj & m* northeast.

nórdico, -a 1 *adj (del norte)* northern; *(escandinavo)* Nordic. **2** *mf* Nordic person.

noreste *adj & m* northeast.

norma *f* norm.

normal *adj* normal; **lo n.** the usual.

normalizar [40] **1** *vt* to normalize. **2 normalizarse** *vr* to return to normal.

noroeste *adj & m* northwest.

norte *m* north; **al n. de** to the north of.

norteafricano, -a *adj & mf* North African.

norteamericano, -a *adj & mf* (North) American.

noruego, -a 1 adj Norwegian. **2** mf Norwegian. **3** m (idioma) Norwegian.

nos pron pers us; (con verbo reflexivo) ourselves; (con verbo recíproco) each other; **n. hemos divertido mucho** we enjoyed ourselves a lot; **n. queremos mucho** we love each other very much.

nosotros, -as pron pers (sujeto) we; (complemento) us; **con n.** with us.

nostalgia f nostalgia; (morriña) homesickness.

nota f note; (de examen) mark, grade; **sacar buenas notas** to get good grades.

notable 1 adj (apreciable) noticeable; (digno de notar) outstanding. **2** m (nota) very good.

notar 1 vt (percibir) to notice. **2 notarse** vr (percibirse) to show; **no se nota** it doesn't show.

notaría f (despacho) notary's office.

notario, -a mf notary (public).

noticia f news sing; **una n.** a piece of news; **una buena n.** (some) good news.

noticiario, Am **noticiero** m television news sing.

notificar [44] vt to notify.

novato, -a 1 adj (persona) inexperienced. **2** mf (principiante) novice.

novecientos, -as adj & mf nine hundred.

novedad f (cosa nueva) novelty; (cambio) change; (cualidad) newness.

novela f novel; (corta) story.

novelista mf novelist.

noveno, -a adj & m ninth; **novena parte** ninth.

noventa adj & m inv ninety.

novia f (amiga) girlfriend; (prometida) fiancée; (en boda) bride.

noviembre m November.

novillada f bullfight with young bulls.

novillo, -a mf (toro) young bull;

(vaca) young cow; **hacer novillos** to play hooky.

novio m (amigo) boyfriend; (prometido) fiancé; (en boda) bridegroom; **los novios** the bride and groom.

nube f cloud.

nublado, -a adj cloudy, overcast.

nublarse vr to cloud over.

nuboso, -a adj cloudy.

nuca f back of the neck.

nuclear adj nuclear; **central n.** nuclear power station.

núcleo m nucleus; (parte central) core.

nudillo m knuckle.

nudista adj & mf nudist.

nudo m knot; **hacer un n.** to tie a knot.

nuera f daughter-in-law.

nuestro, -a 1 adj pos our; **un amigo n.** a friend of ours. **2** pron pos ours; **este libro es n.** this book is ours.

nuevamente adv again.

nueve adj & m nine.

nuevo, -a adj new.

nuez f walnut; **n. (de Adán)** Adam's apple.

nulo, -a adj (sin valor) null and void, invalid; (inepto) useless; **voto n.** invalid vote; **crecimiento n.** zero growth.

numérico, -a adj digital.

número m number; (de zapatos) size; **n. de matrícula** license number.

numeroso, -a adj numerous.

nunca adv never; (enfático) not … ever; **no he estado n. en España** I've never been to Spain; **yo no haría n. eso** I wouldn't ever do that; **casi n.** hardly ever; **más que n.** more than ever; **n. jamás** never ever; (futuro) never again.

nupcial adj wedding, nuptial; **marcha n.** wedding march.

nutrición f nutrition.

nutrir 1 vt to nourish, to feed. **2 nutrirse** vr to feed (de, con on).

nutritivo, -a adj nutritious; **valor n.** nutritional value.

ñame *m Am* yarn.

ñapa *f Am* bonus.

ñato, -a *adj Am* snub-nosed.

ñoño, -a 1 *adj Am (soso)* dull. **2** *mf* dullard.

O

o *conj* or; **o ... o** either ... or; **o sea** in other words.

oasis *m inv* oasis.

obedecer [33] *vt* to obey.

obediencia *f* obedience.

obediente *adj* obedient.

obesidad *f* obesity.

obeso, -a *adj* obese.

obispo *m* bishop.

objetar 1 *vt* **no tengo nada que o.** I've got no objections. **2** *vi* to be a conscientious objector.

objetivo, -a 1 *m (fin, meta)* objective; *(de cámara)* lens. **2** *adj* objective.

objeto *m* object; *(fin)* purpose; **con o. de ...** in order to ....

obligación *f (deber)* obligation; **por o.** out of a sense of duty.

obligar [42] *vt* to force.

obligatorio, -a *adj* obligatory.

obra *f (trabajo)* work; **o. maestra** masterpiece; *(acto)* deed; *(construcción)* building site; **'carretera en o.'** 'roadworks'.

obrar *vi (proceder)* to act; **o. bien/ mal** to do the right/wrong thing.

obrero, -a 1 *mf* worker. **2** *adj* working; **clase obrera** working class.

obsceno, -a *adj* obscene.

obscuro, -a *adj* dark; *(origen, idea)* obscure.

obsequio *m* gift.

observador, -a 1 *mf* observer. **2** *adj* observant.

observar *vt (mirar)* to watch; *(notar)* to notice; *(cumplir)* to observe.

observatorio *m* observatory.

obsesión *f* obsession.

obsesionarse *vr* to get obsessed.

obsesivo, -a *adj* obsessive.

obsoleto, -a *adj* obsolete.

obstaculizar [40] *vt* to obstruct, to get in the way of.

obstáculo *m* obstacle.

obstante: no obstante *adv* nevertheless.

obstinado, -a *adj* obstinate.

obstinarse *vr* to persist (en in).

obstruir [37] **1** *vt (salida, paso)* to block. **2 obstruirse** *vr* to get blocked up.

obtener [24] *vt (alcanzar)* to obtain, to get.

obvio, -a *adj* obvious.

oca *f* goose.

ocasión *f (momento)* occasion; *(oportunidad)* opportunity; *(saldo)* bargain; **en cierta o.** once; **aprovechar la o.** to make the most of an opportunity.

ocasional *adj (eventual)* occasional; **de forma o.** occasionally.

ocasionar *vt* to cause.

occidental *adj* western.

occidente *m* West.

océano *m* ocean.

ochenta *adj & m inv* eighty.

ocho *adj & m inv* eight.

ochocientos, -as *adj & mf* eight hundred.

ocio *m* leisure.

ocioso, -a *adj (inactivo)* idle; *(inútil)* pointless.

octavilla *f (panfleto)* hand-out, leaflet.

octavo, -a *adj & mf* eighth.

octubre *m* October.

oculista *mf* ophthalmologist.

ocultar 1 *vt* to conceal; **o. algo a algn** to hide sth from sb. **2 ocultarse** *vr* to hide.

oculto, -a *adj* concealed, hidden.

ocupación *f (tarea)* occupation.

ocupado, -a *adj (persona)* busy;

(asiento) taken; *(aseos, teléfono)* engaged; *(puesto de trabajo)* filled.

ocupante *mf* occupant; *(ilegal)* squatter.

ocupar 1 *vt* to occupy; *(espacio, tiempo)* to take up; *(cargo)* to hold. **2 ocuparse** *vr* **ocuparse de** *(cuidar)* to look after; *(encargarse)* to see to.

ocurrencia *f (agudeza)* witty remark; *(idea)* idea.

ocurrente *adj* witty.

ocurrir 1 *v impers* to happen; **¿qué te ocurre?** what's the matter with you? **2 ocurrirse** *vr* **no se me ocurre nada** I can't think of anything.

odiar [43] *vt* to hate.

odio *m* hatred.

odioso, -a *adj* hateful.

odontólogo, -a *mf* dental surgeon.

oeste *adj & m* west.

ofender 1 *vt* to offend. **2 ofenderse** *vr* to take offence (**con, por** at).

ofensa *f* offense.

ofensiva *f* offensive.

ofensivo, -a *adj* offensive.

oferta *f* offer; *(presupuesto)* bid.

ofertar *vt* to offer.

oficial, -a 1 *adj* official. **2** *m (rango)* officer; *(obrero)* skilled worker.

oficialismo *m Am (gobierno)* government.

oficialista *Am* **1** *adj* pro-government. **2** *mf* government supporter.

oficina *f* office; **o. de turismo** tourist office; **o. de correos** post office.

oficinista *mf* office worker.

oficio *m (ocupación)* occupation; *(profesión)* trade.

ofimática *f* office automation.

ofrecer [33] **1** *vt* to offer; *(aspecto)* to present. **2 ofrecerse** *vr (prestarse)* to offer; *(situación)* to present itself.

ofrezco *indic pres de* **ofrecer**.

oftalmólogo, -a *mf* ophthalmologist.

oídas: de oídas *adv* by hearsay.

oído *m (sentido)* hearing; *(órgano)* ear.

oír [17] *vt* to hear; **¡oye!** hey!; **¡oiga!** excuse me!

ojal *m* buttonhole.

ojalá 1 *interj* let's hope so! **2** *conj +* *subj* **¡o. sea cierto!** I hope it is true!

ojeada *f* **echar una o.** to have a quick look (**a** at).

ojeras *fpl* bags under the eyes.

ojo 1 *m* eye; *(de cerradura)* keyhole; **calcular a o.** to guess. **2** *interj* careful!

ojota *f Méx (sandalia)* sandal; *RP (chancleta)* thong.

ola *f* wave.

oleaje *m* swell.

óleo *m* oil; **pintura** *o* **cuadro al ó.** oil painting.

oleoducto *m* pipeline.

oler [4] **1** *vt* to smell. **2** *vi (exhalar)* to smell; **o. a** to smell of; **o. bien/mal** to smell good/bad.

olfatear *vt (oler)* to sniff; *fig (indagar)* to pry into.

olfato *m* sense of smell.

olimpiada *f* Olympic Games *pl*; **las olimpiadas** the Olympic Games.

olímpicamente *adv* **paso o. de estudiar** I don't give a damn about studying.

olímpico, -a *adj* Olympic.

oliva *f* olive; **aceite de o.** olive oil.

olivo *m* olive (tree).

olla *f* saucepan; **o. exprés** *o* **a presión** pressure cooker.

olmo *m* elm.

olor *m* smell.

olvidadizo, -a *adj* forgetful.

olvidar 1 *vt* to forget; *(dejar)* to leave. **2 olvidarse** *vr* **olvidarse de algo** to forget sth.

olvido *m (desmemoria)* oblivion; *(lapsus)* oversight.

ombligo *m* navel.

omisión *f* omission.

omitir *vt* to omit.

omnipotente *adj* almighty.

omoplato, omóplato *m* shoulder blade.

once *adj & m inv* eleven.

onda f wave; **o. larga/media/corta** long/medium/short wave; fam **¡qué buena o.!** that's cool! Méx, RP fam **¿qué o.?** (¿qué tal?) how's it going?, how are things?

ondulado, -a adj (pelo) wavy; (paisaje) rolling.

ONU f abr de **Organización de las Naciones Unidas** United Nations (Organization), UN(O).

opaco, -a adj opaque.

opcional adj optional.

ópera f opera. -

operación f operation; (financiera) transaction.

operador, -a mf operator; (de la cámara) (hombre) cameraman; (mujer) camerawoman.

operar 1 vt to operate (a on). **2 operarse** vr to have an operation (**de** for); (producirse) to take place.

opinar vi (pensar) to think; (declarar) to give one's opinion.

opinión f opinion; **cambiar de o.** to change one's mind.

oponente mf opponent.

oponer [19] (pp **opuesto**) **1** vt (resistencia) vr to offer. **2 oponerse** vr (estar en contra) to be against.

oporto m (vino) port. -

oportunidad f opportunity.

oportuno, -a adj timely; (conveniente) appropriate.

oposición f opposition; (examen) competitive examination.

opresión f oppression.

oprimir vt (pulsar) to press; (subyugar) to oppress.

optar vi (elegir) to choose (**entre** between); (aspirar) to apply (**a** for); **opté por ir yo mismo** I decided to go myself; **puede o. a medalla** he's in with a chance of winning a medal.

optativo, -a adj optional.

óptica f (tienda) optician's (shop).

óptico, -a 1 adj optical. **2** mf optician.

optimista 1 adj optimistic. **2** mf optimist.

óptimo, -a adj excellent; (condiciones) optimum.

opuesto, -a adj (contrario) contrary; (de enfrente) opposite; **en direcciones opuestas** in opposite directions.

opuse pt indef de **oponer.**

oración f (plegaria) prayer.

oral adj oral; **por vía o.** to be taken orally.

órale interj Méx fam (vamos) come on!; (de acuerdo) right!, sure!

orar vi to pray.

orden 1 m order; **o. público** law and order; **por o. alfabético** in alphabetical order; **del o. de** in the order of. **2** f order; (judicial) warrant; **¡a la o.!** sir!

ordenado, -a adj tidy.

ordenador m computer; **o. de sobremesa** desktop (computer); **o. doméstico** home computer.

ordenanza 1 m (empleado) office boy. **2** f regulations pl.

ordenar vt (organizar) to put in order; (habitación) to tidy up; (mandar) to order; Am (encargar) to order.

ordeñar vt to milk.

ordinario, -a adj (corriente) ordinary; (grosero) common.

orégano m oregano.

oreja f ear.

orfanato, orfelinato m orphanage.

orgánico, -a adj organic.

organismo m organism; (institución) body.

organización f organization.

organizador, -a 1 adj organizing. **2** mf organizer.

organizar [40] **1** vt to organize. **2 organizarse** vr (armarse) to happen.

órgano m organ.

orgullo m (propia estima) pride; (arrogancia) arrogance.

orgulloso, -a adj estar o. (satisfecho) to be proud; ser o. (arrogante) to be arrogant.

orientación f (dirección) orientation; (guía) guidance.

oriental 1 *adj* eastern. **2** *mf* Oriental.

orientar 1 *vt (indicar camino)* to give directions to; **una casa orientada al sur** a house facing south. **2 orientarse** *vr (encontrar el camino)* to get one's bearings.

oriente *m* East; **el Extremo** *o* **Lejano/Medio/Próximo O.** the Far/Middle/Near East.

orificio *m* hole; *(del cuerpo)* orifice.

origen *m* origin; **dar o. a** to give rise to.

original *adj & mf* original.

originar 1 *vt* to cause, to give rise to. **2 originarse** *vr* to originate.

orilla *f (borde)* edge; *(del río)* bank; *(del mar)* shore.

orinal *m* chamberpot; *fam* potty.

orinar 1 *vi* to urinate. **2 orinarse** *vr* to wet oneself.

oriundo, -a *adj* native of; **ser o. de** to come from.

oro *m* gold; **de o.** golden; **o. de ley** fine gold.

orquesta *f* orchestra; *(de verbena)* dance band.

ortiga *f* (stinging) nettle.

ortodoxo, -a *adj* orthodox.

ortografía *f* spelling.

ortográfico, -a *adj* spelling.

ortopédico, -a *adj* orthopedic.

oruga *f* caterpillar.

orzuelo *m* sty(e).

os *pron pers (complemento directo)* you; *(complemento indirecto)* (to) you; *(con verbo reflexivo)* yourselves; *(con verbo recíproco)* each other; **os veo mañana** I'll see you tomorrow; **os daré el dinero** I'll give you the money; **os escribiré** I'll write to you.

osadía *f (audacia)* daring; *(desvergüenza)* impudence.

osado, -a *adj (audaz)* daring; *(desvergonzado)* shameless.

osar *vi* to dare.

oscilar *vi (variar)* to fluctuate.

oscuras: a oscuras *adv* in the dark.

oscurecer [33] **1** *vi impers* to get dark. **2** *vt (ensombrecer)* to darken. **3 oscurecerse** *vr (nublarse)* to become cloudy.

oscuridad *f* darkness; *fig* obscurity.

oscuro, -a *adj* dark; *(origen, idea)* obscure.

osito *m* **o. (de peluche)** teddy bear.

oso *m* bear; **o. polar** polar bear.

ostentación *f* ostentation.

osteópata *mf* osteopath.

ostra *f* oyster; **aburrirse como una o.** to be bored stiff.

OTAN *f abr de* **Organización del Tratado del Atlántico Norte** North Atlantic Treaty Organization, NATO.

otoño *m* autumn, fall.

otorgar [42] *vt (premio)* to award (**a** to).

otorrinolaringólogo, -a *mf* ear, nose and throat specialist.

otro, -a 1 *adj indef* otro/otra ... another ...; **otros/otras ...** other ...; **el otro/la otra ...** the other ...; **otra cosa** something else; **otra vez** again. **2** *pron indef* another (one); **otros/otras** others; **el otro/la otra** the other (one); **los otros/las otras** the others.

ovacionar *vt* to give an ovation to.

oval, ovalado, -a *adj* oval.

oveja *f* sheep; *(hembra)* ewe; **la o. negra** the black sheep.

overol *m Am* overalls *pl*.

ovillo *m* ball (of wool).

OVNI *m abr de* **objeto volador no identificado** UFO.

oxidado, -a *adj* rusty.

oxidar 1 *vt (metales)* to rust. **2 oxidarse** *vr (metales)* to rust.

oxígeno *m* oxygen.

oye *indic pres & imperativo de* **oír.**

ozono *m* ozone; **capa de o.** ozone layer.

P

pabellón m (en feria) stand; (bloque) wing; **p. de deportes** sports center.

paciencia f patience.

paciente adj & mf patient.

pacificar [44] vt to pacify.

pacotilla f de p. second-rate.

pactar vt to agree.

padecer [33] vti to suffer; **padece del corazón** he suffers from heart trouble.

padrastro m stepfather; (pellejo) hangnail.

padre 1 m father; **padres** parents. **2** adj Méx (genial) great.

padrenuestro m Lord's Prayer.

padrino m (de bautizo) godfather; (de boda) best man; **padrinos** godparents.

padrón m census.

paella f paella (rice dish made with vegetables, meat and/or seafood).

pág abr de **página**, page, p.

paga f (salario) wage; **p. extra** bonus.

pagar [42] vti to pay; (recompensar) to repay; **p. en metálico** o **al contado** to pay cash.

página f page.

pago m payment; **p. adelantado** o **anticipado** advance payment.

paila f Am (frying) pan.

país m country; **P. Vasco** Basque Country; **P. Valenciano** Valencia.

paisaje m landscape.

paisano, -a 1 adj of the same country. **2** mf (hombre) fellow countryman; (mujer) fellow countrywoman; **en traje de p.** in plain clothes.

paja f straw.

pajar m (almacén) straw loft; (en el exterior) straw rick.

pajarita f bow tie; (de papel) paper bird.

pájaro m bird; **p. carpintero** woodpecker.

pajita, pajilla f (drinking) straw.

pakistaní adj & mf (pl pakistaníes) Pakistani.

pala f shovel; (de jardinero) spade; (de ping-pong, frontón) bat; (de remo) blade.

palabra f word; **dirigir la p. a algn** to address sb; **juego de palabras** pun; **p. de honor** word of honor.

palabrota f swearword.

palacio m (grande) palace; (más pequeño) mansion.

paladar m palate.

paladear vt to savor.

palanca f lever; (manecilla) handle; **p. de cambio** gearshift.

palangana f washbasin.

palco m box.

palestino, -a adj & mf Palestinian.

paleta f (espátula) slice; (de pintor) palette; (de albañil) trowel; (de ping-pong) bat.

paletilla f shoulder blade.

paleto, -a 1 adj boorish. **2** mf country bumpkin.

paliar [43] vt to alleviate.

palidecer [33] vi (persona) to turn pale.

palidez f paleness.

pálido, -a adj pale.

palillero m toothpick case.

palillo m (mondadientes) toothpick; **palillos chinos** chopsticks; (de tambor) drumstick.

paliza f beating; **darle a algn una p.** to give sb a thrashing.

palma f palm; (árbol) palm tree; **hacer palmas** to applaud.

palmada f (golpe) slap.

palmera f palm tree.

palmo m **p. a p.** inch by inch.

palo m stick; (vara) rod; (de escoba) broomstick; (golpe) blow; (madera) wood; (de portería) woodwork; (de golf) club.

paloma f pigeon; (como símbolo) dove.

palomar *m* pigeon house.

palomitas (de maíz) *fpl* popcorn *sing*.

palpable *adj* palpable.

palpar *vt* to feel.

palpitar *vi* to palpitate.

palurdo, -a *adj* boorish.

pamela *f* broad-brimmed hat.

pampa *f* pampa, pampas *pl*.

pan *m* bread; **p. de molde** loaf of sliced bread; **p. integral** wholewheat bread; **p. rallado** breadcrumbs *pl*.

pana *f* corduroy.

panadería *f* bakery.

panameño, -a *adj & mf* Panamanian.

pancarta *f* placard; *(en manifestación)* banner.

panda[1] *m* panda.

panda[2] *f* (de amigos) gang.

pandereta *f* tambourine.

pandilla *f* gang.

panecillo *m* bread roll.

panera *f* breadbasket.

panfleto *m* pamphlet.

pánico *m* panic; **sembrar el p.** to cause panic.

panorama *m* panorama.

pantaletas *fpl Am* panties.

pantalla *f* (monitor) screen; *(de lámpara)* shade.

pantalones *mpl* trousers *pl*; **p. vaqueros** jeans *pl*.

pantano *m* (natural) marsh; *(artificial)* reservoir.

pantera *f* panther.

pantorrilla *f* calf.

pantufla *f* slipper.

panty *m* (pair of) tights *pl*.

panza *f* fam belly.

pañal *m* diaper.

paño *m* cloth.

pañuelo *m* handkerchief; *(pañoleta)* shawl.

Papa *m* el P. the Pope.

papa *f* (patata) potato.

papá *m* fam dad, daddy.

papada *f* double chin.

papagayo *m* parrot.

papel *m* paper; *(hoja)* piece of paper; *(rol)* role; **papeles** *(documentos)* identification papers; **p. higiénico** toilet paper; **p. de aluminio** aluminum foil; **p. pintado** wallpaper.

papelera *f* (en despacho) wastepaper basket; *(en calle)* trash can.

papelería *f* (tienda) stationer's.

papeleta *f* (de rifa) ticket; *(de votación)* ballot.

paperas *fpl* mumps *sing*.

papilla *f* mush; *(de niños)* baby food.

paquete *m* packet; *(postal)* parcel.

paquistaní *adj & mf* (pl paquistaníes) Pakistani.

par 1 *adj* (número) even. **2** *m* (pareja) pair; *(dos)* couple; **de p. en p.** wide open.

para *prep* for; *(finalidad)* to, in order to; *(tiempo)* by; *(a punto de)* **está p. salir** it's about to leave; **p. terminar antes** (in order) to finish earlier; **p. entonces** by then; **¿p. qué?** what for?; **ir p. viejo** to be getting old; **no es p. tanto** it's not as bad as all that; **p. mí** in my opinion.

parabólico, -a *adj* antena parabólica satellite dish.

parabrisas *m inv* windshield.

paracaidista *mf* parachutist; *(soldado)* paratrooper.

parachoques *m inv* bumper, fender.

parada *f* stop; **p. de autobús** bus stop; **p. de taxis** taxi rank.

paradero *m* (lugar) whereabouts *pl*; *(apeadero)* stop.

parado, -a 1 *adj* stopped; *(quieto)* still; *(fábrica)* at a standstill; *(desempleado)* unemployed; *Am (de pie)* standing; *fig* salir bien/mal p. to come off well/badly. **2** *mf* unemployed person.

parador *m* roadside inn; **p. nacional** *o* **de turismo** luxury hotel.

paraguas *m inv* umbrella.

paraíso *m* paradise.

paraje *m* spot, place.

paralelo, -a *adj & m* parallel.

paralítico, -a *adj & mf* paralytic.

paralizar [40] **1** *vt* to paralyze; *(circulación)* to stop. **2 paralizarse** *vr* to come to a standstill.

parapente *m* paragliding, parapenting.

parapeto *m* parapet; *(de defensa)* barricade.

parar 1 *vt* to stop; *(balón)* to save. **2** *vi* to stop; **sin p.** nonstop; **fue a parar a la cárcel** he ended up in jail. **3 pararse** *vr* to stop; *Am (ponerse en pie)* to stand up.

pararrayos *m inv* lightning rod.

parásito, -a *adj & m* parasite.

parcela *f* plot.

parche *m* patch; *(emplasto)* plaster.

parchís *m* ≃ ludo.

parcial *adj (partidario)* biased; *(no completo)* partial; **a tiempo p.** part-time.

parcialmente *adv* partly.

pardo, -a *adj (marrón)* brown; *(gris)* dark gray.

parecer [33] **1** *vi* to seem; **parece que no arranca** it looks as if it won't start; **como te parezca** whatever you like; **¿te parece?** is that okay with you?; **¿qué te parece?** what do you think of it? **2 parecerse** *vr* to be alike; **parecerse a** to look like.

parecido, -a 1 *adj* similar; **bien p.** good-looking. **2** *m* resemblance.

pared *f* wall.

pareja *f* pair; *(hombre y mujer)* couple; *(de baile, juego)* partner; **por parejas** in pairs; **hacen buena p.** they make a nice couple.

parentesco *m* relationship.

paréntesis *m inv* bracket; **entre p.** in brackets.

parezco *indic pres de* **parecer**.

pariente *mf* relative, relation.

parir 1 *vt* to give birth to. **2** *vi* to give birth.

parlamento *m* parliament.

paro *m (huelga)* strike; *(desempleo)* unemployment; **estar en p.** to be unemployed; **cobrar el p.** to be on the dole.

parpadear *vi (ojos)* to blink; *(luz)* to flicker.

párpado *m* eyelid.

parque *m* park; *(de niños)* playpen; **p. de atracciones** amusement park; **p. zoológico** zoo; **p. nacional/natural** national park/nature reserve.

parqueadero *m Carib, Col, Pan* parking lot.

parquear *vti Am* to park.

parquímetro *m* parking meter.

parra *f* grapevine.

párrafo *m* paragraph.

parranda *f fam* spree.

parrilla *f* grill; **pescado a la p.** grilled fish.

párroco *m* parish priest.

parroquia *f* parish; *(iglesia)* parish church.

parte 1 *f (sección)* part; *(en una repartición)* share; *(lugar)* place; *(en juicio)* party; **en o por todas partes** everywhere; **por mi p.** as far as I am concerned; **de p. de ...** on behalf of ...; **¿de p. de quién?** who's calling?; **en gran p.** to a large extent; **en p.** partly; **la mayor p.** the majority; **por otra p.** on the other hand. **2** *m (informe)* report.

participación *f* participation; *(acción)* share; *(notificación)* notification.

participante 1 *adj* participating. **2** *mf* participant.

participar 1 *vi* to take part, participate (en in). **2** *vt (notificar)* to notify.

participio *m* participle.

particular 1 *adj (concreto)* particular; *(privado)* private; *(raro)* peculiar. **2** *mf (individuo)* private individual.

partida *f (salida)* departure; *(remesa)* batch; *(juego)* game; *(certificado)* certificate; **p. de nacimiento** birth certificate.

partidario, -a 1 *adj* **ser/no ser p. de algo** to be for/against sth. **2** *mf* supporter.

partido *m* party; *(fútbol)* match, game; **sacar p. de** to profit from.

partir 1 *vt* to break; *(dividir)* to split; *(cortar)* to cut. **2** *vi (marcharse)* to leave; **a p. de** from. **3 partirse** *vr* to split (up); **partirse de risa** to split one's sides laughing.

partitura *f* score.

parto *m* labor, childbirth.

pasa *f* raisin.

pasadizo *m* corridor.

pasado, -a 1 *adj (último)* last; *(anticuado)* old-fashioned; *(alimento)* bad; *(cocido)* cooked; **p. (de moda)** out of date; **p. mañana** the day after tomorrow. **2** *m* past.

pasaje *m* passage; *(calle)* alley; *(pasajeros)* passengers *pl*; *(billete)* ticket.

pasajero, -a 1 *adj* passing. **2** *mf* passenger.

pasamanos *m inv (barra)* handrail; *(de escalera)* banister.

pasaporte *m* passport.

pasar 1 *vt* to pass; *(página)* to turn; *(trasladar)* to move; *(tiempo)* to spend, to pass; *(padecer)* to suffer; *(cruzar)* to cross; *(límite)* to go beyond; **p. hambre** to go hungry. **2** *vi* to pass; *(entrar)* to come in; **p. a** *(continuar)* to go on to; **p. de largo** to go by (without stopping). **3** *v impers (suceder)* to happen; **¿qué pasa aquí?** what's going on here?; **¿qué te pasa?** what's the matter?; **pase lo que pase** come what may. **4 pasarse** *vr (comida)* to go off; *(excederse)* to go too far; **se me pasó la ocasión** I missed my chance; **se le pasó llamarme** he forgot to phone me; **pasarse el día haciendo algo** to spend the day doing sth; **pasárselo bien/mal** to have a good/bad time.

pasarela *f (puente)* footbridge; *(de barco)* gangway; *(de moda)* catwalk.

pasatiempo *m* pastime, hobby.

pascua *f* Easter; **pascuas** *(Navidad)* Christmas *sing*; **¡Felices Pascuas!** Merry Christmas!

pasear 1 *vi* to go for a walk. **2** *vt (perro)* to walk. **3 pasearse** *vr* to go for a walk.

paseo *m* walk; *(en bicicleta, caballo)* ride; *(en coche)* drive; *(avenida)* avenue; **dar un p.** to go for a walk/ride/drive.

pasillo *m* corridor.

pasión *f* passion.

pasivo, -a *adj* passive; *(inactivo)* inactive.

pasmado, -a *adj (asombrado)* astounded, amazed; *(atontado)* flabbergasted; **dejar p.** to astonish; **quedarse p.** to be amazed.

paso *m* step; *(modo de andar)* gait; *(ruido al andar)* footstep; *(camino)* way; *(acción)* passage; *(de montaña)* mountain pass; **abrirse p.** to force one's way through; **'ceda el p.'** 'give way'; **'prohibido el p.'** 'no entry'; **p. de peatones** pedestrian crossing, crosswalk; **el p. del tiempo** the passage of time; **estar de p.** to be just passing through.

pasta *f* paste; *(italiana)* pasta; *(galleta)* biscuit; *fam (dinero)* dough; **p. de dientes** *o* **dentífrica** toothpaste.

pastel *m* cake; *(de carne, fruta)* pie.

pastelería *f* pastry shop, bakery.

pastilla *f* tablet; *(de jabón)* bar; **pastillas para la tos** cough drops.

pastor *m* **1** *mf (hombre)* shepherd; *(mujer)* shepherdess; **p. alemán** Alsatian. **2** *m (sacerdote)* pastor.

pastoso, -a *adj* pasty; *(lengua)* furry.

pata *f* leg; **patas arriba** upside down; **mala p.** bad luck; **meter la p.** to put one's foot in it.

patada *f* kick; *(en el suelo)* stamp.

patalear *vi* to stamp one's feet (with rage).

patán *m* bumpkin.

patata *f* potato; **patatas fritas** French fries; *(de bolsa)* potato chips.

paté *m* pâté.

patentar *vt* to patent.

patente 1 *f (de invención)* patent;

(autorización) license; *CSur (matrícula)* license plate. **2** *adj (evidente)* patent, obvious.

paternal *adj* paternal.

paterno, -a *adj* paternal.

patilla *f (de gafas)* leg; **patillas** *(pelo)* sideburns.

patín *m* skate; *(hidropedal)* pedal boat; **p. de ruedas/de hielo** roller/ ice skate.

patinaje *m* skating; **p. artístico** figure skating; **p. sobre hielo/ruedas** ice-/roller-skating.

patinar *vi* to skate; *(sobre ruedas)* to roller-skate; *(sobre hielo)* to ice-skate; *(deslizarse)* to slide; *(resbalar)* to slip; *(vehículo)* to skid.

patinete *m* scooter.

patio *m (de una casa)* patio; *(de recreo)* playground; **p. de butacas** stalls.

pato *m* duck.

patoso, -a *adj* clumsy, awkward.

patria *f* homeland.

patrimonio *m (bienes)* wealth; *(heredado)* inheritance.

patriotismo *m* patriotism.

patrocinador, -a 1 *adj* sponsoring. **2** *mf* sponsor.

patrocinar *vt* to sponsor.

patrón, -ona 1 *mf (jefe)* boss; *(de pensión) (hombre)* landlord; *(mujer)* landlady. **2** *m* pattern.

patronal 1 *adj* employers'. **2** *f* employers' organization.

patrono, patronazgo *m (institución benéfica)* foundation; *(protección)* patronage.

patrono, -a *mf* boss; *(empresario)* employer.

patrulla *f* patrol.

paulatino, -a *adj* gradual.

pausa *f* pause; *(musical)* rest.

pauta *f* guidelines *pl.*

pavimento *m (de calle)* paving.

pavo *m* turkey.

pavor *m* terror.

payaso *m* clown.

payo, -a *mf* non-Gipsy.

paz *f* peace; *(sosiego)* peacefulness; **¡déjame en p.!** leave me alone!

peaje *f* toll; **autopista de p.** turnpike.

peatón *m* pedestrian.

peca *f* freckle.

pecado *m* sin.

pecador, -a *mf* sinner.

pecar [44] *vi* to sin.

pecera *f* fishtank.

pecho *m* chest; *(de mujer, animal)* breast; **dar el p. (a un bebé)** to breast-feed (a baby).

pechuga *f (de ave)* breast.

pectoral *adj* chest.

peculiar *adj (raro)* peculiar; *(característico)* characteristic.

pedagógico, -a *adj* pedagogical.

pedal *m* pedal.

pedante 1 *adj* pedantic. **2** *mf* pedant.

pedazo *m* piece, bit; **hacer pedazos** to smash to pieces; *(papel, tela)* to tear to pieces.

pediatra *mf* pediatrician.

pedido *m (remesa)* order.

pedir [6] *vt* to ask (for); *(en bar etc)* to order; *(mendigar)* to beg; **p. algo a algn** to ask sb for sth; **p. prestado** to borrow; **p. cuentas** to ask for an explanation.

pedrada *f (golpe)* blow from a stone; *(lanzamiento)* throw of a stone.

pega *f fam (objeción)* objection; **de p.** *(falso)* sham.

pegajoso, -a *adj (pegadizo)* sticky.

pegamento *m* glue.

pegar [42] **1** *vt (adherir)* to stick; *(con pegamento)* to glue; *(golpear)* to hit; *fam* **no pegó ojo** he didn't sleep a wink; **p. un grito** to shout; **p. un salto** to jump. **2** *vi (adherirse)* to stick; *(armonizar)* to match; *(sol)* to beat down. **3 pegarse** *vr (adherirse)* to stick; *(pelearse)* to fight; *(comida)* to get burnt; *(arrimarse)* to get close; **pegarse un tiro** to shoot oneself; **se me ha pegado el sol** I've got a touch of the sun.

pegatina f sticker.

peinado m hairstyle, fam hairdo.

peinar 1 vt (pelo) to comb. **2 peinarse** vr to comb one's hair.

peine m comb.

pelado, -a adj (fruta, patata) peeled; (cabeza) shorn.

pelapatatas m inv potato peeler.

pelar 1 vt (cortar el pelo a) to cut the hair of; (fruta, patata) to peel. **2 pelarse** vr (cortarse el pelo) to get one's hair cut.

peldaño m step; (de escalera de mano) rung.

pelea f fight; (riña) row.

pelear 1 vi to fight; (reñir) to quarrel. **2 pelearse** vr to fight; (reñir) to quarrel; (enemistarse) to fall out.

peletería f (tienda) fur shop.

película f movie; (fotográfica) film; **p. de miedo** o **terror** horror movie; **p. del Oeste** Western.

peligrar vi to be in danger; **hacer p.** to endanger, to jeopardize.

peligro m danger; (riesgo) risk; **correr (el) p. de ...** to run the risk of ...; **poner en p.** to endanger.

peligroso, -a adj dangerous.

pelirrojo, -a 1 adj red-haired; (anaranjado) ginger-haired. **2** mf redhead.

pellejo m (piel) skin; **jugarse el p.** to risk one's neck.

pellizco m pinch.

pelma mf, **pelmazo, -a** mf (persona) bore.

pelo m hair; (de animal) coat; **cortarse el p.** (uno mismo) to cut one's hair; (en la peluquería) to have one's hair cut; **tomar el p. a algn** to pull sb's leg; **por los pelos** by the skin of one's teeth.

pelota f ball; **hacer la p. a algn** to suck up to sb.

pelotón m squad.

pelotudo, -a adj Am slack.

peluca f wig.

peluche m osito de p. teddy bear.

peludo, -a adj hairy.

peluquería f hairdresser's (shop).

peluquero, -a mf hairdresser.

pelusa, pelusilla f fluff; (de planta) down; fam jealousy (among children).

pena f (tristeza) sorrow; **¡qué p.!** what a pity!; **no merece** o **vale la p. (ir)** it's not worthwhile (going); **a duras penas** with great difficulty; **p. de muerte** o **capital** death penalty.

penalti m (pl **penaltis**) penalty.

pendejo m Am jerk.

pendiente 1 adj (por resolver) pending; (colgante) hanging (de from); **asignatura p.** (en colegio) subject not yet passed; **estar p. de** (esperar) to be waiting for; (vigilar) to be on the lookout for. **2** m (joya) earring. **3** f slope.

penetrante adj penetrating; (frío, voz, mirada) piercing.

penetrar 1 vt to penetrate. **2** vi (entrar) to enter (en).

penicillina f penicillin.

península f peninsula.

penique m penny, pl pence.

penitenciario, -a adj prison.

penoso, -a adj (lamentable) sorry, distressing; (laborioso) laborious, difficult; CAm, Carib, Col, Méx (vergonzoso) shy.

pensamiento m thought; (flor) pansy.

pensar [1] 1 vi to think (**en** of, about; **sobre** about, over); **sin p.** (con precipitación) without thinking; (involuntariamente) involuntarily. **2** vt (considerar) to think about; (proponerse) to intend; (concebir) to make; fam **¡ni pensarlo!** not on your life!

pensativo, -a adj thoughtful.

pensión f (residencia) boarding house; (hotel) guesthouse; (paga) allowance; **media p.** half board; **p. completa** full board.

pensionista mf pensioner.

penúltimo, -a adj & mf penultimate.

penumbra f half-light.

penuria f scarcity, shortage.

peña f rock; (de amigos) club.

peñón m rock; **el P. de Gibraltar** the Rock of Gibraltar.

peón m unskilled laborer; (en ajedrez) pawn.

peor adj & adv (comparativo) worse; (superlativo) worst; **en el p. de los casos** if the worst comes to the worst.

pepinillo m gherkin.

pepino m cucumber.

pepita f (de fruta) pip, seed; (de metal) nugget.

pequeño, -a 1 adj small, little; (bajo) short. **2** mf child; **de p.** as a child.

pera f pear.

peral m pear tree.

percance m mishap.

percatarse vr **p. de** to realize.

percepción f perception.

percha f (colgador) (coat)hanger.

perchero m clothes rack.

percibir vt (notar) to perceive; (cobrar) to receive.

percusión f percussion.

perdedor, -a 1 adj losing. **2** mf loser.

perder [3] **1** vt to lose; (tren, autobús, oportunidad) to miss; (tiempo) to waste. **2** vi to lose; **echar (algo) a p.** to spoil (sth); **echarse a p.** to be spoiled; **salir perdiendo** to come off worst. **3 perderse** vr (extraviarse) (persona) to get lost; **se me ha perdido la llave** I've lost my key.

pérdida f loss; (de tiempo, esfuerzos) waste.

perdiz f partridge.

perdón m pardon; ¡p.! sorry!; **pedir p.** to apologize.

perdonar vt to forgive; (eximir) to pardon; ¡perdone! sorry!; **perdonarle la vida a algn** to spare sb's life.

perecedero, -a adj perishable; **artículos perecederos** perishables.

perecer [33] vi to perish.

peregrino, -a 1 mf pilgrim. **2** adj **ideas peregrinas** crazy ideas.

perejil m parsley.

perenne adj perennial.

pereza f laziness.

perezoso, -a adj lazy.

perfección f perfection; **a la p.** to perfection.

perfeccionar vt to perfect; (mejorar) to improve.

perfeccionista adj & mf perfectionist.

perfectamente adv perfectly; ¡p.! (de acuerdo) agreed!, all right!

perfecto, -a adj perfect.

perfil m profile; (contorno) outline; **de p.** in profile.

perfilar 1 vt (dar forma) to shape, to outline. **2 perfilarse** vr to take shape.

perforar vt to perforate.

perfumar 1 vt to perfume. **2 perfumarse** vr to put on perfume.

perfume m perfume.

pericia f expertise.

periferia f periphery; (alrededores) outskirts pl.

periférico m peripheral.

perilla f (barba) goatee; fam **venir de perilla(s)** to be very handy, to be just the thing.

periódico, -a 1 m newspaper. **2** adj periodic.

periodista mf journalist.

periodo, período m period.

periquito m budgerigar, fam budgie.

perjudicar [44] vt to harm; (intereses) to prejudice.

perjudicial adj harmful.

perjuicio m damage.

perla f pearl.

permanecer [33] vi to remain, to stay.

permanente 1 adj permanent. **2** f (de pelo) perm; **hacerse la p.** to have one's hair permed.

permiso m (autorización) permission; (licencia) license; **p. de conducir** driver's license.

permitir 1 vt to permit, to allow. **permitirse** vr (costearse) to afford; **'no**

se **permite fumar'** 'no smoking'.
pero *conj* but.
perpendicular *adj & f* perpendicular.
perpetrar *vt* to perpetrate, to commit.
perpetuo, -a *adj* perpetual; **cadena perpetua** life imprisonment.
perplejo, -a *adj* perplexed.
perra *f* bitch.
perrera *f* kennel; *(para muchos perros)* kennels *pl.*
perro *m* dog; *fam* **vida de perros** dog's life; **p. caliente** hot dog.
persecución *f* pursuit; *(represión)* persecution.
perseguir [6] *vt* to pursue; *(seguir)* to run after; *(reprimir)* to persecute.
perseverar *vi* to persevere; *(durar)* to last.
persiana *f* blinds *pl.*
persignarse *vr* to cross oneself.
persistente *adj* persistent.
persistir *vi* to persist.
persona *f* person; *fam* **p. mayor** grown-up.
personaje *m* character; *(celebridad)* celebrity.
personal 1 *adj* personal. **2** *m (plantilla)* personnel.
personalidad *f* personality.
perspectiva *f* perspective; *(futuro)* prospect.
perspicaz *adj* perspicacious.
persuadir *vt* to persuade.
persuasión *f* persuasion.
pertenecer [33] *vi* to belong (**a** to).
pertinaz *adj* persistent; *(obstinado)* obstinate.
perturbación *f* disturbance.
perturbado, -a *adj* (mentally) deranged *o* unbalanced.
perturbar *vt (el orden)* to disturb.
peruano, -a *adj & mf* Peruvian.
perverso, -a *adj* perverse.
pervertir [5] *vt* to pervert.
pesa *f* weight; **levantamiento de pesas** weightlifting.
pesadez *f* heaviness; *(de estómago)*

fullness; *(fastidio)* drag.
pesadilla *f* nightmare.
pesado, -a *adj* heavy; *(aburrido)* tedious.
pésame *m* **dar el p.** to offer one's condolences.
pesar 1 *vt* to weigh; *(entristecer)* to grieve. **2** *vi* to weigh; *(ser pesado)* to be heavy. **3** *m (pena)* sorrow; *(arrepentimiento)* regret; **a p. de** in spite of.
pesca *f* fishing.
pescadería *f* fish shop.
pescadilla *f* young hake.
pescado *m* fish.
pescador, -a 1 *adj* fishing. **2** *mf (hombre)* fisherman; *(mujer)* fisherwoman.
pescar [44] *vti* to fish.
pescuezo *m fam* neck.
pese: pese a (que) *prep* in spite of (the fact that).
peseta *f* peseta.
pesimismo *m* pessimism.
pesimista 1 *adj* pessimistic. **2** *mf* pessimist.
pésimo, -a *adj* awful.
peso *m* weight; **p. bruto/neto** gross/net weight; **de p.** *(razón)* convincing.
pestaña *f* eyelash.
peste *f (hedor)* stench; *(epidemia)* plague.
pesticida *m* pesticide.
pestillo *m* bolt.
petaca *f (para cigarrillos)* cigarette case; *(para bebidas)* flask; *Am (maleta)* suitcase.
pétalo *m* petal.
petardo *m* firecracker.
petición *f* request.
petróleo *m* oil.
petrolero *m* oil tanker.
pez *m* fish.
pezón *m* nipple.
pezuña *f* hoof.
piadoso, -a *adj (devoto)* pious; *(compasivo)* compassionate; **mentira piadosa** white lie.

pianista *mf* pianist.

piano *m* piano.

pibe, -a *mf Am (niño)* kid.

picadero *m* riding school.

picado, -a 1 *adj (carne)* ground; *(fruta)* bad; *(diente)* decayed; *(mar)* choppy. **2** *m* **caer en p.** to plummet.

picador *m* picador.

picadora *f* mincer.

picadura *f (de insecto, serpiente)* bite; *(de avispa, abeja)* sting; *(en fruta)* spot.

picante *adj* hot; *(chiste etc)* risqué.

picaporte *m (aldaba)* door knocker; *(pomo)* door handle.

picar [44] **1** *vt (insecto, serpiente)* to bite; *(avispas, abejas)* to sting; *(comer) (aves)* to peck (at); *(persona)* to pick at; *(anzuelo)* to bite; *(perforar)* to prick; *(carne)* to mince. **2** *vi (escocer)* to itch; *(herida)* to smart; *(el sol)* to burn; *(estar picante)* to be hot; *(pez)* to bite; *fig (dejarse engañar)* to swallow it. **3 picarse** *vr (fruta)* to spot; *(dientes)* to decay; *(enfadarse)* to get cross.

pícaro, -a 1 *adj (travieso)* mischievous; *(astuto)* crafty. **2** *mf* rogue.

pico *m (de ave)* beak, bill; *(punta)* corner; *(de montaña)* peak; *(herramienta)* pick; **cincuenta y p.** fifty odd; **las dos y p.** a little after two.

picor *m* tingling.

pie *m* foot; *(de instrumento)* stand; *(de copa)* stem; *(de una ilustración)* caption; **a p.** on foot; **de p.** standing up; **de pies a cabeza** from head to foot; **en p.** standing; **hacer p.** to touch the bottom; **perder p.** to get out of one's depth; **al p. de la letra** to the letter.

piedad *f* piety; *(compasión)* pity.

piedra *f* stone; *(de mechero)* flint.

piel *f* skin; *(de patata)* peel; *(cuero)* leather; *(con pelo)* fur; **p. de gallina** goose pimples *pl*.

pienso *m* fodder.

pierna *f* leg.

pieza *f* piece, part; *(habitación)* room; *(teatral)* play; **p. de recambio** spare part.

pijama *m* pajamas *pl*.

pila *f* battery; *(montón)* pile; *(de la cocina)* sink; **nombre de p.** Christian name.

píldora *f* pill.

pileta *f (pila)* sink; *Am (piscina)* swimming pool.

pillar 1 *vt (coger)* to catch; *(alcanzar)* to catch up with; **lo pilló un coche** he was run over by a car. **2 pillarse** *vr* to catch; **pillarse un dedo/una mano** to catch one's finger/hand.

pillo, -a 1 *adj (travieso)* naughty; *(astuto)* cunning. **2** *mf* rogue.

piloto 1 *mf (de avión, barco)* pilot; *(de coche)* driver; *(de moto)* rider **2** *m (luz)* pilot lamp **3** *adj inv* **piso p.** show apartment.

pimentón *m* red pepper.

pimienta *f* pepper.

pimiento *m (fruto)* pepper; *(planta)* pimiento.

pinar *m* pine wood.

pincel *m* paintbrush.

pinchadiscos *mf inv* disc jockey, DJ.

pinchar 1 *vt (punzar)* to jag; *(balón, globo)* to burst; *(rueda)* to puncture. **2** *vi (coche)* to get a puncture.

pinchazo *m (punzadura)* prick; *(de rueda)* puncture; *(de dolor)* sharp pain.

pincho *m (púa)* barb; **p. moruno** shish kebab.

ping-pong *m* table tennis.

pingüino *m* penguin.

pino *m* pine; *fig* **hacer el p.** to do a handstand.

pinole *m Am* corn drink.

pinta *f (medida)* pint; *fam (aspecto)* look.

pintada *f* graffiti.

pintar 1 *vt (dar color)* to paint; *(dibujar)* to draw. **2 pintarse** *vr (maquillarse)* to put make-up on.

pintor, -a *mf* painter.

pintoresco, -a *adj (lugar)* picturesque; *(persona)* eccentric.

pintura f painting; *(materia)* paint.

pinza f *(para depilar)* tweezers pl; *(para tender)* clothes pin; *(de animal)* pincer.

piña f *(de pino)* pine cone; *(ananás)* pineapple.

piñón m pine seed.

piojo m louse.

pipa f *(de fumar)* pipe; *(de fruta)* seed; *(de girasol)* sunflower seed.

pipí m fam pee, wee-wee; **hacer p.** to pee, to wee-wee.

piragua f canoe.

piragüismo m canoeing.

pirámide f pyramid.

piraña f piranha.

pirata adj & mf pirate.

piratear vt to pirate.

piropo m **echar un p.** to pay a compliment.

pis m fam wee-wee, pee; **hacer p.** to wee-wee, to have a pee.

pisada f footstep; *(huella)* footprint.

pisapapeles m inv paperweight.

pisar vt to step on.

piscifactoría f fish farm.

piscina f swimming pool.

piscolabis m inv fam snack.

piso m apartment; *(planta)* floor; *(de carretera)* surface.

pisotear vt *(aplastar)* to stamp on; *(pisar)* to trample on.

pisotón m **me dio un p.** he stood on my foot.

pista f track; *(rastro)* trail; *(indicio)* clue; **p. de baile** dance floor; **p. de esquí** ski slope; **p. de patinaje** ice rink; **p. de tenis** tennis court; **p. de aterrizaje** landing strip; **p. de despegue** runway.

pistacho m pistachio (nut).

pistola f pistol.

pitar 1 vt *(silbato)* to blow. **2** vi to whistle; *(coche)* to toot one's horn.

pitido m whistle.

pitillo m cigarette.

pito m whistle; *(de vehículo)* horn.

pizarra f *(encerado)* blackboard; *(piedra)* slate.

pizarrón m Am blackboard.

pizca f little bit; **ni p.** not a bit.

placa f plate; *(conmemorativa)* plaque.

placentero, -a adj pleasant, agreeable.

placer [33] m pleasure; **tengo el p. de ...** it gives me great pleasure to ....

plácido, -a adj placid, easy-going.

plaga f plague.

plagiar [43] vt *(copiar)* to plagiarize; *Andes, CAm, Méx (secuestrar)* to kidnap.

plagiario, -a mf Am *(secuestrador)* kidnapper.

plagio m plagiarism.

plan m *(proyecto)* plan; *(programa)* program; **p. de estudios** syllabus; **estar a p.** to be on a diet.

plana f page; **primera p.** front page.

plancha f iron; *(de metal)* plate; *(de cocina)* hotplate; **sardinas a la p.** grilled sardines.

planchar vt to iron.

planeta m planet.

planificación f planning.

planificar [44] vt to plan.

planilla f Am application form.

plano, -a 1 m *(de ciudad)* map; *(proyecto)* plan. **2** adj flat.

planta f plant; *(del pie)* sole; *(piso)* floor, story; **p. baja** first floor.

plantado, -a adj fam **dejar a algn p.** to stand sb up.

plantar 1 vt *(árboles, campo)* to plant; *(poner)* to put, to place. **2 plantarse** vr to stand; *(llegar)* to arrive.

planteamiento m approach.

plantear 1 vt *(problema)* to raise; *(proponer)* to put forward; *(exponer)* to present. **2 plantearse** vr *(considerar)* to consider; *(problema)* to arise.

plantilla f *(personal)* staff; *(de zapato)* insole.

plantón m fam **dar un p. a algn** to stand sb up.

plasmar 1 vt (reproducir) to capture; (expresar) to express. **2 plasmarse** vr **plasmarse en** to take the shape of.

plástico, -a adj & m plastic.

plastificar [44] vt to coat o cover with plastic.

plastilina® f Plasticine®.

plata f silver; (objetos de plata) silverware; Am money; **p. de ley** sterling silver.

plataforma f platform.

plátano m (fruta) banana; (árbol) plane tree.

plática f CAm, Méx chat, talk.

platicar [44] vi CAm, Méx to chat, to talk.

platillo m saucer; **p. volante** flying saucer.

platina f (de tocadiscos) deck.

plato m plate, dish; (parte de una comida) course; (guiso) dish; (de balanza) tray; (de tocadiscos) turntable; **de primer p.** for starters; **p. combinado** one-course meal.

playa f beach; (costa) seaside; Am **p. de estacionamiento** parking lot.

playera f sneaker; Am (camiseta) teeshirt.

plaza f square; (mercado) marketplace; (de vehículo) seat; (laboral) post; **p. de toros** bullring.

plazo m (periodo) period; (término) deadline; **a corto/largo p.** in the short term/in the long run; **comprar a plazos** buy on an installment plan.

plegable adj folding.

plegar [1] vt to fold.

plegaria f prayer.

pleito m lawsuit; **poner un p. (a algn)** to sue (sb).

pleno, -a 1 adj full. **2** m plenary meeting.

pliego m sheet of paper.

pliegue m fold; (de vestido) pleat.

plomero m Am plumber.

plomo m (metal) lead; (fusible) fuse.

pluma f feather; (de escribir) fountain pen.

plumero m feather duster.

plumier m pencil box.

plural adj & m plural.

pluriempleo m moonlighting.

población f (ciudad) town; (pueblo) village; (habitantes) population.

poblado, -a 1 adj populated. **2** m village.

pobre 1 adj poor; ¡p.! poor thing! **2** mf poor person; **los pobres** the poor.

pobreza f (indigencia) poverty; (escasez) scarcity.

pocho, -a adj (fruta) overripe.

pocillo m Am cup.

poco, -a 1 m un **p.** a little; **un p. de** azúcar a little sugar. **2** adj not much, little; **p. sitio/tiempo** not much space/time, little space/time; **pocos, -as** not many, few; **pocas personas** not many people, few people; **unos, -as pocos, -as** a few. **3** pron not much; **pocos, -as** few, not many; **queda p.** there isn't much left. **4** adv (con verbo) not (very) much, little; (con adj) not very; **p. generoso** not very generous; **un p. tarde/frío** a little late/cold; **dentro de p.** soon; **p. a p.** little by little; **p. antes/después** shortly before/afterwards; **por p.** almost.

poder¹ m power.

poder² [18] **1** vt to be able to; **no puede hablar** she can't speak; **no podré llamar** I won't be able to phone. ▪ (permiso) may, can; ¿**se puede (entrar)?** may o can I (come in)?; **aquí no se puede fumar** you can't smoke here. ▪ (posibilidad) may, might; **puede que no lo sepan** they may o might not know; **no puede ser** that's impossible; **puede (ser) (que sí)** maybe, perhaps. ▪ (deber) **podrías haberme advertido** you might have warned me. **2** vi to cope (**con** with).

poderoso, -a adj powerful.

podré indic fut de **poder**.

podrido, -a adj rotten.

podrir vt defectivo de **pudrir**.

poesía f (*género*) poetry; (*poema*) poem.

poeta mf poet.

póker m poker.

polaco, -a 1 adj Polish. **2** mf Pole. **3** m (*idioma*) Polish.

polea f pulley.

polémica f controversy.

polémico, -a adj controversial.

polen m pollen.

policía 1 f police(force). **2** mf (*hombre*) policeman; (*mujer*) policewoman.

policíaco, -a, policiaco, -a, policial adj police; **novela/película policíaca** detective story/film.

polideportivo m sports center.

poliéster m polyester.

polietileno m polyethylene.

polígono m polygon; **p. industrial** industrial estate.

polilla f moth.

politécnico, -a adj & m polytechnic.

política f politics sing; (*estrategia*) policy.

político, -a 1 adj political; (*pariente*) in-law; **su familia política** her in-laws. **2** mf politician.

póliza f (*sello*) stamp; **p. de seguros** insurance policy.

pollera f RP (*occidental*) skirt; *Andes* (*indígena*) = long skirt worn by Indian women.

polo m pole; (*helado*) Popsicle®; (*deporte*) polo; **P. Norte/Sur** North/South Pole.

polución f pollution.

polvera f powder compact.

polvo m dust; **limpiar** o **quitar el p.** to dust; **en p.** powdered; **polvo(s) de talco** talcum powder; *fam* **estar hecho p.** (*deprimido*) to be depressed.

pólvora f gunpowder.

polvoriento, -a adj dusty.

polvorón m sweet pastry.

pollo m chicken.

pomada f ointment.

pomelo m (*fruto*) grapefruit; (*árbol*) grapefruit tree.

pómez adj inv **piedra p.** pumice (stone).

pomo m (*de puerta*) knob.

pómulo m cheekbone.

ponche m punch.

poncho m poncho.

pondré indic fut de **poner**.

poner [19] (*pp puesto*) **1** vt to put; (*mesa, huevo*) to lay; (*gesto*) to make; (*multa*) to impose; (*telegrama*) to send; (*negocio*) to set up; (*encender*) to switch on; (*película*) to put on; (+ *adjetivo*) to make; **p. triste a algn** to make sb sad; **¿qué llevaba puesto?** what was he wearing?; (*decir*) **¿qué pone aquí?** what does it say here? **2 ponerse** vr to put oneself; (*vestirse*) to put on; (+ *adjetivo*) to become; (*sol*) to set; **ponerse al teléfono** to answer the phone; **ponerse a** to start to; **ponerse a trabajar** to get down to work.

poney m pony.

pongo indic pres de **poner**.

poniente m (*occidente*) West.

popa f stern.

popular adj (*música, costumbre*) folk; (*famoso*) popular.

popularidad f popularity.

póquer m poker.

por prep (*agente*) by; **pintado p. Picasso** painted by Picasso; **p. qué** why. ▪ (*causa*) because of; **p. necesidad/amor** out of need/love. ▪ (*tiempo*) **p. la mañana/noche** in the morning/at night; **p. ahora** for the time being. ▪ (*en favor de*) for; **lo hago p. mi hermano** I'm doing it for my brother('s sake). ▪ (*lugar*) **pasamos p. Córdoba** we went through Cordoba; **p. ahí** over there; **¿p. dónde vamos?** which way are we taking?; **mirar p. la ventana** to look out of the window; **entrar p. la ventana** to get in through the window. ▪ (*medio*) by **p. avión/correo** by plane/post. ▪ (*a cambio de*) for; **cambiar**

algo p. algo to exchange sth for sth.
▪ *(distributivo)* **p. cabeza** per person; **p. hora/mes** per hour/month.
▪ *(multiplicación)* **dos p. tres, seis** two times three is six; **un diez p. ciento** ten percent. ▪ *(con infinitivo)* in order to. ▪ **p. más/muy … que sea** no matter how … he/she is; **p. mí** as far as I'm concerned.

porcelana *f* porcelain.

porcentaje *m* percentage.

porche *m* porch.

porción *f* portion.

pormenor *m* detail; **venta al p.** retail.

porno *adj inv* porn.

pornográfico, -a *adj* pornographic.

poro *m* pore.

porque *conj* because; **¡p. no!** just because!

porqué *m* reason.

porquería *f* *(suciedad)* dirt; *(birria)* garbage.

porra *f* *(de policía)* nightstick; *fam* **¡vete a la p.!** get lost!

porrazo *m* thump.

porrón *m* glass bottle with a spout coming out of its base, used for drinking wine.

portada *f* *(de libro etc)* cover; *(de periódico)* front page; *(de disco)* sleeve; *(fachada)* facade.

portaequipajes *m inv* *(maletero)* trunk; *(baca)* roof rack.

portal *m* entrance hall; *(porche)* porch; *(puerta de la calle)* main door.

portaminas *m inv* propelling pencil.

portamonedas *m inv* purse.

portarse *vr* to behave.

portátil *adj* portable.

portazo *m* slam of a door; **dar un p.** to slam the door.

portento *m* *(cosa)* marvel; *(persona)* genius.

portería *f* porter's lodge; *(de fútbol etc)* goal.

portero, -a 1 *mf* *(de vivienda)* caretaker; *(guardameta)* goalkeeper **2** *m* **p. automático** entryphone.

portorriqueño, -a *adj & mf* Puerto Rican.

portugués, -a *adj & mf* Portuguese.

porvenir *m* future.

posada *f* inn.

posar 1 *vi* *(para retrato etc)* to pose. **2** *vt* to put down. **3 posarse** *vr* to settle.

posdata *f* postscript.

poseer [36] *vt* to possess.

posibilidad *f* possibility; *(oportunidad)* chance.

posible *adj* possible; **de ser p.** if possible; **lo antes p.** as soon as possible; **es p. que venga** he might come.

posición *f* position.

positivo, -a *adj* positive.

posponer [19] *vt* *(aplazar)* to postpone; *(relegar)* to relegate.

postal 1 *adj* postal. **2** *f* postcard.

poste *m* pole; *(de portería)* post.

póster *m* poster.

posterior *adj* *(lugar)* rear; *(tiempo)* subsequent (**a** to).

posteriormente *adv* subsequently.

postgraduado, -a *adj & mf* postgraduate.

postigo *m* *(de puerta)* wicket; *(de ventana)* shutter.

postizo, -a *adj* false; **dentadura postiza** dentures *pl.*

postre *m* dessert.

póstumo, -a *adj* posthumous.

postura *f* position.

potable *adj* drinkable; **agua p./no p.** drinking water/not drinking water.

potaje *m* hotpot.

potencia *f* power; **en p.** potential.

potencial *adj & m* potential.

potenciar [43] *vt* to promote, to strengthen.

potente *adj* powerful.

potro *m* colt; *(de gimnasia)* horse.

poyo *m* stone bench.

pozo *m* well; *(minero)* shaft.

práctica *f* practice; **en la p.** in practice.

practicante 1 *adj (de religión)* practicing. **2** *mf* medical assistant.

practicar [44] *vti* to practice; *(operación)* to carry out.

práctico, -a *adj* practical; *(útil)* handy.

pradera *f*, **prado** *m* meadow.

pragmático, -a 1 *adj* pragmatic. **2** *mf* pragmatist.

preámbulo *m (introducción)* preamble; *(rodeo)* circumlocution.

precalentamiento *m* warm-up.

precario, -a *adj* precarious.

precaución *f (cautela)* caution; *(medida)* precaution; **con p.** cautiously.

precaver 1 *vt* to guard against. **2 precaverse** *vr* to take precautions (**de**, **contra** against).

precavido, -a *adj* cautious.

precedente 1 *adj* preceding. **2** *m* precedent; **sin p.** unprecedented.

preceder *vt* to precede.

precepto *m* precept.

precintar *vt* to seal off.

precinto *m* seal.

precio *m* price.

preciosidad *f (cosa)* lovely thing; *(persona)* darling.

precioso, -a *adj (hermoso)* lovely, beautiful; *(valioso)* precious.

precipicio *m* precipice.

precipitación *f (prisa)* haste; *(lluvia)* rainfall.

precipitado, -a *adj (apresurado)* hurried; *(irreflexivo)* rash.

precipitar 1 *vt (acelerar)* to hurry; *(arrojar)* to hurl down. **2 precipitarse** *vr (persona)* to hurl oneself; *(acontecimientos)* to gather speed; *(actuar irreflexivamente)* to rush.

precisamente *adv (con precisión)* precisely; *(exactamente)* exactly.

precisar *vt (especificar)* to specify; *(necesitar)* to require.

precisión *f (exactitud)* precision;

(aclaración) clarification; **con p.** precisely.

preciso, -a *adj (necesario)* necessary; *(exacto)* accurate; *(claro)* clear.

precoz *adj (persona)* precocious.

predecesor, -a *mf* predecessor.

predecir [12] *(pp* **predicho)** *vt* to predict.

predicado *m* predicate.

predicar [44] *vt* to preach.

predicción *f* prediction.

predigo *indic pres de* **predecir**.

predije *pt indef de* **predecir**.

predilecto, -a *adj* favorite.

predisponer [19] *(pp* **predispuesto)** *vt* to predispose.

predominante *adj* predominant.

predominar *vi* to predominate.

predominio *m* predominance.

preescolar *adj* preschool.

preferencia *f* preference.

preferible *adj* preferable; **es p. que no vengas** you'd better not come.

preferido, -a *adj & mf* favorite.

preferir [5] *vt* to prefer.

prefijo *m (telefónico)* area code; *(gramatical)* prefix.

pregunta *f* question; **hacer una p.** to ask a question.

preguntar 1 *vti* to ask; **p. algo a algn** to ask sb sth; **p. por algn** to ask about sb. **2 preguntarse** *vr* to wonder.

prehistórico, -a *adj* prehistoric.

prejuicio *m* prejudice.

preliminar *adj & m* preliminary.

prematuro, -a *adj* premature.

premeditado, -a *adj* premeditated.

premiar [43] *vt* to award a prize (**a** to); *(recompensar)* to reward.

premio *m* prize; *(recompensa)* reward.

prenatal *adj* prenatal.

prenda *f* garment.

prender 1 *vt (sujetar)* to fasten; *(con alfileres)* to pin; **p. fuego a** to set fire to. **2** *vi (fuego)* to catch; *(madera)* to catch fire. **2 prenderse** *vr* to catch fire.

prensa *f* press.

prensar *vt* to press.

preñado, -a *adj* pregnant.

preocupación *f* worry.

preocupado, -a *adj* worried.

preocupar 1 *vt* to worry. **2 preocuparse** *vr* to worry (**por** about); **no te preocupes** don't worry.

preparación *f* preparation; *(formación)* training.

preparado, -a 1 *adj* *(dispuesto)* ready, prepared; *(capacitado)* trained, qualified; **comidas preparadas** ready-cooked meals. **2** *m* preparation.

preparar 1 *vt* to prepare. **2 prepararse** *vr* to get ready.

preparativo *m* preparation.

preposición *f* preposition.

presa *f* prey; *(embalse)* dam; *fig* **ser p. de** to be a victim of.

presagiar [43] *vt* to predict.

presagio *m* *(señal)* omen; *(premonición)* premonition.

prescindir *vi* **p. de** to do without.

presencia *f* presence; **p. de ánimo** presence of mind.

presenciar [43] *vt* to witness.

presentación *f* presentation; *(de personas)* introduction.

presentador, -a *mf* presenter.

presentar 1 *vt* to present; *(una persona a otra)* to introduce. **2 presentarse** *vr* *(comparecer)* to present oneself; *(inesperadamente)* to turn up; *(ocasión, oportunidad)* to arise; *(candidato)* to stand; *(darse a conocer)* to introduce oneself (**a** to).

presente 1 *adj* present; **tener p.** *(tener en cuenta)* to bear in mind. **2** *m* present.

presentimiento *m* premonition.

preservar *vt* to preserve (**de** from; **contra** against).

preservativo *m* condom.

presidente, -a *mf* president; *(de una reunión)* chairperson.

presidiario, -a *mf* prisoner.

presidio *m* prison.

presidir *vt* to head; *(reunión)* to chair.

presión *f* pressure; **a** o **bajo p.** under pressure.

presionar *vt* to press; *fig* to pressurize.

préstamo *m* loan.

prestar 1 *vt* to lend, to loan; **¿me prestas tu pluma?** can I borrow your pen?; *(atención)* to pay; *(ayuda)* to give; *(servicio)* to do. **2 prestarse** *vr* *(ofrecerse)* to offer oneself (**a** to); **prestarse a** *(dar motivo)* to cause; **se presta a (crear) malentendidos** it makes for misunderstandings.

prestidigitador, -a *mf* conjuror.

prestigio *m* prestige.

presumido, -a 1 *adj* conceited. **2** *mf* vain person.

presumir 1 *vt* *(suponer)* to presume. **2** *vi* *(ser vanidoso)* to show off.

presunto, -a *adj* supposed; *(culpable)* alleged.

presuntuoso, -a *adj* *(vanidoso)* conceited; *(pretencioso)* pretentious.

presuponer [19] *(pp presupuesto)* *vt* to presuppose.

presupuesto *m* budget; *(cálculo)* estimate.

pretender *vt* *(intentar)* to try; *(aspirar a)* to try for; *(cortejar)* to court.

pretendiente, -a 1 *mf* *(al trono)* pretender **2** *m* *(amante)* suitor.

pretérito *m* preterite.

pretexto *m* pretext.

prevenir [27] *vt* *(precaver)* to prevent; *(evitar)* to avoid; *(advertir)* to warn.

prever [28] *(pp previsto)* *vt* to forecast.

previo, -a *adj* prior; **sin p. aviso** without notice.

previsible *adj* predictable.

previsión *f* *(predicción)* forecast; *(precaución)* precaution; **p. del tiempo** weather forecast; **en p. de**

as a precaution against; *Andes, RP* **p. social** social security.

previsto, -a *adj* forecast.

primario, -a *adj* primary.

primavera *f* spring.

primer *adj (delante de m)* first.

primera *f (en tren)* first class; *(marcha)* first (gear).

primero, -a 1 *adj* first; **de primera necesidad** basic. **2** *mf* first; **a primero(s) de mes** at the beginning of the month. **3** *adv* first.

primitivo, -a *adj* primitive; *(tosco)* rough.

primo, -a 1 *mf* cousin. **p. hermano** first cousin. **2** *adj* **materia prima** raw material.

primogénito, -a *adj & mf* first-born.

primoroso, -a *adj* exquisite.

princesa *f* princess.

principal *adj* main, principal; **puerta p.** front door.

príncipe *m* prince.

principiante 1 *adj* novice. **2** *mf* beginner.

principio *m* beginning, start; *(fundamento)* principle; **a principio(s) de** at the beginning of; **al p., en un p.** at first; **en p.** in principle; **principios** basics.

pringar [42] **1** *vt (ensuciar)* to make greasy. **2 pringarse** *vr (ensuciarse)* to get greasy.

pringoso, -a *adj (grasiento)* greasy.

prioridad *f* priority.

prisa *f* hurry; **date p.** hurry up; **tener p.** to be in a hurry; **de o a p.** in a hurry.

prisión *f* prison.

prisionero, -a *mf* prisoner.

prismáticos *mpl* binoculars.

privado, -a *adj* private.

privar 1 *vt (despojar)* to deprive (**de** of). **2 privarse** *vr (abstenerse)* to go without.

privilegio *m* privilege.

pro 1 *m* advantage; **los pros y los contras** the pros and cons. **2** *prep* in favor of.

proa *f* prow.

probable *adj* probable, likely; **es p. que llueva** it'll probably rain.

probador *m* fitting room.

probar [2] **1** *vt* to try; *(comprobar)* to check; *(demostrar)* to prove. **2** *vi* to try. **3 probarse** *vr (ropa)* to try on.

probeta *f* test tube.

problema *m* problem.

procedente *adj (adecuado)* appropriate; *(en juicio)* proper; **p. de** coming from.

proceder 1 *vi (actuar)* to act; *(ser oportuno)* to be advisable; **p. de** *(provenir)* to come from; **p. a** *(continuar)* to go on to. **2** *m (comportamiento)* behavior.

procedimiento *m* procedure.

procesador *m* processor; **p. de textos** word processor.

procesar *vt* to prosecute; *(información)* to process.

procesión *f* procession.

proceso *m* process; *(juicios)* trial; **p. de datos** data processing.

proclamar *vt* to proclaim.

procurar *vt (intentar)* to attempt; *(proporcionar)* (to manage) to get; **procura que no te vean** make sure they don't see you.

prodigio *m* prodigy, miracle; **hacer prodigios** to work wonders; **niño p.** child prodigy.

prodigioso, -a *adj (sobrenatural)* prodigious; *(maravilloso)* wonderful.

producción *f (acción)* production; *(producto)* product; **p. en cadena/serie** assembly-line/mass production.

producir [10] **1** *vt* to produce; *(fruto, cosecha, rendir)* to yield; *(originar)* to bring about. **2 producirse** *vr* to take place.

productivo, -a *adj* productive; *(beneficioso)* profitable.

producto *m* product; *(producción)* produce.

productor, -a 1 *adj* producing. **2** *mf* producer.

profesión f profession.
profesional adj & mf professional.
profesor, -a mf teacher; (de universidad) lecturer.
profesorado m (grupo de profesores) staff.
profetizar [40] vt to prophesy.
prófugo, -a adj & mf fugitive.
profundidad f depth; **un metro de p.** one meter deep.
profundizar [40] vt (cavar) to deepen; fig (examinar) to study in depth.
profundo, -a adj deep; (idea, sentimiento) profound.
progenitor, -a mf **progenitores** (padres) parents.
programa m program; (informático) program; (de estudios) syllabus.
programación f programming.
programar vt to program; (para ordenador) to program.
progresar vi to make progress.
progresista adj & mf progressive.
progresivamente adv progressively.
progresivo, -a adj progressive.
progreso m progress.
prohibido, -a adj forbidden; 'prohibida la entrada' 'no admittance'; **p. aparcar/fumar** no parking/smoking.
prohibir vt to forbid.
prójimo, -a mf one's fellow man.
proliferar vi to proliferate.
prólogo m prologue.
prolongar [42] **1** vt (alargar) to extend. **2 prolongarse** vr (continuar) to carry on.
promedio m average.
promesa f promise.
prometedor, -a adj promising.
prometer **1** vt to promise. **2** vi to be promising. **3 prometerse** vr to get engaged.
prometido, -a **1** adj promised. **2** mf (hombre) fiancé; (mujer) fiancée.
promocionar vt to promote.
promover [4] vt (cosas, personas)

to promote; (juicio, querella) to initiate; (causar) to cause, to give rise to.
pronombre m pronoun.
pronosticar [44] vt to forecast.
pronóstico m (del tiempo) forecast; (médico) prognosis.
pronto, -a 1 adj quick, prompt. **2** adv (deprisa) quickly; (temprano) early; **de p.** suddenly; **por de o lo p.** (para empezar) to start with; **¡hasta p.!** see you soon!
pronunciación f pronunciation.
pronunciar [43] vt to pronounce; (discurso) to deliver.
propaganda f (política) propaganda; (comercial) advertising.
propagar [42] **1** vt to spread. **2 propagarse** vr to spread.
propiamente adv **p. dicho** strictly speaking.
propiedad f (posesión) ownership; (cosa poseída) property; **con p.** properly.
propietario, -a mf owner.
propina f tip.
propio, -a adj (de uno) own; (correcto) suitable; (característico) typical; (mismo) (hombre) himself; (mujer) herself; (animal, cosa) itself; **el p. autor** the author himself; **propios, -as** themselves.
proponer [19] (pp propuesto) **1** vt to propose. **2 proponerse** vr to intend.
proporción f proportion; **proporciones** (tamaño) size sing.
proporcional adj proportional.
proporcionar vt (dar) to give; (suministrar) to supply.
proposición f (propuesta) proposal.
propósito m (intención) intention; **a p.** (por cierto) by the way; (adrede) on purpose.
propuesta f suggestion.
propuse pt indef de **proponer**.
prórroga f (prolongación) extension; (en partido) overtime; (aplazamiento) postponement.

prorrogar [42] *vt (prolongar)* to extend; *(aplazar)* to postpone.

prosa *f* prose.

proseguir [6] *vti* to carry on.

prospecto *m* leaflet.

prosperar *vi (negocio, país)* to prosper; *(propuesta)* to be accepted.

próspero, -a *adj* prosperous.

prostitución *f* prostitution.

prostituta *f* prostitute.

protagonista *mf* main character.

protección *f* protection; **p. de escritura** write protection.

protector, -a 1 *adj* protective. **2** *mf* protector.

proteger [53] *vt* to protect.

protesta *f* protest.

protestante *adj & mf* Protestant.

protestar *vi* to protest; *(quejarse)* to complain.

protocolo *m* protocol.

protuberante *adj* bulging.

provecho *m* benefit; ¡**buen p.!** enjoy your meal!; **sacar p. de algo** to benefit from sth.

proveedor, -a *mf* supplier; **p. de acceso (a Internet)** Internet access provider.

proveer [36] *(pp provisto) vt* to supply.

provenir [27] *vi* **p. de** to come from.

proverbio *m* proverb.

provincia *f* province.

provisional *adj* provisional.

provisto, -a *adj* **p. de** equipped with.

provocación *f* provocation.

provocador, -a 1 *mf* instigator. **2** *adj* provocative.

provocar [44] *vt (causar)* to cause; *(instigar)* to provoke; *Am* **si no le provoca** if he doesn't feel like it.

provocativo, -a *adj* provocative.

próximamente *adv* soon.

proximidad *f* closeness; **en las proximidades de** in the vicinity of.

próximo, -a *adj (cercano)* near, close; *(siguiente)* next.

proyección *f* projection; *(de película)* showing.

proyectar *vt (luz)* to project; *(planear)* to plan; *(película)* to show.

proyectil *m* projectile.

proyecto *m* project.

proyector *m* projector.

prudencia *f* prudence; *(moderación)* care.

prudente *adj* prudent; *(conductor)* careful.

prueba *f (argumento)* proof; *(examen etc)* test; **a p. de agua/balas** waterproof/bullet-proof.

psicoanálisis *m inv* psychoanalysis.

psicología *f* psychology.

psicológico, -a *adj* psychological.

psicólogo, -a *mf* psychologist.

psicópata *mf* psychopath.

psiquiatra *mf* psychiatrist.

psiquiátrico, -a 1 *adj* psychiatric. **2** *m* mental hospital.

psíquico, -a *adj* psychic.

pta(s)., pts *abr de* **peseta(s)** peseta(s).

púa *f (de planta)* thorn; *(de animal)* spine; *(de peine)* tooth.

pub *m (pl pubs, pubes)* pub.

publicación *f* publication.

publicar [44] *vt* to publish; *(divulgar)* to publicize.

publicidad *f* advertising; *(conocimiento público)* publicity.

público, -a 1 *adj* public. **2** *m* public; *(de teatro)* audience; *(de estadio)* spectators *pl*.

puchero *m (olla)* cooking pot; *(cocido)* stew; **hacer pucheros** to pout.

pucho *m Am* dog-end.

pude *pt indef de* **poder.**

pudiente *adj* rich, wealthy.

pudor *m* modesty.

pudoroso, -a *adj* modest.

pudrir *vt defectivo*, **pudrirse** *vr* to rot.

pueblo *m* village; *(small) town*; *(gente)* people.

puente *m* bridge; **p. aéreo** *(civil)* air shuttle service.

puerco, -a 1 *adj* filthy. **2** *m* pig; *f* sow.

puericultura *f* pediatrics *sing.*

pueril *adj* childish.

puerro *m* leek.

puerta *f* door; *(verja)* gate.

puerto *m (de mar, ordenador)* port; *(de montaña)* (mountain) pass; **p. deportivo** marina.

puertorriqueño, -a *adj & mf* Puerto Rican.

pues *conj (puesto que)* as, since; *(por lo tanto)* therefore; *(entonces)* so; *(para reforzar)* ¡**p. claro que sí!** but of course!; **p. como iba diciendo** well, as I was saying; ¡**p. no!** certainly not!

puestero, -a *mf Am* stallholder.

puesto, -a 1 *conj* **p. que** since, as. **2** *m (lugar)* place; *(empleo)* post; *(tienda)* stall; **p. de trabajo** job. **3** *adj (colocado)* put; **llevar p.** *(ropa)* to have on, to wear.

pugna *f* fight.

pulcro, -a *adj* (extremely) neat.

pulga *f* flea.

pulgada *f* inch.

pulgar *m* thumb.

pulir *vt (metal, madera)* to polish.

pulmón *m* lung.

pulpería *f Am* store.

pulpo *m* octopus.

pulsación *f* pulsation; *(en mecanografía)* keystroke.

pulsar *vt (timbre, botón)* to press; *(tecla)* to hit.

pulsera *f (aro)* bracelet; **reloj de p.** wristwatch.

pulso *m* pulse; *(mano firme)* steady hand; **echarse un p.** to arm-wrestle.

pulverizador *m* spray, atomizer.

puma *m* puma.

puna *f Am* high moor; *(mal)* mountain sickness.

punta *f (extremo)* tip; *(extremo afilado)* point; *(de cabello)* end; **sacar p. a un lápiz** to sharpen a pencil; **tecnología p.** state-of-the-art technology; **hora p.** rush hour.

puntapié *m* kick.

puntería *f* aim; **tener buena/mala p.** to be a good/bad shot.

puntiagudo, -a *adj* sharp.

puntilla *f (encaje)* lace; **dar la p.** to finish (the bull) off; **de puntillas** on tiptoe.

punto *m* point; *(marca)* dot; *(lugar)* point; *(de costura, sutura)* stitch; **a p.** ready; **a p. de** on the point of; **hasta cierto p.** to a certain extent; **p. muerto** neutral; **p. de vista** point of view; **p. y seguido** period; **p. y coma** semicolon; **dos puntos** colon; **p. y aparte** full stop, new paragraph; **las ocho en p.** eight o'clock sharp; **hacer p.** to knit.

puntuación *f (ortográfica)* punctuation; *(deportiva)* score; *(nota)* mark.

puntual 1 *adj* punctual. **2** *adv* punctually.

puntualidad *f* punctuality.

puntualizar [40] *vt* to make it clear.

puntuar [30] **1** *vt (al escribir)* to punctuate; *(calificar)* to mark. **2** *vi (marcar)* to score; *(ser puntuable)* to count.

punzante *adj (objeto)* sharp; *(dolor)* acute, piercing.

puñado *m* handful.

puñal *m* dagger.

puñalada *f* stab.

puñetazo *m* punch.

puño *m* fist; *(de camisa etc)* cuff; *(de herramienta)* handle.

pupa *f (herida)* sore.

pupila *f* pupil.

pupitre *m* desk.

puré *m* purée; **p. de patata** mashed potatoes *pl.*

pureza *f* purity.

purificar [44] *vt* to purify.

puritano, -a 1 *adj* puritanical. **2** *mf* puritan.

puro, -a 1 *adj (sin mezcla)* pure; *(mero)* sheer; **aire p.** fresh air; **la pura verdad** the plain truth. **2** *m (cigarro)* cigar.

púrpura *adj inv* purple.

puse *pt indef de* **poner**.

puzzle *m* jigsaw puzzle.

P.V.P. *m abr de* **precio de venta al público** recommended retail price.

Pza., Plza. *abr de* **plaza** square, Sq.

Q

que¹ *pron rel (sujeto, persona)* who, that; *(cosa)* that, which. ▪ *(complemento, persona)* no se traduce o that; *(cosa)* no se traduce o that, which; **la chica q. conocí** the girl (that) I met; **el coche q. compré** the car (that o which) I bought. ▪ **lo q.** what. ▪ *(con infinitivo)* **hay mucho q. hacer** there's a lot to do.

que² *conj* no se traduce o that; **dijo que llamaría** he said (that) he would call. ▪ *(consecutivo)* no se traduce o that; **habla tan bajo q. no se le oye** he speaks so quietly (that) he can't be heard. ▪ *(en comparativas)* than; **mejor q. tú** better than you. ▪ *(causal)* because; **date prisa q. no tenemos mucho tiempo** hurry up, because we haven't got much time. ▪ *(enfático)* **¡q. no!** no! ▪ *(deseo, mandato)* (+ subj) **¡q. te diviertas!** enjoy yourself! ▪ *(final)* so that; **ven q. te dé un beso** come and let me give you a kiss. ▪ *(disyuntivo)* whether; **me da igual q. suba o no** I couldn't care whether he comes up or not. ▪ *(locuciones)* **q. yo sepa** as far as I know; **yo q. tú** if I were you.

qué 1 *pron interr* what; **¿q. quieres?** what do you want? ▪ *(exclamativo)* (+ adj) how; (+ n) what a; **¡q. bonito!** how pretty!; **¡q. lástima!** what a pity! **2** *adj interr* which; **¿q. libro quieres?** which book do you want?

quebrada *f Am* stream.

quebrar [l] **1** *vt (romper)* to break. **2** *vi (empresa)* to go bankrupt. **2 quebrarse** *vr* to break.

quedar 1 *vi (restar)* to be left; *(con amigo)* to arrange to meet; *(acordar)* to agree (**en** to); *(estar situado)* to be; **quedan dos** there are two left; **quedaría muy bien allí** it would look very nice there; **q. en ridículo** to make a fool of oneself; **q. bien/mal** to make a good/bad impression. **2 quedarse** *vr (permanecer)* to stay; **quedarse sin dinero/pan** to run out of money/bread; **quedarse con hambre** to be still hungry; **quedarse (con)** *(retener)* to keep; **quédese (con) el cambio** keep the change.

quehacer *m* chore.

queja *f* complaint; *(de dolor)* groan.

quejarse *vr* to complain (**de** about).

quemadura *f* burn.

quemar 1 *vt* to burn. **2** *vi* to be burning hot. **3 quemarse** *vr fig* to burn oneself out.

quemazón *f* smarting.

quepo *indic pres de* **caber**.

querella *f* lawsuit.

querer [20] **1** *vt* to want; *(amar)* to love; **sin q.** without meaning to; **¡por lo que más quieras!** for heaven's sake!; **¿quiere pasarme el pan?** would you pass me the bread?; **q. decir** to mean; **no quiso darme permiso** he refused me permission. **2 quererse** *vr* to love each other.

querido, -a *adj* dear.

querré *indic fut de* **querer**.

queso *m* cheese.

quicio *m (de puerta)* doorpost; **sacar de q. (a algn)** to infuriate (sb).

quien *pron rel* **el hombre con q. vino** the man she came with; *(formal)* the man with whom she came. ▪ *(indefinido)* **q. quiera venir** whoever wants to come; **hay q. dice lo contrario** thre are some people who say the opposite.

quién *pron interr* who; **¿q. es?** who is it?; **¿para q. es?** who is it for?; **¿de q. es esa bici?** whose bike is that?

quienquiera *pron indef* (*pl* **quienesquiera**) whoever.

quieto, -a *adj* still; ¡estáte q.! keep still!

quilo *m* = **kilo**.

química *f* (*ciencia*) chemistry.

químico, -a 1 *adj* chemical. **2** *mf* (*científico*) chemist.

quince *adj & m inv* fifteen.

quiniela *f* sports lottery.

quinientos, -as *adj & mf* five hundred.

quinqué *m* oil lamp.

quintal *m* (*medida*) 46 kg; **q. métrico** = 100 kg.

quinto, -a *adj & mf* fifth.

quiosco *m* kiosk; **q. de periódicos** newspaper stand.

quirófano *m* operating room.

quirúrgico, -a *adj* surgical.

quise *pt de* **querer**.

quitaesmaltes *m inv* nail varnish remover.

quitamanchas *m inv* stain remover.

quitanieves *m* (*máquina*) q. snowplow.

quitar 1 *vt* to remove, to take away; (*ropa*) to take off; (*dolor*) to relieve; (*sed*) to quench; (*hambre*) to take away; (*robar*) to steal; (*tiempo*) to take up; (*asiento*) to take. **2** *vi* ¡quita! get out of the way! **3** **quitarse** *vr* (*apartarse*) to move away; (*mancha*) to come out; (*dolor*) to go away; (*ropa, gafas*) to take off; **quitarse de fumar** to give up smoking; **quitarse a algn de encima** to get rid of sb.

quizá(s) *adv* perhaps, maybe.

R

rábano *m* radish.

rabia *f* (*ira*) rage; (*enfermedad*) rabies *sing*; ¡qué r.! how annoying!; **me da r.** it makes me mad.

rabiar [43] *vi* (*enfadarse*) to rage; **hacer r. a algn** to make sb see red.

rabioso, -a *adj* rabid; (*enfadado*) furious.

rabo *m* (*de animal*) tail; (*de fruta*) stalk.

racha *f* (*período*) spell; (*de viento*) gust.

racial *adj* racial.

racimo *m* bunch.

ración *f* portion.

racionar *vt* to ration.

racismo *m* racism.

racista *adj & mf* racist.

radar *m* (*pl* **radares**) radar.

radiación *f* radiation.

radiactividad *f* radioactivity.

radiactivo, -a *adj* radioactive.

radiador *m* radiator.

radiante *adj* radiant (**de** with).

radical *adj* radical.

radio[1] *f* (*aparato*) radio.

radio[2] *m* (*de circunferencia*) radius; (*de rueda*) spoke.

radioactividad *f* radioactivity.

radiocasete *m* radio cassette.

radiografía *f* (*imagen*) X-ray.

ráfaga *f* (*de viento*) gust; (*de disparos*) burst.

raído, -a *adj* (*gastado*) worn.

raíz *f* (*pl* **raíces**) root; **r. cuadrada** square root; **a r. de** as a result of.

raja *f* (*corte*) cut; (*hendidura*) crack.

rajar 1 *vt* (*tela*) to tear; (*hender*) to crack. **2** **rajarse** *vr* (*tela*) to tear; (*partirse*) to crack; *fam* (*echarse atrás*) to back out; (*acobardarse*) to chicken out.

rallado, -a *adj* **queso r.** grated

cheese; **pan r.** breadcrumbs *pl.*

rallador *m* grater.

rallar *vt* to grate.

ralo, -a *adj* thin.

rama *f* branch.

ramillete *m (de flores)* posy.

ramo *m (de flores)* bunch; *(sector)* branch.

rampa *f* ramp.

rana *f* frog.

rancho *m (granja)* ranch.

rancio, -a *adj (comida)* stale.

rango *m* rank; *(jerarquía elevada)* high social standing.

ranura *f* slot; **r. de expansión** expansion slot.

rapar *vt* to crop.

rapaz 1 *adj* predatory; **ave r.** bird of prey. **2** *mf (muchacho)* lad; *(muchacha)* lass.

rape *m (pez)* angler fish; **cortado al r.** close-cropped.

rapidez *f* speed.

rápido, -a 1 *adj* quick, fast. **2** *adv* quickly. **3** *m (tren)* fast train.

raptar *vt* to kidnap.

rapto *m (secuestro)* kidnapping.

raqueta *f (de tenis)* racket; *(de ping-pong)* paddle.

raquítico, -a *adj (delgado)* emaciated; *fam (escaso)* meager.

raro, -a *adj* rare; *(extraño)* strange.

rascacielos *m inv* skyscraper.

rascar [44] *vt (con las uñas)* to scratch.

rasgar [42] *vt* to tear.

rasgo *m* feature.

rasguño *m* scratch.

raso, -a 1 *adj (llano)* flat; *(cielo)* clear. **2** *m* satin.

raspa *f (de pescado)* bone.

raspar 1 *vt (limar)* to scrape (off). **2** *vi (ropa, tela)* to chafe.

rastrear *vt (zona)* to comb.

rastrillo *m* rake; *(mercadillo)* flea market.

rastro *m* trace; *(en el suelo)* trail.

rasurar *vt*, **rasurarse** *vr* to shave.

rata *f* rat.

ratero, -a *mf* pickpocket.

ratificar [44] *vt* to ratify.

rato *m (momento)* while; **a ratos** at times; **al poco r.** shortly after; **pasar un buen/mal r.** to have a good/bad time; **ratos libres** free time *sing.*

ratón *m (también de ordenador)* mouse.

raya *f (línea)* line; *(del pantalón)* crease; *(del pelo)* part; **camisa a rayas** striped shirt.

rayar *vt* to scratch.

rayo *m* ray; *(relámpago)* (flash of) lightning.

raza *f (humana)* race; *(de animal)* breed.

razón *f* reason; *(proporción)* rate; **uso de r.** power of reasoning; **dar la r. a algn** to say that sb is right; **tener r.** to be right.

razonable *adj* reasonable.

razonar 1 *vt (argumentar)* to reason out. **2** *vi (discurrir)* to reason.

reacción *f* reaction; **avión de r.** jet (plane).

reaccionar *vi* to react.

reactor *m* reactor; *(avión)* jet (plane).

reajuste *m* readjustment.

real¹ *adj (efectivo, verdadero)* real.

real² *adj (regio)* royal.

realidad *f* reality; **en r.** in fact.

realismo *m* realism.

realizador, -a *mf* producer.

realizar [40] **1** *vt (hacer)* to carry out; *(ambición)* to achieve. **2 realizarse** *vr (persona)* to fulfill oneself; *(sueño)* to come true.

realmente *adv* really.

realzar [40] *vt (recalcar)* to highlight; *(belleza, importancia)* to heighten.

reanimar *vt*, **reanimarse** *vr* to revive.

reanudar 1 *vt* to renew. **2 reanudarse** *vr* to resume.

rebaja *f (descuento)* reduction; **rebajas** sales.

rebajar 1 *vt (precio)* to cut; *(tanto por ciento)* to take off. **2 rebajarse**

vr (humillarse) to humble oneself.
rebanada *f* slice.
rebaño *m* herd; *(de ovejas)* flock.
rebasar *vt (exceder)* to exceed.
rebeca *f* cardigan.
rebelarse *vr* to rebel.
rebelde 1 *mf* rebel. **2** *adj* rebellious.
rebelión *f* rebellion.
rebobinar *vt* to rewind.
rebosar *vi* to overflow.
rebotar *vi (pelota)* to bounce; *(bala)* to ricochet.
rebuznar *vi* to bray.
recado *m (mandado)* errand; *(mensaje)* message; **dejar un r.** to leave a message.
recalcar [44] *vt* to stress.
recalentar [1] *vt (comida)* to reheat.
recámara *f (de rueda)* tube; *(habitación)* dressing room; *CAm, Col, Méx (dormitorio)* bedroom.
recambio *m (repuesto)* spare (part); *(de pluma etc)* refill; **rueda de r.** spare wheel.
recapacitar *vt* to think over.
recargado, -a *adj (estilo)* over-elaborate.
recargar [42] *vt (batería)* to recharge; *(adornar mucho)* to over-elaborate.
recatado, -a *adj (prudente)* cautious; *(modesto)* modest.
recaudador, -a *mf* tax collector.
recaudar *vt* to collect.
recelar *vi* r. de to distrust.
receloso, -a *adj* suspicious.
recepción *f* reception.
recepcionista *mf* receptionist.
receptor, -a 1 *mf (persona)* recipient. **2** *m (aparato)* receiver.
receta *f* recipe; **r. (médica)** prescription.
recetar *vt* to prescribe.
rechazar [40] *vt* to reject.
rechinar *vi (metal)* to squeak; *(dientes)* to chatter.
rechoncho, -a *adj* chubby.
recibidor *m* entrance hall.
recibimiento *m* reception.

recibir 1 *vt* to receive; *(acoger)* to welcome. **2 recibirse** *vr Am* recibirse de to qualify as.
recibo *m (factura)* bill; *(resguardo)* receipt.
reciclar *vt* to recycle.
recién *adv* recently; *Am (hace poco)* recently. **r. casados** newlyweds; **r. nacido** newborn baby.
reciente *adj* recent.
recientemente *adv* recently.
recinto *m (cercado)* enclosure; **r. comercial** shopping precinct.
recio, -a *adj (robusto)* sturdy; *(grueso)* thick; *(voz)* loud.
recipiente *m* container.
recíproco, -a *adj* reciprocal.
recitar *vt* to recite.
reclamación *f (demanda)* claim; *(queja)* complaint.
reclamar 1 *vt* to claim. **2** *vi* to protest *(contra against)*.
reclinar 1 *vt* to lean *(sobre on)*. **2 reclinarse** *vr* to lean back.
recluir [37] *vt* to shut away.
recluso, -a *mf* inmate.
recobrar 1 *vt* to recover; *(conocimiento)* to regain; **r. el aliento** to get one's breath back. **2 recobrarse** *vr* to recover.
recodo *m* bend.
recoger [53] **1** *vt* to pick up; *(datos etc)* to collect; *(ordenar, limpiar)* to clean; *(cosecha)* to gather. **2 recogerse** *vr* **r. el pelo** to put one's hair up
recogida *f* collection; *(cosecha)* harvest.
recomendación *f* recommendation; *(para persona)* reference.
recomendar [1] *vt* to recommend.
recompensa *f* reward.
reconciliar [43] **1** *vt* to reconcile. **2 reconciliarse** *vr* to be reconciled.
reconfortante *adj* comforting.
reconocer [34] *vt* to recognize; *(admitir)* to admit; *(paciente)* to examine.
reconocimiento *m* recognition; *(médico)* examination.

reconstituyente *m* tonic.
reconstruir [37] *vt* to reconstruct.
recopilación *f* compilation.
recopilar *vt* to compile.
récord *m* record.
recordar [2] *vt* to remember; **r. algo a algn** to remind sb of sth.
recorrer *vt* (*distancia*) to travel; (*país*) to tour; (*ciudad*) to walk round.
recorrido *m* (*trayecto*) journey; (*itinerario*) route.
recortar *vt* to cut out.
recorte *m* cutting; (*de pelo*) trim.
recostar [2] **1** *vt* to lean. **2 recostarse** *vr* (*tumbarse*) to lie down.
recreo *m* recreation; (*en colegio*) break, playtime.
recriminar *vt* to recriminate; (*reprochar*) to reproach.
recrudecer [33] *vt*, **recrudecerse** *vr* to worsen.
recta *f* (*de carretera*) straight stretch.
rectangular *adj* rectangular.
rectángulo *m* rectangle.
rectificar [44] *vt* to rectify; (*corregir*) to remedy.
recto, -a 1 *adj* (*derecho*) straight; (*ángulo*) right. **2** *adv* straight (on).
rector, -a *mf* rector.
recuerdo *m* (*memoria*) memory; (*regalo etc*) souvenir; **recuerdos** regards.
recuperación *f* recovery.
recuperar 1 *vt* (*salud*) to recover; (*conocimiento*) to regain; (*tiempo, clases*) to make up. **2 recuperarse** *vr* to recover.
recurrir *vi* (*sentencia*) to appeal; **r. a** (*a algn*) to turn to; (*a algo*) to resort to.
recurso *m* resource; (*de sentencia*) appeal.
red *f* net; (*sistema*) network; **r. local** local area network, LAN.
redacción *f* (*escrito*) composition; (*acción*) writing.
redactar *vt* to draft.
redactor, -a *mf* editor.
redondel *m* (*círculo*) ring.

redondo, -a *adj* round; (*rotundo*) categorical.
reducción *f* reduction.
reducir [10] **1** *vt* (*disminuir*) to reduce. **2 reducirse** *vr* (*disminuirse*) to diminish; (*limitarse*) to confine oneself (**a** to).
reembolso *m* reimbursement; **contra r.** cash on delivery.
reemplazar [40] *vt* to replace (**con** with).
ref. *abr de* **referencia** reference, ref.
refaccionar *vt Am* to repair.
refectorio *m* refectory.
referencia *f* reference.
referéndum *m* (*pl* **referéndums**) referendum.
referente *adj* **r. a** concerning, regarding.
referir [5] **1** *vt* to tell. **2 referirse** *vr* (*aludir*) to refer (**a** to).
refilón: de refilón *adv* briefly.
refinería *f* refinery.
reflector *m* spotlight.
reflejar 1 *vt* to reflect. **2 reflejarse** *vr* to be reflected (**en** in).
reflejo, -a 1 *m* (*imagen*) reflection; (*destello*) gleam; **reflejos** (*en el cabello*) highlights. **2** *adj* (*movimiento*) reflex.
reflexión *f* reflection.
reflexionar *vi* to think (**sobre** about).
reflexivo, -a *adj* (*persona*) thoughtful; (*verbo etc*) reflexive.
reforma *f* reform; (*reparación*) repair.
reformar *vt* to reform; (*edificio*) to renovate.
reformatorio *m* reform school.
reforzar [2] *vt* to strengthen.
refrán *m* saying.
refregar [1] *vt* to rub vigorously.
refrescante *adj* refreshing.
refrescar [44] **1** *vt* to refresh. **2** *vi* (*bebida*) to be refreshing. **3 refrescarse** *vr* to cool down.
refresco *m* soft drink.
refrigeración *f* refrigeration; (*aire*

acondicionado) air conditioning.

refrigerado, -a *adj (local)* air-conditioned.

refrigerador *m* refrigerator, fridge.

refrigerio *m* snack, refreshments *pl.*

refuerzo *m* strengthening.

refugiarse [43] *vr* to take refuge.

refugio *m* refuge.

refunfuñar *vi* to grumble.

regadera *f* watering can.

regalar *vt (dar)* to give (as a present).

regaliz *m* licorice.

regalo *m* present.

regañadientes: a regañadientes *adv* reluctantly.

regañar 1 *vt* to tell off. **2** *vi* to nag.

regar [1] *vt* to water.

regata *f* regatta.

regatear *vi* to haggle; *(en fútbol)* to dribble.

regazo *m* lap.

regeneración *f* regeneration.

régimen *m (pl regímenes)* regime; *(dieta)* diet; **estar a r.** to be on a diet.

regio, -a *adj (real)* regal; *Am (magnífico)* majestic.

región *f* region.

regional *adj* regional.

regir [58] **1** *vt* to govern. **2** *vi* to be in force. **3 regirse** *vr* to be guided, to go *(por* by).

registrado, -a *adj* **marca registrada** registered trademark.

registrar 1 *vt (examinar)* to inspect; *(cachear)* to frisk; *(inscribir)* to register. **2 registrarse** *vr (detectarse)* to be recorded; *(inscribirse)* to register.

registro *m* inspection; *(inscripción)* registration.

regla *f (norma)* rule; *(instrumento)* ruler; *(periodo)* period; **por r. general** as a (general) rule.

reglamentario, -a *adj* statutory.

reglamento *m* regulations *pl.*

regocijar *vt* to delight.

regocijo *m (placer)* delight; *(alborozo)* rejoicing.

regresar *vi* to return.

regreso *m* return.

regular 1 *vt* to regulate; *(ajustar)* to adjust. **2** *adj* regular; *(mediano)* so-so; **vuelo r.** scheduled flight. **3** *adv* so-so.

regularidad *f* regularity; **con r.** regularly.

regularizar [40] *vt* to regularize.

rehabilitar *vt* to rehabilitate; *(edificio)* to convert.

rehacer [15] *(pp rehecho)* **1** *vt* to redo. **2 rehacerse** *vr (recuperarse)* to recover.

rehén *m* hostage.

rehogar [42] *vt* to brown.

rehuir [37] *vt* to shun.

rehusar *vt* to refuse.

reina *f* queen.

reinar *vi* to reign.

reincidir *vi* to relapse (**en** into).

reincorporarse *vr* **r. al trabajo** to return to work.

reino *m* kingdom; **el R. Unido** the United Kingdom.

reinserción *f* reintegration.

reinsertar *vt,* **reinsertarse** *vr* to reintegrate.

reír [56] *vi,* **reírse** *vr* to laugh (**de** at).

reiterar *vt* to reiterate.

reivindicación *f* demand.

reivindicar [44] *vt* to demand.

reja *f (de ventana)* grating.

rejilla *f* grill; *(de horno)* gridiron; *(por equipaje)* luggage rack.

rejoneador, -a *mf* bullfighter on horseback.

relación *f* relationship; *(conexión)* connection; **relaciones públicas** public relations.

relacionado, -a *adj* related (**con** to).

relacionar 1 *vt* to relate (**con** to). **2 relacionarse** *vr* to be related; *(alternar)* to get acquainted.

relajación *f* relaxation.

relajante *adj* relaxing.

relajar *vt,* **relajarse** *vr* to relax.

relamerse *vr* to lick one's lips.

relámpago *m* flash of lightning.

relatar *vt* to tell, to relate.

relativo, -a *adj* relative (**a** to).

relato *m* story.

relax *m* relaxation.

relegar [42] *vt* to relegate.

relevante *adj* important.

relevar *vt* (*sustituir*) to take over from.

relevo *m* relief; (*en carrera*) relay.

religión *f* religion.

religioso, -a 1 *adj* religious. **2** *mf* (*hombre*) monk; (*mujer*) nun.

relinchar *vi* to neigh.

rellano *m* landing.

rellenar *vt* (*impreso etc*) to fill in; (*llenar*) to pack (**de** with).

relleno, -a 1 *m* (*de aves*) stuffing; (*de pasteles*) filling. **2** *adj* stuffed.

reloj *m* clock; (*de pulsera*) watch.

relojería *f* (*tienda*) watchmaker's.

reluciente *adj* shining.

relucir [35] *vi* to shine.

reluzco *indic pres de* **relucir**.

remache *m* rivet.

remangar [42] *vt*, **remangarse** *vr* (*mangas, pantalones*) to roll up; (*camisa*) to tuck up.

remar *vi* to row.

rematar *vt* to finish off.

remate *m* (*final*) finish; (*en fútbol*) shot at goal; **para r.** to crown it all; **de r.** utter.

remediar [43] *vt* to remedy; (*enmendar*) to repair; **no pude remediarlo** I couldn't help it.

remedio *m* (*cura*) remedy; (*solución*) solution; **¡qué r.!** what else can I do!; **no hay más r.** there's no choice; **sin r.** without fail.

remendar [1] *vt* (*ropa*) to patch.

remesa *f* (*de mercancías*) consignment.

remiendo *m* (*arreglo*) mend; (*parche*) patch.

remilgado, -a *adj* (*melindroso*) fussy.

remite *m* (*en carta*) sender's name and address.

remitente *mf* sender.

remitir 1 *vt* (*enviar*) to send. **2** *vi* (*fiebre, temporal*) to subside.

remo *m* oar.

remodelación *f* (*modificación*) reshaping; (*reorganización*) reorganization.

remojar *vt* to soak (**en** in).

remojón *m fam* **darse un r.** to go for a dip.

remolacha *f* red beet.

remolcador *m* tug.

remolcar [44] *vt* to tow.

remolino *m* (*de agua*) whirlpool; (*de aire*) whirlwind.

remolón, -ona *adj* **hacerse el r.** to shirk, to slack.

remolonear *vi* to shirk, to slack.

remolque *m* (*acción*) towing; (*vehículo*) trailer.

remordimiento *m* remorse.

remoto, -a *adj* remote.

remover [4] *vt* (*tierra*) to turn over; (*líquido*) to shake up; (*comida etc*) to stir.

remplazar [40] *vt* = **reemplazar**.

remuneración *f* remuneration.

remunerar *vt* to remunerate.

renacer [60] *vi* to be reborn; *fig* (*revivir*) to revive, to come back to life.

renacuajo *m* tadpole; *fam* (*niño pequeño*) shrimp.

rencor *m* resentment; **guardar r. a algn** to have a grudge against sb.

rencoroso, -a *adj* resentful.

rendido, -a *adj* (*muy cansado*) exhausted.

rendija *f* crack.

rendimiento *m* (*de máquina, motor*) performance.

rendir [6] **1** *vt* (*fruto, beneficios*) to yield; (*cansar*) to exhaust. **2** *vi* (*dar beneficios*) to pay. **3 rendirse** *vr* to surrender.

RENFE *f abr de* **Red Nacional de Ferrocarriles Españoles** Spanish railroad network.

renglón *m* line.

reno *m* reindeer.

renombre *m* renown.

renovación *f (de contrato, pasaporte)* renewal.

renovar [2] *vt* to renew; *(edificio)* to renovate.

renta *f (ingresos)* income; *(beneficio)* interest; *(alquiler)* rent.

rentable *adj* profitable.

renunciar [43] *vi (dimitir)* to resign; *(no aceptar)* to decline; **r. a** to give up.

reñido, -a *adj (disputado)* hard-fought.

reñir [6] **1** *vt (regañar)* to tell off. **2** *vi (discutir)* to argue; *(pelear)* to fight.

reo *mf (acusado)* accused; *(culpable)* culprit.

reojo: de reojo *adv* mirar algo de **r.** to look at sth out of the corner of one's eye.

reparar 1 *vt* to repair. **2** *vi* **r. en** *(darse cuenta de)* to notice.

reparo *m* no tener reparos en not to hesitate to; **me da r.** I am embarrassed.

repartidor, -a *mf* distributor.

repartir *vt (dividir)* to share out; *(regalo, premio)* to give out; *(correo)* to deliver.

reparto *m* distribution; *(distribución)* handing out; *(de mercancías)* delivery; *(de actores)* cast.

repasar *vt* to revise.

repaso *m* revision.

repecho *m* short steep slope.

repeler *vt (repugnar)* to disgust.

repente: de repente *adv* suddenly.

repentino, -a *adj* sudden.

repercutir 1 *vt (subida de precio)* to pass on. **2** *vi* **r. en** to affect.

repertorio *m* repertoire.

repetición *f* repetition.

repetir [6] **1** *vt* to repeat; *(plato)* to have a second helping of. **2** *vi (en colegio)* to repeat a year. **3 repetirse** *vr (hecho)* to recur.

repicar [44] *vti (campanas)* to ring.

repisa *f* shelf.

replegarse [1] *vr* to fall back.

repleto, -a *adj* full (up); **r. de** packed with.

réplica *f* answer; *(copia)* replica.

replicar [44] **1** *vt (objetar)* to argue. **2** *vi* to reply.

repoblar [2] *vt* to repopulate; *(bosque)* to reforest.

repollo *m* cabbage.

reponer [19] **1** *vt* to replace. **2 reponerse** *vr* **reponerse de** to recover from.

reportaje *m* report; *(noticias)* news item.

reportar 1 *vt (beneficios)* to bring; *Am (informar)* to report. **2 reportarse** *vr Am (presentarse)* to report (a to).

reportero, -a *mf* reporter.

reposar *vti* to rest (**en** on).

reposo *m* rest.

repostar *vti (gasolina)* to fill up.

repostería *f* confectionery.

reprender *vt* to reprimand.

represalia *f (usu pl)* reprisals *pl*, retaliation.

representante *mf* representative.

representar *vt* to represent; *(significar)* to mean; *(obra)* to perform.

represión *f* repression.

represivo, -a *adj* repressive.

reprimenda *f* reprimand.

reprimir *vt* to repress.

reprochar *vt* **r. algo a algn** to reproach sb for sth.

reproducción *f* reproduction.

reproducir [10] *vt*, **reproducirse** *vr* to reproduce.

reptil *m* reptile.

república *f* republic.

repuesto *m (recambio)* spare (part); **rueda de r.** spare wheel.

repugnante *adj* disgusting.

repugnar *vt* to disgust.

repulsivo, -a *adj* repulsive.

repuse *pt indef de* **reponer**.

reputación *f* reputation.

requesón *m* cottage cheese.

requisar *vt* to requisition.

requisito *m* requirement.

res *f* animal.

resaca *f* hangover.

resaltar *vi (sobresalir)* to project; *fig* to stand out.

resbaladizo, -a *adj* slippery.

resbalar *vi,* **resbalarse** *vr* to slip.

resbalón *m* slip.

rescatar *vt (liberar)* to rescue.

rescate *m* rescue; *(dinero pagado)* ransom.

rescindir *vt (contrato)* to cancel.

rescoldo *m* embers *pl.*

resecarse [44] *vr* to dry up, to become parched.

reseco, -a *adj* parched.

resentido, -a *adj* resentful.

resentimiento *m* resentment.

reserva *f (de entradas etc)* booking; *(provisión)* reserve.

reservado, -a *adj* reserved.

reservar *vt (billetes etc)* to reserve, to book; *(guardar)* to keep.

resfriado, -a 1 *m (catarro)* cold; **coger un r.** to catch (a) cold. **2** *adj* **estar r.** to have a cold.

resfriarse *vr* to catch (a) cold.

resguardo *m (recibo)* receipt.

residencia *f* residence; **r. de ancianos** old people's home.

residencial *adj* residential.

residente *adj & mf* resident.

residir *vi* to reside (**en** in).

resignado, -a *adj* resigned.

resignarse *vr* to resign oneself (**a** to).

resina *f* resin.

resistencia *f* resistance; *(aguante)* endurance; *(de bombilla etc)* element.

resistente *adj* resistant (**a** to); *(fuerte)* tough, hardy.

resistir 1 *vi* to resist; *(soportar)* to hold (out). **2** *vt (situación, persona)* to put up with; *(tentación)* to resist. **2 resistirse** *vr* to resist; *(oponerse)* to offer resistance; *(negarse)* to refuse.

resolver [4] *(pp* **resuelto) 1** *vt (solucionar)* to solve; *(asunto)* to settle. **2**

resolverse *vr (solucionarse)* to be solved.

resonar [2] *vi* to resound; *(tener eco)* to echo.

resoplar *vi (respirar)* to breathe heavily; *(de cansancio)* to puff and pant.

resorte *m (muelle)* spring; *(medio)* means.

respaldar *vt* to support, to back (up).

respaldo *m (de asiento)* back.

respecto *m* **al r., a este r.** in this respect; **con r. a, r. a** with regard to.

respetable *adj* respectable.

respetar *vt* to respect.

respeto *m* respect.

respetuoso, -a *adj* respectful.

respingo *m* start.

respiración *f (acción)* breathing; *(aliento)* breath.

respirar *vti* to breathe.

resplandecer [33] *vi* to shine.

resplandor *m (brillo)* brightness; *(muy intenso)* brilliance; *(de fuego)* blaze.

responder 1 *vt* to answer. **2** *vi (a una carta)* to reply; *(reaccionar)* to respond; *(corresponder)* to answer; *(protestar)* to answer back.

responsabilidad *f* responsibility.

responsabilizar [40] **1** *vt* to make responsible (**de** for); *(culpar)* hold responsible (**de** for). **2 responsabilizarse** *vr* to claim responsibility (**de** for).

responsable 1 *adj* responsible. **2** *mf* **el/la r.** *(de robo etc)* the perpetrator.

respuesta *f* answer, reply; *(reacción)* response.

resquicio *m* chink.

resta *f* subtraction.

restablecer [33] **1** *vt* to re-establish; *(el orden)* to restore. **2 restablecerse** *vr (mejorarse)* to recover.

restaguardia *f* rearguard.

restante *adj* remaining.

restar *vt* to subtract.

restaurante *m* restaurant.

restaurar *vt* to restore.

resto *m* rest; *(en resta)* remainder; **restos** remains; *(de comida)* leftovers.

restregar [1] *vt* to scrub.

restricción *f* restriction.

restringir [57] *vt* to restrict.

resucitar *vti* to revive.

resuello *m* gasp.

resultado *m* result; *(consecuencia)* outcome.

resultar *vi (ser)* to turn out; **me resultó fácil** it turned out to be easy for me.

resumen *m* summary; **en r.** in short.

resumir *vt* to sum up.

resurgir [57] *vi* to reappear.

retahíla *f* series *sing*.

retal *m (pedazo)* scrap.

retar *vt* to challenge.

retardarse *vr* to be delayed.

retazo *m (pedazo)* scrap.

retención *f* retention; **r. de tráfico** (traffic) hold-up.

retener [24] *vt (conservar)* to retain; *(detener)* to detain.

reticente *adj* reticent, reserved.

retirada *f* withdrawal.

retirar 1 *vt (apartar, alejar)* to take away; *(dinero)* to withdraw. **2 retirarse** *vr (apartarse)* to withdraw; *(irse, jubilarse)* to retire.

retiro *m (lugar tranquilo)* retreat.

reto *m* challenge.

retoque *m* final touch.

retorcer [41] **1** *vt (cuerda, hilo)* to twist; *(ropa)* to wring (out). **2 retorcerse** *vr* to become twisted.

retorcido, -a *adj fig* twisted.

retornar 1 *vt* to return, to give back. **2** *vi* to return, to come back, to go back.

retorno *m* return.

retortijón *m (dolor)* stomach cramp.

retraído, -a *adj* reserved.

retransmisión *f* broadcast.

retrasado, -a 1 *adj (tren etc)* late; *(reloj)* slow; **estar r.** *(en el colegio)* to be behind. **2** *mf* **r. (mental)** mentally retarded person.

retrasar 1 *vt (retardar)* to slow down; *(atrasar)* to postpone; *(reloj)* to put back. **2 retrasarse** *vr* to be delayed; *(reloj)* to be slow.

retraso *m (demora)* delay; **con r.** late; **una hora de r.** an hour behind schedule.

retratar 1 *vt (pintar)* to paint a portrait of; *(fotografiar)* to take a photograph of; *fig (describir)* to describe, to depict. **2 retratarse** *vr* to have one's photograph taken.

retrato *m (pintura)* portrait; *(fotografía)* photograph.

retrete *m* toilet.

retribución *f (pago)* pay; *(recompensa)* reward.

retroceder *vi* to back away.

retroceso *m (movimiento)* backward movement.

retrógrado, -a *adj & mf (reaccionario)* reactionary.

retrospectivo, -a *adj & f* retrospective.

retrovisor *m* rear-view mirror.

retumbar *vi (resonar)* to resound; *(tronar)* to thunder.

retuve *pt indef de* **retener**.

reúma, reumatismo *m* rheumatism.

reunión *f* meeting.

reunir 1 *vt* to gather together; *(dinero)* to raise; *(cualidades)* to possess; *(requisitos)* to fulfill. **2 reunirse** *vr* to meet.

revalorizar [40] *vt*, **revalorizarse** *vr (moneda)* to revalue.

revancha *f* revenge; *(partido)* return match.

revelar *vt* to reveal; *(película)* to develop.

reventa *f (de entradas)* touting.

reventar [1] *vti*, **reventarse** *vr* to burst.

reventón *m (de neumático)* blow-out.

reverencia f (de hombre) bow; (de mujer) curtsy.

reversible adj reversible.

reverso m back.

revés m (reverso) reverse; (contrariedad) setback; **al** o **del r.** (al contrario) the other way round; (la parte interior en el exterior) inside out; (boca abajo) upside down; (la parte de detrás delante) back to front.

revisar vt to check; (coche) to service.

revisión f checking; (de coche) service; **r. médica** checkup.

revisor, -a mf corrector, inspector.

revista f magazine.

revitalizar [40] vt to revitalize.

revivir vti to revive.

revolcarse vr to roll about.

revoltijo, revoltillo m jumble.

revoltoso, -a adj (travieso) mischievous.

revolución f revolution.

revolucionar vt to revolutionize.

revolver [4] (pp **revuelto**) **1** vt (desordenar) to mess up; **me revuelve el estómago** it turns my stomach. **2** revolverse vr (agitarse) to roll; (el mar) to become rough.

revólver m (pl **revólveres**) revolver.

revuelo m (agitación) stir.

revuelta f revolt.

revuelto, -a adj (desordenado) in a mess; (tiempo) unsettled; (mar) rough; (huevos) scrambled.

rey m king; (**el día de**) **Reyes** Epiphany, January 6.

rezagarse vr to fall behind.

rezar [40] **1** vi (orar) to pray. **2** vt (oración) to say.

rezumar vt to ooze.

ría f estuary.

riada f flood.

ribera f (de río) bank; (zona) riverside.

rico, -a 1 adj ser r. to be rich; estar r. (delicioso) to be delicious. **2** mf rich person; **los ricos** the rich.

ridiculizar [40] vt to ridicule.

ridículo, -a 1 adj ridiculous. **2** m ridicule; **hacer el r., quedar en r.** to make a fool of oneself; **poner a algn en r.** to make a fool of sb.

riego m irrigation.

rienda f rein.

riesgo m risk; **correr el r. de** to run the risk of.

rifa f raffle.

rifar vt to raffle (off).

rifle m rifle.

rigidez f rigidity; (severidad) inflexibility.

rígido, -a adj rigid, stiff; fig (severo) strict, inflexible.

rigor m rigor; (severidad) severity.

rigurosamente adv rigorously; (meticulosamente) meticulously; (severamente) severely.

riguroso, -a adj rigorous; (severo) severe.

rimar vti to rhyme (**con** with).

rímel m mascara.

rincón m corner.

rinoceronte m rhinoceros.

riña f (pelea) fight; (discusión) row.

riñón m kidney.

río m river; **r. abajo** downstream; **r. arriba** upstream.

riqueza f wealth.

risa f laugh; (carcajadas) laughter; **me da r.** it makes me laugh; **morirse** o **mondarse de r.** to die laughing.

risueño, -a adj (sonriente) smiling.

ritmo m rhythm; (paso) rate.

rito m rite; (ritual) ritual.

ritual adj & m ritual.

rival adj & mf rival.

rivalizar [40] vi to rival (**en** in).

rizado, -a adj (pelo) curly; (mar) choppy.

rizar [40] vt, **rizarse** vr (pelo) to curl.

rizo m (de pelo) curl.

robar vt (objeto) to steal; (banco, persona) to rob; (casa) to burgle.

roble m oak (tree).

robo m robbery, theft; (en casa) burglary; **r. a mano armada** armed robbery.

robot m (pl robots) robot; **r. de cocina** food processor.

robustecer [33] vt to strengthen.

robusto, -a adj robust.

roca f rock.

roce m (fricción) friction; (en la piel) chafing; (contacto ligero) brush.

rociar [29] vt to sprinkle.

rocío m dew.

rocoso, -a adj rocky.

rodaja f slice.

rodaje m shooting.

rodar [64] **1** vt (película etc) to shoot. **2** vi to roll.

rodear 1 vt to surround. **2 rodearse** vr to surround oneself (**de** with).

rodeo m (desvío) detour; (al hablar) evasiveness; rodeo; **no andarse con rodeos** to get straight to the point.

rodilla f knee; **de rodillas** kneeling; **hincarse o ponerse de rodillas** to kneel down.

rodillera f (de pantalón) knee patch; (para la rodilla) knee pad.

roer [38] vt (hueso) to gnaw; (galleta) to nibble at.

rogar [2] vt (pedir) to ask; (implorar) to beg; **hacerse de r.** to play hard to get.

roído, -a adj gnawed, eaten away.

rojizo, -a adj reddish.

rojo, -a 1 adj red; **estar en números rojos** to be in the red. **2** m (color) red.

rollizo, -a adj chubby.

rollo m roll; fam (pesadez) drag.

romance m (aventura amorosa) romance.

romántico, -a adj & mf romantic.

rombo m diamond; (en geometría) rhombus.

rompecabezas m inv (juego) (jigsaw) puzzle.

rompeolas m inv breakwater, jetty.

romper (pp roto) **1** vt to break; (papel, tela) to tear; (vajilla, cristal) to smash; (pantalones) to split; (relaciones) to break off. **2** vi to break; **r. a llorar** to burst out crying. **3 romperse** vr to break; (papel, tela) to

tear; **romperse la cabeza** to rack one's brains.

ron m rum.

roncar [44] vi to snore.

roncha f (en la piel) swelling.

ronco, -a adj hoarse; **quedarse r.** to lose one's voice.

ronda f round; (patrulla) patrol; (carretera) ring road; (paseo) avenue.

rondar vti (merodear) to prowl around; (estar cerca de) to be about.

ronquido m snore.

ronronear vi to purr.

roñoso, -a adj (mugriento) filthy; (tacaño) mean.

ropa f clothes pl, clothing; **r. interior** underwear.

ropero m (armario) r. wardrobe, closet.

rosa 1 adj inv (color) pink; **novela r.** romantic novel. **2** f (flor) rose. **3** m (color) pink.

rosado, -a 1 adj (color) pink; (vino) rosé. **2** m (vino) rosé.

rosal m rosebush.

rosbif m roast beef.

rosco m (pastel) ring-shaped pastry.

rosquilla f ring-shaped pastry; **venderse como rosquillas** to sell like hot cakes.

rostro m (cara) face; fam **tener mucho r.** to have a lot of nerve.

roto, -a 1 adj broken; (papel) torn; (gastado) worn out; (ropa) in tatters. **2** m (agujero) hole.

rótula f kneecap.

rotulador m felt-tip pen.

rótulo m (letrero) sign; (titular) heading.

rotundo, -a adj categorical; **éxito r.** resounding success.

rotura f (ruptura) breaking; (de hueso) fracture.

rozadura f scratch.

rozar [40] **1** vt to brush against. **2** vi to rub. **3 rozarse** vr to brush (**con** against).

Rte. *abr de* **remite, remitente**
sender.

rubí *m* (*pl* **rubíes**) ruby.

rubio, -a 1 *adj* (*pelo, persona*)
blond; **tabaco r.** Virginia tobacco. **2**
mf blond; *f* blonde.

ruborizarse [40] *vr* to blush.

rudimentario, -a *adj* rudimen-
tary.

rudo, -a *adj* rough.

rueda *f* wheel; **r. de recambio** spare
wheel; **r. de prensa** press conference.

ruedo *m* bullring.

ruego *m* request.

rugido *m* (*de animal*) roar.

rugir [57] *vi* to roar.

rugoso, -a *adj* rough.

ruido *m* noise; (*sonido*) sound; **hacer r.** to make a noise.

ruidoso, -a *adj* noisy.

ruin *adj* (*vil*) vile; (*tacaño*) mean.

ruina *f* ruin.

ruiseñor *m* nightingale.

ruleta *f* roulette.

rulo *m* (*para el pelo*) roller.

rumba *f* rumba.

rumbo *m* direction; (**con**) **r. a** bound
for.

rumor *m* rumor; (*murmullo*) murmur.

rumorearse *v impers* to be
rumored.

ruptura *f* breaking; (*de relaciones*)
breaking-off.

rural *adj* rural.

ruso, -a *adj & mf* Russian.

rústico, -a *adj* rustic.

ruta *f* route.

rutina *f* routine.

S

S.A. *abr de* **Sociedad Anónima** ≃
PLC, ≃ Ltd, ≃ Inc.

sábado *m* Saturday.

sábana *f* sheet; *fam* **se pegaron las
sábanas** I overslept.

sabañón *m* chilblain.

sabelotodo *mf inv* know-all.

saber[1] *m* knowledge.

saber[2] [21] *vt* to know; (*tener habilidad*) to be able to; (*enterarse*) to
learn; **que yo sepa** as far as I know;
vete tú a s. goodness knows; **a s.**
namely; **¿sabes cocinar?** can you
cook? **2** *vi* (*tener sabor*) to taste (**a**
of); (*soler*) to be accustomed to; **sabe
a fresa** it tastes of strawberries.

sabiduría *f* wisdom.

sabiendas: a sabiendas *adv* **lo
hizo a s.** he did it in the full knowledge of what he was doing; **a s. de
que ...** knowing full well that ...

sabio, -a 1 *adj* (*prudente*) wise. **2** *mf*
scholar.

sable *m* sabre.

sabor *m* (*gusto*) flavor; **con s. a limón** lemon-flavored.

saborear *vt* (*degustar*) to taste.

sabotaje *m* sabotage.

sabotear *vt* to sabotage.

sabré *indic fut de* **saber**.

sabroso, -a *adj* tasty; (*delicioso*)
delicious.

sacacorchos *m inv* corkscrew.

sacapuntas *m inv* pencil sharp-
ener.

sacar [44] **1** *vt* to take out; (*con más
fuerza*) to pull out; (*obtener*) to get;
(*conclusiones*) to draw; (*entrada*) to
buy; (*libro, disco*) to bring out; (*fotografía*) to take; **s. la lengua** to stick
one's tongue out; **s. provecho de algo** to benefit from sth.

sacarina *f* saccharin.

sacerdote m priest.

saciar [43] vt (sed) to quench; (deseos, hambre) to satisfy.

saciedad f satiety; **repetir algo hasta la s.** to repeat sth ad nauseam.

saco m sack; Am (chaqueta) jacket; **s. de dormir** sleeping bag.

sacrificar [44] **1** vt to sacrifice. **2 sacrificarse** vr to make sacrifices.

sacrificio m sacrifice.

sacudida f shake; (espasmo) jolt; (de terremoto) tremor.

sacudir vt (agitar) to shake; (alfombra, sábana) to shake out; (arena, polvo) to shake off; (golpear) to beat.

sádico, -a 1 adj sadistic. **2** mf sadist.

saeta f (dardo) dart.

safari m (cacería) safari; (parque) safari park.

sagaz adj (listo) clever; (astuto) shrewd.

sagrado, -a adj sacred.

sal¹ f salt; **s. de mesa** table salt; **s. gorda** cooking salt.

sal² imperativo de **salir**.

sala f room; (en un hospital) ward; **s. de estar** living room; **s. de espera** waiting room; **s. de exposiciones** exhibition hall; **s. de fiestas** nightclub.

salado, -a adj (con sal) salted; (con exceso de sal) salty; (infortunado) unlucky; **agua salada** salt water.

salario m salary.

salchicha f sausage.

salchichón m (salami-type) sausage.

saldar vt (cuenta) to settle; (deuda) to pay off.

saldo m (de cuenta) balance; **saldos** sales.

saldré indic fut de **salir**.

salero m (recipiente) saltcellar.

salgo indic pres de **salir**.

salida f (partida) departure; (puerta etc) exit, way out; (de carrera) start; (de un astro) rising; (perspectiva) opening; (en ordenador) output;

callejón sin s. dead end; **s. de emergencia** emergency exit; **te vi a la s. del cine** I saw you leaving the cinema; **s. del sol** sunrise.

salir [22] **1** vi (de un sitio, tren etc) to leave; (venir de dentro, revista, disco) to come out; (novios) to go out; (aparecer) to appear; (ley) to come in; (trabajo, vacante) to come up; (resultar) to turn out (to be); (problema) to work out; **salió de la habitación** she left the room; **¿cómo te salió el examen?** how did your exam go?; **s. ganando** to come out on top; **s. barato/caro** to work out cheap/expensive; **esta cuenta no me sale** I can't work this calculation out. **2 salirse** vr (líquido, gas) to leak (out); **salirse de lo normal** to be out of the ordinary; **salirse con la suya** to get one's own way.

saliva f saliva.

salivar vi to salivate.

salmón 1 m (pescado) salmon. **2** adj inv (color) salmon pink.

salmonete m (pescado) red mullet.

salobre adj (agua) brackish; (gusto) salty.

salón m (en una casa) lounge; **s. de actos** assembly hall; **s. de belleza** beauty salon; **s. del automóvil** motor show.

salpicar [44] vt (rociar) to splash; **me salpicó el abrigo de barro** he splashed mud on my coat.

salsa f sauce; (de carne) gravy.

saltamontes m inv grasshopper.

saltar 1 vt (obstáculo, valla) to jump (over). **2** vi to jump; (romperse) to break; (plomos) to blow; (desprenderse) to come off; **s. a la vista** to be obvious. **2 saltarse** vr (omitir) to skip; (no hacer caso) to ignore; **saltarse el semáforo** to run the lights; **se me saltaron las lágrimas** tears came to my eyes.

salto m (acción) jump, leap; **a saltos** in leaps and bounds; **dar** o **pegar un s.** to jump, to leap; **de un s.** in a flash;

s. de altura high jump; **s. de longitud** long jump; **s. mortal** somersault.

salud *f* health; **beber a la s. de algn** to drink to sb's health; **¡s.!** cheers!

saludable *adj (sano)* healthy.

saludar *vt (decir hola a)* to say hello to; **saluda de mi parte a** give my regards to; **le saluda atentamente** *(en una carta)* yours faithfully.

saludo *m* greeting; **un s. de** best wishes from.

salvado *m* bran.

salvaguardar *vt* to safeguard (**de** from).

salvajada *f* brutal act.

salvaje *adj (planta, animal)* wild; *(pueblo, tribu)* savage.

salvam(i)ento *m* rescue.

salvar 1 *vt* to save (**de** from); *(obstáculo)* to clear; *(dificultad)* to overcome. **2 salvarse** *vr (sobrevivir)* to survive; *(escaparse)* to escape (**de** from); **¡sálvese quien pueda!** every man for himself!

salvavidas *m inv* life preserver.

salvo, -a 1 *adj* safe; **a s.** safe. **2** *adv (exceptuando)* except (for). **3** *conj* **s. que** unless.

san *adj* saint; *ver* **santo**.

sanar 1 *vt (curar)* to heal. **2** *vi (persona)* to recover; *(herida)* to heal.

sanción *f* sanction.

sancionar *vt (castigar)* to penalize.

sancochar *vt* to parboil; *Am* to boil meat in water and salt.

sandalia *f* sandal.

sándalo *m* sandalwood.

sandía *f* watermelon.

sandwich *m* sandwich.

sanear *vt (terrenos)* to drain; *(empresa)* to reorganize.

sangrar *vi* to bleed.

sangre *f* blood; **donar s.** to give blood; **a s. fría** in cold blood.

sangría *f (bebida)* sangria.

sangriento, -a *adj (cruel)* cruel.

sanguíneo, -a *adj* blood; **grupo s.** blood group.

sanidad *f* health; **Ministerio de S.** Department of Health.

sano, -a *adj* healthy; **s. y salvo** safe and sound.

santería *f (religión)* santería, = form of religion common in the Caribbean in which people allegedly have contact with the spirit world; *Am (tienda)* = shop selling religious mementoes such as statues of saints.

santiguarse [45] *vr* to cross oneself.

santo, -a 1 *adj* holy. **2** *mf* saint; *(día onomástico)* saint's day; **se me fue el s. al cielo** I completely forgot; **¿a s. de qué?** why on earth?

santuario *m* shrine.

sapo *m* toad.

saque *m (en tenis)* service; *(en fútbol)* **s. inicial** kick-off; **s. de esquina** corner kick.

saquear *vt (casas y tiendas)* to loot.

sarampión *m* measles.

sarcástico, -a *adj* sarcastic.

sardina *f* sardine.

sargento *m* sergeant.

sarpullido *m* rash.

sarro *m (en los dientes)* tartar; *(en la lengua)* fur.

sartén *f* frying pan, skillet.

sastre *m* tailor.

satélite *m* satellite; **televisión vía s.** satellite television.

satén *m* satin.

sátira *f* satire.

satisfacción *f* satisfaction.

satisfacer [15] *(pp* **satisfecho)** *vt* to satisfy; *(deuda)* to pay.

satisfecho, -a *adj* satisfied; **me doy por s.** that's good enough for me.

sauce *m* willow; **s. llorón** weeping willow.

sauna *f* sauna.

saxofón *m* saxophone.

sazonar *vt* to season.

se¹ *pron (reflexivo) (a él mismo)* himself; *(a ella misma)* herself; *(animal)* itself; *(a usted mismo)* yourself; *(a ellos/ellas mismos/mismas)* themselves; *(a ustedes mismos)* yourselves;

se afeitó he shaved; **se compró un nuevo coche** he bought himself a new car. ▪ *(recíproco)* one another, each other. ▪ *(voz pasiva)* **el vino se guarda en cubas** wine is kept in casks. ▪ *(impersonal)* **nunca se sabe** you never know; **se habla inglés** English spoken; **se dice que…** it is said that….

se² *pron pers (a él)* (to o for) him; *(a ella)* (to o for) her; *(a usted o ustedes)* (to o for) you; *(a ellos)* (to o for) them; **se lo diré en cuanto les vea** I'll tell them as soon as I see them; **¿se lo explico?** shall I explain it to him/her *etc*?

sé¹ *indic pres de* **saber**.

sé² *imperativo de* **ser**.

sea *subj pres de* **ser**.

secador *m* dryer; **s. de pelo** hairdryer.

secadora *f* tumble dryer.

secar [44] **1** *vt* to dry. **2 secarse** *vr* to dry; *(marchitarse)* to dry up; **secarse las manos** to dry one's hands.

sección *f* section.

seco, -a *adj* dry; *(tono)* curt; *(golpe, ruido)* sharp; *(frutos secos* dried fruit; **limpieza en s.** dry-cleaning; **frenar en s.** to pull up sharply.

secretaría *f (oficina)* secretary's office.

secretario, -a *mf* secretary.

secreto, -a 1 *adj* secret; **en s.** in secret. **2** *m* secret.

secta *f* sect.

sector *m* sector; *(zona)* area.

secuencia *f* sequence.

secuestrar *vt (persona)* to kidnap; *(avión)* to hijack.

secuestro *m (de persona)* kidnapping; *(de avión)* hijacking.

secundar *vt* to back.

secundario, -a *adj* secondary.

sed *f* thirst; **tener s.** to be thirsty.

seda *f* silk.

sedal *m* fishing line.

sedante *adj & m* sedative.

sede *f* headquarters; *(de gobierno)* seat.

sedentario, -a *adj* sedentary.

sedimento *m* sediment.

sedoso, -a *adj* silky.

seducir [10] *vt* to seduce.

seductor, -a 1 *adj* seductive. **2** *mf* seducer.

segar [1] *vt* to cut.

seglar 1 *adj* secular. **2** *mf* lay person; *m* layman; *f* laywoman.

segmento *m* segment.

seguida: en seguida *adv* immediately, straight away.

seguido *adv* straight; *Am (a menudo)* often; **todo s.** straight ahead.

seguir [6] **1** *vt* to follow; *(camino)* to continue. **2** *vi* to follow; **siguió hablando** he went on o kept on speaking; **sigo resfriado** I've still got the cold.

según 1 *prep* according to; *(en función de)* depending on; *(tal como)* just as; **estaba s. lo dejé** it was just as I had left it. **2** *conj (a medida que)* as; **s. iba leyendo** as I read. **3** *adv* **¿vendrás? — s.** are you coming? — it depends.

segundo, -a¹ *adj* second.

segundo² *m (tiempo)* second.

seguramente *adv (probablemente)* most probably; *(seguro)* surely.

seguridad *f* security; *(física)* safety; *(confianza)* confidence; *(certeza)* sureness; **s. en carretera** road safety; **s. en sí mismo** self-confidence; **con toda s.** most probably; **tener la s. de que** to be certain that; **S. Social** ≃ Social Security.

seguro, -a 1 *adj (cierto)* sure; *(libre de peligro)* safe; *(protegido)* secure; *(fiable)* reliable; *(firme)* steady; **estoy s. de que…** I am sure that…; **está segura de ella misma** she has self-confidence. **2** *m (de accidentes etc)* insurance; *(dispositivo)* safety device; **s. de vida** life insurance. **3** *adv* definitely.

seis *adj & m inv* six.

seiscientos, -as *adj & mf* six hundred.

seleccionador, -a *mf* selector; *(en fútbol)* manager.

seleccionar *vt* to select.

selecto, -a *adj* select.

self-service *m* self-service restaurant.

sello *m (de correos)* stamp; *(para documentos)* seal.

selva *f* jungle.

semáforo *m* traffic lights *pl.*

semana *f* week; **S. Santa** HolyWeek.

semanal *adj & m* weekly.

semanario *m* weekly magazine.

sembrar [1] *vt* to sow; **s. el pánico** to spread panic.

semejante 1 *adj (parecido)* similar. **2** *m (prójimo)* fellow being.

semestre *m* semester.

semifinal *f* semifinal.

semilla *f* seed.

seminario *m (en colegio)* seminar; *(para sacerdotes)* seminary.

sémola *f* semolina.

senado *m* senate.

senador, -a *mf* senator.

sencillo, -a *adj (fácil)* simple; *(natural)* unaffected; *(billete)* single; *(sin adornos)* plain.

senda *f,* **sendero** *m* path.

seno *m (pecho)* breast; *(interior)* heart.

sensación *f* sensation; **tengo la s. de que...** I have a feeling that...; **causar s.** to cause a sensation.

sensacional *adj* sensational.

sensato, -a *adj* sensible.

sensible *adj* sensitive; *(perceptible)* perceptible.

sensiblemente *adv* noticeably.

sensiblero, -a *adj* over-sentimental, mawkish.

sensualidad *f* sensuality.

sentar [1] **1** *vt* to sit; *(establecer)* to establish. **2** *vi (color, ropa)* to suit; **el pelo corto te sienta mal** short hair doesn't suit you; **s. bien/mal a** *(comida)* to agree/disagree with; **la sopa te sentará bien** the soup will do you good. **3 sentarse** *vr* to sit (down).

sentencia *f (condena)* sentence.

sentido *m* sense; *(significado)* meaning; *(dirección)* direction; *(conciencia)* consciousness; **s. común** common sense; **no tiene s.** it doesn't make sense; **(de) s. único** one-way; **perder el s.** to faint.

sentimental 1 *adj* sentimental; **vida s.** love life. **2** *mf* sentimental person.

sentimiento *m* feeling; *(pesar)* sorrow.

sentir [5] **1** *vt* to feel; *(lamentar)* to regret; **lo siento (mucho)** I'm very sorry; **siento molestarle** I'm sorry to bother you. **2 sentirse** *vr* to feel; **me siento mal** I feel ill.

seña *f* mark; *(gesto, indicio)* sign; **hacer señas a algn** to signal to sb; **señas** *(dirección)* address.

señal *f* sign; *(marca)* mark; *(vestigio)* trace; **s. de llamada** dial tone; **s. de tráfico** road sign.

señalar *vt (indicar)* to indicate; *(identificar, comunicar)* to point out; **s. con el dedo** to point at.

señor *m (hombre)* man; *(caballero)* gentleman; *(con apellido)* Mr; *(tratamiento de respeto)* sir; **el Sr. Gutiérrez** Mr Gutiérrez.

señora *f (mujer)* woman; *(trato formal)* lady; *(con apellido)* Mrs; *(tratamiento de respeto)* madam; *(esposa)* wife; **¡señoras y señores!** ladies and gentlemen!; **la Sra. Salinas** Mrs Salinas.

señorita *f (joven)* young woman; *(trato formal)* young lady; *(tratamiento de respeto)* Miss; **la S. Padilla** Miss Padilla.

sepa *subj pres de* **saber**.

separación *f* separation; *(espacio)* space.

separar 1 *vt* to separate; *(desunir)* to detach; *(dividir)* to divide; *(apartar)* to move away. **2 separarse** *vr* to separate; *(apartarse)* to move away (**de** from).

septentrional *adj* northern.

septiembre *m* September.

séptimo, -a *adj & mf* seventh.

sepultura *f* grave.

sequía *f* drought.

séquito *m* entourage.

ser¹ *m* being; **s. humano** human being; **s. vivo** living being.

ser² [23] *vi* to be; **ser músico** to be a musician; **s. de** *(procedencia)* to be from; *(+ material)* to be made of; *(+ poseedor)* to belong to; **el perro es de Miguel** the dog belongs to Miguel; **hoy es dos de noviembre** today is the second of November; **son las cinco de la tarde** it's five o'clock; **¿cuántos estaremos en la fiesta?** how many of us will there be at the party?; **¿cuánto es?** how much is it?; **el estreno será mañana** tomorrow is the opening night; **es que...** it's just that...; **como sea** anyhow; **lo que sea** whatever; **o sea** that is (to say); **por si fuera poco** to top it all; **sea como sea** be that as it may; **a no s. que** unless; **de no s. por...** had it not been for.... ▪ *(auxiliar en pasiva)* to be; **fue asesinado** he was murdered.

sereno, -a *adj* calm.

serial *m* serial.

serie *f* series *sing*; **fabricación en s.** mass production.

seriedad *f (severidad)* seriousness; *(gravedad)* gravity; **falta de s.** irresponsibility.

serio, -a *adj* serious; **en s.** seriously.

sermón *m* sermon.

seropositivo, -a *adj* HIV-positive.

serpiente *f* snake; **s. de cascabel** rattlesnake; **s. pitón** python.

serrín *m* sawdust.

serrucho *m* handsaw.

servicial *adj* helpful.

servicio *m* service; *(retrete)* rest room; **s. a domicilio** delivery service; **s. militar** military service.

servidor, -a **1** *m* server. **2** *mf (criado)* servant.

servilleta *f* napkin.

servilletero *m* serviette ring, napkin ring.

servir [6] **1** *vt* to serve. **2** *vi* to serve; *(valer)* to be suitable; **ya no sirve** it's no use; **¿para qué sirve esto?** what is this (used) for?; **s. de** to serve as. **3 servirse** *vr (comida etc)* to help oneself.

sesenta *adj & m inv* sixty.

sesión *f (reunión)* session; *(pase)* showing.

seso *m* brain.

seta *f (comestible)* mushroom; **s. venenosa** toadstool.

setecientos, -as *adj & mf* seven hundred.

setenta *adj & m inv* seventy.

setiembre *m* September.

seto *m* hedge.

seudónimo *m* pseudonym; *(de escritor)* pen name.

severidad *f* severity; *(rigurosidad)* strictness.

sexo *m* sex; *(órgano)* genitals *pl*.

sexto, -a *adj & mf* sixth.

sexual *adj* sexual; **vida s.** sex life.

si *conj* if; **como si** as if; **si no** if not; **me preguntó si me gustaba** he asked me if *o* whether I liked it.

sí¹ *pron pers (sing) (él)* himself; *(ella)* herself; *(cosa)* itself; *(pl)* themselves; *(uno mismo)* oneself; **por sí mismo** by himself.

sí² *adv* yes; **porque sí** just because; **¡que sí!** yes, I tell you!; **un día sí y otro no** every other day; *(uso enfático)* **sí que me gusta** of course I like it; **¡eso sí que no!** certainly not!

sico- = **psico-**.

sida *m* AIDS.

siderúrgico, -a *adj* iron and steel.

sidra *f* cider.

siempre 1 *adv* always; **como s.** as usual; **a la hora de s.** at the usual time; **para s.** forever. **2** *conj* **s. que** *(cada vez que)* whenever; *(a condición de que)* provided, as long as; **s. y cuando** provided, as long as.

sien *f* temple.

sierra *f* saw; *(montañosa)* mountain range.

siesta *f* siesta; **dormir la s.** to have a siesta.

siete *adj & m inv* seven.

sigilo *m* secrecy.

sigilosamente *adv (secretamente)* secretly.

sigiloso, -a *adj* secretive.

sigla *f* acronym.

siglo *m* century.

significado *m* meaning.

significar [44] *vt* to mean.

significativo, -a *adj* significant; *(expresivo)* meaningful.

signo *m* sign; **s. de interrogación** question mark.

sigo *indic pres de* **seguir**.

siguiente *adj* following, next; **al día s.** the following day.

sílaba *f* syllable.

silbar *vi* to whistle.

silbato *m* whistle.

silbido *m* whistle.

silencio *m* silence.

silencioso, -a *adj (persona)* quiet; *(motor etc)* silent.

silicona *f* silicone.

silla *f* chair; *(de montura)* saddle; **s. de ruedas** wheelchair.

sillín *m* saddle.

sillón *m* armchair.

silueta *f* silhouette; *(de cuerpo)* figure.

silvestre *adj* wild.

símbolo *m* symbol.

simétrico, -a *adj* symmetrical.

simiente *f* seed.

similar *adj* similar.

similitud *f* similarity.

simio *m* monkey.

simpatía *f (de persona, lugar)* charm; **tenerle s. a algn** to like sb.

simpático, -a *adj* nice.

simpatizar [40] *vi* to sympathize (**con** with); *(llevarse bien)* to hit it off (**con** with), to get along well (**con** with).

simple 1 *adj* simple; *(mero)* mere. **2**

m (persona) simpleton.

simulacro *m* sham.

simular *vt* to simulate.

simultanear *vt* to combine; **simultanea el trabajo y los estudios** he's working and studying at the same time.

simultáneo, -a *adj* simultaneous.

sin *prep* without; **cerveza s.** alcohol-free beer; **s. más ni más** without further ado.

sinagoga *f* synagogue.

sinceridad *f* sincerity.

sincero, -a *adj* sincere.

sincronizar [40] *vt* to synchronize.

sindicato *m* labor union.

sinfonía *f* symphony.

singular 1 *adj* singular; *(excepcional)* exceptional; *(raro)* odd. **2** *m (número)* singular; **en s.** in the singular.

siniestro, -a 1 *adj* sinister. **2** *m* disaster.

sino *conj* but; **nadie s. él** no one but him; **no quiero s. que me oigan** I only want them to listen (to me).

sinónimo, -a 1 *adj* synonymous. **2** *m* synonym.

sinsabor *m (usu pl)* trouble, worry.

sintético, -a *adj* synthetic.

sintetizar [40] *vt* to synthesize.

síntoma *m* symptom.

sintonía *f (de programa)* tuning.

sintonizador *m (de radio)* tuning knob.

sintonizar [40] *vt (radio)* to tune in.

sinuoso, -a *adj (camino)* winding.

sinvergüenza 1 *adj (desvergonzado)* shameless; *(descarado)* rude. **2** *mf (desvergonzado)* rogue; *(caradura)* cheeky devil.

siquiera *adv (por lo menos)* at least; **ni s.** not even.

sirena *f* mermaid; *(señal acústica)* siren.

sirviente, -a *mf* servant.

sistema *m* system; **por s.** as a rule; **s. nervioso** nervous system; **s. operativo** operating system.

sitio *m (lugar)* place; *(espacio)* room;

en cualquier s. anywhere; **hacer s.** to make room.

situación *f* situation; *(ubicación)* location.

situar [30] **1** *vt* to locate. **2 situarse** *vr* to be situated.

slogan *m* slogan.

smoking *m* tuxedo.

s/n. *abr de* sin número.

snob *adj & mf* = **esnob**.

sobaco *m* armpit.

soberanía *f* sovereignty.

soberano, -a *adj & mf* sovereign.

soberbia *f* pride.

soberbio, -a *adj* proud; *(magnífico)* splendid.

sobornar *vt* to bribe.

soborno *m (acción)* bribery; *(dinero etc)* bribe.

sobra *f* de s. *(no necesario)* superfluous; **tener de s.** to have plenty; **saber algo de s.** to know sth only too well; **sobras** *(restos)* leftovers.

sobrante **1** *adj* remaining. **2** *m* surplus.

sobrar *vi* to be more than enough; *(quedar)* to be left over; **sobran tres sillas** there are three chairs too many; **ha sobrado carne** there's still some meat left (over).

sobrasada *f* sausage spread.

sobre¹ *m (para carta)* envelope; *(de sopa etc)* packet.

sobre² *prep (encima)* on, on top of; *(por encima)* over, above; *(acerca de)* about, on; *(aproximadamente)* about; **s. todo** above all.

sobrecogedor, -a *adj* awesome.

sobrecoger [53] *vt (conmover)* to shock.

sobredosis *f inv* overdose.

sobreentenderse *vr* **se sobreentiende** that goes without saying.

sobrehumano, -a *adj* superhuman.

sobrellevar *vt* to endure, to bear.

sobrenatural *adj* supernatural.

sobrenombre *m* nickname.

sobrepasar **1** *vt* to exceed. **2**

sobrepasarse *vr* to go too far.

sobreponerse *vr (superar)* to overcome; *(animarse)* to pull oneself together.

sobresaliente **1** *m (nota)* A. **2** *adj (que destaca)* excellent.

sobresalir [22] *vi* to protrude; *fig (destacar)* to stand out.

sobresaltar **1** *vt* to startle. **2 sobresaltarse** *vr* to be startled, to start.

sobresalto *m (movimiento)* start; *(susto)* fright.

sobrevenir [27] *vi* to happen unexpectedly.

sobreviviente **1** *adj* surviving. **2** *mf* survivor.

sobrevivir *vi* to survive.

sobrevolar [2] *vt* to fly over.

sobrina *f* niece.

sobrino *m* nephew.

sobrio, -a *adj* sober.

socarrón, -ona *adj (sarcástico)* sarcastic.

socavón *m (bache)* pothole.

sociable *adj* sociable.

social *adj* social.

socialista *adj & mf* socialist.

sociedad *f* society; *(empresa)* company.

socio, -a *mf (miembro)* member; *(de empresa)* partner; **hacerse s. de un club** to join a club.

sociológico, -a *adj* sociological.

socorrer *vt* to assist.

socorrista *mf* lifeguard.

socorro *m* assistance; **¡s.!** help!; **puesto de s.** first-aid post.

soda *f (bebida)* soda water.

soez *adj* vulgar.

sofá *m (pl sofás)* sofa; **s. cama** sofa bed.

sofisticado, -a *adj* sophisticated.

sofocado, -a *adj* suffocated; **estar s.** to be out of breath; *(preocupado)* to be upset.

sofocante *adj* stifling.

sofocar [44] **1** *vt (ahogar)* to suffocate; *(incendio)* to extinguish. **2 sofocarse** *vr (ahogarse)* to suffocate;

(*irritarse*) to get upset.

sofoco *m fig* (*vergüenza*) embarrassment; **le dio un s.** (*disgusto*) it gave her quite a turn.

sofocón *m fam* shock; **llevarse un s.** to get upset.

soga *f* rope.

soja *f* soybean.

sol *m* sun; (*luz*) sunlight; (*luz y calor*) sunshine; **hace s.** it's sunny; **tomar el s.** to sunbathe; **al** o **bajo el s.** in the sun.

solamente *adv* only; **no s.** not only; **s. que** except that.

solapa *f* (*de chaqueta*) lapel; (*de sobre, bolsillo, libro*) flap.

solar¹ *adj* solar; **luz s.** sunlight.

solar² *m* (*terreno*) plot; (*en obras*) building site.

soldado *m* soldier.

soldar [2] *vt* (*cable*) to solder; (*chapa*) to weld.

soleado, -a *adj* sunny.

soledad *f* (*estado*) solitude; (*sentimiento*) loneliness.

solemne *adj* (*majestuoso*) solemn.

soler [4] *vi defectivo* to be in the habit of; **solemos ir en coche** we usually go by car; **solía pasear por aquí** he used to walk round here.

solicitar *vt* (*información etc*) to request; (*trabajo*) to apply for.

solicitud *f* (*petición*) request; (*de trabajo*) application.

solidaridad *f* solidarity.

sólido, -a *adj* solid.

solitario, -a *adj* (*que está solo*) solitary; (*que se siente solo*) lonely.

sollozar [40] *vi* to sob.

sollozo *m* sob.

solo, -a 1 *adj* only; (*solitario*) lonely; **una sola vez** only once; **se enciende s.** it switches itself on automatically; **a solas** alone, by oneself. **2** *m* (*musical*) solo.

sólo *adv* only; **tan s.** only; **no s.... sino** (**también**) not only... but (also); **con s.,** (**tan**) **s. con** just by.

solomillo *m* sirloin.

soltar [2] **1** *vt* (*desasir*) to let go of; (*prisionero*) to release; (*humo, olor*) to give off; (*carcajada*) to let out; **¡suéltame!** let me go! **2 soltarse** *vr* (*desatarse*) to come loose; (*perro etc*) to get loose; (*desprenderse*) to come off.

soltero, -a 1 *adj* single. **2** *m* (*hombre*) bachelor. **3** *f* (*mujer*) single woman.

solterón, -ona 1 *m* (*hombre*) old bachelor. **2** *f* (*mujer*) old maid.

soltura *f* (*agilidad*) agility; (*seguridad*) confidence, assurance; **habla italiano con s.** he speaks Italian fluently.

soluble *adj* soluble; **café s.** instant coffee.

solución *f* solution.

solucionar *vt* to solve; (*arreglar*) to settle.

solvencia *f* (*financiera*) solvency; (*fiabilidad*) reliability; **fuentes de toda s.** completely reliable sources.

sombra *f* shade; (*silueta proyectada*) shadow; **s. de ojos** eyeshadow.

sombrero *m* (*prenda*) hat; **s. de copa** top hat; **s. hongo** derby hat.

sombrilla *f* sunshade.

sombrío, -a *adj* (*oscuro*) dark; (*tenebroso*) gloomy.

someter 1 *vt* to subject; (*rebeldes*) to put down; **s. a prueba** to put to the test. **2 someterse** *vr* (*subordinarse*) to submit; (*rendirse*) to surrender; **someterse a un tratamiento** to undergo treatment.

somnífero *m* sleeping pill.

somnoliento, -a *adj* sleepy.

sonar [2] **1** *vi* to sound; (*timbre, teléfono*) to ring; **suena bien** it sounds good; **tu nombre/cara me suena** your name/face rings a bell. **2 sonarse** *vr* **sonarse** (**la nariz**) to blow one's nose.

sondeo *m* (*encuesta*) poll.

sonido *m* sound.

sonoro, -a *adj* (*resonante*) resounding; **banda sonora** soundtrack.

sonreír [56] *vi*, **sonreírse** *vr* to smile; **me sonrió** he smiled at me.

sonrisa *f* smile.

sonrojarse *vr* to blush.

sonso, -a *adj Am* foolish, silly.

soñador, -a *mf* dreamer.

soñar [2] *vti* to dream; **s. con** to dream of *o* about.

soñoliento, -a *adj* sleepy.

sopa *f* soup.

sopera *f* soup tureen.

sopesar *vt* to try the weight of; *fig* to weigh up.

soplar 1 *vi (viento)* to blow. **2** *vt (polvo etc)* to blow away; *(para enfriar)* to blow on; *(para apagar)* to blow out; *(para inflar)* to blow up.

soplo *m (acción)* puff; *(de viento)* gust.

soplón, -ona *mf fam (niño)* telltale; *(delator)* informer.

soportable *adj* bearable.

soportar *vt (sostener)* to support; *(tolerar)* to endure; *(aguantar)* to put up with.

soporte *m* support.

sorber *vt (beber)* to sip; *(absorber)* to soak up.

sorbete *m* sorbet.

sorbo *m* sip; *(trago)* gulp.

sórdido, -a *adj* sordid.

sordo, -a 1 *adj (persona)* deaf; *(ruido, dolor)* dull. **2** *mf* deaf person.

sordomudo, -a 1 *adj* deaf and dumb. **2** *mf* deaf and dumb person.

sorprender *vt* to surprise; *(coger desprevenido)* to take by surprise.

sorpresa *f* surprise; **coger por s.** to take by surprise.

sorpresivo, -a *adj Am* unexpected.

sortear *vt* to draw lots for; *(rifar)* to raffle (off).

sorteo *m* draw; *(rifa)* raffle.

sortija *f* ring.

sosegado, -a *adj (tranquilo)* calm, quiet; *(pacífico)* peaceful.

sosegar [1] **1** *vt* to calm. **2 sosegarse** *vr* to calm down.

soso, -a *adj* lacking in salt; *(persona)* dull.

sospecha *f* suspicion.

sospechar 1 *vi (desconfiar)* to suspect; **s. de algn** to suspect sb. **2** *vt (pensar)* to suspect.

sospechoso, -a 1 *adj* suspicious. **2** *mf* suspect.

sostén *m (apoyo)* support; *(prenda)* bra, brassiere.

sostener [24] **1** *vt* to hold; *(sustentar)* to hold up; **s. que...** to maintain that...... **2 sostenerse** *vr (mantenerse)* to support oneself; *(permanecer)* to remain.

sostuve *pt indef de* **sostener**.

sota *f (de baraja)* jack.

sotana *f* cassock.

sótano *m* basement.

soviético, -a *adj & mf* Soviet; **la Unión Soviética** the Soviet Union.

soy *indic pres de* **ser**.

spray *m (pl* **sprays**) spray.

Sr. *abr de* **Señor** Mister, Mr.

Sra. *abr de* **Señora** Mrs, Ms.

Srta. *abr de* **Señorita** Miss.

standard *adj & m* standard.

su *adj pos (de él)* his; *(de ella)* her; *(de usted, ustedes)* your; *(de animales o cosas)* its; *(impersonal)* one's; *(de ellos)* their.

suave *adj* smooth; *(luz, voz etc)* soft; *(templado)* mild.

suavidad *f* smoothness; *(dulzura)* softness; *(de tiempo)* mildness.

suavizante *m (para el pelo)* (hair) conditioner; *(para la ropa)* fabric softener.

suavizar [40] **1** *vt* to smooth (out). **2 suavizarse** *vr (temperatura)* to get milder.

subalterno, -a *adj & mf* subordinate.

subasta *f* auction.

subcampeón, -ona *mf* runner-up.

subconsciente *adj & m* subconscious.

subdesarrollado, -a *adj* underdeveloped.

subdirector, -a *mf* assistant director.

súbdito, -a *mf* subject.

subestimar *vt* to underestimate.

subir 1 *vt* to go up; *(llevar arriba)* to take up, to bring up; *(precio, salario, voz)* to raise; *(volumen)* to turn up. **2** *vi (ir arriba)* to go/come up; *(al autobús, barco etc)* to get on; *(aumentar)* to go up; **s. a** *(un coche)* to get into. **3** **subirse** *vr* to climb up; *(al autobús, avión, tren, bici)* to get on; *(cremallera)* to do up; *(mangas)* to roll up; **subirse a** *(un coche)* to get into.

súbitamente *adv* suddenly.

súbito, -a *adj* sudden.

subjetivo, -a *adj* subjective.

sublevarse *vr* to rebel.

sublime *adj* sublime.

submarinismo *m* skin-diving.

submarino, -a 1 *adj* underwater. **2** *m* submarine.

subnormal 1 *adj* mentally handicapped. **2** *mf* mentally handicapped person.

subordinado, -a *adj & mf* subordinate.

subrayar *vt* to underline; *fig (recalcar)* to stress.

subscribir *(pp* **subscrito)** *vt =* **suscribir.**

subscripción *f* subscription.

subsecretario, -a *mf* undersecretary.

subsidiario, -a *adj* subsidiary.

subsidio *m* allowance; **s. de desempleo** unemployment benefit.

subsistencia *f* subsistence.

subterráneo, -a *adj* underground.

suburbio *m (barrio pobre)* slum; *(barrio periférico)* suburb.

subvención *f* subsidy.

suceder 1 *vi (ocurrir) (uso impers)* to happen; **¿qué sucede?** what's going on?; **s. a** *(seguir)* to follow. **2** **sucederse** *vr* to follow one another.

sucesión *f (serie)* succession.

sucesivamente *adv* **y así s.** and so on.

sucesivo, -a *adj (siguiente)* following; **en lo s.** from now on.

suceso *m (acontecimiento)* event; *(incidente)* incident.

sucesor, -a *mf* successor.

suciedad *f* dirt; *(calidad)* dirtiness.

sucio, -a *adj* dirty.

suculento, -a *adj* succulent.

sucumbir *vi* to succumb.

sucursal *f (de banco etc)* branch.

sudadera *f* sweatshirt.

sudafricano, -a *adj & mf* South African.

sudamericano, -a *adj & mf* South American.

sudar *vti* to sweat.

sudeste *adj & m* southeast.

sudoeste *adj & m* southwest.

sudor *m* sweat.

sudoroso, -a *adj* sweaty.

sueco, -a 1 *adj* Swedish. **2** *mf (persona)* Swede. **3** *m (idioma)* Swedish.

suegra *f* mother-in-law.

suegro *m* father-in-law; **mis suegros** my in-laws.

suela *f* sole.

sueldo *m* wages *pl.*

suelo *m (superficie)* ground; *(de interior)* floor.

suelto, -a 1 *adj* loose; *(en libertad)* free; *(huido)* at large; *(desatado)* undone; **dinero s.** loose change. **2** *m (dinero)* (loose) change.

sueño *m* sleepiness; *(cosa soñada)* dream; **tener s.** to be sleepy.

suerte *f (fortuna)* luck; **por s.** fortunately; **tener s.** to be lucky; **¡que tengas s.!** good luck!

suéter *m* sweater.

suficiente 1 *adj (bastante)* sufficient, enough. **2** *m (nota)* pass.

suficientemente *adv* sufficiently; **no es lo s.** rico como para... he isn't rich enough to....

sufragar [42] **1** *vt (gastos)* to pay, to defray. **2** *vi Am* to vote (**por** for).

sufragio *m (voto)* vote.

sufrido, -a *adj (persona)* long-suffering.

sufrimiento *m* suffering.

sufrir 1 *vi* to suffer. **2** *vt (accidente)* to have; *(dificultades, cambios)* to experience; *(aguantar)* to put up with.

sugerencia *f* suggestion.

sugerir [5] *vt* to suggest.

sugestión *f* suggestion.

suicida 1 *mf (persona)* suicide. **2** *adj* suicidal.

suicidarse *vr* to commit suicide.

suicidio *m* suicide.

suizo, -a 1 *adj* Swiss. **2** *mf (persona)* Swiss. **3** *m (pastel)* eclair.

sujetador *m* bra, brassiere.

sujetar 1 *vt (agarrar)* to hold; *(fijar)* to hold down; *(someter)* to restrain. **2 sujetarse** *vr (agarrarse)* to hold on.

sujeto, -a 1 *m* subject; *(individuo)* fellow. **2** *adj (atado)* secure.

suma *f (cantidad)* sum; *(cálculo)* addition.

sumamente *adv* extremely, highly.

sumar *vt (cantidades)* to add (up).

sumergir [57] **1** *vt* to submerge; *(hundir)* to sink. **2 sumergirse** *vr* to submerge; *(hundirse)* to sink.

sumidero *m* drain.

suministrar *vt* to supply; **s. algo a algn** to supply sb with sth.

suministro *m* supply.

sumiso, -a *adj* submissive.

supe *pt indef de* **saber**.

súper *m (gasolina)* premium; *fam (supermercado)* supermarket.

superar *vt (obstáculo etc)* to overcome; *(prueba)* to pass; *(aventajar)* to surpass.

superdotado, -a 1 *adj* exceptionally gifted. **2** *mf* genius.

superficial *adj* superficial.

superficie *f* surface; *(área)* area.

superfluo, -a *adj* superfluous.

superior 1 *adj (posición)* top, upper; *(cantidad)* greater (**a** than); *(calidad)* superior; *(estudios)* higher. **2** *m (jefe)* superior.

supermercado *m* supermarket.

superponer [19] *vt* to superimpose.

supersónico, -a *adj* supersonic.

supersticioso, -a *adj* superstitious.

supervisar *vt* to supervise.

supervivencia *f* survival.

súpito, -a *adj Am* sudden.

suplantar *vt* to supplant.

suplementario, -a *adj* supplementary.

suplemento *m* supplement.

suplente *adj & mf (sustituto)* substitute, deputy; *(jugador)* substitute.

suplicar [44] *vt* to beg.

suplicio *m (tortura)* torture; *(tormento)* torment.

suplir *vt (reemplazar)* to replace; *(compensar)* to make up for.

suponer [19] *(pp* **supuesto**) *vt* to suppose; *(significar)* to mean; *(implicar)* to entail; **supongo que sí** I suppose so.

supositorio *m* suppository.

supremo, -a *adj* supreme.

suprimir *vt (ley)* to abolish; *(restricción)* to lift; *(palabra)* to delete.

supuesto, -a *adj (asumido)* supposed; *(presunto)* alleged; **¡por s.!** of course!; **dar algo por s.** to take sth for granted.

supuse *pt indef de* **suponer**.

sur *adj & m* south.

suramericano, -a *adj & mf* South American.

surco *m (en tierra)* furrow; *(en disco)* groove.

sureste *adj & m* southeast.

surf(ing) *m* surfing.

surfista *mf* surfer.

surgir [57] *vi (problema, dificultad)* to crop up; *(aparecer)* to arise.

suroeste *adj & m* southwest.

surtido, -a 1 *adj (variado)* assorted. **2** *m* selection.

surtidor *m* spout; **s. de gasolina** gas pump.

surtir *vt* to supply, to provide; **s. efecto** to have the desired effect.

susceptible *adj* susceptible; *(quisquilloso)* touchy; **s. de** *(capaz)* capable of.

suscitar *vt (provocar)* to cause; *(rebelión)* to stir up; *(interés etc)* to arouse.

suscribir (*pp* **suscrito**) **1** *vt* to subscribe to, to endorse; *fml (firmar)* to sign. **2 suscribirse** *vr* to subscribe (**a** to).

suscripción *f* subscription.

suspender 1 *vt (reunión)* to adjourn; *(examen)* to fail; *(colgar)* to hang; **me han suspendido** I've failed (the exam). **2** *vi (en colegio)* **he suspendido** I've failed.

suspense *m* suspense; **novela/película de s.** thriller.

suspensión *f (levantamiento)* hanging (up); *(de coche)* suspension.

suspenso *m (nota)* fail.

suspicacia *f* suspiciousness.

suspicaz *adj* suspicious; *(desconfiado)* distrustful.

suspirar *vi* to sigh.

suspiro *m* sigh.

sustancia *f* substance.

sustantivo *m* noun.

sustento *m (alimento)* sustenance.

sustituir [37] *vt* to substitute.

sustituto, -a *mf* substitute.

susto *m* fright; **llevarse** *o* **darse un s.** to be frightened.

sustraer [25] *vt* to subtract; *(robar)* to steal.

susurrar *vi* to whisper.

sutil *adj (diferencia, pregunta)* subtle; *(aroma)* delicate.

suyo, -a *adj & pron pos (de él)* his; *(de ella)* hers; *(de animal o cosa)* its; *(de usted, ustedes)* yours; *(de ellos, ellas)* theirs.

T

tabaco *m* tobacco; *(cigarrillos)* cigarretes *pl*; **t. rubio** Virginia tobacco.

taberna *f* bar.

tabique *m (pared)* partition (wall).

tabla *f* board; *(de vestido)* pleat; *(de sumar etc)* table; **t. de surf** surfboard; **t. de windsurf** sailboard.

tablero *m (tablón)* panel; *(en juegos)* board; **t. de mandos** *(de coche)* dash(board).

tableta *f (de chocolate)* bar.

tablón *m* plank; *(en construcción)* beam; **t. de anuncios** notice bulletin board.

taburete *m* stool.

tacaño, -a 1 *adj* mean. **2** *mf* miser.

tachar *vt* to cross out.

tacho *m Am* bucket.

taco *m (tarugo)* plug; *(de jamón, queso)* cube; *(palabrota)* swearword.

tacón *m* heel; **zapatos de t.** high-heeled shoes.

táctica *f* tactics *pl.*

táctico, -a *adj* tactical.

tacto *m (sentido)* touch; *(delicadeza)* tact.

tajada *f* slice.

tajante *adj* incisive.

tal 1 *adj (semejante)* such; *(más sustantivo singular contable)* such a; *(indeterminado)* such and such; **en tales condiciones** in such conditions; **nunca dije t. cosa** I never said such a thing; **t. vez** perhaps, maybe; **como si t. cosa** as if nothing had happened. **2** *adv* **t. (y) como** just as; **¿qué t.?** how are things?; **¿qué t. ese vino?** how do you find this wine? **3** *conj* as; **con t. (de) que** + *subj* so long as, provided. **4** *pron (cosa)* something; *(persona)* someone, somebody.

taladrar *vt* to drill; *(pared)* to bore

through; *(papeles)* to punch.

taladro m *(herramienta)* drill.

talante m *(carácter)* disposition; **de mal t.** unwillingly.

talar vt *(madera, piedra)* to fell.

talco m talc; **polvos de t.** talcum powder.

talega f sack.

talento m talent.

Talgo m fast passenger train.

talla f *(de prenda)* size; *(estatura)* height.

tallar vt *(madera, piedra)* to carve; *(piedras preciosas)* to cut; *(metales)* to engrave.

tallarines mpl noodles, tagliatelle sing.

talle m *(cintura)* waist.

taller m *(obrador)* workshop; **t. de reparaciones** *(garaje)* garage.

tallo m stem.

talón m heel; *(cheque)* check.

talonario m *(de cheques)* check book.

tamaño m size; **de gran t.** large; **del t. de** as big as.

tambalearse vr *(persona)* to stagger; *(mesa)* to wobble.

también adv too, also; **yo t.** me too.

tambor m drum.

tampoco adv *(en afirmativas)* nor, neither; *(en negativas)* not either; **no lo sé, yo t.** I don't know, neither o nor do I.

tampón m tampon.

tan adv so; **¡es t. listo!** he's so clever; **¡qué gente t. agradable!** such nice people; **¡qué vestido t. bonito!** such a beautiful dress. ▪ *(consecutivo)* so (that); **iba t. deprisa que no lo ví** he was going so fast that I couldn't see him. ▪ *(comparativo)* **t. ... como** as ... as; **t. alto como tú** as tall as you (are). ▪ **t. sólo** only.

tango m tango.

tanque m tank.

tantear vt *fig* **t. a algn** to sound sb out; **t. el terreno** to see how the land lies. **2** vi to (keep) score.

tanto, -a 1 m *(punto)* point; **un t. para cada uno** so much for each; **t. por ciento** percentage; **estar al t.** *(informado)* to be informed; *(pendiente)* to be on the lookout. **2** adj *(en singular)* so much; **tantos, -as** so many; **t. dinero** so much money; **¡ha pasado t. tiempo!** it's been so long!; **tantas manzanas** so many apples; **cincuenta y tantas personas** fifty odd people; **t. ... como** as much ... as; **tantos, -as... como** as many ... as. **3** pron *(en singular)* so much; **tantos, -as** so many; **otro t.** the same again; **no es o hay para t.** it's not that bad; **otros tantos** as many again; **uno de tantos** run-of-the-mill. **4** adv *(cantidad)* as much; *(tiempo)* so long; *(frecuencia)* so often; **t. mejor/peor** so much the better/worse; **t. ... como** both... and; **t. tú como yo** both you and I; **por lo t.** therefore.

tapa f *(cubierta)* lid; *(de libro)* cover; *(aperitivo)* appetizer.

tapadera f cover.

tapar **1** vt to cover; *(botella etc)* to put the lid on; *(con ropas o mantas)* to wrap up; *(ocultar)* to hide; *(vista)* to block. **2 taparse** vr *(cubrirse)* to cover oneself; *(abrigarse)* to wrap up.

tapete m *(table)* cover.

tapia f wall; *(cerca)* garden wall.

tapizar [40] vt to upholster.

tapón m *(de lavabo etc)* plug; *(de botella)* cap; *(de tráfico)* traffic jam.

taponar **1** vt *(tubería, hueco)* to plug; *(herida)* to tampon. **2 taponarse** vr **se me han taponado los oídos** my ears are blocked up.

taquigrafía f shorthand.

taquilla f ticket office; *(de cine, teatro)* box-office.

tararear vt to hum.

tardar **1** vt **tardé dos horas en venir** it took me two hours to get here. **2** vi *(demorar)* to take long; **no tardes** don't be long; **a más t.** at the latest. **3 tardarse** vr ¿**cuánto se tarda**

en llegar? how long does it take to get there?

tarde 1 f (hasta las cinco) afternoon; (después de las cinco) evening. **2** adv late; **(más) t. o (más) temprano** sooner or later.

tarea f task; **tareas** (de ama de casa) housework sing; (de estudiante) homework sing.

tarifa f (precio) rate; (en transportes) fare; (lista de precios) price list.

tarjeta f card; **t. postal** postcard; **t. de crédito** credit card.

tarro m (vasija) jar; Am (lata) tin.

tarta f tart; (pastel) cake.

tartamudear vi to stutter, to stammer.

tartamudo, -a 1 adj stuttering, stammering. **2** mf stutterer, stammerer.

tartera f lunch box.

tasa f (precio) fee; (impuesto) tax; (índice) rate; **tasas académicas** course fees; **t. de natalidad/mortalidad** birth/death rate.

tasar vt (valorar) to value; (poner precio) to fix the price of.

tasca f bar.

tatarabuelo, -a mf (hombre) great-great-grandfather; (mujer) great-great-grandmother; **tatarabuelos** great-great-grandparents.

tataranieto, -a mf (hombre) great-great-grandson; (mujer) great-great-granddaughter; **tataranietos** great-great-grandchildren.

tatuaje m tattoo.

tatuar [30] vt to tattoo.

taurino, -a adj bullfighting.

taxi m taxi.

taxista mf taxi driver.

taza f cup; **una t. de café** (recipiente) a coffee cup; (contenido) a cup of coffee.

tazón m bowl.

te pron pers **1** (complemento directo) you; (complemento indirecto) (to o for) you; (reflexivo) yourself; **no quiero verte** I don't want to see you;

te compraré uno I'll buy you one; **te lo dije** I told you so; **lávate** wash yourself; **no te vayas** don't go.

té m (pl tés) tea.

teatro m theatre; **obra de t.** play.

tebeo m children's comic.

techo m (de habitación) ceiling; (tejado) roof.

tecla f key.

teclado m keyboard; **t. numérico** numeric keypad.

técnica f (tecnología) technology; (método) technique; (habilidad) skill.

técnico, -a 1 adj technical. **2** mf technician.

tecnología f technology.

tedio m tedium.

teja f tile.

tejado m roof.

tejanos mpl jeans.

tejer vt (en el telar) to weave; (hacer punto) to knit.

tejido m fabric.

tela f cloth; **t. de araña** cobweb; **t. metálica** gauze.

telaraña f spider's web.

tele f fam TV, telly.

telecabina f cable car.

telediario m television news bulletin.

telefax m fax.

teleférico, -a m cable car.

telefilm(e) m TV film.

telefonear vti to telephone, to phone.

teléfono m telephone, phone; **t. portátil** portable telephone; **t. móvil** car phone; **te llamó por t.** she phoned you; **al t.** on the phone.

telegrama m telegram.

telenovela f television serial.

teleobjetivo m telephoto lens.

telescopio m telescope.

telesilla m chair lift.

telespectador, -a mf TV viewer.

telesquí m ski lift.

teletienda f home shopping program.

televidente *mf* TV viewer.

televisión *f* television; **t. digital** digital television; **t. por cable** cable television; **ver la t.** to watch television.

televisivo, -a *adj* television.

televisor *m* television set.

télex *m inv* telex.

telón *m* curtain.

tema *m* subject.

temblar [1] *vi (de frío)* to shiver; *(de miedo)* to tremble (**de** with); *(voz, pulso)* to shake.

temblor *m* tremor; **t. de tierra** earth tremor.

temer 1 *vt* to fear. **2** *vi* to be afraid. **3 temerse** *vr* to fear; **¡me lo temía!** I was afraid this would happen!

temerario, -a *adj* reckless.

temible *adj* fearful, frightful.

temor *m* fear; *(recelo)* worry.

témpano *m* ice block.

temperamento *m* temperament.

temperatura *f* temperature.

tempestad *f* storm.

templado, -a *adj (agua)* lukewarm; *(clima)* mild.

templo *m* temple.

temporada *f* season; *(período)* period; **t. alta** high season; **t. baja** low season.

temporal 1 *adj* temporary. **2** *m* storm.

temprano, -a *adj & adv* early.

tenaz *adj* tenacious.

tenaza *f*, **tenazas** *fpl (herramienta)* pliers.

tendencia *f* tendency.

tender [3] **1** *vt (extender)* to spread out; *(para secar)* to hang out; *(trampa)* to set; *(mano)* to hold out; *Am (cama)* to make; *Am (mesa)* to set, to lay. **2** *vi* **t. a** to tend to. **3 tenderse** *vr* to stretch out.

tendero, -a *mf* shopkeeper.

tendón *m* tendon.

tenebroso, -a *adj (sombrío)* dark; *(siniestro)* sinister.

tenedor *m* fork.

tener [24] **1** *vt* to have, to have got; **va a t. un niño** she's going to have a baby. ■ *(sostener)* to hold; **tenme el bolso un momento** hold my bag a minute. ■ **t. calor/frío** to be hot/cold; **t. cariño a algn** to be fond of sb; **t. miedo** to be frightened. ■ *(edad)* to be; **tiene dieciocho (años)** he's eighteen (years old); ■ *(medida)* **la casa tiene cien metros cuadrados** the house is 100 square meters. ■ *(contener)* to hold. ■ *(mantener)* to keep; **me tuvo despierto toda la noche** he kept me up all night. ■ *(considerar)* to consider; **ten por seguro que lloverá** you can be sure it'll rain. ■ **t. que** to have (got) to; **tengo que...** I have to..., I must.... **2 tenerse** *vr* **tenerse en pie** to stand (up).

tenga *subj pres de* **tener.**

tengo *indic pres de* **tener.**

teniente *mf* lieutenant.

tenis *m* tennis.

tenista *mf* tennis player.

tenor *m* tenor.

tensión *f* tension; *(eléctrica)* voltage; **t. arterial** blood pressure.

tenso, -a *adj (cuerda, cable)* taut; *(persona, relaciones)* tense.

tentación *f* temptation.

tentar [1] *vt (incitar)* to tempt; *(atraer)* to attract.

tentativa *f* attempt.

tentempié *m (pl* tentempiés*) (comida)* snack; *(juguete)* tumbler.

tenue *adj (luz, sonido)* faint.

teñir [6] **1** *vt (pelo etc)* to dye. **2 teñirse** *vr* **teñirse el pelo** to dye one's hair.

teoría *f* theory; **en t.** theoretically.

terapia *f* therapy.

tercer *adj* third; **el t. mundo** the third world.

tercero, -a *adj & mf* third.

tercio *m (one) third; (cerveza)* medium-sized bottle of beer.

terciopelo *m* velvet.

terco *adj* stubborn.

tergiversar *vt* to distort; *(declaraciones)* to twist.

terminal 1 *adj* terminal. **2** *f* terminal; *(de autobús)* terminal. **3** *m (de ordenador)* terminal.

terminar 1 *vt* to finish. **2** *vi (acabarse)* to finish; *(ir a parar)* to end up (en in); **terminó por comprarlo** he ended up buying it. **3 terminarse** *vr* to finish; *(vino, comida)* to run out.

término *m (final)* end; *(palabra)* term; **en términos generales** generally speaking; **por t. medio** on average.

termo *m* thermos (flask).

termómetro *m* thermometer.

termostato *m* thermostat.

ternera *f* calf; *(carne)* veal.

ternura *f* tenderness.

terraplén *m* embankment.

terremoto *m* earthquake.

terreno *m (tierra)* land; *(campo)* field; *(deportivo)* ground; *(ámbito)* field.

terrestre *adj (de la tierra)* terrestrial; *(transporte, ruta)* by land.

terrible *adj* terrible.

territorio *m* territory.

terrón *m (de azúcar)* lump.

terror *m* terror; **película de t.** horror film.

terrorismo *m* terrorism.

terrorista *adj & mf* terrorist.

terso, -a *adj (liso)* smooth.

tertulia *f* get-together.

tesis *f inv* thesis; *(opinión)* point of view.

tesoro *m* treasure.

test *m* test.

testamento *m* will; **hacer t.** to make one's will.

testarudo, -a *adj* obstinate.

testificar [44] *vi* to testify.

testigo *mf* witness.

testimonio *m* testimony; *(prueba)* evidence.

tétano *m* tetanus.

tetera *f* teapot.

tetina *f* (rubber) teat.

texto *m* text; **libro de t.** textbook.

tez *f* complexion.

ti *pron pers* you; **es para ti** it's for you; **piensas demasiado en ti mismo** you think too much about yourself.

tía *f* aunt; *fam (mujer)* woman.

tibio, -a *adj* tepid.

tiburón *m* shark.

tic *m (pl* tics*)* twitch; **t. nervioso** nervous twitch.

tiempo *m* time; *(meteorológico)* weather; *(de partido)* half; *(verbal)* tense; **a t.** in time; **a su (debido) t.** in due course; **al mismo t.** at the same time; **al poco t.** soon afterwards; **con t.** in advance; **¿cuánto t.?** how long?; **¿cuánto t. hace?** how long ago?; **estar a t. de** to still have time to; **¿nos da t. de llegar?** have we got (enough) time to get there?; **t. libre** free time; **¿qué t. hace?** what's the weather like?; **hace buen/mal t.** the weather is good/bad.

tienda *f* store; **ir de tiendas** to go shopping; **t. (de campaña)** tent.

tienta *f* a tientas by touch; **andar a tientas** to feel one's way; **buscar (algo) a tientas** to grope (for sth).

tierno, -a *adj* tender; *(reciente)* fresh.

tierra *f* land; *(planeta)* earth; *(suelo)* ground; **tocar t.** to land.

tieso, -a *adj (rígido)* stiff; *(erguido)* upright.

tiesto *m* flowerpot.

tifus *m inv* typhus (fever).

tigre *m* tiger; *Am* jaguar.

tijeras *fpl* pair of scissors *sing*, scissors.

tila *f* lime tea.

timar *vt* to swindle.

timbre *m (de puerta)* bell; *(sonido)* timbre.

timidez *f* shyness.

tímido, -a *adj* shy.

timo *m* swindle.

timón *m (de barco, avión)* rudder; *(de coche)* steering wheel.

tímpano *m* eardrum.

tinieblas *fpl* darkness *sing.*

tino *m* (puntería) **tener buen t.** to be a good shot.

tinta *f* ink; **t. china** Indian ink.

tinte *m* dye.

tintero *m* inkwell.

tintinear *vi* (vidrio) to clink; (campana) to tinkle.

tinto 1 *adj* (vino) red. **2** *m* (vino) red.

tintorería *f* dry-cleaner's.

tío *m* uncle; *fam* guy; **mis tíos** (tío y tía) my uncle and aunt.

tiovivo *m* merry-go-round.

típico, -a *adj* typical; (baile, traje) traditional.

tipo *m* (clase) type, kind; *fam* (persona) guy; (figura) (de hombre) build; (de mujer) figure; **jugarse el t.** to risk one's neck; **t. bancario** *o* **de descuento** bank rate; **t. de cambio/interés** exchange/interest rate.

tira *f* strip.

tirabuzón *m* ringlet.

tirachinas *m inv* slingshot.

tirada *f* printrun.

tiranía *f* tyranny.

tirante 1 *adj* (cable etc) taut. **2** *m* (de vestido etc) strap; **tirantes** suspenders.

tirar 1 *vt* (echar) to throw, to fling; (dejar caer) to drop; (desechar) to throw away; (derribar) to knock down. **2** *vi* **t. de** (cuerda, puerta) to pull; (disparar) to shoot; **ir tirando** to get by; **tira a la izquierda** turn left. **3 tirarse** *vr* (lanzarse) to throw oneself; (tumbarse) to lie down; **tirarse de cabeza al agua** to dive into the water.

tirita® *f* Band-Aid®.

tiritar *vi* to shiver.

tiro *m* (lanzamiento) throw; (disparo, ruido) shot; (de chimenea) draft; **t. al blanco** target shooting; **t. al plato** clay pigeon shooting.

tirón *m* pull; (de bolso) snatch; *fam* **de un t.** in one go.

tiroteo *m* shooting.

titubear *vi* (dudar) to hesitate.

titulado, -a *adj* (licenciado) graduate; (diplomado) qualified.

titular¹ 1 *mf* (persona) holder. **2** *m* (periódico) headline.

titular² 1 *vt* (poner título) to call. **2 titularse** *vr* (película etc) to be called.

título *m* title; (diploma) diploma; (titular) headline.

tiza *f* chalk.

tiznar *vt* to blacken (with soot).

toalla *f* towel.

toallero *m* towel rail.

tobillo *m* ankle.

tobogán *m* slide; (en piscina) chute.

tocadiscos *m inv* record player.

tocador *m* (mueble) dressing table; (habitación) dressing room.

tocar [44] **1** *vt* to touch; (instrumento, canción) to play; (timbre, campana) to ring; (bocina) to blow; (tema, asunto) to touch on. **2** *vi* (entrar en contacto) to touch; **¿a quién le toca?** (en juegos) whose turn is it?; **me tocó el gordo** (en rifa) I won the jackpot. **3 tocarse** *vr* (una cosa con otra) to touch each other.

tocino *m* lard; **t. de cielo** sweet made with egg yolk.

tocólogo, -a *m* obstetrician.

todavía *adv* (aún) still; (en negativas) yet; (para reforzar) even, still; **t. la quiere** he still loves her; **t. no** not yet; **t. más/menos** even more/less.

todo, -a 1 *adj* all; (cada) every; **t. el mundo** everybody; **t. el día** all day, the whole day; **t. ciudadano de más de dieciocho años** every citizen over eighteen years of age; **todos, -as** all; **t. los niños** all the children; **t. los martes** every Tuesday. **2** *pron* all, everything; **t. aquél** *o* **el que quiera** anybody who wants (to); **todos, -as** all of them; **hablé con todos** I spoke to everybody; **todos aprobamos** we all passed; **ante t.** first of all; **del t.** completely; **después de t.** after all;

eso es t. that's all; **hay de t.** there are all sorts; **lo sé t.** I know all about it; **t. lo contrario** quite the opposite; **t. lo más** at the most. **3** *adv* completely; **t. sucio** all dirty.

toldo *m (cubierta)* awning; *(en la playa)* sunshade; *Am (cabaña)* tent.

tolerante *adj* tolerant.

tolerar *vt* to tolerate.

toma *f (acción)* taking; **t. de corriente** socket.

tomado, -a *adj Am (borracho)* drunk.

tomar 1 *vt* to take; *(comer, beber)* to have; **toma** here (you are); **t. el sol** to sunbathe; **t. en serio/broma** to take seriously/as a joke. **2 tomarse** *vr (comer)* to eat; *(beber)* to drink; **no te lo tomes así** don't take it like that.

tomate *m* tomato; **salsa de t.** *(de lata)* tomato sauce; *(de botella)* ketchup.

tómbola *f* tombola.

tomo *m* volume.

tonel *m* cask.

tonelada *f* ton; **t. métrica** tonne.

tónico, -a 1 *m* tonic. **2** *f (bebida)* tonic (water); **tónica general** overall trend.

tono *m* tone; **un t. alto/bajo** a high/low pitch.

tontería *f* silliness; *(dicho, hecho)* silly thing; *(insignificancia)* trifle.

tonto, -a 1 *adj* silly. **2** *mf* fool.

topacio *m* topaz.

toparse *vr* **t. con** to bump into; *(dificultades)* to run up against.

tope *m (límite)* limit; **estar hasta los topes** to be full up; **fecha t.** deadline.

tópico *m* cliché.

topo *m (animal)* mole; *(espía)* spy, inside informer.

topónimo *m* place name.

torbellino *m (de viento)* whirlwind.

torcer [41] **1** *vt (tobillo)* to sprain; *(esquina)* to turn; *(inclinar)* to slant. **2** *vi* to turn. **3 torcerse** *vr (doblarse)* to twist; *(tobillo, mano)* to sprain; *(desviarse)* to go off to the side.

torear *vi* to fight.

torero, -a *mf* bullfighter.

tormenta *f* storm.

tormento *m (tortura)* torture; *(padecimiento)* torment.

tornillo *m* screw.

torno *m (de alfarero)* wheel; **en t. a** around.

toro *m* bull; **¿te gustan los toros?** do you like bullfighting?

toronja *f* grapefruit.

torpe *adj (sin habilidad)* clumsy; *(tonto)* thick; *(movimiento)* slow.

torre *f* tower; *(en ajedrez)* rook.

torrente *m* torrent.

tórrido, -a *adj* torrid.

torso *m* torso.

torta *f (pastel)* cake; *(golpe)* slap.

tortazo *m (bofetada)* slap.

tortícolis *f inv* crick in the neck.

tortilla *f* omelet; *Am* tortilla; **t. francesa/española** (plain)/potato omelet.

tortuga *f* turtle.

tortuoso, -a *adj* tortuous.

tortura *f* torture.

tos *f* cough; **t. ferina** whooping cough.

tosco, -a *adj (basto)* rough; *(persona)* uncouth.

toser *vi* to cough.

tostada *f* **una t.** some toast, a slice of toast.

tostador *m* toaster.

tostar [2] *vt (pan)* to toast; *(café)* to roast.

total 1 *adj* total. **2** *m (todo)* whole; *(cantidad)* total; **en t.** in all. **3** *adv* anyway; *(para resumir)* in short.

totalidad *f* whole; **la t. de** all of; **en su t.** as a whole.

tóxico, -a 1 *adj* toxic. **2** *m* poison.

toxicómano, -a 1 *adj* addicted to drugs. **2** *mf* drug addict.

tozudo, -a *adj* stubborn.

traba *f (obstáculo)* hindrance.

trabajador, -a 1 *mf* worker. **2** *adj* hard-working.

trabajar 1 *vi* to work; **t. de camarera**

to work as a waitress. **2** *vt* to work (on).

trabajo *m* work; *(esfuerzo)* effort; **un t.** a job; **t. eventual** casual labor; **trabajos manuales** arts and crafts.

trabalenguas *m inv* tongue twister.

trabar 1 *vt (conversación, amistad)* to start. **2 trabarse** *vr* **se le trabó la lengua** he got tongue-tied.

tractor *m* tractor.

tradición *f* tradition.

tradicional *adj* traditional.

traducción *f* translation.

traducir [10] **1** *vt* to translate (**a** into). **2 traducirse** *vr* to result (**en** in).

traductor, -a *mf* translator.

traer [25] **1** *vt* to bring; *(llevar consigo)* to carry; *(problemas)* to cause; *(noticia)* to feature; **trae** give it to me. **2 traerse** *vr (llevar consigo)* to bring along.

traficante *mf (de drogas etc)* trafficker.

traficar [44] *vi (ilegalmente)* to traffic (**con** in).

tráfico *m* traffic; **t. de drogas** drug traffic.

tragaperras *f inv (máquina)* **t.** slot machine.

tragar [42] *vt,* **tragarse** *vr* to swallow.

tragedia *f* tragedy.

trágico, -a *adj* tragic.

trago *m (bebida)* swig; **de un t.** in one go; **pasar un mal t.** to have a bad time.

traición *f* betrayal.

traicionar *vt* to betray.

traidor, -a 1 *adj* treacherous. **2** *mf* traitor.

traigo *indic pres de* **traer.**

traje¹ *m (de hombre)* suit; *(de mujer)* dress; **t. de baño** swimsuit; **t. de chaqueta** two-piece suit; **t. de novia** wedding dress.

traje² *pt indef de* **traer.**

trama *f* plot.

tramar *vt* to plot.

trámite *m (paso)* step; *(formalidad)* formality.

tramo *m (de carretera)* stretch; *(de escalera)* flight.

trampa *f (de caza)* trap; *(engaño)* fiddle; **hacer trampa(s)** to cheat.

trampilla *f* trap door.

trampolín *m* springboard.

tramposo, -a 1 *adj* deceitful. **2** *mf* cheat.

tranquilizante *m* tranquillizer.

tranquilizar [40] **1** *vt* to calm down; **lo dijo para tranquilizarme** he said it to reassure me. **2 tranquilizarse** *vr (calmarse)* to calm down.

tranquilo, -a *adj (persona, lugar)* calm; *(agua)* still; *(conciencia)* clear; *(despreocupado)* placid, easy-going; *fam* **tú t.** don't you worry.

transatlántico, -a 1 *m* (ocean) liner. **2** *adj* transatlantic.

transbordador *m* (car) ferry; **t. espacial** space shuttle.

transbordo *m (de trenes)* **hacer t.** to change.

transcurrir *vi (tiempo)* to pass, to go by; *(acontecer)* to take place.

transcurso *m* **en el t. de** in the course of.

transeúnte *mf (peatón)* passer-by.

transferencia *f* transference; *(de dinero)* transfer; **t. bancaria** bank transfer.

transferir [5] *vt* to transfer.

transformación *f* transformation.

transformador *m* transformer.

transformar 1 *vt* to transform. **2 transformarse** *vr* to turn (**en** into).

transfusión *f* transfusion.

transición *f* transition.

transistor *m* transistor.

transitado, -a *adj (carretera)* busy.

transitivo, -a *adj* transitive.

tránsito *m (tráfico)* traffic; *(movimiento)* passage; **pasajeros en t.** passengers in transit.

transitorio, -a *adj* transitory.

transmisión *f* transmission; *(emisión)* broadcast.

transmisor *m* transmitter.

transmitir *vt* to pass on; *(emitir)* to transmit.

transparentarse *vr* to be transparent; **se le transparentaban las bragas** you could see her panties.

transparente *adj* transparent.

transpiración *f* perspiration.

transplante *m* transplant.

transportar *vt* to transport; *(pasajeros)* to carry; *(mercancías)* to ship.

transporte *m* transport.

transversal *adj* cross.

tranvía *m* streetcar.

trapo *m (viejo, roto)* rag; *(bayeta)* cloth; **t. de cocina** dishcloth; **t. del polvo** duster.

tráquea *f* trachea.

tras *prep (después de)* after; *(detrás)* behind.

trascendencia *f (importancia)* significance.

trascendental, trascendente *adj* significant.

trascurrir *vi* = **transcurrir**.

trasero, -a 1 *adj* back, rear; **en la parte trasera** at the back. **2** *m fam* bottom.

trasladar 1 *vt (cosa)* to move; *(trabajador)* to transfer. **2 trasladarse** *vr* to move.

traslado *m (de casa)* move; *(de personal)* transfer.

trasmano: a trasmano *adv* out of reach; **(me) coge a t.** it's out of my way.

trasnochar *vi* to stay up (very) late.

traspapelarse *vr* to get mislaid o misplaced.

trasparentarse *vr* = **transparentarse**.

traspasar *vt (atravesar)* to go through; *(río)* to cross; *(negocio, local)* to transfer; **'se traspasa'** 'for sale'.

traspié *m (pl traspiés)* stumble; **dar un t.** to trip.

trastero *m (cuarto)* **t.** junk room.

trastienda *f* back room.

trasto *m* thing; *(cosa inservible)* piece of junk.

trastocar [44] *vt* = **trastornar**.

trastornado, -a *adj (loco)* mad, unhinged.

trastornar 1 *vt (planes)* to disrupt; *fig (persona)* to unhinge. **2 trastornarse** *vr (enloquecer)* to go mad.

trastorno *m (molestia)* trouble; **t. mental** mental disorder.

tratado *m (pacto)* treaty; *(estudio)* treatise.

tratamiento *m* treatment; *(de textos etc)* processing.

tratar 1 *vt* to treat; *(asunto)* to discuss; *(manejar)* to handle; *(textos etc)* to process; **me trata de 'tú'** he calls me 'tu'. **2** *vi* **t. de** *(intentar)* to try to; **t. de** o **sobre** o **acerca** to be about. **3 tratarse** *vr (relacionarse)* to be on speaking terms; **se trata de** *(es cuestión de)* it's a question of; *(es)* it is.

tratativas *fpl CSur* negotiation.

trato *m (contacto)* contact; *(acuerdo)* agreement; *(comercial)* deal; **malos tratos** ill-treatment *sing*; **¡t. hecho!** it's a deal!

traumático, -a *adj* traumatic.

través *prep* **a t. de** *(superficie)* across, over; *(agujero etc)* through; *(por medio de)* through; **a t. del periódico** through the newspaper. **2** *adv* **de t.** *(transversalmente)* crosswise; *(de lado)* sideways.

travesaño *m* crosspiece; *(en fútbol)* crossbar.

travesía *f (viaje)* crossing.

travestí, travestí *mf* transvestite.

travesura *f* mischief.

travieso, -a *adj* mischievous.

trayecto *m (distancia)* distance; *(recorrido)* route; *(viaje)* journey.

trazar [40] *vt (línea)* to draw; *(plano)* to design.

trébol *m* trefoil; *(en naipes)* club.

trece *adj & m inv* thirteen.

trecho *m (distancia)* distance; *(tramo)* stretch.

tregua *f* truce.

treinta *adj & m inv* thirty.

tremendo, -a *adj (terrible)* terrible; *(muy grande)* enormous; *(excelente)* tremendous.

tren *m* train.

trenca *f (prenda)* duffle coat.

trenza *f (de pelo)* braid.

trepar *vt* to climb.

tres *adj & m inv* three; **t. en raya** tick-tack-toe.

trescientos, -as *adj & mf* three hundred.

tresillo *m* three-piece suite.

treta *f* ruse.

triángulo *m* triangle; *fig* **t. amoroso** love triangle.

tribu *f* tribe.

tribuna *f (plataforma)* dais; *(en estadio)* stand.

tribunal *m* court; *(de examen)* board of examiners; **T. Supremo** Supreme Court.

tributo *m* tribute; *(finanzas)* tax.

triciclo *m* tricycle.

trienio *m* three-year period.

trigésimo, -a *adj & mf* thirtieth; **t. primero** thirty-first.

trigo *m* wheat.

trimestral *adj* quarterly.

trimestre *m* quarter; *(escolar)* term.

trinchar *vt (carne)* to carve.

trinchera *f* trench.

trineo *m* sledge; *(grande)* sleigh.

tripa *f (intestino)* gut; *fam* tummy; **dolor de t.** stomachache.

triple *adj & m* triple.

triplicar [44] *vt* to triple, to treble.

trípode *m* tripod.

tripulación *f* crew.

tripulante *mf* crew member.

tripular *vt* to man.

triquiñuela *f* dodge.

triste *adj (infeliz)* sad; *(sombrío)* gloomy.

tristeza *f* sadness.

triturar *vt* to grind (up).

triunfador, -a 1 *adj* winning. **2** *mf* winner.

triunfar *vi* to triumph.

triunfo *m (victoria)* triumph; *(deportiva)* win; *(éxito)* success.

trivial *adj* trivial.

triza *f* **hacer trizas** to tear to shreds.

trocar [64] *vt* to transform, to turn (en into).

trocear *vt* to cut up (into pieces).

trofeo *m* trophy.

tromba *f* **t. de agua** violent downpour.

trombón *m* trombone.

trompa *f (instrumento)* horn; *(de elefante)* trunk; *fam* **estar t.** to be sloshed.

trompeta *f* trumpet.

tronchar **1** *vt (rama, tronco)* to cut down. **2 troncharse** *vr* **troncharse de risa** to split one's sides laughing.

tronco *m (torso, de árbol)* trunk; *(leño)* log.

trono *m* throne.

tropa *f* **tropas** troops.

tropel *m* **en t.** in a mad rush.

tropezar [1] *vi (tropicar)* to stumble (con on); **t. con algn/dificultades** to run into sb/difficulties.

tropezón *m (traspié)* stumble; **dar un t.** to trip.

tropical *adj* tropical.

trópico *m* tropics *pl.*

tropiezo¹ *m (obstáculo)* trip.

tropiezo² *indic pres de* **tropezar**.

trotar *vi* to trot.

trote *m* trot; **al t.** at a trot.

trozo *m* piece.

trucha *f* trout.

truco *m (ardid)* trick; *(manera de hacer algo)* knack; **coger el t. (a algo)** to get the knack o hang (of sth).

trueno *m* thunder; **un t.** a thunderclap.

trufa *f* truffle.

tu *adj pos* your; **tu libro** your book; **tus libros** your books.

tú *pron pers* you.

tubería *f (de agua)* pipes *pl;* *(de gas, petróleo)* pipeline.

tubo *m* tube; *(tubería)* pipe; **t. de**

ensayo test tube; **t. de escape** exhaust (pipe).

tuerca *f* nut.

tuerto, -a 1 *adj* blind in one eye. **2** *mf* person who is blind in one eye.

tuerzo *indic pres de* **torcer**.

tulipán *m* tulip.

tullido, -a *adj* crippled.

tumba *f* grave.

tumbar 1 *vt* to knock down. **2 tumbarse** *vr* (*acostarse*) to lie down.

tumbona *f* easy chair; (*de lona*) deckchair.

tumor *m* tumor.

tumulto *m* commotion.

túnel *m* tunnel; **el t. del Canal de la Mancha** the Channel Tunnel.

túnica *f* tunic.

tupé *m* (*pl* **tupés**) (*flequillo*) fringe.

tupido, -a *adj* thick.

turba *f* (*combustible*) peat.

turbado, -a *adj* (*alterado*) disturbed; (*desconcertado*) confused.

turbar 1 *vt* (*alterar*) to unsettle; (*desconcertar*) to baffle. **2 turbarse** *vr* (*preocuparse*) to become upset; (*desconcertarse*) to become confused.

turbio, -a *adj* (*agua*) cloudy; (*negocio etc*) dubious.

turbulencia *f* turbulence.

turco, -a 1 *adj* Turkish. **2** *mf* (*persona*) Turk; *fig* **cabeza de t.** scapegoat. **3** *m* (*idioma*) Turkish.

turismo *m* tourism; (*coche*) car; **ir de t.** to go touring.

turista *mf* tourist.

turístico, -a *adj* tourist; **de interés t.** of interest to tourists.

turnarse *vr* to take turns.

turno *m* (*en juegos etc*) turn; (*de trabajo*) shift; **t. de día/noche** day/night shift.

turquesa *adj & f* turquoise.

turrón *m* nougat.

tutear 1 *vt* to address as 'tú'. **2 tutearse** *vr* to call (each other) 'tú'.

tutela *f* guidance.

tutor, -a *mf* (*de huérfano*) guardian; (*de estudiante*) tutor.

tuve *pt indef de* **tener**.

tuyo, -a 1 *adj pos* (*con personas*) of yours; (*con objetos*) one of your; **¿es amigo t.?** is he a friend of yours?; **un libro t.** one of your books. **2** *pron pos* yours.

U

u *conj* (*before words beginning with* o *or* ho) or.

ubicación *f* location.

ubicar [44] **1** *vt* (*situar*) to locate. **2 ubicarse** *vr* (*en un lugar*) to be located.

Ud. *abr de* **usted** you.

Uds. *abr de* **ustedes** you.

UE *f abr de* **Unión Europea** European Union, EU.

úlcera *f* ulcer.

últimamente *adv* recently.

ultimar *vt* (*terminar*) to finalize; (*matar*) to finish off.

ultimátum *m* (*pl* **ultimátums**) ultimatum.

último, -a *adj* last; (*más reciente*) latest; (*más alto*) top; (*más bajo*) lowest; (*definitivo*) final; (*más lejano*) back; **por ú.** finally; **a. últimos de mes** at the end of the month; **últimas noticias** latest news; **el u. piso** the top apartment; **el u. de la lista** the lowest on the list; **la última fila** the back row.

ultraderecha *f* extreme right.

ultramarinos *mpl* groceries; **tienda de u.** greengrocer.

ultrasónico, -a *adj* ultrasonic.

ultravioleta *adj inv* ultraviolet.

ulular *vi* (*viento*) to howl; (*búho*) to hoot.

umbral *m* threshold.

un, -a 1 *art indef* a, (*antes de vocal*) an; **unos, -as** some. **2** *adj* (*delante de* *m sing)* one; **un chico y dos chicas** one boy and two girls.

unánime *adj* unanimous.

unanimidad *f* unanimity; **por u.** unanimously.

undécimo, -a *adj* eleventh.

únicamente *adv* only.

único, -a *adj (solo)* only; *(extraordinario)* unique; **hijo ú.** only child; **lo ú. que quiero** the only thing I want.

unidad *f* unit; *(cohesión)* unity; **u. de disquete** disk drive.

unido, -a *adj* united; **están muy unidos** they are very attached to one another; **una familia muy unida** a very close family.

unificación *f* unification.

uniforme 1 *m (prenda)* uniform. **2** *adj* uniform; *(superficie)* even.

unilateral *adj* unilateral.

unión *f* union.

unir *vt*, **unirse** *vr* to unite.

unísono *m* **al u.** in unison.

universal *adj* universal.

universidad *f* university.

universitario, -a 1 *adj* university. **2** *mf* university student.

universo *m* universe.

uno, -a 1 *m inv* one; **el u. de mayo** the first of May. **2** *f (hora)* **es la una** it's one o'clock. **3** *adj* **unos, -as** some; **unas cajas** some boxes; **debe haber unos/unas veinte** there must be around twenty. **4** *pron* one; *(persona)* someone, somebody; *(impers)* you, one; **u. (de ellos), una (de ellas)** one of them; **unos cuantos** a few; **se miraron el u. al otro** they looked at each other; **de u. en u.** one by one; **u. tras otro** one after the other; **vive con u.** she's living with some man; **u. tiene que...** you have to....

untar *vt* to smear; *(mantequilla)* to spread.

uña *f* nail; **morderse** *o* **comerse las uñas** to bite one's nails.

uperizado, -a *adj* **leche uperizada** UHT milk.

urbanismo *m* town planning.

urbanización *f (barrio)* housing estate; *(proceso)* urbanization.

urbano, -a *adj* urban.

urbe *f* large city.

urgencia *f* urgency; *(emergencia)* emergency.

urgente *adj* urgent; **correo u.** express mail.

urgir [57] *vi* to be urgent.

urna *f (para votos)* ballot box.

urraca *f* magpie.

uruguayo, -a *adj & mf* Uruguayan.

usado, -a *adj (ropa)* second-hand.

usar 1 *vt* to use; *(prenda)* to wear. **2 usarse** *vr* to be used.

usina *f Am (central eléctrica)* power station.

uso *m* use; **u. externo** for external use only; **u. tópico** local application; **haga u. del casco** wear a helmet.

usted *(pl* ustedes*)* *pron pers* you; **¿quién es u.?, ¿quiénes son ustedes?** who are you?

usual *adj* usual.

usuario, -a *mf* user.

utensilio *m* utensil; *(herramienta)* tool.

útil *adj* useful; *(día)* working.

utilidad *f* utility; **tener u.** to be useful.

utilitario, -a 1 *m (coche)* utility vehicle. **2** *adj* utilitarian.

utilización *f* use.

utilizar [40] *vt* to use.

utópico, -a *adj & mf* utopian.

uva *f* grape; **u. blanca** green grape.

UVI *f abr de* **unidad de vigilancia intensiva** intensive care unit.

V

vaca *f* cow; *(carne)* beef.

vacaciones *fpl* vacation; *(viaje)* holiday; **estar/irse de v.** to be/go on holiday.

vacante 1 *adj* vacant. **2** *f* vacancy.

vaciar [29] *vt*, **vaciarse** *vr* to empty.

vacilar *vi (dudar)* to hesitate; *(voz)* to falter; **sin v.** without hesitation.

vacío, -a 1 *adj* empty; *(hueco)* hollow; *(sin ocupar)* vacant. **2** *m* void; *(hueco)* gap; *(espacio)* (empty) space.

vacuna *f* vaccine.

vacunación *f* vaccination.

vacunar 1 *vt* to vaccinate (**contra** against); *fig* to inure. **2 vacunarse** *vr* to get oneself vaccinated.

vacuno, -a *adj* bovine; **ganado v.** cattle.

vado *m (de un río)* ford; **v. permanente** keep clear.

vagabundo, -a 1 *adj (errante)* wandering. **2** *mf* wanderer; *(sin casa)* hobo.

vagar [42] *vi* to wander about.

vago, -a 1 *adj (perezoso)* lazy; *(indefinido)* vague. **2** *mf (holgazán)* layabout.

vagón *m (para pasajeros)* car; *(para mercancías)* freight car.

vaho *m (de aliento)* breath; *(vapor)* vapor.

vaina *f (de guisante etc)* pod; *Am (molestia)* nuisance.

vainilla *f* vanilla.

vajilla *f* dishes *pl*.

valdré *indic fut de* **valer**.

vale¹ *interj* all right, OK.

vale² *m (comprobante)* voucher; *(pagaré)* IOU (I owe you).

valer [26] **1** *vt* to be worth; *(costar)* to cost; **no vale nada** it is worthless; **no vale la pena (ir)** it's not worthwhile

(going); **¿cuánto vale?** how much is it? **2** *vi (servir)* to be useful; *(ser válido)* to count; **más vale** it is better; **más vale que te vayas ya** you had better leave now. **3 valerse** *vr* **valerse por sí mismo** to be able to manage on one's own.

valgo *indic pres de* **valer**.

válido, -a *adj* valid.

valiente *adj (valeroso)* brave.

valioso, -a *adj* valuable.

valla *f (cerca)* fence; *(muro)* wall; **v. publicitaria** billboard.

valle *m* valley.

valor *m* value; *(precio)* price; *(valentía)* courage; **objetos de v.** valuables; **sin v.** worthless.

valoración *f* appraisal.

valorar *vt* to value.

vals *m* waltz.

válvula *f* valve; **v. de seguridad** safety valve.

vampiro *m* vampire.

vandalismo *m* vandalism.

vanguardia *f* vanguard; *(artística)* avant-garde.

vanidad *f* vanity.

vanidoso, -a *adj* conceited.

vano, -a *adj (vanidoso)* vain; *(esfuerzo, esperanza)* futile; **en v.** in vain.

vapor *m (de agua hirviendo)* steam; *(gas)* vapor; **al v.** steamed; **v. de agua** water vapor.

vaporizador *m* vaporizer.

vaquero, -a 1 *m* cowboy. **2** *adj* **pantalón v.** jeans *pl*. **3** *mpl* **vaqueros** *(prenda)* jeans.

vara *f* rod.

variable *adj & f* variable.

variado, -a *adj* varied.

variante *f (carretera)* detour.

variar [29] *vti* to vary; *(con ironía)* **para v.** just for a change.

varicela *f* chickenpox.

variedad *f* variety; *(espectáculo)* **variedades** variety show.

varilla *f (vara)* rod; *(de abanico, paraguas)* rib.

varios, -as adj several.

variz f varicose vein.

varón m (hombre) man; (chico) boy.

vas indic pres de **ir**.

vascuence m (idioma) Basque.

vaselina f Vaseline®.

vasija f pot.

vaso m (para beber) glass.

vaticinar vt to predict.

vatio m watt.

vaya¹ interj ¡v. lío! what a mess!

vaya² subj pres de **ir**.

Vd., Vds. abr de usted, ustedes you.

ve 1 imperativo de **ir**. **2** indic pres de **ver**.

vecindad f, **vecindario** m (área) neighborhood; (vecinos) residents pl.

vecino, -a 1 m f (persona) neighbor; (residente) resident. **2** adj neighboring.

vega f fertile plain.

vegetación f vegetation; (en nariz) vegetaciones adenoids.

vegetal adj & m vegetable.

vegetariano, -a adj & m f vegetarian.

vehemente adj vehement.

vehículo m vehicle.

veinte adj & m inv twenty.

vejez f old age.

vejiga f bladder.

vela¹ f candle; **pasar la noche en v.** to have a sleepless night.

vela² f (de barco) sail.

velador m Am (mesilla de noche) bedside table.

velar 1 vt (difunto) to hold a wake; (enfermo) to watch over. **2** vi (no dormir) to stay awake. **3 velarse** vr to blur.

velatorio m vigil.

velero m sailing boat.

veleta f weather vane.

vello m hair.

velo m veil.

velocidad f (rapidez) speed; (marcha) gear; **v. máxima** speed limit.

velocímetro m speedometer.

veloz adj rapid.

vena f vein.

venado m deer; (carne) venison.

vencedor, -a 1 m f winner. **2** adj winning.

vencer [49] **1** vt to defeat; (dificultad) to overcome. **2** vi (pago, deuda) to be payable; (plazo) to expire.

vencido, -a adj (derrotado) defeated; (equipo etc) beaten; **darse por v.** to give up.

venda f bandage.

vendaje m dressing.

vendar vt to bandage; **v. los ojos a algn** to blindfold sb.

vendaval m gale.

vendedor, -a m f seller; (hombre) salesman; (mujer) saleswoman.

vender vt, **venderse** vr to sell; **se vende** for sale.

vendimia f grape harvest.

vendré indic fut de **venir**.

veneno m poison; (de serpiente) venom.

venenoso, -a adj poisonous.

venéreo, -a adj venereal.

venezolano, -a adj & m f Venezuelan.

venga subj pres de **venir**.

venganza f vengeance, revenge.

vengarse [42] vr to avenge oneself; **v. de algn** to take revenge on sb.

vengo indic pres de **venir**.

venir [27] **1** vi to come; **el año que viene** next year; fam **¡venga ya!** (expresa incredulidad) come off it!; (vamos) come on!; **v. grande/pequeño** (ropa) to be too big/small; **v. mal/bien** to be inconvenient/convenient. ▪ (en pasivas) **esto vino provocado por...** this was brought about by... ▪ **esto viene ocurriendo desde hace mucho tiempo** this has been going on for a long time now. **2 venirse** vr **venirse abajo** to collapse.

venta f sale; (posada) country inn; **en v.** for sale; **a la v.** on sale; **v. a plazos/al contado** credit/cash sale; **v.**

al por mayor/al por menor wholesale/retail.

ventaja f advantage; **llevar v. a** to have the advantage over.

ventana f window; *(de la nariz)* nostril.

ventanilla f window; *(de la nariz)* nostril.

ventilador m ventilator; *(de coche)* fan.

ventilar vt to ventilate.

ventisca f blizzard; *(de nieve)* snowstorm.

ver [28] **1** vt to see; *(televisión)* to watch; **a v.** let's see; **a v. si escribes** I hope you'll write; **(ya) veremos** we'll see; **no tener nada que v. con** to have nothing to do with. **2 verse** vr *(imagen etc)* to be seen; *(encontrarse con algn)* to see each other; **¡nos vemos!** see you later!; *Am* **te ves divina** you look divine.

veraneante mf vacationist, tourist.

veranear vi to spend one's summer vacation.

veraniego, -a adj summer.

verano m summer.

veras: de veras adv really.

verbena f street o night party.

verbo m verb.

verdad f truth; **es v.** it is true; **¡de v!** really!; truly!; **un amigo de v.** a real friend; *(en frase afirmativa)* **está muy bien, ¿(no es) v?** it is very good, isn't it?; *(en frase negativa)* **no te gusta, ¿v.?** you don't like it, do you?

verdaderamente adv truly.

verdadero, -a adj true.

verde 1 adj green; *(fruta)* unripe; *(chiste, película)* blue. **2** m *(color)* green.

verdoso, -a adj greenish.

verdura f vegetables pl.

vereda f path; *Am (acera)* sidewalk.

veredicto m verdict.

vergonzoso, -a adj *(penoso)* disgraceful; *(tímido)* shy

vergüenza f shame; *(timidez)*

shyness; **¿no te da v.?** aren't you ashamed?; **es una v.** it's a disgrace; **me da v.** I'm too embarrassed.

verificar [44] vt to check.

verja f *(reja)* grating; *(cerca)* railing; *(puerta)* iron gate.

vermut, vermú m *(pl vermús)* vermouth.

verosímil adj probable, likely; *(creíble)* credible.

verruga f wart.

versión f version.

verso m *(poesía)* verse.

vertebrado, -a adj & m vertebrate.

vertedero m *(de basura)* tip.

verter [3] vt to pour (out); *(basura)* to dump.

vertical adj vertical.

vertiente f *(de montaña, tejado)* slope; *Am (manantial)* spring.

vertiginoso, -a adj *(velocidad)* breakneck.

vértigo m vertigo; **me da v.** it makes me dizzy.

vespa® f (motor) scooter.

vespino® m moped.

vestíbulo m *(de casa)* hall; *(de edificio público)* foyer.

vestido, -a 1 m *(de mujer)* dress. **2** adj dressed.

vestigio m trace.

vestir [6] **1** vt *(a alguien)* to dress; *(llevar puesto)* to wear. **2** vi to dress; **ropa de (mucho) v.** formal dress. **3 vestirse** vr to get dressed, to dress; **vestirse de** to wear; *(disfrazarse)* to dress up as.

vestuario m *(conjunto de vestidos)* wardrobe; *(para teatro)* costumes pl; *(camerino)* dressing room; *(en estadio)* changing room.

veterano, -a adj & mf veteran.

veterinario, -a 1 mf vet, veterinarian. **2** f veterinary medicine.

veto m veto.

vez f time; *(turno)* turn; **una v.** once; **dos veces** twice; **cinco veces** five times; **a** o **algunas veces** sometimes; **cada v.** each o every time; **cada v.**

más more and more; **de v. en cuando** now and again; **¿le has visto alguna v.?** have you ever seen him?; **otra v.** again; **a la v.** at the same time; **tal v.** perhaps, maybe; **de una v.** in one go; **en v. de** instead of.

vía 1 f (del tren) track; (camino) road; (por) v. oral to be taken orally; por v. aérea/marítima by air/sea. **2** prep (a través de) via.

viajar vi to travel.

viaje m journey, trip; (largo, en barco) voyage; **¡buen v.!** have a good trip!; **estar de v.** to be away (on a trip); **v. de negocios** business trip; **v. de novios** honeymoon.

viajero, -a mf traveler; (en transporte público) passenger.

víbora f viper.

vibración f vibration.

vibrar vti to vibrate.

vicepresidente, -a mf vice president; (de compañía, comité) vice-chairman, vice president.

viceversa adv vice versa.

vicio m vice; (mala costumbre) bad habit.

vicioso, -a 1 adj (persona) depraved; **círculo v.** vicious circle. **2** mf depraved person.

víctima f victim.

victoria f victory.

vid f vine.

vida f life; **en mi v.** never in my life; **ganarse la v.** to earn one's living; **¿qué es de tu v.?** how's life?

vídeo m video; **grabar en v.** to video.

videocámara f video camera.

videoclub m video club.

videojuego m video game.

vidriera f stained-glass window; Am (escaparate) shop window.

vidrio m glass.

viejo, -a 1 adj old; **hacerse v.** to grow old; **un v. amigo** an old friend. **2** mf (hombre) old man; (mujer) old woman; **los viejos** old people; fam **mis viejos** my parents.

viento m wind; **hace** o **sopla mucho v.** it is very windy.

vientre m belly.

viernes m inv Friday; **V. Santo** Good Friday.

vietnamita adj & mf Vietnamese.

viga f (de madera) beam; (de hierro) girder.

vigencia f validity; **entrar en v.** to come into force.

vigésimo, -a adj & mf twentieth.

vigilante m guard; (nocturno) night watchman.

vigilar 1 vt to watch; (lugar) to guard. **2** vi to keep watch.

vigor m vigor; (fuerza) strength; **en v.** in force.

vil adj vile.

villa f (población) town; (casa) villa.

villancico m (Christmas) carol.

vinagre m vinegar.

vinagreras fpl oil and vinegar cruets.

vinagreta f vinaigrette.

vincha f Am headband.

vínculo m link.

vine pt indef de **venir.**

vino m wine; **v. blanco/tinto** white/red wine; **v. rosado** rosé.

viña f vineyard.

viñedo m vineyard.

viñeta f illustration.

violación f (de persona) rape; (de ley, derecho) violation.

violar vt (persona) to rape; (ley, derecho) to violate.

violencia f violence.

violento, -a adj violent; (situación) embarrassing; **sentirse v.** to feel awkward.

violeta 1 adj violet. **2** m (color) violet. **3** f (flor) violet.

violín m violin.

violonc(h)elo m cello.

virar vt to turn round.

virgen adj (persona, selva) virgin; (aceite, lana) pure; (cinta) blank.

viril adj virile.

virtud f virtue; (propiedad) ability.

virtuoso, -a *adj* virtuous; *(músico)* virtuoso.

viruela *f* smallpox.

virus *m inv* virus.

visa *f Am* visa.

visado *m* visa.

visera *f (de gorra)* peak; *(de casco)* visor.

visibilidad *f* visibility.

visible *adj* visible.

visillo *m* small net curtain.

visión *f* vision; *(vista)* sight.

visita *f* visit; *(invitado)* visitor; **hacer una v.** to pay a visit; **estar de v.** to be visiting.

visitante 1 *mf* visitor. **2** *adj (equipo)* away.

visitar *vt* to visit.

vislumbrar *vt* to glimpse.

visón *m* mink.

víspera *f (día anterior)* day before; *(de festivo)* eve.

vista *f* sight; *(panorama)* view; **a la v.** visible; **a primera o simple v.** on the face of it; **en v. de** in view of, considering; **corto de v.** short-sighted; **conocer a algn de v.** to know sb by sight; **perder de v. a** to lose sight of; **¡hasta la v.!** see you!; **con vista(s) al mar** overlooking the sea.

vistazo *m* glance; **echar un v. a algo** *(ojear)* to have a (quick) look at sth.

visto, -a **1** *adj* **está v. que** it is obvious that ; **por lo v.** apparently; **estar bien v.** to be well looked upon; **estar mal v.** to be frowned upon. **2** *m* **v. bueno** approval.

vitalicio, -a *adj* lifelong.

vitalidad *f* vitality.

vitamina *f* vitamin.

viticultor, -a *mf* wine grower.

vitorear *vt* to cheer.

vitrina *f (aparador)* display cabinet; *(de exposición)* showcase; *Am (escaparate)* shop window.

viudo, -a *mf (hombre)* widower; *(mujer)* widow.

viva *interj* hurrah!

vivaracho, -a *adj* lively.

vivaz *adj* vivacious; *(perspicaz)* quick-witted.

víveres *mpl* provisions.

vivero *m (de plantas)* nursery.

vivienda *f* housing; *(casa)* house; *(piso)* apartment.

vivir 1 *vi* to live. **2** *vt (guerra, experiencia)* to live through.

vivo, -a *adj* alive; *(vivaz)* lively; *(listo)* clever; *(color)* vivid; **en v.** *(programa)* live; **al rojo v.** red-hot.

vocabulario *m* vocabulary.

vocación *f* vocation.

vocal 1 *f* vowel. **2** *m* member. **3** *adj* vocal.

voceador, -a *mf Am* vendor.

vocero, -a *mf Am* spokesperson; *(hombre)* spokesman; *(mujer)* spokeswoman.

vociferar *vi* to shout.

vodka *m* vodka.

volandas: en vandas *adv* flying through the air.

volante 1 *m* steering wheel; *(de vestido)* frill; **ir al v.** to be at the wheel. **2** *adj* flying; **platillo v.** flying saucer.

volantín *m Am (cometa)* small kite.

volar [2] **1** *vi* to fly; *fam* **lo hizo volando** he did it in a flash. **2** *vt (explotar)* to blow up; *(caja fuerte)* to blow open; *(terreno)* to blast. **3 volarse** *vr (papel etc)* to be blown away.

volcán *m* volcano.

volcar [2] **1** *vt (cubo etc)* to knock over; *(barco, bote)* to capsize; *(vaciar)* to empty out. **2** *vi (coche)* to turn over; *(barca)* to capsize. **3 volcarse** *vr (vaso, jarra)* to fall over; *(coche)* to turn over; *(barca)* to capsize.

voleibol *m* volleyball.

voltaje *m* voltage.

voltear 1 *vt CSur (derribar)* to knock over; *Andes, CAm, Carib, Méx (cabeza)* to turn; **v. la espalda a alguien** to turn one's back on sb. **2 voltearse** *vr Andes, CAm, Carib, Méx (volverse)* to turn around.

voltereta *f* somersault.

voltio *m* volt.

volumen *m* volume.

voluminoso, -a *adj* voluminous; *(enorme)* massive.

voluntad *f* will; **fuerza de v.** will-power; **tiene mucha v.** he is very strong-willed.

voluntario, -a 1 *adj* voluntary; **ofrecerse v.** to volunteer. **2** *mf* volunteer.

volver [4] *(pp vuelto)* **1** *vi* to return; *(venir de vuelta)* to come back; *(ir de vuelta)* to go back; **v. en sí** to come round; **v. a hacer algo** to do sth again. **2** *vt (convertir)* to make; *(dar vuelta a)* to turn; *(boca abajo)* to turn upside down; *(de fuera adentro)* to turn inside out; *(de atrás adelante)* to turn back to front; *(cinta, disco)* to turn over; **volverle la espalda a algn** to turn one's back on sb; **al v. la esquina** on turning the corner. **3 volverse** *vr* to turn; *(venir de vuelta)* to come back; *(ir de vuelta)* to go back; *(convertirse)* to become; **volverse loco** to go mad.

vomitar 1 *vi* to vomit; **tengo ganas de v.** I feel sick. **2** *vt* to bring up.

voraz *adj* voracious.

vos *pron pers pl Am* you.

vosotros, -as *pron pers pl* you.

votación *f (voto)* vote; *(acción)* voting.

votante *mf* voter.

votar *vi* to vote; **v. a algn** to vote for sb.

voto *m* vote.

voy *indic pres de* **ir**.

voz *f* voice; *(grito)* shout; **en v. alta** aloud; **en v. baja** in a low voice; **a media v.** in a low voice; **a voces** shouting; **dar voces** to shout; **no tener ni v. ni voto** to have no say in the matter.

vuelo *m* flight; **v. chárter/regular** charter/scheduled flight; **una falda de v.** a full skirt.

vuelta *f (regreso)* return; *(viaje)* return journey; *(giro)* turn; *(en carreras)* lap; *(ciclista)* tour; *(dinero)* change; **a v. de correo** by return

post; **estar de v.** to be back; **dar media v.** to turn round; **la cabeza me da vueltas** my head is spinning; **no le des más vueltas** stop worrying about it; **dar una v.** *(a pie)* to go for a walk; *(en coche)* to go for a drive.

vuelto *m Am* change.

vuestro, -a 1 *adj pos (antes del sustantivo)* your; *(después del sustantivo)* of yours. **2** *pron pos* yours; **lo v.** what is yours.

vulgar *adj* vulgar.

vulnerable *adj* vulnerable.

W

walkman® *m* Walkman®.

wáter *m (pl wáteres)* toilet.

whisky *m* whiskey.

windsurf(ing) *m* windsurfing.

X

xenofobia *f* xenophobia.

Y

y *conj* and; **son las tres y cuarto** it's a quarter past three; **¿y qué?** so what?; **¿y tú?** what about you?; **¿y eso?** how come?; *ver* **e**.

ya 1 *adv* already; *(ahora mismo)* now; **ya lo sabía** I already knew; **¡hazlo ya!** do it at once!; **ya mismo** right away; **ya hablaremos luego** we'll talk about it later; **ya verás** you'll see; **ya no** no longer; **ya no viene por aquí** he doesn't come round here any more; **ya era hora** about time too; **ya lo creo** I should think so; **¡ya voy!** coming!; **¡ya está!** that's it! **2** *conj* **ya que** since.

yacaré *m Am* alligator.

yacer [61] *vi* to lie.

yacimiento *m* deposit.

yanqui 1 *adj* Yankee. **2** *mf* Yank.

yarda *f* yard.

yate *m* yacht.

yedra *f* ivy.

yegua *f* mare.

yema *f (de huevo)* yolk; *(de planta)* bud; *(pastel)* sweet made from sugar and egg yolk; **y. del dedo** fingertip.

yendo *gerundio de* **ir**.

yerba *f* = **hierba**.

yerbatero, -a *mf Am (curandero)* witch doctor who uses herbs.

yerno *m* son-in-law.

yerro *indic pres de* **errar**.

yeso *m* plaster.

yo *pron pers* I; **entre tú y yo** between you and me; **¿quién es? — soy yo** who is it? — it's me; **yo no** not me; **yo que tú** if I were you; **yo mismo** I myself.

yoga *m* yoga.

yogur *m* yogurt.

yuca *f* yucca.

yudo *m* judo.

yugo(e)slavo, -a *adj & mf* Yugoslav, Yugoslavian.

Z

zafarse *vr* to get away (**de** from).

zafiro *m* sapphire.

zalamero, -a *mf* crawler. **2** *adj* crawling.

zamarra *f (prenda)* sheepskin jacket.

zambo, -a *adj* knock-kneed; *Am* half Indian and half Negro.

zambullirse *vr* to jump.

zanahoria *f* carrot.

zancada *f* stride.

zancadilla *f* **ponerle la z. a algn** to trip sb up.

zanco *m* stilt.

zancudo *m Am* mosquito.

zanja *f* ditch.

zapatería *f* shoe shop.

zapatero, -a *m (vendedor)* shoe shop owner; *(fabricante)* shoemaker; *(reparador)* cobbler.

zapatilla *f* slipper; **zapatillas de deporte** trainers.

zapato *m* shoe.

zarandear *vt* to shake.

zarcillo *m (pendiente)* earring.

zarpa *f* claw.

zarpar *vi* to set sail.

zarza *f* bramble.

zarzamora *f (zarza)* blackberry bush; *(fruto)* blackberry.

zarzuela *f* Spanish operetta; **la Z.** royal residence in Madrid.

zigzag *m (pl* zigzags *o* zigzagues) zigzag.

zócalo *m (de pared)* baseboard.

zodiaco, zodíaco *m* zodiac; **signo del z.** sign of the zodiac.

zona *f* zone.

zoo *m* zoo.

zoológico, -a 1 *adj* zoological; **parque z.** zoo. **2** *m* zoo.

zopilote *m Am* buzzard.

zoquete *m fam* blockhead.

zorra *f* vixen.

zorro *m* fox.

zueco *m* clog.

zumbar *vi* to buzz; **me zumban los oídos** my ears are buzzing.

zumbido *m* buzzing.

zumo *m* juice.

zurcir [52] *vt* to darn.

zurdo, -a 1 *mf (persona)* left-handed person. **2** *adj* left-handed.

SPANISH VERBS

Models for regular conjugation

TOMAR to take

INDICATIVE

PRESENT	FUTURE	CONDITIONAL
1. tomo	tomaré	tomaría
2. tomas	tomarás	tomarías
3. toma	tomará	tomaría
1. tomamos	tomaremos	tomaríamos
2. tomáis	tomaréis	tomaríais
3. toman	tomarán	tomarían

IMPERFECT	PRETERITE	PERFECT
1. tomaba	tomé	he tomado
2. tomabas	tomaste	has tomado
3. tomaba	tomó	ha tomado
1. tomábamos	tomamos	hemos tomado
2. tomabais	tomasteis	habéis tomado
3. tomaban	tomaron	han tomado

FUTURE PERFECT	CONDITIONAL PERFECT	PLUPERFECT
1. habré tomado	habría tomado	había tomado
2. habrás tomado	habrías tomado	habías tomado
3. habrá tomado	habría tomado	había tomado
1. habremos tomado	habríamos tomado	habíamos tomado
2. habréis tomado	habríais tomado	habíais tomado
3. habrán tomado	habrían tomado	habían tomado

SUBJUNCTIVE

PRESENT	IMPERFECT	PERFECT/PLUPERFECT
1. tome	tom-ara/ase	haya/hubiera* tomado
2. tomes	tom-aras/ases	hayas/hubieras tomado
3. tome	tom-ara/ase	haya/hubiera tomado

* the alternative form 'hubiese' etc is also possible.

1. tomemos	tom-áramos/ásemos	hayamos/hubiéramos tomado
2. toméis	tom-arais/aseis	hayáis/hubierais tomado
3. tomen	tom-aran/asen	hayan/hubieran tomado

IMPERATIVE	INFINITIVE	PARTICIPLE
(tú) toma	**PRESENT**	**PRESENT**
(Vd) tome	tomar	tomando
(nosotros) tomemos		
(vosotros) tomad	**PERFECT**	**PAST**
(Vds) tomen	haber tomado	tomado

COMER to eat

INDICATIVE

PRESENT	FUTURE	CONDITIONAL
1. como	comeré	comería
2. comes	comerás	comerías
3. come	comerá	comería
1. comemos	comeremos	comeríamos
2. coméis	comeréis	comeríais
3. comen	comerán	comerían

IMPERFECT	PRETERITE	PERFECT
1. comía	comí	he comido
2. comías	comiste	has comido
3. comía	comió	ha comido
1. comíamos	comimos	hemos comido
2. comíais	comisteis	habéis comido
3. comían	comieron	han comido

FUTURE PERFECT	CONDITIONAL PERFECT	PLUPERFECT
1. habré comido	habría comido	había comido
2. habrás comido	habrías comido	habías comido
3. habrá comido	habría comido	había comido
1. habremos comido	habríamos comido	habíamos comido
2. habréis comido	habríais comido	habíais comido
3. habrán comido	habrían comido	habían comido

PRESENT	IMPERFECT	PERFECT/PLUPERFECT
1. coma	com-iera/iese	haya/hubiera* comido
2. comas	com-ieras/ieses	hayas/hubieras comido
3. coma	com-iera/iese	haya/hubiera comido
1. comamos	com-iéramos/iésemos	hayamos/hubiéramos comido
2. comáis	com-ierais/ieseis	hayáis/hubierais comido
3. coman	com-ieran/iesen	hayan/hubieran comido

* the alternative form 'hubiese' etc is also possible

IMPERATIVE	INFINITIVE	PARTICIPLE
(tú) come	**PRESENT**	**PRESENT**
(Vd) coma	comer	comiendo
(nosotros) comamos		
(vosotros) comed	**PERFECT**	**PAST**
(Vds) coman	haber comido	comido

PARTIR to leave

INDICATIVE

PRESENT	FUTURE	CONDITIONAL
1. parto	partiré	partiría
2. partes	partirás	partirías
3. parte	partirá	partiría
1. partimos	partiremos	partiríamos
2. partís	partiréis	partiríais
3. parten	partirán	partirían

IMPERFECT	PRETERITE	PERFECT
1. partía	partí	he partido
2. partías	partiste	has partido
3. partía	partió	ha partido
1. partíamos	partimos	hemos partido
2. partíais	partisteis	habéis partido
3. partían	partieron	han partido

FUTURE PERFECT	CONDITIONAL PERFECT	PLUPERFECT
1. habré partido	habría partido	había partido
2. habrás partido	habrías partido	habías partido
3. habrá partido	habría partido	había partido
1. habremos partido	habríamos partido	habíamos partido
2. habréis partido	habríais partido	habíais partido
3. habrán partido	habrían partido	habían partido

SUBJUNCTIVE

PRESENT	IMPERFECT	PERFECT/PLUPERFECT
parta	parti-era/ese	haya/hubiera* partido
partas	parti-eras/eses	hayas/hubieras partido
parta	parti-era/ese	haya/hubiera partido
partamos	parti-éramos/ésemos	hayamos/hubiéramos partido
partáis	parti-erais/eseis	hayáis/hubierais partido
partan	parti-eran/esen	hayan/hubieran partido

*the alternative form 'hubiese' etc is also possible

IMPERATIVE	INFINITIVE	PARTICIPLE
(tú) parte	**PRESENT**	**PRESENT**
(Vd) parta	partir	partiendo
(nosotros) partamos	**PERFECT**	**PAST**
(vosotros) partid	haber partido	partido
(Vds) partan		

Models for irregular conjugation

[1] pensar PRES pienso, piensas, piensa, pensamos, pensáis, piensan; PRES SUBJ piense, pienses, piense, pensemos, penséis, piensen; IMPERAT piensa, piense, pensemos, pensad, piensen

[2] contar PRES cuento, cuentas, cuenta, contamos, contáis, cuentan; PRES SUBJ cuente, cuentes, cuente, contemos, contéis, cuenten; IMPERAT cuenta, cuente, contemos, contad, cuenten

[3] perder PRES pierdo, pierdes, pierde, perdemos, perdéis, pierden; PRES SUBJ pierda, pierdas, pierda, perdamos, perdáis, pierdan; IMPERAT pierde, pierda, perdamos, perded, pierdan

[4] morder PRES muerdo, muerdes, muerde, mordemos, mordéis, muerden; PRES SUBJ muerda, muerdas, muerda, mordamos, mordáis, muerdan; IMPERAT muerde, muerda, mordamos, morded, muerdan

[5] sentir PRES siento, sientes, siente, sentimos, sentís, sienten; PRES SUBJ sienta, sientas, sienta, sintamos, sintáis, sientan; PRES P sintiendo; IMPERAT siente, sienta, sintamos, sentid, sientan

[6] vestir PRES visto, vistes, viste, vestimos, vestís, visten; PRES SUBJ vista, vistas, vista, vistamos, vistáis, vistan; PRES P vistiendo; IMPERAT viste, vista, vistamos, vestid, vistan

[7] dormir PRES duermo, duermes, duerme, dormimos, dormís, duermen; PRES SUBJ duerma, duermas, duerma, durmamos, durmáis, duerman; PRES P durmiendo; IMPERAT duerme, duerma, durmamos, dormid, duerman

[8] andar PRET anduve, anduviste, anduvo, anduvimos, anduvisteis, anduvieron; IMPERF SUBJ anduviera/anduviese

[9] caber PRES quepo, cabes, cabe, cabemos, cabéis, caben; PRES SUBJ quepa, quepas, quepa, quepamos, quepáis, quepan; FUT cabré; COND cabría; PRET cupe, cupiste, cupo, cupimos, cupisteis, cupieron; IMPERF SUBJ cupiera/cupiese; IMPERAT cabe, quepa, quepamos, cabed, quepan

[10] conducir PRES conduzco, conduces, conduce, conducimos, conducís, conducen; PRES SUBJ conduzca, conduzcas, conduzca, conduzcamos, conduzcáis, conduzcan; PRET conduje, condujiste, condujo, condujimos, condujisteis, condujeron; IMPERF SUBJ condujera/condujese; IMPERAT conduce, conduzca, conduzcamos, conducid, conduzcan

[11] dar PRES doy, das, da, damos, dais, dan; PRES SUBJ dé, des, dé, demos, deis, den; PRET di, diste, dio, dimos, disteis, dieron; IMPERF SUBJ diera/diese; IMPERAT da, dé, demos, dad, den

[12] decir PRES digo, dices, dice, decimos, decís, dicen; PRES SUBJ diga, digas, diga, digamos, digáis, digan; FUT diré; COND diría; PRET dije, dijiste, dijo, dijimos, dijisteis, dijeron; IMPERF SUBJ dijera/dijese; PRES P diciendo; PP dicho; IMPERAT di, diga, digamos, decid, digan

[13] ESTAR to be

INDICATIVE

PRESENT	FUTURE	CONDITIONAL
1. estoy	estaré	estaría
2. estás	estarás	estarías
3. está	estará	estaría
1. estamos	estaremos	estaríamos
2. estáis	estaréis	estaríais
3. están	estarán	estarían

IMPERFECT	PRETERITE	PERFECT
1. estaba	estuve	he estado
2. estabas	estuviste	has estado
3. estaba	estuvo	ha estado
1. estábamos	estuvimos	hemos estado
2. estabais	estuvisteis	habéis estado
3. estaban	estuvieron	han estado

FUTURE PERFECT	CONDITIONAL PERFECT	PLUPERFECT
1. habré estado	habría estado	había estado
2. habrás estado	habrías estado	habías estado
3. habrá estado	habría estado	había estado
1. habremos estado	habríamos estado	habíamos estado
2. habréis estado	habríais estado	habíais estado
3. habrán estado	habrían estado	habían estado

SUBJUNCTIVE

PRESENT	IMPERFECT	PERFECT/PLUPERFECT
1. esté	estuv-iera/iese	haya/hubiera* estado
2. estés	estuv-ieras/ieses	hayas/hubieras estado
3. esté	estuv-iera/iese	haya/hubiera estado
1. estemos	estuv-iéramos/iésemos	hayamos/hubiéramos estado
2. estéis	estuv-ierais/ieseis	hayáis/hubierais estado
3. estén	estuv-ieran/iesen	hayan/hubieran estado

IMPERATIVE

(tú) está
(Vd) esté
(nosotros) estemos
(vosotros) estad
(Vds) estén

INFINITIVE

PRESENT
estar

PERFECT
haber estado

PARTICIPLE

PRESENT
estando

PAST
estado

* the alternative form 'hubiese' etc is also possible

[14] HABER to have (*auxiliary*)

INDICATIVE

PRESENT	FUTURE	CONDITIONAL
1. he	habré	habría
2. has	habrás	habrías
3. ha/hay*	habrá	habría
1. hemos	habremos	habríamos
2. habéis	habréis	habríais
3. han	habrán	habrían

IMPERFECT	PRETERITE	PERFECT
1. había	hube	
2. habías	hubiste	
3. había	hubo	ha habido*
1. habíamos	hubimos	
2. habíais	hubisteis	
3. habían	hubieron	

FUTURE PERFECT	CONDITIONAL PERFECT	PLUPERFECT
1.		
2.		
3. habrá habido*	habría habido*	había habido*
1.		
2.		
3.		

SUBJUNCTIVE

PRESENT	IMPERFECT	PERFECT/PLUPERFECT
1. haya	hub-iera/iese	
2. hayas	hub-ieras/ieses	
3. haya	hub-iera/iese	haya/hubiera** habido*
1. hayamos	hub-iéramos/iésemos	
2. hayáis	hub-ierais/ieseis	
3. hayan	hub-ieran/iesen	

INFINITIVE

	PARTICIPLE
PRESENT	**PRESENT**
haber	habiendo
PERFECT	**PAST**
haber habido*	habido

* 'haber' is an auxiliary verb used with the participle of another verb to form compound tenses (eg he bebido – I have drunk). 'hay' means 'there is/are' and all third person singular forms in their respective tenses have this meaning. The forms highlighted with an asterisk are used only for this latter construction.

** the alternative form 'hubiese' is also possible.

(7)

[15] hacer PRES hago, haces, hace, hacemos, hacéis, hacen; PRES SUBJ haga, hagas, haga, hagamos, hagáis, hagan; FUT haré; COND haría; PRET hice, hiciste, hizo, hicimos, hicisteis, hicieron; IMPERF SUBJ hiciera/hiciese; PP hecho; IMPERAT haz, haga, hagamos, haced, hagan

[16] ir PRES voy, vas, va, vamos, vais, van; PRES SUBJ vaya, vayas, vaya, vayamos, vayáis, vayan; IMPERF iba, ibas, iba, íbamos, ibais, iban; PRET fui, fuiste, fue, fuimos, fuisteis, fueron; IMPERF SUBJ fuera/fuese; PRES P yendo; IMPERAT ve, vaya, vamos, id, vayan

[17] oír PRES oigo, oyes, oye, oímos, oís, oyen; PRES SUBJ oiga, oigas, oiga, oigamos, oigáis, oigan; PRET oí, oíste, oyó, oímos, oísteis, oyeron; IMPERF SUBJ oyera/oyese; PRES P oyendo; PP oído; IMPERAT oye, oiga, oigamos, oíd, oigan

[18] poder PRES puedo, puedes, puede, podemos, podéis, pueden; PRES SUBJ pueda, puedas, pueda, podamos, podáis, puedan; FUT podré; COND podría; PRET pude, pudiste, pudo, pudimos, pudisteis, pudieron; IMPERF SUBJ pudiera/pudiese; PRES P pudiendo; IMPERAT puede, pueda, podamos, poded, puedan

[19] poner PRES pongo, pones, pone, ponemos, ponéis, ponen; PRES SUBJ ponga, pongas, ponga, pongamos, pongáis, pongan; FUT pondré; PRET puse, pusiste, puso, pusimos, pusisteis, pusieron; IMPERF SUBJ pusiera/pusiese; PP puesto; IMPERAT pon, ponga, pongamos, poned, pongan

[20] querer PRES quiero, quieres, quiere, queremos, queréis, quieren; PRES SUBJ quiera, quieras, quiera, queramos, queráis, quieran; FUT querré; COND querría; PRET quise, quisiste, quiso, quisimos, quisisteis, quisieron; IMPERF SUBJ quisiera/quisiese; IMPERAT quiere, quiera, queramos, quered, quieran

[21] saber PRES sé, sabes, sabe, sabemos, sabéis, saben; PRES SUBJ sepa, sepas, sepa, sepamos, sepáis, sepan; FUT sabré; COND sabría; PRET supe, supiste, supo, supimos, supisteis, supieron; IMPERF SUBJ supiera/supiese; IMPERAT sabe, sepa, sepamos, sabed, sepan

[22] salir PRES salgo, sales, sale, salimos, salís, salen; PRES SUBJ salga, salgas, salga, salgamos, salgáis, salgan; FUT saldré; COND saldría; IMPERAT sal, salga salgamos, salid, salgan

[23] ser PRES soy, eres, es, somos, sois, son; PRES SUBJ sea, seas, sea, seamos, seáis, sean; IMPERF era, eras, era, éramos, erais, eran; PRET fui, fuiste, fue, fuimos, fuisteis, fueron; IMPERF SUBJ fuera/fuese; IMPERAT sé, sea, seamos, sed, sean

[24] tener PRES tengo, tienes, tiene, tenemos, tenéis, tienen; PRES SUBJ tenga, tengas, tenga, tengamos, tengáis, tengan; FUT tendré; COND tendría; PRET tuve, tuviste, tuvo, tuvimos, tuvisteis, tuvieron; IMPERF SUBJ tuviera/tuviese; IMPERAT ten, tenga, tengamos, tened, tengan

[25] traer PRES traigo, traes, trae, traemos, traéis, traen; PRES SUBJ traiga, traigas, traiga, traigamos, traigáis, traigan; PRET traje, trajiste, trajo, trajimos, trajisteis, trajeron; IMPERF SUBJ trajera/trajese; IMPERAT trae, traiga, traigamos, traed, traigan

[26] valer PRES valgo, vales, vale, valemos, valéis, valen; PRES SUBJ valga, valgas, valga, valgamos, valgáis, valgan; FUT valdré; COND valdría; IMPERAT vale, valga, valemos, valed, valgan

[27] venir PRES vengo, vienes, viene, venimos, venís, vienen; PRES SUBJ venga, vengas, venga, vengamos, vengáis, vengan; FUT vendré; COND vendría; PRET vine, viniste, vino, vinimos, vinisteis, vinieron; IMPERF SUBJ viniera/viniese; PRES P viniendo; IMPERAT ven, venga, vengamos, venid, vengan

[28] ver PRES veo, ves, ve, vemos, veis, ven; PRES SUBJ vea, veas, vea, veamos, veáis, vean; IMPERF veía, veías, veía, veíamos, veíais, veían; PRET vi, viste, vio, vimos, visteis, vieron; IMPERF SUBJ viera/viese; IMPERAT ve, vea, veamos, ved, vean

[29] desviar PRES desvío, desvías, desvía, desviamos, desviáis, desvían; PRES SUBJ desvíe, desvíes, desvíe, desviemos, desviéis, desvíen; IMPERAT desvía, desvíe, desviemos, desviéis, desvíen

[30] continuar PRES continúo, continúas, continúa, continuamos, continuáis, continúan; PRES SUBJ continúe, continúes, continúe, continuemos, continuéis, continúen; IMPERAT continúa, continúe, continuemos, continuad, continúen

[31] adquirir PRES adquiero, adquieres, adquiere, adquirimos, adquirís, adquieren; PRES SUBJ adquiera, adquiras, adquiera, adquiramos, adquiráis, adquieran; IMPERAT adquiere, adquiera, adquiramos, adquirid, adquieran

[32] jugar PRES juego, juegas, juega, jugamos, jugáis, juegan; PRES SUBJ juegue, juegues, juegue, juguemos, juguéis, jueguen; IMPERAT juega, juegue, juguemos, jugad, jueguen

[33] agradecer PRES agradezco, agradeces, agradece, agradecemos, agradecéis, agradecen; PRES SUBJ agradezca, agradezcas, agradezca, agradezcamos, agradezcáis, agradezcan; IMPERAT agradece, agradezca, agradezcamos, agradeced, agradezcan

[34] conocer PRES conozco, conoces, conoce, conocemos, conocéis, conocen; PRES SUBJ conozca, conozcas, conozca, conozcamos, conozcáis, conozcan; IMPERAT conoce, conozca, conozcamos, conoced, conozcan

[35] lucir PRES luzco, luces, luce, lucimos, lucís, lucen; PRES SUBJ luzca, luzcas, luzca, luzcamos, luzcáis, luzcan; IMPERAT luce, luzca, luzcamos, lucid, luzcan

[36] leer PRET leí, leíste, leyó, leímos, leísteis, leyeron; IMPERF SUBJ leyera/leyese; PRES P leyendo; PP leído; IMPERAT lee, lea, leamos, leed, lean

[37] huir PRES huyo, huyes, huye, huimos, huís, huyen; PRES SUBJ huya, huyas, huya, huyamos, huyáis, huyan; PRET huí, huiste, huyó, huimos, huisteis, huyeron; IMPERF SUBJ huyera/huyese; PRES P huyendo; PP huido; IMPERAT huye, huya, huyamos, huid, huyan

[38] roer PRES roo/roigo/royo, roes, roe, roemos, roéis, roen; PRES SUBJ roa/roiga/roya, roas, roa, roamos, roáis, roan; PRET roí, roíste, royó, roímos, roísteis, royeron; IMPERF SUBJ royera/royese; PRES P royendo; PP roído; IMPE-RAT roe, roa, roamos, roed, roan

[39] caer PRES caigo, caes, cae, caemos, caéis, caen; PRES SUBJ caiga, caigas, caiga, caigamos, caigáis, caigan; PRES P cayendo; PP caído; IMPERAT cae, caiga, caigamos, caed, caigan

[40] cazar PRET cacé, cazaste, cazó, cazamos, cazasteis, cazaron; PRES SUBJ cace, caces, cacen, cacemos, cacéis, cacen

[41] cocer PRES cuezo, cueces, cuece, cocemos, cocéis, cuecen; PRES SUBJ cueza, cuezas, cueza, cozamos, cozáis, cuezan; IMPERAT cuece, cueza, cozamos, cozed, cuezan

[42] llegar PRET llegué, llegaste, llegó, llegamos, llegasteis, llegaron; PRES SUBJ llegue, llegues, llegue, lleguemos, lleguéis, lleguen

[43] cambiar PRES cambio, cambias, cambia, cambiamos, cambiáis, cambian; PRES SUBJ cambie, cambies, cambie, cambiemos, cambiéis, cambien; IMPERAT cambia, cambie, cambiemos, cambiad, cambien

[44] sacar PRET saqué, sacaste, sacó, sacamos, sacasteis, sacaron; PRES SUBJ saque, saques, saque, saquemos, saquéis, saquen; IMPERAT saca, saque, saquemos, sacad, saquen

[45] averiguar PRET averigüé, averiguaste, averiguó, averiguamos, averiguasteis, averiguaron; PRES SUBJ averigüe, averigües, averigüe, averigüemos, averigüéis, averigüen; IMPERAT averigua, averigüe, averigüemos, averiguad, averigüen

[46] asir PRES asgo, ases, ase, asimos, asís, asen; PRES SUBJ asga, asgas, asga, asgamos, asgáis, asgan; IMPERAT ase, asga, asgamos, asid, asgan

[47] adecuar PRES adecuo, adecuas, adecua, adecuamos, adecuáis, adecuan; PRES SUBJ adecue, adecues, adecue, adecuemos, adecuéis, adecuen; IMPERAT adecua, adecuen, adecuemos, adecuad, adecuen

[48] delinquir PRES delinco, delinques, delinque, delinquimos, delinquís, delinquen; PRES SUBJ delinca, delincas, delinca, delincamos, delincáis, delincan; IMPERAT delinque, delinca, delincamos, delinquid, delincan

[49] mecer PRES mezo, meces, mece, mecemos, mecéis, mecen; PRES SUBJ meza, mezas, meza, mezamos, mezáis, mezan; IMPERAT mece, meza, mezamos, meced, mezan

[50] errar PRES yerro, yerras, yerra, erramos, erráis, yerran; PRES SUBJ yerre, yerres, yerre, erremos, erréis, yerren; IMPERAT yerra, yerre, erremos, errad, yerren

[51] comenzar PRES comienzo, comienzas, comienza, comenzamos, comenzáis, comienzan; PRES SUBJ comience, comiences, comience, comencemos, comencéis, comiencen; IMPERAT comienza, comience, comencemos, comenzad, comiencen

[52] zurcir PRES zurzo, zurces, zurce, zurcimos, zurcís, zurcen; PRES SUBJ zurza, zurzas, zurza, zurzamos, zurzáis, zurzan; **IMPERAT** zurce, zurza, zurzamos, zurcid, zurzan

[53] proteger PRES protejo, proteges, protege, protegemos, protegéis, protegen; **PRES SUBJ** proteja, protejas, proteja, protejamos, protejáis, protejan; **IMPERAT** protege, proteja, protejamos, proteged, protejan

[54] discernir PRES discierno, disciernes, discierne, discernimos, discernís, disciernen; **PRES SUBJ** discierna, disciernas, discierna, discernamos, discernáis, disciernan; **IMPERAT** discierne, discierna, discernamos, discernid, disciernan

[55] erguir PRES irgo/yergo, irgues/yergues, irgue/yergue, erguimos, erguís, irguen/yerguen; **PRET** erguí, erguiste, irguió, erguimos, erguisteis, irguieron; **PRES SUBJ** irga/yerga, irgas/yergas, irga/yerga, irgamos/yergamos, irgáis/yergáis, irgan/yergan; **IMPERF SUBJ** irguiera/irguiese; **IMPERAT** irgue/yergue, irga/yerga, irgamos/yergamos, erguid, irgan/yergan

[56] reír PRES río, ríes, ríe, reímos, reís, ríen; **PRET** reí, reíste, rió, reímos, reísteis, rieron; **PRES SUBJ** ría, rías, ría, riamos, riáis, rían; **IMPERF SUBJ** riera/riese; **IMPERAT** ríe, ría, riamos, reíd, rían

[57] dirigir PRES dirijo, diriges, dirige, dirigimos, dirigís, dirigen; **PRES SUBJ** dirija, dirijas, dirija, dirijamos, dirijáis, dirijan; **IMPERAT** dirige, dirija, dirijamos, dirigid, dirijan

[58] regir PRES rijo, riges, rige, regimos, regís, rigen; **PRES SUBJ** rija, rijas, rija, rijamos, rijáis, rijan; **IMPERAT** rige, rija, rijamos, regid, rijan

[59] distinguir PRES distingo, distingues, distingue, distinguimos, distinguís, distinguen; **PRES SUBJ** distinga, distingas, distinga, distingamos, distingáis, distingan; **IMPERAT** distingue, distinga, distingamos, distinguid, distingan

[60] nacer PRES nazco, naces, nace, nacemos, nacéis, nacen; **PRES SUBJ** nazca, nazcas, nazca, nazcamos, nazcáis, nazcan; **IMPERAT** nace, nazca, nazcamos, naced, nazcan

[61] yacer PRES yazco/yazgo/yago, yaces, yace, yacemos, yacéis, yacen; **PRES SUBJ** yazca/yazga/yaga; **IMPERAT** yace/yaz, yazca/yazga/yaga, yazcamos/yazgamos/yagamos, yaced, yazcan/yazgan/yagan

[62] argüir PRES arguyo, arguyes, arguye, argüimos, argüís, arguyen; **PRET** argüí, argüiste, arguyó, argüimos, argüisteis, arguyeron; **PRES SUBJ** arguya, arguyas, arguya, arguyamos, arguyáis, arguyan; **IMPERF SUBJ** arguyera/arguyese; **IMPERAT** arguye, arguya, arguyamos, argüid, arguyan

[63] avergonzar PRES avergüenzo, avergüenzas, avergüenza, avergonzamos, avergonzáis, avergüenzan; **PRET** avergoncé, avergonzaste, avergonzó, avergonzamos, avergonzasteis, avergonzaron; **PRES SUBJ** avergüence, avergüences, avergüence, avergoncemos, avergoncéis, avergüencen; **IMPERAT** avergüenza, avergüence, avergoncemos, avergonzad, avergüencen

[64] trocar PRES trueco, truecas, trueca, trocamos, trocáis, truecan; **PRET**

troqué, trocaste, trocó, trocamos, trocasteis, trocaron; PRES SUBJ trueque, trueques, trueque, troquemos, troquéis, truequen; IMPERAT trueca, trueque, troquemos, trocad, truequen

[65] oler PRES huelo, hueles, huele, olemos, oléis, huelen; PRES SUBJ huela, huelas, huela, olamos, oláis, huelan; IMPERAT huele, huela, olamos, oled, huelan

VERBOS IRREGULARES INGLESES

INFINITIVE	PAST SIMPLE	PAST PARTICIPLE
arise	arose	arisen
awake	awoke	awoken
be	was, were	been
bear	bore	borne
beat	beat	beaten
become	became	become
begin	began	begun
bend	bent	bent
bet	bet, betted	bet, betted
bid *(offer)*	bid	bid
bind	bound	bound
bite	bit	bitten
bleed	bled	bled
blow	blew	blown
break	broke	broken
breed	bred	bred
bring	brought	brought
broadcast	broadcast	broadcast
build	built	built
burn	burnt, burned	burnt, burned
burst	burst	burst
buy	bought	bought
cast	cast	cast
catch	caught	caught
choose	chose	chosen
cling	clung	clung
come	came	come
cost	cost	cost
creep	crept	crept
cut	cut	cut
deal	dealt	dealt
dig	dug	dug
dive	dove	dived
do	did	done
draw	drew	drawn

INFINITIVE	PAST SIMPLE	PAST PARTICIPLE
dream	dreamt, dreamed	dreamt, dreamed
drink	drank	drunk
drive	drove	driven
eat	ate	eaten
fall	fell	fallen
feed	fed	fed
feel	felt	felt
fight	fought	fought
find	found	found
flee	fled	fled
fling	flung	flung
fly	flew	flown
forbid	forbad(e)	forbidden
forecast	forecast	forecast
foresee	foresaw	foreseen
forget	forgot	forgotten
forgive	forgave	forgiven
freeze	froze	frozen
get	got	gotten
give	gave	given
go	went	gone
grind	ground	ground
grow	grew	grown
hang	hung, hanged	hung, hanged
have	had	had
hear	heard	heard
hide	hid	hidden
hit	hit	hit
hold	held	held
hurt	hurt	hurt
keep	kept	kept
kneel	knelt, kneeled	knelt, kneeled
know	knew	known
lay	laid	laid
lead	led	led
lean	leant, leaned	leant, leaned
leap	leapt, leaped	leapt, leaped
learn	learnt, learned	learnt, learned
leave	left	left
lend	lent	lent
let	let	let
lie	lay	lain

INFINITIVE	PAST SIMPLE	PAST PARTICIPLE
light	lit, lighted	lit, lighted
lose	lost	lost
make	made	made
mean	meant	meant
meet	met	met
mislay	mislaid	mislaid
mislead	misled	misled
mistake	mistook	mistaken
misunderstand	misunderstood	misunderstood
mow	mowed	mown, mowed
outdo	outdid	outdone
overcome	overcame	overcome
overdo	overdid	overdone
overtake	overtook	overtaken
pay	paid	paid
put	put	put
quit	quit	quit
read	read	read
redo	redid	redone
rend	rent	rent
rewind	rewound	rewound
ride	rode	ridden
ring	rang	rung
rise	rose	risen
run	ran	run
saw	sawed	sawn, sawed
say	said	said
see	saw	seen
seek	sought	sought
sell	sold	sold
send	sent	sent
set	set	set
sew	sewed	sewn, sewed
shake	shook	shaken
shear	sheared	shorn, sheared
shed	shed	shed
shine	shone	shone
shoot	shot	shot
show	showed	shown, showed
shrink	shrank, shrunk	shrunk
shut	shut	shut
sing	sang	sung

INFINITIVE	PAST SIMPLE	PAST PARTICIPLE
sink	sank	sunk
sit	sat	sat
sleep	slept	slept
slide	slid	slid
sling	slung	slung
slink	slunk	slunk
slit	slit	slit
smell	smelt, smelled	smelt, smelled
sneak	sneaked, snuck	sneaked, snuck
sow	sowed	sown, sowed
speak	spoke	spoken
speed	sped, speeded	sped, speeded
spell	spelt, spelled	spelt, spelled
spend	spent	spent
spill	spilt, spilled	spilt, spilled
spin	spun	spun
spit	spat	spat
split	split	split
spoil	spoilt, spoiled	spoilt, spoiled
spread	spread	spread
spring	sprang	sprung
stand	stood	stood
steal	stole	stolen
stick	stuck	stuck
sting	stung	stung
stink	stank	stunk
stride	strode	stridden
strike	struck	struck, stricken
string	strung	strung
strive	strove	striven
swear	swore	sworn
sweep	swept	swept
swell	swelled	swollen, swelled
swim	swam	swum
swing	swung	swung
take	took	taken
teach	taught	taught
tear	tore	torn
tell	told	told
think	thought	thought
thrive	thrived, throve	thrived
throw	threw	thrown
thrust	thrust	thrust

INFINITIVE	PAST SIMPLE	PAST PARTICIPLE
tread	trod	trodden
undergo	underwent	undergone
understand	understood	understood
undertake	undertook	undertaken
undo	undid	undone
upset	upset	upset
wake	woke	woken
wear	wore	worn
weave	wove	woven
weep	wept	wept
wet	wet, wetted	wet, wetted
win	won	won
wind	wound	wound
withdraw	withdrew	withdrawn
withhold	withheld	withheld
wring	wrung	wrung
write	wrote	written

COUNTRIES AND REGIONS
PAÍSES Y REGIONES

Africa *(African)*	África f *(africano, -a)*
Albania *(Albanian)*	Albania f *(albanés, -esa)*
Algeria *(Algerian)*	Argelia f *(argelino, -a)*
America *(American)*	América f *(americano, -a)*
Central/North/South America *(Central/North/South American)*	América f Central/del Norte/ del Sur
Antarctica, the Antarctic *(Antarctic)*	Antártida f, Antártico m *(antártico, -a)*
Arabia *(Arab, Arabic)*	Arabia f *(árabe)*
the Arctic *(Arctic)*	el Ártico m *(ártic, -a)*
Argentina *(Argentinian, Argentine)*	Argentina f *(argentino, -a)*
Asia *(Asian)*	Asia f *(asiático, -a)*
Australia *(Australian)*	Australia f *(australiano, -a)*
Austria *(Austrian)*	Austria f *(austríaco, -a)*
Belgium *(Belgian)*	Bélgica f *(belga)*
Bolivia *(Bolivian)*	Bolivia f *(boliviano, -a)*
Brazil *(Brazilian)*	Brasil m *(brasileño, -a, brasilero, -a)*
Bulgaria *(Bulgarian)*	Bulgaria f *(búlgaro, -a)*

Burma (*Burmese*)	Birmania *f* (*birmano, -a*)
Canada (*Canadian*)	Canadá *m* (*canadiense*)
Central America (*Central American*)	Centroamérica *f* (*centroamericano, -a*)
Chile (*Chilean*)	Chile *m* (*chileno, -a*)
China (*Chinese*)	China *f* (*chino, -a*)
Colombia (*Colombian*)	Colombia *f* (*colombiano, -a*)
Costa Rica (*Costa Rican*)	Costa Rica *f* (*costarricense, costarriqueño, -a*)
Crete (*Cretan*)	Creta *f* (*cretense*)
Cuba (*Cuban*)	Cuba *f* (*cubano, -a*)
Cyprus (*Cypriot*)	Chipre *m* (*chipriota*)
Czech Republic (*Czech*)	República Checa *f* (*checo, -a*)
Denmark (*Danish*)	Dinamarca *f* (*danés, -esa*)
Dominican Republic (*Dominican*)	República Dominicana *f* (*dominicano, -a*)
Ecuador (*Ecuadorian*)	Ecuador *m* (*ecuatoriano, -a*)
Egypt (*Egyptian*)	Egipto *m* (*egipcio, -a*)
El Salvador (*Salvadoran, Salvadorian*)	El Salvador *m* (*salvadoreño, -a*)
England (*English*)	Inglaterra *f* (*inglés, -esa*)
Ethiopia (*Ethiopian*)	Etiopía *f* (*etiope, etíope*)
Europe (*European*)	Europa *f* (*europeo, -a*)
Finland (*Finnish*)	Finlandia *f* (*finlandés, -a*)
France (*French*)	Francia *f* (*francés, -esa*)
Germany (*German*)	Alemania *f* (*alemán, -ana*)
Gibraltar (*Gibraltarian*)	Gibraltar *m* (*gibraltaneño, -a*)
Great Britain (*British*)	Gran Bretaña *f* (*británico, -a*)
Greece (*Greek*)	Grecia *f* (*griego, -a*)
Holland (*Dutch*)	Holanda *f* (*holandés, -esa*)
Honduras (*Honduran*)	Honduras *f* (*hondureño, -a*)
Hungary (*Hungarian*)	Hungría *f* (*húngaro, -a*)
Iceland (*Icelandic*)	Islandia *f* (*islandés, -esa*)
India (*Indian*)	India *f* (*indio, -a*)
Indonesia (*Indonesian*)	Indonesia *f* (*indonesio, -a*)
Iran (*Iranian*)	Irán *m* (*iraní*)
Iraq (*Iraqi*)	Irak, Iraq *m* (*iraquí*)
Ireland (*Irish*)	Irlanda *f* (*irlandés, -esa*)
Israel (*Israeli*)	Israel *m* (*israelí*)
Italy (*Italian*)	Italia *f* (*italiano, -a*)
Jamaica (*Jamaican*)	Jamaica *f* (*jamaicano, -a*)
Japan (*Japanese*)	Japón *m* (*japonés, -esa*)
Kenya (*Kenyan*)	Kenia *f* (*keniano, -a*)
Korea (*Korean*)	Corea *f* (*coreano, -a*)

Latin America (*Latin American*)	Latinoamérica *f* (*latinoaméricano, -a*); Hispanoamérica *f* (*hispanoamericano, -a*); Iberoamérica *f* (*iberoamericano, -a*)
Latvia (*Latvian*)	Letonia *f* (*letón, -ona*)
the Lebanon (*Lebanese*)	Líbano *m* (*libanés, -esa*)
Libya (*Libyan*)	Libia *f* (*libio, -a*)
Lithuania (*Lithuanian*)	Lituania *f* (*lituano, -a*)
Luxembourg	Luxemburgo *m* (*luxemburgués*)
Malaysia (*Malay*)	Malasia *f* (*malasio, -a*)
Mexico (*Mexican*)	México, Méjico *m* (*mexicano, -a, mejicano, -a*)
Mongolia (*Mongolian*)	Mongolia *f* (*mongol*)
Morocco (*Moroccan*)	Marruecos *m* (*marroquí*)
the Netherlands, the Low Countries (*Dutch*)	Países Bajos *mpl* (*neerlandés, -esa*)
Nicaragua (*Nicaraguan*)	Nicaragua *f* (*nicaragüense, nicaragüeño, -a*)
North Africa (*North African*)	África *f* del Norte (*norteafricano, -a*)
North America (*North American*)	Norteamérica *f* (*norteamericano, -a*)
Northern Ireland (*Northern Irish*)	Irlanda del Norte *f*
Norway (*Norwegian*)	Noruega *f* (*noruego, -a*)
Pakistan (*Pakistani*)	Pakistán, Paquistán *m* (*paquistaní*)
Palestine (*Palestinian*)	Palestina *f* (*palestino, -a*)
Panama (*Panamanian*)	Panamá *m* (*panameño, -a*)
Paraguay (*Paraguayan*)	Paraguay *m* (*paraguayo, -a*)
Peru (*Peruvian*)	Perú *m* (*peruano, -a*)
(the) Philippines (*Philippine, Filipino*)	Filipinas *fpl* (*filipino, -a*)
Poland (*Polish*)	Polonia *f* (*polaco, -a*)
Portugal (*Portuguese*)	Portugal *m* (*portugués, -esa*)
Puerto Rico (*Puerto Rican*) .	Puerto Rico *m* (*portorriqueño, -a, puertorriqueño, -a*)
Rumania, Romania (*R(o)umanian*)	Rumanía *f* (*rumano, -a*)
Russia (*Russian*)	Rusia *f* (*ruso, -a*)
Saudi Arabia (*Saudi Arabian, Saudi*)	Arabia Saudita *f* (*saudita, saudí*)
Scandinavia (*Scandinavian*)	Escandinavia *f* (*escandinavo, -a*)
Scotland (*Scottish, Scots*)	Escocia *f* (*escocés, -esa*)
Slovakia (*Slovak*)	Eslovaquia *f* (*eslovaco, -a*)
South Africa (*South African*)	Sudáfrica *f* (*sudafricano, -a*)

South America (*South American*)	Sudamérica *f (sudamericano, -a);*	
	Suramérica *f (suramericano, -a)*	
Spain (*Spanish*),	España *f (español, -a)*	
Sweden (*Swedish*)	Suecia *f (sueco, -a)*	
Switzerland (*Swiss*)	Suiza *f (suizo, -a)*	
Syria (*Syrian*)	Siria *f (sirio, -a)*	
Thailand (*Thai*)	Tailandia *f (tailandés, -esa)*	
Tunisia (*Tunisian*)	Túnez *m (tunecino, -a)*	
Turkey (*Turkish*)	Turquía *f (turco, -a)*	
Ukraine (*Ukrainian*)	Ucrania *f (ucraniano, -a)*	
the United States (*United States,*	Estados Unidos *mpl*	
American)	*(estadounidense)*	
Uruguay (*Uruguayan*)	Uruguay *m (uruguayo, -a)*	
Venezuela (*Venezuelan*)	Venezuela *f (venezolano, -a)*	
Vietnam (*Vietnamese*)	Vietnam *m (vietnamita)*	
Wales (*Welsh*)	Gales *m* (el país *m* de) (*galés, -esa*)	
the West Indies (*West Indian*)	Antillas *f (antillano, -a)*	

NUMBERS
LOS NÚMEROS

zero	0	cero
one	1	uno, una
two	2	dos
three	3	tres
four	4	cuatro
five	5	cinco
six	6	seis
seven	7	siete
eight	8	ocho
nine	9	nueve
ten	10	diez
eleven	11	once
twelve	12	doce
thirteen	13	trece
fourteen	14	catorce
fifteen	15	quince
sixteen	16	dieciséis
seventeen	17	diecisiete
eighteen	18	dieciocho

nineteen	19	diecinueve
twenty	20	viente
twenty-one	21	veintiuno
twenty-two	22	veintidós
thirty	30	treinta
thirty-one	31	treinta y uno
thirty-two	32	treinta y dos
forty	40	cuarenta
fifty	50	cincuenta
sixty	60	sesenta
seventy	70	setenta
eighty	80	ochenta
ninety	90	noventa
a *or* one hundred	100	cien
a *or* one hundred and one	101	ciento uno
a *or* one hundred and ten	110	ciento diez
two hundred	200	doscientos/doscientas
five hundred	500	quinientos/quinientas
seven hundred	700	setecientos/setecientas
a *or* one thousand	1,000	mil
two hundred thousand	200,000	doscientos/ doscientas mil
one million	1,000,000	un millón

English–Spanish
Inglés–Español

A

a *indef art* (*before vowel or silent h* **an**) un, una; **he has a big nose** tiene la nariz grande; **half a liter/an hour** medio litro/media hora; **he's a teacher** es profesor; **60 cents a kilo** 60 centavos el kilo; **three times a week** tres veces a la semana.

a·ban·don *vt* abandonar.

ab·bey abadía *f.*

ab·bre·vi·a·tion abreviatura *f.*

a·bil·i·ty capacidad *f.*

a·ble *adj* (*capable*) capaz; **to be a. to do sth** poder hacer algo.

a·ble-bod·ied *adj* sano, -a.

ab·nor·mal *adj* anormal.

ab·nor·mal·ly *adv* anormalmente.

a·board 1 *adv* a bordo; **to go a.** (*ship*) embarcarse; (*train*) subir. **2** *prep* a bordo de.

a·bol·ish *vt* abolir.

a·bor·tion aborto *m*; **to have an a.** abortar.

a·bout 1 *adv* (*approximately*) más o menos; **he's a. 40** tendrá unos 40 años; **it's a. time you got up** ya es hora de que te levantes. **2** *prep* (*concerning*) acerca de; **a program a. New York** un programa sobre Nueva York; **to speak a. sth** hablar de algo; **what's it all a.?** ¿de qué se trata?; **how a. a game of tennis?** ¿qué te parece un partido de tenis? ▪ **it's a. to start** está a punto de empezar.

a·bove 1 *adv* arriba; **the apartment a.** el piso de arriba; **a policy imposed from a.** una política impuesta desde arriba. **2** *prep* (*higher than*) encima de; (*greater than*) superior a; **100 meters a. sea level** 100 metros sobre el nivel del mar; **it's a. the door** está encima de la puerta; **a. all** sobre todo; **he's not a. stealing** es capaz incluso de robar.

a·bove-men·tioned *adj* susodicho, -a.

a·breast *adv* **to keep a. of things** mantenerse al día.

a·broad *adv* en el extranjero; **to go a.** irse al extranjero.

a·brupt *adj* (*manner*) brusco, -a; (*change*) súbito, -a.

ab·rupt·ly *adv* (*act*) bruscamente; (*speak*) con aspereza.

ab·scess absceso *m.*

ab·sence (*of person*) ausencia *f*, (*of thing*) falta *f.*

ab·sent *adj* ausente.

ab·sent-mind·ed *adj* distraído, -a.

ab·so·lute *adj* absoluto, -a; (*failure*) total; (*truth*) puro, -a.

ab·so·lute·ly *adv* completamente; **a. not** en absoluto; **you're a. right** tienes toda la razón; **a.!** ¡desde luego!

ab·sorb *vt* (*liquid*) absorber; **to be absorbed in sth** estar absorto, -a en algo.

ab·surd *adj* absurdo, -a.

a·buse 1 *n* (*ill-treatment*) malos tratos *mpl*; (*misuse*) abuso *m*; (*insults*) injurias *fpl*. **2** *vt* (*ill-treat*) maltratar; (*misuse*) abusar de; (*insult*) injuriar.

a·bu·sive *adj* (*insulting*) grosero, -a.

ac·a·dem·ic 1 *adj* académico, -a; (*career*) universitario, -a; **a. year** año *m* escolar. **2** *n* académico, -a *mf.*

ac·cel·er·ate *vi* acelerar.

ac·cel·er·a·tor acelerador *m.*

ac·cent acento *m.*

ac·cept *vt* aceptar; (*theory*) admitir.

ac·cept·a·ble *adj* admisible. ▪

ac·cess acceso *m.*

ac·ces·si·ble *adj* accesible; (*person*) asequible.

ac·ces·so·ry (*to crime*) cómplice *mf*, **accessories** accesorios *mpl*; (*for outfit*) complementos *mpl.*

ac·cess time tiempo *m* de acceso.

ac·ci·dent accidente *m*; **by a.** por casualidad.

ac·ci·den·tal *adj* fortuito, -a; (*unintended*) imprevisto, -a.

ac·ci·den·tal·ly *adv (by chance)* por casualidad.

ac·com·mo·date *vt (guests)* alojar; **to a. sb's wishes** complacer a algn.

ac·com·mo·da·tion(s) alojamiento *m*.

ac·com·pa·ny *vt* acompañar.

ac·com·plish *vt (aim)* conseguir; *(task, mission)* llevar a cabo.

ac·cord of his own a. espontáneamente.

ac·cor·dance in a. with de acuerdo con.

ac·cord·ing·ly *adv* en consecuencia.

ac·cord·ing to *prep* según.

ac·cor·di·on acordeón *m*.

ac·count *(report)* informe *m*; *(at bank, in business)* cuenta *f*; **on a.** a causa de; **to take a. of, to take into a.** tener en cuenta; **accounts department** servicio *m* de contabilidad; **current a.** cuenta *f* corriente.

▸ **account for** *vt (explain)* explicar.

ac·count·ant contable *mf*.

ac·cu·mu·late 1 *vt* acumular. **2** *vi* acumularse.

ac·cu·rate *adj (number)* exacto, -a; *(answer)* correcto, -a; *(observation)* acertado, -a; *(translation)* fiel.

ac·cu·rate·ly *adv* con precisión.

ac·cu·sa·tion acusación *f*.

ac·cuse *vt* acusar.

ac·cused *n* **the a.** el/la acusado(a).

ac·cus·tomed *adj* **to be a. to sth** estar acostumbrado a algo; **to get a. to sth** acostumbrarse a algo.

ace *(card & fig)* as *m*; *(in tennis)* ace *m*.

ache 1 *n* dolor *m*. **2** *vi* doler; **my back aches** me duele la espalda.

a·chieve *vt (attain)* conseguir; *(accomplish)* llevar a cabo.

a·chieve·ment *(attainment)* logro *m*; *(feat)* hazaña *f*.

a·cid 1 *adj* ácido, -a. **2** *n* ácido *m*.

a·cid rain lluvia *f* ácida.

ac·knowl·edge *vt (recognize)* reconocer; *(letter)* acusar recibo de; *(greet)* saludar.

ac·ne acné *m*.

a·corn bellota *f*.

a·cous·tics *npl* acústica *f sing*.

ac·quaint *vt* **to be acquainted with sb** conocer a algn; **to be acquainted with sth** estar al corriente de algo.

ac·quain·tance conocimiento *m*; *(person)* conocido, -a *mf*; **to make sb's a.** conocer a algn.

ac·quire *vt* adquirir.

a·cre acre *m (approx 40,47 áreas).*

ac·ro·bat·ic *adj* acrobático, -a.

a·cross 1 *adv* a través; **to go a.** atravesar; **to run a.** atravesar corriendo. **2** *prep* a través de; *(at the other side of)* al otro lado de; **they live a. the road** viven enfrente; **to go a. the street** cruzar la calle.

a·cryl·ic *adj* acrílico, -a.

act 1 *n (action)* acto *m*; *(parliamentary)* ley *f*; *(of play)* acto *m*; **a. of God** caso *m* de fuerza mayor. **2** *vt (part)* interpretar; *(character)* representar; **to a. like a fool** hacer el tonto. **3** *vi (pretend)* fingir; *(behave)* comportarse; *(take action)* actuar; *(work)* funcionar.

▸ **act for** *vt* obrar en nombre de.

▸ **act out** *vt* exteriorizar.

▸ **act up** *vi fam (machine)* funcionar mal; *(child)* dar guerra.

ac·tion *(deed)* acción *f*; *(in war)* acción *f* de combate; **to be out of a.** *(person)* estar fuera de servicio; *(machine)* estar estropeado, -a; **to take a.** tomar medidas.

ac·tive *adj* activo, -a; *(energetic)* vigoroso, -a; *(interest)* vivo, -a.

ac·tiv·i·ty actividad *f*; *(on street etc)* bullicio *m*.

ac·tor actor *m*.

ac·tress actriz *f*.

ac·tu·al *adj* verdadero, -a.

ac·tu·al·ly *adv (really)* en efecto; *(even)* incluso.

a·cute *adj* agudo, -a; *(pain)* intenso, -a; *(hearing)* muy fino, -a.

AD *abbr* of **Anno Domini** después de Cristo, d.C.

ad *fam* anuncio *m*.

a·dapt 1 *vt* adaptar (**to** a). **2** *vi* adaptarse.

a·dapt·a·ble *adj* he's very a. se amolda fácilmente a las circunstancias.

a·dap·ter, a·dap·tor *(plug)* ladrón *m*.

add 1 *vt (numbers)* sumar; *(one thing to another)* añadir. **2** *vi (count)* sumar.

▸ **add in** *vt (include)* incluir.

▸ **add to** *vt* aumentar.

▸ **add together** *vt (numbers)* sumar.

▸ **add up 1** *vt (numbers)* sumar. **2** *vi* it doesn't a. up no tiene sentido.

ad·dict adicto, -a *mf*; **drug a.** drogadicto, -a *mf*; **television a.** teleadicto, -a *mf*.

ad·dict·ed *adj* adicto, -a.

ad·dic·tion *(to gambling etc)* vicio *m*; *(to drugs)* adicción *f*.

ad·di·tion adición *f*; **in a. to** además de.

ad·di·tion·al *adj* adicional.

ad·di·tive aditivo *m*.

ad·dress 1 *n (on letter)* dirección *f*, *(speech)* discurso *m*. **2** *vt (letter)* dirigir; *(speak to)* dirigirse (**to** a).

ad·e·noids *npl* vegetaciones *fpl* (adenoideas).

ad·e·quate *adj (enough)* suficiente; *(satisfactory)* adecuado, -a.

ad·e·quate·ly *adv* suficientemente.

ad·here *vi (stick)* pegarse (**to** a).

▸ **adhere to** *vt (policy)* adherirse a; *(contract)* cumplir con.

ad·he·sive 1 *adj* adhesivo, -a. **2** *n* adhesivo *m*.

ad·ja·cent *adj (building)* contiguo, -a; *(land)* colindante; **a. to** contiguo, -a a.

ad·jec·tive adjetivo *m*.

ad·just 1 *vt (machine etc)* ajustar; *(methods)* variar. **2** *vi (person)* adaptarse (**to** a).

ad·just·a·ble *adj* ajustable.

ad·just·ment *(by person)* adapta-

ción *f*, *(change)* modificación *f*.

ad·lib *vi* improvisar.

ad·min·is·ter *vt (country)* gobernar; *(justice)* administrar.

ad·min·is·tra·tion *(of country)* gobierno *m*; *(of justice)* administración *f*.

ad·min·is·tra·tive *adj* administrativo, -a.

ad·mi·ral almirante *m*.

ad·mi·ra·tion admiración *f*.

ad·mire *vt* admirar.

ad·mis·sion *(to school etc)* ingreso *m*; *(price)* entrada *f*, *(of fact)* reconocimiento *m*.

ad·mit *vt (person)* dejar entrar; *(crime, guilt)* confesar.

ad·mit·tance *(entry)* entrada *f*.

ad·o·les·cent adolescente *mf*.

a·dopt *vt* adoptar.

a·dopt·ed *adj* **a. child** hijo, -a *mf* adoptivo, -a.

a·dop·tion adopción *f*.

a·dor·a·ble *adj* adorable.

a·dore *vt* adorar.

a·dult 1 *n (person)* adulto, -a *mf*. **2** *adj (film, education)* para adultos.

ad·vance 1 *n (movement)* avance *m*; *(progress)* progreso *m*; **in a.** de antemano. **2** *adj (before time)* adelantado, -a; **a. payment** pago *m* por adelantado. **3** *vt (troops)* avanzar; *(time, date)* adelantar; *(idea)* proponer; *(loan)* prestar. **4** *vi (move forward, make progress)* avanzar.

ad·vanced *adj (developed)* avanzado, -a; *(student)* adelantado, -a; *(course)* superior.

ad·van·tage ventaja *f*; **to take a. of sb** abusar de algn; **to take a. of sth** aprovechar algo.

ad·ven·ture aventura *f*.

ad·ven·tur·ous *adj (character)* aventurero, -a; *(bold)* atrevido, -a.

ad·verb adverbio *m*.

ad·ver·tise 1 *vt* anunciar. **2** *vi* hacer publicidad; *(in newspaper)* poner un anuncio; **to a. for sth/sb** buscar algo/a algn mediante un anuncio.

ad·ver·tise·ment anuncio *m*; **advertisements** publicidad *f sing*.

ad·vice consejos *mpl*; **a piece of a.** un consejo.

ad·vis·a·ble *adj* aconsejable.

ad·vise *vt* aconsejar; *(on business etc)* asesorar.

▸ **advise against** *vt* desaconsejar.

ad·vis·er consejero, -a *mf*; *(in business etc)* asesor, -a *mf*.

ad·vo·cate 1 *n (supporter)* defensor, -a *mf*. **2** *vt* abogar por.

aer·i·al antena *f*.

aer·o·bics aerobic *m*.

aer·o·plane avión *m*.

aer·o·sol aerosol *m*.

aes·thet·ic *adj* estético, -a.

af·fair *(matter)* asunto *m*; **business affairs** negocios *mpl*; **love a.** aventura *f* amorosa.

af·fect *vt (person, health)* afectar; *(prices, future)* influir en.

af·fec·tion afecto *m*.

af·fec·tion·ate *adj* cariñoso, -a.

af·flu·ent *adj (society)* opulento, -a; *(person)* rico, -a.

af·ford *vt (be able to buy)* permitirse el lujo de.

af·ford·a·ble *adj (price etc)* asequible.

a·float *adv* **to keep a.** mantenerse a flote.

a·fraid *adj* **to be a.** tener miedo *(of sb* a algn; *of sth* de algo); **I'm a. of it** me da miedo; **I'm a. not/so** me temo que no/sí.

Af·ri·can *adj & n* africano, -a *(mf)*.

af·ter 1 *adv* después; **the day a.** el día siguiente. **2** *prep (later)* después de; *(behind)* detrás de; **the day a. tomorrow** pasado mañana; **a. you!** ¡pase usted!; **they asked a. you** preguntaron por ti; **what's he a.?** ¿qué pretende?; **he takes a. his uncle** se parece a su tío. **3** *conj* después (de) que; **a. it happened** después de que ocurrió.

af·ter·ef·fects *npl* consecuencias *fpl*; *(of drug)* efectos *mpl* secundarios.

af·ter·noon tarde *f*; **good a.!** ¡buenas tardes!; **in the a.** por la tarde.

after-sales ser·vice servicio *m* posventa.

af·ter·shave loción *f* para después del afeitado.

af·ter·wards *adv* después.

a·gain *adv* otra vez; **a. and a.** repetidas veces; **to do sth a.** volver a hacer algo; **never a.!** ¡nunca más!; **now and a.** de vez en cuando.

a·gainst *prep* contra; **a. the law** ilegal.

age 1 *n* edad *f*, *fam (long time)* eternidad *f*, **underage** menor de edad; **old a.** vejez *f*, **the Iron A.** la Edad del Hierro. **2** *vti* envejecer.

ag·ed¹ *adj* de or a la edad de; *(old)* anciano, -a.

ag·ed² *npl* **the a.** los ancianos.

a·gen·cy agencia *f*.

a·gen·da orden *m* del día.

a·gent agente *mf*, *(representative)* representante *mf*.

ag·gra·vate *vt (worsen)* agravar; *(annoy)* molestar.

ag·gres·sion agresión *f*.

ag·gres·sive *adj* agresivo, -a.

ag·ile *adj* ágil.

ag·i·tat·ed *adj* inquieto, -a.

a·go *adv* **a week a.** hace una semana; **how long a.?** ¿hace cuánto tiempo?

ag·o·ny dolor *m* muy fuerte; *(mental)* angustia *f*.

a·gree *vi (be in agreement)* estar de acuerdo; *(reach agreement)* ponerse de acuerdo; **to a. to do sth** consentir en hacer algo; **onions don't a. with me** la cebolla no me sienta bien.

▸ **agree (up)on** *vt (decide)* ponerse de acuerdo en.

a·gree·a·ble *adj (pleasant)* agradable; *(person)* simpático, -a; *(in agreement)* de acuerdo.

a·greed *adj (time, place)* acordado, -a.

a·gree·ment *(arrangement)* acuerdo *m*; *(contract etc)* contrato *m*.

ag·ri·cul·tur·al *adj* agrícola.

ag·ri·cul·ture agricultura *f*.

a·head *adv* delante; *(early)* antes; **go a.!** ¡adelante!; **to be a.** *(in race etc)* llevar la ventaja; **to look a.** pensar en el futuro.

aid 1 *n* ayuda *f*, *(rescue)* auxilio *m*; **in a. of** a beneficio de. **2** *vt* ayudar.

AIDS SIDA *m*.

aim 1 *n* *(with weapon)* puntería *f*, *(objective)* propósito *m*. **2** *vti* *(gun)* apuntar (**at** a, hacia).

▶ **aim at** *vt (target)* apuntar a.

▶ **aim to** *vt* **to a. to do sth** tener la intención de hacer algo.

air 1 *n* aire *m*; **to travel by a.** viajar en avión; **to be on the a.** *(program)* estar emitiendo. **2** *vt (bed, clothes)* airear; *(room)* ventilar.

air·con·di·tioned *adj* climatizado, -a.

air con·di·tion·ing aire *m* acondicionado.

air·craft *inv* avión *m*.

air·craft car·ri·er portaaviones *m inv*.

air·fare precio *m* de billete de avión.

air force fuerzas *fpl* aéreas.

air fresh·en·er ambientador *m*.

air·line línea *f* aérea.

air·line tick·et billete *m* de avión.

air·mail correo *m* aéreo; **by a.** por avión.

air·plane avión *m*.

air·port aeropuerto *m*.

air raid ataque *m* aéreo.

air·sick·ness mareos *mpl* (en avión).

air·tight *adj* hermético, -a.

air traf·fic con·trol control *m* de tráfico aéreo.

air traf·fic con·trol·ler controlador *m* aéreo.

aisle *(in church)* nave *f*, *(in theater)* pasillo *m*.

a·jar *adj & adv* entreabierto, -a.

a·larm 1 *n* alarma *f*, *(fear)* inquietud *f*. **2** *vt* alarmar.

a·larm clock despertador *m*.

al·bum álbum *m*.

al·co·hol alcohol *m*.

al·co·hol·ic *adj & n* alcohólico, -a *(mf)*.

a·lert 1 *adj* alerta; *(lively)* despabilado, -a. **2** *n* alerta *m*.

al·ge·bra álgebra *f*.

Al·ge·ri·an *adj & n* argelino, -a *(mf)*.

a·li·as 1 *n* *(pl aliases)* alias *m*. **2** *adv* alias.

al·i·bi coartada *f*.

a·li·en *adj & n* extranjero, -a *(mf)*; *(from space)* extraterrestre *mf*.

a·light *adj (on fire)* ardiendo, -a.

a·like 1 *adj (similar)* parecidos, -as; *(the same)* iguales. **2** *adv (in the same way)* de la misma manera, igualmente.

a·live *adj* vivo, -a; *fig (teeming)* lleno, -a (**with** de).

all 1 *adj* todo, -a, todos, -as; **a. year** *(during)* todo el año; **a. kinds of things** todo tipo de cosas; **at a. times** siempre; **a. six of us were there** los seis estábamos allí. **2** *pron* todo, -a, todos, -as; **after a.** al fin y al cabo; **a. who saw it** todos los que lo vieron; **it's a. you can do** es lo único que puedes hacer; **I don't like it at a.** no me gusta en absoluto; **most of a., above a.** sobre todo; **once and for a.** de una vez para siempre; **thanks — not at a.** gracias — de nada; **a. in a.** en conjunto; **that's a.** ya está; **the score was one a.** empataron a uno; **it's still 3 a.** siguen empatados a tres. **3** *adv* **a. by myself** completamente solo, -a; **a. at once** *(suddenly)* de repente; *(altogether)* de una vez; **a. the better** tanto mejor; **a. the same** de todos modos; **if it's a. the same to you** si no te importa. **4** *n* **to give one's a.** darse por completo.

all-a·round *adj (athlete etc)* completo, -a.

al·le·giance lealtad *f* (**to** a).

al·ler·gic *adj* alérgico, -a (**to** a).

al·ley callejón *m*.

al·ley·way callejón *m*.

al·li·ance alianza *f.*

al·lied *adj (country)* aliado, -a; *(matters)* afín.

al·li·ga·tor caimán *m.*

al·lo·cate *vt* destinar (**to** para).

al·lot·ment *(land)* parcela *f.*

all-out *(effort)* supremo, -a; *(attack)* concentrado, -a.

al·low *vt (permit)* permitir; *(a request)* acceder a; *(allot) (time)* dejar; *(money)* destinar; **you're not allowed to do that** no puedes hacer eso; **I wasn't allowed to go** no me dejaron ir.

▶ **allow for** *vt* tener en cuenta.

al·low·ance *(payment)* subsidio *m*; *(discount)* descuento *m*; **to make allowances for sb** disculpar a algn; **travel a.** dietas *fpl* de viaje.

all-pur·pose *adj (tool)* multiuso, de uso universal.

all-right 1 *adj (okay)* bien; **thank you very much — that's a.** muchas gracias — de nada. **2** *adv (well)* bien; *(definitely)* sin duda; *(okay)* de acuerdo.

al·ly aliado, -a *mf.*

al·mond almendra *f.*

al·most *adv* casi.

a·lone 1 *adj* solo, -a; **let a.** ni mucho menos; **leave it a.!** ¡no lo toques!; **leave me a.** déjame en paz. **2** *adv* solamente.

a·long 1 *adv* **come a.!** ¡anda, ven!; **a. with** junto con. **2** *prep (the length of)* a lo largo de; **to walk a. the street** andar por la calle.

a·long·side 1 *adv* de costado. **2** *prep* al lado de.

a·loud *adv* en voz alta.

al·pha·bet alfabeto *m.*

al·pha·bet·i·cal *adj* alfabético, -a.

al·pha·bet·i·cal·ly *adv* por orden alfabético.

Alps *npl* **the A.** los Alpes.

al·read·y *adv* ya.

al·right *adj & adv* = **all right**.

al·so *adv* también.

al·tar altar *m.*

al·ter 1 *vt (plan)* cambiar; *(law, draft etc)* modificar. **2** *vi* cambiar(se).

al·ter·a·tion *(to plan)* cambio *m*; *(to law etc)* modificación *f*; *(to timetable)* revisión *f.*

al·ter·nate 1 *adj* alterno, -a; **on a. days** cada dos días. **2** *vt* alternar; **a alternates with b** a alterna con b.

al·ter·nate·ly *adv* **a. hot and cold** ahora caliente, ahora frío.

al·ter·na·tive 1 *adj* alternativo, -a. **2** *n* alternativa *f*, **I have no a.** no tengo más remedio.

al·ter·na·tive·ly *adv* o bien.

al·though *conj* aunque.

al·to·geth·er *adv (in total)* en total; *(completely)* completamente.

a·lu·mi·num aluminio *m.*

al·ways *adv* siempre.

am *1st person sing pres of* **be**.

a.m. *abbr of* **ante meridiem** de la mañana; **2 a.m.** las dos de la mañana.

am·a·teur 1 *n* aficionado, -a *mf.* **2** *adj* aficionado, -a; *(pejorative)* chapucero, -a.

a·maze *vt* asombrar; **to be amazed at sth** quedar pasmado, -a de algo.

a·maz·ing *adj* asombroso, -a.

am·bas·sa·dor embajador, -a *mf.*

am·ber 1 *adj (traffic light)* amarillo, -a, ámbar. **2** *n* ámbar.

am·big·u·ous *adj* ambiguo, -a.

am·bi·tion ambición *f.*

am·bi·tious *adj* ambicioso, -a.

am·bu·lance ambulancia *f*; **a. driver** ambulanciero *m.*

a·mend *vt (law)* enmendar; *(error)* subsanar.

A·mer·i·can *adj & n (of USA)* norteamericano, -a *(mf)*, estadounidense *(mf)*; *(of continent)* americano, -a *(mf).*

a·mid(st) *prep* entre, en medio de.

am·mu·ni·tion municiones *fpl.*

a·mong(st) *prep* entre.

am·o·rous *adj (person)* ligón, -ona; *(feelings, relationship)* amoroso.

a·mount cantidad *f*, *(of money)*

suma *f*; *(of bill)* importe *m*.

▸ **amount to** *vt* ascender a; *(be equivalent to)* equivaler a.

am·ple *adj (enough)* bastante; *(more than enough)* abundante; *(large)* amplio, -a.

am·pli·fi·er amplificador *m*.

am·pu·tate *vt* amputar.

a·muse *vt* divertir.

a·muse·ment diversión *f*.

a·muse·ment park parque *m* de atracciones.

a·mus·ing *adj* divertido, -a.

an *indef art* see **a**.

a·nal·y·sis *(pl* analyses) análisis *m inv*.

an·a·lyst *n* analista *mf*; *(psychoanalyst)* psicoanalista *mf*.

an·a·lyze *vt* analizar.

an·ar·chy anarquía *f*.

a·nat·o·my anatomía *f*.

an·ces·tor antepasado *m*.

an·chor 1 *n* ancla *f*. 2 *vt* anclar; *fig (fix securely)* sujetar.

an·cho·vy anchoa *f*.

an·cient *adj* antiguo, -a.

and *conj*; *(before stressed i-, hi-)* e; **a hundred a. one** ciento uno; **a. so on** etcétera; **come a. see us** ven a vernos; **she cried a. cried** no paró de llorar; **try a. help me** trata de ayudarme; **wait a. see** espera a ver; **worse a. worse** cada vez peor.

an·es·thet·ic anestesia *f*.

an·gel ángel *m*.

an·ger cólera *f*.

an·gle ángulo *m*; *(point of view)* punto *m* de vista.

an·gler pescador, -a *mf* de caña.

an·gling pesca *f* con caña.

an·gri·ly *adv* furiosamente.

an·gry *adj* enfadado, -a; **to get a.** enfadarse.

an·i·mal *adj & n* animal *(m)*.

an·kle tobillo *m*; **a. socks** calcetines *mpl* cortos.

an·nex *(building)* (edificio *m)* anexo *m*.

an·ni·ver·sa·ry aniversario *m*.

an·nounce *vt* anunciar; *(news)* comunicar.

an·nounce·ment anuncio *m*; *(news)* comunicación *f*, *(statement)* declaración *f*.

an·nounc·er *(on TV)* locutor, -a *mf*.

an·noy *vt* molestar; **to get annoyed** molestarse.

an·noy·ing *adj* molesto, -a.

an·nu·al 1 *adj* anual. **2** *n (book)* anuario *m*.

an·nu·al·ly *adv* anualmente.

a·non·y·mous *adj* anónimo *f*.

an·o·rak anorak *m*.

an·oth·er 1 *adj* otro, -a; **a. one** otro, -a; **a. 15** otros quince. **2** *pron* otro, -a; **to love one a.** quererse el uno al otro.

an·swer 1 *n (to letter etc)* contestación *f*, *(to question)* respuesta *f*, *(to problem)* solución *f*; **there's no a.** *(on telephone)* no contestan; *(at door)* no abren. **2** *vt* contestar a; *(problem)* resolver; *(door)* abrir; *(phone)* contestar. **3** *vi* contestar.

▸ **answer back** *vi* replicar; **don't a. back!** ¡no repliques!

▸ **answer for** *vt* responder de; **he's got a lot to a. for** es responsable de muchas cosas.

▸ **answer to** *vt (name)* responder a; *(description)* corresponder a.

an·swer·ing ma·chine contestador *m* automático.

ant hormiga *f*.

Ant·arc·tic 1 *adj* antártico, -a; **A. Ocean** océano *m* Antártico. **2** *n* the **A.** La Antártida.

an·te·lope antílope *m*.

an·ten·na *(pl* antennae) antena *f*.

an·them national a. himno *m* nacional.

an·thol·o·gy antología *f*.

an·ti·bi·ot·ic *adj & n* antibiótico, -a *(m)*.

an·ti·bod·y anticuerpo *m*.

an·tic·i·pate *vt (expect)* esperar; *(problems)* anticipar.

an·tic·i·pa·tion *(excitement)* ilusión *f.*

an·tics *npl* payasadas *fpl; (naughtiness)* travesuras *fpl.*

an·ti·freeze anticongelante *m.*

an·ti·his·ta·mine *n* antihistamínico *m.*

an·tique 1 *adj* antiguo, -a. **2** *n* antigüedad *f.*

an·tique deal·er anticuario, -a *mf.*

an·tique shop tienda *f* de antigüedades.

an·ti·sep·tic *adj & n* antiséptico, -a *(m).*

anx·i·e·ty *(concern)* inquietud *f; (worry)* preocupación *f, (eagerness)* ansia *f.*

anx·ious *adj (concerned)* inquieto, -a; *(worried)* preocupado, -a; *(fearful)* angustiado, -a; *(eager)* ansioso, -a.

anx·ious·ly *adv (to wait)* con impaciencia.

an·y 1 *adj (in questions, conditionals)* algún, -una; **are there a. seats left?** ¿quedan plazas?; **is there a. water left?** ¿queda agua?; **if you see a. blouses you like** si ves algunas blusas que te gusten. ▪ *(in negative clauses)* ningún, -una; **there aren't a. others** no hay otros. ▪ *(no matter which)* cualquier, -a; *(every)* todo, -a; **a. doctor will say the same** cualquier médico te dirá lo mismo; **at a. moment** en cualquier momento; **in a. case** de todas formas. **2** *pron (in questions, conditionals)* alguno, -a; **do they have a.?** ¿tienen alguno?; **I need some paper, do you have a.?** necesito papel, ¿tienes?; **if you see a., let me know** si ves alguno, -a, dímelo. ▪ *(in negative clauses)* ninguno, -a; **I don't want a.** no quiero ninguno, -a. ▪ *(no matter which)* cualquiera; **a. of them will do** cualquiera vale. **3** *adv* **is there a. more?** ¿hay más?; **not a. more/longer** ya no; **is that a. better?** ¿está mejor así?

an·y·bod·y *pron (in questions,*

conditionals) alguien; *(in negative clauses)* nadie; *(no matter who)* cualquiera; **bring a. you like** trae a quien quieras.

an·y·how *adv (in spite of that)* de todas formas; *(changing the subject)* bueno; *(carelessly)* de cualquier forma.

an·y·one *pron* **= anybody.**

an·y·place *adv* **= anywhere.**

an·y·thing *pron (in questions, conditionals)* algo, alguna cosa; *(in negative clauses)* nada; *(no matter what)* cualquier cosa; **a. but that** cualquier cosa menos eso; **a. else?** ¿algo más?; **hardly a.** casi nada; **to run/work like a.** correr/trabajar a más no poder.

an·y·way *adv* **= anyhow.**

an·y·where *adv (in questions, conditionals) (position)* en alguna parte; *(movement)* a alguna parte; **could it be a. else?** ¿podría estar en otro sitio? ▪ *(in negative clauses) (position)* en ninguna parte; *(movement)* a ninguna parte. ▪ *(no matter where)* en cualquier parte; **go a. you like** ve a donde quieras.

a·part *adv* **you should keep them a.** debes mantenerlos aparte; **to fall a.** deshacerse; **to take sth a.** desmontar algo; **with his feet a.** con los pies separados; **a. from** aparte de.

a·part·ment piso *m;* **a. complex** bloque *m* de pisos.

ape mono *m.*

a·pé·ri·tif aperitivo *m.*

a·pol·o·get·ic *adj* **he was very a.** pidió mil perdones.

a·pol·o·gize *vi* disculparse *(for* por*).*

a·pol·o·gy disculpa *f.*

a·pos·tro·phe apóstrofo *m.*

ap·pall·ing *adj (horrifying)* horroroso, -a; *(very bad)* fatal.

ap·pa·ra·tus aparato *m; (equipment)* equipo *m.*

ap·par·ent adj (obvious) evidente; (seeming) aparente; **to become a.** ponerse de manifiesto.

ap·par·ent·ly adv (seemingly) por lo visto.

ap·peal 1 n (request) solicitud f; (plea) súplica f; (interest) interés m; (in law) apelación f. **2** vi (plead) rogar (**to** a); **to a. for help** solicitar ayuda; **it doesn't a. to me** no me dice nada.

ap·pear vi (become visible) aparecer; (publicly) presentarse; (seem) parecer; **so it appears** según parece.

ap·pear·ance (becoming visible) aparición f; (publicly) presentación f; (of book etc) publicación f; (look) aspecto m; **to all appearances** al parecer.

ap·pen·di·ci·tis apendicitis f.

ap·pen·dix (pl **appendices**) apéndice m.

ap·pe·tite apetito m; (sexual) deseo m; **he's lost his a. for this sort of job** se le han quitado las ganas de un trabajo de este tipo.

ap·pe·tiz·ing adj apetitoso.

ap·plaud vti aplaudir.

ap·plause aplausos mpl, aplauso m.

ap·ple manzana f; **a. pie** tarta f de manzana; **a. tree** manzano m.

ap·pli·ance dispositivo m.

ap·pli·ca·ble adj aplicable (**to** a).

ap·pli·cant (for post) candidato, -a mf.

ap·pli·ca·tion (of cream) aplicación f; (for post etc) solicitud f; **a. form** solicitud f.

ap·ply 1 vt aplicar; (brake) echar; (law) recurrir a; (force) usar; **to a. oneself to sth** dedicarse a algo. **2** vi (for job) presentar una solicitud.

▸**apply for** vt (post, information) solicitar.

ap·point·ment (to post) nombramiento m; (meeting) cita f.

ap·prais·al evaluación f.

ap·pre·ci·ate 1 vt (be thankful for) agradecer; (understand) entender; (value) apreciar. **2** vi (increase in value) apreciarse.

ap·pre·ci·a·tion (of help, advice) agradecimiento m; (of difficulty) comprensión f; (increase in value) apreciación f.

ap·pren·tice aprendiz, -a mf.

ap·pren·tice·ship aprendizaje m.

ap·proach 1 n (coming near) acercamiento m; (to town) acceso m; (to problem) enfoque m. **2** vt (come near to) acercarse a; (problem) abordar. **3** vi acercarse.

ap·pro·pri·ate adj (suitable) apropiado, -a; (convenient) oportuno, -a.

ap·pro·pri·ate·ly adv adecuadamente.

ap·prov·al aprobación f; **on a.** sin compromiso de compra.

ap·prove vt aprobar.

▸**approve of** vt (conduct, decision, idea) aprobar.

ap·prox·i·mate adj aproximado, -a.

ap·prox·i·mate·ly adv aproximadamente.

a·pri·cot albaricoque m.

A·pril abril m; **A. Fools' Day** día m uno de abril, ≃ día de los Inocentes (28 de diciembre).

a·pron delantal m.

apt adj (suitable) apropiado, -a; (description) exacto, -a; **to be a. to do sth** (liable) tener tendencia a hacer algo.

ap·ti·tude capacidad f.

a·quar·i·um acuario m.

Ar·ab adj & n árabe (mf).

A·ra·bi·an adj árabe.

Ar·a·bic 1 adj árabe; **A. numerals** numeración f arábiga. **2** n (language) árabe m.

ar·bi·trar·y adj arbitrario, -a.

arc arco m.

ar·cade arcada f; **shopping a.** galerías fpl (comerciales); **amusement a.** salón m de juegos.

arch 1 n (of bridge etc) arco m; (roof)

bóveda *f.* **2** *vt (back)* arquear.
arch·er arquero, -a *mf.*
arch·er·y tiro *m* con arco.
ar·chi·tect arquitecto, -a *mf.*
ar·chi·tec·ture arquitectura *f.*
Arc·tic the A. el Ártico.
are *2nd person sing pres, 1st, 2nd, 3rd person pl pres of* **be**.
ar·e·a zona *f; (of surface)* superficie *f.*
ar·e·a code prefijo *m* local.
a·re·na *n (stadium)* estadio *m; (circus)* pista *f.*
Ar·gen·tin·i·an *adj & n* argentino, -a *(mf).*
ar·gue 1 *vi (quarrel)* discutir; *(reason)* argumentar. **2** *vt* discutir; *(point of view)* mantener; **to a. that ...** sostener que ....*
ar·gu·ment *(quarrel)* discusión *f,* disputa *f; (reason)* argumento *m* **(for** a favor de; **against** en contra de).
a·rise* *vi (get up)* levantarse; *(problem, need)* surgir.
a·rith·me·tic aritmética *f.*
arm 1 *n* brazo *m; (of garment)* manga *f,* **arms** *(weapons)* armas *fpl.* **2** *vt* armar.
arm·band brazalete *m; (for swimming)* manguito *m.*
arm·chair sillón *m.*
ar·mor *(of tank etc)* blindaje *m;* **(suit of)** a. armadura *f.*
ar·mored car coche *m* blindado.
arm·pit axila *f.*
ar·my ejército *m.*
a·round 1 *adv* alrededor; **all a.** por todos lados. **2** *prep* alrededor de; *(approximately)* aproximadamente; **a. the corner** a la vuelta de la esquina; **a. here** por aquí; **there's nobody a.** no hay nadie; **to rush a.** correr de un lado para otro.
a·rouse *vt* despertar; *(sexually)* excitar.
ar·range 1 *vt (order)* ordenar; *(hair, flowers)* arreglar; *(music)* adaptar; *(plan)* organizar; *(agree on)* quedar en; **to a. a time** fijar una hora. **2** *vi* l

shall a. **for him to be there** lo arreglaré para que pueda asistir.
ar·range·ment *(display)* colocación *f; (of music)* adaptación *f; (agreement)* acuerdo *m;* **arrangements** *(plans)* planes *mpl.*
ar·rears *npl* atrasos *mpl;* **to be paid in a.** cobrar con retraso; **salaries are paid monthly in a.** los salarios se pagan mensualmente con un mes de retraso.
ar·rest 1 *n* detención *f;* **to be under a.** estar detenido, -a. **2** *vt (criminal)* detener.
ar·ri·val llegada *f.*
ar·rive *vi* llegar **(at, in** a).
ar·row flecha *f.*
art arte *m; (drawing)* dibujo *m;* **arts** *(branch of knowledge)* letras *fpl.*
ar·ter·y arteria *f.*
ar·thri·tis artritis *f.*
ar·ti·cle artículo *m.*
ar·tic·u·late¹ *adj (speech)* claro, -a; *(person)* que se expresa bien.
ar·tic·u·late² *vti* articular; *(words)* pronunciar.
ar·ti·fi·cial *adj* artificial.
art·ist artista *mf; (painter)* pintor, -a *mf.*
ar·tis·tic *adj* artístico, -a.
as *adv & conj (comparison)* **as ... as ...** tan ... como ...; **as far as** hasta; **as far as I'm concerned** por lo que a mí respecta; **as many as** tantos, -as como; **as much as** tanto, -a como; **as opposed to** a diferencia de; **as little as $5** tan sólo cinco dólares; **as soon as they arrive** en cuanto lleguen; **I'll stay as long as I can** me quedaré todo el tiempo que pueda; **just as big** igual de grande; **three times as fast** tres veces más rápido; **the same as** igual que. ▪ *(manner)* como; **as you like** como quieras; **leave it as it is** déjalo tal como está; **do as I say** haz lo que yo te digo; **it serves as a table** sirve de mesa; **she was dressed as a gypsy** iba vestida de gitana; **to act as if** actuar

como si (+ *subjunctive*). ▪ *(time)* mientras; **as a child** de niño, -a; **as I was eating** mientras comía; **as we were leaving** we saw Pat al salir vimos a Pat; **as from, as of** a partir de. ▪ *(because)* como, ya que; **as it is getting late** ya que se está haciendo tarde. ▪ *(and so)* igual que; **as I do** igual que yo; **as well** también. ▪ *(concerning)* **as for my brother** en cuanto a mi hermano.

ASAP *abbr of* as soon as possible lo antes posible.

as·cer·tain *vt (establish)* precisar, determinar; *(find out)* averiguar.

ash[1] *(tree)* fresno *m*.

ash[2] ceniza *f*.

a·shamed *adj* avergonzado, -a; **you ought to be a. of yourself!** ¿no te da vergüenza?

a·shore *adv* en tierra; **to go a.** desembarcar.

ash·tray cenicero *m*.

Ash Wednes·day miércoles *m inv* de ceniza.

A·sian *adj & n* asiático, -a *(mf)*.

a·side 1 *adv* aparte; **to stand a.** apartarse. **2** *prep* **a. from** *(apart from)* aparte de; *(as well as)* además de. **3** *n* aparte *m*.

ask 1 *vt* preguntar; *(request)* pedir; *(invite)* invitar; **to a. sb a question** preguntar algo a algn; **to a. sb how to do sth** preguntar a algn cómo se hace algo. **2** *vi (inquire)* preguntar; *(request)* pedir.

▸**ask after** *vt* preguntar por.

▸**ask for** *vt (help)* pedir; *(person)* preguntar por; **to a. sb for sth** pedir algo a algn.

a·sleep *adj* dormido, -a; **to fall a.** quedarse dormido, -a.

as·par·a·gus *inv* espárrago *m*.

as·pect aspecto *m*.

as·pi·rin aspirina *f*.

as·sault 1 *n* ataque *m* (on a); *(crime)* agresión *f*. **2** *vt* atacar; *(sexually)* violar.

as·sem·ble 1 *vt (people)* reunir;

(furniture) montar. **2** *vi (people)* reunirse.

as·sem·bly assamblea *f*; *(of machinery etc)* montaje *m*; **morning a.** servicio *m* matinal.

as·sert *vt* afirmar; **to a. oneself** imponerse; **to a. one's rights** hacer valer sus derechos.

as·sess *vt (estimate value)* valorar; *(damages, price)* calcular; *(effect)* evaluar.

as·set ventaja *f*; **to be an a.** *(person)* ser de gran valor; **assets** activo *m*.

as·sign *vt* asignar.

as·sign·ment *(task)* tarea *f*.

as·sist *vti* ayudar.

as·sis·tance ayuda *f*.

as·sis·tant ayudante *mf*; **a. manager** subdirector, -a *mf*; **shop a.** dependiente, -a *mf*.

as·so·ci·ate[1] *vt (ideas)* relacionar. **2** *vi* **to a. with** tratar con.

as·so·ci·ate[2] *(colleague)* colega *mf*; *(partner)* socio, -a *mf*; *(accomplice)* cómplice *mf*.

as·so·ci·a·tion asociación *f*; *(company)* sociedad *f*.

as·sort·ed *adj* surtido, -a.

as·sort·ment surtido *m*.

as·sume *vt (suppose)* suponer; *(power)* asumir; *(attitude, name)* adoptar.

as·sur·ance *(guarantee)* garantía *f*; *(confidence)* confianza *f*; *(insurance)* seguro *m*.

as·sure *vt* asegurar.

as·ter·isk asterisco *m*.

asth·ma asma *f*.

asth·mat·ic *adj & n* asmático, -a *(mf)*.

a·ston·ish *vt* asombrar.

a·ston·ish·ing *adj* asombroso, -a.

a·stray *adv* **to go a.** extraviarse; *fig* equivocarse.

a·strol·o·gy astrología *f*.

as·tro·naut astronauta *mf*.

as·tron·o·my astronomía *f*.

a·sy·lum *(protection)* asilo *m*; **to seek political a.** pedir asilo político;

mental a. manicomio m.

at prep (position) en, a; **at school/work** en el colegio/trabajo; **at the window** a la ventana; **at the top** en lo alto. ▪ (direction) a; **to look at sth/sb** mirar algo/a algn; **to shout at sb** gritarle a algn. ▪ (time) a; **at Easter/Christmas** en Semana Santa/Navidad; **at six o'clock** a las seis. ▪ **at best/worst** en el mejor/peor de los casos; **not at all** en absoluto; (don't mention it) de nada. ▪ (rate) a; **at 100 dollars each** a 100 dólares la unidad; **two at a time** de dos en dos.

ath·lete atleta mf.

ath·let·ic adj atlético, -a; (sporty) deportista.

ath·let·ics npl atletismo m sing.

At·lan·tic the A. (Ocean) el (océano) Atlántico.

at·las atlas m.

at·mos·phere (air) atmósfera f, (ambience) ambiente m.

at·om átomo m; **a. bomb** bomba f atómica.

a·tom·ic adj atómico, -a.

at·tach vt (stick) pegar; (document) adjuntar; **to be attached to** (be fond of) tener cariño a.

at·ta·ché agregado, -a mf; **a. case** maletín m.

at·tack 1 n ataque m. **2** vt (assault) atacar; (problem) abordar.

at·tack·er agresor, -a mf.

at·tain vt (aim) lograr; (rank, age) llegar a.

at·tempt 1 n intento m; **at the second a.** a la segunda. **2** vt intentar.

at·tend 1 vt (school) frecuentar; (meeting) asistir a. **2** vi (at meeting) asistir.

▸**attend to** vt (business) ocuparse de; (in shop) atender a.

at·ten·dance asistencia f.

at·ten·dant (in museum) guía mf; (in parking lot) vigilante, -a mf.

at·ten·tion atención f; **for the a. of** a la atención de.

at·ten·tive adj (listener) atento, -a; (helpful) solícito, -a.

at·tic ático m.

at·ti·tude actitud f, (position of body) postura f.

at·tor·ney abogado, -a mf; **A. General** ≈ Ministro, -a mf de Justicia; **district a.** fiscal mf.

at·tract vt atraer; **to a. attention** llamar la atención.

at·trac·tion (attractive thing) atractivo m; (charm) encanto m.

at·trac·tive adj (person) atractivo, -a; (idea, proposition) atrayente.

at·trib·ute¹ n (quality) atributo m.

at·trib·ute² vt atribuir (**to** a).

auc·tion 1 n subasta f. **2** vt subastar.

auc·tion·eer subastador, -a mf.

au·di·ble adj audible.

au·di·ence (spectators) público m; (at concert, conference) auditorio m; (television) telespectadores mpl; (meeting) audiencia f.

au·di·o de sonido.

au·di·o·vis·u·al adj audiovisual.

au·dit 1 n revisión f de cuentas. **2** vt revisar, intervenir.

Au·gust agosto m.

aunt (also fam **auntie, aunty**) tía f.

au pair a. (girl) au pair f.

Aus·tra·lian adj & n australiano, -a (mf).

Aus·tri·an adj & n austríaco, -a (mf).

au·then·tic adj auténtico, -a.

au·thor autor, -a mf.

au·thor·i·ty autoridad f; **local a.** ayuntamiento m.

au·thor·ize vt autorizar; (payment etc) aprobar.

au·to·bi·og·ra·phy autobiografía f.

au·to·graph 1 n autógrafo m. **2** vt (book, photo) dedicar.

au·to·mat·ic 1 adj automático, -a. **2** n (car) coche m automático.

au·to·mat·i·cal·ly adv automáticamente.

au·to·mo·bile automóvil m, Am carro m.

au·ton·o·mous *adj* autónomo, -a.

au·tumn otoño *m*.

aux·il·ia·ry *adj* auxiliar.

a·vail·a·ble *adj (thing)* disponible; *(person)* libre.

av·a·lanche avalancha *f*.

av·e·nue avenida *f*, *fig* vía *f*.

av·er·age 1 *n* promedio *m*; **on a.** por término medio. **2** *adj* medio, -a; *(middle)* regular.

a·vi·a·tion aviación *f*.

av·o·ca·do *(also* **avocado pear***)* aguacate *m*.

a·void *vt* evitar; **to a. doing sth** evitar hacer algo.

a·void·a·ble *adj* evitable.

a·wake 1 *adj* despierto, -a. **2** *vi** despertarse.

a·ward 1 *n (prize)* premio *m*; *(medal)* condecoración *f*, *(grant)* beca *f*. **2** *vt (prize)* otorgar; *(medal)* dar; *(damages)* adjudicar.

a·ware *adj (informed)* enterado, -a; **not that I'm a. of** que yo sepa no; **to become a. of sth** darse cuenta de algo.

a·way *adv* **far a.** lejos; **go a.!** ¡lárgate!; **it's 3 miles a.** está a 3 millas (de distancia); **keep a. from the fire!** ¡no te acerques al fuego!; **right a.** en seguida; **to be a.** *(absent)* estar ausente; **to go a.** irse; **to play a.** *(in sport)* jugar fuera; **to turn a.** volver la cara; **to chatter/work a.** hablar/trabajar sin parar.

aw·ful *adj* espantoso, -a; *fam* **an a. lot of work** muchísimo trabajo.

aw·ful·ly *adv fam* terriblemente.

awk·ward *adj (clumsy)* torpe; *(difficult)* pesado, -a; *(moment)* inoportuno, -a.

awn·ing *(on shop)* marquesina *f*.

ax 1 *n* hacha *f*. **2** *vt (jobs)* suprimir; *(cut back)* reducir; *(plan)* cancelar.

ax·is *(pl* **axes***)* eje *m*.

ax·le eje *m*.

B

BA *abbr of* **Bachelor of Arts**.

ba·by bebé *m*; *(young child)* niño, -a *mf*.

ba·by car·riage cochecito *m* de niño.

ba·by·sit *vi* hacer de canguro.

ba·by·sit·ter canguro *mf*.

bach·e·lor soltero *m*, **B. of Arts/Science** licenciado, -a *mf* en Filosofía y Letras/Ciencias.

back 1 *n (of person)* espalda *f*; *(of chair)* respaldo *m*; *(of hand)* dorso *m*; *(of house, car)* parte *f* de atrás; *(of stage, cupboard)* fondo *m*; **b. to front** al revés. **2** *adj* trasero, -a; **b. door** puerta *f* de atrás; **b. seat** asiento *m* de detrás; **b. wheel** rueda *f* trasera; **b. number** número *m* atrasado. **3** *adv (at the rear)* atrás; *(towards the rear)* hacia atrás. **4** *vt (support)* apoyar; *(financially)* financiar; *(bet on)* apostar por.

▸ **back out** *vi (withdraw)* volverse atrás.

▸ **back up** *vt (support)* apoyar a.

back·ache dolor *m* de espalda.

back·fire *vi (car)* petardear.

back·ground fondo *m*; *(origin)* origen *m*; *(past)* pasado *m*; *(education)* formación *f*; *(circumstances)* antecedentes *mpl*; **b. music** hilo *m* musical.

back·ing *(support)* apoyo *m*; *(financial)* respaldo *m* financiero.

back·log **to have a b. of work** tener un montón de trabajo atrasado.

back·pack mochila *f*.

back·side *fam* trasero *m*.

back·stage *adv* entre bastidores.

back·up *(of disk)* copia *f* de seguridad.

back·ward 1 *adj (movement)* hacia atrás; *(child, country)* retrasado, -a. **2** *adv* (hacia) atrás.

back·wards *adv* hacia atrás; **to walk b.** andar de espaldas.

back·yard jardín *m* trasero.

ba·con tocino *m*, beicon *m*.

bac·te·ri·a *npl* bacterias *fpl*.

bad *adj* malo, -a; *(decayed)* podrido, -a; *(accident)* grave; *(headache)* fuerte; *(ill)* enfermo, -a.

badge insignia *f*, *(metal disc)* chapa *f*.

badg·er tejón *m*.

bad·ly *adv* mal; *(seriously)* gravemente; *(very much)* mucho; **we need it b.** nos hace mucha falta; **to be b. off** *(financially)* andar mal de dinero.

bad-man·nered *adj* maleducado.

bad·min·ton bádminton *m*.

bad-tem·pered *adj* **to be b.** *(temperament)* tener mal genio; *(temporarily)* estar de mal humor.

baf·fle *vt* desconcertar.

bag *(plastic, paper, shopping)* bolsa *f*, *(handbag)* bolso *m*; *fam* **bags of** montones de; **bags** *(under eyes)* ojeras *fpl*.

bag·gage equipaje *m*.

bag·gy *adj* holgado, -a; **b. trousers** pantalones *mpl* anchos.

bag·pipes *npl* gaita *f sing*.

bail fianza *f*; **on b.** bajo fianza.

bait cebo *m*.

bake *vt* cocer al horno.

baked *adj* al horno; **b. potato** patata *f* asada.

baked beans alubias *fpl* cocidas en salsa de tomate.

bak·er panadero, -a *mf*.

bak·er·y panadería *f*.

bal·ance 1 *n* *(equilibrium)* equilibrio *m*; *(financial)* saldo *m*; *(remainder)* resto *m*. **2** *vt* poner en equilibrio **(on** en); *(budget)* equilibrar. **3** *vi* guardar el equilibrio.

bal·ance sheet balance *m*.

bal·co·ny balcón *m*.

bald *adj* calvo, -a.

bald·ness calvicie *f*.

Bal·kans *npl* **the B.** los Balcanes.

ball¹ *(in baseball, tennis etc)* pelota *f*;

(football) balón *m*; *(in billiards, golf etc)* bola *f*, *(of wool)* ovillo *m*; **to be on the b.** *fam* ser un espabilado.

ball² *(dance)* baile *m*.

bal·le·ri·na bailarina *f*.

bal·let ballet *m*.

bal·loon globo *m*.

bal·lot votación *f*.

ball·point (pen) bolígrafo *m*.

ball·room salón *m* de baile.

ban 1 *n* prohibición *f*. **2** *vt* *(prohibit)* prohibir; *(exclude)* excluir.

ba·nan·a plátano *m*, *Am* banana *f*.

band *(strip)* tira *f*, *(stripe)* raya *f*, *(group)* grupo *m*; *(of musicians)* banda *f*.

band·age 1 *n* venda *f*. **2** *vt* vendar.

Band-Aid® tirita® *f*.

bang *n* *(blow)* golpe *m*; *(noise)* ruido *m*; *(explosion)* estallido *m*; *(of gun)* estampido *m*.

▶ **bang into** *vt* golpearse contra.

bang·er *fam* *(firework)* petardo *m*; **old b.** *(car)* coche *m* destartalado.

ban·gle brazalete *m*.

ban·is·ter(s) pasamanos *m inv*.

bank¹ *(for money)* banco *m*.

bank² *(of river)* ribera *f*, orilla *f*.

▶ **bank on** *vt* contar con.

bank ac·count cuenta *f* bancaria.

bank card tarjeta *f* bancaria.

bank·er banquero, -a *mf*.

bank·ing banca *f*.

bank·rupt *adj* en quiebra; **to go b.** quebrar.

bank·rupt·cy bancarrota *f*.

ban·ner *(in demonstration)* pancarta *f*.

bar 1 *n* *(of gold)* barra *f*, *(of chocolate)* tableta *f*, *(of cage)* barrote *m*; *(pub)* bar *m*; *(counter)* barra *f*, *(of soap)* pastilla *f*. **2** *vt* *(door)* atrancar; *(road)* cortar; *(exclude)* excluir *(from* de); *(prohibit)* prohibir.

bar·be·cue barbacoa *f*.

barbed *adj* **b. wire** alambre *m* de espino.

bar·ber barbero, -a *mf*; **b.'s (shop)** barbería *f*.

bare *adj* desnudo, -a; *(head)* descubierto, -a; *(foot)* descalzo, -a; *(room)* sin muebles; **with his b. hands** sólo con las manos.

bare·foot *adj & adv* descalzo, -a.

bare·ly *adv* apenas.

bar·gain 1 *n (deal)* negocio *m*; *(cheap purchase)* ganga *f*; **b. price** precio *m* de oferta. **2** *vi* negociar.

▸**bargain for** *vt* esperar; **I hadn't bargained for this** no contaba con esto.

barge gabarra *f*.

▸**barge in** *vi (go in)* entrar sin permiso.

▸**barge into** *vt (room)* irrumpir en; *(person)* tropezar con.

bark¹ *vi (dog)* ladrar.

bark² *(of tree)* corteza *f*.

bark·ing ladridos *mpl*.

bar·ley cebada *f*.

barn granero *m*.

ba·rom·e·ter barómetro *m*.

bar·racks *npl* cuartel *m sing*.

bar·rage *(dam)* presa *f*.

bar·rel *(of wine)* tonel *m*; *(of beer, oil)* barril *m*; *(of firearm)* cañón *m*.

bar·ren estéril; *(land)* yermo, -a.

bar·rette pasador *m* (del pelo).

bar·ri·cade 1 *n* barricada *f*. **2** *vt* cerrar con barricadas.

bar·ri·er barrera *f*.

bar·tend·er camarero *m*.

base 1 *n* base *f*; *(foot)* pie *m*; *(of column)* basa *f*. **2** *vt* basar **(on** en).

base·ball béisbol *m*.

base·ment sótano *m*.

bash 1 *n (heavy blow)* golpetazo *m*; *(dent)* bollo *m*. **2** *vt* golpear.

▸**bash up** *vt* **to b. sb up** darle a algn una paliza.

ba·sic 1 *adj* básico, -a; **b. pay** sueldo *m* base. **2** *npl* **basics** lo fundamental.

ba·si·cal·ly *adv* fundamentalmente.

ba·sin *(washbowl)* palangana *f*; *(for washing up)* barreño *m*; *(in bathroom)* lavabo *m*.

ba·sis *(pl* bases) base *f*; **on the b. of** en base a.

bask *vi (in sunlight)* tostarse.

bas·ket *(big)* cesta *f*; *(small)* cesto *m*.

bass 1 *n (singer)* bajo *m*; *(notes)* graves *mpl*; **b. drum** bombo *m*; **b. guitar** bajo *m*. **2** *adj* bajo, -a.

bat¹ *(in baseball)* bate *m*.

bat² *(animal)* murciélago *m*.

bat³ *vt* **without batting an eyelid** sin pestañear.

batch *(of bread)* hornada *f*; *(of goods)* lote *m*.

bath 1 *n* baño *m*; *(tub)* bañera *f*; **to have a b.** bañarse. **2** *vt* bañar.

bathe *vi* bañarse.

bath·ing baño *m*.

bath·ing suit traje *m* de baño.

bath·ing trunks *npl* bañador *m*.

bath·robe albornoz *m*.

bath·room cuarto *m* de baño.

bath·tub bañera *f*.

bat·ter 1 *n* pasta para rebozar. **2** *vt (baby)* maltratar.

▸**batter down** *vt (door)* derribar.

bat·tered *adj (car)* desvencijado, -a.

bat·ter·y *(for radio)* pila *f*, *(for car)* batería *f*.

bat·tle 1 *n* batalla *f*; *fig* lucha *f*. **2** *vi* luchar.

bat·tle·ship acorazado *m*.

baud baudio *m*.

bawl *vi* gritar.

bay bahía *f*; *(large)* golfo *m*.

BC *abbr of* **before Christ** a.C.

be* **1** *vi (permanent state)* ser; **he is very tall** es muy alto; **Washington is the capital** Washington es la capital; **sugar is sweet** el azúcar es dulce. ▪ *(temporary state, location)* estar; **how are you?** ¿cómo estás?; **this soup is cold** esta sopa está fría. ▪ *(cost)* **a return ticket is $24** un billete de ida y vuelta cuesta 24 dólares; **how much is it?** ¿cuánto es? ▪ *(weather)* **it's foggy** hay niebla; **it's cold/hot** hace frío/calor. ▪ *(time, date)* ser; **it's one o'clock** es la una; **it's four o'clock** son las cuatro; **it's**

the 11th/Tuesday today hoy es 11/ martes. ▪ **to be cold/afraid/hungry** tener frío/miedo/hambre; **she is thirty (years old)** tiene treinta. años. **2** v aux estar; **he is writing a letter** está escribiendo una carta; **she was singing** cantaba; **they are leaving next week** se van la semana que viene; **we have been waiting for a long time** hace mucho que estamos esperando. ▪ *(passive)* ser; **he was murdered** fue asesinado. ▪ *(obligation)* **I am to see him this afternoon** debo verle esta tarde. ▪ *(in tag questions)* ¿verdad?; **there is, there are** hay; **there was, there were** había; **there will be** habrá; **there would be** habría; **there have been a lot of complaints** ha habido muchas quejas; **there were ten of us** éramos diez. ▪ *(in tag questions)* ¿verdad?, ¿no?; **you're happy, aren't you?** estás contento, ¿verdad?

beach playa f.

bea·con baliza f, *(lighthouse)* faro m.

bead *(of necklace etc)* cuenta f; *(of liquid)* gota f.

beak *(of bird)* pico m.

beam *(in building)* viga f; *(of light)* rayo m.

beam·ing adj *(smiling)* radiante.

bean alubia f, judía f; Am frijol m; **broad b.** haba f; **coffee b.** grano m de café; **green** or **runner b.** judía f verde.

bear¹* **1** vt *(carry)* llevar; *(endure)* soportar; **to b. in mind** tener presente. **2** vi **to b. left** girar a la izquierda.

▸ **bear out** vt confirmar.

bear² *(animal)* oso m.

bear·a·ble adj soportable.

beard barba f.

beard·ed adj barbudo, -a.

bear·ing *(relevance)* relación f; **to have a b. on** estar relacionado, -a con; **to get one's bearings** orientarse.

beast bestia f.

beast·ly adj fam asqueroso, -a.

beat 1 vt* *(hit)* pegar; *(drum)* tocar; *(in cooking)* batir; *(defeat)* vencer. **2** vi* *(heart)* latir. **3** n *(of heart)* latido m; *(of policeman)* ronda f.

▸ **beat down** vi *(sun)* caer a plomo.

▸ **beat off** vt rechazar.

▸ **beat up** vt dar una paliza a.

beat·ing *(thrashing)* paliza f; *(defeat)* derrota f.

beau·ti·ful adj hermoso, -a, bello, -a.

beau·ty belleza f, hermosura f.

beau·ty spot *(on face)* lunar m; *(place)* lugar m pintoresco.

bea·ver castor m.

be·cause 1 conj porque. **2** prep b. of a.causa de.

be·come* vi *(doctor, priest)* hacerse; *(mayor, officer)* llegar a ser; *(angry, sad)* ponerse; **what has b. of him?** ¿qué ha sido de él?

bed cama f; **to get out of b.** levantarse de la cama; **to go to b.** acostarse; **b. and breakfast** *(service)* cama f y desayuno m; *(sign)* 'pensión'.

bed·ding ropa f de cama.

bed·room dormitorio m.

bed·side b. table mesilla f de noche.

bed·time hora f de acostarse.

bee abeja f.

beech haya f.

beef carne f de vaca, Am carne f de res.

been pp of **be**.

beep 1 n pitido m. **2** vi pitar.

beep·er busca(personas) m inv.

beer cerveza f; **a glass of b.** una caña.

beet red b. remolacha f.

bee·tle escarabajo m.

be·fore 1 conj *(earlier than)* antes de que (+ subjunctive), antes de (+ infinitive); **b. she goes** antes de que se vaya; **b. leaving** antes de salir. **2** prep *(place)* delante de; *(in the presence of)* ante; *(order, time)* antes de.

3 adv (time) antes; (place) (por) delante; **I have met him b.** ya lo conozco; **the night b.** la noche anterior.

be·friend vt trabar amistad con.

beg 1 vt (money etc) pedir; (beseech) rogar. **2** vi (solicit) mendigar; **to b. for money** pedir limosna.

beg·gar mendigo, -a mf.

be·gin* vti empezar, comenzar; **to b. doing** or **to do sth** empezar a hacer algo; **to b. with ...** para empezar ...

be·gin·ner principiante mf.

be·gin·ning principio m, comienzo m; **at the b. of May** a principios de mayo.

be·grudge vt dar de mala gana; (envy) envidiar; **to b. sb sth** envidiarle algo a algn.

be·half nombre m; **on b. of, in b. of** de parte de.

be·have vi (person) (com)portarse; **b. yourself!** ¡pórtate bien!

be·hav·ior comportamiento m, conducta f; (of machine) funcionamiento m.

be·hind 1 prep detrás de. **2** adv (in the rear) detrás, atrás; **I've left my umbrella b.** se me ha olvidado el paraguas; **to be b. with one's payments** estar atrasado, -a en los pagos. **3** n fam (bottom) trasero m.

beige adj & n beige (m).

belch 1 vi eructar. **2** n eructo m.

Bel·gian adj & n belga (mf).

be·lief creencia f; (opinion) opinión f; (faith) fe f; (confidence) confianza f (in en).

be·liev·a·ble adj creíble.

be·lieve vti creer; **I b. so** creo que sí; **to b. in sb/sth** creer en algn/algo.

be·liev·er (religious) creyente mf.

be·lit·tle vt (person) restar importancia a.

bell (of church) campana f; (small) campanilla f; (of school, door, bicycle) timbre m; (on animal) cencerro m.

bell·boy botones m inv.

bel·ly (of person) barriga f, tripa f.

bel·ly·ache fam dolor m de barriga.

be·long vi pertenecer (**to** a); (be a member) ser socio, -a (**to** de).

be·long·ings npl efectos mpl personales.

be·low 1 prep debajo de. **2** adv abajo.

belt cinturón m; (in machine) correa f; (area) zona f.

▸ **belt along** vi fam ir a todo gas.

bench (seat) banco m.

bend 1 vt* doblar; (back) encorvar; (head) inclinar. **2** vi* torcerse; (road) torcerse; **to b. (over)** inclinarse. **3** n (in river, road) curva f; (in pipe) recodo m.

▸ **bend down** vi inclinarse.

be·neath 1 prep (below) bajo, debajo de. **2** adv debajo.

ben·e·fi·cial adj (doing good) benéfico, -a; (advantageous) beneficioso, -a.

ben·e·fit 1 vt beneficiar. **2** vi sacar provecho (**from** or **by** de). **3** n (advantage) beneficio m; (allowance) subsidio m; **I did it for your b.** lo hice por tu bien.

bent adj (curved) curvado, -a; **to be b. on doing sth** (determined) estar empeñado, -a en hacer algo.

be·reave·ment duelo m.

ber·ry baya f.

ber·serk adj **to go b.** volverse loco, -a.

berth (bed) litera f.

be·side prep (next to) al lado de, junto a; (compared with) comparado con; **that's b. the point** eso no viene al caso.

be·sides 1 prep (in addition to) además de; (except) excepto. **2** adv además.

best 1 adj mejor; **the b. thing would be to phone them** lo mejor sería llamarles; **the b. part of a year** casi un año. **2** adv mejor; **as b. I can** lo mejor que pueda. **3** n lo mejor; **to do one's b.** hacer todo lo posible; **to make the**

b. of sth sacar el mejor partido de algo.

best man ≃ padrino *m* de boda.

best·sell·er best-seller *m*.

bet 1 *n* apuesta *f*. **2** *vti** apostar (**on** a).

be·tray *vt* traicionar.

be·tray·al traición *f*.

bet·ter 1 *adj* mejor; **that's b.!** ¡eso es!; **to get b.** mejorar; *(healthier)* mejor; **b. off** *(richer)* más rico, -a; **the b. part of the day** la mayor parte del día. **2** *adv* mejor; **we had b. leave** más vale que nos vayamos. **3** *vt (improve)* mejorar; *(surpass)* superar.

bet·ting apuestas *fpl*.

be·tween 1 *prep* entre; **b. you and me** entre nosotros; **closed b. 1 and 3** cerrado de la 1 a 3. **2** *adv* en medio; **in b.** *(position)* en medio; *(time)* mientras (tanto).

bev·er·age bebida *f*.

be·ware *vi* tener cuidado (**of** con); **b.!** ¡cuidado!

be·wil·der *vt* desconcertar.

be·yond 1 *prep* más allá de; **it is b. me why ...** no comprendo por qué ...; **this task is b. me** no puedo con esta tarea. **2** *adv* más allá.

bi·as *(tendency)* tendencia *f* (**towards** hacia); *(prejudice)* prejuicio *m*.

bi·as(s)ed *adj* parcial; **to be b. against sth/sb** tener prejuicio en contra de algo/algn.

bib *(for baby)* babero *m*.

Bi·ble Biblia *f*.

bi·cy·cle bicicleta *f*.

bid 1 *vti** *(at auction)* pujar (**for** por). **2** *n (offer)* oferta *f*; *(at auction)* puja *f*.

big *adj* grande (gran *before sing noun*); **a b. clock** un reloj grande; **a b. surprise** una gran sorpresa; **my b. brother** mi hermano mayor; *fam* **b. deal!** ¡y qué?

big·head *fam* engreído, -a *mf*.

bike *(bicycle)* bici *f*; *(motorcycle)* moto *f*.

bike path carril *m* bici.

bi·ki·ni bikini *m*.

bile bilis *f*.

bi·lin·gual *adj* bilingüe.

bill *(for gas etc)* factura *f*; *(in restaurant)* cuenta *f*; *(in Congress)* proyecto *m* de ley; *(currency)* billete *m* (de banco).

bill·board cartelera *f*.

bill·fold billetero *m*.

bil·liards billar *m*.

bil·lion *(thousand million)* mil millones *mpl*.

bin *(for storage)* cajón *m*; *(garbage)* **b.** cubo *m* de la basura.

bind* *vt (tie up)* atar; *(book)* encuadernar.

bind·er *(file)* carpeta *f*.

bin·go bingo *m*.

bin·oc·u·lars *npl* prismáticos *mpl*.

bi·o·log·i·cal *adj* biológico, -a.

bi·ol·o·gy biología *f*.

birch *(tree)* abedul *m*.

bird *(small)* pájaro *m*; *(large)* ave *f*.

bird's-eye view vista *f* de pájaro.

birth nacimiento *m*; **to give b. to a child** dar a luz a un niño.

birth cer·tif·i·cate partida *f* de nacimiento.

birth·day cumpleaños *m inv*.

birth·mark antojo *m*.

bis·cuit bizcocho *m*.

bish·op obispo *m*; *(chess)* alfil *m*.

bit *(small piece)* trozo *m*; *(small quantity)* poco *m*; **a b. of sugar** un poco de azúcar; **b. by b.** poco a poco; **a b.** *(slightly)* un poco.

bitch 1 *n (dog)* perra *f*, *fam (spiteful woman)* bruja *f*. **2** *vi fam* **to b.** *(about)* *(criticize)* criticar.

bite 1 *n (act)* mordisco *m*; *(wound)* mordedura *f*; *(mouthful, snack)* bocado *m*; *(insect)* **b.** picadura *f*. **2** *vti** morder; *(insect)* picar; **to b. one's nails** morderse las uñas.

bit·ter *adj* amargo, -a; *(weather)* glacial; *(wind)* cortante; *(person)* amargado, -a; *(struggle)* enconado, -a; *(hatred)* implacable.

bit·ter·ness amargura *f*; *(of weather)* crudeza *f*; *(of person)* rencor *m*.

bi·zarre *adj (odd)* extraño, -a; *(eccentric)* estrafalario, -a.

black 1 *adj (color)* negro, -a; *fig* **b. and blue** amoratado, -a. **2** *n (color)* negro *m*; *(person)* negro, -a *mf*.

▶ **black out** *vi (faint)* desmayarse.

black·ber·ry zarzamora *f*.

black·bird mirlo *m*.

black·board pizarra *f*, encerado *m*.

black·cur·rant grosella *f* negra.

black eye ojo *m* amoratado.

black·list lista *f* negra.

black·mail 1 *n* chantaje *m*. **2** *vt* chantajear.

black·mail·er chantajista *mf*.

black·out *(of lights)* apagón *m*; *(fainting)* pérdida *f* de conocimiento.

blad·der vejiga *f*.

blade *(of grass)* brizna *f*; *(of knife etc)* hoja *f*.

blame 1 *n* culpa *f*. **2** *vt* echar la culpa a; **he is to b.** él tiene la culpa.

blame·less *adj (person)* inocente; *(conduct)* intachable.

bland *adj (food)* soso, -a.

blank 1 *adj (without writing)* en blanco; **b. check** cheque *m* en blanco. **2** *n (space)* espacio *m* en blanco.

blan·ket manta *f*.

blare *vi* resonar.

▶ **blare out** *vt* pregonar.

blast 1 *n (of wind)* ráfaga *f*; *(of horn etc)* toque *m*; *(explosion)* explosión *f*; *(shock wave)* onda *f* de choque. **2** *vt fam* **b. (it)!** ¡maldito sea!

blast·ed *adj* maldito, -a.

blast·off despegue *m*.

blaze 1 *n (burst of flame)* llamarada *f*; *(fierce fire)* incendio *m*; *(of sun)* resplandor *m*. **2** *vi (fire)* arder; *(sun etc)* brillar.

blaz·er chaqueta *f* sport.

bleach *(household)* lejía *f*.

bleak *adj (countryside)* desolado, -a.

bleed* *vti* sangrar.

blem·ish *(flaw)* defecto *m*; *(on fruit)*

maca *f*, *fig* **without b.** sin tacha.

blend 1 *n* mezcla *f*. **2** *vt (mix)* mezclar; *(match)* armonizar. **3** *vi (mix)* mezclarse.

blend·er *(for food)* licuadora *f*.

bless *vt* bendecir; **b. you!** *(after sneeze)* ¡Jesús!

bless·ing bendición *f*; *(advantage)* ventaja *f*.

blew *pt of* **blow**.

blind 1 *adj* ciego, -a; **a b. man** un ciego; **a b. woman** una ciega. **2** *n (on window)* persiana *f*; *pl* **the b.** los ciegos.

blind·fold 1 *n* venda *f*. **2** *vt* vendar los ojos a.

blind·ly *adv* a ciegas; *(love)* ciegamente.

blind·ness ceguera *f*.

blink *vi (eyes)* pestañear; *(lights)* parpadear.

bliss felicidad *f*.

blis·ter *(on skin)* ampolla *f*.

bliz·zard ventisca *f*.

blob *(drop)* gota *f*; *(spot)* mancha *f*.

block 1 *n* bloque *m*; *(of wood)* taco *m*; *(group of buildings)* manzana *f*; **a b. of apartments** un bloque de pisos. **2** *vt (obstruct)* obstruir.

▶ **block up** *vt* bloquear; **to get blocked up** *(pipe)* obstruirse.

block·age bloqueo *m*.

bloke *fam* tío *m*, tipo *m*.

blond *adj & n* rubio (*m*).

blonde *adj & n* rubia (*f*).

blood sangre *f*; **b. donor** donante *mf* de sangre; **b. group** grupo *m* sanguíneo; **b. pressure** tensión *f* arterial; **high/low b. pressure** hipertensión *f*/hipotensión *f*.

blood·shed derramamiento *m* de sangre.

blood·shot *adj* inyectado, -a de sangre.

blood·y *adj (battle)* sangriento, -a; *(bloodstained)* manchado, -a de sangre.

bloom 1 *n (flower)* flor *f*, **in full b.** en flor. **2** *vi (blossom)* florecer.

blos·som 1 n (flower) flor f. **2** vi florecer.

blot (of ink) borrón m.

blotch·y adj (skin) enrojecido, -a; (paint) cubierto, -a de manchas.

blouse blusa f.

blow¹ golpe m.

blow²* 1 vi (wind) soplar. **2** vt (trumpet etc) tocar; (smoke) echar; (of wind) llevarse; **to b. one's nose** sonarse la nariz.

▸**blow away** vt **the wind blew it away** el viento se lo llevó.

▸**blow down** vt derribar.

▸**blow off 1** vt (remove) quitar. **2** vi (hat) salir volando.

▸**blow out 1** vt apagar. **2** vi apagarse.

▸**blow up 1** vt (building) volar; (inflate) inflar. **2** vi (explode) explotar.

blow dry 1 vt secar con secador, marcar. **2** n marcado m.

blow·torch soplete m.

blue 1 adj azul; (sad) triste. **2** n azul m.

blue·ber·ry arándano m.

blue·print proyecto m.

bluff 1 n (deception) farol m. **2** vi tirarse un farol.

blun·der 1 n metedura f de pata, fam patinazo m. **2** vi meter la pata.

blunt adj (knife) embotado, -a; (pencil) despuntado, -a; (frank) directo, -a; (statement) tajante.

blur 1 n **he was just a b.** apenas se le veía. **2** vt (shape) desdibujar; (memory) enturbiar.

blurred adj borroso, -a.

blush vi ruborizarse.

blus·ter·y adj borrascoso, -a.

board 1 n (plank) tabla f; (meals) pensión f; **full b.** pensión completa; **room and b.** casa f y comida; **b. of directors** consejo m de administración; **on b.** a bordo. **2** vt (ship, plane etc) embarcarse en.

board·er (in boarding house) huésped mf; (at school) interno, -a mf.

board·ing (embarkation) embarque m.

board·ing house pensión f.

board·ing pass tarjeta f de embarque.

board·ing school internado m.

boast vi jactarse (**about** de).

boat barco m; (small) barca f; (large) buque m.

bod·i·ly adj físico, -a.

bod·y cuerpo m; (corpse) cadáver m; (organization) organismo m.

bod·y·guard guardaespaldas mf inv.

bod·y·work carrocería f.

bo·gus adj falso, -a.

boil¹ 1 n **to come to a b.** empezar a hervir. **2** vt (water, egg) hervir; (food) cocer. **3** vi hervir.

▸**boil over** vi (milk) salirse.

boil² (on skin) furúnculo m.

boiled adj **b. egg** huevo m pasado por agua.

boil·er caldera f.

boil·ing adj (water) hirviente; **it's b. hot** (food) quema; (weather) hace un calor agobiante.

bold adj (courageous) valiente; (dress, proposition etc) audaz, atrevido.

bold·ness audacia f, descaro m, osadía f.

Bo·liv·i·an adj & n boliviano, -a (mf).

bolt 1 n (on door) cerrojo m; (small) pestillo m; (with nut) tornillo m. **2** vt (lock) cerrar con cerrojo; (food) engullir. **3** vi (person) largarse; (horse) desbocarse.

bomb 1 n bomba f. **2** vt (city etc) bombardear; (by terrorists) volar.

bomb·er bombardero m.

bomb·ing bombardeo m.

bond (link) vínculo m; (financial) bono m.

bone hueso m; (in fish) espina f.

bon·fire hoguera f.

bon·net (child's) gorro m.

bo·nus plus m; (on wages) prima f; (on shares) dividendo m extraordinario.

bon·y *adj (person)* huesudo, -a; *(fish)* lleno, -a de espinas.

boo 1 *interj* ¡bu! **2** *vt* abuchear.

boo·by trap trampa *f; (bomb etc)* trampa *f* explosiva.

book 1 *n* libro *m; (of stamps)* carpeta *f; (in commerce)* **books** cuentas *fpl.* **2** *vt (reserve)* reservar.

book·case estantería *f.*

booked up *adj* completo, -a.

book·ing *(reservation)* reserva *f.*

book·ing of·fice taquilla *f.*

book·keep·er contable *mf.*

book·keep·ing contabilidad *f.*

book·let *(pamphlet)* folleto *m.*

book·mak·er corredor, -a *mf* de apuestas.

book·sell·er librero, -a *mf.*

book·shelf estantería *f.*

book·store librería *f.*

boom *(noise)* estampido *m; (sudden prosperity)* auge *m.*

boost 1 *n* estímulo *m.* **2** *vt (increase)* aumentar; *(tourism, exports)* fomentar; **to b. sb's confidence** subirle la moral a algn.

boot *n* bota *f; (short)* botín *m; fam* **she got the b.** la echaron (del trabajo).

▸**boot out** *vt fam* echar a patadas.

booth *(in language lab etc)* cabina *f;* **telephone b.** cabina *f* telefónica.

booze *fam* **1** *n* priva *f.* **2** *vi* privar.

bor·der *n* borde *m; (frontier)* frontera *f.*

▸**border on** *vt (country)* lindar con.

bor·der·line 1 *adj (case etc)* dudoso, -a. **2** *n* línea *f* divisoria, frontera *f.*

bore 1 *vt* aburrir. **2** *n (person)* pesado, -a *mf; (thing)* lata *f;* **what a b.!** ¡qué rollo!

bore·dom aburrimiento *m.*

bor·ing *adj* aburrido, -a, pesado, -a.

born *adj* nacido, -a; **to be b.** nacer; **I was b. in 1969** nací en 1969.

bor·ough municipio *m.*

bor·row *vt* pedir prestado; **can I b. your pen?** ¿me dejas tu bolígrafo?

boss *n (head)* jefe, -a *mf; (factory owner etc)* patrón, -ona *mf.*

▸**boss around** *vt* ser mandón, -ona con.

boss·y *adj* mandón, -ona.

botch 1 *vt* chapucear; **a botched job** una chapuza. **2** *n* chapuza *f.*

both 1 *adj* ambos, -as, los/las dos; **b. men are teachers** ambos son profesores; **hold it with b. hands** sujétalo con las dos manos. **2** *pron* **b. (of them)** ambos, -as, los/las dos; **b. of you** vosotros dos. **3** *adv* a la vez; **b. New York and Ohio are in the U.S.** tanto Nueva York como Ohio están en los Estados Unidos.

both·er 1 *vt (disturb)* molestar; *(be a nuisance to)* dar la lata a; *(worry)* preocupar; **I can't be bothered** no tengo ganas; **he didn't b. shaving** no se molestó en afeitarse. **2** *vi* **don't b.** no te molestes. **3** *n (disturbance)* molestia *f; (nuisance)* lata *f; (trouble)* problemas *mpl.* **4** *interj* ¡maldito sea!

bot·tle botella *f; (of perfume, ink)* frasco *m;* **baby's b.** biberón *m.*

bot·tle o·pen·er abrebotellas *m inv.*

bot·tom 1 *adj (lowest)* más bajo, -a. **2** *n* parte *f* inferior; *(of sea, garden, street, box, bottle)* fondo *m; (of page, hill)* pie *m; (buttocks)* trasero *m;* **to be at the b. of the class** ser el último/la última de la clase.

boul·der canto *m* rodado.

bounce 1 *vi (ball)* rebotar; *(check)* ser rechazado, -a (por el banco). **2** *vt (ball)* botar.

bound¹ *adj* **he's b. to know it** seguro que lo sabe; **it's b. to happen** sucederá con toda seguridad; **it was b. to fail** estaba destinado al fracaso.

bound² *adj* **to be b. for** dirigirse a.

bound·a·ry límite *m.*

bounds *npl* **the river is out of b.** está prohibido bajar al río.

bou·quet *(of flowers)* ramillete *m.*

bou·tique boutique *f.*

bow¹ 1 *vi* hacer una reverencia. **2** *n (with head, body)* reverencia *f.*

bow² *(for violin, arrows)* arco *m;* *(knot)* lazo *m.*

bow·els *npl* entrañas *fpl.*

bowl¹ *(dish)* cuenco *m;* *(for soup)* tazón *m;* *(for washing clothes, dishes)* barreño *m.*

bowl² *vi (in cricket)* lanzar la pelota.

bowl·er *(hat)* bombín *m.*

bowl·ing *(game)* bolos *mpl.*

bowl·ing alley bolera *f.*

bowl·ing pin bolo *m.*

bowls *npl* bolos *mpl.*

bow tie pajarita *f.*

box¹ caja *f; (large)* cajón *m.*

box² **1** *vi* boxear. **2** *vt (hit)* pegar.

▶**box in** *vt (enclose)* aprisionar.

box·er boxeador *m; (dog)* bóxer *m.*

box·ing boxeo *m;* **b. ring** cuadrilátero *m.*

box of·fice taquilla *f.*

boy *(child)* chico *m; (youth)* joven *m.*

boy·cott **1** *n* boicot *m.* **2** *vt* boicotear.

boy·friend novio *m; (live-in)* compañero *m.*

bra sostén *m.*

brace·let pulsera *f.*

brack·et *(round)* paréntesis *m; (square)* corchete *m.*

brag *vi* jactarse **(about** de).

brag·ging fanfarronería *f.*

braid **1** *vt* trenzar. **2** *n* trenza *f.*

brain cerebro *m;* **brains** inteligencia *f;* **to have brains** ser inteligente.

brain·storm *(brilliant idea)* genialidad *f.*

brain·wash *vt* lavar el cerebro a.

brain·y *adj fam* inteligente.

brake **1** *n* freno *m.* **2** *vi* frenar.

brake light luz *f* de freno.

branch **1** *n (of tree)* rama *f; (of road)* bifurcación *f;* **b. (office)** sucursal *f.* **2** *vi (road)* bifurcarse.

▶**branch off** *vi* desviarse.

▶**branch out** *vi* diversificarse.

brand marca *f;* **b. name** marca *f* de fábrica.

brand-new *adj* flamante.

bran·dy brandy *m.*

brass latón *m.*

brave *adj* valiente.

brav·er·y valentía *f.*

brawl reyerta *f.*

brawn·y *adj* fornido, -a.

Bra·zil·i·an *adj & n* brasileño, -a *(mf).*

bread pan *m;* **b. and butter** pan con mantequilla.

bread-box panera *f.*

bread·crumb miga *f* de pan; **breadcrumbs** pan *m sing* rallado.

breadth *(width)* anchura *f; (extent)* amplitud *f.*

bread·win·ner cabeza *mf* de familia.

break **1** *vt** romper; *(fail to keep)* faltar a: *(destroy)* destrozar; *(financially)* arruinar; *(journey)* interrumpir; *(record)* batir; **to b. a leg** romperse la pierna; **to b. the law** violar la ley; **she broke the news to him** le comunicó la noticia. **2** *vi** romperse; *(storm)* estallar; *(story)* divulgarse. **3** *n (fracture)* rotura *f; (crack)* grieta *f; (opening)* abertura *f; (in a relationship)* ruptura *f; (pause)* pausa *f; (at school)* recreo *m; fam (chance)* oportunidad *f;* **to take a b.** descansar un rato; *(holiday)* tomar unos días libres; **a lucky b.** un golpe de suerte.

▶**break away** *vi (become separate)* desprenderse **(from** de).

▶**break down** **1** *vt (door)* derribar; *(resistance)* acabar con. **2** *vi (in car)* tener una avería; *(weep)* ponerse a llorar.

▶**break in** *vi (burglar)* entrar a la fuerza.

▶**break into** *vt (house)* allanar; *(safe)* forzar.

▶**break loose** *vi* escaparse.

▶**break off** **1** *vt (relations)* romper. **2** *vi (become detached)* desprenderse; *(talks)* interrumpirse; *(stop)* pararse.

▶**break out** *vi (prisoners)* escaparse; *(war etc)* estallar.

▶**break up** **1** *vt (object)* romper; *(car*

desguazar; (crowd) disolver. **2** vi romperse; (crowd) disolverse; (meeting) levantarse; (relationship) fracasar; (couple) separarse; (at end of term) terminar.

break·down avería f; (in communications) ruptura f; **(nervous) b.** crisis f nerviosa.

break·fast desayuno m; **to have b.** desayunar.

break-in robo m (con allanamiento de morada).

break·through avance m.

break·up (in marriage) separación f.

breast (chest) pecho m; (of chicken etc) pechuga f.

breast·feed vt dar el pecho a.

breast·stroke braza f.

breath aliento m; **out of b.** sin aliento.

Breath·a·lyz·er® alcoholímetro m.

breathe vti respirar.

▸ **breathe in** vi aspirar.

▸ **breathe out** vi espirar.

breath·ing respiración f; **b. space** respiro m.

breath·tak·ing adj impresionante.

breed 1 n (of animal) raza f. **2** vt* (animals) criar. **3** vi* (animals) reproducirse.

breed·er (person) criador, -a mf.

breed·ing (of animals) cría f; (of person) educación f; **b. ground** caldo m de cultivo.

breeze brisa f.

breez·y adj (weather) ventoso, -a.

brew 1 vt (beer) elaborar; (hot drink) preparar. **2** vi (tea) reposar; **a storm is brewing** se prepara una tormenta; **something's brewing** algo se está cociendo.

brew·er·y cervecería f.

bribe 1 vt sobornar. **2** n soborno m.

brick ladrillo m.

brick·lay·er albañil m.

bride novia f; **the b. and groom** los novios.

bride·groom novio m.

brides·maid dama f de honor.

bridge puente m.

brief 1 adj (short) breve; (concise) conciso, -a. **2** n briefs (for men) calzoncillos mpl; (for women) bragas fpl. **3** vt (inform) informar; (instruct) dar instrucciones a.

brief·case cartera f.

brief·ing (meeting) reunión f informativa.

brief·ly adv brevemente.

bright adj (light, sun, eyes) brillante; (color) vivo, -a; (day) claro, -a; (cheerful) alegre; (clever) listo, -a.

bright·en vi (prospects) mejorar; (face) iluminarse.

▸ **brighten up 1** vt (room etc) hacer más alegre. **2** vi (weather) despejarse; (person) animarse.

bright·ly adv brillantemente.

bright·ness (of sun) resplandor m; (of color) viveza f.

bril·liance (of light) brillo m; (of color) viveza f; (of person) brillantez f.

bril·liant adj brillante; (idea) genial; (very good) estupendo, -a.

bring* vt traer; (take to a different position) llevar; (cause) provocar; **could you b. that book?** ¿podrías traerme el libro?

▸ **bring about** vt provocar.

▸ **bring along** vt traer.

▸ **bring around** vt (revive) hacer volver en sí; (persuade) convencer.

▸ **bring back** vt (return) devolver; (reintroduce) volver a introducir; (make one remember) traer a la memoria.

▸ **bring down** vt (from upstairs) bajar (algo); (government) derribar; (reduce) rebajar.

▸ **bring forward** vt (meeting etc) adelantar.

▸ **bring in** vt (yield) dar; (show in) hacer entrar; (law etc) introducir.

▸ **bring out** vt (publish) publicar; (emphasize) recalcar.

▸ **bring to** vt reanimar.

▸ **bring together** vt (reconcile) reconciliar.

►**bring up** vt (educate) educar; (subject) plantear; (vomit up) vomitar.

brink (edge) borde m.

brisk adj (energic) enérgico, -a; (pace) rápido, -a; (trade) activo, -a.

brisk·ly adv (to walk) rápidamente.

bris·tle cerda f.

Brit·ish 1 adj británico, -a; **the B. Isles** las Islas Británicas. **2** npl **the B.** los británicos.

Brit·on británico, -a mf.

brit·tle adj quebradizo, -a.

broad adj (road, river) ancho, -a; (not detailed) general; **in b. daylight** a plena luz del día.

broad·cast 1 n emisión f. **2** vt* emitir.

broad·en vt ensanchar.

broc·co·li brécol m.

bro·chure folleto m.

broke adj **to be (flat) b.** estar sin blanca.

bro·ken adj roto, -a; (machinery) averiado, -a; (leg) fracturado, -a; **a b. home** una familia deshecha.

bro·ken-down adj (machine) averiado, -a.

bron·chi·tis bronquitis f.

bronze bronce m.

brooch broche m.

brood 1 n (of birds) cría f. **2** vi (ponder) rumiar; **to b. over a problem** darle vueltas a un problema.

brood·y adj (pensive) pensativo, -a; (moody) melancólico, -a; fam (woman) con ganas de tener hijos.

brook arroyo m.

broom escoba f, (plant) retama f.

broom·stick palo m de escoba.

broth·er hermano m; **brothers and sisters** hermanos.

broth·er-in-law cuñado m.

brought pt & pp of **bring**.

brow (forehead) frente f, (eyebrow) ceja f, (of hill) cima f.

brown 1 adj marrón, (hair) castaño, -a; (tanned) moreno, -a. **2** n marrón m.

browse vi (person in shop) mirar; (through book) hojear.

bruise 1 n morado m, cardenal m. **2** vt contusionar.

bruised adj amoratado, -a.

brunch combinación f de desayuno y almuerzo.

bru·nette adj & n morena (f).

brush 1 n (for hair, teeth) cepillo m; (artist's) pincel m; (for house-painting) brocha f. **2** vt cepillar; **to b. one's hair/teeth** cepillarse el pelo/los dientes.

►**brush aside** vt dejar de lado.

►**brush off** vt ignorar.

►**brush up (on)** vt repasar.

bru·tal adj brutal, cruel.

bru·tal·i·ty brutalidad f.

brute (animal) bruto m; (person) bestia f.

BS abbr of **Bachelor of Science**.

bub·ble burbuja f.

►**bubble over** vi rebosar.

buck fam dólar m.

buck·et cubo m.

buck·le 1 n hebilla f. **2** vt abrochar (con hebilla). **3** vi (wall, metal) combarse.

►**buck up 1** vt **b. your ideas up!** ¡espabílate! **2** vi (cheer up) animarse.

bud 1 n (shoot) brote m; (flower) capullo m. **2** vi brotar.

Bud·dhist adj & n budista (mf).

bud·dy fam Am compadre m, Esp colega m.

budge vi (move) moverse.

budg·er·i·gar periquito m.

budg·et 1 n presupuesto m; **the B.** (of the state) los presupuestos del Estado. **2** vi hacer un presupuesto (**for** para).

buf·fa·lo (pl **buffaloes**) búfalo m.

buff·er n (device) parachoques m inv; (in computer) memoria f intermedia.

buf·fet (snack bar) bar m; (self-service meal) bufet m libre.

bug 1 n (insect) bicho m; (microbe) microbio m; **I've got a b.** tengo alguna infección; (hidden microphone) micrófono *m* oculto; *(in computer program)* error *m*. **2** *vt fam (annoy)* fastidiar.

bug·gy *(baby's stroller)* cochecito *m* de niño.

bu·gle bugle *m*.

build 1 *vt** construir. **2** *n (physique)* físico *m*.

build·er constructor, -a *mf*; *(contractor)* contratista *mf*.

build·ing edificio *m*.

built-in *adj (cupboard)* empotrado, -a; *(incorporated)* incorporado, -a.

built-up *adj* urbanizado, -a.

bulb *(of plant)* bulbo *m*; *(lightbulb)* bombilla *f*.

Bul·gar·i·an *adj & n* búlgaro, -a *(mf)*.

bulge 1 *n* protuberancia *f*; *(in pocket)* bulto *m*. **2** *vi (swell)* hincharse; *(be full)* estar repleto, -a.

bulg·ing *adj* abultado, -a; *(eye)* saltón.

bulk *(mass)* masa *f*, volumen *m*; *(greater part)* mayor parte *f*.

bulk·y *adj* voluminoso, -a.

bull toro *m*.

bull·dog buldog *m*.

bull·doz·er bulldozer *m*.

bul·let bala *f*.

bul·le·tin boletín *m*.

bul·le·tin board tablón *m* de anuncios.

bul·let·proof *adj* a prueba de balas; **b. vest** chaleco *m* antibalas.

bull·fight corrida *f* de toros.

bull·fight·er torero, -a *mf*.

bull·fight·ing los toros *mpl*; *(art)* tauromaquia *f*.

bull·ring plaza *f* de toros.

bul·ly 1 *n* matón *m*. **2** *vt* intimidar.

bum *fam (tramp)* vagabundo *m*; *(idler)* holgazán, -ana *mf*.

▶**bum around** *vi fam* vaguear.

bum·ble·bee abejorro *m*.

bump 1 *n (swelling)* chichón *m*; *(on road)* bache *m*; *(blow)* golpe *m*; *(jolt)* sacudida *f*. **2** *vt* golpear; **to b. one's head** darse un golpe en la cabeza.

▶**bump into** *vt (meet)* tropezar con.

bump·er *(on vehicle)* parachoques *m inv*.

bump·y *adj (road)* con muchos baches.

bun *(bread)* panecillo *m*; *(sweet)* magdalena *f*.

bunch *(of keys)* manojo *m*; *(of flowers)* ramo *m*; *(of grapes)* racimo *m*; *(of people)* grupo *m*.

bun·dle 1 *n (of clothes)* bulto *m*; *(of papers)* fajo *m*. **2** *vt (make bundle of)* liar; *(push)* empujar.

bun·ga·low bungalow *m*.

bunk *(bed)* litera *f*.

bun·ny *fam* **b.** *(rabbit)* conejito *m*.

buoy boya *f*.

bur·den 1 *n* carga *f*. **2** *vt* cargar *(with* con).

bu·reau *(pl* bureaux) *(office)* agencia *f*, oficina *f*; *(chest of drawers)* cómoda *f*.

bu·reauc·ra·cy burocracia *f*.

burg·er *fam* hamburguesa *f*.

bur·glar ladrón, -ona *mf*.

bur·glar a·larm alarma *f* antirrobo.

bur·glar·ize *vt* robar.

bur·gla·ry robo *m* en una casa.

bur·gle *vt* robar.

bur·i·al entierro *m*.

burn 1 *n* quemadura *f*. **2** *vt** quemar. **3** *vi* (fire)* arder; *(building, food)* quemarse; *(ointment etc)* escocer.

▶**burn down 1** *vt* incendiar. **2** *vi* incendiarse.

burn·er *(on stove)* quemador *m*.

burn·ing *adj (on fire)* ardiendo, -a en llamas.

burp 1 *n* eructo *m*. **2** *vi* eructar.

burst 1 *n (explosion)* estallido *m*; *(of tire)* reventón *m*; **b. of laughter** carcajada *f*. **2** *vt* (balloon)* reventar. **3** *vi** reventarse; *(shell)* estallar.

▶**burst into** *vi* **b. into laughter/tears** echarse a reír/llorar; **to b. into a room** irrumpir en una habitación.

▶**burst out** *vi* **to b. out laughing** echarse a reír.

burst·ing adj the bar was b. with people el bar estaba atestado de gente.

bur·y vt enterrar; (hide) ocultar; **to be buried in thought** estar absorto en pensamientos.

bus (pl buses or busses) autobús m; **b. shelter** marquesina f (de autobús); **b. station** estación f de autobuses.

bush (shrub) arbusto m.

bush·y adj espeso, -a.

busi·ness (commerce) negocios mpl; (firm) empresa f; (matter) asunto m; **on b.** de negocios; **b. hours** horas fpl de oficina; **b. trip** viaje m de negocios; **it's no b. of mine** no es asunto mío; **mind your own b.** no te metas en donde no te llaman.

busi·ness·man hombre m de negocios.

busi·ness·wom·an mujer f de negocios.

bus stop parada f de autobús.

bust¹ (of woman) pecho m; (sculpture) busto m.

bust² adj fam **to go b.** quebrar.

bus·tle (activity, noise) bullicio m.

▸**bustle about** vi ir y venir.

bus·tling adj bullicioso, -a.

bus·y adj ocupado, -a; (life) ajetreado, -a; (street) concurrido, -a; (telephone) ocupado, -a; **b. signal** señal f de comunicando.

bus·y·bod·y entrometido, -a mf, cotilla mf.

but 1 conj pero; (after negative) sino; **not two b. three** no dos sino tres. **2** prep menos; **everyone b. her** todos menos ella.

butch·er carnicero, -a mf; **b.'s (shop)** carnicería f.

but·ler mayordomo m.

butt (of cigarette) colilla f; fam (bottom) culo m.

but·ter 1 n mantequilla f. **2** vt untar con mantequilla.

but·ter·cup botón m de oro.

but·ter·fly mariposa f.

but·tock nalga f; **buttocks** nalgas fpl.

but·ton 1 n botón m. **2** vt **to b. (up) one's jacket** abotonarse la chaqueta.

but·ton·hole ojal m.

buy 1 n **a good b.** una ganga. **2** vt* comprar; **she bought that car from a neighbor** compró ese coche a un vecino.

buy·er comprador, -a mf.

buzz 1 n (of bee) zumbido m; (of conversation) rumor m. **2** vi zumbar.

▸**buzz off** vi fam largarse.

by 1 prep (indicating agent) por; **composed by Bach** compuesto, -a por Bach; **a film by Almodóvar** una película de Almodóvar. ■ (via) por; **he left by the back door** salió por la puerta trasera. ■ (manner) en, con, por; **by car/train** en coche/ tren; **by credit card** con tarjeta de crédito; **by chance** por casualidad; **by oneself** solo, -a; **you can obtain a ticket by filling in the coupon** puede conseguir una entrada rellenando el cupón. ■ (amount) por; **little by little** poco a poco; **they are sold by the dozen** se venden por docenas; **to be paid by the hour** cobrar por horas; **he won by a foot** ganó por un pie. ■ (beside) al lado de, junto a; **side by side** juntos. ■ (past) to walk by a building pasar por delante de un edificio. ■ (time) para; **by now** ya; **by then** para entonces; **we have to be there by nine** tenemos que estar allí para las nueve; **by the time we arrive** (para) cuando lleguemos. ■ (during) de; **by day/night** de día/noche. ■ (according to) según; **is that O.K. by you?** ¿te viene bien? **2** adv **to go by** (past) pasar; **she just walked by** pasó de largo; **by and by** con el tiempo; **by and large** en conjunto.

bye(-bye) ¡adiós!, ¡hasta luego!

by·e·lec·tion elección f parcial.

by·pass 1 n (road) carretera f de

circunvalación. **2** *vt* evitar.

by·stand·er mirón, -ona *mf.*

C

cab taxi *m.*

cab·bage col *f.*

cab·in *(hut)* choza *f*, *(on ship)* camarote *m.*

cab·i·net *(furniture)* armario *m*; *(glass-fronted)* vitrina *f*, *(in government)* gabinete *m.*

cab·i·net meet·ing consejo *m* de ministros.

ca·ble cable *m.*

ca·ble car teleférico *m.*

ca·ble TV televisión *f* por cable.

cac·tus *(pl* cacti*)* cactus *m.*

ca·fé, caf·e·te·ria cafetería *f*, bar *m.*

caf·feine cafeína *f.*

cage jaula *f.*

cake pastel *m.*

cal·cu·late *vt* calcular.

cal·cu·la·tion cálculo *m.*

cal·cu·la·tor calculadora *f.*

cal·en·dar calendario *m.*

calf *(pl* calves*) (of cattle)* becerro, -a *mf*, ternero, -a *mf*, *(part of leg)* pantorrilla *f.*

call 1 *vt* llamar; *(meeting etc)* convocar; **what's he called?** ¿cómo se llama? **2** *vi* llamar; **to c. at sb's (house)** pasar por casa de algn. **3** *n* llamada *f*, *(visit)* visita *f*, **(phone) c.** llamada *f.*

▸**call back** *vti (phone again)* llamar otra vez.

▸**call in 1** *vt (doctor)* llamar. **2** *vi* entrar; **to call in on sb** ir a ver a algn.

▸**call on** *vt* visitar; **to c. on sb for support** recurrir a algn en busca de apoyo.

▸**call out 1** *vt (shout)* gritar; *(doctor)* hacer venir. **2** *vi* gritar.

▸**call (up)** *vt* llamar (por teléfono).

call box cabina *f* telefónica.

calm 1 *adj (weather, sea)* en calma; *(relaxed)* tranquilo, -a; **keep c.!** ¡tranquilo, -a! **2** *n (of weather, sea)* calma *f.* **3** *vt* calmar.

▸**calm down** *vi* calmarse.

calm·ly *adv* con calma, tranquilamente.

cal·o·rie caloría *f.*

cam·cord·er videocámara *f.*

came *pt of* **come**.

cam·el camello, -a *mf.*

cam·er·a cámara *f.*

camp 1 *n* campamento *m.* **2** *vi* **to go camping** ir de camping.

cam·paign campaña *f.*

camp bed cama *f* plegable.

camp·er *(person)* campista *mf*, *(vehicle)* caravana *f.*

camp·fire fogata *f.*

camp(·ing) site camping *m.*

cam·pus campus *m*, ciudad *f* universitaria.

can[1] *v aux (pt* could*)* poder; *(know how to)* saber; **I'll phone you as soon as I c.** te llamaré en cuanto pueda; **she can't do it** no puede hacerlo; **I cannot understand why** no entiendo por qué; **he could have come** podría haber venido; **c. you ski?** ¿sabes esquiar?; **she could have forgotten** puede (ser) que lo haya olvidado; **they can't be very poor** no deben ser muy pobres; **what c. it be?** ¿qué será?

can[2] *(tin)* lata *f.*

Ca·na·di·an *adj & n* canadiense *(mf).*

ca·nal canal *m.*

ca·nar·y canario *m.*

can·cel *vt (train, booking)* cancelar; *(contract)* anular; *(permission)* retirar.

can·cel·la·tion cancelación *f*, *(of contract)* anulación *f.*

can·cer cáncer *m.*

can·did *adj* franco, -a.

can·di·date candidato, -a *mf*, *(in*

state exam) opositor, -a *mf.*

can·dle vela *f*; *(in church)* cirio *m.*

can·dle·stick palmatoria *f*; *(in church)* cirial *m.*

can·dy caramelo *m.*

cane 1 *n (walking stick)* bastón *m*; *(for punishment)* palmeta *f.* **2** *vt* castigar con la palmeta.

can·na·bis canabis *m.*

canned *adj* enlatado, -a; **c. foods** conservas *fpl.*

can·ni·bal *adj & n* caníbal *(mf).*

ca·noe canoa *f*; *(for sport)* piragua *f.*

ca·noe·ing piragüismo *m.*

can o·pen·er abrelatas *m.*

can·o·py *(awning)* toldo *m.*

can·teen *(restaurant)* comedor *m,* cantina *f.*

can·vas lona *f*; *(painting)* lienzo *m.*

can·yon cañón *m.*

cap gorro *m*; *(soldier's)* gorra *f*; *(of pen)* capuchón *m*; *(of bottle)* chapa *f.*

ca·pa·bil·i·ty habilidad *f.*

ca·pa·ble *adj (skillful)* hábil; *(able)* capaz **(of** de).

ca·pac·i·ty capacidad *f*; *(position)* puesto *m*; **in her c. as manageress** en calidad de gerente.

cape *(garment)* capa *f.*

cap·i·tal 1 *(town)* capital *f*; *(money)* capital *m*; *(letter)* mayúscula *f.*

cap·size 1 *vt* hacer zozobrar. **2** *vi* zozobrar.

cap·sule cápsula *f.*

cap·tain capitán *m.*

cap·ture *vt* capturar; *(of troops) (town)* tomar.

car coche *m,* Am carro *m*; **by c.** en coche.

car·a·mel azúcar *m* quemado; *(sweet)* caramelo *m.*

car·a·van *(vehicle)* caravana *f.*

car·bon carbono *m*; **c. copy** copia *f* al papel carbón.

car·bu·re·tor carburador *m.*

card tarjeta *f*; *(of cardboard)* cartulina *f*; *(in file)* ficha *f.*

card·board cartón *m.*

car·di·gan rebeca *f.*

car·di·nal 1 *n* cardenal *m.* **2** *adj* **c. numbers** números *mpl* cardinales.

care 1 *vi (be concerned)* preocuparse (**about** por); **I don't c.** no me importa; **who cares?** ¿qué más da? **2** *n (attention, protection)* cuidado *m*; *(worry)* preocupación *f*; **to take c. of** cuidar; *(business)* ocuparse de; **take c.** *(be careful)* ten cuidado; *(as farewell)* ¡cuídate!; **to take c. not to do sth** guardarse de hacer algo.

▸ **care about** *vt (something)* preocuparse de; *(somebody)* tener cariño a.

▸ **care for** *vt (look after)* cuidar; **I don't c. for that sort of thing** no me hace gracia una cosa así; **would you c. for a coffee?** ¿te apetece un café?

ca·reer carrera *f.*

care-free *adj* despreocupado, -a.

care·ful *adj* cuidadoso, -a; *(cautious)* prudente; **to be c.** tener cuidado; **be c.!** ¡ojo!

care·ful·ly *adv (painstakingly)* cuidadosamente; *(cautiously)* con cuidado.

care·less *adj* descuidado, -a; *(about clothes)* desaliñado, -a; *(driving)* negligente.

car fer·ry transbordador *m* para coches.

car·ing *adj* humanitario, -a, afectuoso, -a.

car·na·tion clavel *m.*

car·ni·val carnaval *m.*

car·ol villancico *m.*

carp *(fish)* carpa *f.*

car·pen·ter carpintero, -a *mf.*

car·pen·try carpintería *f.*

car·pet alfombra *f*; *(fitted)* moqueta *f.*

car·pet·ing (wall to wall) **c.** moqueta *f.*

car·pet sweep·er barredora *f* para alfombras.

car·riage *(horse-drawn)* carruaje *m*; *(on train)* vagón *m,* coche *m.*

car·ri·er *(company)* transportista *mf*; *(of disease)* portador, -a *mf*

car·rot zanahoria f.

car·ry 1 vt llevar; (goods) transportar; (stock) tener; (responsibility, penalty) conllevar; (disease) ser portador, -a de. **2** vi (sound) oírse.

▸ **carry away** vt llevarse; **to get carried away** entusiasmarse.

▸ **carry off** vt (prize) llevarse; **to c. it off** salir airoso, -a.

▸ **carry on 1** vt continuar; (conversation) mantener. **2** vi continuar; **c. on!** ¡adelante!

▸ **carry out** vt (plan) llevar a cabo; (order) cumplir; (repairs) hacer.

▸ **carry through** vt (plan) completar.

carryon (baggage) bolsa f de viaje.

cart 1 n (horse-drawn) carro m; (handcart) carretilla f. **2** vt acarrear.

▸ **cart around** vt fam llevar y traer.

car·ton (of cream etc) paquete m.

car·toon (strip) tira f cómica; (animated) dibujos mpl animados.

car·tridge cartucho m; (for pen) recambio m.

carve vt (wood) tallar; (stone, metal) esculpir; (meat) trinchar.

car wash túnel m or tren m de lavado.

case¹ (instance, medical) caso m; (legal) causa f, **in any c.** en cualquier caso; **just in c.** por si acaso.

case² (suitcase) maleta f, (small) estuche m; (soft) funda f.

cash 1 dinero m efectivo; **to pay c.** pagar al contado or en efectivo. **2** vt (check) cobrar.

cash·box caja f.

cash·ier cajero, -a mf.

cash price precio m al contado.

cash reg·is·ter caja f registradora.

ca·si·no casino m.

cas·se·role (container) cacerola f, (food) guisado m.

cas·sette casete f.

cas·sette play·er casete m.

cas·sette re·cord·er casete m.

cast 1 vt* (net, fishing line) echar; (light) proyectar; (glance) lanzar; (vote) emitir; **to c. suspicion on sb** levantar sospechas sobre algn; (play, film) hacer el reparto de. **2** n (plaster) c. escayola f, (of play) reparto m.

cast-i·ron adj (pan) de hierro fundido; (alibi) a toda prueba.

cas·tle castillo m; (in chess) torre f.

cas·tor ruedecilla f.

ca·su·al adj informal; (worker) eventual; (clothes) (de) sport; (unimportant) casual.

ca·su·al·ty (injured) herido, -a mf; **casualties** víctimas fpl.

cat gato, -a mf.

cat·a·log catálogo m.

cat·a·pult tirachinas m inv.

ca·tas·tro·phe catástrofe f.

catch 1 vt* (thief, bus etc) coger, Am agarrar; (fish) pescar; (mouse etc) atrapar; (surprise) sorprender; (hear) entender; **to c. fire** (log) prenderse; (building) incendiarse; **to c. one's breath** (recover) recuperar el aliento. **2** vi* (sleeve etc) engancharse (on en); (fire) encenderse. **3** n (of ball) parada f, (of fish) presa f, (on door) pestillo m; (drawback) pega f.

▸ **catch on** vi (become popular) ganar popularidad; (understand) caer en la cuenta.

▸ **catch up** vti **to c. up (with) sb** (reach) alcanzar a algn; (with news) ponerse al corriente (on de); **to c. up with work** ponerse al día con el trabajo.

catch·ing adj (disease) contagioso, -a.

cat·e·go·ry categoría f.

▸ **cater for, cater to** vt (need, taste) atender a.

cat·er·pil·lar oruga f.

ca·the·dral catedral f.

Cath·o·lic adj & n católico, -a (mf).

cau·li·flow·er coliflor f.

cause 1 n (of event etc) causa f, (reason) motivo m. **2** vt provocar; **to c. sb to do sth** hacer que algn haga algo.

cau·tion (care) cautela f, (warning) aviso m.

cau·tious *adj* cauteloso, -a.

cau·tious·ly *adv* con precaución.

cave cueva *f.*

▶**cave in** *vi (roof etc)* derrumbarse.

cav·i·ty *(hole)* cavidad *f.*

CD *abbr of* **compact disc** CD *m.*

cease 1 *vt* to c. doing *or* to do sth dejar de hacer algo. **2** *vi* cesar.

cease-fire alto *m* el fuego.

ceil·ing techo *m.*

cel·e·brate 1 *vt* celebrar. **2** *vi* divertirse.

cel·e·bra·tion celebración *f.*

ce·leb·ri·ty celebridad *f.*

cel·er·y apio *m.*

cell *(in prison)* celda *f; (in organism)* célula *f.*

cel·lar sótano *m; (for wine)* bodega *f.*

cel·lo·phane celofán *m.*

ce·ment 1 *n* cemento *m.* **2** *vt (fix with cement)* unir con cemento.

ce·ment mix·er hormigonera *f.*

cem·e·ter·y cementerio *m.*

cen·sus censo *m.*

cent centavo *m,* céntimo *m.*

cen·ter 1 *n* centro *m;* **town c.** centro de la ciudad. **2** *vt (attention, interest)* centrar (**on** en).

cen·ti·grade *adj* centígrado, -a.

cen·ti·me·ter centímetro *m.*

cen·ti·pede ciempiés *m inv.*

cen·tral *adj* central.

Cen·tral A·mer·i·can *adj & n* centro-americano, -a *(mf).*

cen·tral·ize *vt* centralizar.

cen·tu·ry siglo *m.*

ce·ram·ic *adj* de cerámica.

ce·re·al cereal *m.*

cer·e·mo·ny ceremonia *f.*

cer·tain 1 *adj (sure)* seguro, -a; *(true)* cierto, -a; **to make c. of sth** asegurarse de algo; **to a c. extent** hasta cierto punto. **2** *adv* **for c.** a ciencia cierta.

cer·tain·ly *adv* desde luego; **c. not** de ninguna manera.

cer·tain·ty certeza *f, (assurance)* seguridad *f.*

cer·tif·i·cate certificado *m; (from college)* diploma *m.*

cer·ti·fy *vt* certificar.

chain 1 *n* cadena *f; (of events)* serie *f;* **c. of mountains** cordillera *f.* **2** *vt* **to c. (up)** encadenar.

chair silla *f, (with arms)* sillón *m; (of meeting)* presidente *mf.*

chair lift telesilla *m.*

chair·man presidente *m.*

cha·let chalet *m,* chalé *m.*

chalk *(for writing)* tiza *f.*

chal·lenge 1 *vt* desafiar; *(authority etc)* poner a prueba; *(statement)* poner en duda; **to c. sb to do sth** retar a algn a que haga algo. **2** *n* desafío *m.*

chal·leng·ing *adj (idea)* desafiante; *(task)* que presenta un desafío.

cham·ber **C. of Commerce** Cámara *f* de Comercio.

cham·pagne *(French)* champán *m; (from Catalonia)* cava *m.*

cham·pi·on campeón, -ona *mf.*

cham·pi·on·ship campeonato *m.*

chance 1 *n (fortune)* azar *m; (opportunity)* oportunidad *f;* **by c.** por casualidad; **to take a c.** arriesgarse; **(the) chances are that …** lo más probable es que …. **2** *vt* arriesgar.

chan·cel·lor *(head of state, in embassy)* canciller *m.*

chan·de·lier araña *f* (de luces).

change 1 *vt* cambiar; **to c. gear** cambiar de marcha; **to c. one's mind/the subject** cambiar de opinión/de tema; **to c. trains** hacer trasbordo; **to get changed** cambiarse de ropa. **2** *vi* cambiar(se); **I think he's changed** lo veo cambiado. **3** *n* cambio *m; (money after purchase)* vuelta *f,* **for a c.** para variar; **c. of scene** cambio de aires; **small c.** suelto *m.*

▶**change over** *vi* **to c. over to sth** cambiar a algo, adoptar algo.

change·a·ble *adj (weather)* variable; *(person)* inconstante.

change·o·ver conversión *f.*

chang·ing room vestuario *m.*

chan·nel canal *m*; *(administrative)* vía *f*; **the English C.** el Canal de la Mancha.

chant 1 *n (of demonstrators)* eslogan *m*. **2** *vti (demonstrators)* corear.

cha·os caos *m*.

cha·ot·ic *adj* caótico, -a.

chap·el capilla *f*.

chapped *adj* agrietado, -a.

chap·ter capítulo *m*.

char *vt* carbonizar.

char·ac·ter carácter *m*; *(in play)* personaje *m*; *(person)* tipo *m*.

char·ac·ter·is·tic 1 *n* característica *f*. **2** *adj* característico, -a.

charge 1 *vt* cobrar; *(the enemy)* cargar contra; *(battery)* cargar; **to c. sb with a crime** acusar a algn de un crimen. **2** *vi (battery, troops)* cargar; **to c. about** andar a lo loco. **3** *n (cost)* precio *m*; *(in court)* acusación *f*; **bank charges** comisión *f*; **free of c.** gratis; **service c.** servicio *m*; **to be in c. of** estar a cargo de; **to take c. of** hacerse cargo de.

char·i·ty *(organization)* institución *f* benéfica.

charm 1 *n (quality)* encanto *m*; **lucky c.** amuleto *m*. **2** *vt* encantar.

charm·ing *adj* encantador, -a.

chart *(giving information)* tabla *f*; *(graph)* gráfico *m*; *(map)* carta *f* de navegación; *(of hit records)* **the charts** la lista de éxitos.

char·ter 1 *n (of institution)* estatutos *mpl*; *(of rights)* carta *f*; **c. flight** vuelo *m* chárter. **2** *vt (plane, boat)* fletar.

chase *vt* perseguir; *(hunt)* cazar.

▸**chase after** *vt (someone)* correr detrás de; *(something)* andar tras.

▸**chase away, chase off** *vt* ahuyentar.

chasm sima *f*; *fig* abismo *m*.

chas·sis chasis *m inv*.

chat 1 *n* charla *f*. **2** *vi* charlar.

chat·ter 1 *n (person)* parlotear; *(teeth)* castañetear. **2** *n (of person)* parloteo *m*; *(of teeth)* castañeteo *m*.

chat·ter·box parlanchín, -ina *mf*.

chat·ty *adj* hablador, -a.

chauf·feur chófer *m*.

cheap 1 *adj* barato, -a; *(fare)* económico, -a; *(contemptible)* bajo, -a. **2** *adv* barato.

cheap·ly *adv* en plan económico.

cheat 1 *vt* engañar; **to c. sb out of sth** estafar algo a algn. **2** *vi (at games)* hacer trampa; *(on an exam etc)* copiar(se). **3** *n (trickster)* tramposo, -a *mf*.

check 1 *vt* verificar; *(facts)* comprobar; *(tickets)* controlar; *(tires, oil)* revisar; *(stop)* detener; *(in chess)* dar jaque a. **2** *vi* comprobar. **3** *n (of documents etc)* revisión *f*; *(of facts)* comprobación *f*; *(in chess)* jaque *m*; *(in restaurant etc)* cuenta *f*.

▸**check in** *vi (at airport)* facturar; *(at hotel)* registrarse **(at** en).

▸**check off** *vt (names on list etc)* tachar.

▸**check on** *vt* verificar.

▸**check out 1** *vi (of hotel)* dejar el hotel. **2** *vt (facts)* verificar.

▸**check up** *vi* **to c. up on sth** comprobar algo.

check·book talonario *m* de cheques.

check·ers *(game)* damas *fpl*.

check in c. desk *(at airport)* mostrador *m* de facturación.

check·mate jaque mate *m*.

check·out *(counter)* caja *f*.

check·room guardarropa *f*; *(for luggage)* consigna *f*.

check·up *(medical)* chequeo *m*.

ched·dar queso *m* cheddar.

cheek mejilla *f*; *(nerve)* cara *f*; **what c.!** ¡vaya jeta!

cheek·y *adj* fresco, -a.

cheer 1 *vi* aclamar. **2** *vt (applaud)* aclamar. **3** *n* viva *m*; **cheers** aplausos *mpl*; **cheers!** *(before drinking)* ¡salud!

▸**cheer up 1** *vi* animarse. **2** *vt* **to c. sb up** animar a algn.

cheer·ful *adj* alegre.

cheer·ing ovación *f*.

cheese queso *m.*

cheese·burg·er hamburguesa *f* de queso.

cheese·cake tarta *f* de queso.

chef chef *m.*

chem·i·cal 1 *n* sustancia *f* química. **2** *adj* químico, -a.

chem·ist farmacéutico, -a *mf*; *(scientist)* químico, -a *mf.*

chem·is·try química *f.*

cher·ry cereza *f.*

cher·ry bran·dy licor *m* de cerezas.

chess ajedrez *m.*

chess·board tablero *m* de ajedrez.

chest pecho *m*; *(for linen)* arca *f*; *(for valuables)* cofre *m*; **c. of drawers** cómoda *f.*

chest·nut *(nut)* castaña *f.*

chew *vt* masticar.

chew·ing gum chicle *m.*

chick pollito *m.*

chick·en *n* pollo *m*; *fam (coward)* gallina *mf.*

▸ **chicken out** *vi* rajarse (por miedo).

chick·en·pox varicela *f.*

chick·pea garbanzo *m.*

chic·o·ry achicoria *f.*

chief 1 *n* jefe *m.* **2** *adj* principal.

chief·ly *adv (above all)* sobre todo; *(mainly)* principalmente.

chil·blain sabañón *m.*

child *(pl* **children)** niño, -a *mf*; *(son)* hijo *m*; *(daughter)* hija *f.*

child care *(for working parents)* servicio *m* de guardería.

child·hood infancia *f*, niñez *f.*

child·ish *adj* pueril.

Chi·le·an *adj & n* chileno, -a *(mf).*

chill 1 *n (illness)* resfriado *m*; *(coldness)* fresco *m.* **2** *vt (meat)* refrigerar; *(wine)* enfriar.

chilled *adj (wine)* frío, -a.

chil·(l)i chile *m.*

chill·y *adj* frío, -a.

chime *vi* repicar, sonar.

chim·ney chimenea *f.*

chim·ney flue cañón *m.*

chim·pan·zee chimpancé *m.*

chin barbilla *f.*

chi·na loza *f*; **bone c.** porcelana *f.*

Chi·nese 1 *adj* chino, -a. **2** *n (person)* chino, -a *mf*; *(language)* chino *m.*

chip 1 *n (in cup)* mella *f*; *(microchip)* chip *m*; *(in gambling)* ficha *f*; **chips** patatas *fpl* fritas. **2** *vt (china, glass)* mellar.

chi·ro·po·dist pedicuro, -a *mf.*

chis·el cincel *m.*

chives *npl* cebollino *m sing.*

choc·ice *(ice cream)* helado *m* cubierto de chocolate.

chock-a-block, chock-full *adj* hasta los topes.

choc·o·late 1 *n* chocolate *m*; **chocolates** bombones *mpl.* **2** *adj* de chocolate.

choice elección *f*; **a wide c.** un gran surtido; **there's no c.** no hay más remedio.

choir coro *m.*

choke 1 *vt (person)* ahogar; *(obstruct)* obstruir. **2** *vi* ahogarse.

cho·les·ter·ol colesterol *m.*

choose* 1 *vt* elegir; *(decide on)* optar por. **2** *vi* elegir.

choos·(e)y *adj* exigente.

chop 1 *vt (wood)* cortar; *(tree)* talar; *(food)* cortar a pedacitos. **2** *n (of lamb, pork etc)* chuleta *f.*

▸ **chop down** *vt (tree)* talar.

▸ **chop off** *vt (branch, finger etc)* cortar.

▸ **chop up** *vt* cortar en pedazos.

chop·per *fam (helicopter)* helicóptero *m.*

chop·sticks *npl* palillos *mpl.*

chord *(musical)* acorde *m.*

chore tarea *f.*

cho·rus coro *m*; *(in song)* estribillo *m.*

chris·ten *vt* bautizar.

chris·ten·ing bautizo *m.*

Chris·tian *adj & n* cristiano, -a *(mf).*

Chris·tian name nombre *m* de pila.

Christ·mas Navidad *f*; **Merry C.** feliz Navidad; **C. Day** (día *m* de)

Navidad *f*; **C. Eve** Nochebuena *f*.
chrome cromo *m*.
chron·ic *adj* crónico, -a.
chry·san·the·mum crisantemo *m*.
chub·by *adj* rellenito, -a.
chuck *vt fam* tirar.
chum compañero, -a *mf*.
chunk pedazo *m*.
church iglesia *f*.
chute *(for refuse)* conducto *m*; *(slide)* tobogán *m*.
ci·der sidra *f*.
ci·gar puro *m*.
cig·a·rette cigarrillo *m*.
cig·a·rette butt colilla *f*.
cig·a·rette light·er mechero *m*.
cin·e·ma cine *m*.
cin·na·mon canela *f*.
cir·cle 1 *n* círculo *m*; *(of people)* corro *m*; **in business circles** en el mundo de los negocios. **2** *vt (move round)* dar la vuelta a. **3** *vi* dar vueltas.
cir·cuit circuito *m*.
cir·cu·lar *adj & n* circular *(f)*.
cir·cu·late 1 *vt (news)* hacer circular. **2** *vi* circular.
cir·cu·la·tion *(of blood)* circulación *f*; *(of newspaper)* tirada *f*.
cir·cum·fer·ence circunferencia *f*.
cir·cum·stance circunstancia *f*; **under no circumstances** en ningún caso.
cir·cus circo *m*.
cite *vt (quote)* citar.
cit·i·zen ciudadano, -a *mf*.
cit·y ciudad *f*.
cit·y cen·ter centro *m* urbano.
cit·y hall ayuntamiento *m*.
civ·ic *adj (authority, building)* municipal; *(duty, rights)* cívico, -a.
civ·il *adj* civil; *(polite)* educado, -a; **c. rights** derechos *mpl* civiles.
ci·vil·ian *adj & n* civil *(mf)*.
civ·i·li·za·tion civilización *f*.
civ·il ser·vant funcionario, -a *mf*.
civ·il ser·vice administración *f* pública.

claim 1 *vt (benefit, rights)* reclamar; *(assert)* afirmar. **2** *n (demand)* reclamación *f*; *(right)* derecho *m*; *(assertion)* pretensión *f*; **to put in a c.** pedir una indemnización.
clam almeja *f*.
clamp wheel c. cepo *m*.
clap *vi* aplaudir.
clap·ping aplauso(s) *m(pl)*.
clar·i·fy *vt* aclarar.
clar·i·net clarinete *m*.
clash 1 *vi (disagree)* estar en desacuerdo; *(colors)* desentonar; *(dates)* coincidir. **2** *n (sound)* sonido *m*; *(fight)* choque *m*; *(conflict)* conflicto *m*.
clasp 1 *n (on belt)* cierre *m*; *(on necklace)* broche *m*. **2** *vt (object)* agarrar.
class 1 *n* clase *f*; **second c. ticket** billete *m* de segunda (clase). **2** *vt* clasificar.
clas·sic 1 *adj* clásico, -a.
clas·si·fy *vt* clasificar.
class·mate compañero, -a *mf* de clase.
class·room aula *f*.
clause oración *f*.
claw *(of bird, lion)* garra *f*; *(of cat)* uña *f*; *(of crab)* pinza *f*.
clay arcilla *f*.
clean 1 *adj* limpio, -a; *(unmarked, pure)* sin defecto. **2** *adv* por completo; **it went c. through the middle** pasó justo por el medio. **3** *vt (room)* limpiar; **to c. one's teeth** lavarse los dientes.
clean·er limpiador, -a *mf*.
clean·ing limpieza *f*.
clean·ing wom·an señora *f* de la limpieza.
clean·ly *adv (to break, cut)* limpiamente.
cleans·ing c. lotion leche *f* limpiadora.
clear 1 *adj* claro, -a; *(road, day)* despejado, -a; *(obvious)* claro, -a; *(majority)* absoluto, -a; *(profit)* neto, -a; **to make sth c.** aclarar algo. **2** *adv* **stand c.!** ¡apártese!; **to stay c. of**

evitar. **3** vt (room) vaciar; (authorize) autorizar; (hurdle) salvar; **to c. one's throat** aclararse la garganta; **to c. the table** quitar la mesa; **to c. sb of a charge** exculpar a algn de un delito. **4** vi (sky) despejarse.

▸**clear away** vt quitar.

▸**clear off** vi fam largarse; **c. off!** ¡largo!

▸**clear out** vt (room) limpiar a fondo; (cupboard) vaciar.

▸**clear up 1** vt (tidy) recoger; (arrange) ordenar; (mystery) resolver. **2** vi (weather) despejarse.

clear·ance (of area) despeje m.

clear·ance sale liquidación f (de existencias).

clear-cut adj claro, -a.

clear·ing (in wood) claro m.

clear·ly adv claramente; (at start of sentence) evidentemente.

clear·way carretera f donde está prohibido parar.

clem·en·tine clementina f.

clench vt (teeth, fist) apretar.

cler·gy clero m.

cler·i·cal adj (of an office) de oficina.

clerk (office worker) oficinista mf; (civil servant) funcionario, -a mf; (in shop) dependiente, -a mf.

clev·er adj (person) inteligente; (argument) ingenioso, -a; **to be c. at sth** tener aptitud para algo.

click (sound) clic m.

cli·ent cliente mf.

cliff acantilado m.

cli·mate clima m.

cli·max (peak) punto m culminante.

climb 1 vt (ladder) subir por; (mountain) escalar; (tree) subir a. **2** vi subir; (plants) trepar; fig (socially) ascender. **3** n subida f, ascensión f.

▸**climb down** vi bajar.

climb·er alpinista mf, Am andinista mf.

cling* vi (hang on) agarrarse (**to** a); (clothes) ajustarse; **to c. together** unirse.

clin·ic (in state hospital) ambulatorio

m; (specialized) clínica f.

clip¹ vt (cut) cortar; (ticket) picar.

clip² n (for hair) pasador m; (for paper) sujetapapeles m inv; (brooch) clip m.

▸**clip on** vt (brooch) prender (**to** a); (documents) sujetar (**to** a).

clip·pers npl (for hair) maquinilla f para rapar; (for nails) cortauñas m inv; (for hedge) tijeras fpl de podar.

clip·ping (newspaper) recorte m.

cloak (garment) capa f.

cloak·room guardarropa m; (toilets) servicios mpl.

clock reloj m; **to be open round the c.** estar abierto las 24 horas (del día).

clock·wise adj & adv en el sentido de las agujas del reloj.

close¹ 1 adj (in space, time) cercano, -a; (contact) directo, -a; **c.** to cerca de; (relationship) estrecho, -a; (friend) íntimo, -a; (weather) bochornoso, -a; **c. together** juntos. **2** adv cerca; **they live c. by** or **c. at hand** viven cerca.

close² 1 vt cerrar; (bring to a close) concluir; (meeting) levantar. **2** vi (shut) cerrar(se). **3** n fin m, final m.

▸**close down** vti (business) cerrar para siempre.

▸**close in** vi **to c. in on sb** rodear a algn.

▸**close up 1** vt cerrar del todo. **2** vi cerrarse; (ranks) apretarse.

closed adj cerrado, -a; **c.-circuit television** televisión f en circuito cerrado.

close·ly adv (listen) con atención; **c. contested/connected** muy reñido, -a/relacionado, -a; **to follow (events) c.** seguir de cerca (los acontecimientos).

clos·et armario m.

clos·ing time hora f de cierre.

clo·sure cierre m.

clot 1 n (of blood) coágulo m. **2** vi coagularse.

cloth paño m; (rag) trapo m; (tablecloth) mantel m.

clothes *npl* ropa *f sing.*

clothes hang·er percha *f.*

clothes·line tendedero *m.*

clothes peg pinza *f.*

clothes shop tienda *f* de ropa.

cloth·ing ropa *f.*

cloud *n* nube *f.*

▸**cloud over** *vi* nublarse.

cloud·y *adj (sky)* nublado, -a.

clove *(of garlic)* diente *f.*

clown payaso *m.*

club *(society)* club *m; (for golf)* palo *m; (in cards)* trébol *m.*

clue *(sign)* indício *m; (to mystery)* pista *f; (in crossword)* clave *f,* fam **I haven't a c.** no tengo (ni) idea.

clum·sy *adj* torpe; *(awkward)* tosco, -a.

clus·ter 1 *n* grupo *m.* **2** *vi* agruparse.

clutch 1 *vt* agarrar. **2** *n (in vehicle)* embrague *m.*

clut·ter *vt* **to c. (up)** llenar de cosas.

Co *abbr of* **Company** C., Cª, Cía.

coach 1 *n* autocar *m; (carriage)* carruaje *m; (of train)* coche *m,* vagón *m.* **2** *vt (student)* dar clases particulares a; *(team)* entrenar.

coal carbón *m.*

coal mine mina *f* de carbón.

coarse *adj (material)* basto, -a; *(language)* grosero, -a.

coast costa *f.*

coat 1 *n (overcoat)* abrigo *m; (short)* chaquetón *m; (of animal)* pelo *m; (of paint)* capa *f.* **2** *vt* cubrir **(with** de); *(with liquid)* bañar **(with** en).

coat hang·er percha *f.*

coat·ing capa *f.*

cob mazorca *f.*

cob·bled *adj* adoquinado, -a.

cob·web telaraña *f.*

co·caine cocaína *f.*

cock *(bird)* gallo *m.*

cock·le berberecho *m.*

cock·pit cabina *f* del piloto.

cock·roach cucaracha *f.*

cock·tail cóctel *m.*

co·coa cacao *m.*

co·co·nut coco *m.*

cod bacalao *m.*

code código *m; (symbol)* clave *f; (for telephone)* prefijo *m.*

cod-liv·er oil aceite *m* de hígado de bacalao.

co·ed 1 *adj* mixto, -a. **2** *n* colegio *m* mixto.

cof·fee café *m.*

cof·fee bar cafetería *f.*

cof·fee break pausa *f* para el café.

cof·fee·pot cafetera *f.*

cof·fee ta·ble mesita *f* de café.

cof·fin ataúd *m.*

co·gnac coñac *m.*

co·her·ent *adj* coherente.

coil 1 *vt (up)* enrollar. **2** *n (loop)* vuelta *f; (of rope)* rollo *m.*

coin moneda *f.*

co·in·cide *vi* coincidir **(with** con).

co·in·ci·dence coincidencia *f.*

Coke® *abbr of* **Coca-Cola**® coca-cola *f.*

col·an·der colador *m.*

cold 1 *adj* frío, -a; **I'm c.** tengo frío; **it's c.** *(weather)* hace frío. **2** *n* frío *m; (illness)* resfriado *m;* **to catch a c.** resfriarse, acatarrarse; **to have a c.** estar resfriado, -a.

cold·ness frialdad *f.*

cole·slaw ensalada *f* de col.

col·lab·o·rate *vi* colaborar **(with** con).

col·lab·o·ra·tion colaboración *f.*

col·lapse 1 *vi (fall down)* derrumbarse; *(cave in)* hundirse. **2** *n (falling down)* derrumbamiento *m; (caving in)* hundimiento *m.*

col·lar *n (of garment)* cuello *m; (for dog)* collar *m.*

col·lar·bone clavícula *f.*

col·league colega *mf.*

col·lect 1 *vt (gather)* recoger; *(stamps etc)* coleccionar; *(taxes)* recaudar. **2** *vi (for charity)* hacer una colecta **(for** para). **3** *adv* **to call c.** llamar a cobro revertido.

col·lec·tion *(of mail)* recogida *f; (of money)* colecta *f; (of stamps)* colección *f; (of taxes)* recaudación *f.*

col·lec·tor *(of stamps)* coleccionista *mf.*

col·lege ≃ centro *m* de enseñanza superior, ≃ politécnico *m*; **to go to c.** seguir estudios superiores.

col·lide *vi* chocar.

col·li·sion choque *m.*

col·lo·qui·al *adj* coloquial.

co·logne (agua *f* de) colonia *f.*

Co·lom·bi·an *adj & n* colombiano, -a *(mf).*

co·lon *(punctuation)* dos puntos *mpl.*

colo·nel coronel *m.*

co·lo·ni·al *adj* colonial.

col·o·ny colonia *f.*

col·or 1 *n* color *m*; **c. film/television** película *f*/televisión *f* en color. **2** *vt* colorear.

col·ored *adj (pencil)* de color; *(photograph)* en color.

col·or·ful *adj (with color)* lleno, -a de color; *(person)* pintoresco, -a.

col·umn columna *f.*

co·ma coma *m*; **to go into a c.** entrar en coma.

comb 1 *n* peine *m.* **2** *vt* **to c. one's hair** peinarse.

com·bi·na·tion combinación *f.*

com·bine 1 *vt* combinar. **2** *vi* combinarse; *(companies)* asociarse.

come* *vi* venir; *(arrive)* llegar; *(happen)* suceder; **to c. apart/undone** desatarse/soltarse; **that's what comes of being too impatient** es lo que pasa por ser demasiado impaciente.

▸**come about** *vi* ocurrir, suceder.

▸**come across** *vt (thing)* encontrar por casualidad; **to c. across sb** tropezar con algn.

▸**come along** *vi (arrive)* venir; *(make progress)* progresar; **c. along!** ¡venga!

▸**come around 1** *vt (corner)* dar la vuelta a. **2** *vi (visit)* venir; *(regain consciousness)* volver en sí.

▸**come away** *vi (leave)* salir; *(part)* desprenderse (**from** de).

▸**come back** *vi (return)* volver.

▸**come by 1** *vt (acquire)* adquirir. **2** *vi (visit)* **why don't you c. by?** ¿por qué no te pasas por casa?

▸**come down** *vi* bajar; *(rain)* caer; **to c. down with the flu** pillar la gripe.

▸**come forward** *vi (advance)* avanzar; *(volunteer)* ofrecerse.

▸**come in** *vi (enter)* entrar; *(arrive) (train)* llegar; *(tide)* subir.

▸**come into** *vt (enter)* entrar en; *(inherit)* heredar.

▸**come off 1** *vt (fall from)* caerse de. **2** *vi (button)* caerse; *(succeed)* salir bien.

▸**come on** *vi (make progress)* progresar; **c. on!** *(hurry)* ¡venga!

▸**come out** *vi* salir (**of** de); *(book)* aparecer; *(stain)* quitarse; **to c. out (on strike)** declararse en huelga.

▸**come over 1** *vi* venir. **2** *vt* **what's c. over you?** ¿qué te pasa?

▸**come through** *vt (cross)* cruzar; *(illness)* recuperarse de; *(accident)* sobrevivir a.

▸**come to 1** *vi (regain consciousness)* volver en sí. **2** *vt (amount to)* ascender a; *(arrive at)* llegar a.

▸**come up** *vi (rise)* subir; *(sun)* salir; *(approach)* acercarse (**to** a); *(difficulty, question)* surgir.

▸**come up against** *vt (problems etc)* encontrarse con.

▸**come upon** *vt* = **come across**.

▸**come up to** *vt (equal)* igualar.

▸**come up with** *vt (solution etc)* encontrar.

come·back **to make a c.** reaparecer.

co·me·di·an cómico *m.*

com·e·dy comedia *f.*

com·fort 1 *n* comodidad *f*, *(consolation)* consuelo *m.* **2** *vt* consolar.

com·fort·a·ble *adj* cómodo, -a; *(temperature)* agradable.

com·fort·er edredón *m.*

com·ic 1 *adj* cómico, -a. **2** *n* tebeo *m*, comic *m.*

com·ic strip tira *f* cómica.

com·ing comings and goings idas y venidas *fpl*.

com·ma coma *f*.

com·mand 1 *vt* mandar. **2** *n (order)* orden *f*; *(authority)* mando *m*; *(of language)* dominio *m*.

com·mand·er comandante *mf*.

com·mem·o·rate *vt* conmemorar.

com·mence *vti* comenzar.

com·ment *n* comentario *m*.

▶**comment** *vt (event etc)* comentar.

com·men·tar·y comentario *m*.

com·men·ta·tor comentarista *mf*.

com·merce comercio *m*.

com·mer·cial *adj* comercial.

com·mis·sion comisión *f*.

com·mit *vt (crime)* cometer; **to c. suicide** suicidarse.

com·mit·ment compromiso *m*.

com·mit·tee comisión *f*, comité *m*.

com·mod·i·ty artículo *m*.

com·mon *adj* común; *(ordinary)* corriente.

com·mon·ly *adv (generally)* en general.

com·mon·place *adj* corriente.

com·mon sense sentido *m* común.

com·mo·tion alboroto *m*.

com·mu·nal *adj (bathroom etc)* comunitario, -a.

com·mu·ni·cate 1 *vi* comunicarse (**with** con). **2** *vt* comunicar.

com·mu·ni·ca·tion comunicación *f*.

com·mun·ion comunión *f*.

com·mu·ni·ty comunidad *f*; *(people)* colectividad *f*.

com·mu·ni·ty cen·ter centro *m* social.

com·mute *vi* viajar diariamente al lugar de trabajo.

com·mut·er persona *f* que viaja diariamente al lugar de trabajo.

com·mut·ing desplazarse diariamente al lugar de trabajo.

com·pact 1 *adj* compacto, -a; *(style)* conciso, -a. **2** *n (for powder)* polvera *f*.

com·pact disc disco *m* compacto.

com·pan·ion compañero, -a *mf*.

com·pa·ny compañía *f*; *(business)* empresa *f*; **to keep sb c.** hacer compañía a algn.

com·pa·ra·ble *adj* comparable (**to**, **with** con).

com·par·a·tive 1 *adj* comparativo, -a; *(relative)* relativo, -a. **2** *n (in grammar)* comparativo *m*.

com·para·tive·ly *adv* relativamente.

com·pare 1 *vt* comparar (**to**, **with** con); **(as) compared with** en comparación con. **2** *vi* compararse.

com·par·i·son comparación *f*.

com·part·ment *(on train)* departamento *m*.

com·pass brújula *f*; **(pair of) compasses** compás *m*.

com·pat·i·ble *adj* compatible.

com·pel *vt (oblige)* obligar; **to c. sb to do sth** obligar a algn a hacer algo.

com·pen·sate *vti* compensar; **to c. sb for sth** indemnizar a algn de algo.

com·pen·sa·tion *(for loss)* indemnización *f*.

com·pete *vi* competir.

com·pe·tent *adj* competente.

com·pe·ti·tion competencia *f*; *(contest)* concurso *m*.

com·pet·i·tive *adj* competitivo, -a.

com·pet·i·tor competidor, -a *mf*.

com·pile *vt* compilar.

com·plain *vi* quejarse (**of**, **about** de).

com·plaint queja *f*; *(formal)* reclamación *f*; *(illness)* enfermedad *f*.

com·ple·ment 1 *n* complemento *m*. **2** *vt* complementar.

com·plete 1 *adj (entire)* completo, -a; *(absolute)* total. **2** *vt* completar; *(form)* rellenar.

com·plete·ly *adv* completamente, por completo.

com·plex 1 *adj* complejo, -a. **2** *n* complejo *m*.

com·plex·ion tez *f*; *fig* aspecto *m*.

com·pli·cate *vt* complicar.

com·pli·cat·ed *adj* complicado, -a.

com·pli·ca·tion complicación *f*.

com·pli·ment cumplido *m*.

com·pli·men·ta·ry *adj (praising)* elogioso, -a; *(free)* gratuito, -a.

com·ply *vi* obedecer; **to c. with** *(order)* cumplir con.

com·pose *vti* componer; **to be composed of** componerse de; **to c. oneself** calmarse.

com·posed *adj (calm)* sereno, -a.

com·pos·er compositor, -a *mf*.

com·po·si·tion *(essay)* redacción *f*.

com·pound compuesto *m*.

com·pre·hen·sive *adj* completo, -a; *(insurance)* a todo riesgo; **c. school** escuela *f* secundaria.

com·prise *vt (include)* comprender; *(consist of)* constar de; *(constitute)* constituir.

com·pro·mise acuerdo *m*.

com·pul·sive *adj* compulsivo, -a.

com·pul·so·ry *adj* obligatorio, -a.

com·put·er ordenador *m*.

com·put·er·ized *adj* informatizado, -a.

com·put·er pro·gram·mer programador, -a *mf* de ordenadores.

com·put·er sci·ence informática *f*.

com·put·ing informática *f*.

con *vt fam* estafar.

con·ceal *vt* ocultar; *(emotions)* disimular.

con·cede *vt* conceder.

con·ceit·ed *adj* presuntuoso, -a.

con·ceiv·a·ble *adj* concebible.

con·ceive *vti* concebir.

con·cen·trate 1 *vt* concentrar. **2** *vi* **to c. on sth** concentrarse en algo.

con·cen·tra·tion concentración *f*.

con·cern 1 *vt* concernir; *(worry)* preocupar. **2** *n (worry)* preocupación *f*, *(business)* negocio *m*.

con·cerned *adj (worried)* preocupado, -a **(about** por).

con·cern·ing *prep* con respecto a.

con·cert concierto *m*.

con·ces·sion concesión *f*.

con·cise *adj* conciso, -a.

con·clude *vti* concluir.

con·clu·sion conclusión *f*.

con·crete 1 *n* hormigón *m*. **2** *adj (made of concrete)* de hormigón; *(definite)* concreto, -a.

con·demn *vt* condenar.

con·den·sa·tion condensación *f*.

con·di·tion condición *f*; **on c. that ...** a condición de que ...

con·di·tion·er acondicionador *m*.

con·dom preservativo *m*.

con·duct 1 *n (behavior)* conducta *f*. **2** *vt (lead)* guiar; *(business, orchestra)* dirigir.

con·duct·ed tour visita *f* guiada.

con·duc·tor *(on bus)* cobrador, -a *mf*; *(on train)* revisor, -a *mf*, *(of orchestra)* director, -a *mf*.

cone cono *m*; **ice-cream c.** cucurucho *m*.

con·fer 1 *vt* **to c. a title on sb** condecer un título a algn. **2** *vi (discuss)* deliberar.

con·fer·ence congreso *m*.

con·fess *vti* confesar; *(to priest)* confesarse.

con·fes·sion confesión *f*.

con·fet·ti confeti *m*.

con·fi·dence confianza *f*; **in c.** en confianza.

con·fi·dent *adj* seguro, -a.

con·fi·den·tial *adj (secret)* confidencial; *(entrusted)* de confianza.

con·fi·dent·ly *adv* con seguridad.

con·fine *vt* limitar.

con·firm *vt* confirmar.

con·fir·ma·tion confirmación *f*.

con·firmed *adj* empedernido, -a.

con·fis·cate *vt* confiscar.

con·flict 1 *n* conflicto *m*. **2** *vi* chocar **(with** con).

con·flict·ing *adj* contradictorio, -a.

con·form *vi* conformarse; **to c. to or with** *(customs)* amoldarse a; *(rules)* someterse a.

con·front *vt* hacer frente a.

con·fron·ta·tion confrontación f.

con·fuse vt (person) despistar; (thing) confundir (**with** con); **to get confused** confundirse.

con·fused adj (person) confundido, -a; (mind, ideas) confuso, -a.

con·fus·ing adj confuso, -a.

con·fu·sion confusión f.

con·gest·ed adj (street) repleto, -a de gente.

con·ges·tion congestión f.

con·grat·u·late vt felicitar.

con·grat·u·la·tions npl felicitaciones fpl; **c.!** ¡enhorabuena!

con·gre·gate vi congregarse.

con·gress congreso m.

con·gress·man diputado m, miembro m del Congreso.

con·gress·wom·an diputada f, miembro f del Congreso.

con·ju·gate vt conjugar.

con·ju·ga·tion conjugación f.

con·junc·tion conjunción f.

con·jur·er prestidigitador, -a mf.

con·jur·ing trick juego m de manos.

con man estafador m.

con·nect 1 vt unir; (wires) empalmar; (install) instalar; (electricity) conectar; (on phone) poner. **2** vi (train, flight) enlazar (**with** con).

con·nect·ed adj unido, -a; (events) relacionado, -a.

con·nec·tion conexión f; (installation) instalación f; (rail, flight) enlace m; (of ideas) relación f; (person) contacto m; **in c. with** (regarding) con respecto a.

con·quer vt (enemy, bad habit) vencer; (country) conquistar.

con·quest conquista f.

con·science conciencia f.

con·sci·en·tious adj concienzudo, -a.

con·scious adj (aware) consciente; (choice etc) deliberado, -a.

con·sen·sus consenso m.

con·sent 1 n consentimiento m. **2** vi consentir (**to** en).

con·se·quence consecuencia f.

con·se·quent·ly adv por consiguiente.

con·ser·va·tion conservación f.

con·ser·va·tive adj & n conservador, -a (mf).

con·ser·va·to·ry (greenhouse) invernadero m.

con·serve 1 vt conservar. **2** n conserva f.

con·sid·er vt (ponder on, regard) considerar; (keep in mind) tener en cuenta; **to c. doing sth** pensar hacer algo.

con·sid·er·a·ble adj considerable.

con·sid·er·ate adj considerado, -a.

con·sid·er·a·tion consideración f.

con·sid·er·ing prep teniendo en cuenta.

con·sign·ment envío m.

con·sist vi **to c. of** consistir en.

con·sis·ten·cy (of actions) coherencia f, (of mixture) consistencia f.

con·sis·tent adj (quality, results) constante; (behaviour) coherente.

con·so·la·tion consuelo m; **c. prize** premio m de consolación.

con·sole¹ vt consolar.

con·sole² consola f.

con·so·nant consonante f.

con·spic·u·ous adj (striking) llamativo, -a; (easily seen) visible.

con·spir·a·cy conjura f.

con·sta·ble policía m.

con·stant adj constante; (continuous) incesante; (loyal) fiel.

constant·ly adv constantemente.

con·sti·pat·ed adj estreñido, -a.

con·sti·tu·tion constitución f.

con·straint coacción f.

con·struct vt construir.

con·struc·tion construcción f.

con·struc·tive adj constructivo, -a.

con·sul cónsul mf.

con·su·late consulado m.

con·sult vti consultar (**about** sobre).

con·sul·tan·cy (firm) asesoría f, consulting m.

con·sult·ant *(doctor)* especialista *mf*; *(in business)* asesor, -a *mf.*

con·sul·ta·tion consulta *f.*

con·sume *vt* consumir.

con·sum·er consumidor, -a *mf.*

con·sump·tion consumo *m.*

con·tact 1 *n* contacto *m.* **2** *vt* ponerse en contacto con.

con·tact lens·es lentes *fpl* de contacto.

con·ta·gious *adj* contagioso, -a.

con·tain *vt* contener.

con·tain·er *(box, package)* recipiente *m*; *(for shipping)* contenedor *m.*

con·tem·po·rar·y *adj & n* contemporáneo, -a *(mf).*

con·tempt desprecio *m.*

▸**con·tend with** *vt (problem, person)* enfrentarse a.

con·tent[1] contenido *m*; **table of contents** índice *m* de materias.

con·tent[2] *adj* contento, -a.

con·tent·ed *adj* satisfecho, -a.

con·test prueba *f.*

con·tes·tant concursante *mf.*

con·text contexto *m.*

con·ti·nent continente *m*; **(on) the C.** (en) Europa.

con·ti·nen·tal *adj* continental; *(European)* **C.** europeo, -a.

con·tin·u·al *adj* continuo, -a, constante.

con·tin·u·al·ly *adv* continuamente.

con·tin·ue *vt* continuar, seguir; **to c. to do sth** seguir *or* continuar haciendo algo.

con·tin·u·ous *adj* continuo, -a.

con·tin·u·ous·ly *adv* continuamente.

con·tra·cep·tion anticoncepción *f.*

con·tra·cep·tive *adj & n* anticonceptivo *(m).*

con·tract contrato *m.*

con·trac·tor contratista *mf.*

con·tra·dict *vt* contradecir.

con·tra·dic·tion contradicción *f.*

con·trar·y 1 *n* **on the c.** todo lo contrario. **2** *adv* **c. to** en contra de.

con·trast contraste *m.*

con·trast·ing *adj* opuesto, -a.

con·trib·ute 1 *vt (money)* contribuir; *(ideas, information)* aportar. **2** *vi* contribuir; *(in discussion)* participar; *(to publication)* colaborar (**to** en).

con·tri·bu·tion *(of money)* contribución *f*, *(to publication)* colaboración *f.*

con·trive *vi* **to c. to do sth** buscar la forma de hacer algo.

con·trived *adj* artificial.

con·trol 1 *vt* controlar; *(person, animal)* dominar; *(vehicle)* manejar; **to c. one's temper** controlarse. **2** *n (power)* control *m*; *(authority)* autoridad *f*; *(in car, plane)* device) mando *m*; *(on TV)* botón *m* de control; **out of c.** fuera de control; **to be in c.** estar al mando; **to be under c.** *(situation)* estar bajo control; **to go out of c.** descontrolarse; **to lose c.** perder los estribos.

con·trol tow·er torre *f* de control.

con·va·lesce *vi* convalecer.

con·va·les·cence convalecencia *f.*

con·va·les·cent home clínica *f* de reposo.

con·ven·ience comodidad *f.*

con·ven·ience food comida *f* precocinada.

con·ven·ient *adj (arrangement)* conveniente; *(time)* oportuno, -a; *(place)* bien situado, -a.

con·vent convento *m.*

con·ver·sa·tion conversación *f.*

con·verse *vi* conversar.

con·ver·sion conversión *f* (**to** a; **in·to** en).

con·vert *vt* convertir (**into** en).

con·vert·i·ble 1 *adj* convertible. **2** *n (car)* descapotable *m.*

con·vey *vt (carry)* transportar; *(sound)* transmitir; *(idea)* comunicar.

con·vey·or belt cinta *f* transportadora.

con·vict vt declarar culpable a.

con·vic·tion (belief) creencia f, convicción f; (for crime) condena f.

con·vince vt convencer.

con·vinc·ing adj convincente.

con·voy convoy m.

cook 1 n vt cocinar, guisar; (dinner) preparar. **2** vi (person) cocinar, guisar; (food) cocerse. **3** n cocinero, -a mf.

cook·book libro m de cocina.

cook·er cocina f.

cook·er·y cocina f.

cook·ie galleta f.

cook·ing cocina f.

cook·ing ap·ple manzana f ácida para cocinar.

cool 1 adj fresco, -a; (calm) tranquilo, -a; (reserved) frío, -a; **it's c.** (weather) hace fresquito. **2** n (coolness) fresco m; **to lose one's c.** perder la calma. **3** vt (air) refrescar; (drink) enfriar.

▸**cool down, cool off** vi (something hot) enfriarse; fig calmarse; (feelings) enfriarse.

cool·er (for food) nevera f portátil.

cool·ness (calmness) calma f, (composure) aplomo m.

co·op·er·ate vi cooperar.

co·op·er·a·tion cooperación f.

coop up vt encerrar.

co·or·di·nate 1 vt coordinar. **2** n coordinates (clothes) coordinados mpl.

cope vi arreglárselas; **to c. with** (person, work) poder con; (problem) hacer frente a.

cop·per (metal) cobre m.

cop·y 1 n copia f, (of book) ejemplar m. **2** vti copiar.

▸**copy down** vt (letter etc) pasar a limpio.

cord (string) cuerda f, (electrical) cordón m.

cor·dial (drink) licor m.

cor·don off vt acordonar.

cor·du·roy pana f.

core (of fruit) corazón m; fig centro m.

cork corcho m.

cork·screw sacacorchos m inv.

corn¹ (maize) maíz m; (grain) granos mpl; (seed) cereal m.

corn² (on foot) callo m.

corned beef carne f acecinada.

cor·ner 1 n (of street) esquina f; (bend in road) curva f; (of room) rincón m; (in soccer) **c. (kick)** córner m. **2** vt (enemy) arrinconar; (market) acaparar.

cor·net (for ice cream) cucurucho m.

corn·flakes npl copos mpl de maíz, cornflakes mpl.

corn·starch harina f de maíz.

corn·y adj gastado, -a.

cor·po·ral cabo m.

corps (pl corps) cuerpo m.

corpse cadáver m.

cor·rect 1 vt (mistake) corregir; (child) reprender. **2** adj correcto, -a; (behavior) formal.

cor·rec·tion corrección f.

cor·rect·ly adv correctamente.

cor·re·spond vi corresponder; (by letter) escribirse; **to c.** to equivaler a.

cor·re·spon·dence correspondencia f, **c. course** curso m por correspondencia.

cor·re·spond·ing adj (matching) correspondiente.

cor·ri·dor pasillo m.

cor·ru·gat·ed adj **c. iron** hierro m ondulado.

cor·rupt adj (person) corrupto, -a; (actions) deshonesto, -a.

cor·rup·tion corrupción f.

cos·met·ic cosmético m.

cos·mo·naut cosmonauta mf.

cost 1 n (price) precio m; coste m; **at all costs** a toda costa. **2** vti* costar, valer; **how much does it c.?** ¿cuánto te cuesta?

Cos·ta Ri·can adj & n costarricense (mf).

cost·ly adj costoso, -a.

cos·tume traje m; **c. jewelery** bisutería f.

cot cuna f.

cot·tage casa *f* de campo.

cot·tage cheese requesón *m*.

cot·ton algodón *m*; *(thread)* hilo *m*.

cot·ton wool algodón *m* hidrófilo.

couch sofá *m*.

cou·chette litera *f*.

cough 1 *vi* toser. **2** *n* tos *f*.

▶ **cough up** *vt fam* **to c. up the money** soltar la pasta.

cough syr·up jarabe *m* para la tos.

could *v aux of* **can¹**.

coun·cil *(body)* consejo *m*; **town c.** consejo municipal.

coun·cil house ≃ vivienda *f* de protección oficial.

coun·cil·or concejal *mf*.

count¹ 1 *vt* contar. **2** *vi* contar; **that doesn't c.** eso no vale.

▶ **count in** *vt* incluir a, contar con.

▶ **count on** *vt* contar con.

▶ **count out** *vt (banknotes)* contar uno por uno.

count² *(nobleman)* conde *m*.

count·down cuenta *f* atrás.

coun·ter *(in shop)* mostrador *m*; *(in bank)* ventanilla *f*; *(in board games)* ficha *f*.

coun·ter- *prefix* contra-.

coun·ter·at·tack contraataque *m*.

coun·ter·clock·wise *adj & adv* en sentido inverso a las agujas del reloj.

coun·ter·foil *(of check)* matriz *f*.

coun·ter·part homólogo, -a *mf*.

coun·try *(state)* país *m*; *(rural area)* campo *m*; **native c.** patria *f*.

coun·try·side *(area)* campo *m*; *(scenery)* paisaje *m*.

coun·ty condado *m*.

coup golpe *m*; **c. d'état** golpe de estado.

cou·ple *(of people)* pareja *f*; *(of things)* par *m*; **a married c.** un matrimonio; **a c. of times** un par de veces.

cou·pon cupón *m*.

cour·age valor *m*.

cou·ra·geous *adj* valiente.

cou·ri·er *(messenger)* mensajero, -a *mf*; *(guide)* guía *mf* turístico, -a.

course *(of river)* curso *m*; *(of ship,*

plane) rumbo *m*; *(series)* ciclo *m*; *(for golf)* campo *m*; *(of meal)* plato *m*; *(degree)* carrera *f*; *(in single subject)* curso *m*; *(short course)* cursillo *m*; **in the c. of construction** en vías de construcción; **a c. of treatment** un tratamiento; **of c.** claro, por supuesto; **of c. not!** ¡claro que no!

court *(of law)* tribunal *m*; *(royal)* corte *f*; *(for sport)* pista *f*, cancha *f*.

cour·te·ous *adj* cortés.

cour·te·sy cortesía *f*, educación *f*.

court·room sala *f* de justicia.

court·yard patio *m*.

cous·in primo, -a *mf*.

cov·er 1 *vt* cubrir (**with** de); *(with lid)* tapar; *(hide)* disimular; *(protect)* abrigar; *(include)* abarcar. **2** *n* cubierta *f*; *(of chair etc)* funda *f*; *(of magazine)* portada *f*; *(in restaurant)* cubierto *m*; **full c.** *(in insurance)* cobertura *f* completa; **to take c.** refugiarse.

▶ **cover over** *vt (floor etc)* recubrir.

▶ **cover up 1** *vt* cubrir; *(crime)* encubrir. **2** *vi (person)* abrigarse; **to c. up for sb** encubrir a algn.

cov·er·age cobertura *f*.

cov·er·alls *npl* mono *m sing*.

cov·er charge *(in restaurant)* precio *m* del cubierto.

cov·er·ing 1 *n* cubierta *f*. **2** *adj (letter)* explicatorio, -a.

cow vaca *f*.

cow·ard cobarde *mf*.

cow·ard·ice cobardía *f*.

cow·ard·ly *adj* cobarde.

cow·boy vaquero *m*.

co·zy *adj (atmosphere)* acogedor, -a; *(bed)* calentito, -a.

crab cangrejo *m*.

crack 1 *vt (cup)* partir; *(nut)* cascar; *(whip)* hacer restallar; *(joke)* contar. **2** *vi (glass)* partirse; *(wall)* agrietarse; *fam* **to get cracking on sth** ponerse a hacer algo. **3** *n (in cup)* raja *f*, *(in wall, ground)* grieta *f*; *(of whip)* restallido *m*; *(of gun)* detonación *f*; *fam (drug)* crack *m*.

crack up vi (go insane) desquiciarse; (with laughter) partirse de risa.

crack·er galleta f seca; (firework) petardo m.

crack·pot fam chiflado, -a mf.

cra·dle (baby's) cuna f.

craft (occupation) oficio m; (art) arte m; (skill) destreza f.

crafts·man artesano m.

craft·y adj astuto, -a.

cram 1 vt atiborrar; crammed with atestado, -a de. **2** vi (for exam) empollar.

cramp (in leg etc) calambre m.

cramped adj apretado, -a.

crane (device) grúa f.

crank (handle) manivela f; fam (eccentric) tipo m raro.

crash 1 vt to c. one's car tener un accidente con el coche. **2** vi (car, plane) estrellarse; (collide) chocar; **to c. into** estrellarse contra. **3** n (noise) estrépito m; (collision) choque m; (of market) quiebra f; **car/plane c.** accidente m de coche/avión.

crash course curso m intensivo.

crash hel·met casco m protector.

crash-land vi hacer un aterrizaje forzoso.

crate caja f (para embalaje).

crav·ing ansia f.

crawl 1 vi (baby) gatear; (vehicle) avanzar lentamente. **2** n (swimming) crol m.

cray·on cera f.

craze manía f; (fashion) moda f.

cra·zy adj loco, -a.

creak vi (hinge) chirriar.

cream (of milk) nata f; **c. colored** color crema.

cream cheese queso m crema.

cream·y adj cremoso, -a.

crease 1 n (wrinkle) arruga f; (on trousers) raya f. **2** vt (clothes) arrugar. **3** vi arrugarse.

cre·ate vt crear.

cre·a·tion creación f.

cre·a·tive adj (person) creativo, -a.

crea·ture (animal) criatura f.

crèche guardería f.

cred·i·ble adj creíble.

cred·it 1 n (financial) crédito m; (merit) honor m; **on c.** a crédito; **to be a c. to** hacer honor a. **2** vt **to c. sb's account** abonar en cuenta a algn.

cred·it card tarjeta f de crédito.

cred·it fa·cil·i·ties facilidades fpl de pago.

cred·it·wor·thy adj solvente.

creek cala f; riachuelo m.

creep* vi (insect) arrastrarse; (cat) deslizarse; (person) arrastrarse.

creep·y adj fam espeluznante.

cre·mate vt incinerar.

cre·ma·to·ri·um crematorio m.

crepe pa·per papel m crespón.

cress berro m.

crest (of cock, wave) cresta f; (of hill) cima f.

crew (of plane, yacht) tripulación f.

crib 1 n (for baby) cuna f. **2** vt (copy) copiar.

crick·et¹ (insect) grillo m.

crick·et² (game) cricket m.

crime delincuencia f; (offence) delito m.

crim·i·nal adj & n criminal (mf).

crip·ple lisiado, -a mf.

cri·sis (pl crises) crisis f inv.

crisp adj crujiente; (lettuce) fresco, -a.

cri·te·ri·on (pl criteria) criterio m.

crit·ic crítico, -a mf.

crit·i·cal adj crítico, -a.

crit·i·cal·ly adv **c. ill** gravemente enfermo, -a.

crit·i·cism crítica f.

crit·i·cize vt criticar.

cro·chet ganchillo m.

crock·er·y loza f.

croc·o·dile cocodrilo m.

cro·cus crocus m.

crook fam caco m.

crook·ed adj (stick, picture) torcido, -a; (path) tortuoso, -a.

crop cultivo m; (harvest) cosecha f.

▸**crop up** vi surgir.
cro·quet croquet m.
cross 1 n cruz f; (of breeds) cruce m; **c. section** sección f transversal. **2** vt cruzar. **3** vi cruzar; (roads) cruzarse. **4** adj (angry) enfadado, -a.
▸**cross off, cross out** vt tachar.
▸**cross over** vi cruzar.
cross-coun·try race cros m.
cross-eyed adj bizco, -a.
cross·ing pedestrian c. paso m de peatones; **sea c.** travesía f.
cross-ref·er·ence referencia f cruzada.
cross·roads cruce m; fig encrucijada f.
cross·walk paso m de peatones.
cross·word (puz·zle) crucigrama m.
crouch vi **to c. (down)** agacharse.
crow cuervo m.
crow·bar palanca f.
crowd 1 n muchedumbre f; (gang) pandilla f; **the c.** el vulgo; **there was such a c. there** había tantísima gente allí. **2** vi **to c. in/out** entrar/salir en tropel.
▸**crowd round** vt apiñarse alrededor de.
crowd·ed adj lleno, -a, atestado, -a.
crown corona f.
cru·cial adj decisivo, -a.
crude adj (manners, style) grosero, -a.
cru·el adj cruel (**to** con).
cru·el·ty crueldad f (**to** hacia).
cru·et c. set vinagreras fpl.
cruise 1 vi (ship) hacer un crucero; (car) viajar a velocidad constante; (plane) viajar a velocidad de crucero. **2** n (on ship) crucero m.
crumb miga f.
crum·ble 1 vt desmigar. **2** vi (wall) desmoronarse; (bread) desmigajarse.
crum·bly adj que se desmigaja.
crum·my adj fam chungo, -a.
crum·ple vt (clothes) arrugar.
crunch 1 vt (food) mascar. **2** n crujido m.

crunch·y adj crujiente.
crush 1 vt aplastar; (wrinkle) arrugar; (grind) moler. **2** n (of people) gentío m.
crust corteza f.
crutch (for walking) muleta f.
cry 1 vi gritar; (weep) llorar. **2** n grito m; (weep) llanto m.
▸**cry off** vi rajarse.
▸**cry out** vi gritar; **to c. out for sth** pedir algo a gritos.
▸**cry over** vt llorar por.
crys·tal cristal m.
cub (young animal) cachorro, -a mf; (junior scout) niño m explorador.
Cu·ban adj & n cubano, -a (mf).
cube cubo m; (of sugar) terrón m.
cu·bic adj cúbico, -a.
cuck·oo cuco m.
cu·cum·ber pepino m.
cud·dle 1 vt abrazar. **2** vi abrazarse.
▸**cuddle up to** vt acurrucarse contra.
cuddly toy muñeco m de peluche.
cue (in play) pie m; indicación f.
cuff (of sleeve) puño m; (of trousers) dobladillo m.
cuff-links npl gemelos mpl.
cul-de-sac callejón m sin salida.
cul·prit culpable mf.
cult culto m; **c. film** película f de culto.
cul·ti·vate vt cultivar.
cul·ti·vat·ed adj (person) culto, -a.
cul·tur·al adj cultural.
cul·ture cultura f.
cul·tured adj (person) culto, -a.
cum·ber·some adj (bulky) voluminoso, -a.
cun·ning 1 adj astuto, -a. **2** n astucia f.
cup taza f; (trophy) copa f.
cup·board armario m; (on wall) alacena f.
cur·a·ble adj curable.
curb bordillo m.
cure 1 vt curar. **2** n (remedy) cura f, remedio m.
cu·ri·os·i·ty curiosidad f.

cu·ri·ous adj (inquisitive) curioso, -a; (odd) extraño, -a.

curl 1 vt (hair) rizar. **2** vi rizarse. **3** n (of hair) rizo m.

▸ **curl up** vi (cat etc) enroscarse; (person) hacerse un ovillo.

curl·y adj rizado, -a.

cur·rant pasa f (de Corinto).

cur·ren·cy moneda f; **foreign c.** divisas fpl.

cur·rent adj actual; (opinion) general; (year) en curso.

cur·rent ac·count cuenta f corriente.

cur·rent af·fairs actualidad f sing (política).

cur·rent·ly adv actualmente.

cur·ric·u·lum (pl curricula) plan m de estudios; **c. vitae** (resume) currículum m (vitae).

cur·ry curry m.

curse vi blasfemar.

cur·sor cursor m.

cur·tain cortina f.

curt·s(e)y 1 n reverencia f. **2** vi hacer una reverencia (**to** a).

curve 1 n curva f. **2** vi (road, river) describir una curva.

cush·ion cojín m; (large) almohadón m.

cus·tard natillas fpl.

cus·to·dy custodia f; **to take into c.** detener.

cus·tom (habit) costumbre f.

cus·tom·ar·y adj habitual.

cus·tom·er cliente mf.

cus·toms n sing or pl aduana f.

cus·toms du·ty derechos mpl de aduana.

cus·toms of·fi·cer agente mf de aduana.

cut 1 vt* cortar; (stone) tallar; (reduce) reducir; (divide up) dividir (**into** en). **2** vi* cortar. **3** n corte m; (in skin) cortadura f; (wound) herida f; (with knife) cuchillada f; (of meat) clase f de carne; (reduction) reducción f.

▸ **cut away** (remove) cortar.

▸ **cut back** vt (expenses) reducir; (production) disminuir.

▸ **cut down** vt (tree) talar.

▸ **cut down on** vt reducir.

▸ **cut off** vt (water etc) cortar; (place) aislar; (heir) excluir.

▸ **cut out** vt (from newspaper) recortar; (delete) suprimir; (person) **to be c. out for sth** estar hecho, -a para algo; fam **c. it out!** ¡basta ya! **2** vi (engine) calarse.

▸ **cut up** vt cortar en pedazos.

cut·back reducción f (**in** de).

cute adj mono, -a, lindo, -a.

cut·ler·y cubiertos mpl.

cut·let chuleta f.

cut·ting 1 n (from newspaper) recorte m; (plant) esqueje m. **2** adj (wind) cortante; (remark) mordaz.

CV, cv abbr of **curriculum vitae** currículum m (vitae).

cy·cle 1 n ciclo m; (bicycle) bicicleta f; (motorcycle) moto f. **2** vi ir en bicicleta.

cy·cling ciclismo m.

cy·clist ciclista mf.

cyl·in·der cilindro m; (for gas) bombona f.

cym·bal platillo m.

cyn·i·cal adj (sceptical) descreído, -a, suspicaz; (unscrupulous) desaprensivo, -a, sin escrúpulos.

Czech 1 adj checo, -a. **2** n (person) checo, -a mf; (language) checo m.

D

dab vt (apply) aplicar; (touch lightly) tocar ligeramente.

dad, dad·dy fam papá m, papi m.

daf·fo·dil narciso m.

daft adj (idea) tonto, -a.

dai·ly 1 adj diario, -a. **2** adv diariamente. **3** n (newspaper) diario m.

dair·y lechería f; **d. farming** industria f lechera; **d. produce** productos mpl lácteos.

dai·sy margarita f.

dam (barrier) dique m; (lake) presa f.

dam·age 1 n daño m; (to health, reputation) perjuicio m. **2** vt (harm) dañar; (spoil) estropear.

dam·ag·ing adj perjudicial.

damn fam **1** interj **d. (it)!** ¡maldito, -a sea! **2** n **I don't give a d.** me importa un bledo. **3** adj maldito, -a. **4** adv (very) muy, sumamente.

damp 1 adj (humid) húmedo, -a; (wet) mojado, -a. **2** n humedad f.

damp·en vt humedecer.

damp·ness humedad f.

dance 1 n baile m; (classical, tribal) danza f. **2** vti bailar.

dance hall salón m de baile.

danc·er (by profession) bailarín, -ina mf; **she's a good d.** baila muy bien.

dan·de·li·on diente m de león.

dan·druff caspa f.

Dane danés, -esa mf.

dan·ger (peril) peligro m; (risk) riesgo m; (of war etc) amenaza f; **out of d.** fuera de peligro.

dan·ger·ous adj peligroso, -a; (risky) arriesgado, -a; (harmful) nocivo, -a; (illness) grave.

danger·ous·ly adv peligrosamente.

Dan·ish 1 adj danés, -esa. **2** n (language) danés m.

dare 1 vi atreverse, osar. **2** vt (challenge) desafiar; **to d. to do sth** atreverse a hacer algo.

dar·ing adj osado, -a.

dark 1 adj (unlit, color) oscuro, -a; (hair, complexion) moreno, -a; (eyes, future) negro, -a. **2** n (darkness) oscuridad f.

dark-haired adj moreno, -a.

dark·ness oscuridad f.

dark-skinned adj de piel oscura.

dar·ling adj & n querido, -a (mf).

dart (missile) dardo m; **darts** sing (game) dardos mpl.

dart·board diana f.

dash 1 n (hyphen) guión m. **2** vi (rush) correr.

▸ **dash off** vi salir corriendo.

dash·board salpicadero m.

da·ta npl datos mpl.

da·ta·base base m de datos.

data proc·ess·ing (act) proceso m de datos; (science) informática f.

date¹ n fecha f; (social event) compromiso m; (with girl, boy) cita f; (person dated) ligue m; **what's the d. today?** ¿qué día es hoy?; **out of d.** (ideas) anticuado, -a; (expression) desusado, -a; (invalid) caducado, -a; **to be up to d.** estar al día.

▸ **date back to, date from** vt datar de; (origins etc) remontarse a.

date² (fruit) dátil m.

dat·ed adj (idea) anticuado, -a; (fashion) pasado, -a de moda; (expression) desusado, -a.

daugh·ter hija f.

daugh·ter-in-law nuera f.

daw·dle vi (walking) andar despacio; (waste time) perder el tiempo.

dawn amanecer m.

day día m; **(on)** the next or following d. al or al día siguiente; **the d. after tomorrow** pasado mañana; **the d. before yesterday** anteayer.

day·break amanecer m.

day·light luz f del día.

day re·turn (ticket) billete m de ida y vuelta para el mismo día.

day·time día m.

dead 1 adj muerto, -a; **he was shot d.** le mataron a tiros. **2** adv fam (tired, easy) muy.

dead-end (street) callejón m sin salida.

dead·line (date) fecha f tope; (time) hora f tope.

dead·ly 1 adj mortal; (weapon) mortífero, -a; (aim) certero, -a. **2** adv (extremely) terriblemente, sumamente.

deaf 1 adj sordo, -a; **d. mute** sordomudo, -a mf. **2** npl **the d.** los sordos.

deaf·ness sordera f.

deal (in business, politics) trato m; (amount) cantidad f; (at cards) reparto m; business d. contrato m; to do a d. with sb (transaction) cerrar un trato con algn; (agreement) pactar algo con algn; it's a d.! ¡trato hecho!; a good d. (of sth) una gran parte (de algo); a good d. slower mucho más despacio.

▸**deal* in** vt (goods) comerciar en; (drugs) traficar con.

▸**deal* out** vt repartir.

▸**deal* with** vt (firm, person) tratar con; (subject, problem) abordar; (in book etc) tratar de.

deal·er (in goods) comerciante mf; (in drugs) traficante mf.

deal·ings npl (relations) trato m sing; (in business) negocios mpl.

dear 1 adj (loved) querido, -a; (expensive) caro, -a; (in letter) D. Andrew Querido Andrew; D. Madam Estimada señora; D. Sir(s) Muy señor(es) mío(s). **2** n querido, -a mf; my d. mi vida. **3** interj oh d.!, d. me! (surprise) ¡vaya por Dios!; (disappointment) ¡qué pena!

death muerte f.

death cer·tif·i·cate certificado m de defunción.

de·bate 1 n debate m. **2** vti discutir.

deb·it 1 n débito m. **2** vt to d. sb's account cargar una suma en la cuenta de algn.

debt deuda f.

debt·or deudor, -a mf.

de·but debut m; to make one's d. debutar.

dec·ade década f, decenio m.

de·caf·fein·at·ed adj descafeinado, -a.

de·cay (of food, body) descomposición f; (of teeth) caries f inv; (of buildings) desmoronamiento m.

de·ceive vt (mislead) engañar; (lie to) mentir.

De·cem·ber diciembre m.

de·cent adj decente; (person) honrado, -a; (kind) simpático, -a.

de·cep·tion engaño m.

de·cide 1 vt decidir; to d. to do sth decidir hacer algo. **2** vi (reach decision) decidirse.

▸**decide on** vt (choose) optar por.

dec·i·mal 1 adj decimal; d. point coma f (de fracción decimal). **2** n decimal m.

de·ci·sion decisión f.

de·ci·sive adj (resolute) decidido, -a; (conclusive) decisivo, -a.

deck (of ship) cubierta f.

deck-chair tumbona f.

de·clare vt declarar; (winner, innocence) proclamar.

de·cline vi (decrease) disminuir; (amount) bajar; (business) decaer; (deteriorate) deteriorarse; (health) empeorar.

dec·o·rate vt (adorn) decorar (with con); (paint) pintar; (wallpaper) empapelar.

dec·o·ra·tion (decor) decoración f.

dec·o·ra·tive adj decorativo, -a.

dec·o·ra·tor decorador, -a mf; (painter) pintor, -a mf; (paper-hanger) empapelador, -a mf.

de·crease 1 n disminución f; (in speed, size, price) reducción f. **2** vi disminuir; (price, temperature) bajar; (speed, size) reducirse. **3** vt disminuir; (price, temperature) bajar.

de·cree 1 n decreto m; (by court) sentencia f. **2** vt decretar.

ded·i·cate vt consagrar, dedicar.

ded·i·cat·ed adj dedicado, -a, entregado, -a.

de·duct vt descontar (from de).

de·duc·tion (conclusion) conclusión f; (subtraction) descuento m.

deed (act) acto m; (legal document) escritura f.

deep adj profundo, -a; (breath, sigh) hondo, -a; (voice) bajo, -a; it's ten meters d. tiene diez metros de profundidad.

deep-freeze 1 n congelador m. **2** vt congelar.

deer *n inv* ciervo *m.*

de·fault *n* **by d.** por defaut, por omisión; **to win by d.** ganar por incomparecencia del adversario.

de·feat 1 *vt* derrotar. **2** *n (of army, team)* derrota *f.*

de·fect defecto *m.*

de·fec·tive *adj (faulty)* defectuoso, -a.

de·fend *vt* defender.

de·fen·dant acusado, -a *mf.*

de·fense defensa *f.*

de·fen·sive 1 *adj* defensivo, -a. **2** *n* **to be on the d.** estar a la defensiva.

de·fi·ant *adj (behavior)* desafiante; *(person)* insolente.

de·fi·cien·cy falta *f,* carencia *f.*

de·fi·cient *adj* deficiente; **to be d. in sth** carecer de algo.

def·i·cit déficit *m.*

de·fine *vt* definir; *(duties, powers)* delimitar.

def·i·nite *adj (clear)* claro, -a; *(progress)* notable; *(date, place)* determinado, -a.

def·i·nite·ly *adv* sin duda.

def·i·ni·tion definición *f.*

de·formed *adj* deforme.

de·frost *vt (freezer, food)* descongelar.

de·fy *vt* desafiar; *(law, order)* contravenir.

de·gen·er·ate *vi* degenerar *(into* en).

de·gree grado *m; (qualification)* título *m;* **to some d.** hasta cierto punto; **to have a d. in science** ser licenciado en ciencias.

de·icer anticongelante *m.*

de·ject·ed *adj* deprimido, -a.

de·lay 1 *vt (flight, train)* retrasar; *(person)* entretener; *(postpone)* aplazar. **2** *n* retraso *m.*

del·e·gate 1 *n* delegado, -a *mf.* **2** *vt* delegar **(to** en); **to d. sb to do sth** encargar a algn que haga algo.

del·e·ga·tion delegación *f.*

de·lete *vt* suprimir; *(cross out)* tachar.

de·lib·er·ate *adj (intentional)* deliberado, -a.

de·lib·er·ate·ly *adv (intentionally)* a propósito; *(unhurriedly)* pausadamente.

del·i·ca·cy *(food)* manjar *m* (exquisito).

del·i·cate *adj* delicado, -a; *(handwork)* fino, -a; *(instrument)* sensible; *(flavor)* fino, -a.

del·i·ca·tes·sen delicatessen *m.*

de·li·cious *adj* delicioso, -a.

de·light 1 *n (pleasure)* placer *m; (source of pleasure)* encanto *m;* **he took d. in it** le encantó. **2** *vt* encantar.

de·light·ed *adj* encantado, -a.

de·light·ful *adj (person)* encantador, -a; *(view)* muy agradable; *(meal, weather)* delicioso, -a.

de·lin·quent *adj & n* delincuente *(mf).*

de·liv·er *vt (goods, letters)* repartir; *(parcel, manuscript etc)* entregar; *(speech, verdict)* pronunciar; *(baby)* dar a luz.

de·liv·er·y *(of goods)* reparto *m; (of package, manuscript etc)* entrega *f, (of baby)* parto *m.*

de·lude *vt* engañar; **don't d. yourself** no te hagas ilusiones.

de·lu·sion *(state, act)* engaño *m; (false belief)* ilusión *f* (vana); **delusions of grandeur** delirios *mpl* de grandeza.

de luxe *adj* de lujo *inv.*

de·mand 1 *n (request)* petición *f; (for pay rise, rights)* reclamación *f; (need)* necesidad *f, (claim)* exigencia *f; (economic)* demanda *f;* **to be in d.** ser solicitado, -a. **2** *vt* exigir; *(rights)* reclamar; **to d. that …** insistir en que … *(+ subjunctive).*

de·mand·ing *adj (hard to please)* exigente; *(job)* agotador, -a.

dem·er·a·ra (su·gar) azúcar *m* moreno.

dem·o *fam (demonstration)* manifestación *f,* **d. tape** maqueta *f.*

de·moc·ra·cy democracia f.

dem·o·crat·ic adj democrático, -a.

de·mol·ish vt (building) derribar.

dem·o·li·tion demolición f.

de·mon demonio m.

dem·on·strate 1 vt demostrar. **2** vi (politically) manifestarse.

dem·on·stra·tion (proof) demostración f, (explanation) explicación f, (political) manifestación f.

dem·on·stra·tive adj franco, -a.

dem·on·stra·tor manifestante mf.

de·mor·al·ize vt desmoralizar.

den (of animal) guarida f, (study) estudio m.

de·ni·al (of charge) desmentido m; (of rights) denegación f.

den·im dril m; **denims** tejanos mpl, vaqueros mpl.

de·nounce vt denunciar.

dent 1 n abolladura f. **2** vt abollar.

den·tal adj dental.

den·tist dentista mf.

den·tures npl dentadura f postiza.

de·ny vt (refuse) negar; (rumor, report) desmentir; (charge) rechazar; **to d. sb sth** negarle algo a algn.

de·o·dor·ant desodorante m.

de·part vi marcharse, irse; (from subject) desviarse (**from** de).

de·part·ment sección f, (in university) departamento m; (in government) ministerio m.

de·part·ment store grandes almacenes mpl.

de·par·ture partida f, (of plane, train) salida f.

de·pend 1 vi (rely) fiarse (**on, upon** de). **2** v impers (be determined by) depender (**on** de); **it depends on the weather** según el tiempo que haga; **that depends** según.

de·pend·a·ble adj (person) fiable.

de·pen·dent 1 adj dependiente; **to be d. on sth** depender de algo. **2** n his/her d. la persona a su cargo.

de·pict vt (in painting) representar; (describe) describir.

de·plor·a·ble adj lamentable.

de·plore vt deplorar.

de·pos·it 1 n (in bank, on rented car) depósito m; (in river, test tube) sedimento m; (in wine) poso m; (on purchase) señal f, (on house) entrada f. **2** vt depositar; (into account) ingresar.

de·pot almacén m; (bus garage) cochera f (de autobuses).

de·press vt (discourage) deprimir.

de·pressed adj (person) deprimido, -a; **to get d.** deprimirse.

de·pres·sion depresión f.

de·prive vt privar (**of** de).

de·prived adj necesitado, -a.

depth profundidad f, (of emotion) intensidad f.

dep·u·ty (substitute) suplente mf; **d. head** subdirector, -a mf.

de·rail·ment descarrilamiento m.

der·e·lict adj abandonado, -a.

de·rive vt sacar, obtener.

de·scend 1 vi descender; **to d. from** (be related to) descender de. **2** vt (stairs) bajar.

▸**descend upon** vt (area) invadir.

de·scen·dant descendiente mf.

de·scent descenso m.

de·scribe vt describir.

de·scrip·tion descripción f, (type) clase f.

des·ert¹ desierto m.

de·sert² vt (place, family) abandonar.

de·serve vt (rest, punishment) merecer; (prize, praise) ser digno, -a de.

de·sign 1 n diseño m; (of building etc) plano m; (of room) disposición f, (pattern) dibujo m. **2** vt diseñar.

des·ig·nate vt designar, nombrar.

de·sign·er diseñador, -a mf; **d. jeans** vaqueros mpl de marca.

de·sign·er clothes ropa f de marca.

de·sir·a·ble adj deseable; (asset, offer) atractivo, -a.

de·sire 1 n deseo m; **I haven't the slightest d. to go** no me apetece nada ir. **2** vt desear.

desk (in school) pupitre m; (in office) escritorio m; (reception) d. recepción f.

desk clerk recepcionista mf.

desk·top escritorio m; d. publishing autoedición f.

de·spair 1 n desesperación f. **2** vi desesperar(se) (of de).

des·patch vt = dispatch.

des·per·ate adj (person, situation, action) desesperado, -a; (need) apremiante; to be d. for sth necesitar algo con urgencia.

des·per·ate·ly adv (need) urgentemente; (bad, busy) terriblemente.

des·pi·ca·ble adj despreciable; (behavior) indigno, -a.

de·spise vt despreciar.

de·spite prep a pesar de.

des·sert postre m.

des·sert spoon cuchara f de postre.

des·ti·na·tion destino m.

des·ti·tute adj indigente.

de·stroy vt destruir; (vehicle, old furniture) destrozar.

de·struc·tion destrucción f.

de·struc·tive adj (gale etc) destructor, -a.

de·tach vt (remove) separar.

de·tach·a·ble adj separable (from de).

de·tached adj (separated) separado, -a.

de·tached house casa f independiente.

de·tail detalle m, pormenor m.

detailed adj detallado, -a.

de·tain vt (police etc) detener; (delay) retener.

de·tect vt (error, movement) advertir; (difference) notar; (smell, sound) percibir; (discover) descubrir.

de·tec·tive detective mf; d. story novela f policíaca.

de·tec·tor aparato m detector.

de·ten·tion (of suspect etc) detención f.

de·ter vt (dissuade) disuadir (from

de); to d. sb from doing sth impedir a algn hacer algo.

de·ter·gent detergente m.

de·te·ri·o·rate vi deteriorarse.

de·te·ri·o·ra·tion empeoramiento m; (of substance, friendship) deterioro m.

de·ter·mi·na·tion (resolution) resolución f.

de·ter·mine vt determinar.

de·ter·mined adj (person) decidido, -a; (effort) enérgico, -a.

de·ter·rent fuerza f disuasoria.

de·tour desvío m.

dev·as·tat·ing adj (news, results) demoledor, -a.

de·vel·op 1 vt desarrollar; (trade) fomentar; (plan) elaborar; (illness, habit) contraer; (interest) mostrar; (natural resources) aprovechar; (build on) (site) urbanizar. **2** vi (body, industry) desarrollarse; (system) perfeccionarse; (interest) crecer.

▸**develop into** vt transformarse en.

de·vel·op·ment desarrollo m; (of trade) fomento m; (of skill) perfección f; (of character) formación f; (advance) avance m; (exploitation) explotación f; (of land, site) urbanización f; there are no new developments no hay ninguna novedad.

de·vi·ate vi desviarse (from de).

de·vice aparato m; (mechanism) mecanismo m.

dev·il diablo m, demonio m; fam where the d. did you put it? ¿dónde demonios lo pusiste?

de·vise vt idear.

de·vote vt dedicar.

de·vot·ed adj dedicado, -a (to a).

de·vo·tion devoción f; (to cause) dedicación f.

dew rocío m.

di·a·be·tes diabetes f.

di·a·bet·ic adj & n diabético, -a (mf).

di·ag·nose vt diagnosticar.

di·ag·no·sis (pl diagnoses) diagnóstico m.

di·ag·o·nal adj & n diagonal (f).

di·ag·o·nal·ly adv en diagonal, diagonalmente.

di·a·gram diagrama m; (of process, system) esquema m; (of workings) gráfico m.

di·al 1 n (of clock) esfera f; (on machine) botón m selector; (on radio) dial m; **d. tone** señal f de marcar. **2** vt marcar.

di·a·lect dialecto m.

di·a·log diálogo m.

di·am·e·ter diámetro m.

di·a·mond diamante m; (shape) rombo m.

di·a·per pañal m.

di·ar·rhe·a diarrea f.

di·a·ry diario m; (for appointments) agenda f.

dice 1 n dado m. **2** vt (food) cortar en cuadritos.

dic·tate 1 vt (letter, order) dictar. **2** vi (order about) dar órdenes.

dic·ta·tion dictado m.

dic·tion·ar·y diccionario m.

did pt of **do**.

die vi morir(se); **to be dying for sth/ to do sth** morirse por algo/de ganas de hacer algo.

▶**die down** vi (wind) amainar; (noise, excitement) disminuir.

die out vi extinguirse.

die·sel (oil) gasoil m; **d. engine** motor m diesel.

di·et 1 n (normal food) dieta f; (selected food) régimen m. **2** vi estar a régimen.

dif·fer vi (be unlike) ser distinto, -a; (disagree) discrepar.

dif·fer·ence diferencia f; (disagreement) desacuerdo m; **it makes no d. (to me)** (me) da igual; **what d. does it make?** ¿qué más da?

dif·fer·ent adj distinto, -a.

dif·fer·ent·ly adv de otra manera.

dif·fi·cult adj difícil.

dif·fi·cul·ty dificultad f; (problem) problema m.

dig* 1 vt (earth) cavar; (tunnel) excavar; (hole) hacer. **2** vi cavar.

▶**dig out** vt fig (find) sacar; (information) descubrir.

▶**dig up** vt (weeds) arrancar; (buried object) desenterrar.

di·gest vt (food) digerir; (facts) asimilar.

di·ges·tion digestión f.

dig·ger excavadora f.

dig·it (number) dígito m.

dig·i·tal adj digital.

dig·ni·ty dignidad f.

di·lap·i·dat·ed adj en mal estado.

di·lem·ma dilema m.

di·lute vt diluir; (wine, milk) aguar.

dim 1 adj (light) tenue; (room) oscuro, -a; (outline) borroso, -a; (memory) vago, -a; fam (stupid) torpe. **2** vt (light) bajar.

dime moneda f de diez centavos.

di·men·sion dimensión f.

di·min·ish vti disminuir.

din estrépito m.

dine vi (formal use) cenar.

din·er (person) comensal mf; (restaurant) restaurante m barato.

din·ghy bote m; **(rubber) d.** bote m neumático.

din·gy adj (street, house) oscuro, -a; (dirty) sucio, -a; (colour) desteñido, -a.

din·ing car vagón m restaurante.

din·ing room comedor m.

din·ner (at midday) comida f; (in evening) cena f.

din·ner jack·et smoking m.

din·ner par·ty cena f.

din·ner ser·vice vajilla f.

di·no·saur dinosaurio m.

dip 1 n (bathe) chapuzón m; (of road) pendiente f. **2** vi (road) bajar.

▶**dip into** vt (savings) echar mano de.

diph·thong diptongo m.

di·plo·ma diploma m.

dip·lo·mat diplomático, -a mf.

dip·lo·mat·ic adj diplomático, -a.

di·rect 1 adj directo, -a. **2** adv directamente. **3** vt dirigir; **can you d. me to a bank?** ¿me puede indicar dónde hay un banco?

di·rec·tion dirección f; **directions** (to place) señas fpl; **directions for use** modo m de empleo.

di·rect·ly 1 adv (above etc) justo; (speak) directamente; (at once) en seguida. **2** conj en cuanto.

di·rec·tor director, -a mf.

di·rec·to·ry (for telephone) guía f telefónica.

di·rec·to·ry as·sis·tance (servicio m de) información f.

dirt suciedad f.

dirt-cheap adv & adj fam tirado, -a.

dirt·y 1 adj sucio, -a; (joke) verde; (mind) pervertido, -a; **d. word** palabrota f; **to get sth d.** ensuciar algo. **2** vt ensuciar.

dis·a·bil·i·ty discapacidad f.

dis·a·bled 1 adj minusválido, -a. **2** npl **the d.** los minusválidos mpl.

dis·ad·van·tage desventaja f; (obstacle) inconveniente m.

dis·a·gree vi (differ) no estar de acuerdo (with con); (quarrel) reñir (about por); **garlic disagrees with me** el ajo no me sienta bien.

dis·a·gree·a·ble adj desagradable.

dis·a·gree·ment desacuerdo m; (argument) riña f.

dis·ap·pear vi desaparecer.

dis·ap·pear·ance desaparición f.

dis·ap·point vt decepcionar.

dis·ap·point·ing adj decepcionante.

dis·ap·point·ment decepción f.

dis·ap·prove vi **to d. of** desaprobar.

dis·arm 1 vt desarmar. **2** vi desarmarse.

dis·as·ter desastre m.

dis·as·trous adj desastroso, -a.

disc disco m.

dis·card vt (old things) deshacerse de; (plan) descartar.

dis·charge vt (prisoner) soltar; (patient) dar de alta; (soldier) licenciar; (dismiss) despedir.

dis·con·tin·ued adj (article) que no se fabrica más.

dis·ci·pline 1 n disciplina f. **2** vt (child) castigar; (worker) sancionar.

disc jock·ey disc-jockey mf, pinchadiscos mf inv.

dis·close vt revelar.

dis·co discoteca f.

dis·com·fort (pain) malestar m.

dis·con·nect vt desconectar (from de); (gas, electricity) cortar.

dis·con·tent·ed adj descontento, -a.

dis·co·theque discoteca f.

dis·count descuento m.

dis·cour·age vt (dishearten) desanimar; (advances) rechazar.

dis·cov·er vt descubrir; (missing person, object) encontrar.

dis·cov·er·y descubrimiento m.

dis·creet adj discreto, -a.

dis·crim·i·nate vi distinguir (between entre); **to d. against sth/sb** discriminar algo/a algn.

dis·crim·i·na·tion (bias) discriminación f.

dis·cuss vt discutir; (in writing) tratar de.

dis·cus·sion discusión f.

dis·ease enfermedad f.

dis·em·bark vti desembarcar.

dis·fig·ured adj desfigurado, -a.

dis·grace 1 n desgracia f. **2** vt deshonrar.

dis·grace·ful adj vergonzoso, -a.

dis·guise 1 n disfraz m; **in d.** disfrazado, -a. **2** vt (person) disfrazar (as de).

dis·gust 1 n repugnancia f, asco m. **2** vt (revolt) dar asco a.

dis·gust·ed adj disgustado, -a, indignado, -a.

dis·gust·ing adj repugnante; (behavior, state of affairs) intolerable.

dish (for serving) fuente f; (course) plato m; **to wash** or **do the dishes** fregar los platos.

▶ **dish up** vt (meal) servir.

dish·cloth trapo m de fregar.

di·shev·eled adj (hair) despeinado, -a; (appearance) fraudulento, -a.

dis·hon·est adj (person) poco honrado, -a.

dis·hon·es·ty (of person) falta f de honradez.

dish·tow·el paño m de cocina.

dish·wash·er lavaplatos m inv.

dis·il·lu·sioned adj desilusionado, -a.

dis·in·cen·tive freno m.

dis·in·fect vt desinfectar.

dis·in·fec·tant desinfectante m.

disk disco m; (for computer) disquete m; **d. drive** unidad f de disquete, disquetera f.

dis·like 1 n antipatía f (**for, of** a, hacia). **2** vt tener antipatía hacia.

dis·lo·cate vt (joint) dislocar.

dis·mal adj (prospect) sombrío, -a; (place, weather) deprimente; (person) triste.

dis·man·tle vt desmontar.

dis·may 1 n consternación f. **2** vt consternar.

dis·miss vt (employee) despedir.

dis·miss·al (of employee) despido m.

dis·o·be·di·ence desobediencia f.

dis·o·be·di·ent adj desobediente.

dis·o·bey vt desobedecer; (law) violar.

dis·or·der (untidiness) desorden m; (riot) disturbio m; (illness) trastorno m.

dis·or·gan·ized adj desorganizado, -a.

dis·patch vt (mail) enviar; (goods) expedir.

dis·pel vt disipar.

dis·pens·er (device) máquina f expendedora; **cash d.** cajero m automático.

dis·perse 1 vt dispersar. **2** vi dispersarse.

dis·play 1 n (exhibition) exposición f, (on computer screen) visualización f. **2** vt mostrar; (goods) exponer; (on computer screen) visualizar; (feelings) manifestar.

dis·pleased adj contrariado, -a.

dis·pos·a·ble adj desechable.

dis·pos·al at my d. a mi disposición.

dis·pose vi **to d. of** (trash) tirar; (unwanted object) deshacerse de.

dis·pute 1 n (disagreement) discusión f, (quarrel) disputa f; **industrial d.** conflicto m laboral. **2** vt refutar.

dis·qual·i·fy vt (team) descalificar; (make ineligible) incapacitar.

dis·re·gard vt (ignore) ignorar.

dis·re·spect·ful adj irrespetuoso, -a.

dis·rupt vt (meeting, traffic) interrumpir; (order) trastornar; (schedule etc) desbaratar.

dis·rup·tion (of meeting, traffic) interrupción f, (of schedule etc) desbaratamiento m.

dis·sat·is·fac·tion descontento m.

dis·sat·is·fied adj descontento, -a.

dis·sent 1 n disconformidad f. **2** vi disentir.

dis·solve 1 vt disolver. **2** vi disolverse.

dis·suade vt disuadir (**from** de).

dis·tance distancia f; **in the d.** a lo lejos.

dis·tant adj (place, time) lejano, -a; (look) distraído, -a; (aloof) distante.

dis·taste aversión f.

dis·taste·ful adj desagradable.

dis·tinct adj (different) diferente; (smell, change) marcado, -a; (idea, intention) claro, -a; **as d. from** a diferencia de.

dis·tinc·tion (difference) diferencia f, (excellence) distinción f, (in exam) sobresaliente m.

dis·tinc·tive adj distintivo, -a.

dis·tinct·ly adv (clearly) claramente; (definitely) sensiblemente.

dis·tin·guish vt distinguir.

dis·tin·guished adj distinguido, -a.

dis·tort vt (misrepresent) deformar.

dis·tract vt distraer.

dis·trac·tion (interruption) distracción f; **to drive sb to d.** volver loco a algn.

dis·tress (mental) angustia f; (physical) dolor m.

dis·tress·ing adj penoso, -a.

dis·trib·ute vt distribuir.

dis·tri·bu·tion distribución f.

dis·trib·u·tor distribuidor, -a mf; (in car engine) delco m.

dis·trict (of country) región f; (of town) barrio m; **d. attorney** fiscal mf.

dis·trust vt desconfiar de.

dis·turb vt (inconvenience) molestar; (silence) romper; (sleep) interrumpir; (worry) perturbar; (papers) desordenar.

dis·tur·bance (commotion) disturbio m.

dis·turb·ing adj inquietante.

ditch zanja f; (at roadside) cuneta f; (for irrigation) acequia f.

dit·to ídem.

di·van diván m.

dive 1 n (into water) zambullida f; (of diver) buceo m; (of plane) picado m; (in sport) salto m. **2** vi* zambullirse; (diver) bucear; (plane) bajar en picado; (in sport) saltar; **he dived for the phone** se precipitó hacia el teléfono.

div·er (person) buceador, -a mf; (professional) buzo m; (from diving board) saltador, -a mf.

di·ver·sion (distraction) distracción f.

di·vert vt desviar.

di·vide 1 vt dividir. **2** vi (road, stream) bifurcarse.

▸**divide off** vt separar.

▸**divide up** vt (share out) repartir.

div·i·dend dividendo m.

di·vine adj divino, -a.

div·ing submarinismo m; (sport) salto m de trampolín.

div·ing board trampolín m.

di·vi·sion división f; (sharing) reparto m; (of organization) sección f.

di·vorce 1 n divorcio m. **2** vt **she divorced him** se divorció de él.

di·vorced divorciado, -a; **to get d.** divorciarse.

diz·zi·ness vértigo m.

diz·zy adj (person) (unwell) mareado, -a.

DJ abbr of **disc jockey**.

do* 1 v aux (in negatives and questions) (not translated in Spanish) **do you drive?** ¿tienes carnet de conducir?; **don't you want to come?** ¿no quieres venir?; **he doesn't smoke** no fuma. ■ (emphatic) (not translated in Spanish) **do come with us!** ¡ánimo, vente con nosotros!; **I do like your bag** me encanta tu bolso. ■ (substituting main verb) (not translated in Spanish) **I don't believe him — neither do I** no le creo — yo tampoco; **I'll go if you do** si vas tú, voy yo; **I think it's dear, but he doesn't** a mí me parece caro pero a él no; **who went? — I did** ¿quién asistió? — yo. ■ (in question tags) **he refused, didn't he?** dijo que no, ¿verdad?; **I don't like it, do you?** a mí no me gusta, ¿y a ti? **2** vt hacer; (task) realizar; (duty) cumplir con; (distance) recorrer; **what can I do for you?** ¿en qué puedo servirle?; **what do you do (for a living)?** ¿a qué te dedicas?; **he's done it!** ¡lo ha conseguido!; **we were doing eighty** íbamos a ochenta. **3** vi (act) hacer; **do as I tell you** haz lo que te digo; **how are you doing?** ¿qué tal?; **to do well** (person) tener éxito; (business) ir bien; **five dollars will do** con cinco dólares será suficiente; **that will do!** ¡basta ya!; **this cushion will do as a pillow** este cojín servirá de almohada.

▸**do away with** vt (abolish) abolir; (discard) deshacerse de.

▸**do for** vt (destroy, ruin) arruinar; **I'm done for if I don't finish this** estoy perdido, -a si no acabo esto.

▸**do in** vt **I'm done in** (exhausted) estoy hecho, -a polvo.

▸**do out** vt (clean) limpiar a fondo.

do over vt (repeat) repetir.

do up vt (wrap) envolver; (belt etc) abrochar; (laces) atar; (dress up) arreglar; (redecorate) renovar.

do with vt I could do with a rest (need) un descanso no me vendría nada mal; **to have** or **be to do with** (concern) tener que ver con.

do without vt pasar sin, prescindir de.

dock 1 n the docks el muelle. **2** vi (ship) atracar.

dock·er estibador m.

dock·yard astillero m.

doc·tor médico, -a mf; (academic) doctor, -a mf.

doc·tor·ate doctorado m.

doc·trine doctrina f.

doc·u·ment documento m.

doc·u·men·ta·ry adj & n documental (m).

dodge vt (blow) esquivar; (pursuer) despistar; (tax) evadir.

dodg·em coche m de choque.

does 3rd person sing pres of **do**.

dog perro, -a mf.

dog·gy bag (in restaurant) bolsita f para llevarse los restos de la comida.

dog·house perrera f; fam **to be in the d.** estar en desgracia.

do·ing it was none of my d. yo no tuve nada que ver.

do-it-your·self bricolaje m.

doll (toy) muñeca f.

dol·lar dólar m.

doll·house casa f de muñecas.

dol·phin delfín m.

do·main (sphere) campo m, esfera f; (territory) dominio m; **d. name** nombre m de dominio.

dome cúpula f.

do·mes·tic adj (appliance, pet) doméstico, -a f; (flight, news) nacional; (trade, policy) interior.

dom·i·nant adj dominante.

dom·i·nate vti dominar.

Do·min·i·can adj & n dominicano, -a (mf).

dom·i·no (pl dominoes) (piece) ficha f de dominó; **dominoes** (game) dominó m sing.

do·nate vt donar.

do·na·tion donativo m.

done 1 pp of **do**. **2** adj (finished) terminado, -a; (meat) hecho, -a; (vegetables) cocido, -a.

don·key burro, -a mf.

do·nor donante mf.

door puerta f.

door·bell timbre m (de la puerta).

door·knob pomo m.

door knock·er picaporte m.

door·man portero m.

door·mat felpudo m.

door·step peldaño m.

door·way entrada f.

dope 1 n fam (drug) chocolate m. **2** adj tonto, -a.

dor·mi·to·ry (in school) dormitorio m; (in university) colegio m mayor.

dos·age (amount) dosis f inv.

dose dosis f inv.

dot punto m.

dot·ted line línea f de puntos.

dou·ble 1 adj doble. **2** adv doble; **folded d.** doblado, -a por la mitad; **it's d. the price** cuesta dos veces más. **3** n to earn d. ganar el doble.

double back vi to d. back on one's tracks volver sobre sus pasos.

double up vi (bend) doblarse.

dou·ble bed cama f de matrimonio.

dou·ble-breast·ed adj cruzado, -a.

dou·ble-cross vt engañar, traicionar.

dou·ble glaz·ing doble acristalamiento m.

doubt 1 n duda f; **no d.** sin duda; **to be in d. about sth** dudar algo. **2** vt dudar.

doubt·ful adj I'm a bit d. about it no me convence del todo; **it's d. whether ...** no se sabe seguro si ....

doubt·less adv sin duda, seguramente.

dough (for bread) masa f; (for

pastries) pasta f; fam (money) pasta f.
dough·nut rosquilla f, dónut® m.
dove paloma f.
down 1 adv (to or at lower level) abajo; (to floor) al suelo; (to ground) a tierra; **to go d.** (price, person) bajar; **d. there** allí abajo; **to be d. with a cold** estar resfriado, -a; **to feel d.** estar deprimido, -a. **2** prep (along) por; **to go d. the road** bajar la calle.
down-and-out vagabundo, -a mf.
down·fall (of régime) caída f; (of person) perdición f.
down·hill adv **to go d.** ir cuesta abajo.
down pay·ment entrada f, fianza f.
down·pour chaparrón m.
down·right 1 adj (liar, rogue) declarado, -a; (lie) manifiesto, -a. **2** adv (totally) completamente.
down·stairs 1 adv abajo; (to first floor) a la planta baja; **to go d.** bajar la escalera. **2** adj (on first floor) de la planta baja.
down-to-earth adj realista.
down·town adv en el centro (de la ciudad).
down·ward(s) adv hacia abajo.
doze 1 vi dormitar. **2** n cabezada f; **to have a d.** echar una cabezada.
▶ **doze off** vi quedarse dormido, -a.
doz·en docena f; **half a d./a d. eggs** media docena/una docena de huevos.
Dr abbr of **Doctor** Doctor, -a mf, Dr., Dra.
drab adj (dreary) gris; (color) pardo, -a.
draft (of cold air) corriente f (de aire); **d. (beer)** cerveza f de barril.
draft·y adj **this room is very d.** en esta habitación hay mucha corriente.
drag 1 vt (pull) arrastrar. **2** vi (trail) arrastrarse; (person) rezagarse.
▶ **drag along** vt arrastrar.
▶ **drag on** vi (war, strike) hacerse interminable.

▶ **drag out** vt (speech etc) alargar.
drag·on dragón m.
drain 1 n (for water) desagüe m; (grating) sumidero m. **2** vt (marsh etc) avenar; (reservoir) desecar. **3** vi **to d. (away)** (liquid) irse.
drain·ing board escurridero m.
drain·pipe tubo m de desagüe.
dra·ma (play) obra f de teatro; (subject) teatro m; (tense situation) drama m.
dra·mat·ic adj (change) impresionante; (moment) emocionante; (of the theater) dramático, -a.
dra·mat·i·cal·ly adv (to change) de forma espectacular.
drapes npl cortinas fpl.
dras·tic adj (severe) drástico, -a; (change) radical.
dras·ti·cal·ly adv radicalmente.
draw 1 vt* (picture) dibujar; (line) trazar; (curtains) (open) descorrer; (close) correr; (attract) atraer; (attention) llamar. **2** vi* (sketch) dibujar; **they drew two all** empataron a dos. **3** n (score) empate m.
▶ **draw in** vi (days) acortarse.
▶ **draw near (to)** vt acercarse (a).
▶ **draw on** vt (savings) recurrir a; (experience) aprovecharse de.
▶ **draw out** vt (withdraw) sacar.
▶ **draw up** vt (contract) preparar; (plan) esbozar.
draw·back inconveniente m.
draw·er cajón m.
draw·ing dibujo m.
draw·ing pin chincheta f.
draw·ing room sala f de estar.
dread 1 vt temer. **2** n temor m.
dread·ful adj (shocking) espantoso, -a; (awful) fatal.
dread·ful·ly adv (horribly) terriblemente; (very) muy.
dream 1 n sueño m; (marvel) maravilla f. **2** vti* soñar (of, about con).
▶ **dream up** vt (excuse) inventarse; (plan) idear.
drea·ry adj (gloomy) triste; (boring) aburrido, -a.

drench vt empapar.

dress 1 n vestido m; (clothing) ropa f. **2** vt (person) vestir; (wound) vendar; (salad) aliñar; **he was dressed in a gray suit** llevaba (puesto) un traje gris. **3** vi vestirse.

▸**dress up** vi (in disguise) disfrazarse (as de); (in best clothes) vestirse elegante.

dress·er (in bedroom) tocador m.

dress·ing (bandage) vendaje m; (salad) d. aderezo m, aliño m; **d. room** (in theater) camerino m; **d. table** tocador m.

dress·mak·er modista mf.

drew pt of **draw**.

drib·ble 1 vi (baby) babear; (liquid) gotear. **2** vt (ball) regatear.

dried adj (fruit) seco, -a; (milk) en polvo.

drier = **dryer**.

drift vi (boat) ir a la deriva; (person) ir sin rumbo, vagar; **they drifted away** se marcharon poco a poco.

drill 1 n (handtool) taladro m; **dentist's d.** fresa f, **pneumatic d.** martillo m neumático. **2** vt (wood etc) taladrar.

drink 1 vti* beber; **to have sth to d.** tomarse algo; **to d. to sth/sb** brindar por algo/algn. **2** n bebida f; (alcoholic) copa f.

▸**drink up 1** vt beberse todo. **2** vi **d. up!** ¡bébelo todo!

drink·a·ble adj potable; (not unpleasant) agradable.

drink·ing wa·ter agua f potable.

drip 1 n goteo m; fam (person) necio, -a mf. **2** vi gotear; **he was dripping with sweat** le caía el sudor a gotas.

drip-dry adj que no necesita planchado.

drive 1 vt* (vehicle) conducir, Am manejar; (person) llevar; (stake) hincar; (nail) clavar; (compel) forzar; **to d. sb mad** volver loco, -a a algn. **2** vi* (in car) conducir, Am manejar. **3** n camino m de entrada; (energy) energía f; **to go for a d.** dar una vuelta en coche; **left-hand d.** conducción f por la izquierda.

▸**drive along** vti (in car) conducir.

▸**drive back 1** vt (enemy) rechazar; (passenger) llevar de vuelta a. **2** vi volver en coche.

▸**drive in** vt (nail) clavar.

▸**drive off** vi salir (en coche).

▸**drive on** vi (after stopping) continuar.

▸**drive out** vt expulsar.

▸**drive up** vi llegar en coche.

driv·el tonterías fpl.

driv·er (of car, bus) conductor, -a mf; (of train) maquinista mf, (of lorry) camionero, -a mf.

driv·er's li·cense carnet m de conducir.

drive·way n camino m de entrada.

driv·ing les·son clase f de conducir.

driv·ing school autoescuela f.

driv·ing test examen m de conducir.

driz·zle 1 n llovizna f. **2** vi lloviznar.

droop vi (flower) marchitarse.

drop 1 n (liquid) gota f; (descent) desnivel m; (in price) bajada f; (in temperature) descenso m. **2** vt (let fall) dejar caer; (lower) bajar; (reduce) disminuir; (abandon) (subject, charge etc) abandonar. **3** vi (object) caerse; (voice, price, temperature) bajar; (speed) disminuir.

▸**drop behind** vi quedarse atrás.

▸**drop in, drop round** vi (visit) pasarse (at por).

▸**drop off 1** vi (fall asleep) quedarse dormido, -a. **2** vt (deliver) dejar en casa (de algn).

▸**drop out** vi (of college) dejar los estudios; (of society) marginarse; (of competition) retirarse.

drought sequía f.

drown 1 vt ahogar; (place) inundar. **2** vi ahogarse; **he drowned** murió ahogado.

drows·y adj soñoliento, -a; **to feel d.** tener sueño.

drug 1 n (medicine) medicamento m; (narcotic) droga f; **to be on drugs** drogarse. **2** vt (person) drogar; (food, drink) adulterar con drogas.

drug ad·dict drogadicto, -a mf.

drug·store establecimiento m donde se compran medicamentos, periódicos etc.

drum tambor m; (container) bidón m; **to play the drums** tocar la batería.

drum·mer (in band) tambor mf; (in pop group) batería mf.

drunk 1 adj borracho, -a; **to get d.** emborracharse. **2** n borracho, -a mf.

drunk·ard borracho, -a mf.

drunk·en adj (driver) borracho, -a; **d. driving** conducir en estado de embriaguez.

dry 1 adj seco, -a. **2** vt secar. **3** vi to **d.** (off) secarse.

▸**dry up 1** vt secar. **2** vi secarse.

dry-clean vt lavar en seco.

dry-clean·er (shop) tintorería f.

dry·er secadora f.

du·al adj doble, dual.

dub vt (subtitle) doblar (into a).

du·bi·ous adj (morals etc) dudoso, -a; (doubting) indeciso, -a.

duch·ess duquesa f.

duck[1] pato, -a mf; (as food) pato m.

duck[2] vi (bow down) agacharse. **2** vt (evade) esquivar.

due 1 adj (expected) esperado, -a; (money) pagadero, -a; **the train is d. (to arrive) at ten** el tren debe llegar a las diez; **in d. course** a su debido tiempo; **to be d. to** deberse a. **2** adv (north etc) derecho hacia.

du·el duelo m.

duf·fel coat trenca f.

duke duque m.

dull adj (boring) pesado, -a; (place) sin interés; (light) apagado, -a; (weather) gris; (sound, ache) sordo, -a.

du·ly adv (properly) debidamente; (as expected) como era de esperar.

dumb adj mudo, -a; (stupid) tonto, -a.

dump 1 n (tip) vertedero m; fam (place) lugar m de mala muerte; (town) poblacho m; (dwelling) tugurio m. **2** vt (garbage) verter.

dump truck volquete m.

dun·ga·rees npl mono m sing.

du·plex casa f adosada; **d. apartment** dúplex m inv.

du·pli·cate duplicado m; **in d.** por duplicado.

du·ra·ble adj duradero, -a.

du·ra·tion duración f.

dur·ing prep durante.

dusk crepúsculo m; **at d.** al anochecer.

dust 1 n polvo m. **2** vt (furniture) quitar el polvo a.

dust·er (for housework) trapo m (del polvo).

dust·y adj polvoriento, -a.

Dutch 1 adj holandés, -esa. **2** n (language) holandés m; **the D.** los holandeses mpl.

Dutch·man holandés m.

Dutch·wom·an holandesa f.

du·ty deber m; (task) función f, (tax) impuesto m; **to be on d.** estar de servicio; (doctor, soldier) estar de guardia; **d. chemist** farmacia f de guardia; **customs d.** derechos mpl de aduana.

du·ty-free adj libre de impuestos.

du·vet edredón m.

DVD abbr of **d**igital **v**ersatile **d**isk, **d**igital **v**ideo **d**isk DVD m; **D. player** reproductor m or lector m de DVD.

dwarf (pl **dwarves**) enano, -a mf.

dye 1 n tinte m. **2** vt teñir; **to d. one's hair black** teñirse el pelo de negro.

dy·nam·ic adj dinámico, -a.

dy·na·mite dinamita f.

dy·na·mo dínamo f.

dys·lex·ic adj disléxico, -a.

E

each 1 *adj* cada; **e. day/month** todos los días/meses. **2** *pron* cada uno, -a; **we bought one e.** nos compramos uno cada uno; **e. other** el uno al otro; **they hate e. other** se odian.

ea·ger *adj (anxious)* impaciente (**to** por); *(keen)* deseoso, -a.

ea·ger·ly *adv (anxiously)* con impaciencia; *(keenly)* con ilusión.

ea·ger·ness impaciencia *f* (**to do** por hacer); *(keenness)* afán *m*.

ea·gle águila *f*.

ear oreja *f*, *(inner ear)* oído *m*; *(of corn)* espiga *f*.

ear·ache dolor *m* de oídos.

ear·ly 1 *adj (before usual time)* temprano, -a; **to have an e. night** acostarse pronto; **you're e.!** ¡qué pronto has venido! ▪ *(at first stage, period)* **in her e. forties** a los cuarenta y pocos; **in e. July** a principios de julio. ▪ *(in the near future)* **an e. reply** una respuesta pronta. **2** *adv (before the expected time)* temprano; **to leave e.** irse pronto; **e. on** al principio; **earlier on** antes; **five minutes e.** con cinco minutos de adelanto; **as e. as possible** tan pronto como sea posible; **to book e.** reservar con tiempo; **at the earliest** cuanto antes.

earn *vt* ganarse; *(money)* ganar; **to earn one's living** ganarse la vida.

ear·nest 1 *adj* serio, -a, formal. **2** *n* **in e.** de veras, en serio.

earn·ings *npl* ingresos *mpl*.

ear·phones *npl* auriculares *mpl*, cascos *mpl*.

ear·plug tapón *m* para los oídos.

ear·ring pendiente *m*.

earth *n* tierra *f*, *(electric)* toma *f* de tierra; **to be down to e.** ser práctico, -a; *fam* **where/why on e. …?** ¿pero

dónde/por qué demonios …?

earth·quake terremoto *m*.

ease 1 *n (lack of difficulty)* facilidad *f*, *(affluence)* comodidad *f*, *(freedom from discomfort)* tranquilidad *f*; **at e.** relajado, -a. **2** *vt (pain)* aliviar; *(move gently)* deslizar con cuidado.

▸**ease off, ease up** *vi (decrease)* disminuir; *(slow down)* ir más despacio.

ea·sel caballete *m*.

eas·i·ly *adv* fácilmente; **e. the best** con mucho el mejor.

east 1 *n* este *m*. **2** *adj* del este, oriental. **3** *adv* al este.

east·bound *adj* (con) dirección este.

Eas·ter Semana Santa *f*; **E. Sunday** Domingo *m* de Resurrección.

east·ern *adj* oriental, del este.

east·ward(s) *adv* hacia el este.

eas·y 1 *adj* fácil; *(comfortable)* cómodo, -a; *fam* **I'm e.!** me da lo mismo; **e. chair** butacón *m*. **2** *adv* **go e. on the wine** no te pases con el vino; **to take things e.** tomarse las cosas con calma; **take it e.!** ¡tranquilo!

eas·y-go·ing *adj (calm)* tranquilo, -a; *(lax)* despreocupado, -a; *(undemanding)* poco exigente.

eat* *vt* comer.

▸**eat away** *vt* desgastar; *(metal)* corroer.

▸**eat out** *vi* comer fuera.

▸**eat up** *vt (meal)* terminar; *(petrol)* consumir; *(miles)* tragar.

eau de Co·logne colonia *f*.

ec·cen·tric *adj & n* excéntrico, -a *(mf)*.

ech·o 1 *n (pl* echoes*)* eco *m*. **2** *vt (repeat)* repetir. **3** *vi* resonar.

ec·o·nom·ic *adj* económico, -a; *(profitable)* rentable.

ec·o·nom·i·cal *adj* económico, -a.

e·con·o·mize *vi* economizar (**on** en).

e·con·o·my *(national)* economía *f*, *(saving)* ahorro *m*; **e. class** (clase *f*) turista *f*.

edge 1 *n* borde *m*; *(of knife)* filo *m*; *(of*

water) orilla *f*; **on the e. of town** en las afueras de la ciudad; **to have the e. on sb** llevar ventaja a algn; **to be on e.** tener los nervios de punta. **2** *vt* **to e. closer** acercarse lentamente; **to e. forward** avanzar poco a poco.

ed·i·ble *adj* comestible.

ed·it *vt* editar; *(proofs)* corregir; *(newspaper)* ser redactor, -a de; *(film, TV program)* montar; *(cut)* cortar.

▸ **edit out** *vt* suprimir.

e·di·tion edición *f*.

ed·i·tor *(of book)* editor, -a *mf*; *(of newspaper)* redactor, -a *mf*; *(of film, TV program)* montador, -a *mf*.

ed·i·to·ri·al 1 *adj* **e. staff** redacción *f*. **2** *n* editorial *m*.

ed·u·cate *vt* educar.

ed·u·cat·ed *adj* culto, -a.

ed·u·ca·tion *(schooling)* enseñanza *f*, *(training)* formación *f*, *(studies)* estudios *mpl*; *(culture)* cultura *f*.

ed·u·ca·tion·al *adj* educativo, -a.

eel anguila *f*.

ef·fect efecto *m*; *(impression)* impresión *f*; **in e.** efectivamente; **to come into e.** entrar en vigor; **to have an e. on** afectar a; **to no e.** sin resultado alguno; **effects** *(possessions)* efectos *mpl*.

ef·fec·tive *adj (successful)* eficaz; *(impressive)* impresionante.

ef·fec·tive·ly *adv (successfully)* eficazmente; *(in fact)* en efecto.

ef·fi·cien·cy *(of person)* eficacia *f*, *(of machine)* rendimiento *m*.

ef·fi·cient *adj* eficaz; *(person)* eficiente; *(machine)* de buen rendimiento.

ef·fi·cient·ly *adv* eficazmente; **to work e.** tener buen rendimiento.

ef·fort esfuerzo *m*; *(attempt)* intento *m*; **to make an e.** hacer un esfuerzo.

eg *abbr* p. ej.

egg 1 *n* huevo *m*. **2** *vt* **to e. sb on (to do sth)** empujar a algn (a hacer algo).

egg cup huevera *f*.

egg·plant berenjena *f*.

egg tim·er reloj *m* de arena.

egg white clara *f* de huevo.

e·go ego *m*; *fam* amor propio; *fam* **e. trip** autobombo *m*.

E·gyp·tian *adj & n* egipcio, -a *(mf)*.

ei·der·down edredón *m*.

eight *adj & n* ocho *(m)* inv.

eight·een *adj & n* dieciocho *(m)* inv.

eighth *adj & n* octavo, -a *(mf)*.

eight·y *adj & n* ochenta *(m)* inv.

ei·ther 1 *pron (affirmative)* cualquiera; *(negative)* ninguno, ninguna, ni el uno ni el otro, ni la una ni la otra; **e. of them** cualquiera de los dos; **I don't want e. of them** no quiero ninguno de los dos. **2** *adj (both)* cada, los dos, las dos; **on e. side** en ambos lados. **3** *conj* o; **e. ... or ...** o ... o ...; **e. Friday or Saturday** o (bien) el viernes o el sábado. **4** *adv (after negative)* tampoco; **I don't want to do it e.** yo tampoco quiero hacerlo.

e·lab·o·rate 1 *vt (devise)* elaborar; *(explain)* explicar detalladamente. **2** *vi* explicarse; **to e. on sth** explicar algo con más detalles. **3** *adj (complicated)* complicado, -a; *(detailed)* detallado, -a; *(style)* esmerado, -a.

e·las·tic *adj* elástico, -a; *fig* flexible; **e. band** goma elástica. **2** *n* elástico *m*.

el·bow 1 *n* codo *m*. **2** *vt* **to e. sb** dar un codazo a algn.

eld·er *adj* mayor.

eld·er·ly 1 *adj* anciano, -a. **2** *npl* **the e.** los ancianos.

eld·est 1 *adj* mayor. **2** *n* el/la mayor.

e·lect *vt* elegir.

e·lec·tion 1 *n* elección *f*; **general e.** elecciones *fpl* generales. **2** *adj* electoral.

e·lec·tor·ate electorado *m*.

e·lec·tric *adj* eléctrico, -a; *fig* electrizante.

e·lec·tri·cal *adj* eléctrico, -a.

e·lec·tric blan·ket manta *f* eléctrica.

e·lec·tric chair silla *f* eléctrica.

e·lec·tri·cian electricista *mf.*

e·lec·tric·i·ty electricidad *f*; **e. bill** recibo *m* de la luz.

e·lec·tric shock electrochoque *m.*

e·lec·tro·cute *vt* electrocutar.

e·lec·tron·ic *adj* electrónico, -a.

e·lec·tron·ics *(science)* electrónica *f*; *(of machine)* componentes *mpl* electrónicos.

el·e·gance elegancia *f.*

el·e·gant *adj* elegante.

el·e·gant·ly *adv* con elegancia.

el·e·ment elemento *m*; *(electrical)* resistencia *f.*

el·e·men·ta·ry *adj (not developed)* rudimentario, -a; *(easy)* fácil; **e. school** escuela *f* primaria.

el·e·phant elefante *m.*

el·e·va·tor ascensor *m.*

e·lev·en *adj & n* once *(m) inv.*

e·lev·enth *adj & n* undécimo, -a *(mf).*

el·i·gi·ble *adj* apto, -a; **he isn't e. to vote** no tiene derecho al voto.

e·lim·i·nate *vt* eliminar.

e·lite elite *f.*

else *adv* **anything e.?** ¿algo más?; **everything e.** todo lo demás; **no-one e.** nadie más; **someone e.** otro, -a; **something e.** otra cosa; **somewhere e.** en otra parte; **what e.?** ¿qué mas?; **where e.?** ¿en qué otro sitio?; **or e.** si no.

else·where *adv* en otra parte.

e·lude *vt (avoid)* esquivar; **his name eludes me** no consigo acordarme de su nombre.

em·bark *vi* embarcar(se); **to e. upon sth** emprender algo.

em·bar·rass *vt* avergonzar.

em·bar·rass·ing *adj* embarazoso, -a; *(situation)* violento, -a.

em·bar·rass·ment vergüenza *f.*

em·bas·sy embajada *f.*

em·blem emblema *m.*

em·brace **1** *vt* abrazar; *(include)* abarcar. **2** *vi* abrazarse. **3** *n* abrazo *m.*

em·broi·der *vt* bordar; *(story, truth)* adornar.

em·broi·der·y bordado *m.*

em·bry·o embrión *m.*

em·er·ald esmeralda *f.*

e·merge *vi* salir; *(problem)* surgir; **it emerged that ...** resultó que ....

e·mer·gen·cy emergencia *f*; *(medical)* urgencia *f*; **in an e.** en caso de emergencia; **e. exit** salida *f* de emergencia; **e. landing** aterrizaje *m* forzoso; **state of e.** estado *m* de excepción.

em·i·grate *vi* emigrar.

e·mo·tion emoción *f.*

e·mo·tion·al *adj* emocional; *(moving)* conmovedor, -a.

em·per·or emperador *m.*

em·pha·sis énfasis *m*; **to place e. on sth** hacer hincapié en algo.

em·pha·size *vt* subrayar.

em·pire imperio *m.*

em·ploy *vt* emplear; *(time)* ocupar.

em·ploy·ee empleado, -a *mf.*

em·ploy·er empresario, -a *mf.*

em·ploy·ment empleo *m.*

em·ploy·ment a·gen·cy agencia *f* de colocaciones.

emp·ty **1** *adj* vacío, -a; **e. promises** promesas *fpl* vanas. **2** *vt* vaciar. **3** *vi* vaciarse. **4** *npl* **empties** envases *mpl.*

emp·ty-hand·ed *adv* con las manos vacías.

e·mul·sion **e. (paint)** pintura *f* mate.

en·a·ble *vt* **to e. sb to do sth** permitir a algn hacer algo.

e·nam·el esmalte *m.*

en·chant·ing *adj* encantador, -a.

en·close *vt (surround)* rodear; *(fence in)* cercar; *(in envelope)* adjuntar; **please find enclosed** le enviamos adjunto.

en·clo·sure *(fenced area)* cercado *m*; *(in envelope)* documento *m* adjunto.

en·coun·ter **1** *n* encuentro *m.* **2** *vt* encontrarse con; *(problems)* tropezar con.

en·cour·age *vt (urge)* animar; *(help*

to develop) fomentar.

en·cour·age·ment estímulo *m.*

en·cy·clo·pe·dia enciclopedia *f.*

end 1 *n (of stick)* punta *f; (of street)* final *m; (conclusion)* fin *m,* final *m; (aim)* objetivo *m;* **in the e.** al final; **for hours on e.** hora tras hora; **to put an e. to** acabar con; **it makes my hair stand on e.** me pone el pelo de punta. **2** *vt* acabar, terminar. **3** *vi* acabarse, terminarse.

▸**end up** *vi* terminar; **to e. up doing sth** terminar por hacer algo.

en·dan·ger *vt* poner en peligro.

end·ing final *m.*

en·dive escarola *f.*

end·less *adj* interminable.

en·dorse *vt (check etc)* endosar; *(approve)* aprobar; *(support)* apoyar.

en·dorse·ment *(on check etc)* endoso *m; (approval)* aprobación *f.*

en·dur·ance resistencia *f.*

en·dure *vt (bear)* aguantar. **2** *vi* perdurar.

en·e·my *adj & n* enemigo, -a *(mf).*

en·er·get·ic *adj* enérgico, -a.

en·er·gy 1 *n* energía *f.* **2** *adj* energético, -a.

en·force *vt (law)* hacer cumplir.

en·gaged *adj* prometido, -a; *(busy)* ocupado, -a; **to get e.** prometerse; **it's e.** *(phone)* está comunicando.

en·gage·ment *(to marry)* noviazgo *m; (appointment)* cita *f.*

en·gage·ment ring anillo *m* de compromiso.

en·gine motor *m; (of train)* locomotora *f.*

en·gine driv·er maquinista *mf.*

en·gi·neer ingeniero, -a *mf; (on train)* maquinista *mf.*

en·gi·neer·ing ingeniería *f.*

Eng·lish 1 *adj* inglés, -esa. **2** *n (language)* inglés *m;* **the E.** los ingleses *mpl.*

Eng·lish·man inglés *m.*

Eng·lish-speak·ing *adj* de habla inglesa.

Eng·lish·wom·an inglesa *f.*

en·grave *vt* grabar.

en·grav·ing grabado *m.*

en·joy *vt* disfrutar; **to e. oneself** pasarlo bien; **he enjoys swimming** le gusta nadar.

en·joy·able *adj* agradable.

en·joy·ment disfrute *m.*

en·large *vt* ampliar.

en·light·en *vt* iluminar.

en·list 1 *vt (recruit)* reclutar; **to e. sb's help** conseguir ayuda de algn. **2** *vi (in the army)* alistarse.

e·nor·mous *adj* enorme.

e·nor·mous·ly *adv* enormemente; **I enjoyed myself e.** lo pasé genial.

e·nough 1 *adj* bastante, suficiente; **e. books** bastantes libros; **have we got e. gas?** ¿tenemos suficiente gasolina? **2** *adv* bastante; **sure e.** en efecto. **3** *n* lo suficiente; **e. to live on** lo suficiente para vivir; **it isn't e.** no basta; **I've had e.!** ¡estoy harto!

en·quire = **inquire**.

en·quir·y = **inquiry**.

en·roll 1 *vt* matricular. **2** *vi* matricularse.

en·roll·ment matrícula *f.*

en·sure *vt* asegurar.

en·tail *vt* suponer.

en·ter 1 *vt (go into)* entrar en; *(data into computer)* introducir; *(join)* ingresar en; **to e. one's name for a course** matricularse en un curso. **2** *vi* entrar.

▸**enter into** *vt (agreement)* firmar; *(negotiations)* iniciar.

en·ter·prise empresa *f;* **free e.** libre empresa.

en·ter·pris·ing *adj* emprendedor, -a.

en·ter·tain 1 *vt (amuse)* divertir; *(consider)* considerar. **2** *vi (have guests)* tener invitados.

en·ter·tain·er artista *mf.*

en·ter·tain·ing *adj* divertido, -a.

en·ter·tain·ment diversión *f; (show)* espectáculo *m.*

en·thu·si·asm entusiasmo *m.*

en·thu·si·ast entusiasta *mf.*

en·thu·si·as·tic *adj* entusiasta; *(praise)* caluroso, -a; **to be e. about sth** entusiasmarse por algo.

en·thu·si·as·ti·cal·ly *adv* con entusiasmo.

en·tire *adj* todo, -a; **the e. family** toda la familia.

en·tire·ly *adv (completely)* totalmente; *(solely)* exclusivamente.

en·ti·tle *vt (permit)* dar derecho a; **to be entitled to** tener derecho a.

en·trance entrada *f*; *(admission)* ingreso *m*; **e. examination** examen *m* de ingreso.

en·trant *(in competition)* participante *mf*.

en·try *(entrance)* entrada *f*; **no e.** dirección prohibida.

en·try form hoja *f* de inscripción.

en·ve·lope sobre *m*.

en·vi·ous *adj* envidioso, -a; **to feel e.** tener envidia.

en·vi·ron·ment entorno *m*; *(natural)* medio ambiente m.

en·vi·ron·men·tal *adj* medio ambiental.

en·vis·age, en·vi·sion *vt (imagine)* imaginarse; *(foresee)* prever.

en·vy 1 *n* envidia *f*. **2** *vt* envidiar.

ep·i·dem·ic 1 *n* epidemia *f*. **2** *adj* epidémico, -a.

ep·i·sode episodio *m*.

e·qual 1 *adj* igual; **to be e. to the occasion** estar a la altura de las circunstancias. **2** *n* igual *mf*; **to treat sb as an e.** tratar a algn de igual a igual. **3** *vt* equivaler a.

e·qual·i·ty igualdad *f*.

e·qual·ize *vi (in sport)* empatar.

e·qual·ly *adv* igualmente; **e. pretty** igual de bonito; **to share sth e.** dividir algo en partes iguales.

e·qua·tion ecuación *f*.

e·qua·tor ecuador *m*.

e·quip *vt (supply)* equipar; *(person)* proveer.

e·quip·ment *(materials)* equipo *m*.

e·quiv·a·lent *adj & n* equivalente *(m)*.

e·ra era *f*.

e·rase *vt* borrar.

e·ras·er goma *f* de borrar.

e·rect 1 *adj (upright)* erguido, -a. **2** *vt (monument)* erigir.

e·ro·sion *(of land)* erosión *f*.

er·rand recado *m*.

er·rat·ic *adj (performance, behavior)* irregular; *(weather)* muy variable; *(person)* caprichoso, -a.

er·ror error *m*.

e·rupt *vi (volcano)* entrar en erupción; *(violence)* estallar.

e·rup·tion erupción *f*.

es·ca·la·tor escalera *f* mecánica.

es·cape 1 *n* fuga *f*; *(of gas)* escape *m*; **e. route** vía *f* de escape. **2** *vi* escaparse. **3** *vt (avoid)* evitar; **the name escapes me** se me escapa el nombre.

es·cort 1 *n (bodyguard etc)* escolta *f*. **2** *vt (protect)* escoltar.

Es·ki·mo *adj & n* esquimal *(mf)*.

es·pe·cial·ly *adv* especialmente.

es·pres·so café *m* exprés.

es·say *(at school)* redacción *f*.

es·sen·tial *adj* esencial.

es·sen·tial·ly *adv* esencialmente.

es·tab·lish *vt (found)* establecer; *(business)* montar; **to e. the truth** demostrar la verdad.

es·tab·lished *adj (person)* establecido, -a; *(fact)* conocido, -a.

es·tab·lish·ment establecimiento *m*; **the E.** el sistema.

es·tate *(land)* finca *f*, *(property)* bienes *mpl*; *(inheritance)* herencia *f*; **(housing) e.** urbanización *f*.

es·ti·mate 1 *n (calculation)* cálculo *m*; *(likely cost of work)* presupuesto *m*. **2** *vt* calcular.

etch·ing aguafuerte *m*.

e·ter·nal *adj* eterno, -a, incesante.

ethics ética *f*.

et·i·quette etiqueta *f*.

EU *abbr of* **European Union** UE.

Euro- *prefix* Euro-.

Eu·ro·pe·an *adj & n* europeo, -a *(mf)*.

e·vac·u·ate vt evacuar.

e·vade vt evadir.

e·val·u·ate vt evaluar.

e·vap·o·rate 1 vi evaporarse. **2** vt evaporar.

eve víspera f; **on the e. of** en vísperas de.

e·ven 1 adj (smooth) liso, -a; (regular) uniforme; (equally balanced) igual; (number) par; (in football game etc) to be e. ir empatados, -as; **to get e. with sb** desquitarse con algn. **2** adv aun; **e. now** incluso ahora; **e. the children knew** hasta los niños lo sabían; **e. as** mientras; **e. if** incluso si; **e. though** aunque. ▪ (with negative) si siquiera; **she can't e.** write her name ni siquiera sabe escribir su nombre. ▪ (before comparative) aun, todavía; **e. worse** aun peor.

eve·ning (early) tarde f; (late) noche f; **in the e.** por la tarde/noche; **tomorrow e.** mañana por la tarde/noche.

eve·ning class clase f nocturna.

e·ven·ly adv (uniformly) de modo uniforme; (fairly) equitativamente.

e·vent (happening) suceso m; (in sport) prueba f; **at all events** en todo caso; **in the e. of fire** en caso de incendio.

e·ven·tu·al adj (ultimate) final; (resulting) consiguiente.

e·ven·tu·al·ly adv finalmente.

ev·er adv (always) siempre; **for e.** para siempre; **stronger than e.** más fuerte que nunca; **have you e. been there?** ¿has estado allí alguna vez?; **how e. did you manage it?** ¿cómo diablos lo conseguiste?; fam **e. so ... muy ...; thank you e. so much** muchísimas gracias.

eve·ry adj (each) cada; (all) todos, -as; **e. now and then** de vez en cuando; **e. day** todos los días; **e. other day** cada dos días; **e. one of you** todos, -as vosotros, -as; **e. citizen** todo ciudadano.

eve·ry·bod·y pron todo el mundo, todos, -as; **e. who ...** todos los que ...

eve·ry·day adj de todos los días; **an e. occurrence** un suceso cotidiano.

eve·ry·one pron = **everybody.**

eve·ry·place adv en todos sitios.

eve·ry·thing pron todo; **he eats e.** come de todo; **e. I have** todo lo que tengo.

eve·ry·where adv por or en todas partes; **e. I go** por todas partes adonde voy.

ev·i·dence n (proof) evidencia f; (in court case) testimonio m; (sign) indicio m; **to give e.** prestar declaración.

ev·i·dent adj evidente.

ev·i·dent·ly adv evidentemente.

e·vil 1 n (wicked) malvado, -a; (harmful) nocivo, -a. **2** n mal m.

e·voke vt evocar.

ewe oveja f.

ex her e. su ex marido; **his e.** su ex mujer.

ex- prefix ex-; **ex-minister** ex ministro m.

ex·act adj exacto, -a; **this e. spot** ese mismo lugar.

ex·act·ly adv exactamente; **e.!** ¡exacto!

ex·ag·ger·ate vti exagerar.

ex·ag·ger·a·tion exageración f.

ex·am examen m.

ex·am·i·na·tion examen m; (medical) reconocimiento m; **to sit an e.** hacer un examen.

ex·am·ine vt examinar; (customs) registrar; (medically) reconocer a.

ex·am·in·er examinador, -a mf.

ex·am·ple ejemplo m; **for e.** por ejemplo.

ex·ceed vt exceder.

ex·ceed·ing·ly adv extremadamente.

ex·cel vi sobresalir.

ex·cel·lent adj excelente.

ex·cept prep excepto; **e. for the little ones** excepto los pequeños; **e. that ...** salvo que ...

ex·cep·tion excepción f; **with the e. of** a excepción de; **to take e. to sth** ofenderse por algo.

ex·cep·tion·al adj excepcional.

ex·cep·tion·al·ly adv excepcionalmente.

ex·cerpt extracto m.

ex·cess 1 n exceso m. **2** adj excedente; **e. baggage** exceso m de equipaje; **e. fare** suplemento m.

ex·ces·sive adj excesivo, -a.

ex·ces·sive·ly adv excesivamente, en exceso.

ex·change 1 n cambio m; (telephone) **e.** central f telefónica; **in e. for** a cambio de. **2** vt intercambiar; **to e. blows** golpearse.

ex·change rate tipo m de cambio.

ex·cite vt (enthuse) entusiasmar; (arouse) provocar; **to get excited** entusiasmarse.

ex·cit·ed adj ilusionado, -a; emocionado, -a.

ex·cite·ment (emotion) emoción f.

ex·cit·ing adj emocionante.

ex·claim vi exclamar.

ex·cla·ma·tion exclamación f.

ex·cla·ma·tion point signo m de admiración.

ex·clude vt excluir; (from club) no admitir.

ex·clu·sive 1 adj exclusivo, -a; (select) selecto, -a. **2** n (in newspaper) exclusiva f.

ex·clu·sive·ly adv exclusivamente.

ex·cur·sion excursión f.

ex·cuse 1 vt disculpar; (exempt) dispensar; (justify) justificar; **e. me!** con permiso. **2** n excusa f; **to make excuses** dar excusas.

ex·e·cute vt (order) cumplir; (task) realizar; (person) ejecutar.

ex·e·cu·tion (of order) cumplimiento m; (of task) realización f; (of person) ejecución f.

ex·ec·u·tive adj & n ejecutivo, -a (mf).

ex·empt 1 vt eximir (from de). **2** adj

exento, -a; **e. from tax** libre de impuesto.

ex·emp·tion exención f.

ex·er·cise 1 n ejercicio m; **e. book** cuaderno m. **2** vt (rights, duties) ejercer; (dog) sacar de paseo. **3** vi hacer ejercicio.

ex·er·cise book cuaderno m.

ex·ert vt (influence) ejercer; **to e. oneself** esforzarse.

ex·er·tion esfuerzo m.

ex·haust 1 vt agotar. **2** n (gas) gases mpl de combustión; **e. pipe** tubo m de escape.

ex·haust·ed adj agotado, -a.

ex·haust·ing adj agotador, -a.

ex·hib·it 1 n objeto m expuesto. **2** vt exponer; (manifest) mostrar.

ex·hi·bi·tion exposición f.

ex·hib·i·tor expositor, -a mf.

ex·ile 1 n (banishment) exilio m; (person) exiliado, -a mf. **2** vt exiliar.

ex·ist vi existir; (stay alive) subsistir.

ex·is·tence existencia f.

ex·ist·ing adj actual.

ex·it salida f.

ex·or·bi·tant adj exorbitante.

ex·pand 1 vt ampliar. **2** vi (grow) ampliarse; (metal) dilatarse.

▶**expand on** vt ampliar.

ex·panse extensión f.

ex·pan·sion (in size) expansión f; (of gas, metal) dilatación f.

ex·pan·sion slot ranura f de expansión.

ex·pect 1 vt (anticipate) esperar; (suppose) suponer; **to e. sth from sb/sth** esperar algo de algn/algo; **to e. to do sth** contar con hacer algo; **she's expecting a baby** está esperando un niño. **2** vi **to be expecting** estar embarazada.

ex·pec·ta·tion esperanza f; **contrary to e.** contrariamente a lo que se esperaba.

ex·pe·di·tion expedición f.

ex·pel vt expulsar.

ex·pen·di·ture desembolso m.

ex·pense gasto m; **to spare no e.**

no escatimar gastos; *fig* **at the e. of** a costa de.

ex·pen·sive *adj* caro, -a.

ex·pe·ri·ence 1 *n* experiencia *f.* **2** *vt* (*sensation*) experimentar; (*difficulty, loss*) sufrir.

ex·pe·ri·enced *adj* experimentado, -a.

ex·per·i·ment 1 *n* experimento *m.* **2** *vi* experimentar (**on, with** con).

ex·pert *adj & n* experto, -a (*mf*).

ex·per·tise pericia *f.*

ex·pi·ra·tion vencimiento *m.*

ex·pi·ra·tion date fecha *f* de caducidad.

ex·pire *vi* (*come to an end*) terminar; (*policy, contract*) vencer; (*ticket*) caducar.

ex·pired *adj* (*ticket*) caducado, -a.

ex·plain *vt* explicar; (*clarify*) aclarar; **to e. oneself** justificarse.

▸**explain away** *vt* justificar.

ex·pla·na·tion explicación *f*; (*clarification*) aclaración *f.*

ex·plic·it *adj* explícito, -a.

ex·plode 1 *vt* hacer explotar. **2** *vi* (*bomb*) explotar; **to e. with anger** montar en cólera.

ex·ploit 1 *n* hazaña *f.* **2** *vt* explotar.

ex·plo·ra·tion exploración *f.*

ex·plore *vt* explorar.

ex·plor·er explorador, -a *mf.*

ex·plo·sion explosión *f.*

ex·plo·sive 1 *adj* explosivo, -a. **2** *n* explosivo *m.*

ex·port 1 *vt* exportar. **2** *n* exportación *f.*

ex·pose *vt* (*uncover*) exponer; (*secret*) revelar; (*plot*) descubrir.

ex·press 1 *adj* (*explicit*) expreso, -a; (*letter*) urgente. **2** *n* (*train*) expreso *m.* **3** *vt* expresar.

ex·pres·sion expresión *f.*

ex·press·way autopista *f.*

ex·tend 1 *vt* (*enlarge*) ampliar; (*lengthen*) alargar; (*prolong*) prolongar; (*increase*) aumentar. **2** *vi* (*stretch*) extenderse; (*last*) prolongarse.

ex·ten·sion extensión *f*; (*of time*) prórroga *f*; (*of building*) anexo *m.*

ex·ten·sive *adj* extenso, -a.

ex·ten·sive·ly *adv* extensamente; (*frequently*) con frecuencia.

ex·tent (*area*) extensión *f*; **to some e.** hasta cierto punto; **to a large e.** en gran parte; **to such an e.** hasta tal punto.

ex·te·ri·or *adj & n* exterior (*m*).

ex·ter·nal *adj* externo, -a.

ex·tin·guish·er extintor *m.*

ex·tra 1 *adj* extra; (*spare*) de sobra. **2** *adv* extra; **e. fine** extra fino. **3** *n* (*additional charge*) suplemento *m*; (*in film*) extra *mf.*

ex·tract 1 *n* extracto *m.* **2** *vt* (*tooth, information*) extraer.

ex·tra·cur·ric·u·lar *adj* extracurricular.

ex·traor·di·nar·y *adj* extraordinario, -a; (*strange*) raro, -a.

ex·trav·a·gant *adj* (*wasteful*) derrochador, -a; (*excessive*) exagerado, -a.

ex·treme 1 *adj* extremo, -a; **an e. case** un caso excepcional. **2** *n* extremo *m*; **in the e.** en sumo grado.

ex·treme·ly *adv* extremadamente; **I'm e. sorry** lo siento de veras.

eye *n* ojo *m*; **I couldn't believe my eyes** no podía creerlo; **not to take one's eyes off sb/sth** no quitar la vista de encima a algn/algo; **to catch sb's e.** llamar la atención de algn; **to turn a blind e.** hacer la vista gorda (**to** a); **with an e. to** con miras a; **to keep an e. on sb/sth** vigilar a algn/algo.

eye·brow ceja *f.*

eye·glasses *npl* gafas *fpl.*

eye·lash pestaña *f.*

eye·lid párpado *m.*

eye·lin·er lápiz *m* de ojos.

eye·shad·ow sombra *f* de ojos.

eye·sight vista *f.*

F

fab·ric *(cloth)* tejido *m.*

fab·u·lous *adj* fabuloso, -a.

face 1 *n* cara *f; (surface)* superficie *f;* **f. to f.** cara a cara; **she slammed the door in my f.** me dio con la puerta en las narices; **in the f. of danger** ante el peligro; **to pull faces** hacer muecas; **f. down/up** boca abajo/arriba; **to save f.** salvar las apariencias. **2** *vt (look onto)* dar a; *(be opposite)* estar enfrente de; *(problem)* hacer frente a; **to f. up to** hacer cara a; *(tolerate)* aguantar. **3** *vi* **to f. on to** dar a; **to f. towards** mirar hacia.

fa·cil·i·tate *vt* facilitar.

fa·cil·i·ty *(ease)* facilidad *f;* **facilities** *(means)* facilidades *fpl; (rooms, equipment)* instalaciones *fpl.*

fact hecho *m; (reality)* realidad *f;* **as a matter of f.** de hecho; **in f.** en realidad.

fac·tor factor *m.*

fac·to·ry fábrica *f.*

fac·tu·al *adj* **a f. error** un error de hecho.

fade *vi (colour)* desteñirse; *(flower)* marchitarse; *(light)* apagarse.

▸**fade away, fade out** *vi* desvanecerse.

▸**fade in** *vt* hacer aparecer gradualmente.

fail 1 *n (at school)* suspenso *m;* **without f.** sin falta. **2** *vt (exam)* suspender; **to f. to do sth** *(be unable)* no poder hacer algo; *(neglect)* dejar de hacer algo. **3** *vi (show, film)* fracasar; *(brakes)* fallar; *(at school)* suspender; *(health)* deteriorarse.

failed *adj (attempt, poet)* fracasado, -a.

fail·ing 1 *n (shortcoming)* defecto *m; (weakness)* punto *m* débil. **2** *prep* a falta de.

fail·ure fracaso *m; (at school)* suspenso *m; (person)* fracasado, -a *mf; (breakdown)* avería *f;* **power f.** apagón *m;* **heart f.** paro *m* cardíaco; **her f. to answer** el hecho de que no contestara.

faint 1 *adj (sound)* débil; *(color)* pálido, -a; *(outline)* borroso, -a; *(recollection)* vago, -a; *(giddy)* mareado, -a; **I haven't the faintest idea** no tengo la más mínima idea. **2** *n* desmayo *m.* **3** *vi* desmayarse.

faint·ly *adv (with little strength)* débilmente; *(unclearly)* vagamente.

fair¹ *adj (impartial)* imparcial; *(just)* justo, -a; *(hair)* rubio, -a; *(weather)* bueno, -a; **it's not f.** no hay derecho; **f. enough!** ¡vale!; **a f. number** un buen número. **2** *adv* **to play f.** jugar limpio.

fair² feria *f;* **trade f.** feria *f* de muestras.

fair-haired *adj* rubio, -a.

fairly *adv (justly)* justamente; *(moderately)* bastante.

fair play juego *m* limpio.

fair-sized *adj* bastante grande.

fair·y hada *f;* **f. tale** cuento *m* de hadas.

faith fe *f; (trust)* confianza *f.*

faith·ful *adj* fiel.

faith·ful·ly *adv* **yours f.** *(in letter)* le saluda atentamente.

fake 1 *adj* falso, -a. **2** *n (object)* falsificación *f; (person)* impostor, -a *mf.* **3** *vt (forge)* falsificar; *(feign)* fingir.

fall 1 *n* caída *f; (decrease)* baja *f;* otoño *m;* **falls** *(waterfall)* cascada *f;* **Niágara Falls** las cataratas del Niágara. **2** *vi* caer, caerse; *(temperature, prices)* bajar; **night was falling** anochecía; **to f. asleep** dormirse; **to f. ill** caer enfermo, -a; **to f. in love** enamorarse.

▸**fall apart** *vi (of machine)* deshacerse.

▸**fall back on** *vt (as last resort)* recurrir a.

▸**fall behind** *vi (in race)* quedarse

atrás; **to f. behind with one's work** retrasarse en el trabajo.

▸**fall down** vi (picture etc) caerse; (building) derrumbarse.

▸**fall for** vt (person) enamorarse de; (trick) dejarse engañar por.

▸**fall in** vi (roof) desplomarse.

▸**fall off** vi (drop off) caer; (part) desprenderse; (diminish) disminuir.

▸**fall out** vi (hair) caerse; (quarrel) pelearse.

▸**fall over** vi caerse.

▸**fall through** vi (plan) fracasar.

false adj falso, -a; **f. teeth** dentadura f postiza; **f. alarm** falsa alarma f.

fame fama f.

fa·mil·iar adj (common) conocido, -a; **his face is f.** su cara me suena; **to be on f. terms with sb** (know well) tener confianza con algn.

fa·mil·i·ar·i·ty familiaridad f (**with** con); (intimacy) confianza f.

fa·mil·iar·ize vt (make acquainted) familiarizar (**with** con); **to become familiarized with sth** familiarizarse con algo.

fam·i·ly familia f; **f. doctor** médico m de cabecera; **f. planning** planificación f familiar; **f. tree** árbol m genealógico.

fa·mous adj famoso, -a (**for** por).

fan (held in hand) abanico m; (electric) ventilador m; (person) aficionado, -a mf; (of pop star etc) fan mf; **football f.** hincha mf.

fan·cy 1 adj de fantasía; **f. goods** artículos mpl de fantasía. **2** n (whim) capricho m; **to take a f. to sth** encapricharse con algo; **what takes your f.?** ¿qué se te antoja? **3** vt (imagine) imaginar; (like, want) apetecer; **fam f. that!** ¡fíjate!; **do you f. a drink?** ¿te apetece una copa?

fan heat·er estufa f de aire.

fan·tas·tic adj fantástico, -a.

fan·ta·sy fantasía f.

far 1 adj (distant) lejano, -a; **at the f. end** en el otro extremo. **2** adv (distant) lejos; **f. off** a lo lejos; **farther**

back más atrás; **how f. is it to Chicago?** ¿cuánto hay de aquí a Chicago?; **as f. as I can** en lo que puedo; **as f. as I know** que yo sepa; **as f. as possible** en lo posible; **f. from complaining, he seemed pleased** lejos de quejarse, parecía contento; **in so f. as ...** en la medida en que ...; **to go too f.** pasarse de la raya; **f. into the night** hasta muy entrada la noche; **so f.** (in time) hasta ahora; **by f.** con mucho; **f. cleverer** mucho más listo, -a; **f. too much** demasiado.

far·a·way adj lejano, -a.

farce farsa f.

fare (ticket price) tarifa f, precio m del billete; (for boat) pasaje m; (passenger) pasajero, -a mf.

fare·well 1 interj (old use) ¡adiós! **2** n despedida f.

far-fetched adj rebuscado, -a.

farm 1 n granja f, Am hacienda f. **2** vt cultivar.

▸**farm out** vt encargar fuera.

farm·er granjero, -a mf, Am hacendado, -a mf.

farm·house granja f, Am hacienda f.

farm·ing 1 n (agriculture) agricultura f; (of land) cultivo m. **2** adj agrícola.

farm·yard corral m.

far-off adj lejano, -a.

far-reach·ing adj de gran alcance.

far·ther adv más lejos.

far·thest 1 adj más lejano, -a. **2** adv más lejos.

fas·ci·nate vt fascinar.

fas·ci·nat·ing adj fascinante.

fas·ci·na·tion fascinación f.

fash·ion (manner) manera f; (latest style) moda f; **to go/be out of f.** pasar/no estar de moda; **f. parade** desfile m de modelos.

fash·ion show pase m de modelos.

fast 1 adj (quick) rápido, -a; (clock) adelantado, -a. **2** adv rápidamente, deprisa; **how f.?** ¿qué velocidad?; **f. asleep** profundamente dormido, -a.

fas·ten vt (attach) sujetar; (fix) fijar; (belt) abrochar; (bag) asegurar; (shoelaces) atar.

fas·ten·er cierre m.

fat 1 adj gordo, -a; (thick) grueso, -a; (meat) poco magro, -a. **2** n grasa f; cooking f. manteca f de cerdo.

fa·tal adj (accident, illness) mortal; (ill-fated) funesto, -a.

fa·tal·ly adv f. wounded mortalmente herido, -a.

fate destino m.

fa·ther padre m; my f. and mother mis padres.

Fa·ther Christ·mas Papá m Noel.

fa·ther-in-law suegro m.

fa·tigue fatiga f.

fat·ten·ing adj que engorda.

fat·ty 1 adj (food) graso, -a. **2** n fam (person) gordinflón, -ona mf.

fau·cet grifo m.

fault (defect) defecto m; (in merchandise) desperfecto m; (blame) culpa f; to find f. with poner reparos a; to be at f. tener la culpa.

fault·y adj defectuoso, -a.

fa·vor 1 n favor m; in f. of a favor de; to ask sb a f. pedirle un favor a algn. **2** vt (treat favorably) favorecer; (approve) estar a favor de.

fa·vor·a·ble adj favorable.

fa·vor·ite adj & n favorito, -a (mf).

fax 1 n fax m. **2** vt (document) mandar por fax; to f. sb mandar un fax a algn.

fear 1 n miedo m; for f. of por temor a. **2** vt temer; I f. it's too late me temo que ya es tarde.

fear·ful adj (person) temeroso, -a; (frightening) espantoso, -a.

fear·less adj intrépido, -a.

feast banquete m.

feat hazaña f.

feath·er pluma f; f. duster plumero m.

fea·ture 1 n (of face) facción f; (characteristic) característica f; f. film largometraje m. **2** vi figurar.

Feb·ru·ar·y febrero m.

fed·er·al adj federal.

fed up adj fam harto, -a (with de).

fee (of lawyer, doctor) honorarios mpl.

fee·ble adj débil.

feed* 1 vt (give food to) dar de comer a; to f. a baby (breastfeed) amamantar a un bebé; (with bottle) dar el biberón a un bebé. **2** vi comer; (cows, sheep) pacer.

feed·back feedback m; fig reacción f.

feel 1 vi* (have emotion, sensation) sentirse; (have opinion) opinar; how do you f.? ¿qué tal te encuentras?; I f. bad about it me da pena; to f. happy sentirse feliz; to f. cold/sleepy tener frío/sueño; I feel that ... me parece que ...; it feels like summer parece verano; I f. sure that ... estoy seguro, -a de que ...; I f. like an ice cream me apetece un helado; to f. like doing sth tener ganas de hacer algo. **2** vt* (touch) tocar; (sense) sentir; (the cold) notar; she feels like a failure se siente inútil. **3** n (touch, sensation) tacto m.

▸**feel for** vt (have sympathy for) compadecer.

▸**feel up to** vt tener ánimos para.

feel·ing (emotion) sentimiento m; (physical) sensación f; (opinion) opinión f; I had the f. that ... (impression) tuve la impresión de que ...; to express one's feelings expresar sus opiniones.

feet npl see foot.

fell pt of fall.

fel·low 1 n tipo m, tío m. **2** f. citizen conciudadano, -a mf; f. countryman/countrywoman compatriota mf.

fel·o·ny crimen m, delito m mayor.

felt¹ pt & pp of feel.

felt² fieltro m.

felt-tip(ped) pen rotulador m.

fe·male 1 adj femenino, -a; (animal) hembra. **2** n (animal) hembra f; (woman) mujer f; (girl) chica f.

fem·i·nine *adj* femenino, -a.

fence 1 *n* cerca *f*. **2** *vi* *(in sport)* practicar la esgrima.

▶ **fence in** *vt* meter en un cercado.

fenc·ing *(sport)* esgrima *f*.

fend *vi* to f. for oneself valerse por sí mismo.

▶ **fend off** *vt* *(blow)* parar; *(attack)* rechazar.

fend·er *(on car)* parachoques *m inv*.

fern helecho *m*.

fe·ro·cious *adj* feroz.

fer·ry 1 *n* *(small)* barca *f* de pasaje; *(large, for cars)* ferry *m*. **2** *vt* transportar.

fer·tile *adj* fértil.

fer·til·iz·er abono *m*.

fes·ti·val festival *m*.

fes·tive *adj* festivo, -a; the f. season las fiestas de Navidad.

fes·tiv·i·ty the festivities las fiestas.

fetch *vt* *(go for)* ir a buscar; *(bring)* traer.

fete fiesta *f*.

feud 1 *n* enemistad *f* duradera. **2** *vi* pelear.

fe·ver fiebre *f*.

fe·ver·ish *adj* febril.

few 1 *adj* *(not many)* pocos, -as; as f. as solamente; a f. unos, -as, algunos, -as; in the next f. days dentro de unos días; she has fewer books than I thought tiene menos libros de lo que pensaba; quite a f. un buen número. **2** *pron* *(not many)* pocos, -as; there are too f. no hay suficientes; a f. *(some)* algunos, -as; who has the fewest? ¿quién tiene menos?

fi·an·cé prometido *m*.

fi·an·cée prometida *f*.

fi·ber fibra *f*.

fic·tion ficción *f*.

fid·dle *fam* *n* *(musical instrument)* violín *m*.

▶ **fiddle about** *vi* juguetear *(with con)*.

fidg·et *vi* moverse; stop fidgeting!

¡estáte quieto!; to f. with sth jugar con algo.

field 1 *n* campo *m*; *(oil field, coal field etc)* yacimiento *m*. **2** *vt* *(in sport)* *(ball)* parar y devolver; *(team)* presentar.

field trip viaje *m* de estudios.

field·work trabajo *m* de campo.

fierce *adj* *(animal)* feroz; *(argument)* acalorado, -a; *(heat, competition)* intenso, -a.

fif·teen *adj & n* quince *(m) inv*.

fif·teenth *adj & n* decimoquinto, -a *(mf)*.

fifth *adj & n* quinto, -a *(mf)*.

fif·ti·eth *adj & n* quincuagésimo, -a *(mf)*.

fif·ty 1 *adj* cincuenta *inv*; a f.-f. chance una probabilidad del cincuenta por ciento; to go f.-f. ir a medias. **2** *n* cincuenta *m inv*.

fig *(fruit)* higo *m*.

fight 1 *vt** combatir; *(bull)* lidiar. **2** *vi** pelear(se); *(quarrel)* reñir; *fig (struggle)* luchar *(for/against* por/contra). **3** *n* pelea *f*; *(boxing)* combate *m*; *(quarrel)* riña *f*; *fig (struggle)* lucha *f*.

▶ **fight back 1** *vt* *(tears)* contener. **2** *vi* *(recover ground)* resistir.

▶ **fight off** *vt* *(attack)* rechazar.

▶ **fight out** *vt* arreglar discutiendo *or* peleando.

fight·er *(person)* combatiente *mf*; *(boxing)* púgil *m*; *fig* luchador, -a *mf*. f. (plane) avión *m* de caza *m*.

fig·ure¹ 1 *n* *(numeral)* cifra *f*; *(form, outline)* forma *f*; *(shape, statue, character)* figura *f*; she has a good f. tiene buen tipo; f. of speech figura retórica. **2** *vt* *fam* imaginarse. **3** *vi* *(appear)* figurar; *fam* that figures eso tiene sentido.

fig·ure² *vt* *(guess)* imaginar.

▶ **figure on** *vt* to f. on doing sth esperar hacer algo.

▶ **figure out** *vt* comprender; I can't f. it out no me lo explico.

file 1 *n* *(tool)* lima *f*; *(folder)* carpeta *f*;

(archive) archivo *m*; *(of computer)* fichero *m*; *(line)* fila *f*; **on f.** archivado, -a; **in single f.** en fila india. **2** *vt* *(smooth)* limar; *(put away)* archivar. **3** *vi* **to f. past** desfilar.

▸ **file away** *vt (put away)* archivar; *(in card catalog)* clasificar.

▸ **file down** *vt* limar.

fil·ing clasificación *f*.

fil·ing cab·i·net archivador *m*; *(for cards)* fichero *m*.

fill 1 *vt (space, time)* llenar **(with** de); *(post, requirements)* cubrir. **2** *vi* llenarse **(with** de).

▸ **fill in 1** *vt (space, form)* rellenar; *(time)* pasar; *(inform)* fam poner al corriente **(on** de). **2** *vi* **to f. in for sb** sustituir a algn.

▸ **fill out** *vt (form)* rellenar.

▸ **fill up 1** *vt* llenar hasta arriba; **f. her up!** ¡llénelo! **2** *vi* llenarse.

fil·let filete *m*; **f. steak** filete *m*.

fill·ing 1 *adj (of food)* que llena mucho. **2** *n (stuffing)* relleno *m*; *(in tooth)* empaste *m*.

fill·ing sta·tion gasolinera *f*.

film 1 *n* película *f*. **2** *vt* filmar. **3** *vi* rodar.

film star estrella *f* de cine.

fil·ter 1 *n* filtro *m*; **f. lane** carril *m* de acceso. **2** *vt* filtrar. **3** *vi (traffic)* **to f. to the right** girar a la derecha.

filth *(dirt)* porquería *f*, fig porquerías *fpl*.

filth·y *adj (dirty)* asqueroso, -a; *(obscene)* obsceno, -a.

fin *(of fish)* aleta *f*.

fi·nal 1 *adj* último, -a; *(definitive)* definitivo, -a. **2** *n (sport)* final *f*.

fi·nal·ize *vt* ultimar; *(date)* fijar.

fi·nal·ly *adv* finalmente.

fi·nance 1 *n* finanzas *fpl*; **finances** fondos *mpl*. **2** *vt* financiar.

fi·nan·cial *adj* financiero, -a.

find *vt* (locate, think)* encontrar; *(discover)* descubrir; **it has been found that ...** se ha comprobado que ...; **I found it impossible to**

get away me resultó imposible irme. **2** *n* hallazgo *m*.

▸ **find out 1** *vt (inquire)* averiguar; *(discover)* descubrir. **2** *vi* **to f. out about sth** informarse sobre algo; *(discover)* enterarse de algo.

fine¹1 *n (sum of money)* multa *f*. **2** *vt* multar.

fine²1 *adj (delicate etc)* fino, -a; *(excellent)* excelente; *(weather)* bueno, -a; **it was f.** hacía buen tiempo. **2** *adv* muy bien. **3** *interj* ¡vale!

fin·ger dedo *m* (de la mano); **to keep one's fingers crossed** esperar que todo salga bien.

fin·ger·nail uña *f*.

fin·ger·print huella *f* dactilar.

fin·ger·tip punta *f* or yema *f* del dedo.

fin·ish 1 *n* fin *m*; *(of race)* llegada *f*. **2** *vt (complete)* acabar, terminar; *(use up)* agotar; **to f. doing sth** terminar de hacer algo. **3** *vi* acabar, terminar.

▸ **finish off** *vt (complete)* terminar completamente; *(kill)* rematar.

▸ **finish up 1** *vt* acabar; **to f. up doing sth** acabar haciendo algo. **2** *vi* **to f. up in jail** ir a parar a la cárcel.

fin·ished *adj (product)* acabado, -a; *fam (exhausted)* rendido, -a.

Finn finlandés, -esa *mf*.

Finn·ish 1 *adj* finlandés, -esa. **2** *n (language)* finlandés *m*.

fir abeto *m*.

fire 1 *n* fuego *m*; *(accident etc)* incendio *m*; *(heater)* estufa *f*; *(gunfire)* fuego *m*; **to open f.** abrir fuego. **2** *vt (gun)* disparar **(at** a); *(dismiss)* despedir. **3** *vi (shoot)* disparar **(at** sobre).

fire a·larm alarma *f* de incendios.

fire bri·gade (cuerpo *m* de) bomberos *mpl*.

fire·crack·er petardo *m*.

fire ex·it salida *f* de emergencia.

fire ex·tin·guish·er extintor *m*.

fire·man bombero *m*.

fire·place chimenea *f*; *(hearth)* hogar *m*.

fire·wood leña f.

fire·works npl fuegos mpl artificiales.

firm 1 adj firme. **2** n empresa f.

first 1 adj primero, -a; (before masculine singular noun) primer; **for the f. time** por primera vez; **in the f. place** en primer lugar. **2** adv (before anything else) primero; **f. and foremost** ante todo; **at f.** al principio. **3** n the f. el primero, la primera; **the f. of April** el uno or el primero de abril; **from the (very) f.** desde el principio.

first aid primeros auxilios.

first-class 1 adj de primera clase. **2** adv **to travel f.** viajar en primera.

first·ly adv en primer lugar.

fish 1 n (pl fish) pez m; (as food) pescado m. **2** vi pescar.

fish·er·man pescador m.

fish·ing pesca f; **to go f.** ir de pesca.

fish·ing rod caña f de pescar.

fish shop pescadería f.

fish stick palito m de pescado.

fist puño m.

fit¹ 1 vt (clothes) ir bien a; (slot) encajar; (install) colocar; **that suit doesn't f. you** ese traje no te queda bien; **a car fitted with a radio** un coche provisto de radio; **she doesn't f. the description** no responde a la descripción. **2** vi (be of right size) caber; (be suitable) encajar; (facts etc) cuadrar. **3** adj (suitable) apto, -a (for para); (healthy) en (plena) forma; **are you f. to drive?** ¿estás en condiciones de conducir?; **to keep f.** mantenerse en forma. **4** n to be a good f. encajar bien.

fit² (attack) ataque m; fig arrebato m; **by fits and starts** a trompicones.

▸ **fit in 1** vi (tally) cuadrar (**with** con); **he didn't f. in with his colleagues** no encajó con sus compañeros de trabajo. **2** vt (find time for) encontrar un hueco para.

▸ **fit on** vt to f. sth on(to) sth colocar or encajar algo en algo.

▸ **fit out** vt equipar.

fit·ness (health) (buen) estado m físico.

fit·ted adj empotrado, -a; **f. carpet** moqueta f.

fit·ting adj apropiado, -a.

fit·ting room probador m.

fit·tings npl accesorios mpl; **light f.** apliques mpl eléctricos.

five adj & n cinco (m) inv; **f. hundred** quinientos, -as.

fix 1 n to be in a f. estar en un apuro. **2** vt (fasten) fijar; (date, price) fijar; (repair) arreglar; (food, drink) preparar; **he'll f. it with the boss** (arrange) se las arreglará con el jefe.

▸ **fix on** vt (lid etc) encajar.

▸ **fix up** vt (arrange) arreglar; **to f. sb up with sth** proveer a algn de algo.

fix·ture (in sport) encuentro m; fixtures (in building) accesorios mpl.

fizzy adj (water) con gas.

flag 1 n bandera f; (on ship) pabellón m. **2** vi (interest) decaer; (conversation) languidecer.

flake 1 n (of snow) copo m; (of skin, soap) escama f. **2** vi (paint) desconcharse.

flame llama f; **to go up in flames** incendiarse.

flam·ma·ble adj inflamable.

flan tarta f rellena; **fruit f.** tarta f de fruta.

flan·nel (material) franela f.

flap 1 n (of wings, arms) batir. **2** vi (wings) aletear; (flag) ondear. **3** n (of envelope, pocket) solapa f; **to get into a f.** ponerse nervioso, -a.

flare 1 n (distress signal) bengala f. **2** vi (fire) llamear; (trouble) estallar.

flash 1 n (of light) destello m; (of lightning) relámpago m; (for camera) flash m. **2** vt (torch) dirigir; **he flashed his card** enseñó rápidamente su carnet. **3** vi (sudden light) destellar; (shine) brillar; **a car flashed past** un coche pasó como un rayo.

flash·light linterna f.

flask frasco m; (thermos) **f.** termo m.

flat 1 *adj (surface)* llano, -a; *(beer)* sin gas; *(battery)* descargada, -a; *(tire)* desinflado, -a; *(dull)* soso, -a; *(in music)* B f. si m bemol. **2** *adv* to fall f. on one's face caerse de bruces; **to go f. out** ir a todo gas. **3** *n (flat tire)* pinchazo m.

flat·ly *adv* rotundamente.

flat·ten *vt (make level)* allanar; *(crush)* aplastar.

flat·ter *vt* halagar; *(clothes, portrait)* favorecer.

fla·vor 1 *n* sabor m. **2** *vt (food)* sazonar (**with** con).

fla·vor·ing condimento m; **artificial f.** aroma m artificial.

flaw *(failing)* defecto m; *(fault)* desperfecto m.

flea pulga f.

flea mar·ket rastro m.

flee* 1 *vt* huir. **2** *vi* huir (**from** de).

fleet flota f.

Flem·ish 1 *adj* flamenco, -a. **2** *n (language)* flamenco m.

flesh carne f; *(of fruit)* pulpa f; **in the f.** en persona.

flex *vt (muscles)* flexionar.

flex·i·ble *adj* flexible.

flick 1 *n (of finger)* capirotazo m. **2** *vt (finger)* dar un capirotazo a.

▸**flick off** *vt (piece of fluff)* quitar con un dedo.

▸**flick through** *vt* hojear.

flick·er *vi (eyes)* parpadear; *(flame)* vacilar.

flies *npl (on trousers)* bragueta f.

flight vuelo m; *(escape)* huida f; *(of stairs)* tramo m; **to take f.** darse a la fuga.

flight at·ten·dant azafata f.

flim·sy *adj (cloth)* ligero, -a; *(structure)* poco sólido, -a; *(excuse)* poco convincente.

fling* *vt* arrojar.

flint *(in lighter)* piedra f de mechero.

flip 1 *n (flick)* capirotazo m. **2** *vt (toss)* tirar (al aire); **to f. a coin** echar a cara o cruz.

▸**flip through** *vt (book)* hojear.

flip-flop *(footwear)* chancleta f.

float 1 *n* flotador m; *(in procession)* carroza f. **2** *vi* flotar.

flock 1 *n* rebaño m; *(of birds)* bandada f. **2** *vi* acudir en masa.

flood 1 *n* inundación f; *(of river)* riada f. **2** *vt* inundar. **3** *vi (river)* desbordarse.

flood·light foco m.

floor *(of room)* suelo m; *(storey)* piso m; **first f.** planta f baja.

floor·board tabla f (del suelo).

flop 1 *n (failure)* fracaso m. **2** *vi* fracasar.

flop·py *adj* flojo, -a.

flop·py disk disquete m, disco m flexible.

flo·rist florista mf; **f.'s** floristería f.

floun·der *inv (fish)* platija f.

flour harina f.

flour·ish 1 *n (gesture)* ademán m (teatral). **2** *vt (brandish)* agitar. **3** *vi (thrive)* florecer; *(plant)* crecer.

flow 1 *n* flujo m; *(of traffic)* circulación f; *(of people, goods)* movimiento m. **2** *vi (blood, river)* fluir; *(traffic)* circular.

flow chart organigrama m.

flow·er 1 *n* flor f. **2** *vi* florecer.

flow·er bed arriate m.

flow·er shop floristería f.

flu gripe f.

flu·ent *adj (eloquent)* fluido, -a; **he speaks f. German** habla el alemán con soltura.

flu·ent·ly *adv (to speak)* con soltura.

fluff *(down)* pelusa f.

flu·id líquido m.

flunk *vt fam* catear.

flu·o·res·cent *adj* fluorescente.

flush 1 *adj* **f. with** *(level)* a ras de. **2** *n (blush)* rubor m. **3** *vt* **to f. the lavatory** tirar de la cadena. **4** *vi (blush)* ruborizarse.

flute flauta f.

flut·ter *vi (leaves, birds)* revolotear; *(flag)* ondear.

fly¹* 1 *vt (plane)* pilotar. **2** *vi (bird,*

plane) volar; *(go by plane)* ir en avión; *(flag)* ondear.

▸**fly over** *vt (country etc)* sobrevolar.

fly² *(insect)* mosca *f;* **f. spray** spray *m* matamoscas.

fly³ *(on trousers)* bragueta *f.*

fly·ing 1 *adj (soaring)* volante; *(rapid)* rápido, -a. **2** *n (action)* vuelo *m; (aviation)* aviación *f.*

fly·ing sau·cer platillo *m* volante.

fly-o·ver paso *m* elevado.

foam espuma *f;* **f. rubber** goma *f* espuma.

fo·cus 1 *vt* centrar **(on** en). **2** *vi* to **f. on sth** enfocar algo; *fig* centrarse en algo. **3** *n* foco *m.*

fog niebla *f; (at sea)* bruma *f.*

fog·gy *adj* **it is f.** hay niebla.

foil 1 *n* **aluminum f.** papel *m* de aluminio. **2** *vt (plot)* frustrar.

fold 1 *n (crease)* pliegue *m.* **2** *vt* doblar; **to f. one's arms** cruzar los brazos. **3** *vi* **to f. (up)** *(chair etc)* plegarse.

▸**fold away** *vt* plegar.

fold·er carpeta *f.*

fold·ing *adj (chair etc)* plegable.

folk *npl (people)* gente *f.*

folk mu·sic música *f* folk.

fol·low 1 *vt* seguir; *(understand)* comprender. **2** *vi (come after)* seguir; *(result)* resultar; *(understand)* entender; **that doesn't f.** eso no es lógico.

▸**follow around** *vt* **to f. sb around** seguir a algn por todas partes.

▸**follow on** *vi (come after)* venir detrás.

▸**follow up** *vt (idea)* llevar a cabo; *(clue)* investigar.

follower seguidor, -a *mf.*

fol·low·ing 1 *adj* siguiente. **2** *n* seguidores *mpl.*

fond *adj* **to be f. of sb** tenerle mucho cariño a algn; **to be f. of doing sth** ser aficionado, -a a hacer algo.

font *(of characters)* fuente *f.*

food comida *f.*

food poi·son·ing intoxicación *f* alimenticia.

fool 1 *n* tonto, -a *mf;* **to play the f.** hacer el tonto. **2** *vt (deceive)* engañar. **3** *vi (joke)* bromear.

▸**fool around** *vi* hacer el tonto.

fool·ish *adj (silly)* tonto, -a; *(unwise)* estúpido, -a.

fool·ish·ly *adv* estúpidamente.

foot 1 *n (pl feet)* pie *m; (of animal)* pata *f;* **on f.** a pie; **to put one's f. in it** meter la pata. **2** *vt* **to f. the bill** *(pay)* pagar la cuenta.

foot·ball fútbol americano *m; (ball)* balón *m.*

foot·bridge puente *m* para peatones.

foot·path sendero *m.*

foot·print pisada *f.*

foot·step paso *m.*

for *prep (purpose)* para; **what's this f.?** ¿para qué sirve esto?; **f. sale** en venta. ■ *(because of, on behalf of)* por; **famous f. its cuisine** famoso, -a por su cocina; **will you do it f. me?** ¿lo harás por mí? ■ *(instead of)* por; **can you go f. me?** ¿puede ir por mí? ■ *(during)* por, durante; **I was ill f. a month** estuve enfermo durante un mes; **I've been here f. three months** hace tres meses que estoy aquí. ■ *(distance)* por; **I walked f. ten kilometers** caminé diez kilómetros. ■ *(at a point in time)* para; **I can do it f. next Monday** puedo hacerlo para el lunes que viene; **f. the last time** por última vez. ■ *(in exchange for)* por; **I got the car f. five hundred dollars** conseguí el coche por quinientos dólares. ■ *(in favor of)* a favor de; **are you f. or against?** ¿estás a favor o en contra? ■ *(towards)* hacia, por; **affection f. sb** cariño hacia algn. ■ **it's time f. you to go** es hora de que os marchéis.

for·bid* *vt* prohibir; **to f. sb to do sth** prohibirle a algn hacer algo.

force 1 *n* fuerza *f;* **to come into f.** entrar en vigor; **the (armed) forces** las fuerzas armadas. **2** *vt* forzar; **to f. sb**

to do sth forzar a algn a hacer algo.
fore·cast 1 n pronóstico m, previsión f. **2** vt* pronosticar.
fore·head frente f.
for·eign adj extranjero, -a; (trade, policy) exterior.
for·eign·er extranjero, -a mf.
fore·man capataz m.
fore·most adj principal; **first and f.** ante todo.
fore·run·ner precursor, -a mf.
fore·see* vt prever.
for·est bosque m.
for·ev·er adv (constantly) siempre; (for good) para siempre.
forge vt (counterfeit) falsificar; (metal) forjar.
▶**forge ahead** vi hacer grandes progresos.
for·ger·y falsificación f.
for·get* 1 vt olvidar; **I forgot to close the window** se me olvidó cerrar la ventana. **2** vi olvidarse.
▶**forget about** vt olvidar.
for·get·ful adj olvidadizo, -a.
for·give* vt perdonar; **to f. sb for sth** pendonarle algo a algn.
fork 1 n (cutlery) tenedor m; (farming) horca f; (in road) bifurcación f. **2** vi (roads) bifurcarse.
▶**fork out** vt fam (money) soltar.
form 1 n forma f; (type) clase f; (document) formulario m; (at school) clase f; **on/on top/off f.** en/en plena/en baja forma. **2** vt formar. **3** vi formarse.
for·mal adj (official) oficial; (party, dress) de etiqueta; (person) formalista.
for·mal·i·ty formalidad f.
for·mal·ly adv oficialmente.
for·mat 1 n formato m. **2** vt (computer disk) formatear.
for·ma·tion formación f.
for·mer adj (time) anterior; (onetime) antiguo, -a; (first) aquél/aquélla; **the f. champion** el ex-campeón.
for·mer·ly adv antes, antiguamente.

for·mu·la fórmula f.
for·mu·late vt formular.
fort fortaleza f.
forth adv fml **and so f.** y así sucesivamente; **to go back and f.** ir de acá para allá.
forth·com·ing adj (event) próximo, -a; (communicative) comunicativo, -a; **no money was f.** no hubo oferta de dinero.
for·ti·eth adj & n cuadragésimo, -a (mf).
fort·night quincena f.
for·tress fortaleza f.
for·tu·nate adj afortunado, -a; **it was f. that he came** fue una suerte que viniera.
for·tu·nate·ly adv afortunadamente.
for·tune (luck, fate) suerte f; (money) fortuna f.
for·ty adj & n cuarenta (m) inv.
fo·rum foro m.
for·ward 1 adv (also **forwards**) (direction and movement) hacia adelante; **from this day f.** de ahora en adelante. **2** adj (person) fresco, -a. **3** n (in sport) delantero, -a mf. **4** vt (send on) remitir; (goods) expedir.
fos·sil fósil m.
fos·ter adj **f. child** niño(a) mf en régimen de acogida; **f. home** hogar m de acogida; **f. parents** padres mpl de acogida.
foul 1 adj (smell) fétido, -a; (taste) asqueroso, -a; (language) grosero, -a. **2** n (in football etc) falta f.
found¹ pt & pp of **find**.
found² vt (establish) fundar.
found·er fundador, -a mf.
foun·tain fuente f.
foun·tain pen pluma estilográfica.
four adj & n cuatro (m) inv; **on all fours** a gatas.
four·teen adj & n catorce (m) inv.
fourth adj & n cuarto, -a (mf).
fowl aves fpl de corral.
fox zorro, -a mf.
foy·er vestíbulo m.

frac·tion fracción f.
frac·ture 1 n fractura f. **2** vt fracturar.
frag·ile adj frágil.
frag·ment fragmento m.
fra·grance fragancia f.
frail adj frágil.
frame 1 n (of window, door, picture) marco m; (of machine) armazón m; **f. of mind** estado m de ánimo. **2** vt (picture) enmarcar; (question) formular; (innocent person) incriminar.
frame·work within the f. of ... dentro del marco de ....
franc franco m.
fran·chise (right to vote) derecho m al voto; (right to sell product) concesión f, licencia f.
frank adj franco, -a.
frank·ly adv francamente.
frank·ness franqueza f.
fran·tic adj (anxious) desesperado, -a; (hectic) frenético, -a.
fran·ti·cal·ly adv desesperadamente.
fraud fraude m; (person) impostor, -a mf.
fray vi (cloth) deshilacharse.
freck·le peca f.
freck·led adj pecoso, -a.
free 1 adj libre; **f. (of charge)** gratuito, -a; (generous) generoso, -a. **2** adv (for) gratis. **3** vt (liberate) poner en libertad.
free·dom libertad f.
free·way autopista f.
freeze* 1 vt congelar. **2** vi (liquid) helarse; (food) congelarse.
▸**freeze up, freeze over** vi helarse; (windshield) cubrirse de hielo.
freez·er congelador m.
freez·ing adj glacial; **above/below f. point** sobre/bajo cero.
freight (transport) transporte m; (goods, price) flete m; **f. train** tren m de mercancías.
French 1 adj francés, -esa. **2** n (language) francés m; pl **the F.** los franceses.

French fries npl patatas fpl fritas.
French·man francés m.
French·wom·an francesa f.
fre·quent adj frecuente.
fre·quent·ly adv frecuentemente.
fresh adj fresco, -a; (new) nuevo, -a; **in the f. air** al aire libre.
fresh·en up vi asearse.
fret vi preocuparse (**about** por).
Fri·day viernes m.
fridge nevera f, frigorífico m.
fried adj frito, -a.
friend amigo, -a mf; **a f. of mine** un, -a amigo, -a mío, -a.
friend·ly adj (person) simpático, -a; (atmosphere) acogedor, -a.
friend·ship amistad f.
fright (fear) miedo m; (shock) susto m; **to get a f.** pegarse un susto.
fright·en vt asustar.
▸**frighten away, frighten off** vt ahuyentar.
fright·ened adj asustado, -a; **to be f. of sb** tenerle miedo a algn.
fright·en·ing adj espantoso, -a.
frill (dress) volante m.
fringe (edge) borde m; fig **on the f. of society** al margen de la sociedad.
frog rana f.
from prep (time) desde, a partir de; **f. the eighth to the seventeenth** desde el ocho hasta el diecisiete; **f. time to time** de vez en cuando. ▪ (price, number) desde, de; **dresses f. ten dollars** vestidos desde diez dólares. ▪ (origin) de; **he's f. Malaga** es de Málaga; **the train f. Bilbao** el tren procedente de Bilbao. ▪ (distance) de; **the town is four miles f. the coast** el pueblo está a cuatro millas de la costa. ▪ (remove, subtract) a; **he took the book f. the child** le quitó el libro al niño. ▪ (according to) según, por; **f. what the author said** según lo que dijo el autor. ▪ (position) desde, de; **f. here** desde aquí.
front 1 n parte f delantera; (of building) fachada f; (military, political, of

weather) frente *m;* **in f. (of)** delante (de). **2** *adj* delantero, -a.

front door puerta *f* principal.

fron·tier frontera *f.*

frost *n (covering)* escarcha *f; (freezing)* helada *f.*

frost·bite congelación *f.*

frost·y *adj fig* glacial; **it will be a f. night tonight** esta noche habrá helada.

froth espuma *f.*

frown *vi* fruncir el ceño.

▸**frown upon** *vt* desaprobar.

fro·zen *adj (liquid, feet etc)* helado, -a; *(food)* congelado, -a.

fruit fruta *f;* **fruits** *(rewards)* frutos *mpl.*

fruit sal·ad macedonia *f* de frutas.

frus·trate *vt* frustrar.

frus·trat·ed *adj* frustrado, -a.

frus·trat·ing *adj* frustrante.

frus·tra·tion frustración *f.*

fry *vt* freír.

fry·ing pan sartén *f.*

fu·el combustible *m; (for engines)* carburante *m.*

fu·gi·tive fugitivo, -a *mf.*

ful·fill *vt (task, ambition)* realizar; *(promise)* cumplir; *(wishes)* satisfacer.

ful·fill·ing *adj* que llena.

full 1 *adj* lleno, -a **(of** de); *(complete)* completo, -a; **I'm f. (up)** no puedo más. **2** *n* **in f.** en su totalidad.

full board pensión *f* completa.

full-scale *adj (model)* de tamaño natural.

full stop punto *m.*

full-time 1 *adj* de jornada completa. **2** *adv* **to work f.** trabajar a jornada completa.

ful·ly *adv* completamente.

fumes *npl* humo *m.*

fun *(amusement)* diversión *f;* **in or for f.** en broma; **to have f.** pasarlo bien; **to make f. of sb** reírse de algn.

func·tion 1 *n* función *f; (ceremony)* acto *m; (party)* recepción *f.* **2** *vi* funcionar.

func·tion·al *adj* funcional.

fund 1 *n* fondo *m;* **funds** fondos *mpl.* **2** *vt (finance)* financiar.

fu·ner·al funeral *m;* **f. home** funeraria *f.*

fun·nel *(for liquids)* embudo *m; (of ship)* chimenea *f.*

fun·ny *adj (peculiar)* raro, -a; *(amusing)* divertido, -a; *(ill)* mal; **I found it very f.** me hizo mucha gracia.

fur *(of living animal)* pelo *m; (of dead animal)* piel *f.*

fu·ri·ous *adj (angry)* furioso, -a.

fur·nace horno *m.*

fur·nish *vt (house)* amueblar.

fur·ni·ture muebles *mpl;* **a piece of f.** un mueble.

fur·ther 1 *adj (new)* nuevo, -a; *(additional)* otro, -a. **2** *adv* más lejos; *(more)* más; **f. back** más atrás.

fur·ther ed·u·ca·tion estudios *mpl* superiores.

fur·ther·more *adv* además.

fur·thest *adj* más lejano, -a.

fu·ry furia *f.*

fuse 1 *n* fusible *m; (of bomb)* mecha *f.* **2** *vi* **the lights fused** se fundieron los plomos.

fuss 1 *n (commotion)* jaleo *m;* **to kick up a f.** armar un escándalo; **to make a f. of** *(pay attention to)* mimar a. **2** *vi* preocuparse **(about** por).

▸**fuss over** *vt* consentir a.

fuss·y *adj (nitpicking)* quisquilloso, -a; *(thorough)* exigente.

fu·ture 1 *n* futuro *m;* **in the near f.** en un futuro próximo. **2** *adj* futuro, -a.

fuzz·y *adj (hair)* muy rizado, -a; *(blurred)* borroso, -a.

G

gadg·et aparato *m*.

Gael·ic 1 *adj* gaélico, -a. **2** *n (language)* gaélico *m*.

gag 1 *n* mordaza *f*; *(joke)* chiste *m*. **2** *vt* amordazar.

gai·e·ty regocijo *m*.

gai·ly *adv* alegremente.

gain 1 *n* ganancia *f*; *(increase)* aumento *m*. **2** *vt (obtain)* ganar; *(increase)* aumentar; **to g. weight** aumentar de peso.

▸ **gain on** *vt* ganar terreno a.

ga·la gala *f*.

ga·lax·y galaxia *f*.

gale vendaval *m*.

gal·lant *adj (chivalrous)* galante.

gal·ler·y galería *f*.

gal·li·vant *vi fam* callejear.

gal·lon galón *m*.

gal·lop 1 *n* galope *m*. **2** *vi* galopar.

gam·ble 1 *n (risk)* riesgo *m*; *(bet)* apuesta *f*. **2** *vi (bet)* jugar; *(take a risk)* arriesgarse.

▸ **gamble away** *vt (lose)* perder en el juego.

gam·bler jugador, -a *mf*.

gam·bling juego *m*.

game juego *m*; *(match)* partido *m*; *(of bridge)* partida *f*.

gang *(of criminals)* banda *f*; *(of youths)* pandilla *f*.

▸ **gang up** *vi* confabularse (**on** contra).

gang·ster gángster *m*.

gang·way pasarela *f*.

gap hueco *m*; *(blank space)* blanco *m*; *(in time)* intervalo *m*; *(gulf)* diferencia *f*; *(deficiency)* laguna *f*.

gape *vi (person)* mirar boquiabierto, -a.

ga·rage garaje *m*; *(for repairs)* taller *m* mecánico; *(gas station)* gasolinera *f*.

gar·bage basura *f*; **g. can** cubo *m* de la basura.

gar·ban·zo g. (bean) garbanzo *m*.

gar·den jardín *m*.

gar·den·er jardinero, -a *mf*.

gar·den·ing jardinería *f*.

gar·gle *vi* hacer gárgaras.

gar·land guirnalda *f*.

gar·lic ajo *m*.

gar·ment prenda *f*.

gas 1 *n* gas *m*; gasolina *f*; **g. cooker** cocina *f* de gas; **g. fire** estufa *f* de gas. **2** *vt (asphyxiate)* asfixiar con gas.

gash 1 *n* herida *f* profunda. **2** *vt* **he gashed his forehead** se hizo una herida en la frente.

gas·o·line gasolina *f*.

gasp 1 *n (cry)* grito *m* sordo; *(breath)* bocanada *f*. **2** *vi (in surprise)* quedar boquiabierto, -a; *(breathe)* jadear.

gas sta·tion gasolinera *f*.

gas·sy *adj* gaseoso, -a.

gas tank depósito *m* de gasolina.

gas·works fábrica *f* de gas.

gate puerta *f*; *(at stadium)* entrada *f*.

gate·crash *vti* colarse.

gath·er *vt (collect)* juntar; *(pick up)* recoger; *(bring together)* reunir; *(understand)* suponer; **to g. speed** ir ganando velocidad; **I g. that ...** tengo entendido que .... **2** *vi (come together)* reunirse.

▸ **gather around** *vi* agruparse.

gath·er·ing reunión *f*.

gaud·y *adj* chillón, -ona.

gauge 1 *n (of railway)* ancho *m* de vía; *(calibrator)* indicador *m*. **2** *vt (judge)* juzgar.

gaunt *adj (lean)* demacrado, -a; *(desolate)* lúgubre.

gauze gasa *f*.

gave *pt of* **give**.

gay *adj (homosexual)* gay; *(happy)* alegre.

gaze 1 *n* mirada *f* fija. **2** *vi* mirar fijamente.

▸ **gaze at** *vt* mirar fijamente.

GB *abbr of* **Great Britain**.

gear 1 n (equipment) equipo m; (belongings) bártulos mpl; (clothing) ropa f; (in car etc) marcha f. **2** vt adaptar (**to** a).

gear·box caja f de cambios.

geese npl see **goose**.

gel gel m; (for hair) gomina f.

gem piedra f preciosa.

gen·der género m.

gen·er·al 1 adj general; **in g.** en general; **the g. public** el público. **2** n (in army) general m.

gen·er·al·ly adv generalmente.

gen·er·a·tion generación f.

gen·er·a·tion gap abismo m or conflicto m generacional.

gen·er·a·tor generador m.

gen·er·os·i·ty generosidad f.

gen·er·ous adj generoso, -a; (plentiful) copioso, -a.

gen·er·ous·ly adv generosamente.

gen·ius (person) genio m; (gift) don m.

gen·tle adj dulce; (breeze) suave.

gen·tle·man caballero m.

gen·tle·ness (mildness) ternura f; (kindness) amabilidad f.

gent·ly con cuidado.

gents npl servicio m de caballeros.

gen·u·ine adj auténtico, -a; (sincere) sincero, -a.

gen·u·ine·ly adv auténticamente.

ge·o·graph·i(·)c(al) adj geográfico, -a.

ge·og·ra·phy geografía f.

ge·o·met·ri(·)c(al) adj geométrico, -a.

ge·om·e·try geometría f.

germ microbio m.

Ger·man 1 adj alemán, -ana; **G. measles** rubeola f. **2** n alemán, -ana mf; (language) alemán m.

Ger·man shep·herd (dog) pastor m alemán.

ges·ture gesto m.

get* vt (obtain) obtener, conseguir; (earn) ganar; (fetch) (something) traer; (somebody) ir a por; (receive) recibir; (bus, train, thief etc) coger,

Am agarrar; (understand) entender; (on phone) **g. me Mr Brown** póngame con el Sr. Brown; **can I g. you something to eat?** ¿te traigo algo de comer?; **g. him to call me** dile que me llame; **to g. one's hair cut** cortarse el pelo; **to g. sb to do sth** (ask) persuadir a algn de que haga algo. **2** vi (become) ponerse; **to g. late** hacerse tarde; **to g. married** casarse; **to g. dressed** vestirse; **to g.** (come to) llegar a; **to g. to know sb** llegar a conocer a algn.

▸**get across** vt (idea etc) hacer comprender.

▸**get along** vi (manage) arreglárselas; (two people) llevarse bien.

▸**get around 1** vi (person) salir; (news) difundirse. **2** vt (problem) salvar; (difficulty) vencer.

▸**get around to** vi **if I g. around to it** si tengo tiempo; **I'll g. around to it later** encontraré tiempo para hacerlo más tarde.

▸**get at** vt (reach) alcanzar; (criticize) criticar.

▸**get away** vi escaparse.

▸**get back 1** vi (return) volver; **g. back!** (move backwards) ¡atrás! **2** vt (recover) recuperar.

▸**get by** vi (manage) arreglárselas; **she can g. by in French** sabe defenderse en francés.

▸**get down 1** vt (depress) deprimir. **2** vi (descend) bajar.

▸**get in** vi (arrive) llegar; (politician) ser elegido, -a. **2** vt (buy) comprar; (collect) recoger.

▸**get into** vt (house, car) entrar en; fig **to g. into bad habits** adquirir malas costumbres; **to g. into trouble** meterse en un lío.

▸**get off 1** vt (bus etc) bajarse de; (remove) quitarse. **2** vi bajarse; (escape) escaparse; **to g. off lightly** salir bien librado, -a.

▸**get on 1** vt (board) subir a. **2** vi (board) subirse; (make progress) hacer progresos; **how are you getting** on? ¿cómo te van las cosas?; **to g. on well (with sb)** llevarse bien (con algn); *(continue)* **to g. on with sth** seguir con algo.

▶**get on to** *vt (find) (person)* localizar; *(find out)* descubrir; *(continue)* pasar a.

▶**get out 1** *vt (object)* sacar. **2** *vi (of room etc)* salir (**of** de); *(of train)* bajar (**of** de); *(news)* difundirse; *(secret)* hacerse público.

▶**get over** *vt (illness)* recuperarse de; *(difficulty)* vencer; *(convey)* hacer comprender.

▶**get through 1** *vi (message)* llegar; *(on phone)* **to g. through to sb** conseguir comunicar con algn. **2** *vt (consume)* consumir; **to g. through a lot of work** trabajar mucho.

▶**get together** *vi (people)* reunirse.

▶**get up 1** *vi (rise)* levantarse. **2** *vt (wake up)* despertar.

▶**get up to** *vt* hacer; **to g. up to mischief** hacer de las suyas.

get·to·geth·er reunión *f.*

ghast·ly *adj* espantoso, -a.

gher·kin pepinillo *m.*

ghet·to gueto *m.*

ghost fantasma *m.*

gi·ant *adj & n* gigante *(m).*

gid·dy *adj* mareado, -a; **it makes me g.** me da vértigo; **to feel g.** sentirse mareado, -a.

gift regalo *m; (talent)* don *m.*

gift·ed *adj* dotado, -a.

gig *fam (concert)* actuación *f.*

gi·gan·tic *adj* gigantesco, -a.

gig·gle *vi* reírse tontamente.

gim·mick truco *m; (in advertising)* reclamo *m.*

gin ginebra *f;* **g. and tonic** gin tonic *m.*

gin·ger 1 *adj (hair)* pelirrojo, -a. **2** *n* jengibre *m.*

gi·raffe jirafa *f.*

girl chica *f; (child)* niña *f; (daughter)* hija *f.*

girl·friend novia *f; (female friend)* amiga *f.*

give* *vt* dar; **to g. sth as a present** regalar algo a algn.

▶**give away** *vt (present)* regalar; *(disclose)* revelar.

▶**give back** *vt* devolver.

▶**give in 1** *vi (admit defeat)* darse por vencido, -a; *(surrender)* rendirse. **2** *vt (hand in)* entregar.

▶**give off** *vt (smell etc)* despedir.

▶**give out** *vt* repartir.

▶**give up** *vt (idea)* abandonar; **to g. up smoking** dejar de fumar; **to g. oneself up** entregarse.

giv·en 1 *adj (particular)* dado, -a. **2** *conj (considering)* dado, -a.

glad *adj* contento, -a; **to be g.** alegrarse.

glad·ly *adv* con mucho gusto.

glam·or·ous *adj* atractivo, -a.

glam·our atractivo *m; (charm)* encanto *m.*

glance 1 *n* vistazo *m.* **2** *vi* echar un vistazo (**at** a).

gland glándula *f.*

glare 1 *n (look)* mirada *f* feroz. **2** *vi (look)* lanzar una mirada furiosa (**at** a).

glar·ing *adj (light)* deslumbrante; *(obvious)* evidente.

glass *(material)* vidrio *m; (drinking vessel)* vaso *m;* **pane of g.** cristal *m;* **wine g.** copa *f* (para vino); **glasses** *(spectacles)* gafas *fpl.*

glee gozo *m.*

glide *vi (plane)* planear.

glid·ing vuelo *m* sin motor.

glim·mer *fig (trace)* destello *m.*

glimpse 1 *n* atisbo *m.* **2** *vt* atisbar.

glit·ter·ing *adj* reluciente.

globe globo *m.*

gloom *(obscurity)* penumbra *f; (melancholy)* melancolía *f.*

gloom·y *adj (dismal)* deprimente; *(despondent)* pesimista; *(sad)* triste.

glo·ri·fied *adj fam* con pretensiones; **a g. boarding house** una pensión con pretensiones.

glo·ri·ous *adj (momentous)* glorioso, -a; *(splendid)* espléndido, -a.

glo·ry gloria *f; (splendor)* esplendor *m*.

gloss *(sheen)* brillo *m*; **g. (paint)** esmalte *m*.

gloss·y *adj* lustroso, -a; **g. magazine** revista *f* de lujo.

glove guante *m*; **g. compartment** guantera *f*.

glow 1 *n* brillo *m*. **2** *vi* brillar.

glue 1 *n* pegamento *m*. **2** *vt* pegar **(to** a).

glum *adj* alicaído, -a.

glut·ton glotón, -ona *mf*.

gnat mosquito *m*.

gnaw *vti (chew)* roer.

go* 1 *vi* ir; *(depart)* irse, marcharse; *(bus)* salir; *(disappear)* desaparecer; *(function)* funcionar; *(become)* quedarse, volverse; *(fit)* caber; *(time)* pasar; **how's it going?** ¿qué tal (te van las cosas)?; **to get** *or* **be going to** *(in the future)* ir a; *(on the point of)* estar a punto de; **there are only two weeks to go** sólo quedan dos semanas; **to let sth go** soltar algo. **2** *n (try)* intento *m*; *(turn)* turno *m*; **to have a go at sth** probar suerte con algo; **it's your go** te toca a ti; **to have a go at sb** criticar a algn.

▸ **go about 1** *vt (task)* emprender; **how do you go about it?** ¿cómo hay que hacerlo? **2** *vi (rumor)* correr.

▸ **go after** *vt (pursue)* andar tras.

▸ **go against** *vt (oppose)* ir en contra de; *(be unfavorable to)* ser desfavorable a.

▸ **go ahead** *vi (proceed)* proceder; **we'll go on ahead** iremos adelante.

▸ **go along** *vi (street)* ir por.

▸ **go along with** *vt (agree)* estar de acuerdo con; *(accompany)* acompañar.

▸ **go around** *vi (revolve)* dar vueltas; **to go around to sb's house** pasar por casa de algn.

▸ **go away** *vi* marcharse.

▸ **go back** *vi (return)* volver.

▸ **go back on** *vt* **to go back on one's word** faltar a su palabra.

▸ **go back to** *vt* volver a; *(date from)* datar de.

▸ **go by** *vi* pasar; **as time goes by** con el tiempo.

▸ **go down** *vi (descend)* bajar; *(sun)* ponerse; *(ship)* hundirse; *(diminish)* disminuir; *(temperature)* bajar.

▸ **go down with** *vt (disease)* coger.

▸ **go for** *vt (fetch)* ir por; *(attack)* atacar, lanzarse sobre; **the same goes for you** lo mismo te digo a ti *or* vale para ti

▸ **go in** *vi* entrar.

▸ **go in for** *vt (exam)* presentarse a.

▸ **go into** *vt (enter)* entrar en; *(matter)* investigar.

▸ **go off** *vi (leave)* irse, marcharse; *(bomb)* explotar; *(gun)* dispararse; *(alarm)* sonar; *(food)* pasarse.

▸ **go on** *vi (continue)* seguir, continuar; *(happen)* pasar; *(light)* encenderse; **to go on talking** seguir hablando.

▸ **go out** *vi (leave)* salir; *(fire, light)* apagarse.

▸ **go over** *vt (cross)* atravesar; *(revise)* repasar.

▸ **go over to** *vt (switch to)* pasar a; **to go over to the enemy** pasarse al enemigo.

▸ **go through** *vt (endure)* sufrir; *(examine)* examinar; *(search)* registrar; *(spend)* gastar.

▸ **go under** *vi (ship)* hundirse; *(business)* fracasar.

▸ **go up** *vi* subir.

▸ **go with** *vt (accompany)* ir con; *(colors)* hacer juego con.

▸ **go without** *vt* pasarse sin.

go-a·head to give sb the g. dar luz verde a algn.

goal gol *m*; *(aim, objective)* meta *f*.

goal·keep·er portero, -a *mf*.

goat *(male)* macho cabrío *m*; *(female)* cabra *f*.

god dios *m*.

god·daugh·ter ahijada *f*.

god·fa·ther padrino *m*.

god·moth·er madrina *f*.

god·send to be a g. venir como agua de mayo.
god·son ahijado m.
gog·gles npl (for diving) gafas fpl de bucear; (protective) gafas fpl protectoras.
go·ing adj (price) corriente.
go·ings-on npl tejemanejes mpl.
gold 1 n oro m. 2 adj de oro; (color) dorado, -a.
gold·en adj de oro; (color) dorado, -a.
gold·fish pez m de colores.
gold-plat·ed adj chapado, -a en oro.
golf golf m.
golf·er golfista mf.
gone pp of go.
good 1 adj (before noun) buen, -a; (after noun) bueno, -a; (kind) amable; (generous) generoso, -a; (morally correct) correcto, -a; g. afternoon, g. evening buenas tardes; g. morning buenos días; g. night buenas noches; to have a g. time pasarlo bien; be g.! ¡pórtate bien!; he's g. at languages tiene facilidad para los idiomas; he's in a g. mood está de buen humor. 2 n bien m; for your own g. por tu propio bien; it's no g. waiting no sirve de nada esperar. 3 adv she's gone for g. se ha ido para siempre. 4 interj g.! ¡muy bien!
good-bye interj ¡adiós!
good-look·ing adj guapo, -a.
good·ness bondad f; my g.! ¡Dios mío!
goods npl (possessions) bienes mpl; (commercial) mercancías fpl.
good will buena voluntad f.
goose (pl geese) ganso m, oca f.
goose·ber·ry grosella f espinosa.
goose-flesh, **goose-pim·ples** npl carne f de gallina.
gorge desfiladero m.
gor·geous adj magnífico, -a; (person) atractivo, -a.
go·ril·la gorila m.
gos·pel the G. el Evangelio

gos·sip (rumor) cotilleo m; (person) chismoso, -a mf.
got pt & pp of get.
got·ten pp of get.
gour·met gourmet mf.
gov·ern vt gobernar; (determine) determinar.
gov·ern·ment gobierno m.
gov·er·nor (ruler) gobernador, -a mf; (of school) administrador, -a mf.
gown (dress) vestido m largo; (of lawyer, professor) toga f.
GP abbr of general practitioner médico m de cabecera.
grab vt agarrar; to g. hold of sb agarrarse a algn.
grace gracia f, (elegance) elegancia f.
grace·ful adj elegante; (movement) garboso, -a.
grade 1 n (rank) categoría f, (in army) rango m; (mark) nota f, (class) clase f. 2 vt clasificar.
grad·u·al adj gradual.
grad·u·al·ly adv poco a poco.
grad·u·ate 1 n licenciado, -a mf. 2 vi (from university) licenciarse (in en).
grad·u·a·tion cer·e·mo·ny ceremonia f de entrega de los títulos.
graf·fi·ti npl grafiti mpl.
graft 1 n injerto m. 2 vt injertar (on to en).
grain (cereals) cereales mpl; (particle) grano m.
gram gramo m.
gram·mar gramática f.
gram·mar school ≃ instituto m de Bachillerato.
gram·mat·i·cal adj gramatical.
grand adj (splendid) grandioso, -a; (impressive) impresionante.
grand·child nieto, -a mf.
grand·dad fam abuelo m.
grand-daugh·ter nieta f.
grand-fa·ther abuelo m.
grand·ma fam abuelita f.
grand·moth·er abuela f.
grand·par·ents npl abuelos mpl.

grand·son nieto *m*.

gran·ny *fam* abuelita *f*.

grant 1 *vt* (*give*) conceder; (*accept*) admitir; **to take for granted** dar por sentado. **2** *n* (*for study*) beca *f*; (*subsidy*) subvención *f*.

grape uva *f*, **g. juice** mosto *m*.

grape·fruit pomelo *m*.

graph gráfica *f*.

graph·ic *adj* gráfico, -a; **g. arts** artes *fpl* gráficas.

graph·ics (computer) g. gráficas *fpl*.

grasp 1 *vt* agarrar; (*understand*) comprender. **2** *n* (*grip*) agarrón *m*; (*understanding*) comprensión *f*.

grass hierba *f*, (*lawn*) césped *m*.

grass·hop·per saltamontes *m inv*.

grate 1 *vt* (*food*) rallar. **2** *vi* chirriar. **3** *n* (*fireplace*) rejilla *f*.

grate·ful *adj* agradecido, -a; **to be g. for** agradecer.

grat·er rallador *m*.

grat·i·fy·ing *adj* grato, -a.

grat·i·tude agradecimiento *m*.

grave[1] tumba *f*.

grave[2] *adj* (*situation*) grave.

grav·el gravilla *f*.

grave·yard cementerio *m*.

grav·i·ty gravedad *f*.

gra·vy salsa *f*.

gray *adj* (*color*) gris; (*hair*) cano, -a; (*sky*) nublado, -a.

graze 1 *vt* (*scratch*) rasguñar; (*brush against*) rozar. **2** *vi* (*cattle*) pacer. **3** *n* rasguño *m*.

grease 1 *n* grasa *f*. **2** *vt* engrasar.

grease·proof pa·per papel *m* apergaminado.

greas·y *adj* (*hair, food*) graso, -a.

great *adj* grande; (*before sing noun*) gran; *fam* (*excellent*) estupendo, -a; **a g. many** muchos, -as; **to have a g. time** pasarlo en grande.

great-grand·fa·ther bisabuelo *m*.

great-grand·moth·er bisabuela *f*.

great·ly *adv* (*with adjective*) muy; (*with verb*) mucho.

greed, gree·di·ness (*for food*) gula *f*, (*for money*) codicia *f*.

greed·y *adj* (*for food*) glotón, -ona; (*for money*) codicioso, -a (**for** de).

Greek 1 *adj* griego, -a. **2** *n* (*person*) griego, -a *mf*, (*language*) griego *m*.

green 1 *n* (*color*) verde *m*; (*for golf*) campo *m*; **greens** verduras *fpl*. **2** *adj* verde.

green·house invernadero *m*; **g. effect** efecto *m* invernadero.

greet *vt* saludar.

greet·ing saludo *m*.

gre·nade granada *f*.

grey *adj* = **gray**.

grey·hound galgo *m*.

grid (*on map*) cuadrícula *f*, (*of electricity etc*) red *f* nacional.

grief pena *f*, dolor *m*.

grieve *vi* to g. for sb llorar la muerte de algn.

grill 1 *vt* (*food*) asar a la parrilla. **2** *n* parrilla *f*, (*dish*) parrillada *f*.

grim *adj* (*landscape*) lúgubre; (*manner*) severo, -a; (*unpleasant*) desagradable.

grime mugre *f*.

grim·y *adj* mugriento, -a.

grin 1 *vi* sonreír abiertamente. **2** *n* sonrisa abierta.

grind* *vt* moler; **to g. one's teeth** hacer rechinar los dientes.

grip 1 *n* (*hold*) agarrón *m*; (*handle*) asidero *m*. **2** *vt* agarrar; **to be gripped by fear** ser presa del miedo.

grip·ping *adj* (*film, story*) apasionante.

groan 1 *n* gemido *m*. **2** *vi* gemir.

gro·cer tendero, -a *mf*.

gro·cer·y (*shop*) tienda *f* de ultramarinos; **g. store** supermercado *m*.

groin ingle *f*.

groom (*bridegroom*) novio *m*.

groove (*furrow etc*) ranura *f*, (*of record*) surco *m*.

grope *vi* to g. for sth buscar algo a tientas.

▶**grope about** *vi* andar a tientas; (*looking for sth*) buscar a tientas.

gross *adj* grosero, -à; *(not net)* bruto, -a.

gross·ly *adv* enormemente.

gross na·tion·al prod·uct producto *m* nacional bruto.

ground¹ suelo *m*; *(terrain)* terreno *m*; **grounds** *(gardens)* jardines *mpl*; *(reason)* motivo *m sing*.

ground² *adj (coffee)* molido, -a; *(meat)* picado, -a.

ground·work trabajo *m* preparatorio.

group grupo *m*.

grow* **1** *vt (cultivate)* cultivar; **to g. a beard** dejarse *(crecer)* la barba. **2** *vi* crecer; *(increase)* aumentar; *(become)* volverse.

▸ **grow into** *vt* convertirse en.

▸ **grow out of** *vt (phase etc)* superar; **he's grown out of his shirt** se le ha quedado pequeña la camisa.

▸ **grow up** *vi* crecer.

growl **1** *vi* gruñir. **2** *n* gruñido *m*.

grown *adj* crecido, -a.

grown-up *adj & n* adulto, -a *(mf)*; **the grown-ups** los mayores.

growth crecimiento *m*; *(increase)* aumento *m*; *(development)* desarrollo *m*; *(diseased part)* bulto *m*.

grub *fam (food)* comida *f*.

grub·by *adj* sucio, -a.

grudge **1** *n* rencor *m*; **to bear sb a g.** guardar rencor a algn. **2** *vt* **he grudges me my success** me envidia el éxito.

gru·el·ing *adj* penoso, -a.

grue·some *adj* espantoso, -a.

grum·ble *vi* refunfuñar.

grump·y *adj* gruñón, -ona.

grunt **1** *vi* gruñir. **2** *n* gruñido *m*.

guar·an·tee **1** *n* garantía *f*. **2** *vt* garantizar; *(assure)* asegurar.

guard **1** *vt (protect)* proteger; *(keep watch over)* vigilar; *(control)* guardar. **2** *n (sentry)* guardia *mf*; *(on train)* jefe *m* de tren; **to be on one's g.** estar en guardia; **to stand g.** montar la guardia.

guard·i·an guardián, -ana *mf*; *(of minor)* tutor, -a *mf*.

Gua·te·ma·lan *adj & n* guatemalteco, -a *(mf)*.

guess **1** *vti* adivinar; *fam* suponer. **2** *n* conjetura *f*; *(estimate)* cálculo *m*; **to have** *or* **make a g.** intentar adivinar.

guess·work conjetura *f*.

guest invitado, -a *mf*; *(in hotel)* cliente, -a *mf*, huésped, -a *mf*.

guest·house casa *f* de huéspedes.

guid·ance orientación *f*.

guide **1** *vt* guiar. **2** *n (person)* guía *mf*; *(guidebook)* guía *f*.

guide·line pauta *f*.

guild gremio *m*.

guilt culpabilidad *f*.

guilt·y *adj* culpable *(of* de).

guinea pig conejillo *m* de Indias.

gui·tar guitarra *f*.

gui·tar·ist guitarrista *mf*.

gulf golfo *m*; *fig* abismo *m*.

gull gaviota *f*.

gulp trago *m*.

gum¹ **1** *n* goma *f*. **2** *vt* pegar con goma.

gum² *(around teeth)* encía *f*.

gun *(handgun)* pistola *f*, *(rifle)* fusil *m*; *(cannon)* cañón *m*.

▸ **gun down** *vt* matar a tiros.

gun·fire tiros *mpl*.

gun·man pistolero *m*.

gun·point **at g.** a punta de pistola.

gun·pow·der pólvora *f*.

gun·shot tiro *m*.

gush *vi* brotar.

gust *(of wind)* ráfaga *f*.

gut **1** *n (inside body)* intestino *m*; **guts** *(entrails)* tripas *fpl*; *fam (courage)* agallas *fpl*. **2** *vt (fish)* destripar; *(destroy)* destruir por dentro.

gut·ter *(in street)* cuneta *f*; *(on roof)* canalón *m*.

guy *fam* tipo *m*, tío *m*.

gym *(gymnasium)* gimnasio *m*; *(gymnastics)* gimnasia *f*.

gy·ne·col·o·gist ginecólogo, -a *mf*.

H

hab·it costumbre *f*; **to be in the h. of doing sth** soler hacer algo; **to get into the h. of doing sth** acostumbrarse a hacer algo.

hab·i·tat hábitat *m*.

hack 1 *n (cut)* corte *m*; *(with an ax)* hachazo *m*. **2** *vt (with knife, ax)* cortar.

had *pt & pp of* **have**.

had·dock abadejo *m*.

hag bruja *f*.

hag·gle *vi* regatear.

hail 1 *n* granizo *m*; **a h. of bullets** una lluvia de balas. **2** *vi* granizar.

hail·stone granizo *m*.

hair pelo *m*; *(on arm, leg)* vello *m*; **to have long h.** tener el pelo largo.

hair·brush cepillo *m* (para el pelo).

hair·cut corte *m* de pelo; **to have a h.** cortarse el pelo.

hair·do *fam* peinado *m*.

hair·dress·er peluquero, -a *mf*; **h.'s (shop)** peluquería *f*.

hair·dry·er, hair·dri·er secador *m* (de pelo).

hair·grip horquilla *f*.

hair·pin bend curva *f* muy cerrada.

hair·rais·ing *adj* espeluznante.

hair·spray laca *f* (para el pelo).

hair·style peinado *m*.

hair·y *adj (with hair)* peludo, -a; *fam (frightening)* espeluznante.

half 1 *n (pl* **halves**) mitad *f*; *(period in match)* tiempo *m*; **he's four and a h.** tiene cuatro años y medio; **to cut in h.** cortar por la mitad. **2** *adj* medio, -a; **h. a dozen/an hour** media docena/ hora; **h. fare** media tarifa *f*. **3** *adv* a medias; **h. asleep** medio dormido, -a; **h. past one** la una y media.

half board media pensión *f*.

half·heart·ed *adj* poco entusiasta.

half·hour media hora *f*.

half term *(holiday)* vacación *f* a mitad de trimestre.

half·time descanso *m*.

half·way *adv* a medio camino.

hal·i·but mero *m*.

hall *(lobby)* vestíbulo *m*; *(building)* sala *f*; **h. of residence** colegio *m* mayor.

Hal·low·e('·)en víspera *f* de Todos los Santos.

hall·stand percha *f*.

hall·way vestíbulo *m*.

halt alto *m*; **to call a h. to sth** poner fin a algo.

halve *vt* reducir a la mitad.

ham jamón *m*.

ham·burg·er hamburguesa *f*.

ham·mer 1 *n* martillo *m*. **2** *vt (nail)* clavar; *fig* **to h. home** insistir sobre. **3** *vi* dar golpes.

ham·mer·ing *fam (defeat)* paliza *f*.

ham·mock hamaca *f*.

ham·per¹ cesta *f*.

ham·per² *vt* dificultar.

ham·ster hámster *m*.

hand 1 *n* mano *f*; *(worker)* trabajador, -a *mf*; *(of clock)* aguja *f*; **by h.** a mano; **(close) at h.** a mano; **on the one/other h.** por una/otra parte; **to get out of h.** descontrolarse; **to be on h.** estar a mano; **to have a h. in** intervenir en; **to give sb a h.** echarle una mano a algn; **to give sb a big h.** *(applause)* dedicar a algn una gran ovación. **2** *vt (give)* dar.

▶ **hand back** *vt* devolver.

▶ **hand in** *vt (homework)* entregar.

▶ **hand out** *vt* repartir.

▶ **hand over** *vt* entregar.

hand·bag bolso *m*.

hand·book manual *m*.

hand·brake freno *m* de mano.

hand·cuff 1 *vt* esposar. **2** *npl* **hand·cuffs** esposas *fpl*.

hand·ful puñado *m*.

hand gre·nade granada *f* de mano.

hand·i·cap 1 *n (physical)* minusvalía *f*; *(in sport)* hándicap *m*. **2** *vt* impedir.

hand·i·capped adj (physically) minusválido, -a; (mentally) retrasado, -a; fig desfavorecido, -a.

hand·ker·chief pañuelo m.

han·dle 1 n (of knife) mango m; (of cup) asa f; (of door) pomo m; (of drawer) tirador m. **2** vt manejar; (problem) encargarse de; (people) tratar; 'h. with care' 'frágil'.

han·dle·bars npl manillar m.

hand lug·gage equipaje m de mano.

hand·made adj hecho, -a a mano.

hand·out (leaflet) folleto m; (charity) limosna f.

hand·rail pasamanos m inv.

hand·shake apretón m de manos.

hand·some adj (person) guapo, -a; (substantial) considerable.

hand·writ·ing letra f.

hand·y adj (useful) útil; (nearby) a mano; (dexterous) diestro, -a.

hand·y·man manitas m inv.

hang* 1 vt colgar; (head) bajar. **2** vi colgar (from de); (in air) flotar; (criminal) ser ahorcado, -a; **to h. oneself** ahorcarse.

► **hang around 1** vi fam no hacer nada; (wait) esperar. **2** vt (bar etc) frecuentar.

► **hang on** vi agarrarse; (wait) esperar; **to h. on to sth** (keep) guardar.

► **hang out 1** vt (washing) tender. **2** vi **his tongue was hanging out** le colgaba la lengua.

► **hang up** vt (picture, telephone) colgar.

han·gar hangar m.

hang·er percha f.

hang·glid·er alta f delta.

hang·o·ver resaca f.

hang-up fam (complex) complejo m.

hap·pen vi suceder, ocurrir; **if you h. to see my friend** si por casualidad ves a mi amigo.

hap·pen·ing acontecimiento m.

hap·pi·ly adv (with pleasure) felizmente; (fortunately) afortunadamente.

hap·pi·ness felicidad f.

hap·py adj feliz; **h. birthday!** ¡feliz cumpleaños!

ha·rass vt acosar.

ha·rass·ment hostigamiento m, acoso m.

har·bor 1 n puerto m. **2** vt (criminal) encubrir; (doubts) abrigar.

hard 1 adj duro, -a; (solid) sólido, -a; (difficult) difícil; (harsh) severo, -a; (strict) estricto, -a; **h. of hearing** duro, -a de oído; **to be h. up** estar sin blanca; **to take a h. line** tomar medidas severas; **h. drugs** droga f dura; **a h. worker** un trabajador concienzudo; **h. luck!** ¡mala suerte!; **h. evidence** pruebas definitivas; **h. currency** divisa f fuerte. **2** adv (forcibly) fuerte; (with application) mucho.

hard·ball béisbol m.

hard-boiled adj duro, -a.

hard-core adj irreductible.

hard disk disco m duro.

hard·en 1 vt endurecer. **2** vi endurecerse.

hard·ly adv apenas; **h. anyone/ ever** casi nadie/nunca; **he had h. begun when …** apenas había comenzado cuando ….

hard·ness dureza f; (difficulty) dificultad f.

hard·ship privación f.

hard·ware (goods) ferretería f; (computer equipment) hardware m; **h. store** ferretería f.

hard-wear·ing adj duradero, -a.

hard-work·ing adj muy trabajador, -a.

hare liebre f.

harm 1 n daño m. **2** vt hacer daño a.

harm·ful adj perjudicial (**to** para).

harm·less adj inofensivo, -a.

har·mon·i·ca armónica f.

har·mo·ni·ous adj armonioso, -a.

har·mo·ny armonía f.

har·ness 1 n (for horse) arreos mpl. **2** vt (horse) enjaezar.

harp arpa f.

► **harp on** vi fam hablar sin parar; **to**

h. on about sth hablar sin parar sobre algo.

harsh *adj* severo, -a; *(voice)* áspero, -a; *(sound)* discordante.

harsh·ly *adv* duramente.

harsh·ness dureza *f*, *(discordancy)* discordancia *f*.

har·vest 1 *n* cosecha *f*, *(of grapes)* vendimia *f*. **2** *vt* cosechar, recoger.

has *3rd person sing pres of* **have**.

has·sle *fam* **1** *n (nuisance)* rollo *m*; *(problem)* lío *m*; *(wrangle)* bronca *f*. **2** *vt* fastidiar.

haste prisa *f*.

has·ten *vi* apresurarse.

has·ti·ly *adv (quickly)* de prisa.

hast·y *adj* apresurado, -a; *(rash)* precipitado, -a.

hat sombrero *m*.

hatch[1] escotilla *f*, serving h. ventanilla *f*.

hatch[2] **1** *vt (egg)* empollar. **2** *vi (bird)* salir del huevo.

hatch·back coche *m* de 3/5 puertas.

hate 1 *n* odio *m*. **2** *vt* odiar.

hate·ful *adj* odioso, -a.

ha·tred odio *m*.

haul 1 *n (journey)* trayecto *m*. **2** *vt* tirar; *(drag)* arrastrar.

haunt 1 *n* guarida *f*. **2** *vt (of ghost)* aparecerse en; *fig* atormentar; *(frequent)* frecuentar.

haunt·ed *adj* embrujado, -a.

have* *vt* tener; *(party, meeting)* hacer; **h. you got a car?** ¿tienes coche?; **to h. a cigarette** fumarse un cigarrillo; **to h. breakfast/lunch/tea/dinner** desayunar/comer/merendar/cenar; **what will you h.?** ¿qué quieres tomar?; **can I h. your pen for a moment?** *(borrow)* ¿me dejas tu bolígrafo un momento? ▪ **to h. to** *(obligation)* tener que, deber; **I h. to go now** tengo que irme ya. ▪ *(make happen)* hacer; **I'll h. someone come around** haré que venga alguien. **2** *v aux (compound)* haber; **yes I h.!** ¡que sí!; **you haven't**

seen my book, h. you? no has visto mi libro, ¿verdad?; **he's been to France, hasn't he?** ha estado en Francia, ¿verdad?

▸**have on** *vt (wear)* vestir; *fam* **to h. sb on** tomarle el pelo a algn.

▸**have out** *vt* **to h. it out with sb** ajustar cuentas con algn.

▸**have over** *vt (invite)* recibir.

hav·oc to play h. with hacer estragos en.

hawk halcón *m*.

hay heno *m*.

hay fe·ver fiebre *f* del heno.

hay·stack almiar *m*.

haz·ard 1 *n* peligro *m*, riesgo *m*. **2** *vt* arriesgar; **to h. a guess** intentar adivinar.

haze *(mist)* neblina *f*.

ha·zel·nut avellana *f*.

haz·y *adj* nebuloso, -a.

he *pers pron* él; **he who** el que.

head 1 *n* cabeza *f*; *(mind)* mente *f*; *(of company)* director, -a *mf*; *(of coin)* cara *f*; **to be h. over heels in love** estar locamente enamorado, -a; **to keep one's h.** mantener la calma; **to lose one's h.** perder la cabeza; **heads or tails** cara o cruz. **2** *adj* principal; **h. office** sede *f*. **3** *vt (list etc)* encabezar.

▸**head for** *vt* dirigirse hacia.

head·ache dolor *m* de cabeza; *fig* quebradero *m* de cabeza.

head·band cinta *f* para la cabeza

head·ing título *m*; *(of letter)* membrete *m*.

head·light faro *m*.

head·line titular *m*.

head·mas·ter director *m*.

head·mis·tress directora *f*.

head·phones *npl* auriculares *mpl*.

▸**head·quar·ters** *npl* oficina *f* central; *(military)* cuartel *m* general.

head teach·er director, -a *mf*.

head·wait·er jefe *m* de comedor.

head·way to make h. avanzar.

heal 1 *vi* cicatrizar. **2** *vt* curar.

health salud *f*; *fig* prosperidad *f*; **to**

be in good/bad h. estar bien/mal de salud; **h. foods** alimentos *mpl* naturales; **h. service** ≃ Insalud *m*.

health·y *adj* sano, -a; *(good for health)* saludable.

heap 1 *n* montón *m*. **2** *vt* amontonar; *(praises)* colmar de; **to h. praises on sb** colmar a algn de elogios.

hear* *vt* oír; *(listen to)* escuchar; *(find òut)* enterarse de; *(evidence)* oír; **I won't h. of it!** ¡ni hablar!; **to h. from sb** tener noticias de algn.

hear·ing oído *m*; *(legal)* audiencia *f*.

hear·ing aid audífono *m*.

hearse coche *m* fúnebre.

heart corazón *m*; **hearts** corazones; **al h.** en el fondo; **to lose h.** desanimarse.

heart at·tack infarto *m* (de miocardio).

heart·beat latido *m* del corazón.

heart·break·ing *adj* desgarrador, -a.

heart·en·ing *adj* alentador, -a.

heart·y *adj* (person) francote; *(meal)* abundante; **to have a h. appetite** ser de buen comer.

heat 1 *n* calor *m*; *(in sport)* eliminatoria *f*. **2** *vt* calentar.

▸**heat up** *vi (warm up)* calentarse.

heat·er calentador *m*.

heath *(land)* brezal *m*.

heath·er brezo *m*.

heat·ing calefacción *f*.

heat·wave ola *f* de calor.

heave *vt (lift)* levantar; *(haul)* tirar; *(push)* empujar; *(throw)* arrojar.

heav·en cielo *m*; **for heaven's sake!** ¡por Dios!

heav·i·ly *adv* it rained h. llovió mucho; **to sleep h.** dormir profundamente.

heav·y 1 *adj* pesado, -a; *(rain, meal)* fuerte; *(traffic)* denso, -a; *(loss)* grande; **is it h.?** ¿pesa mucho?; **a h. drinker/smoker** un, -a bebedor, -a/ fumador, -a empedernido, -a.

heav·y·weight peso *m* pesado.

He·brew 1 *adj* hebreo, -a; **2** *n*

(person) hebreo -a *mf*; *(language)* hebreo *m*.

hec·tic *adj* agitado, -a.

hedge 1 *n* seto *m*. **2** *vt* **to h. one's bets** cubrirse.

hedge·hog erizo *m*.

heel talón *m*; *(of shoe)* tacón *m*.

heft·y *adj (person)* fornido, -a; *(package)* pesado, -a.

height altura *f*; *(of person)* estatura *f*; **what h. are you?** ¿cuánto mides?

heir heredero *m*.

heir·ess heredera *f*.

held *pt & pp* of **hold**.

hel·i·cop·ter helicóptero *m*.

hell infierno *m*; *fam* **what the h. are you doing?** ¿qué diablos estás haciendo?; *fam* **go to h.!** ¡vete a hacer puñetas!; *fam* **a h. of a party** una fiesta estupenda; *fam* **she's had a h. of a day** ha tenido un día fatal; *fam* **h.!** ¡demonios!

hel·lo *interj* ¡hola!; *(on phone)* ¡diga!; *(showing surprise)* ¡hala!

helm timón *m*.

hel·met casco *m*.

help 1 *n* ayuda *f*; **h.!** ¡socorro!; **(daily) h.** asistenta *f*. **2** *vt* ayudar; **can I h. you?** *(in shop)* ¿qué desea?; **h. yourself!** *(to food etc)* ¡sírvete!; **I couldn't h. laughing** no pude evitar reírme; **I can't h. it** no lo puedo remediar.

▸**help out** *vt* **to h. sb out** echarle una mano a algn.

help·er ayudante, -a *mf*.

help·ful *adj (person)* amable; *(thing)* útil.

help·ing ración *f*.

help·less *adj (defenseless)* desamparado, -a; *(powerless)* impotente.

hem dobladillo *m*.

▸**hem in** *vt* cercar, rodear.

hem·i·sphere hemisferio *m*.

hem·or·rhage hemorragia *f*.

hen gallina *f*.

hep·a·ti·tis hepatitis *f*.

her 1 *poss adj (one thing)* su; *(more than one)* sus; *(to distinguish male* *from female)* de ella; **are they h. books or his?** ¿los libros son de ella o de él? **2** *object pron (direct object)* la; **I saw h. recently** la vi hace poco. ▪ *(indirect object)* le; *(with other third person pronouns)* se; **he gave h. money** le dio dinero; **they handed it to h.** se lo entregaron. ▪ *(after prep)* ella; **for h.** para ella. ▪ *(emphatic)* ella; **look, it's h.!** ¡mira, es ella!

herb hierba *f*; **herb tea** infusión *f*.

herd *(of cattle)* manada *f*, *(of goats)* rebaño *m*.

here 1 *adv* aquí; **h.!** ¡presente!; **you are!** ¡toma! **2** *interj* **look h., you can't do that!** ¡oiga, no puede hacer eso!

he·red·i·tar·y *adj* hereditario, -a.

her·mit ermitaño, -a *mf*.

he·ro *(pl heroes)* héroe *m*; *(in novel)* protagonista *m*.

he·ro·ic *adj* heroico, -a.

her·o·in heroína *f*.

her·o·ine heroína *f*; *(in novel)* protagonista *f*.

her·ring arenque *m*.

hers *poss pron (attribute) (one thing)* suyo, -a; *(more than one)* suyos, -as; *(to distinguish male from female)* de ella; **they are h.** not his son de ella, no de él. ▪ *(one thing)* el suyo, la suya; *(more than one)* los suyos, las suyas.

her·self *pers pron (reflexive)* se; **she dressed h.** se vistió. ▪ *(alone)* ella misma; **she was by h.** estaba sola. ▪ *(emphatic)* **she told me so h.** eso me dijo ella misma.

hes·i·tant *adj* vacilante.

hes·i·tate *vi* vacilar.

hes·i·ta·tion indecisión *f*.

het up *adj* nervioso, -a.

hey *interj* ¡oye!; ¡oiga!

hi *interj* ¡hola!

hic·cup hipo *m*; *(minor problem)* problemilla *m*; **to have hiccups** tener hipo.

hide¹* 1 *vt (conceal)* esconder;

(obscure) ocultar. **2** *vi* esconderse, ocultarse.

hide² *(skin)* piel *f*.

hide-and-seek escondite *m*.

hid·e·ous *adj (horrific)* horroroso, -a; *(extremely ugly)* espantoso, -a.

hide·ous·ly *adv* horrorosamente.

hide-out escondrijo *m*.

hid·ing a good h. una buena paliza.

hid·ing place escondite *m*.

hi·er·ar·chy jerarquía *f*.

hi-fi hifi *m*.

high 1 *adj* alto, -a; *(price)* elevado, -a; *(drugged)* colocado, -a; **how h. is that wall?** ¿qué altura tiene esa pared?; **it's three feet h.** tiene tres pies de alto; **h. wind** viento *m* fuerte; **to have a h. opinion of sb** tener muy buena opinión de algn. **2** *adv* alto; **to fly h.** volar a gran altura.

high-class *adj* de alta categoría.

high den·si·ty *adj* de alta densidad.

high·er *adj* superior; **h. education** enseñanza *f* superior.

high·lands *npl* tierras *fpl* altas.

high·light 1 *n (in hair)* reflejo *m*; *(of event)* atracción *f* principal. **2** *vt* hacer resaltar; *(with highlighter)* subrayar con marcador.

high·light·er marcador *m*.

high·ly *adv (very)* sumamente; **to speak h. of sb** hablar muy bien de algn.

high-pitched *adj* estridente.

high-pro·file *adj (person)* prominente, destacado(a); *(campaign)* de gran alcance.

high-rise *adj* **h. building** rascacielos *m inv*.

high school instituto *m* de enseñanza media.

high-speed *adj* **h. train** tren *m* de alta velocidad.

high street calle *f* mayor.

high-tech *adj* de alta tecnología.

high·way autopista *f*.

hi·jack 1 *vt* secuestrar. **2** *n* secuestro *m*.

hi·jack·er secuestrador, -a *mf*; *(of planes)* pirata *mf* del aire.

hi·jack·ing secuestro *m*.

hike 1 *n (walk)* excursión *f*. **2** *vi* ir de excursión.

hik·er excursionista *mf*.

hi·lar·i·ous *adj* graciosísimo, -a.

hill colina *f*; *(slope)* cuesta *f*.

hill·side ladera *f*.

hill·y *adj* accidentado, -a.

him *object pron (direct object)* lo, le; **hit h.!** ¡pégale!; **she loves h.** lo quiere. ▪ *(indirect object)* le; *(with other third person pronouns)* se; **give h. the money** dale el dinero; **give it to h.** dáselo. ▪ *(after prep)* él; **it's not like h. to say that** no es propio de él decir eso. ▪ *(emphatic)* él; **it's h.** es él.

him·self *pers pron (reflexive)* se; **he hurt h.** se hizo daño. ▪ *(alone)* por sí mismo; **by h.** solo. ▪ *(emphatic)* él mismo; **he told me so h.** me lo dijo él mismo.

hin·der *vt* dificultar.

Hin·du *adj & n* hindú *(mf)*.

hinge bisagra *f*.

▶**hinge on** *vt* depender de.

hint 1 *n* indirecta *f*, *(clue)* pista *f*; *(advice)* consejo *m*. **2** *vi* lanzar indirectas. **3** *vt (imply)* insinuar.

▶**hint at** *vt* aludir a.

hip cadera *f*.

hip·po·pot·a·mus hipopótamo *m*.

hire *vt (rent)* alquilar; *(employ)* contratar.

his 1 *poss adj (one thing)* su; *(more than one)* sus; *(to distinguish male from female)* de él; **he washed h. face** se lavó la cara; **is it h. dog or hers?** ¿el perro es de él o de ella? **2** *poss pron (attribute) (one thing)* suyo, -a; *(more than one)* suyos, -as; *(to distinguish male from female)* de él. ▪ *(one thing)* el suyo, la suya; *(more than one)* los suyos, las suyas.

His·pan·ic 1 *adj* hispánico, -a. **2** *n* hispano, -a *mf*.

hiss 1 *n* siseo *m*; *(in theater)* silbido *m*. **2** *vti* silbar.

his·tor·ic *adj* histórico, -a.

his·tor·i·cal *adj* histórico, -a.

his·to·ry historia *f*.

hit 1 *n (blow)* golpe *m*; *(success)* éxito *m*. **2** *vt* (strike)* pegar; *(affect)* afectar; **he was h. in the leg** le dieron en la pierna; **the car h. the kerb** el coche chocó contra el bordillo.

▶**hit back** *vi (reply to criticism)* replicar.

▶**hit out** *vi* **to h. out at sb** atacar a algn.

▶**hit (up)on** *vt* dar con; **we h. on the idea of ...** se nos ocurrió la idea de ....

hit-and-run driv·er conductor *m* que atropella a algn y no para.

hitch 1 *n* dificultad *f*. **2** *vi (hitchhike)* hacer autostop.

hitch·hike *vi* hacer autostop.

hitch·hik·er autostopista *mf*.

hitch·hik·ing autostop *m*.

HIV *abbr of* **human immunodeficiency virus** virus *m* de inmunodeficiencia humano, VIH *m*; **to be HIV positive/negative** ser/no ser seropositivo, -a.

hive colmena *f*.

hoard 1 *n (provisions)* reservas *fpl*; *(money etc)* tesoro *m*. **2** *vt (objects)* acumular; *(money)* atesorar.

hoard·ing *(billboard)* valla *f* publicitaria.

hoarse *adj* ronco, -a; **to be h.** tener la voz ronca.

hoax *(joke)* broma *f* pesada; *(trick)* engaño *m*.

hob·by pasatiempo *m*.

ho·bo vagabundo, -a *mf*.

hock·ey hockey *m*.

hold 1 *vt* (keep in hand)* tener (en la mano); *(grip)* agarrar; *(opinion)* sostener; *(contain)* dar cabida a; *(meeting)* celebrar; *(reserve) (ticket)* guardar; *(at police station etc)* detener; *(office)* ocupar; **to h. sb's hand** cogerle la mano a algn; **the jug**

holds a liter en la jarra cabe un litro; **to h. one's breath** contener la respiración; **to h. sb hostage** retener a algn como rehén; **to h. the line** no colgar. **2** vi* (rope) aguantar; (offer) ser válido, -a. **3** n (in ship) bodega f; (control) control m; **to get h. of** (grip) coger; (get in touch with) localizar.

►**hold back** vt (crowd) contener; (feelings) reprimir; (truth) ocultar; (suspect) retener; (store) guardar.

►**hold down** vt (control) dominar; (job) desempeñar.

►**hold on** vi (keep a firm grasp) agarrarse bien; (wait) esperar; **h. on!** (on phone) ¡no cuelgue!

►**hold on to** vt (to stop oneself from falling) agarrarse a; (to stop something from falling) agarrar; (keep) guardar.

►**hold out** **1** vt (hand) tender. **2** vi (last) (things) durar; (person) resistir.

►**hold up** vt (support) apuntalar; (rob) (train) asaltar; (bank) atracar; (delay) retrasar; **we were held up for half an hour** sufrimos media hora de retraso.

hold·er (receptacle) recipiente m; (owner) poseedor, -a mf; (bearer) portador, -a mf; (of passport) titular mf.

hold·up (robbery) atraco m; (delay) retraso m; (in traffic) atasco m.

hole agujero m; (large, in golf) hoyo m.

hol·i·day (one day) día m (de) fiesta f; (several days) vacaciones fpl.

hol·low **1** adj hueco, -a; (cheeks, eyes) hundido, -a. **2** n hueco m.

hol·ly acebo m.

ho·ly adj sagrado, -a; (blessed) bendito, -a.

Ho·ly Ghost Espíritu m Santo.

home 1 n casa f, hogar m; (institution) asilo m; (country) patria f; **at h.** en casa; **make yourself at h.!** ¡estás en tu casa!; **old people's h.** asilo m de ancianos; **to play at h.** jugar en

casa. **2** adj (domestic) del hogar; (political) interior; (native) natal; **h. affairs** asuntos mpl interiores. **3** adv en casa; **to go h.** irse a casa; **to leave h.** irse de casa.

home com·put·er ordenador m doméstico.

home help asistenta f.

home·land patria f; (birthplace) tierra f natal.

home·less 1 adj sin hogar. **2** npl **the h.** los sin hogar.

home·made adj casero, -a.

home·sick adj **to be h.** tener morriña.

home·town ciudad f natal.

home·work deberes mpl.

ho·mo·sex·u·al adj & n homosexual (mf).

Hon·du·ran adj & n hondureño, -a (mf).

hon·est adj honrado, -a; (sincere) sincero, -a; (fair) justo, -a.

hon·est·ly adv honradamente; **h.?** ¿de verdad?

hon·es·ty honradez f.

hon·ey miel f, fam (endearment) cariño m.

hon·ey·moon luna f de miel.

honk vi (person in car) tocar la bocina.

hon·or 1 n honor m. **2** vt (respect) honrar; (obligation) cumplir.

hon·or·a·ble adj (person) honrado, -a; (actions) honroso, -a.

hood (of garment) capucha f; (of car) capota f; (bonnet) capó m.

hoof (pl hoofs or hooves) (of horse) casco m; (of cow, sheep) pezuña f.

hook gancho m; (for fishing) anzuelo m; **to take the phone off the h.** descolgar el teléfono.

►**hook up** vti conectar (with con).

hooked adj (nose) aguileño, -a; (addicted) enganchado, -a (on a); **to get h.** engancharse.

hook·y **to play h.** hacer novillos.

hoo·li·gan gamberro, -a mf.

hoop aro m.

hoot 1 *n (owl)* grito *m*; **hoots of laughter** carcajadas *fpl*. **2** *vi (owl)* ulular; *(train)* silbar; *(siren)* pitar.

Hoo·ver® **1** *n* aspiradora *f*. **2** *vt* to h. pasar la aspiradora a.

hop 1 *vi* saltar; **to h. on one leg** andar a la pata coja. **2** *n (small jump)* brinco *m*.

hope 1 *n* esperanza *f*; *(false)* ilusión *f*; **to have little h. of doing sth** tener pocas posibilidades de hacer algo. **2** *vti* esperar; **I h. so/not** espero que sí/no.

▸ **hope for** *vt* esperar.

hope·ful *adj (confident)* optimista; *(promising)* prometedor, -a.

hope·ful·ly *adv* **h. she won't come** esperemos que no venga.

hope·less *adj* desesperado, -a; **to be h. at sports** ser negado, -a para los deportes.

hope·less·ly *adv* desesperadamente; **h. lost** completamente perdido, -a.

hops *npl* lúpulo *m*.

hop·scotch to play h. jugar al tejo.

ho·ri·zon horizonte *m*.

hor·i·zon·tal *adj* horizontal.

horn cuerno *m*; *(on car)* bocina *f*.

hor·ri·ble *adj* horrible.

hor·ri·bly *adv* horriblemente.

hor·rif·ic *adj* horrendo, -a.

hor·ri·fy *vt* horrorizar.

hor·ror horror *m*; **a little h.** un diablillo.

hor·ror film película *f* de terror.

horse caballo *m*.

horse·back on h. a caballo.

horse·pow·er caballo *m* (de vapor).

horse race carrera *f* de caballos.

horse·shoe herradura *f*.

hose *(pipe)* manguera *f*.

hose·pipe manguera *f*.

hos·pi·ta·ble *adj* hospitalario, -a.

hos·pi·tal hospital *m*.

hos·pi·tal·i·ty hospitalidad *f*.

hos·pi·tal·ize *vt* hospitalizar.

host 1 *n (at home)* anfitrión *m*; *(on TV)* presentador *m*. **2** *vt (TV show etc)* presentar.

hos·tage rehén *m*; **to take sb h.** tomar a algn como rehén.

hos·tel hostal *m*.

host·ess *(at home etc)* anfitriona *f*; *(on TV)* presentadora *f*.

hos·tile *adj* hostil.

hos·til·i·ty hostilidad *f*.

hot *adj* caliente; *(weather)* caluroso, -a; *(spicy)* picante; *(temper)* fuerte; **it's very h.** hace mucho calor; **to feel h.** tener calor; **it's not so h.** *(not very good)* no es nada del otro mundo.

hot·cake crepe *f*, panqueque *m*, *Esp* tortita *f*.

hot dog perrito *m* caliente.

ho·tel hotel *m*.

hot-wa·ter bot·tle bolsa *f* de agua caliente.

hound 1 *n* perro *m* de caza. **2** *vt* acosar.

hour hora *f*; **60 miles an h.** 60 millas por hora; **by the h.** por horas.

hour·ly 1 *adj* cada hora. **2** *adv* por horas.

house 1 *n* casa *f*; *(in theater)* sala *f*; **at my h.** en mi casa. **2** *vt* alojar; *(store)* guardar.

house·hold hogar *m*; **h. products** productos *mpl* domésticos.

house·keep·ing administración *f* doméstica.

house-warm·ing par·ty fiesta *f* que se da al estrenar casa.

house·wife ama *f* de casa.

house·work trabajo *m* doméstico.

hous·ing vivienda *f*.

hous·ing es·tate urbanización *f*.

hov·el casucha *f*.

hov·er *vi (bird)* cernerse; *(helicopter)* permanecer inmóvil (en el aire).

hov·er·craft aerodeslizador *m*.

how *adv* ¿cómo?; **h. are you?** ¿cómo estás?; **h. do you do?** mucho gusto; **h. funny!** ¡qué divertido!; **h. about ...?** ¿y si ...?; **h. about a stroll?** ¿qué te parece un paseo?; **h. old is**

she? ¿cuántos años tiene?; **h. tall are you?** ¿cuánto mides?; ¿h. **many?** ¿cuántos, -as?; **h. much?** ¿cuánto, -a?

how·ev·er adv no obstante, sin embargo; **h. difficult it may be** por difícil que sea; **h. much** por mucho que (+ subjunctive).

howl 1 n aullido m. **2** vi aullar.

HQ abbr of headquarters.

hub·cap tapacubos m inv.

hud·dle 1 n grupo m. **2** vi **to h. (up** or **together)** acurrucarse.

hug 1 vt abrazar. **2** n abrazo m.

huge adj enorme.

hull casco m.

hum 1 vt (tune) tararear. **2** vi (bees, engine) zumbar. **3** n (of bees) zumbido m.

hu·man 1 adj humano, -a; **h. race** raza f humana. **2** n ser m humano.

hu·man be·ing ser m humano.

hu·man·i·ty humanidad f, **the humanities** las humanidades.

hum·ble adj humilde.

hu·mid adj húmedo, -a.

hu·mid·i·ty humedad f.

hu·mil·i·ate vt humillar.

hu·mil·i·a·tion humillación f.

hu·mor humor m.

hu·mor·ous adj (person, story) gracioso, -a; (writer) humorístico, -a.

hump (on back) joroba f, (small hill) montículo m.

hunch (idea) corazonada f.

hun·dred 1 n cien m, ciento m; (rough number) centenar m; **a h. and twenty-five** ciento veinticinco; **five h.** quinientos, -ás. **2** adj cien; **a h. people** cien personas; **a h. per cent** cien por cien; **two h. chairs** doscientas sillas.

hun·dredth adj & n centésimo, -a (mf).

Hun·gar·i·an adj & n húngaro, -a (mf).

hun·ger hambre m; **h. strike** huelga m de hambre.

hun·gry adj **to be h.** tener hambre.

hunt 1 vt cazar. **2** vi (for game)

cazar; (search) buscar. **3** n caza f, (search) búsqueda f.

▶ **hunt down** vt perseguir.

hunt·er cazador, -a mf.

hunt·ing caza f, (expedition) cacería f.

hur·dle (in sport) valla f, fig obstáculo m.

hurl vt lanzar.

hur·rah, hur·ray interj ¡hurra!; **h. for John!** ¡viva John!

hur·ri·cane huracán m.

hur·ry 1 vi darse prisa. **2** vt meter prisa a. **3** n **to be in a h.** tener prisa.

▶ **hurry up** vi (go faster) darse prisa.

hurt 1 vt* hacer daño a; (wound) herir; (mentally) ofender. **2** vi* doler; **my arm hurts** me duele el brazo. **3** adj (physically) herido, -a; (mentally) dolido, -a.

hus·band marido m, esposo m.

hush 1 n silencio m. **2** interj ¡silencio!

hus·tle 1 vt (jostle) empujar; (hurry along) meter prisa a. **2** n **h. and bustle** ajetreo m.

hut cabaña f, (shed) cobertizo m.

hy·dro·gen hidrógeno m.

hy·giene higiene f.

hy·gien·ic adj higiénico, -a.

hymn himno m; **h. book** cantoral m.

hy·per·mar·ket hipermercado m.

hy·phen guión m.

hy·phen·at·ed adj (word) (escrito, -a) con guión.

hyp·no·tize vt hipnotizar.

hy·poc·ri·sy hipocresía f.

hyp·o·crite hipócrita mf.

hy·poth·e·sis (pl hypotheses) hipótesis f.

hys·ter·i·cal adj histérico, -a.

hys·ter·i·cal·ly adv (to cry) histéricamente.

I

I *pers pron* yo.
ice hielo *m*.
ice·berg iceberg *m*.
ice-cold *adj* helado, -a.
ice cream helado *m*.
ice cube cubito *m* de hielo.
ice-skat·ing patinaje *m* sobre hielo.
i·ci·cle carámbano *m*.
ic·ing alcorza *f*.
ic·ing sug·ar azúcar *m* glas.
i·con icono *m*.
ic·y *adj (road etc)* helado, -a; *(smile)* glacial.
ID ID card documento *m* nacional de identidad, DNI *m*.
i·de·a idea *f*.
i·de·al *adj & n* ideal *(m)*.
i·de·al·ly *adv (if possible)* de ser posible.
i·den·ti·cal *adj* idéntico, -a.
i·den·ti·fi·ca·tion identificación *f*; *(papers)* documentación *f*.
i·den·ti·fy 1 *vt* identificar. **2** *vi* identificarse *(with* con).
i·den·ti·ty identidad *f*.
id·i·om modismo *m*.
id·i·ot idiota *mf*.
id·i·ot·ic *adj* idiota.
i·dle *adj* holgazán, -ana; *(not working) (person)* desempleado, -a.
i·dol ídolo *m*.
i·dol·ize *vt* idolatrar.
i.e. *abbr* a saber.
if *conj* si; **if I were rich** si fuera rico, -a; **if I were you** yo en tu lugar.
ig·loo iglú *m*.
ig·no·rance ignorancia *f*.
ig·no·rant *adj* ignorante *(of* de).
ig·nore *vt (warning, remark)* no hacer caso de; *(behavior, fact)* pasar por alto.
ill 1 *adj* enfermo, -a; *(bad)* malo, -a. **2** *n* mal *m*.

il·le·gal *adj* ilegal.
il·leg·i·ble *adj* ilegible.
il·lit·er·ate *adj* analfabeto, -a.
ill·ness enfermedad *f*.
il·lu·sion ilusión *f*.
il·lus·trate *vt* ilustrar.
il·lus·tra·tion ilustración *f*.
im·age imagen *f*.
i·mag·i·nar·y *adj* imaginario, -a.
i·mag·i·na·tion imaginación *f*.
i·mag·ine *vt* imaginarse; *(think)* suponer.
im·be·cile *fam* imbécil *mf*.
im·i·tate *vt* imitar.
im·i·ta·tion 1 *n* imitación *f*. **2** *adj* de imitación.
im·mac·u·late *adj* impecable.
im·ma·ture *adj* inmaduro, -a.
im·me·di·ate *adj* inmediato, -a.
im·me·di·ate·ly 1 *adv* inmediatamente. **2** *conj (as soon as)* en cuanto.
im·mense *adj* inmenso, -a.
im·mensely *adv* sumamente.
im·mi·grant *adj & n* inmigrante *(mf)*.
im·mi·gra·tion inmigración *f*.
im·mi·nent *adj* inminente.
im·mor·tal *adj* inmortal.
im·mune *adj* inmune.
im·mu·nize *vt* inmunizar *(against* contra).
im·pact impacto *m*; *(crash)* choque *m*.
im·pa·tience impaciencia *f*.
im·pa·tient *adj* impaciente.
im·pa·tient·ly *adv* con impaciencia.
im·per·a·tive *(form of verb)* imperativo *m*.
im·per·son·ate *vt* hacerse pasar por; *(famous people)* imitar.
im·per·son·a·tor *(on TV etc)* imitador, -a *mf*.
im·per·ti·nent *adj* impertinente.
im·pe·tus ímpetu *m*; *fig* impulso *m*.
im·ple·ment 1 *n (tool)* herramienta *f*. **2** *vt (decision, plan)* llevar a cabo.
im·pli·ca·tion implicación *f*; *(consequence)* consecuencia *f*.

im·plic·it adj (implied) implícito, -a; (trust) absoluto, -a; (faith) incondicional.

im·ply vt (hint) dar a entender.

im·po·lite adj maleducado, -a.

im·port 1 n importación f. **2** vt importar.

im·por·tance importancia f; **of little i.** de poca importancia.

im·por·tant adj importante; **it's not i.** no importa.

im·port·er importador, -a mf.

im·pose 1 vt imponer (**on, upon** a). **2** vi **to i. on** o **upon** (take advantage of) abusar de.

im·pos·ing adj imponente.

im·po·si·tion would it be an i. if …? ¿le molestaría si …?

im·pos·si·bil·i·ty imposibilidad f.

im·pos·si·ble adj imposible.

im·pos·tor impostor, -a mf.

im·prac·ti·cal adj poco práctico, -a.

im·press vt impresionar.

im·pres·sion impresión f; **to be under the i. that …** tener la impresión de que …

im·pres·sive adj impresionante.

im·pris·on vt encarcelar.

im·prob·a·ble adj improbable.

im·prop·er adj (indecent) indecente.

im·prove 1 vt mejorar. **2** vi mejorarse.

▸ **improve on** vt superar.

im·prove·ment mejora f.

im·pro·vise vti improvisar.

im·pu·dent adj insolente.

im·pulse impulso m.

im·pul·sive adj irreflexivo, -a.

im·pul·sive·ly adv de forma impulsiva.

im·pu·ri·ty impureza f.

in 1 prep (place) en; **in prison** en la cárcel; **in the distance** a lo lejos; **she arrived in New York** llegó a Nueva York. • (time) (during) en, durante; **in May/1945** en mayo/1945; **in spring** en primavera; **in the daytime** durante el día; **in the morning** por la mañana. • (time) (within) dentro de. • (time) (after) al cabo de. • (manner) en, de; **in a loud/quiet voice** en voz alta/baja; **in French** en francés; **dressed in blue** vestido, -a de azul; **in uniform** de uniforme. • (ratio, numbers) de; **one in six** uno de cada seis; **two meters in length** dos metros de largo. • (after superlative) de; **the smallest car in the world** el coche más pequeño del mundo. **2** adv **to be in** (at home) estar (en casa); (in fashion) estar de moda; **the bus is in** el autobús ha llegado.

in·a·bil·i·ty incapacidad f.

in·ac·ces·si·ble adj inaccesible.

in·ac·cu·ra·cy (error) inexactitud f.

in·ac·cu·rate adj incorrecto, -a.

in·ad·e·qua·cy (lack) insuficiencia f; (inability) incompetencia f.

in·ad·e·quate adj (lacking) insuficiente; (unsuitable) inadecuado, -a.

in·ap·pro·pri·ate adj (behavior) poco apropiado, -a.

in·au·gu·rate vt (building) inaugurar.

in·au·gu·ra·tion (of building) inauguración f.

Inc, inc abbr of **Incorporated** ≃ S.A.

in·ca·pa·ble adj incapaz (**of doing sth** de hacer algo).

in·cense 1 vt enfurecer. **2** n incienso m.

in·cen·tive incentivo m.

inch pulgada f (approx 2.54 cm).

in·ci·dent incidente m.

in·ci·den·tal·ly adv por cierto, a propósito.

in·cite vt incitar; **to i. sb to do sth** incitar a algn a hacer algo.

in·cite·ment incitación f.

in·cli·na·tion deseo m; **my i. is to stay** yo prefiero quedarme.

in·cline 1 vt **she's incined to be aggressive** tiende a ser agresiva. **2** vi (slope) inclinarse.

in·clude vt incluir (**in** en); (in price)

comprender (**in** en).

in·clud·ing *prep* incluso, inclusive.

in·clu·sive *adj* inclusivo, -a; **the rent is i.** of bills el alquiler incluye las facturas.

in·come ingresos *mpl*; *(from investment)* réditos *mpl.*

in·come tax impuesto *m* sobre la renta.

in·com·pat·i·ble *adj* incompatible (with con).

in·com·pe·tent *adj* incompetente.

in·com·plete *adj* incompleto, -a.

in·con·ceiv·a·ble *adj* inconcebible.

in·con·sid·er·ate *adj* desconsiderado, -a.

in·con·sis·ten·cy inconsecuencia *f.*

in·con·sis·tent *adj* inconsecuente; **your evidence is i. with the facts** su testimonio no concuerda con los hechos.

in·con·spic·u·ous *adj* que pasa desapercibido, -a.

in·con·ven·ience 1 *n* molestia *f*; *(disadvantage)* inconvenientes *mpl*; **the i. of living out here** los inconvenientes de vivir aquí. **2** *vt* molestar.

in·con·ven·ient *adj* molesto, -a; *(time)* inoportuno, -a.

in·cor·po·rate *vt (include)* incluir; *(contain)* contener.

in·cor·rect *adj* incorrecto, -a.

in·crease 1 *n* aumento *m*; *(in number)* incremento; *(in price etc)* subida *f.* **2** *vt* aumentar; *(price etc)* subir. **3** *vi* aumentar.

in·creas·ing *adj* creciente.

in·creas·ing·ly *adv* cada vez más.

in·cred·i·ble *adj* increíble.

in·cred·i·bly *adv* increíblemente.

in·cu·ba·tor incubadora *f.*

in·cur *vt (blame)* incurrir en; *(debt)* contraer; *(loss)* sufrir.

in·cur·a·ble *adj* incurable.

in·de·cent *adj* indecente.

in·de·ci·sive *adj* indeciso, -a.

in·deed *adv (in fact)* efectivamente;

it's very hard i. es verdaderamente difícil; **thank you very much i.** muchísimas gracias.

in·def·i·nite *adj* indefinido, -a.

in·def·i·nite·ly *adv* indefinidamente.

in·de·pend·ence independencia *f.*

in·de·pend·ent *adj* independiente; **to become i.** independizarse.

in·de·pend·ent·ly *adv* independientemente.

in·dex 1 *n (in book)* índice *m*; *(in library)* catálogo *m.* **2** *vt* catalogar.

in·dex card ficha *f.*

in·dex fin·ger dedo *m* índice.

in·dex-linked *adj* sujeto, -a al aumento de la inflación.

In·di·an *adj & n (of America)* indio, -a *(mf)*; *(of India)* hindú *(mf).*

in·di·cate 1 *vt* indicar. **2** *vi (driving)* poner el intermitente.

in·di·ca·tion indicio *m.*

in·di·ca·tor indicador *m*; *(on car)* intermitente *m.*

in·dif·fer·ence indiferencia *f.*

in·dif·fer·ent *adj (uninterested)* indiferente; *(mediocre)* regular.

in·di·ges·tion indigestión *f*; **to have i.** tener un empacho.

in·dig·nant *adj* indignado, -a; **to get i. about sth** indignarse por algo.

in·di·rect *adj* indirecto, -a.

indi·rect·ly *adv* indirectamente.

in·dis·creet *adj* indiscreto, -a.

in·dis·crim·i·nate *adj* indiscriminado, -a.

in·dis·crim·i·nate·ly *adv (at random)* indistintamente, sin criterio.

in·dis·tin·guish·a·ble *adj* indistinguible.

in·di·vid·u·al 1 *adj (separate)* individual; *(for one)* particular; *(characteristic)* particular. **2** *n (person)* individuo *m.*

in·di·vid·u·al·ly *adv* individualmente.

in·door *adj (plant)* interior; **i. pool** piscina cubierta.

in·doors *adv (inside)* dentro (de casa).

in·duce *vt (persuade)* inducir; *(cause)* producir.

in·dulge 1 *vt (child)* consentir; *(person)* complacer; *(whim)* ceder a, satisfacer; **to i. oneself** darse gusto. **2** *vi* darse el gusto (**in** de).

in·dul·gent *adj* indulgente.

in·dus·tri·al *adj* industrial; *(accident)* laboral; **i. dispute** conflicto *m* laboral; **i. estate** polígono *m* industrial.

in·dus·try industria *f.*

in·ed·i·ble *adj* incomible.

in·ef·fec·tive *adj* ineficaz.

in·ef·fi·cien·cy ineficacia *f; (of person)* incompetencia *f.*

in·ef·fi·cient *adj* ineficaz; *(person)* inepto, -a.

in·ept *adj (person)* inepto, -a; *(remark)* estúpido, -a.

in·e·qual·i·ty desigualdad *f.*

in·ev·i·ta·ble *adj* inevitable.

in·ev·i·ta·bly *adv* inevitablemente.

in·ex·cus·a·ble *adj* inexcusable.

in·ex·pen·sive *adj* económico, -a.

in·ex·pe·ri·enced *adj* inexperto, -a.

in·ex·pli·ca·ble *adj* inexplicable.

in·fal·li·ble *adj* infalible.

in·fa·mous *adj* infame.

in·fan·cy infancia *f.*

in·fant niño, -a *mf.*

in·fan·try infantería *f.*

in·fat·u·at·ed *adj* encaprichado, -a (**with** con).

in·fat·u·a·tion encaprichamiento *m.*

in·fect *vt* infectar.

in·fec·tion infección *f.*

in·fec·tious *adj (disease)* infeccioso, -a; *fig* contagioso, -a.

in·fer *vt* inferir (**from** de).

in·fe·ri·or *adj* inferior (**to** a).

in·fe·ri·or·i·ty inferioridad *f.*

in·fest *vt* infestar (**with** de).

in·fi·nite *adj* infinito, -a.

in·fi·nite·ly *adv* infinitamente.

in·fin·i·tive infinitivo *m.*

in·fin·i·ty infinidad *f.*

in·firm *adj (ailing)* enfermizo, -a; *(weak)* débil.

in·flamed *adj* inflamado, -a; **to become i.** inflamarse.

in·flam·ma·tion inflamación *f.*

in·flate *vt* inflar.

in·fla·tion inflación *f.*

in·flex·i·ble *adj* inflexible.

in·flict *vt (damage)* causar (**on** a); *(defeat)* infligir (**on** a).

in·flu·ence 1 *n* influencia *f*; **to be under the i.** *(of drink)* llevar unas copas de más; *(formally)* estar en estado de embriaguez. **2** *vt* influir en.

in·flu·en·tial *adj* influyente.

in·flu·en·za gripe *f.*

in·flux afluencia *f.*

in·fo *fam* información *f.*

in·form *vt* informar (**of, about** de, sobre).

in·for·mal *adj (occasion, behavior)* informal; *(language, treatment)* familiar; *(unofficial)* no oficial.

in·for·mal·ly *adv (to speak, behave)* de manera informal.

in·for·ma·tion información *f*; **a piece of i.** un dato.

information technology informática *f.*

in·form·a·tive *adj* informativo, -a.

in·fu·ri·ate *vt* poner furioso, -a.

in·fu·ri·at·ing *adj* exasperante.

in·gen·ious *adj* ingenioso, -a.

in·grat·i·tude ingratitud *f.*

in·gre·di·ent ingrediente *m.*

in·hab·it *vt* vivir en, ocupar.

in·hab·i·tant habitante *mf.*

in·hale *vt (gas)* inhalar; *(air)* aspirar.

in·her·it *vt* heredar (**from** de).

in·her·i·tance herencia *f.*

in·hib·it *vt (freedom)* limitar; *(person)* cohibir; **to be inhibited** *(person)* sentirse cohibido, -a.

in·hi·bi·tion cohibición *f.*

in·hos·pi·ta·ble *adj* inhospitalario, -a.

in·hu·man *adj* inhumano, -a.

in·i·tial 1 *adj* inicial. **2** *n* **initials** *(of name)* iniciales *fpl*; *(of abbreviation)* siglas *fpl*.

in·i·tial·ly *adv* al principio.

in·i·ti·ate *vt* iniciar; *(reform)* promover; *(lawsuit)* entablar.

in·ject *vt (drug etc)* inyectar.

in·jec·tion inyección *f*.

in·jure *vt* herir; **to i. oneself** hacerse daño.

in·jured 1 *adj* herido, -a. **2** *npl* **the i.** los heridos.

in·ju·ry herida *f*.

in·jus·tice injusticia *f*.

ink tinta *f*.

ink-jet print·er impresora *f* de chorro de tinta.

in·kling *(idea)* idea *f* vaga, indicio *m*.

in·land 1 *adj* (del) interior. **2** *adv (travel)* tierra adentro.

in-laws *npl* familia *f* política.

in·mate *(of prison)* preso, -a *mf*.

inn *(with lodging)* posada *f*.

in·ner *adj* interior; **i. city** casco *m* urbano.

in·ning *(in baseball)* turno *m* para batear, *Am* inning *m*.

in·no·cence inocencia *f*.

in·no·cent *adj & n* inocente *(mf)*.

in·oc·u·late *vt* inocular.

in·oc·u·la·tion inoculación *f*.

in·put *(of data)* input *m*, entrada *f*.

in·quire 1 *vt* preguntar. **2** *vi* preguntar (**about** por); *(find out)* informarse (**about** de).

▸ **inquire into** *vt* investigar.

in·quir·y pregunta *f*, *(investigation)* investigación *f*; **'inquiries'** 'información'.

in·quis·i·tive *adj* curioso, -a; *(questioning)* preguntón, -ona.

in·sane *adj* loco, -a.

in·san·i·ty locura *f*.

in·scrip·tion *(on stone, coin)* inscripción *f*; *(in book, on photo)* dedicatoria *f*.

in·sect insecto *m*; **i. bite** picadura *f*.

in·sec·ti·cide insecticida *m*.

in·se·cure *adj* inseguro, -a.

in·sen·si·tive *adj* insensible.

in·sen·si·tiv·i·ty insensibilidad *f*.

in·sert *vt* introducir.

in·side 1 *n* interior *m*; **on the i.** por dentro; **to turn sth i. out** volver algo al revés. **2** *adj* interior; **i. lane** carril *m* interior. **3** *adv (be)* dentro, adentro; *(run etc)* (hacia) adentro. **4** *prep (place)* dentro de.

in·sid·er *(of firm)* empleado, -a *mf* de la empresa.

in·sight *(quality)* perspicacia *f*.

in·sig·nif·i·cant *adj* insignificante.

in·sin·cere *adj* poco sincero, -a.

in·sist 1 *vi* insistir (**on** en). **2** *vt* **to i. that …** insistir en que ….

in·sis·tence insistencia *f*.

in·sis·tent *adj* insistente.

in·so·lence insolencia *f*.

in·so·lent *adj* insolente.

in·som·ni·a insomnio *m*.

in·spect *vt* inspeccionar.

in·spec·tion inspección *f*.

in·spec·tor inspector, -a *mf*; *(on bus, train)* revisor, -a *mf*.

in·spi·ra·tion inspiración *f*.

in·spire *vt* inspirar; **to i. respect in sb** infundir respeto a algn.

in·stall *vt* instalar.

in·stall·ment *(of payment)* plazo *m*; *(of novel, program)* entrega *f*.

in·stance caso *m*; **for i.** por ejemplo.

in·stant 1 *n (moment)* instante *m*. **2** *adj* inmediato, -a; *(coffee, meal)* instantáneo, -a.

in·stant·ly *adv* inmediatamente.

in·stant re·play repetición *f*.

in·stead 1 *adv* en cambio. **2** *prep* **i. of** en vez de.

in·stinct instinto *m*.

in·stinc·tive *adj* instintivo, -a.

in·stinc·tive·ly *adv* instintivamente.

in·sti·tu·tion institución *f*.

in·struct *vt* instruir; *(order)* mandar.

in·struc·tion instructions instrucciones *fpl*; **'instructions for use'** 'modo de empleo'.

in·struc·tive adj instructivo, -a.

in·struc·tor instructor, -a mf; (of driving) profesor, -a mf.

in·stru·ment instrumento m.

in·stru·men·tal adj (music) instrumental; **to be i. in sth** contribuir decisivamente a algo.

in·suf·fi·cient adj insuficiente.

in·su·late vt aislar (**against, from** de).

in·su·la·tion aislamiento m.

in·sult 1 n insulto m. **2** vt insultar.

in·sur·ance seguro m; **i. company** compañía f de seguros.

in·sure vt asegurar (**against** contra).

in·tact adj intacto, -a.

in·take (of food) consumo m; (of students, recruits) número m de admitidos.

in·te·grate 1 vt integrar. **2** vi integrarse.

in·teg·ri·ty integridad f, honradez f.

in·tel·lect intelecto m.

in·tel·lec·tu·al adj & n intelectual (mf).

in·tel·li·gence inteligencia f.

in·tel·li·gent adj inteligente.

in·tel·li·gi·ble adj inteligible.

in·tend vt (mean) tener la intención de.

in·tense adj intenso, -a.

in·tense·ly adv (extremely) sumamente.

in·ten·si·fy vt intensificar.

in·ten·si·ty intensidad f.

in·ten·sive adj intensivo, -a; **i. care unit** unidad f de vigilancia intensiva.

in·tent adj **to be i. on doing sth** estar resuelto, -a a hacer algo.

in·ten·tion intención f.

in·ten·tion·al adj deliberado, -a.

in·ten·tion·al·ly adv a propósito.

in·ter·act vi (people) interrelacionarse.

in·ter·ac·tive adj interactivo, -a.

in·ter·cept vt interceptar.

in·ter·change (on motorway) cruce m.

in·ter·change·a·ble adj intercambiable.

in·ter·com (at entrance) portero m automático.

in·ter·con·nect·ed adj (facts etc) interrelacionado, -a.

in·ter·course (sexual) relaciones fpl sexuales.

in·ter·est 1 n interés m; **i. rate** tipo m de interés. **2** vt interesar; **to be interested in** interesarse en; **I'm not interested** no me interesa.

in·ter·est·ing adj interesante.

in·ter·fere vi (meddle) entrometerse (**in** en).

in·ter·fer·ence (meddling) intromisión f; (on radio etc) interferencia f.

in·ter·im 1 n fml **in the i.** en el ínterin. **2** adj interino, -a, provisional.

in·te·ri·or 1 adj interior. **2** n interior m.

in·ter·me·di·ar·y intermediario, -a mf.

in·ter·me·di·ate adj intermedio, -a.

in·ter·mis·sion (at cinema, in theater) intermedio m; (in music) interludio m.

in·tern (doctor) interno, -a mf.

in·ter·nal adj interior; (dispute, injury) interno, -a.

In·ter·nal Rev·e·nue Ser·vice Hacienda f.

in·ter·na·tion·al adj internacional.

in·ter·pret vt interpretar.

in·ter·pret·er intérprete mf.

in·ter·ro·gate vt interrogar.

in·ter·ro·ga·tion interrogatorio m.

in·ter·rupt vti interrumpir.

in·ter·rup·tion interrupción f.

in·ter·sect 1 vt cruzar. **2** vi cruzarse.

in·ter·sec·tion (crossroads) cruce m.

in·ter·state 1 n autopista f interestatal. **2** adj entre estados.

in·ter·val (of time, space) intervalo m.

in·ter·vene *vi (person)* intervenir (**in** en); *(event)* sobrevenir.

in·ter·ven·tion intervención *f.*

in·ter·view 1 *n* entrevista *f.* **2** *vt* entrevistar.

in·ter·view·er entrevistador, -a *mf.*

in·ti·mate *adj* íntimo, -a.

in·tim·i·date *vt* intimidar.

in·to *prep (motion)* en, a; **to get i. a car** subir a un coche; **to go i. a house** entrar a una casa; **to change dollars i. pesos** cambiar dólares en or por pesos; **to translate sth i. French** traducir algo al francés; *fam* **to be i. sth** ser aficionado, -a a algo.

in·tol·er·a·ble *adj* intolerable.

in·tox·i·cate *vt* embriagar.

in·tox·i·cat·ed *adj* borracho, -a.

in·tran·si·tive *adj* intransitivo, -a.

in·tro·duce *vt (person, program)* presentar (**to** a); *(bring in)* introducir (**into**, **to** en).

in·tro·duc·tion *(of person, program)* presentación *f;* *(in book, bringing in)* introducción *f.*

in·trude *vi* entrometerse (**into**, **on** en); *(disturb)* molestar.

in·trud·er intruso, -a *mf.*

in·tru·sion intrusión *f.*

in·tu·i·tion intuición *f.*

in·un·date *vt* inundar (**with** de); **I was inundated with offers** me llovieron las ofertas.

in·vade *vt* invadir.

in·vad·er invasor, -a *mf.*

in·va·lid¹ *(disabled person)* minusválido, -a *mf;* *(sick person)* enfermo, -a *mf.*

in·val·id² *adj* nulo, -a.

in·val·u·a·ble *adj* inestimable.

in·vari·a·bly *adv (always)* invariablemente.

in·va·sion invasión *f.*

in·vent *vt* inventar.

in·ven·tion invento *m.*

in·ven·tor inventor, -a *mf.*

in·ven·to·ry inventario *m.*

in·vert·ed *adj* **(in) i. commas** (entre) comillas *fpl.*

in·vest *vt* invertir (**in** en).

in·ves·ti·gate *vt (crime, subject)* investigar; *(cause, possibility)* estudiar.

in·ves·ti·ga·tion *(of crime)* investigación *f;* *(of cause)* examen *m.*

in·ves·ti·ga·tor investigador, -a *mf.*

in·ves·tor inversor, -a *mf.*

in·vig·or·at·ing *adj* vigorizante.

in·vis·i·ble *adj* invisible.

in·vi·ta·tion invitación *f.*

in·vite *vt* invitar (**to** a); *(comments etc)* solicitar; *(criticism)* provocar.

in·vit·ing *adj (attractive)* atractivo, -a; *(food)* apetitoso, -a.

in·voice 1 *n* factura *f.* **2** *vt* facturar.

in·voke *vt fml* invocar.

in·volve *vt (entail)* suponer; *(concern)* implicar (**in** en); **to be involved in an accident** sufrir un accidente.

in·volved *adj (complicated)* complicado, -a; *(romantically)* enredado, -a.

in·volve·ment *(participation)* participación *f;* *(in crime)* implicación *f;* **emotional i.** relación *f* sentimental.

in·ward 1 *adj* interior. **2** *adv* = **inwards**.

in·wards *adv* hacia dentro.

IQ *abbr of* **intelligence quotient** coeficiente *m* intelectual, CI *m.*

IRA *abbr of* **individual retirement account** cuenta *f* de retiro or jubilación individual.

I·ra·ni·an *adj & n* iraní *(mf).*

I·ra·qi *adj & n* iraquí *(mf).*

i·ris *(of eye)* iris *m inv;* *(plant)* lirio *m.*

I·rish 1 *adj* irlandés, -esa. **2** *npl* **the I.** los irlandeses.

I·rish·man irlandés *m.*

I·rish·wom·an irlandesa *f.*

i·ron 1 *n* hierro *m;* *(for clothes)* plancha *f;* **the i. and steel industry** industria siderúrgica. **2** *vt (clothes)* planchar.

i·ron·i(·)c(al) *adj* irónico, -a.

i·ron·ing **to do the i.** planchar.

i·ron·ing board tabla *f* de planchar.

i·ro·ny ironía *f.*

ir·ra·tion·al *adj* irracional.

ir·reg·u·lar *adj* irregular.

ir·rel·e·vance irrelevancia *f.*

ir·rel·e·vant *adj* no pertinente.

ir·re·sist·i·ble *adj* irresistible.

ir·re·spec·tive *adj* i. of sin tener en cuenta.

ir·ri·gate *vt* regar.

ir·ri·ta·ble *adj* irritable.

ir·ri·tate *vt* (annoy) irritar, fastidiar.

ir·ri·tat·ing *adj* irritante.

ir·ri·ta·tion (annoyance) fastidio *m;* (bad mood) mal humor *m.*

is 3rd person sing pres of **be**.

Is·lam·ic *adj* islámico, -a.

is·land isla *f.*

i·so·late *vt* aislar (**from** de).

i·so·lat·ed *adj* aislado, -a.

i·so·la·tion aislamiento *m.*

is·sue 1 *n* (matter) cuestión *f;* (of journal etc) ejemplar *m.* 2 *vt* (book) publicar; (currency etc) emitir; (passport) expedir; (supplies) repartir; (order, instructions) dar.

it pers pron (subject) él, ella (often omitted); **it's here** está aquí. ▪ (direct object) lo, la; **I don't believe it** no me lo creo. ▪ (indirect object) le; **give it a kick** dale una patada. ▪ (after prep) él, ella, ello; **we'll talk about it later** ya hablaremos de ello. ▪ (impersonal) **it's late** es tarde; **it's me** soy yo; **it's raining** está lloviendo; **who is it?** ¿quién es?

I·tal·ian 1 *adj* italiano, -a. 2 *n* (person) italiano, -a *mf,* (language) italiano *m.*

i·tal·ic *adj* **in italics** en cursiva.

itch 1 *n* picor *m.* 2 *vi* (skin) picar.

itch·y *adj* que pica.

i·tem (in list) artículo *m;* (in collection) pieza *f;* (on agenda) asunto *m;* **i. of clothing** prenda *f* de vestir; **news i.** noticia *f.*

its poss adj (one thing) su; (more than one) sus.

it·self pers pron ▪ (reflexive) se; **the cat scratched i.** el gato se rascó.

▪ (emphatic) él or ella mismo, -a.

i·vo·ry marfil *m.*

i·vy hiedra *f.*

J

jab 1 *n* pinchazo *m;* (poke) golpe *m* seco. 2 *vt* pinchar.

jack (for car) gato *m;* (cards) sota *f.*

jack·et chaqueta *f,* (of suit) americana *f;* **j. potatoes** patatas *fpl* al horno.

ja·cuz·zi jacuzzi *m.*

jag·ged *adj* dentado, -a.

jail 1 *n* cárcel *f.* 2 *vt* encarcelar.

jam¹ mermelada *f.*

jam² 1 *n* (blockage) atasco *m.* 2 *vt* (cram) meter a la fuerza; (block) atascar. 3 *vi* (door) atrancarse; (brakes) agarrotarse.

▸**jam into** *vt* (crowd) apretarse en; **to j. sth into sth** meter algo a la fuerza en algo.

jam jar pote *m* de mermelada.

jam-packed *adj fam* (with people) atestado, -a; (with things) atiborrado, -a.

jan·i·tor portero *m,* conserje *m.*

Jan·u·ar·y enero *m.*

Jap·a·nese 1 *adj* japonés, -esa. 2 *n* (person) japonés, -esa *mf,* (language) japonés *m.*

jar (glass) tarro *m;* (earthenware) tinaja *f.*

jaun·dice ictericia *f.*

jave·lin jabalina *f.*

jaw mandíbula *f.*

jay·walk·ing imprudencia *f* peatonal.

jazz jazz *m.*

jea·lous *adj* celoso, -a; (envious) envidioso, -a; **to be j. of** tener celos de.

jeal·ous·y celos *mpl;* (envy) envidia *f.*

jeans *npl* vaqueros *npl,* tejanos *mpl.*

jeep jeep *m.*

jeer 1 *n (boo)* abucheo *m.* **2** *vi (boo)* abuchear; *(mock)* burlarse.

jeer·ing *adj* burlón, -ona.

Jell-O®, jel·lo gelatina *f.*

jel·ly gelatina *f.*

jeop·ard·ize *vt* poner en peligro; *(agreement etc)* comprometer.

jerk 1 *n (jolt)* sacudida *f*, *fam (idiot)* imbécil *mf.* **2** *vt (shake)* sacudir.

jer·sey jersey *m.*

jet reactor *m*; **j. engine** reactor *m.*

jet lag desfase *m* horario.

Jew judío, -a *mf.*

jew·el joya *f*; *(in watch)* rubí *m.*

jew·el·er joyero, -a *mf.*

jew·el·ry joyas *fpl*, alhajas *fpl.*

Jew·ish *adj* judío, -a.

jig·saw *(puzzle)* rompecabezas *m inv.*

jin·gle *vi* tintinear.

jit·ters *npl* **to get the j.** ponerse nervioso, -a.

job trabajo *m*; *(task)* tarea *f*, *(occupation)* (puesto *m* de) trabajo *m*; **we had a j. to …** nos costó (trabajo) …; **it's a good j. that …** menos mal que …

job cen·ter oficina *f* de empleo.

job·less *adj* parado, -a.

jock·ey jinete *m.*

jog 1 *n* trote *m.* **2** *vt* empujar; *(memory)* refrescar. **3** *vi (run)* hacer footing.

john *fam* meódromo *m.*

join 1 *vt* juntar; *(road)* empalmar con; *(river)* desembocar en; *(meet)* reunirse con; *(group)* unirse a; *(institution)* entrar en; *(army)* alistarse a; *(party)* afiliarse a; *(club)* hacerse socio, -a de. **2** *vi* unirse; *(roads)* empalmar; *(rivers)* confluir; *(become a member)* afiliarse; *(club)* hacerse socio, -a. **3** *n* juntura *f.*

▸**join in 1** *vi* participar. **2** *vt* participar en.

joint 1 *n* articulación *f*, *(of meat)* corte *m* de carne para asar; *(once roasted)* asado *m*, *(drugs)* porro *m.* **2**

adj colectivo, -a; **j. (bank) account** cuenta *f* conjunta.

joint·ly *adv* conjuntamente, en común.

joke 1 *n* chiste *m*; *(prank)* broma *f.* **2** *vi* estar de broma.

jok·er bromista *mf*; *(in cards)* comodín *m.*

jol·ly *adj* alegre.

jolt 1 *n* sacudida *f.* **2** *vi* moverse a sacudidas. **3** *vt* sacudir.

jos·tle 1 *vt* dar empujones a. **2** *vi* dar empujones.

▸**jot down** *vt* apuntar.

jour·nal·ist periodista *mf.*

jour·ney viaje *m*; *(distance)* trayecto *m.*

joy alegría *f.*

joy·ful *adj* alegre.

joy·stick palanca *f* de mando; *(of video game)* joystick *m.*

judge 1 *n* juez *mf*, jueza *f.* **2** *vt* juzgar; *(estimate)* considerar; *(assess)* valorar. **3** *vi* juzgar.

judg(e)·ment sentencia *f*, *(opinion)* opinión *f.*

ju·di·cial *adj* judicial.

ju·do judo *m.*

jug jarra *f*, **milk j.** jarra de leche.

jug·gle *vi* hacer juegos malabares (with con).

jug·gler malabarista *mf.*

juice jugo *m*; *(of citrus fruits)* zumo *m.*

juic·y *adj* jugoso, -a.

Ju·ly julio *m.*

jum·ble 1 *n* revoltijo *m.* **2** *vt* revolver.

jum·bo *adj* gigante.

jum·bo jet jumbo *m.*

jump 1 *n* salto *m*; *(sudden increase)* subida repentina *f.* **2** *vi* saltar; *(start)* sobresaltarse; *(increase)* aumentar de golpe. **3** *vt* saltar; **to j. the line** colarse.

▸**jump in, jump on 1** *vt (train etc)* subirse a. **2** *vi* subir.

jump rope comba *f.*

jump·y *adj fam* nervioso, -a.

junc·tion *(of roads)* cruce *m.*

June junio m.

jun·gle jungla f.

jun·ior 1 adj (lower in rank) subalterno, -a; (younger) menor; **j. team** equipo juvenil. **2** n (of lower rank) subalterno, -a mf, (younger person) menor mf.

jun·ior high school = instituto m de enseñanza secundaria.

junk trastos mpl.

junk shop tienda f de segunda mano.

ju·ry jurado m.

just 1 adj (fair) justo, -a. **2** adv (at this very moment) ahora mismo, en este momento; (only) solamente; (barely) por poco; (exactly) exactamente; **he had j. arrived** acababa de llegar; **he was j. leaving when Rosa arrived** estaba a punto de salir cuando llegó Rosa; **j. as I came in** justo cuando entré; **I only j. caught the bus** cogí el autobús por los pelos; **j. about** casi; **j. as fast as** tan rápido como.

jus·tice justicia f.

jus·ti·fi·ca·tion justificación f.

jus·ti·fy vt justificar.

▸ **jut out** vi sobresalir.

K

kan·ga·roo canguro m.

ka·ra·te kárate m.

ke·bab pincho moruno m.

keen adj (eager) entusiasta, -a; (intense) profundo, -a; (mind, senses) agudo, -a.

keep 1 n to earn one's k. ganarse el pan. **2** vt* mantener; (letters, memories, silence, secret) guardar; (retain possession of) quedarse con; (hold back) entretener; (in prison) detener; (promise) cumplir; (diary, accounts) llevar; **to k. sb waiting**

hacer esperar a algn; **to k. doing sth** seguir haciendo algo; **she keeps forgetting her keys** siempre se olvida las llaves; **to k. going** seguir adelante. **3** vi* (food) conservarse.

▸ **keep away 1** vt mantener a distancia. **2** vi mantenerse a distancia.

▸ **keep back 1** vt (information) callar; (money etc) retener. **2** vi (crowd) mantenerse atrás.

▸ **keep down** vt to k. prices down mantener los precios bajos.

▸ **keep off** vt k. off the grass prohibido pisar la hierba.

▸ **keep on** vt (clothes etc) no quitarse; (continue to employ) mantener a; **it keeps on breaking** siempre se está rompiendo. **2** vi the rain kept on la lluvia siguió/continuó; **he just kept on (talking, complaining)** siguió machacando; **k. straight on** sigue todo derecho.

▸ **keep out 1** vt no dejar pasar. **2** vi no entrar; **k. out (sign)** prohibida la entrada

▸ **keep to** vt (subject) limitarse a; **to k. to one's room** quedarse en el cuarto; **k. to the point!** ¡cíñete a la cuestión!; **to k. to the left** circular por la izquierda.

▸ **keep up 1** vt mantener. **2** vi (in race etc) no rezagarse.

▸ **keep up with** vt to k. up with the times estar al día.

ken·nel caseta f para perros.

Ken·yan adj & n keniano, -a (mf).

kept pt & pp of **keep**.

ker·o·sene queroseno m.

ketch·up ketchup m.

ket·tle hervidor m.

key 1 n (for lock) llave f, (of piano, typewriter) tecla f. **2** adj clave.

key·board teclado m.

key ring llavero m.

kick 1 n (from person) puntapié m. **2** vi (animal) cocear; (person) dar patadas. **3** vt dar un puntapié a.

▸ **kick down, kick in** vt (door etc) derribar a patadas.

▸**kick off** *vi fam* empezar; *(of footballer)* sacar.

▸**kick out** *vt* echar a patadas.

kick·off saque *m* inicial.

kid[1] *fam (child)* niño, -a *mf*; **the kids** los críos.

kid[2] **1** *vt* tomar el pelo a. **2** *vi* tomar el pelo.

kid·nap *vt* secuestrar.

kid·nap·per secuestrador, -a *mf*.

kid·ney riñón *m*.

kill *vt* matar.

kill·er asesino, -a *mf*.

kill·ing *(of person)* asesinato *m*; *(of animal)* matanza *f*.

ki·lo kilo *m*.

kil·o·gram kilogramo *m*.

kil·o·me·ter kilómetro *m*.

kin familiares *mpl*; parientes *mpl*.

kind[1] **1** *n* clase *f*; **what k. of?** ¿qué tipo de? **2** *adv fam* **k. of** en cierta manera.

kind[2] *adj* amable.

kin·der·gar·ten jardín *m* de infancia.

kind·ly 1 *adj* (**kindlier, kindliest**) amable, bondadoso, -a. **2** *adv fml (please)* por favor; **to look k. on** aprobar.

kind·ness amabilidad *f*.

king rey *m*.

king·dom reino *m*.

ki·osk quiosco *m*.

kiss 1 *n* beso *m*. **2** *vt* besar. **3** *vi* besarse.

kit *(gear)* equipo *m*; *(clothing)* ropa *f*; *(toy model)* maqueta *f*.

kitch·en cocina *f*.

kite *(toy)* cometa *f*.

kit·ten gatito, -a *mf*.

klutz *fam (stupid person)* bobo, -a *mf, Esp* chorra *mf*; *(clumsy person)* torpe *mf, Esp* patoso, -a *mf*.

knack **to get the k. of doing sth** cogerle el truquillo a algo.

knee rodilla *f*.

kneel* *vi* **to k. (down)** arrodillarse.

knew *pt of* **know**.

knick·ers *npl* bragas *fpl*.

knife *(pl* **knives**) cuchillo *m*.

knight caballero *m*; *(in chess)* caballo *m*.

knit 1 *vt* tejer; *(join)* juntar. **2** *vi* hacer punto; *(bone)* soldarse.

knit·ting punto *m*.

knit·ting nee·dle aguja *f* de hacer punto.

knob *(of stick)* puño *m*; *(of drawer)* tirador *m*; *(button)* botón *m*.

knock 1 *n* golpe *m*; **there was a k. at the door** llamaron a la puerta. **2** *vt* golpear. **3** *vi* chocar (**against, into** contra); *(at door)* llamar (**at** a).

▸**knock down** *vt (demolish)* derribar; *(car)* atropellar.

▸**knock off** *vt* tirar.

▸**knock out** *vt (make unconscious)* dejar sin conocimiento; *(in boxing)* derrotar por K.O.

▸**knock over** *vt* volcar; *(car)* atropellar.

knock·er *(on door)* aldaba *f*.

knot 1 *n* nudo *m*. **2** *vt* anudar.

know* 1 *vt* saber; *(be acquainted with)* conocer; **she knows how to ski** sabe esquiar; **we got to k. each other at the party** nos conocimos en la fiesta. **2** *vi* saber; **to let sb k.** avisar a algn.

know-how conocimiento *m* práctico.

know-it-all *fam* sabihondo, -a *mf*, sabelotodo *mf*.

knowl·edge conocimiento *m*; *(learning)* conocimientos *mpl*.

known *adj* conocido, -a.

knuck·le nudillo *m*.

Ko·ran Corán *m*.

Ko·re·an *adj & n* coreano, -a *(mf)*.

L

lab *fam* laboratorio *m*.
la·bel 1 *n* etiqueta *f*. **2** *vt* poner etiqueta a.
la·bor 1 *n* (*work*) trabajo *m*; (*workforce*) mano *f* de obra; **to be in l.** estar de parto. **2** *adj* (*market etc*) laboral; **L. day** día *m* de los trabajadores. **3** *vi* (*work*) trabajar (duro).
lab·o·ra·to·ry laboratorio *m*.
la·bor·er peón *m*; **farm l.** peón *m* agrícola.
la·bor un·ion sindicato *m*.
lace *n* (*fabric*) encaje *m*; **laces** cordones *mpl*; **to do up one's laces** atarse los cordones.
lack 1 *n* falta *f*. **2** *vt* carecer de. **3** *vi* carecer (**in** de).
lad chaval *m*.
lad·der escalera *f* (de mano).
la·dle cucharón *m*.
la·dy señora *f*, **'Ladies'** (*restroom*) 'Señoras'.
la·dy·bug mariquita *f*.
la·ger cerveza *f* (rubia).
lake lago *m*.
lamb cordero *m*; (*meat*) carne *f* de cordero.
lame *adj* cojo, -a.
lamp lámpara *f*.
lamp·post farola *f*.
lamp·shade pantalla *f*.
land 1 *n* tierra *f*; (*country*) país *m*; (*property*) tierras *fpl*; **piece of l.** terreno *m*; **by l.** por tierra. **2** *vt* (*plane*) hacer aterrizar. **3** *vi* (*plane*) aterrizar; (*passengers*) desembarcar.
land·ing (*of staircase*) rellano *m*; (*of plane*) aterrizaje *m*.
land·la·dy (*of apartment*) propietaria *f*, casera *f*; (*of boarding house*) patrona *f*; (*of pub*) dueña *f*.
land·lord (*of apartment*) propietario *m*, casero *m*; (*of pub*) dueño *m*.

land·own·er terrateniente *mf*.
land·scape paisaje *m*.
land·slide desprendimiento *m* de tierras.
lane (*in country*) camino *m*; (*in town*) callejón *m*; (*of highway*) carril *m*.
lan·guage idioma *m*, lengua *f*.
lan·guage lab·o·ra·to·ry laboratorio *m* de idiomas.
lan·tern farol *m*.
lap[1] (*knees*) rodillas *fpl*.
lap[2] (*circuit*) vuelta *f*.
la·pel solapa *f*.
lap·top **laptop (computer)** *Esp* ordenador *m* or *Am* computadora *f* portátil.
lar·ce·ny hurto *m*.
lar·der despensa *f*.
large *adj* grande; (*amount*) importante; **by and l.** por lo general.
large·ly *adv* (*mainly*) en gran parte; (*chiefly*) principalmente.
large-scale *adj* (*project, problem etc*) de gran envergadura; (*map*) a gran escala.
lark (*bird*) alondra *f*.
la·ser láser *m*; **l. printer** impresora *f* láser.
last 1 *adj* (*final, most recent*) último, -a; (*past*) pasado, -a; (*previous*) anterior; **l. but one** penúltimo, -a; **l. month** el mes pasado; **l. night** anoche. **2** *adv* (*on final occasion*) por última vez; (*at the end*) en último lugar; (*in race etc*) último; **at (long) l.** por fin. **3** *n* el último, la última. **4** *vi* (*time*) durar; (*hold out*) aguantar.
last·ly *adv* por último.
latch pestillo *m*.
late 1 *adj* (*not on time*) tardío, -a; (*hour*) avanzado, -a; (*far on in time*) tarde; **to be five minutes l.** llegar con cinco minutos de retraso; **in the l. afternoon** a última hora de la tarde. **2** *adv* tarde; **l. at night** a altas horas de la noche.
late·com·er rezagado, -a *mf*.
late·ly *adv* últimamente.
Lat·in 1 *adj* latino, -a; **L. America**

América f Latina, Latinoamérica f; **L. American** f Latinoamericano, -a (mf). **2** n latino, -a mf; (language) latín m.

lat·ter 1 n (last) último, -a; (second of two) segundo, -a. **2** pron éste, -a.

laugh 1 n risa f. **2** vi reír, reírse.

▸**laugh about** vt to l. about sb/sth reírse de algn/algo.

▸**laugh at** vt to l. at sb/sth reírse de algn/algo.

laugh·ter risa f.

launch 1 n (vessel) lancha f; (of product) lanzamiento m. **2** vt (rocket, new product) lanzar; (ship) botar; (film, play) estrenar.

Laun·dro·mat® lavandería f automática.

laun·dry (place) lavandería f; (dirty clothes) ropa f sucia; **to do the l.** lavar la ropa.

lav·a·to·ry retrete m; (room) baño m; **public l.** servicios mpl.

law ley f; (as subject) derecho m.

law court tribunal m de justicia.

lawn césped m.

lawn-mow·er cortacésped m.

law·suit pleito m.

law·yer abogado, -a mf.

lay* vt (place) poner; (cable, trap) tender; (foundations) echar; (table, eggs) poner; (set down) asentar.

▸**lay down** vt (put down) poner.

▸**lay off** vt (dismiss) despedir.

▸**lay on** vt (provide) proveer de; (food) preparar.

▸**lay out** vt (open out) extender; (arrange) disponer; (ideas) exponer; (spend) gastar.

lay·a·bout vago, -a mf.

lay·er capa f.

lay·man lego, -a mf.

lay·out (arrangement) disposición f; (presentation) presentación f.

la·zy adj vago, -a.

lead[1] (metal) plomo m, (in pencil) mina f.

lead[2] **1** n (front position) delantera f; (advantage) ventaja f; (leash) correa f; (electric cable) cable m; **to be in**

the l. ir en cabeza; **to take the l.** (in race) tomar la delantera; (score) adelantarse. **2** vt* (conduct) conducir; (be the leader of) dirigir; (life) llevar; **to l. sb to think sth** hacer a algn pensar algo. **3** vi* (road) llevar (**to** a); (in race) llevar la delantera.

▸**lead away** vt llevar.

▸**lead on** vt (deceive) engañar, timar.

▸**lead to** vt (result in) dar lugar a.

lead·er jefe, -a mf; (political) líder mf.

lead·ing adj (main) principal.

leaf (pl leaves) hoja f.

leaf·let folleto m.

leak 1 n (of gas, liquid) escape m; (of information) filtración f. **2** vi (gas, liquid) escaparse. **3** vt (information) filtrar.

lean* **1** vi inclinarse; (thing) estar inclinado; **to l. on/against** apoyarse en/contra. **2** vt apoyar (**on** en).

▸**lean forward** vi inclinarse hacia delante.

▸**lean over** vi inclinarse.

leap 1 n (jump) salto m. **2** vi* saltar.

leap year año m bisiesto.

learn* **1** vt aprender; (find out about) enterarse de; **to l. (how) to ski** aprender a esquiar. **2** vi aprender; **to l. about** or **of** (find out) enterarse de.

learn·er (beginner) principiante mf.

learn·ing (knowledge) conocimientos mpl; (erudition) saber m.

lease 1 n contrato m de arrendamiento. **2** vt arrendar.

leash correa f.

least 1 adj menor. **2** adv menos. **3** n lo menos; **at l.** por lo menos.

leath·er 1 n (fine) piel f, (heavy) cuero m. **2** adj de piel.

leave[1]* **1** vt dejar; (go away from) abandonar; (go out of) salir de; **I have two cookies left** me quedan dos galletas. **2** vi (go away) irse, marcharse; (go out) salir; **the train leaves in five minutes** el tren sale dentro de cinco minutos.

▸**leave behind** *vt* dejar atrás.

▸**leave on** *vt (clothes)* dejar puesto, -a; *(lights, radio)* dejar encendido, -a.

▸**leave out** *vt (omit)* omitir.

leave² *(time off)* vacaciones *fpl*.

lec·ture 1 *n* conferencia *f*, *(at university)* clase *f*; **to give a l.** dar una conferencia (**on** sobre). **2** *vi (at university)* dar clases.

lec·tur·er conferenciante *mf*, *(at university)* profesor, -a *mf*.

leek puerro *m*.

left¹ 1 *adj* izquierdo, -a. **2** *adv* a la izquierda. **3** *n* izquierda *f*; **on the l.** a mano izquierda.

left² *pt & pp of* **leave¹**

left-hand *adj* **on the l. side** a mano izquierda.

left-hand·ed *adj* zurdo, -a.

left·o·vers *npl* sobras *fpl*.

leg pierna *f*, *(of animal, table)* pata *f*.

le·gal *adj* legal; *(permitted by law)* lícito, -a; *(relating to the law)* jurídico, -a.

le·gal hol·i·day fiesta *f* nacional.

le·gal·ly *adv* legalmente.

leg·end leyenda *f*.

leg·i·ble *adj* legible.

leg·is·la·tion legislación *f*.

leg·is·la·tive *adj* legislativo, -a.

leg·is·la·ture asamblea *f* legislativa.

le·git·i·mate *adj* legítimo, -a.

lei·sure ocio *m*, *(free time)* tiempo *m* libre; **l. activities** pasatiempos *mpl*.

lem·on limón *m*; **l. juice** zumo *m* de limón; **l. tea** té *m* con limón.

lem·on·ade gaseosa *f*.

lend* *vt* prestar.

lend·er entidad *f* de crédito.

length largo *m*; *(duration)* duración *f*; *(section of string etc)* trozo *m*.

length·en 1 *vt* alargar; *(lifetime)* prolongar. **2** *vi* alargarse; *(lifetime)* prolongarse.

length·y *adj* (**lengthier, lengthiest**) largo, -a; *(meeting, discussion)* prolongado, -a.

le·nient *adj* indulgente.

lens *(of spectacles)* lente *f*, *(of camera)* objetivo *m*.

len·til lenteja *f*.

leop·ard leopardo *m*.

le·o·tard mallas *fpl*.

less menos; **l. and l.** cada vez menos; **a year l. two days** un año menos dos días.

les·son clase *f*, *(in book)* lección *f*.

let* 1 *vt* dejar; *(rent out)* alquilar; **to l. sb do sth** dejar a algn hacer algo; **to l. go of sth** soltar algo; **to l. sb know** avisar a algn. **2** *v aux* **l. him wait** que espere; **l.'s go!** ¡vamos!, ¡vámonos!

▸**let down** *vt (lower)* bajar; *(fail)* defraudar.

▸**let in** *vt (admit)* dejar entrar.

▸**let off** *vt (bomb)* hacer explotar; *(fireworks)* hacer estallar; **to l. sb off** *(pardon)* perdonar.

▸**let on** *vi fam* **don't l. on** *(reveal information)* no se lo digas.

▸**let out** *vt (release)* soltar; *(news)* divulgar; *(secret)* revelar; *(cry)* soltar.

▸**let up** *vi (cease)* cesar.

let·down decepción *f*.

let·ter *(of alphabet)* letra *f*, *(written message)* carta *f*.

let·ter-box buzón *m*.

let·tuce lechuga *f*.

lev·el 1 *adj (flat)* llano, -a; *(even)* nivelado, -a; **to be l. with** estar a nivel de. **2** *n* nivel *m*; **to be on a l. with** estar al mismo nivel que.

lev·el crossing paso *m* a nivel.

lev·er palanca *f*.

li·a·ble *adj* **the river is l. to freeze** el río tiene tendencia a helarse.

li·ar mentiroso, -a *mf*.

li·bel 1 *n* libelo *m*. **2** *vt* difamar, calumniar.

lib·er·al 1 *adj* liberal; *(abundant)* abundante; **L. Party** Partido *m* Liberal. **2** *n* **L.** liberal *mf*.

lib·er·ty libertad *f*; **to be at l. to say sth** ser libre de decir algo.

li·brar·i·an bibliotecario, -a *mf*.

li·brar·y biblioteca *f*.

Lib·y·an *adj & n* libio, -a *(mf)*.

lice *npl see* **louse**.

li·cense *(permit)* permiso *m*; **l. plate** *(of car)* (placa *f* de la) matrícula *f*.

lick *vt* lamer.

lic·o·rice regaliz *m*.

lid *(cover)* tapa *f*; *(of eye)* párpado *m*.

lie¹ 1 *vi* mentir. **2** *n* mentira *f*.

lie²* *vi (act)* acostarse; *(state)* estar acostado, -a.

▸ **lie around** *vi (person)* estar tumbado, -a; *(things)* estar tirado, -a.

▸ **lie down** *vi* acostarse.

life *(pl* lives) vida *f*; **to come to l.** cobrar vida.

life belt cinturón *m* salvavidas.

life·boat *(on ship)* bote *m* salvavidas; *(on shore)* lancha *f* de socorro.

life·guard socorrista *mf*.

life in·sur·ance seguro *m* de vida.

life jack·et chaleco *m* salvavidas.

life·style estilo *m* de vida.

life·time vida *f*; **in his l.** durante su vida.

lift 1 *vt* levantar; *(head etc)* alzar; *(pick up)* coger. **2** *n* **to give sb a l.** llevar a algn en coche.

▸ **lift out** *vt (take out)* sacar.

▸ **lift up** *vt* levantar.

light¹ 1 *n* luz *f*; *(lamp)* lámpara *f*; *(headlight)* faro *m*; **to set l. to sth** prender fuego a algo; **have you got a l.?** ¿tiene fuego? **2** *vt* (illuminate)* iluminar; *(ignite)* encender. **3** *adj* claro, -a; *(hair)* rubio, -a.

▸ **light up 1** *vt* iluminar. **2** *vi* iluminarse; *(light cigarette)* encender un cigarrillo.

light² 1 *adj* ligero, -a; *(rain)* fino, -a. **2** *adv* **to travel l.** ir ligero, -a de equipaje.

light bulb bombilla *f*.

light·er *(cigarette)* **l.** mechero *m*.

light·house faro *m*.

light·ing *(act)* iluminación *f*.

light·ning *(flash)* relámpago *m*; *(which hits the earth)* rayo *m*.

like¹ 1 *prep (similar to)* parecido, -a a; *(the same as)* igual que; **l. that** así;

what's he l.? ¿cómo es?; **to feel l.** tener ganas de. **2** *adj* parecido, -a; *(equal)* igual.

like² 1 *vt* **do you l. chocolate?** ¿te gusta el chocolate?; **he likes dancing** le gusta bailar; **I would l. a coffee** quisiera un café; **would you l. to go now?** ¿quieres que nos vayamos ya? **2** *vi* querer; **as you l.** como quieras.

like·a·ble *adj* simpático, -a.

like·li·hood probabilidad *f*.

like·ly 1 *adj* probable; **he's l. to cause trouble** es probable que cause problemas. **2** *adv* probablemente; **not l.!** ¡ni hablar!

like·wise *adv (also)* asimismo.

lik·ing *(for thing)* afición *f*; *(for person)* simpatía *f*; *(for friend)* cariño *m*.

lil·y lirio *m*.

limb miembro *m*.

lime *(fruit)* lima *f*; *(tree)* limero *m*.

lim·it 1 *n* límite *m*; *(maximum)* máximo *m*; *(minimum)* mínimo *m*. **2** *vt (restrict)* limitar **(to** a).

lim·ou·sine limusina *f*.

limp 1 *vi* cojear. **2** *n* cojera *f*.

line¹ línea *f*; *(straight)* raya *f*; *(of writing)* renglón *m*; *(of poetry)* verso *m*; *(row)* fila *f*; *(of trees)* hilera *f*; *(of people waiting)* cola *f*; *(rope)* cuerda *f*; *(telephone)* línea *f*; *(of railway)* vía *f*.

line² *vt (clothes)* forrar.

▸ **line up 1** *vt (arrange in rows)* poner en fila; **he has something lined up for this evening** tiene algo organizado para esta noche. **2** *vi (people)* ponerse en fila; *(in line)* hacer cola.

lin·en *(sheets etc)* ropa *f* blanca.

lin·er transatlántico *m*.

line·up *(of team)* alineación *f*; *(of band)* formación *f*; *(of police suspects)* rueda *f* de reconocimiento or identificación.

lin·ger *vi* tardar; *(dawdle)* rezagarse; *(smell, doubt)* persistir; *fig (memory)* perdurar.

lin·guis·tics lingüística *f*.

lin·ing forro *m*.

link 1 n (of chain) eslabón m; (connection) conexión f. **2** vt unir.

▶**link up** vi unirse; (meet) encontrarse.

lino linóleo m.

lint brush cepillo m de la ropa.

li·on león m.

lip labio m.

lip·stick lápiz m de labios.

li·queur licor m.

liq·uid adj & n líquido, -a (m).

liq·ui·date vt liquidar.

liq·uor bebidas fpl alcohólicas.

list 1 n lista f, (catalog) catálogo m. **2** vt (make a list of) hacer una lista de; (put on a list) poner en una lista.

lis·ten vi escuchar; **to l. to** sth/sb escuchar algo/a algn.

▶**listen out** vi estar atento, -a (**for** a).

lis·ten·er oyente mf.

li·ter litro m.

lit·er·al·ly adv literalmente.

lit·er·ar·y adj literario, -a.

lit·er·a·ture literatura f; (documentation) folleto m informativo.

lit·i·ga·tion litigio m.

lit·ter (trash) basura f; (papers) papeles mpl; (offspring) camada f.

lit·ter bin papelera f.

lit·tle 1 adj pequeño, -a; **a l. dog** un perrito; **a l. house** una casita. **2** pron poco m; **save me a l.** guárdame un poco; **a l. cheese** un poco de queso. **3** adv poco; **l. by l.** poco a poco; **as l. as possible** lo menos posible; **l. milk/money** poca leche/poco dinero.

live¹ vti vivir; **to l. an interesting life** llevar una vida interesante.

live² adj (TV etc) en directo; (wire) con corriente.

▶**live off, live on** vt (food, money) vivir de.

▶**live on** vi (memory) persistir.

▶**live through** vt sobrevivir a, vivir.

▶**live together** vi vivir juntos.

▶**live up to** vt (promises) cumplir con; **to l. up to expectations** estar a la altura de lo que se esperaba.

▶**live with** vt vivir con.

live·ly adj (person) vivo, -a; (place) animado, -a.

liv·er hígado m.

liv·ing 1 adj vivo, -a. **2** n vida f, **to earn** or **make one's l.** ganarse la vida.

living room sala f de estar.

liz·ard (large) lagarto m; (small) lagartija f.

load 1 n (cargo) carga f; (weight) peso m; fam **loads of** montones de; fam **that's a l. of garbage!** ¡no son más que tonterías! **2** vt cargar.

▶**load up** vti cargar.

loaf (pl **loaves**) pan m.

loan 1 n (to individual) préstamo m; (to company etc) empréstito m; **on l.** prestado, -a. **2** vt prestar.

lob·by (hall) vestíbulo m.

lob·ster langosta f.

lo·cal adj local; (person) del pueblo.

lo·cal ar·e·a net·work red f local.

lo·cal·i·ty localidad f.

lo·cal·ly adv en or de la localidad.

lo·cate vt (situate) ubicar; (find) localizar.

lo·ca·tion ubicación f.

lock¹ n (on door etc) cerradura f; (bolt) cerrojo m; (padlock) candado m; (on canal) esclusa f. **2** vt cerrar con llave or cerrojo or candado.

lock² (of hair) mechón m.

▶**lock in** vt (person) encerrar a.

▶**lock out** vt (person) cerrar la puerta a.

▶**lock up** vt (house) cerrar; (in jail) meter en la cárcel.

lock·er armario m ropero.

lock·et medallón m.

lodge 1 n (gamekeeper's) casa f del guarda; (porter's) portería f, (hunter's) refugio m. **2** vt (accommodate) alojar; (complaint) presentar. **3** vi (live) alojarse; (get stuck) meterse (in en).

lodg·er huésped, -a mf.

lodg·ing alojamiento m; **l. house** casa f de huéspedes.

loft desván *m.*

log *(wood)* tronco *m; (for fire)* leño *m.*

log·ic lógica *f.*

log·i·cal *adj* lógico, -a.

lol·li·pop chupachup® *m.*

lone *adj (solitary)* solitario, -a; *(single)* solo, -a.

lone·li·ness soledad *f.*

lone·ly *adj (person)* solo, -a; *(place)* solitario, -a.

long¹ 1 *adj (size)* largo, -a; *(time)* mucho, -a; **it's three meters l.** tiene tres metros de largo; **it's a l. way** está lejos; **at l.** last por fin; **how l. is the film?** ¿cuánto tiempo dura la película? **2** *adv* mucho tiempo; **as l. as the exhibition lasts** mientras dure la exposición; **as l. as** *or* **so l. as you don't mind** con tal de que no te importe; **before l.** dentro de poco; **how l. have you been here?** ¿cuánto tiempo llevas aquí?

long-dis·tance *adj* de larga distancia; **l. call** conferencia *f* interurbana.

long-term *adj* largo plazo.

look 1 *n (glance)* mirada *f; (appearance)* aspecto *m;* **to take a l. at** echar un vistazo a. **2** *vi* mirar; *(seem)* parecer; **he looks well** tiene buena cara; **she looks like her father** se parece a su padre.

▸**look after** *vt* ocuparse de, cuidar de.

▸**look around 1** *vi* mirar alrededor; *(turn head)* volver la cabeza. **2** *vt (house, shop)* ver.

▸**look at** *vt* mirar.

▸**look back** *vi* mirar hacia atrás; **to l. back on sth** *(remember)* recordar algo.

▸**look for** *vt* buscar.

▸**look forward to** *vt* esperar con ilusión; **I l. forward to hearing from you** *(in letter)* espero noticias suyas.

▸**look into** *vt* investigar.

▸**look onto** *vt* dar a.

▸**look out** *vi* **the bedroom looks out onto the garden** el dormitorio da al jardín; **l. out!** ¡cuidado!, ¡ojo!

▸**look over** *vt (examine)* revisar; *(place)* inspeccionar.

▸**look up 1** *vi (glance upwards)* alzar la vista. **2** *vt (look for)* buscar.

lookout *(person)* centinela *mf; (place)* mirador *m;* **to be on the l. for** estar al acecho de.

loom¹ telar *m.*

loom² *vi (of mountain)* alzarse; *(threaten)* amenazar.

loop lazo *m.*

loop·hole *fig* escapatoria *f.*

loose 1 *adj (not secure)* flojo, -a; *(papers, hair, clothes)* suelto, -a; *(baggy)* holgado, -a; *(not packaged)* a granel; **to set sb l.** soltar a algn; **l. change** suelto *m.* **2** *n* **to be on the l.** *(prisoner)* andar suelto.

loos·en *vt* aflojar; *(belt)* desabrochar.

lord señor *m.*

lose* *vti* perder; **to l. to sb** perder contra algn.

los·er perdedor, -a *mf.*

loss pérdida *f.*

lost *adj* perdido, -a; **to get l.** perderse; **get l.!** *fam* ¡vete a la porra!

lost and found oficina *f* de objetos perdidos.

lot **a l. of** *(much)* mucho, -a; *(many)* muchos, -as; **he feels a l. better** se encuentra mucho mejor; **lots of** montones de; **what a l. of bottles!** ¡qué cantidad de botellas!

lo·tion loción *f.*

lot·ter·y lotería *f.*

loud 1 *adj (voice)* alto, -a; *(noise)* fuerte; *(protests, party)* ruidoso, -a. **2** *adv* **to read/think out l.** leer/pensar en voz alta.

loud·ly *adv (to speak etc)* en voz alta.

loud·speak·er altavoz *m.*

lous·y *adj fam* fatal; **a l. trick** una cochinada.

love 1 *n* amor *m;* **to be in l. with sb**

estar enamorado, -a de algn; **to make l.** hacer el amor. **2** *vt (person)* querer; *(sport etc)* ser muy aficionado, -a a; **he loves cooking** le encanta cocinar.

love·ly *adj (charming)* encantador, -a; *(beautiful)* precioso, -a; *(delicious)* riquísimo, -a.

lov·er *(enthusiast)* aficionado, -a *mf.*

lov·ing *adj* cariñoso, -a.

low 1 *adj* bajo, -a; *(poor)* pobre; *(reprehensible)* malo, -a; **to feel l.** sentirse deprimido, -a. **2** *adv* bajo.

low·er 1 *adj* inferior. **2** *vt* bajar; *(reduce)* reducir; *(price)* rebajar.

low-fat *adj (milk)* desnatado, -a; *(food)* light *inv.*

loy·al *adj* leal.

loy·al·ty lealtad *f*, fidelidad *f.*

loz·enge pastilla *f.*

LP LP *m*, elepé *m.*

luck suerte *f*; **bad l.!** ¡mala suerte!; **good l.!** ¡(buena) suerte!

luck·i·ly *adv* afortunadamente.

luck·y *adj (person)* afortunado, -a; *(charm)* de la suerte; **that was l.** ha sido una suerte.

lu·di·crous *adj* ridículo, -a.

lug·gage equipaje *m.*

luke·warm *adj (water etc)* tibio, -a.

lull·a·by nana *f.*

lum·ber maderos *mpl.*

lum·ber·yard almacén *m* maderero, maderería *f*, RP barraca *f* maderera.

lu·mi·nous *adj* luminoso, -a.

lump *(of coal etc)* trozo *m*; *(of sugar, earth)* terrón *m*; *(swelling)* bulto *m.*

lump sum suma *f* global.

lu·na·tic *adj & n* loco, -a *(mf).*

lunch comida *f*, almuerzo *m*; **l. hour** hora *f* de comer.

lung pulmón *m.*

lux·u·ri·ous *adj* lujoso, -a.

lux·u·ry lujo *m.*

M

mac(c)aroni macarrones *mpl.*

ma·chine máquina *f.*

ma·chin·er·y *(machines)* maquinaria *f*, *(workings of machine)* mecanismo *m.*

mack·er·el *inv* caballa *f.*

mad *adj* loco, -a; **to be m. about sth/sb** estar loco, -a por algo/algn; **to be m. at sb** estar enfadado, -a con algn.

Mad·am señora *f.*

made *pt & pp of* **make**.

mad·man loco *m.*

mad·ness locura *f.*

mag·a·zine *(periodical)* revista *f.*

mag·got gusano *m.*

mag·ic 1 *n* magia *f.* **2** *adj* mágico, -a; **m. wand** varita *f* mágica.

mag·i·cal *adj* mágico, -a.

ma·gi·cian *(wizard)* mago, -a *mf*, *(conjuror)* prestidigitador, -a *mf.*

mag·is·trate juez, -a *mf* de paz.

mag·net imán *m.*

mag·nif·i·cent *adj* magnífico, -a.

mag·ni·fy·ing glass lupa *f.*

ma·hog·a·ny caoba *f.*

maid criada *f.*

mail 1 *n* correo *m.* **2** *vt (post)* echar (al buzón).

mail-box buzón *m.*

mail-man cartero *m.*

main *adj (problem, door etc)* principal; *(square, mast, sail)* mayor; *(office)* central; **the m. thing is to keep calm** lo esencial es mantener la calma; **m. road** carretera *f* principal. **2** *n (pipe, wire)* conducto *m* principal; **the mains** *(water or gas system)* la conducción; *(electrical)* la red (eléctrica).

main·land continente *m.*

main·ly *adv* principalmente; *(for the most part)* en su mayoría.

main·tain vt (road, machine) conservar en buen estado; **to m. that** sostener que.

main·te·nance (of vehicle, road) mantenimiento m; (divorce allowance) pensión f.

maî·tre d' jefe m de sala.

maize maíz m.

maj·es·ty majestad f.

ma·jor 1 adj principal; (contribution, operation) importante. **2** n (officer) comandante m.

ma·jor·ette majorette f.

ma·jor·i·ty mayoría f.

make 1 vt* hacer; (manufacture) fabricar; (clothes, curtains) confeccionar; (meal) preparar; (decision) tomar; (earn) ganar; **to be made of** ser de; **to m. sb do sth** obligar a algn a hacer algo; **to m. do with sth** arreglárselas con algo; **I don't know what to m. of it** no sé qué pensar de eso; **we've made it!** (succeeded) ¡lo hemos conseguido! **2** n (brand) marca f.

▸ **make out 1** vt (list, receipt) hacer; (check) extender; (perceive) distinguir; (understand) entender; (claim) pretender. **2** vi **how did you m. out?** ¿qué tal te fue?

▸ **make up 1** vt (list) hacer; (assemble) montar; (invent) inventar; (apply cosmetics to) maquillar; (one's face) maquillarse; (loss) compensar. **2** vi **to m. up (with sb)** hacer las paces (con algn).

▸ **make up for** vt (loss, damage) compensar por; (lost time, mistake) recuperar.

mak·er fabricante mf.

make-up (cosmetics) maquillaje m.

ma·lar·i·a malaria f.

male 1 adj (animal, plant) macho; (person) varón; (sex) masculino. **2** n (person) varón m; (animal, plant) macho m.

mal·ice (wickedness) malicia f.

ma·li·cious adj (wicked) malévolo, -a.

mall (shopping) centro m comercial.

mam·mal mamífero m.

man (pl **men**) hombre m; **old m.** viejo m; **young m.** joven m; (humanity) el hombre; (human being) ser m humano.

man·age 1 vt (company, household) llevar; (money, affairs, person) manejar; (achieve) conseguir; **to m. to do sth** lograr hacer algo. **2** vi (cope physically) poder; (financially) arreglárselas.

man·age·ment dirección f.

man·ag·er (of company, bank) director, -a mf; (of department) jefe, -a mf.

man·ag·ing di·rec·tor director, -a mf gerente.

man·da·rin (fruit) mandarina f.

mane (of horse) crin f; (of lion) melena f.

ma·neu·ver 1 n maniobra f. **2** vt maniobrar; (person) manejar. **3** vi maniobrar.

ma·ni·ac maníaco, -a mf, fam loco, -a mf.

man·kind la humanidad.

man·made adj (lake) artificial; (fibers, fabric) sintético, -a.

man·ner (way, method) manera f, modo m; (way of behaving) forma f de ser; **(good) manners** buenos modales mpl; **bad manners** falta f sing de educación.

man·pow·er mano f de obra.

man·tel·piece (shelf) repisa f de chimenea; (fireplace) chimenea f.

man·u·al adj & n manual (m).

man·u·fac·ture 1 vt fabricar. **2** n fabricación f.

man·u·fac·tur·er fabricante mf.

ma·nure estiércol m.

man·y 1 adj muchos, -as; **a great m.** muchísimos, -as; **as m. ... as ...** tantos, -as ... como ...; **how m. days?** ¿cuántos días?; **not m. books** pocos libros; **so m. flowers!** ¡cuántas flores!; **too m.** demasiados, -as. **2** pron muchos, -as.

map 113 **mattress**

map (of country) mapa m; (of town, bus) plano m.

mar·a·thon maratón m or f.

mar·ble (stone) mármol m; (glass ball) canica f.

March marzo m.

march 1 n marcha f. **2** vi marchar.

mare yegua f.

mar·ga·rine margarina f.

mar·gin margen m.

ma·rine 1 adj marino, -a. **2** n soldado m de infantería de marina; **the M. Corps** la infantería de marina.

mark 1 n (trace) huella f; (stain) mancha f; (symbol) signo m; (sign, token) señal f; (in exam etc) nota f. **2** vt (make mark on) marcar; (stain) manchar; (exam) corregir.

▶**mark out** vt (area) delimitar.

mark·er (pen) rotulador m.

mar·ket mercado m.

mar·ket·ing marketing m.

mar·ma·lade mermelada f (de cítricos).

mar·riage (state) matrimonio m; (wedding) boda f.

mar·ried adj casado, -a.

mar·row (bone) m. médula f; (vegetable) calabacín m.

mar·ry vt casarse con; (priest) casar; **to get married** casarse.

marsh pantano m; **salt m.** marisma f.

mar·shal 1 n (in army) mariscal m; (sheriff) policía mf; (police or fire chief) jefe, -a mf. **2** vt (troops) formar; (facts etc) ordenar.

Mar·tian n & adj marciano, -a (mf).

mar·vel·ous adj maravilloso, -a.

mar·zi·pan mazapán m.

mas·car·a rímel m.

mas·cot mascota f.

mas·cu·line adj masculino, -a.

mash vt to m. (up) machacar; **mashed potatoes** puré m de patatas.

mask máscara f.

mass¹ (in church) misa f; **to say m.** decir misa.

mass² 1 n masa f; (large quantity) montón m; (of people) multitud f. **2** adj masivo, -a.

mas·sa·cre 1 n masacre f. **2** vt masacrar.

mas·sage 1 n masaje m. **2** vt dar masaje a.

mas·seur masajista m.

mas·seuse masajista f.

mas·sive adj enorme.

mast mástil m; (radio etc) torre f.

mas·ter 1 n (dog, servant) amo m; (of household) señor m; (teacher) profesor m; **m.'s degree** ≃ máster m. **2** vt (person, situation) dominar; (subject, skill) llegar a dominar.

mas·ter·piece obra f maestra.

mat (rug) alfombrilla f; (doormat) felpudo m; (rush mat) estera f.

match¹ cerilla f.

match² 1 n (sport) partido m. **2** vt (be in harmony with) armonizar con; (colors, clothes) hacer juego con; **they are well matched** (teams) van iguales; (couple) hacen buena pareja. **3** vi (harmonize) hacer juego.

▶**match up to** vt estar a la altura de.

match·box caja f de cerillas.

match·ing adj a juego.

match·stick cerilla f.

ma·te·ri·al (substance) materia f; (cloth) tejido m; **materials** (ingredients, equipment) materiales mpl.

ma·ter·nal adj maternal; (uncle etc) materno, -a.

ma·ter·ni·ty maternidad f.

ma·ter·ni·ty hos·pi·tal maternidad f.

math matemáticas fpl.

math·e·mat·i·cal adj matemático, -a.

math·e·mat·ics matemáticas fpl.

mat·i·née (cinema) sesión f de tarde; (theater) función f de tarde.

mat·ter 1 n (affair, question) asunto m; (problem) problema m; (substance) materia f; **what's the m.?** ¿qué pasa? **2** vi importar; **it doesn't m.** no importa, da igual.

mat·tress colchón m.

ma·ture *adj* maduro, -a.

max·i·mum 1 *n* máximo *m.* **2** *adj* máximo, -a.

May mayo *m.*

may *v aux (pt* **might)** *(possibility, probability)* poder, ser posible; **he m.** *or* **might come** puede que venga; **you m.** *or* **might as well stay** más vale que te quedes. ▪ *(permission)* poder; **m. I?** ¿me permite?; **you m. smoke** pueden fumar. ▪ *(wish)* ojalá *(+ subjunctive);* **m. you always be happy!** ¡ojalá seas siempre feliz!

may·be *adv* quizá(s), tal vez.

may·on·naise mayonesa *f.*

may·or *(man)* alcalde *m; (woman)* alcaldesa *f.*

maze laberinto *m.*

MBA *abbr of* **Master of Business Administration** MBA *m,* máster *m* en administración de empresas

me *pron (as object)* me; **he gave it to me** me lo dio; **listen to me** escúchame; **she knows me** me conoce. ▪ *(after prep)* mí; **it's for me** es para mí; **with me** conmigo. ▪ *(emphatic)* yo; **it's me soy yo; what about me?** y yo, ¿qué?

mead·ow prado *m.*

meal *(food)* comida *f.*

mean[1]* *vt (signify)* querer decir; *(intend)* pensar; *(wish)* querer; **what do you m. by that?** ¿qué quieres decir con eso?; **I m. it** (te) lo digo en serio; **she was meant to arrive on the 7th** tenía que *or* debía llegar el día 7; **they m. well** tienen buenas intenciones; **I didn't m. to do it** lo hice sin querer.

mean[2] *adj (miserly)* tacaño, -a; *(unkind)* malo, -a; *(bad-tempered)* malhumorado, -a.

mean·ing sentido *m.*

mean·ing·ful *adj* significativo, -a.

mean·ing·less *adj* sin sentido.

mean·ness *(miserliness)* tacañería *f, (nastiness)* maldad *f.*

means *sing or pl (method)* medio *m; (resources, wealth)* recursos *mpl*

(económicos); **by m. of** por medio de, mediante; **by all m.!** ¡por supuesto!; **by no m.** de ninguna manera.

mean·time in the m. mientras tanto.

mean·while *adv* mientras tanto.

mea·sles sarampión *m.*

meas·ure 1 *n* medida *f, (ruler)* regla *f.* **2** *vt (object, area)* medir.

▶ **measure up** *vi* to **m. up to sth** estar a la altura de algo.

meas·ure·ment medida *f.*

meat carne *f.*

me·chan·ic mecánico, -a *mf.*

me·chan·i·cal *adj* mecánico, -a.

mech·a·nism mecanismo *m.*

med·al medalla *f.*

med·al·ist medalla *mf,* **to be a gold m.** ser medalla de oro.

me·di·a *npl* medios *mpl* de comunicación.

med·i·cal *adj (treatment)* médico, -a; *(book)* de medicina.

med·i·ca·tion medicación *f.*

med·i·cine *(science)* medicina *f, (drug etc)* medicamento *m.*

med·i·cine cab·i·net botiquín *m.*

me·di·e·val *adj* medieval.

Med·i·ter·ra·ne·an 1 *adj* mediterráneo, -a. **2** *n* the M. el Mediterráneo.

me·di·um *adj* mediano, -a.

me·di·um-sized *adj* de tamaño mediano.

meet* **1** *vt (by chance)* encontrar; *(by arrangement)* reunirse con; *(pass in street etc)* toparse con; *(get to know)* conocer; *(await arrival of)* esperar; *(collect)* ir a buscar; **pleased to m. you!** ¡mucho gusto! **2** *vi (by chance)* encontrarse; *(by arrangement)* reunirse; *(formal meeting)* entrevistarse; *(get to know each other)* conocerse.

▶ **meet with** *vt (difficulty)* tropezar con; *(loss)* sufrir; *(success)* tener; *(person)* reunirse con.

meet·ing *(prearranged)* cita *f, (formal)* entrevista *f, (of committee etc)*

reunión f; (of assembly) sesión f.
mel·o·dy melodía f.
mel·on melón m.
melt 1 vt (metal) fundir. **2** vi (snow)
derretirse; (metal) fundirse.
mem·ber miembro mf; (of a society)
socio, -a mf; (of party, union) afiliado,
-a mf.
mem·o (official) memorándum m;
(personal) apunte m.
mem·o·ra·ble adj memorable.
me·mo·ri·al 1 adj (plaque etc)
conmemorativo, -a. **2** n monumento
conmemorativo.
mem·o·ry memoria f; (recollection)
recuerdo m.
men npl see **man**.
mend vt reparar; (clothes) remendar; (socks etc) zurcir.
men·tal adj mental; **m. home**, **m.
hospital** hospital m psiquiátrico; **m.
illness** enfermedad f mental.
men·tal·ly adv **to be m. handicapped** ser un, -a disminuido, -a psíquico, -a.
men·tion 1 n mención f. **2** vt mencionar; **don't m. it!** ¡de nada!
men·u (à la carte) carta f; (fixed
meal) menú m; **today's m.** menú del
día; (computer) menú m.
mer·cy misericordia f; **at the m. of**
a la merced de.
mere adj mero, -a.
mere·ly adv simplemente.
merge vi unirse; (roads) converger;
(companies) fusionarse.
merg·er (of companies) fusión f.
mer·it 1 n (of person) mérito m; (of
plan etc) ventaja f. **2** vt merecer.
mer·ry adj alegre; (tipsy) achispado,
-a; **M. Christmas!** ¡Felices Navidades!
mer·ry-go-round tiovivo m.
mesh malla f.
mess (confusion) confusión f; (disorder) desorden m; (mix-up) lío m;
(dirt) suciedad f.
▸ **mess about**, **mess around 1** vt
fastidiar. **2** vi (act the fool) hacer el
tonto.

▸ **mess around with** vt (fiddle with)
manosear.
▸ **mess up** vt (make untidy) desordenar; (dirty) ensuciar; (spoil) estropear.
mes·sage recado m.
mes·sen·ger mensajero, -a mf.
mess·y adj (untidy) desordenado, -a;
(dirty) sucio, -a.
met·al 1 n metal m. **2** adj metálico, -a.
met·a·phor metáfora f.
me·ter¹ contador m.
me·ter² metro m.
meth·od método m.
me·thod·i·cal adj metódico, -a.
met·ric adj métrico, -a.
mew npl see **mouse**.
Mex·i·can adj & n mejicano, -a (mf),
mexicano, -a (mf).
mice npl see **mouse**.
mi·cro·chip microchip m.
mi·cro·phone micrófono m.
mi·cro·scope microscopio m.
mi·cro·wave (ov·en) (horno m)
microondas m inv.
mid adj (in) **m. afternoon** a media
tarde; (in) **m. April** a mediados de
abril.
mid-air adj (collision, explosion) en
el aire.
mid·day mediodía m.
mid·dle 1 adj de en medio; **the M.
Ages** la Edad Media. **2** n medio m;
(waist) cintura f; **in the m. of** en medio de; **in the m. of winter** en pleno
invierno.
mid·dle-aged adj de mediana
edad.
mid·dle-class adj de clase media.
mid·night medianoche f.
midst in the m. of en medio de.
mid·way adv a medio camino.
mid·wife comadrona f.
might v aux see **may**.
might·y 1 adj (mightier, might-
iest) (strong) fuerte; (powerful) poderoso, -a; (great) enorme. **2** adv
fam cantidad de, muy.
mild adj (person, character) apacible;

(climate) templado, -a; *(punishment)* leve; *(tobacco, taste)* suave.

mile milla *f*; *fam* **miles better** muchísimo mejor.

mile·age kilometraje *m*.

mil·i·tar·y *adj* militar.

milk leche *f*.

milk choc·o·late chocolate *m* con leche.

milk·man lechero *m*.

milk shake batido *m*.

mill *(grinder)* molino *m*; *(for coffee)* molinillo *m*; *(factory)* fábrica *f*.

mil·li·me·ter milímetro *m*.

mil·lion millón *m*.

mil·lion·aire millonario, -a *mf*.

mime *vt* imitar.

mim·ic *vt* imitar.

mince(·meat) carne *f* picada.

mincer picadora *f* de carne.

mind 1 *n (intellect)* mente *f*; *(brain)* cabeza *f*; **what kind of car do you have in m.?** ¿en qué clase de coche estás pensando?; **to be in two minds** estar indeciso, -a; **to my m.** a mi parecer. **2** *vt (child)* cuidar; *(house)* vigilar; *(be careful of)* tener cuidado con; *(object to)* tener inconveniente en; **m. the step!** ¡ojo con el escalón!; **I wouldn't m. a cup of coffee** me vendría bien un café; **never m.** no importa. **3** *vi (object)* **do you m. if I open the window?** ¿le importa que abra la ventana?

mine¹ *poss pron* (el) mío, (la) mía, (los) míos, (las) mías; **a friend of m.** un amigo mío; **these gloves are m.** estos guantes son míos; **which is m.?** ¿cuál es el mío?

mine² *(for coal etc)* mina *f*.

min·er minero, -a *mf*.

min·er·al *adj* mineral.

min·er·al wa·ter agua *f* mineral.

min·i- *prefix* mini-.

min·i·a·ture 1 *n* miniatura *f*. **2** *adj* (en) miniatura.

min·i·mum *adj* mínimo, -a.

min·ing 1 *n* minería *f*, explotación *f* de minas. **2** *adj* minero, -a.

min·is·ter ministro, -a *mf*; *(of church)* pastor, -a *mf*.

min·is·try *(political)* ministerio *m*; *(in church)* sacerdocio *m*.

mi·nor *adj (lesser)* menor; *(unimportant)* sin importancia.

mi·nor·i·ty minoría *f*.

mint *(herb)* menta *f*; *(sweet)* pastilla *f* de menta.

mi·nus *prep* **5 m. 3** 5 menos 3; **m. 10 degrees** 10 grados bajo cero.

min·ute¹ minuto *m*; **just a m.** (espera) un momento.

mi·nute² *adj (tiny)* diminuto, -a.

mir·a·cle milagro *m*.

mi·rac·u·lous *adj* milagroso, -a.

mir·ror espejo *m*; **rear-view m.** retrovisor *m*.

mis·be·have *vi* portarse mal.

mis·cel·la·ne·ous *adj* variado, -a.

mis·chief *(naughtiness)* travesura *f*, *(evil)* malicia *f*; **to get up to m.** hacer travesuras.

mis·chie·vous *adj (naughty)* travieso, -a; *(playful)* juguetón, -ona; *(wicked)* malicioso, -a.

mis·de·mean·or delito *m* menor.

mi·ser avaro, -a *mf*.

mis·er·a·ble *adj (sad)* triste; *(wretched)* miserable.

mi·ser·ly *adj* tacaño, -a.

mis·er·y *(sadness)* tristeza *f*, *(wretchedness)* desgracia *f*; *(suffering)* sufrimiento *m*; *(poverty)* miseria *f*.

mis·for·tune desgracia *f*.

mis·hap contratiempo *m*.

mis·lay* *vt* extraviar.

mis·lead* *vt* despistar; *(deliberately)* engañar.

mis·lead·ing *adj (erroneous)* erróneo, -a; *(deliberately)* engañoso, -a.

miss¹ señorita *f*.

miss² **1** *vt (train etc)* perder; *(opportunity)* dejar pasar; *(regret absence of)* echar de menos; **you have missed the point** no has captado la idea. **2** *vi (throw etc)* fallar; *(shot)* errar; **is anything missing?** ¿falta algo?

▸**miss out 1** *vt (omit)* saltarse. **2** *vi* **don't worry, you're not missing out** no te preocupes, no te pierdes nada.

▸**miss out on** *vt* perderse.

mis·sile misil *m*; *(object thrown)* proyectil *m*.

miss·ing *adj (lost)* perdido, -a; *(disappeared)* desaparecido, -a; *(absent)* ausente; **m. person** desaparecido, -a *mf*; **three cups are m.** faltan tres tazas.

mis·sion misión *f*.

mist *(fog)* niebla *f*; *(thin)* neblina *f*; *(at sea)* bruma *f*.

mis·take 1 *n* error *m*; **by m.** por equivocación; *(unintentionally)* sin querer; **to make a m.** cometer un error. **2** *vt (meaning)* malentender; **to m. Jack for Bill** confundir a Jack con Bill.

mis·tak·en *adj* erróneo, -a; **you are m.** estás equivocado, -a.

mis·tak·en·ly *adv* por error.

mis·treat maltratar.

mis·tress *(of house)* ama *f*; *(primary school)* maestra *f*; *(secondary school)* profesora *f*; *(lover)* amante *f*.

mis·trust 1 *n* recelo *m*. **2** *vt* desconfiar de.

mist·y *adj (day)* de niebla; *(window etc)* empañado, -a.

mis·un·der·stand* *vti* malentender.

mis·un·der·stand·ing malentendido *m*; *(disagreement)* desavenencia *f*.

mit·ten manopla *f*.

mix 1 *vt* mezclar. **2** *vi (blend)* mezclarse **(with** con).

▸**mix up** *vt (ingredients)* mezclar bien; *(confuse)* confundir **(with** con); *(papers)* revolver.

mixed *adj (assorted)* surtido, -a; *(varied)* variado, -a; *(school)* mixto, -a.

mix·er *(for food)* batidora *f*.

mix·ture mezcla *f*.

mix-up confusión *f*.

moan 1 *n* gemido *m*. **2** *vi (groan)* gemir; *(complain)* quejarse **(about** de).

mob 1 *n* multitud *f*. **2** *vt* acosar.

mo·bile *adj* móvil.

mo·bile phone teléfono *m* móvil.

mod·el 1 *n* modelo *mf*; **(scale)** m. maqueta *f*. **2** *adj (railway)* en miniatura.

mo·dem módem *m*.

mod·er·ate *adj* moderado, -a; *(reasonable)* razonable; *(average)* regular; *(ability)* mediocre.

mod·er·a·tion moderación *f*.

mod·ern *adj* moderno, -a; **m. languages** lenguas *fpl* modernas.

mod·ern·ize *vt* modernizar.

mod·est *adj* modesto, -a; *(chaste)* púdico, -a; *(price)* módico, -a; *(success)* discreto, -a.

mod·es·ty *(humility)* modestia *f*; *(chastity)* pudor *m*.

mod·i·fi·ca·tion modificación *f*.

mod·i·fy *vt* modificar.

moist *adj* húmedo, -a.

mois·ture humedad *f*.

mold¹ *(fungus)* moho *m*.

mold² 1 *n (shape)* molde *m*. **2** *vt* moldear; *(clay)* modelar.

mold·y *adj* mohoso, -a; **to go m.** enmohecerse.

mole¹ *(beauty spot)* lunar *m*.

mole² *(animal)* topo *m*.

mom *fam* mamá *f*.

mo·ment momento *m*.

Mon·day lunes *m*.

mon·ey dinero *m*.

mon·ey or·der giro *m* postal.

mon·i·tor *(of computer)* monitor *m*.

monk monje *m*.

mon·key mono *m*.

mo·nop·o·lize *vt (attention etc)* acaparar.

mo·not·o·nous *adj* monótono -a.

mo·not·o·ny monotonía *f*.

mon·ster monstruo *m*.

month mes *m*.

month·ly 1 *adj* mensual. **2** *adv* mensualmente.

mon·u·ment monumento *m*.

moo *vi* mugir.

mood humor *m*; **to be in a good/ bad m.** estar de buen/mal humor; **to be in the m. for (doing) sth** estar de humor para (hacer) algo.

mood·y *adj (changeable)* de humor variable; *(bad-tempered)* malhumorado, -a.

moon luna *f.*

moon·light luz *f* de la luna.

moor *(heath)* páramo *m.*

moose *inv* alce *m.*

mop *(for floor)* fregona *f.*

▸ **mop up** *vt (liquids)* limpiar.

mo·ped ciclomotor *m.*

mor·al 1 *adj* moral. **2** *n* moraleja *f*; **morals** moral *f sing*, moralidad *f sing.*

mo·rale moral *f.*

more 1 *adj* más; **and what is m.** y lo que es más; **is there any m. tea?** ¿queda más té?; **I've no m. money** no me queda más dinero. **2** *pron* más; **how many m.?** ¿cuántos más?; **I need some m.** necesito más; **many/much m.** muchos, -as / mucho más; **m. than a hundred** más de cien. **3** *adv* más; **I won't do it any m.** no lo volveré a hacer; **m. and m. difficult** cada vez más difícil; **m. or less** más o menos; **she doesn't live here any m.** ya no vive aquí.

more·o·ver *adv* además.

morn·ing mañana *f*; *(before dawn)* madrugada *f*; **in the m.** por la mañana; **on Monday mornings** los lunes por la mañana; **tomorrow m.** mañana por la mañana.

Mo·roc·can *adj & n* marroquí *(mf).*

mor·tal *adj & n* mortal *(mf).*

mort·gage hipoteca *f.*

mort·gage com·pa·ny sociedad *f* hipotecaria.

Mos·lem *adj & n* musulmán, -ana *(mf).*

mosque mezquita *f.*

mos·qui·to *(pl* **mosquitoes)** mosquito *m.*

moss musgo *m.*

most 1 *adj (greatest in quantity etc)* más; *(the majority of)* la mayor parte de; **this house suffered (the) m. damage** esta casa fue la más afectada; **who made (the) m. mistakes?** ¿quién cometió más errores?; **m. of the time** la mayor parte del tiempo; **m. people** la mayoría de la gente. **2** *pron (greatest part)* la mayor parte; *(greatest number)* lo máximo; *(the majority of people)* la mayoría; **at the (very) m.** como máximo. **3** *adv* más; **the m. intelligent student** el estudiante más inteligente; **what I like m.** lo que más me gusta; **m. of all** sobre todo.

most·ly *adv (chiefly)* en su mayor parte; *(generally)* generalmente; *(usually)* normalmente.

mo·tel motel *m.*

moth mariposa *f* nocturna; **clothes m.** polilla *f.*

moth·er madre *f*; **M.'s Day** Día *m* de la Madre.

moth·er-in-law suegra *f.*

mo·tion 1 *n (movement)* movimiento *m*; *(gesture)* ademán *m.* **2** *vi* **to m. (to) sb to do sth** hacer señas a algn para que haga algo.

mo·ti·vat·ed *adj* motivado, -a.

mo·tive *(reason)* motivo *m.*

mo·tor *(engine)* motor *m.*

mo·tor·boat (lancha) motora *f.*

mo·tor·cy·cle motocicleta *f.*

mo·tor·cy·clist motociclista *mf.*

mo·tor·ist automovilista *mf.*

mount 1 *n (horse)* montura *f*; *(for photograph)* marco *m.* **2** *vt (horse)* subirse *or* montar a; *(photograph)* enmarcar. **3** *vi (go up)* subir; *(get on horse, bike)* montar.

▸ **mount up** *vi (increase)* subir; *(accumulate)* acumularse.

moun·tain montaña *f*; **m. bike** bicicleta *f* de montaña.

moun·tain·eer alpinista *mf, Am* andinista *mf.*

moun·tain·eer·ing alpinismo *m, Am* andinismo *m.*

moun·tain·ous *adj* montañoso, -a.

mourn *vti* to m. (for) sb llorar la muerte de algn.

mourn·ing luto *m*; **in m.** de luto.

mouse (*pl* mice) ratón *m*.

mousse (*dessert*) mousse *f*.

mouth (*pl* mouths) boca *f*, (*of river*) desembocadura *f*.

mouth-wash enjuague *m* bucal.

move 1 *n* (*movement*) movimiento *m*; (*in game*) jugada *f*; (*turn*) turno *m*; (*course of action*) medida *f*; (*to new home*) mudanza *f*. **2** *vt* mover; (*transfer*) trasladar; (*affect emotionally*) conmover; **to m. house** mudarse (de casa); **to m. job** cambiar de trabajo. **3** *vi* (*change position*) moverse; (*change house*) mudarse (de casa); (*change post*) trasladarse; (*leave*) marcharse; (*in game*) hacer una jugada.

▸**move about, move around 1** *vt* cambiar de sitio. **2** *vi* (*be restless*) ir y venir.

▸**move along 1** *vt* (*move forward*) hacer avanzar. **2** *vi* (*move forward*) avanzar.

▸**move away** *vi* (*move aside*) apartarse; (*change house*) mudarse (de casa).

▸**move back 1** *vt* (*to original place*) volver a. **2** *vi* (*withdraw*) retirarse; (*to original place*) volver.

▸**move forward** *vti* avanzar.

▸**move in** *vi* (*into new home*) instalarse.

▸**move on** *vi* (*go forward*) avanzar; (*time*) transcurrir.

▸**move out** *vi* (*leave house*) mudarse.

▸**move over** *vi* correrse hacia un lado.

▸**move up** *vi* (*go up*) subir; (*move along*) correrse hacia un lado, hacer sitio.

move·ment movimiento *m*; (*gesture*) ademán *m*; (*trend*) corriente *f*; (*of goods, capital*) circulación *f*.

mov·ie película *f*.

mov·ing *adj* (*that moves*) móvil; (*car etc*) en marcha; (*touching*) conmovedor, -a.

mow* *vt* (*lawn*) cortar.

mow·er cortacésped *m or f*.

Mr *abbr of* mister señor *m*, Sr.

Mrs *abbr* señora *f*, Sra.

MS *abbr of* Master of Science Licenciado, -a *mf* en Ciencias.

much 1 *adj* mucho, -a; **as m. ... as** tanto, -a ... como; **how m. chocolate?** ¿cuánto chocolate?; **so m.** tanto, -a. **2** *adv* mucho; **as m. as** tanto como; **as m. as possible** todo lo posible; **how m.?** ¿cuánto?; **how m. is it?** ¿cuánto es?; **m. better** mucho mejor; **m. more** mucho más; **too m.** demasiado. **3** *pron* mucho; **I thought as m.** lo suponía; **m. of the town was destroyed** gran parte de la ciudad quedó destruida.

Ms *abbr* señora *f*, Sra.

mud barro *m*.

mud·dle 1 *n* desorden *m*; (*mix-up*) embrollo *m*; **to get into a m.** hacerse un lío. **2** *vt* **to m. (up)** confundir.

mud·dy *adj* fangoso, -a; (*hands*) cubierto, -a de barro; (*liquid*) turbio, -a.

mug¹ (*large cup*) tazón *m*; (*beer*) jarra *f*.

mug² *vt* (*assault*) asaltar.

mug·ger asaltante *mf*.

mule mulo, -a *mf*.

mul·ti·ple 1 *adj* múltiple. **2** *n* múltiplo *m*.

mul·ti·pli·ca·tion multiplicación *f*.

mul·ti·ply *vt* multiplicar (**by** por).

mum·ble 1 *vt* decir entre dientes. **2** *vi* hablar entre dientes.

mum·my *fam* mami *f*.

mumps paperas *fpl*.

mu·nic·i·pal *adj* municipal.

mur·der 1 *n* asesinato *m*. **2** *vt* asesinar.

mur·der·er asesino *m*.

mur·mur 1 *vti* murmurar. **2** *n* murmullo *m*.

mus·cle músculo *m*.

mus·cu·lar *adj* (*person*) musculoso, -a.

mu·se·um museo *m*.

mush·room seta *f*; *(food)* champiñón *m*.

mu·sic música *f*.

mu·si·cal 1 *adj* musical; **to be m.** estar dotado, -a para la música. **2** *n* musical *m*.

mu·si·cian músico, -a *mf*.

Mus·lim *adj* & *n* musulmán, -ana *(mf)*.

mus·sel mejillón *m*.

must *v aux (obligation)* deber, tener que; **you m. arrive on time** tienes que *or* debes llegar a la hora. ■ *(probability)* deber (de); **he m. be ill** debe (de) estar enfermo.

mus·tache bigote *m*.

mus·tard mostaza *f*.

must·y *adj* que huele a cerrado *or* a humedad.

mute 1 *adj* mudo, -a. **2** *n (person)* mudo, -a *mf*; *(for musical instrument)* sordina *f*.

mut·ter *vti* murmurar.

mut·ton *(carne f de)* cordero *m*.

mu·tu·al *adj* mutuo, -a; *(shared)* común.

muz·zle *(for animal)* bozal *m*. •

my *poss* mi; **I washed my hair** me lavé el pelo; **my cousins** mis primos; **my father** mi padre; **one of my friends** un amigo mío.

my·self *pers pron (emphatic)* yo mismo, -a; **my husband and m.** mi marido y yo. ■ *(reflexive)* me; **I hurt m.** me hice daño. ■ *(after prep)* mí (mismo, -a).

mys·te·ri·ous *adj* misterioso, -a.

mys·ter·y misterio *m*.

myth mito *m*.

N

nail 1 *n (of finger, toe)* uña *f*; *(metal)* clavo *m*. **2** *vt* clavar.

▶**nail down** *vt* clavar.

nail-file lima *f* de uñas.

nail pol·ish, nail var·nish esmalte *m or* laca *f* de uñas.

na·ïve *adj* ingenuo, -a.

naked *adj* desnudo, -a.

name 1 *n* nombre *m*; *(surname)* apellido *m*; *(reputation)* reputación *f*; **what's your n.?** ¿cómo te llamas? **2** *vt* llamar; *(appoint)* nombrar.

name·ly *adv* a saber.

nan·ny niñera *f*.

nap *(sleep)* siesta *f*; **to have a n.** echar la *or* una siesta.

nap·kin (table) n. servilleta *f*.

nap·py pañal *m*.

nar·ra·tive 1 *n (genre)* narrativa *f*; *(story)* narración *f*. **2** *adj* narrativo, -a.

nar·row 1 *adj (passage, road etc)* estrecho, -a. **2** *vi* estrecharse.

▶**narrow down** *vt* reducir.

narrow·ly *adv (closely)* de cerca; *(by a small margin)* por poco.

nasti·ly *adv (to behave)* antipáticamente.

nas·ty *adj (unpleasant)* desagradable; *(unfriendly)* antipático, -a; *(malicious)* mal intencionado, -a.

na·tion nación *f*.

na·tion·al *adj* nacional.

na·tion·al·i·ty nacionalidad *f*.

na·tive 1 *adj (place)* natal; **n. language** lengua *f* materna. **2** *n* nativo, -a *mf*.

nat·u·ral *adj* natural; *(normal)* normal; *(born)* nato, -a.

nat·u·ral·ly *adv (of course)* naturalmente; *(by nature)* por naturaleza; *(in a relaxed manner)* con naturalidad.

na·ture naturaleza f; **n. study** historia f natural.

naugh·ty adj (child) travieso, -a.

nau·seous adj **to feel n.** tener ganas de vomitar.

na·val adj naval; **n. officer** oficial mf de marina.

na·vel ombligo m.

nav·i·gate 1 vt (river) navegar por; (ship) gobernar. **2** vi navegar.

nav·i·ga·tion navegación f.

na·vy marina f; **n. blue** azul m marino.

near 1 adj (space) cercano, -a; (time) próximo, -a; **in the n. future** en un futuro próximo; **it was a n. thing** poco faltó. **2** adv (space) cerca; **that's n. enough** ya vale. **3** prep cerca de; **n. the end of the film** hacia el final de la película.

near·by 1 adj cercano, -a. **2** adv cerca.

near·ly adv casi; **very n.** casi, casi; **we haven't n. enough** no alcanza ni con mucho.

neat adj (room, habits etc) ordenado, -a; (appearance) pulcro, -a.

neat·ly adv (carefully) cuidadosamente; (cleverly) hábilmente.

nec·es·sar·i·ly adv necesariamente.

nec·es·sar·y adj necesario, -a; **to do what is n.** hacer lo que haga falta; **if n.** si es preciso.

ne·ces·si·ty necesidad f; (article) requisito m indispensable.

neck cuello m; (of animal) pescuezo m.

neck·lace collar m.

nec·tar·ine nectarina f.

need 1 n necesidad f; (poverty) indigencia f; **if n. be** si fuera necesario; **there's no n. for you to do that** no hace falta que hagas eso. **2** vt necesitar; (require) requerir; **I n. to see him** tengo que verle. **3** v aux tener que, deber; **n. he go?** ¿tiene que ir?; **you needn't wait** no hace falta que esperes.

nee·dle aguja f.

need·less·ly adv innecesariamente.

nee·dle·work (sewing) costura f; (embroidery) bordado m.

neg·a·tive 1 adj negativo, -a. **2** n (in grammar) negación f; (photo) negativo m.

ne·glect vt (not look after) descuidar; **to n. to do sth** (omit to do) no hacer algo.

ne·glect·ed adj (appearance) desarreglado, -a; (garden) descuidado, -a; **to feel n.** sentirse desatendido, -a.

neg·li·gence negligencia f.

neg·li·gent adj negligente.

ne·go·ti·ate vti negociar.

ne·go·ti·a·tion negociación f.

neigh vi relinchar.

neigh·bor vecino, -a mf.

neigh·bor·hood (district) vecindad f, barrio m; (people) vecindario m.

neigh·bor·ing adj vecino, -a.

nei·ther 1 adj & pron ninguno de los dos, ninguna de las dos. **2** adv & conj ni; **n. ... nor** ni ... ni; **it's n. here nor there** no viene al caso; **she was not there and n. was her sister** ella no estaba, ni su hermana tampoco.

ne·on neón m; **n. light** luz f de neón.

neph·ew sobrino m.

nerve nervio m; (courage) valor m; (cheek) descaro m; **to get on sb's nerves** poner los nervios de punta a algn.

nerv·ous adj (apprehensive) nervioso, -a; (afraid) miedoso, -a; (timid) tímido, -a; **to be n.** tener miedo.

nest nido m.

net¹ red f.

net² adj neto, -a.

net·ting (wire) alambrada f.

net·tle ortiga f.

net·work red f.

neu·tral 1 adj neutro, -a. **2** n (gear) punto m muerto.

nev·er adv nunca, jamás; **he n.**

complains no se queja nunca; **n. again** nunca (ja)más.

nev·er·end·ing adj interminable.

nev·er·the·less adv sin embargo, no obstante.

new adj nuevo, -a.

new·born adj recién nacido, -a.

new·com·er recién llegado, -a mf, (to job etc) nuevo, -a mf.

new·ly adv recién.

news noticias fpl; **a piece of n.** una noticia.

news bul·le·tin boletín m informativo.

news·flash noticia f de última hora.

news·let·ter hoja f informativa.

news·pa·per periódico m.

next 1 adj (in position) de al lado; (in time) próximo, -a; (in order) siguiente, próximo, -a; **the n. day** el día siguiente; **n. Friday** el viernes que viene. **2** adv después; (next time) la próxima vez; **what shall we do n.?** ¿qué hacemos ahora? **3** prep **n. to** al lado de.

next-door adj de al lado; **our n. neighbor** el vecino or la vecina de al lado.

nib plumilla f.

nib·ble vti mordisquear.

nice adj (person) simpático, -a; (thing) agradable; (nice-looking) Esp bonito, -a, Am lindo, -a; **n. and cool** fresquito, -a; **to smell/taste n.** oler/saber bien.

nice·ly adv muy bien.

nick·el moneda f de cinco centavos.

nick·el-and-dime store = tienda de productos muy baratos.

nick·name apodo m.

niece sobrina f.

night noche f; **at twelve o'clock at n.** a las doce de la noche; **last n.** anoche; **to have a n. out** salir por la noche.

night·club sala f de fiestas; (disco) discoteca f.

night·gown camisón m.

night·in·gale ruiseñor m.

night·mare pesadilla f.

night·stand mesita f or mesilla f de noche, RP mesa f de luz, Méx buró m.

night·time noche f; **at n.** por la noche.

night watch·man vigilante m nocturno.

nil nada f, (in sport) cero m.

nine adj & n nueve (m) inv; **n. hundred** novecientos, -as.

nine·teen adj & n diecinueve (m) inv.

nine·ty adj & n noventa (m) inv.

ninth adj & n noveno, -a (mf).

nip vt (pinch) pellizcar; (bite) morder.

nip·ple (female) pezón m, (male) tetilla f.

ni·tro·gen nitrógeno m.

no 1 adv no; **no longer** ya no; **no less than** no menos de. **2** adj ninguno, -a; **she has no children** no tiene hijos; **I have no idea** no tengo (ni) idea; **no sensible person** ninguna persona razonable; **'no parking'** 'prohibido aparcar'; **¡no way!** ¡ni hablar!

no·ble adj noble.

no·bod·y pron nadie; **there was n. there** no había nadie; **n. else** nadie más.

nod 1 n (in agreement) señal m de asentimiento. **2** vi (in agreement) asentir con la cabeza. **3** vt **to n. one's head** inclinar la cabeza.

▸**nod off** vi dormirse.

noise ruido m; **to make a n.** hacer ruido.

nois·i·ly adv ruidosamente.

nois·y adj ruidoso, -a.

nom·i·nate vt (appoint) nombrar.

nom·i·na·tion (proposal) propuesta f, (appointment) nombramiento m.

non- prefix no.

none pron ninguno, -a; **n. at all** nada en absoluto.

none·the·less adv no obstante, sin embargo.

non·ex·ist·ent adj inexistente.

non·fic·tion obras *fpl* de no ficción.

non·sense tonterías *fpl*; **that's n.** eso es absurdo.

non·smok·er no fumador, -a *mf.*

non·stick *adj* antiadherente.

non·stop 1 *adj* continuo, -a; *(train)* directo, -a. **2** *adv* sin parar.

noo·dles *npl* fideos *mpl*, tallarines *mpl.*

noon mediodía *m*; **at n.** a mediodía.

nor *conj* ni, ni … tampoco; **neither … n.** ni … ni; **neither you n. I** ni tú ni yo; **n. do I** (ni) yo tampoco.

norm norma *f.*

nor·mal *adj* normal.

nor·mal·ly *adv* normalmente.

north 1 *n* norte *m.* **2** *adv* hacia el norte. **3** *adj* del norte; **n. wind** viento del norte.

north·bound *adj* (con) dirección norte.

north·east nor(d)este *m.*

north·ern *adj* del norte.

north·ern·er norteño, -a *mf.*

north·ward *adj* & *adv* hacia el norte.

north·west noroeste *m.*

Nor·we·gian 1 *adj* noruego, -a. **2** *n* *(person)* noruego, -a *mf*; *(language)* noruego *m.*

nose nariz *f*; **her n. is bleeding** le está sangrando la nariz.

nose·bleed hemorragia *f* nasal.

nos·tril orificio *m* nasal.

nos·y *adj* entrometido, -a.

not *adv* no; **he's n. in today** hoy no está; **n. at all** en absoluto; **thank you — n. at all** gracias — no hay de qué; **n. one (of them) said thank you** nadie me dio las gracias.

no·ta·ble *adj* notable.

no·ta·bly *adv* notablemente.

note 1 *n* *(in music, written)* nota *f*; *(money)* billete *m* (de banco); **to take n. of** *(notice)* prestar atención a; **to take notes** *(at lecture)* tomar apuntes. **2** *vt* *(write down)* anotar; *(notice)* darse cuenta de.

note·book cuaderno *m.*

note·pad bloc *m* de notas.

note·pa·per papel *m* de carta.

noth·ing 1 *n* nada; **I saw n.** no vi nada; **for n. (free)** gratis; **it's n. to do with you** no tiene nada que ver contigo; **n. else** nada más; **n. much** poca cosa. **2** *adv* **she looks n. like her sister** no se parece en nada a su hermana.

no·tice 1 *n* *(warning)* aviso *m*; *(attention)* atención *f*; *(in newspaper etc)* anuncio *m*; *(sign)* aviso *m*; **he gave a month's n.** presentó la dimisión con un mes de antelación; **at short n.** con poca antelación; **until further n.** hasta nuevo aviso; **to take n. of sth** prestar atención a algo. **2** *vt* darse cuenta de.

no·tice·a·ble *adj* obvio, -a, evidente.

no·ti·fi·ca·tion aviso *m.*

no·ti·fy *vt* avisar.

no·tion idea *f.*

no·to·ri·ous *adj pej* tristemente célebre.

nought cero *m.*

noun sustantivo *m.*

nour·ish·ing *adj* nutritivo, -a.

nov·el¹ novela *f.*

nov·el² *adj* original.

nov·el·ist novelista *mf.*

No·vem·ber noviembre *m.*

now 1 *adv* ahora; *(at present, these days)* actualmente; **just n., right n.** ahora mismo; **from n. on** de ahora en adelante; **n. and then, n. and again** de vez en cuando; **n. (then)** ahora bien; **n., n.!** ¡de eso nada! **2** *conj* **n. (that)** ahora que.

now·a·days *adv* hoy (en) día.

no·where *adv* en ninguna parte; **it's n. near ready** no está preparado, ni mucho menos.

noz·zle boquilla *f.*

nu·clear *adj* nuclear.

nude *adj* desnudo, -a; **in the n.** al desnudo.

nudge 1 *vt* dar un codazo a. **2** *n* codazo *m.*

nui·sance pesadez *f*; *(person)* pesado, -a *mf*; **what a n.!** ¡qué lata!

numb *adj (without feeling)* entumecido, -a.

num·ber 1 *n* número *m*; **have you got my (phone) n.?** ¿tienes mi (número de) teléfono?; **a n. of** people varias personas. **2** *vt (put a number on)* numerar.

nu·mer·al número *m*.

nu·mer·ous *adj* numeroso, -a.

nun monja *f*.

nurse 1 *n* enfermera *f*; *(male)* enfermero *m*. **2** *vt (look after)* cuidar.

nurs·er·y guardería *f*; *(in house)* cuarto *m* de los niños; *(garden center)* vivero *m*.

nurs·er·y rhyme canción *f* infantil.

nurs·er·y school jardín *m* de infancia.

nurs·ing n. home clínica *f*.

nut *(fruit)* fruto *m* seco; *(for bolt)* tuerca *f*.

nut·crack·er cascanueces *m inv*.

nut·shell in a n. en pocas palabras.

ny·lon 1 *n* nailon *m*; **nylons** medias *fpl* de nailon. **2** *adj* de nailon.

O

oak roble *m*.

oar remo *m*.

oats avena *f*.

o·be·di·ence obediencia *f*.

o·be·di·ent *adj* obediente.

o·bey *vt* obedecer; *(law)* cumplir.

ob·ject[1] *(thing)* objeto *m*; *(aim, purpose)* objetivo *m*; *(in grammar)* complemento *m*.

ob·ject[2] *vi* oponerse (**to** a); **do you o. to my smoking?** ¿le molesta que fume?

ob·jec·tion objeción *f*.

ob·jec·tive objetivo *m*.

ob·li·ga·tion obligación *f*.

o·blige *vt (compel)* obligar; *(do a favor for)* hacer un favor a; **I'm obliged to do it** me veo obligado, -a a hacerlo.

o·blig·ing *adj* solícito, -a.

o·blique *adj* oblicuo, -a inclinado, -a.

ob·scene *adj* obsceno, -a.

ob·scure 1 *adj* oscuro, -a; *(author, poet)* desconocido, -a. **2** *vt (truth)* ocultar.

ob·ser·vant *adj* observador, -a.

ob·ser·va·tion observación *f*; *(surveillance)* vigilancia *f*.

ob·serve *vt* observar; *(on surveillance)* vigilar; *(remark)* advertir.

ob·ses·sion obsesión *f*.

ob·sta·cle obstáculo *m*.

ob·sti·nate *adj (person)* obstinado, -a.

ob·struct *vt* obstruir; *(pipe etc)* atascar; *(view)* tapar; *(hinder)* estorbar; *(progress)* dificultar.

ob·tain *vt* obtener.

ob·vi·ous *adj* obvio, -a, evidente.

ob·vi·ous·ly *adv* evidentemente; **o.!** ¡claro!

oc·ca·sion ocasión *f*; *(event)* acontecimiento *m*.

oc·ca·sion·al *adj* eventual.

oc·ca·sion·al·ly *adv* de vez en cuando.

oc·cu·pant ocupante *mf*; *(tenant)* inquilino, -a *mf*.

oc·cu·pa·tion *(job, profession)* profesión *f*; *(task)* trabajo *m*.

oc·cu·py *vt (live in)* habitar en; **to o. one's time in doing sth** dedicar su tiempo a hacer algo; **to keep oneself occupied** mantenerse ocupado, -a.

oc·cur *vi (event)* suceder; *(change)* producirse; *(be found)* encontrarse; **it occurred to me that ...** se me ocurrió que ...

oc·cur·rence acontecimiento *m*.

o·cean océano *m*.

o·clock *adv* (it's) one o'c. (es) la una; (it's) two o'c. (son) las dos.

Oc·to·ber octubre *m.*

oc·to·pus pulpo *m.*

odd **1** *adj* (strange) raro, -a; (occasional) esporádico, -a; (extra) adicional; (not even) impar; (unpaired) desparejado, -a; **the o. customer** algún que otro cliente; **o. job** trabajillo *m;* **to be the o. man out** estar de más; **an o. sock** un calcetín suelto. **2** *adv* y pico; **twenty o. people** veinte y pico *or* veintitantas personas.

odd·ly *adv* extrañamente.

odds *npl* (chances) probabilidades *fpl;* (in betting) puntos *mpl* de ventaja; **the o. are that ...** lo más probable es que ... (+ *subjunctive*); **at o. with sb** reñido, -a con algn; **o. and ends** (small things) cositas *fpl.*

o·dor olor *m;* (fragrance) perfume *m.*

of *prep* de; **a friend of mine** un amigo mío; **there are four of us** somos cuatro; **two of them** dos de ellos; **that's very kind of you** es usted muy amable.

off **1** *prep* de; **she fell o. her horse** se cayó del caballo; **a house o. the road** una casa apartada de la carretera; **I'm o. wine** he perdido el gusto al vino. **2** *adv* (absent) fuera; **I have a day o.** tengo un día libre; **to be o. sick** estar de baja por enfermedad. **his arrival is three days o.** faltan tres días para su llegada; **six miles o. a seis millas.** ▪ **I'm o. to New York** me voy a Nueva York; **she ran o.** se fue corriendo. ▪ **ten percent o.** un descuento del diez por ciento. ▪ **with his shoes o.** descalzo. ▪ **on and o.** de vez en cuando. **3** *adj* **to be o.** (meat, fish) estar pasado, -a; (milk) estar agrio, -a; (gas etc) estar apagado, -a; (water) estar cortado, -a; (cancelled) estar cancelado, -a; **on the o. chance** por si acaso; **the o. season** la temporada baja; **you're better o. like that** así estás mejor.

of·fend *vt* ofender.

of·fend·er (criminal) delincuente *mf.*

of·fense (in law) delito *m;* **to take o. at sth** ofenderse por algo.

of·fen·sive **1** *n* (military) ofensiva *f.* **2** *adj* (insulting) ofensivo, -a; (repulsive) repugnante.

of·fer **1** *vt* ofrecer; (propose) proponer; (provide) proporcionar; **to o. to do a job** ofrecerse para hacer un trabajo. **2** *n* oferta *f,* (proposal) propuesta *f;* **on o.** de oferta.

of·fer·ing ofrecimiento *m;* (in religious ceremony) ofrenda *f.*

off·hand **1** *adj* (abrupt) brusco, -a. **2** *adv* de improviso.

of·fice (room) despacho *m;* (building) oficina *f,* (position) cargo *m.*

of·fi·cer oficial *mf;* (police) o. agente *mf* de policía.

of·fi·cial **1** *adj* oficial. **2** *n* funcionario, -a *mf.*

of·fi·cial·ly *adv* oficialmente.

off-line *adj* (computer, user) desconectado, -a.

off·spring *inv* (child) vástago *m;* (children) progenitura *f.*

of·ten *adv* a menudo; **every so o.** de vez en cuando.

oh *interj* ¡oh!

oil **1** *n* aceite *m;* (crude) petróleo *m.* **2** *vt* engrasar.

oil-can aceitera *f.*

oil change cambio *m* de aceite.

oint·ment pomada *f.*

OK, o·kay **1** *interj* ¡vale! **2** *adj* bien; **is it OK if ...?** ¿está bien si ...?

old *adj* viejo, -a; (previous) antiguo, -a; **an o. man** un anciano; **o. age** vejez *f,* **how o. are you?** ¿cuántos años tienes?; **she's five years o.** tiene cinco años.

old-fash·ioned *adj* (outdated) a la antigua; (unfashionable) anticuado, -a.

ol·ive (tree) olivo *m;* (fruit) aceituna *f,* oliva *f.*

O·lym·pic *adj* olímpico, -a; **O. Games** Juegos *mpl* Olímpicos.

om·e·let tortilla f; Spanish o. tortilla española or de patatas.

o·mis·sion omisión f.

o·mit vt omitir; (accidentally) pasar por alto; (forget) olvidarse (**to** de).

on 1 prep (position) sobre, encima de, en; **it's on the table** está encima de or sobre la mesa; **on page four** en la página cuatro; **a town on the coast** un pueblo en la costa; **on the right** a la derecha; **on the way** en el camino. ▪ (time) **on April 3rd** el tres de abril; **on a sunny day** un día de sol; **on Monday** el lunes; **on the following day** al día siguiente; **on his arrival** a su llegada; **on time** a tiempo. ▪ (means) **on the radio** en la radio; **to play sth on the piano** tocar algo al piano; **onTV** en la tele; **on the phone** al teléfono; **on foot** a pie; **on the train/plane** en tren/avión. ▪ (about) sobre; **a lecture on numismatics** una conferencia sobre numismática. **2** adj **to be on** (TV, radio, light) estar encendido, -a; (engine) estar en marcha; (tablecloth) estar puesto; **she had a coat on** llevaba un abrigo puesto; **that film was on last week** pusieron esa película la semana pasada. **3** adv **have you anything on tonight?** ¿tienes algún plan para esta noche?; **he talks on and on** habla sin parar; **to work on** seguir trabajando.

once 1 adv (one time) una vez; (formerly) en otro tiempo; **o. a week** una vez por semana; **o. in a while** de vez en cuando; **o. more** una vez más; **at o.** en seguida; **don't speak all at o.** no habléis todos a la vez. **2** conj una vez que.

one 1 adj un, una; **he'll come back o. day** un día volverá. **2** dem pron **any o.** cualquiera; **that o.** ése, ésa; (distant) aquél, aquélla; **the blue ones** los azules, las azules; **the o. on the table** el or la que está encima de la mesa; **the ones that, the ones who** los or las que; **this o.** éste, ésta.

3 indef pron uno, -a mf; **give me o.** dame uno; **o. by o.** uno tras otro; **o. never knows** nunca se sabe; **to cut o.'s finger** cortarse el dedo; **o. another** el uno al otro; **they love o. another** se quieren. **4** n (digit) uno m; **a hundred and o.** ciento uno.

one·self pron uno, -a mismo, -a mf; (reflexive) sí mismo, -a mf; **to talk to o.** hablar para sí; **by o.** solo, -a.

one-way adj (ticket) de ida; (street) de dirección única.

on·ion cebolla f.

on-line adj (computer, user) conectado, -a.

on·look·er espectador, -a mf.

on·ly 1 adv solamente, sólo; **he has o. just left** acaba de marcharse hace un momento; **o. yesterday** ayer mismo. **2** adj único, -a. **3** conj pero.

on·to prep see **on**.

on·ward(s) adv en adelante; **from this time o.** de ahora en adelante.

o·paque adj opaco, -a.

o·pen 1 adj abierto, -a; **wide o.** abierto de par en par; **in the o. air** al aire libre; **o. ticket** billete m abierto. **2** vt abrir; (exhibition etc) inaugurar; (negotiations, conversation) entablar. **3** vi abrirse. **4** n **in the o.** al aire libre; fig **to bring into the o.** hacer público.

▸**open out 1** vt desplegar. **2** vi (flowers) abrirse; (view) extenderse.

▸**open up 1** vt (market etc) abrir; (possibilities) crear. **2** vi abrirse.

o·pen·ing (act) apertura f; (beginning) comienzo m; (aperture) abertura f; (gap) brecha f; (in market) oportunidad f.

o·pen·ly adv abiertamente.

o·pen-mind·ed adj sin prejuicios.

o·pen·ness (frankness) franqueza f.

op·er·a ópera f.

op·er·ate 1 vi (function) funcionar; (act) actuar; (surgeon) operar. **2** vt (switch on) accionar; (control) manejar; (business) dirigir.

op·er·at·ing sys·tem sistema *m* operativo.

op·er·a·tion *(of machine)* funcionamiento *m*; *(surgical)* operación *f.*

op·er·a·tor *(of machine)* operario, -a *mf*, *(telephone)* operador, -a *mf.*

o·pin·ion opinión *f*; **in my o.** en mi opinión.

op·po·nent adversario, -a *mf.*

op·por·tu·ni·ty oportunidad *f*, *(prospect)* perspectiva *f.*

op·pose *vt* oponerse a.

op·posed *adj* opuesto, -a; **to be o. to sth** estar en contra de algo.

op·pos·ing *adj* adversario, -a.

op·po·site 1 *adj (facing)* de enfrente; *(page)* contiguo, -a; *(contrary)* contrario, -a; **in the o. direction** en dirección contraria. **2** *n* lo contrario *m*; **quite the o.!** ¡al contrario! **3** *prep* enfrente de. **4** *adv* enfrente.

op·po·si·tion oposición *f*, **in o. to** en contra de.

opt *vi* to **o. for** optar por; **to o. to do sth** optar por hacer algo.

op·ti·cal *adj* óptico, -a.

op·ti·cian óptico, -a *mf.*

op·ti·mist optimista *mf.*

op·ti·mis·tic *adj* optimista.

op·tion opción *f*; **I have no o.** no tengo más remedio.

op·tion·al *adj* optativo, -a.

or *conj* o; *(before a word beginning with a stressed o or ho)* u; *(with negative)* ni; **he can't read or write** no sabe leer ni escribir.

o·ral 1 *adj* oral. **2** *n* examen *m* oral.

or·ange 1 *n* naranja *f.* **2** *adj* de color naranja.

or·ange juice zumo *m* de naranja.

or·bit órbita *f.*

or·chard huerto *m.*

or·ches·tra orquesta *f.*

or·deal mala experiencia *f.*

or·der 1 *n (sequence, command)* orden *m*; *(commission)* pedido *m*; **to put in o.** ordenar; **is your passport in o.?** ¿tienes el pasaporte en regla?; **'out of o.'** 'averiado'; **to be on o.** estar pedido; **in o. that** para que *(+ subjunctive)*, a fin de que *(+ subjunctive)*; **in o. to** para *(+ infinitive)*, a fin de *(+ infinitive)*. **2** *vt (command)* ordenar; *(goods)* encargar; **to o. sb to do sth** mandar a algn hacer algo; **to o. a dish** pedir un plato.

or·di·nance *(decree)* ordenanza *f*, decreto *m.*

or·di·nar·y 1 *adj* normal; *(average)* corriente. **2** *n* **out of the o.** fuera de lo común.

ore mineral *m.*

or·gan órgano *m.*

or·gan·ic *adj* orgánico, -a.

or·gan·i·za·tion organización *f.*

or·gan·ize *vt* organizar.

or·gan·iz·er organizador, -a *mf.*

O·ri·en·tal *adj & n* oriental *(mf).*

or·i·gin origen *m.*

o·rig·i·nal 1 *adj* original; *(first)* primero, -a; *(novel)* original. **2** *n* original *m.*

o·rig·i·nal·i·ty originalidad *f.*

o·rig·i·nal·ly *adv (at first)* en un principio.

o·rig·i·nate 1 *vt* originar. **2** *vi* **to o. from** or **in** tener su origen en.

or·na·ment adorno *m.*

or·phan huérfano, -a *mf.*

or·phan·age orfanato *m.*

or·tho·dox *adj* ortodoxo, -a.

os·trich avestruz *f.*

oth·er 1 *adj* otro, -a; **the o. one** el otro, la otra. **2** *pron* otro, -a *mf*; **many others** otros muchos; **the others** los otros, los demás; **we see each o. quite often** nos vemos con bastante frecuencia.

oth·er·wise *adv (if not)* si no; *(differently)* de otra manera; *(in other respects)* por lo demás.

ought *v aux* deber; **I thought I o. to tell you** creí que debía decírtelo; **she o. to do it** debería hacerlo; **you o. to see the exhibition** deberías ver la exposición. ▪ *(expectation)* **he o. to pass the exam** seguramente aprobará el examen; **that o.**

to do con eso bastará.

ounce onza *f*.

our *poss adj* nuestro, -a.

ours *poss pron* (el) nuestro, (la) nuestra, (los) nuestros, (las) nuestras; **a friend of o.** un amigo nuestro.

our·selves *pers pron pl* (*reflexive*) nos; (*emphatic*) nosotros mismos, nosotras mismas; **by o.** a solas.

out 1 *adv*·(*outside, away*) fuera; **o. there** ahí fuera; **to go o.** salir. **2** *prep* **o. of** (*place*) fuera de; (*cause, motive*) por; (*made from*) de; (*short of, without*) sin; **move o. of the way!** ¡quítate de en medio!; **he jumped o. the window** saltó por la ventana; **o. of danger** fuera de peligro; **forty o. of fifty** cuarenta de cada cincuenta. **3** *adj* **to be o.** (*unfashionable*) estar pasado, -a de moda; (*not lit*) estar apagado, -a; (*eliminated from game*) quedar eliminado, -a; **the sun is o.** ha salido el sol; **she's o.** (*not in*) ha salido.

out·break (*of war*) comienzo *m*; (*of disease*) brote *m*; (*of violence*) ola *f*.

out·burst (*of anger*) arrebato *m*.

out·come resultado *m*.

out·dat·ed *adj* anticuado, -a.

out·do* *vt* exceder; **to o. sb** superar a algn.

out·door *adj* al aire libre; (*clothes*) de calle.

out·doors *adv* al aire libre.

out·er *adj* exterior.

out·er space espacio *m* sideral.

out·fit (*kit, equipment*) equipo *m*; (*set of clothes*) conjunto *m*.

out·grow* *vt* he's outgrowing all his clothes toda la ropa se le está quedando pequeña; **he'll o. it** se le pasará con la edad.

out·ing excursión *f*.

out·law 1 *n* proscrito, -a *mf*. **2** *vt* prohibir.

out·let (*for goods*) mercado *m*.

out·line (*draft*) bosquejo *m*; (*outer line*) contorno *m*; (*silhouette*) perfil *m*; (*sketch*) boceto *m*.

out·look (*point of view*) punto *m* de vista; (*prospect*) perspectiva *f*.

out·num·ber *vt* exceder en número.

out-of-doors *adv* al aire libre.

out·put producción *f*; (*of machine*) rendimiento *m*.

out·rage 1 *n* ultraje *m*; **it's an o.!** ¡es un escándalo! **2** *vt* **to be outraged by sth** indignarse por algo.

out·ra·geous *adj* (*behavior*) escandaloso, -a; (*clothes*) extravagante.

out·right *adv* (*completely*) por completo; (*directly*) directamente.

out·set comienzo *m*, principio *m*.

out·side 1 *prep* fuera de; (*beyond*) más allá de; (*other than*) aparte de. **2** *adj* (*exterior*) exterior, externo, -a. **3** *adv* (*exterior*) exterior *m*; **on the o.** por fuera.

out·sid·er (*stranger*) extraño, -a *mf*; (*in election*) candidato, -a *mf* con pocas posibilidades de ganar.

out·skirts *npl* afueras *fpl*.

out·stand·ing *adj* (*exceptional*) destacado, -a; (*unpaid, unresolved*) pendiente.

out·ward *adj* (*appearance*) externo, -a; **the o. journey** el viaje de ida.

out·ward(s) *adv* hacia (a)fuera.

o·val 1 *adj* ovalado, -a. **2** *n* óvalo *m*.

ov·en horno *m*.

o·ver 1 *prep* (*above*) encima de; (*across*) al otro lado de; (*during*) durante; (*more than*) más de; **the bridge o. the river** el puente que cruza el río; **all o. Spain** por toda España; **it's all o. the carpet** está por toda la alfombra; **o. the phone** por teléfono; **men o. twenty-five** hombres mayores de veinticinco años. **2** *adv* (*more*) más; (*again*) otra vez; (*in excess*) de más; **o. there** allá; **all o.** por todas partes; **o. and o.** (*again*) una y otra vez; **there are still some o.** todavía quedan algunos. **3** *adj* (*finished*) acabado, -a; **it's (all) o.** se acabó; **the danger is o.** ha pasado el peligro.

o·ver·all 1 adj total. **2** adv (on the whole) en conjunto. **3** n guardapolvo m; **overalls** mono m sing.

o·ver·board adv por la borda.

o·ver·charge vt (charge too much) cobrar de más.

o·ver·coat abrigo m.

o·ver·come* vt (conquer) vencer; (overwhelm) abrumar; (surmount) superar.

o·ver·do* vt (carry too far) exagerar; (in cooking) cocer or asar demasiado.

o·ver·draft crédito m al descubierto.

o·ver·due adj (rent, train etc) atrasado, -a.

o·ver·eat vi comer en exceso.

o·ver·ex·cit·ed adj sobreexcitado, -a.

o·ver·flow vi (river) desbordarse; (cup etc) derramarse.

o·ver·head adj (por) encima de la cabeza.

o·ver·hear vt oír por casualidad.

o·ver·heat vi recalentarse.

o·ver·joyed adj rebosante de alegría.

o·ver·lap vi superponerse.

ov·er·leaf adv al dorso.

o·ver·load vt sobrecargar.

o·ver·look vt (fail to notice) pasar por alto; (ignore) no hacer caso de; (have a view of) tener vista a.

o·ver·night 1 adv por la noche; **we stayed there o.** pasamos la noche allí. **2** adj (journey) de noche.

o·ver·pass (bridge) paso m elevado.

o·ver·rat·ed adj sobrestimado, -a.

o·ver·seas 1 adv en ultramar; **to live o.** vivir en el extranjero. **2** adj de ultramar; (visitor) extranjero, -a; (trade) exterior.

o·ver·sight descuido m.

o·ver·sleep vi quedarse dormido, -a.

o·ver·spend vi gastar demasiado.

o·ver·take* vt adelantar.

o·ver·time horas fpl extra.

o·ver·turn vti volcar.

o·ver·weight adj **to be o.** ser gordo, -a.

o·ver·whelm vt (defeat) aplastar; (overpower) abrumar.

o·ver·whelm·ing adj (defeat) aplastante; (desire) irresistible.

o·ver·work vi trabajar demasiado.

owe vt deber.

ow·ing adj o. to debido a.

owl búho m.

own 1 adj propio, -a; **it's his o. fault** es culpa suya. **2** pron **my o., your o., his o.** etc lo mío, lo tuyo, lo suyo etc; **to get one's o. back** tomarse la revancha; **on one's o.** (without help) uno, -a mismo, -a; (alone) solo, -a. **3** vt poseer.

▸ **own up** vi to o. up (to) confesar.

own·er propietario, -a mf.

ox·y·gen oxígeno m.

oys·ter ostra f.

o·zone ozono m; **o. layer** capa f de ozono.

P

pace (step) paso m; (speed) ritmo m.

Pa·cif·ic the P. (Ocean) el (océano) Pacífico.

pac·i·fi·er (of baby) chupete m.

pack 1 n paquete m; (rucksack) mochila f; (of cards) baraja f; (of hounds) jauría f. **2** vt (goods) embalar; (in suitcase) poner; (fill) atestar; (press down) (snow) apretar; **to p. one's bags** hacer las maletas; fig marcharse. **3** vi (baggage) hacer las maletas.

▸ **pack away** vt (tidy away) guardar.

▸ **pack up** fam **1** vt (give up) dejar. **2** vi (stop working) terminar; (machine etc) estropearse.

pack·age *(parcel, software)* paquete *m*.

pack·age tour viaje *m* todo incluido.

pack·ag·ing embalaje *m*.

packed *adj (place)* atestado, -a.

packed lunch almuerzo *m* (para tomar fuera).

pack·et paquete *m*.

pack·ing embalaje *m*.

pact pacto *m*.

pad 1 *n* almohadilla *f*; *(of paper)* bloc *m*. **2** *vt (chair)* rellenar.

pad·ded *adj (cell)* acolchado, -a.

pad·dle¹ *(oar)* pala *f*.

pad·dle² *vi* chapotear.

pad·lock candado *m*.

page¹ página *f*.

page² *(at club etc)* botones *m inv*.

pain dolor *m*; *(grief)* sufrimiento *m*; **to take pains over sth** esmerarse en algo.

pain·ful *adj* doloroso, -a.

pain·kill·er analgésico *m*.

paint 1 *n* pintura *f*. **2** *vt* pintar; **to p. sth white** pintar algo de blanco.

paint·brush pincel *m*; *(for walls)* brocha *f*.

paint·er pintor, -a *mf*.

paint·ing cuadro *m*; *(activity)* pintura *f*.

paint strip·per quitapinturas *m inv*.

pair *(of gloves, shoes)* par *m*; *(of people, cards)* pareja *f*.

pa·ja·mas *npl* pijama *m*.

Pak·i·stan·i *adj & n* paquistaní *(mf)*.

pal *fam* amigo, -a *mf*.

pal·ace palacio *m*.

pal·ate paladar *m*.

pale *adj (skin)* pálido, -a; *(color)* claro, -a.

Pal·es·tin·i·an *adj & n* palestino, -a *(mf)*.

pal·ette paleta *f*.

palm *(of hand)* palma *f*, *(tree)* palmera *f*, **p. leaf** palma *f*.

pam·phlet folleto *m*.

pan *(saucepan)* cazuela *f*.

pan·cake crepe *f*.

pane cristal *m*, vidrio *m*.

pan·el *(of wall)* panel *m*; *(of instruments)* tablero *m*; *(jury)* jurado *m*.

pan·ic 1 *n* pánico *m*; **to get into a p.** ponerse histérico, -a. **2** *vi* **he panicked** le entró pánico.

pant *vi* jadear.

pant·ies *npl* bragas *fpl*.

pan·to·mime *(play)* función *f* musical navideña.

pan·try despensa *f*.

pants *npl (underpants) (ladies')* bragas *fpl*; *(men's)* calzoncillos *mpl*; *(trousers)* pantalón *m*.

pant·y·hose panties *mpl*.

pa·per papel *m*; *(newspaper)* periódico *m*; *(exam)* examen *m*; *(essay)* trabajo *m* (escrito).

pa·per·back libro *m* en rústica.

pa·per·clip clip *m*.

pa·per knife cortapapeles *m inv*.

pap·er·work papeleo *m*.

par *(parity)* igualdad *f*, *(in golf)* par *m*.

par·a·chute paracaídas *m inv*.

pa·rade desfile *m*.

par·a·dise paraíso *m*.

par·af·fin parafina *f*.

par·a·graph párrafo *m*.

Par·a·guay·an *adj & n* paraguayo, -a *(mf)*.

par·a·le·gal ayudante *mf* de un abogado, *RP* procurador, -a *mf*.

par·al·lel *adj* paralelo, -a **(to, with** a**)**.

par·a·lyze *vt* paralizar.

par·a·site parásito *m*.

par·a·sol sombrilla *f*.

par·cel paquete *m*.

par·don 1 *n* perdón *m*; **I beg your p.** (Vd.) perdone; **(I beg your) p.?** ¿cómo (dice)? **2** *vt* perdonar; **p. me!** ¡Vd. perdone!

par·ents *npl* padres *mpl*.

par·ish parroquia *f*.

park 1 *n* parque *m*. **2** *vt (car)* estacionar, *Esp* aparcar.

park·ing aparcamiento *m*; **'no p.'** 'prohibido aparcar'.

park·ing light luz f de estacionamiento.

park·ing lot aparcamiento m.

park·ing me·ter parquímetro m.

park·ing space aparcamiento m.

park·ing tick·et multa f de aparcamiento.

par·lia·ment parlamento m.

par·rot loro m.

pars·ley perejil m.

pars·nip chirivía f.

part 1 n parte f; (piece) trozo m; (of machine, engine) pieza f; (in play etc) papel m; **for the most p.** en la mayor parte; **to take p. in sth** participar en algo; **in these parts** por estos lugares. **2** (partly) en parte. **3** vi separarse; (say goodbye) despedirse.

▸**part with** vt separarse de.

par·tial adj parcial; **to be p. to sth** ser aficionado, -a a algo.

par·tic·i·pant participante mf.

par·tic·i·pate vi participar (in en).

par·tic·i·pa·tion participación f.

par·ti·ci·ple participio m.

par·ti·cle board madera f aglomerada.

par·tic·u·lar 1 adj (special) particular; (fussy) exigente; **in this p. case** en este caso concreto. **2** npl particulars pormenores mpl; **to take down sb's particulars** tomar nota de los datos personales de algn.

par·tic·u·lar·ly adv particularmente.

part·ing (in hair) raya f.

par·ti·tion (wall) tabique m.

part·ly adv en parte.

part·ner compañero, -a mf; (in dancing, tennis) pareja f; (in business) socio, -a mf.

part·ner·ship (in business) sociedad f.

par·tridge perdiz f.

part-time 1 adj (work etc) de media jornada. **2** adv a tiempo parcial.

par·ty (celebration) fiesta f; (group) grupo m; (political) partido m.

pass 1 n (of mountain) desfiladero m; (permit) permiso m; (in football etc) pase m. **2** vt pasar; (overtake) adelantar; (exam, law) aprobar. **3** vi pasar; (car) adelantar; (people) cruzarse; (in football etc) hacer un pase; (in exam) aprobar; **we passed on the stairs** nos cruzamos en la escalera.

▸**pass away** vi pasar a mejor vida.

▸**pass by 1** vt pasar de largo. **2** vi pasar cerca; **if you're ever passing by** si alguna vez pasas por aquí.

▸**pass off 1** vt to p. oneself off as sth hacerse pasar por algo. **2** vi (happen) transcurrir.

▸**pass on** vt (hand on) transmitir. **2** vi (die) pasar a mejor vida.

▸**pass out** vi (faint) desmayarse.

▸**pass over** vt (disregard) pasar por alto.

▸**pass through** vi estar de paso.

▸**pass up** vt (opportunity) renunciar a; (offer) rechazar.

pass·a·ble adj (road) transitable; (acceptable) pasable.

pas·sage (hallway) pasillo m; (in music, text) pasaje m.

pas·sage·way (interior) pasillo m; (exterior) pasaje m.

pas·sen·ger pasajero, -a mf.

pas·ser·by transeúnte mf.

pass·ing 1 n (of time) transcurso m; **in p.** de pasada. **2** adj que pasa; **p. grade** (in exam) aprobado m.

pas·sion pasión f.

pas·sion·ate adj apasionado, -a.

pas·sive adj pasivo, -a.

pass·port pasaporte m.

pass·word contraseña f.

past 1 n pasado m; **in the p.** antiguamente. **2** adj pasado, -a; (former) anterior; **in the p. weeks** en las últimas semanas. **3** adv por delante; **to run p.** pasar corriendo. **4** prep (beyond) más allá de; (more than) más de; **it's five p. ten** son las diez y cinco.

pas·ta pasta f.

paste 1 n pasta f; (glue) engrudo m. **2** vt (stick) pegar.

pas·teur·ized adj pasteurizado, -a.

pas·time pasatiempo m.

pas·try (dough) pasta f; (cake) pastel m.

pas·ture pasto m.

pat vt acariciar.

patch (of material) parche m; (of color) mancha f; **to go through a bad p.** pasar por una mala racha.

▸**patch up** vt (garment) poner un parche en; **to p. up a quarrel** hacer las paces (**with** con).

pat·ent 1 n (for product) patente f. **2** adj (obvious) patente, evidente. **3** vt (product) patentar.

path sendero m; (route) camino m.

pa·thet·ic adj patético, -a; (hopeless) malísimo, -a.

path·way sendero m.

pa·tience paciencia f; **to lose one's p. with sb** perder la paciencia con algn.

pa·tient 1 adj paciente. **2** n paciente mf.

pa·tient·ly adv con paciencia.

pat·i·o patio m.

pa·tri·ot·ic adj (person) patriota; (speech, act) patriótico, -a.

pa·trol 1 n patrulla f. **2** vt patrullar por.

pa·tron (of charity) patrocinador, -a mf; (of arts) mecenas m inv; (customer) cliente, -a mf habitual; **p. saint** (santo, -a mf) patrón, -ona mf.

pat·tern (in sewing) patrón m; (design) dibujo m.

pause 1 n pausa f, (in conversation) silencio m. **2** vi hacer una pausa.

pave vt pavimentar; (with stones) empedrar; **to p. the way for sb/ sth** preparar el terreno para algn/ algo.

paved adj pavimentado, -a.

pave·ment acera f; (road surface) calzada f.

pa·vil·ion pabellón m.

pav·ing stone losa f.

paw (foot) pata f; (of cat) garra f.

pawn (in chess) peón m.

pay 1 n (wages) paga f. **2** vt* pagar; (attention) prestar; (visit) hacer; (be profitable for) compensar; **to be or get paid** cobrar; **to p. sb a compliment** halagar a algn. **3** vi* pagar; (be profitable) ser rentable; **to p. for sth** pagar (por) algo.

▸**pay back** vt reembolsar.

▸**pay in** vt (money) ingresar.

▸**pay off** vt (debt) liquidar.

▸**pay out** vt (spend) gastar (**on** en).

▸**pay up** vt (bill) liquidar, saldar. **2** vi pagar.

pay·a·ble adj pagadero, -a.

pay·check sueldo m.

pay·ment pago m.

pay·phone teléfono m público.

pay slip nómina f.

pea guisante m.

peace paz f; (calm) tranquilidad f; **at** or **in p.** en paz; **p. and quiet** tranquilidad.

peace·ful adj (non-violent) pacífico, -a; (calm) tranquilo, -a.

peach melocotón m.

pea·cock pavo m real.

peak (of mountain) pico m; (summit) cima f; **p. hours** horas fpl punta.

peaky adj fam (ill) pálido, -a.

pea·nut cacahuete m.

pear pera f.

pearl perla f.

peb·ble guijarro m; (small) china f.

pe·can (nut) pacana f.

peck vt (bird) picotear.

peck·ish adj **to feel p.** empezar a tener hambre.

pe·cu·liar adj (odd) extraño, -a; (particular) característico, -a.

pe·cu·li·ar·i·ty (characteristic) característica f.

ped·al 1 n pedal m. **2** vi pedalear.

pe·des·tri·an peatón, -ona mf.

pe·des·tri·an cross·ing paso m de peatones.

peek 1 n ojeada f. **2** vi **to p. at sth** mirar algo a hurtadillas.

peel 1 n piel f; (of orange, lemon) cáscara f. **2** vt (fruit) pelar. **3** vi (paint) desconcharse; (skin) pelarse.

▶**peel off** vt (skin of fruit) pelar; (clothes) quitarse.

peel·er potato p. pelapatatas m inv.

peep 1 n (glance) ojeada f; (furtive look) mirada f furtiva. **2** vi to p. at sth echar una ojeada a algo.

peer vi mirar detenidamente.

peg clavija f; (for coat, hat) colgador m.

pen[1] pluma f.

pen[2] (for animals) corral m.

pen·al·ty (punishment) pena f; (in sport) castigo m; (in soccer) penalti m.

pen·cil lápiz m.

pen·cil case estuche m de lápices.

pen·cil sharp·en·er sacapuntas m inv.

pen·du·lum péndulo m.

pen·e·trate vt (break through, grasp) penetrar; (forest, territory) adentrarse en.

pen·guin pingüino m.

pen·i·cil·lin penicilina f.

pen·in·su·la península f.

pen·knife navaja f.

pen·ni·less adj sin dinero.

pen·ny (pl pennies) centavo m.

pen pal amigo, -a mf por carta.

pen·sion pensión f; retirement p. jubilación f.

pen·sion·er jubilado, -a mf.

peo·ple npl gente f sing; (individuals) personas fpl; (nation) pueblo m sing; old p.'s home asilo m de ancianos; p. say that ... se dice que ...

pep·per (spice) pimienta f; (fruit) pimiento m.

pep·per·mint hierbabuena f; (sweet) pastilla f de menta.

per prep por; **5 times p. week** 5 veces a la semana; **p. day/annum** al or por día/año; **p. capita** or **person** per cápita.

per·ceive vt percibir.

percent adv por ciento.

per·cent·age porcentaje m.

perch 1 n (for bird) percha f. **2** vi (bird) posarse (**on** en).

per·co·la·tor cafetera f de filtro.

per·fect 1 adj perfecto, -a; **p. tense** tiempo m perfecto. **2** vt perfeccionar.

per·fec·tion perfección f.

per·fect·ly adv perfectamente; (absolutely) completamente.

per·form 1 vt (task) realizar; (piece of music) interpretar; (play) representar. **2** vi (machine) funcionar; (musician) tocar; (actor) actuar.

per·form·ance (of task) realización f; (of piece of music) interpretación f; (of play) representación f; (in sport) actuación f; (of machine etc) rendimiento m.

per·form·er (singer) intérprete mf; (actor) actor m, actriz f.

per·fume perfume m.

per·haps adv tal vez, quizá(s).

per·il (danger) peligro m.

pe·ri·od período m; (stage) etapa f; (at school) clase f; (full stop) punto m; (menstruation) regla f.

pe·ri·od·i·cal 1 n revista f. **2** adj periódico, -a.

pe·riph·er·al periférico m.

perk extra m.

▶**perk up** vi animarse.

perm 1 n permanente f. **2** vt to p. one's hair permed hacerse la permanente.

per·ma·nent adj permanente; (address, job) fijo, -a.

per·ma·nent·ly adv permanentemente.

per·mis·sion permiso m.

per·mit 1 n permiso m. **2** vt to p. sb to do sth permitir a algn hacer algo.

per·pen·dic·u·lar adj perpendicular.

per·se·cute vt perseguir.

per·se·cu·tion persecución f.

per·se·ver·ance perseverancia f.

per·se·vere vi perseverar.

per·sist vi empeñarse (**in** en).

per·sist·ent *adj (person)* perseverante; *(continual)* constante.

per·son persona *f*; **in p.** en persona.

per·son·al *adj (private)* personal; *(friend)* íntimo, -a; *pej (comment etc)* indiscreto, -a; **he will make a p. appearance** estará aquí en persona.

per·son·al·i·ty personalidad *f*.

per·son·al·ly *adv (for my part)* personalmente; *(in person)* en persona.

per·son·nel personal *m*.

per·suade *vt* persuadir; **to p. sb to do sth** persuadir a algn para que haga algo.

per·sua·sion persuasión *f*.

per·ti·nent *adj (relevant)* pertinente; **p. to** relacionado, -a con, a propósito de.

Pe·ru·vi·an *adj & n* peruano, -a *(mf)*.

pes·si·mist pesimista *mf*.

pes·si·mis·tic *adj* pesimista.

pest *(animal, insect)* plaga *f*; *fam (person)* pelma *mf*; *(thing)* lata *f*.

pes·ter *vt* molestar.

pet 1 *n* animal *m* doméstico. **2** *adj (favorite)* preferido, -a.

pet·al pétalo *m*.

pe·ti·tion petición *f*.

pe·tro·le·um petróleo *m*.

pet·ti·coat enaguas *fpl*.

pet·ty *adj (trivial)* insignificante; *(small-minded)* mezquino, -a.

pet·ty cash dinero *m* para gastos pequeños.

phar·ma·cist farmacéutico, -a *mf*.

phar·ma·cy farmacia *f*.

phase 1 *n* fase *f*. **2** *vt* **to p. sth in/out** introducir/retirar algo progresivamente.

PhD Doctor, -a *mf* en Filosofía.

pheas·ant faisán *m*.

phe·nom·e·nal *adj* fenomenal.

phe·nom·e·non *(pl* **phenomena)** fenómeno *m*.

phi·los·o·pher filósofo, -a *mf*.

phil·o·soph·i·cal *adj* filosófico, -a.

phi·los·o·phy filosofía *f*.

phlegm flema *f*.

phone 1 *n* teléfono *m*. **2** *vt* llamar por teléfono a.

phone book guía *f* telefónica.

phone booth cabina *f* telefónica.

phone call llamada *f* (telefónica).

phone card tarjeta *f* telefónica.

phone numb·er número *m* de teléfono.

pho·net·ic *adj* fonético, -a.

pho·to foto *f*.

pho·to·cop·i·er fotocopiadora *f*.

pho·to·cop·y 1 *n* fotocopia *f*. **2** *vt* fotocopiar.

pho·to·graph 1 *n* fotografía *f*. **2** *vt* fotografiar.

pho·tog·ra·pher fotógrafo, -a *mf*.

pho·tog·ra·phy fotografía *f*.

phrase frase *f*.

phrase·book libro *m* de frases.

phys·i·cal *adj* físico, -a.

phys·i·cal·ly *adv* físicamente; **p. handicapped** minusválido, -a.

phy·si·cian médico, -a *mf*.

phys·ics física *f*.

pi·an·ist pianista *mf*.

pi·an·o piano *m*.

pick 1 *n (tool)* pico *m*; **take your p.** *(choice)* elige el que quieras. **2** *vt (choose)* escoger; *(team)* seleccionar; *(flowers, fruit)* coger; *(lock)* forzar; **to p. one's nose** hurgarse la nariz.

▸ **pick at** *vt* **she picked at her food** picoteó la comida con desgana.

▸ **pick on** *vt (persecute)* meterse con.

▸ **pick out** *vt (choose)* elegir; *(identify)* identificar.

▸ **pick up 1** *vt (object on floor)* recoger; *(telephone)* descolgar; *(collect)* recoger; *(shopping, person)* buscar; *(acquire)* conseguir; *(learn)* aprender; **to p. up speed** ganar velocidad. **2** *vi (improve)* mejorarse.

pick·ax piqueta *f*.

pick·le *vt (food)* conservar en adobo *or* escabeche; **pickled onions** cebollas *fpl* en vinagre.

pick·pock·et carterista *mf*.

pic·nic comida *f* de campo, picnic *m*.

pic·ture 1 n (painting) cuadro m; (drawing) dibujo m; (portrait) retrato m; (photo) foto f; (on TV) imagen f; (at cinema) película f. **2** vt (imagine) imaginarse.

pic·ture frame marco m.

pic·tur·esque adj pintoresco, -a.

pie (fruit) (big) tarta f; (small) pastel m; (meat etc) empanada f; (pasty) empanadilla f.

piece pedazo m; (of paper) trozo m; (part) pieza f; (coin) moneda f; **a p. of news** una noticia; **to break sth into pieces** hacer algo pedazos.

pier embarcadero m, muelle m.

pierce vt perforar.

pierc·ing adj (sound etc) penetrante.

pig cerdo m.

pi·geon paloma f.

pi·geon·hole casilla f.

pig·gy·back to give sb a p. llevar a algn a cuestas.

pig·tail trenza f.

pile 1 n montón m. **2** vt amontonar.

pile·up 1 vt (things) amontonar; (riches, debts) acumular. **2** vi amontonarse.

piles sing (illness) hemorroides fpl.

pile·up choque m en cadena.

pill píldora f; **to be on the p.** estar tomando la píldora (anticonceptiva).

pil·lar pilar m, columna f.

pil·lar box buzón m.

pil·low almohada f.

pil·low·case funda f de almohada.

pi·lot piloto m.

pim·ple espinilla f.

pin 1 n alfiler m. **2** vt (onto board) clavar con chinchetas.

▶**pin up** vt clavar con chinchetas.

pin·a·fore (apron) delantal m.

pin·ball flipper m.

pin·cers npl (tool) tenazas fpl.

pinch 1 n (nip) pellizco m; **a p. of salt** una pizca de sal. **2** vt pellizcar; fam (steal) birlar.

pin·cush·ion acerico m.

pine (tree) pino m.

pine·ap·ple piña f.

pink adj rosa inv.

pink·ie dedo m meñique.

pint pinta f (0,47 litro); **a p. of beer** una cerveza.

pi·o·neer 1 n (settler) pionero, -a mf; (forerunner) precursor, -a mf. **2** vt ser pionero, -a en.

pip (seed) pepita f.

pipe tubería f; (for smoking) pipa f.

pi·rate pirata m.

pi·rat·ed adj (book, record, CD) pirateado, -a.

pis·ta·chi·o pistacho m.

pis·tol pistola f.

pit hoyo m; (large) hoya f; (coal mine) mina f de carbón; (of fruit) hueso m.

pitch 1 vt (throw) lanzar; (tent) armar. **2** n (for sport) campo m; (throw) lanzamiento m.

pitch-black, pitch-dark adj negro, -a como boca de lobo.

pitch·er (container) cántaro m, jarro m.

pit·y 1 n (compassion) compasión f; (shame) lástima f; **what a p.!** ¡qué pena! **2** vt compadecerse de.

piz·za pizza f.

plac·ard pancarta f.

place 1 n sitio m, lugar m; (seat) sitio m; (on bus) asiento m; (position on scale) posición f; (house) casa f; (building) lugar m; **to take p.** tener lugar; **to take sb's p.** sustituir a algn; **in the first p.** en primer lugar; **we're going to his p.** vamos a su casa. **2** vt poner, colocar; (face, person) recordar.

place·mat tapete m individual.

place·ment (for trainee, student) colocación f en prácticas.

place set·ting cubierto m.

plague peste f.

plain 1 adj (clear) claro, -a; (simple) sencillo, -a; (unattractive) poco atractivo, -a; **the p. truth** la verdad lisa y llana. **2** n (land) llanura f.

plain·ly adv claramente; (simply)

sencillamente; **to speak p.** hablar con franqueza.

plait 1 *n* trenza *f*. **2** *vt* trenzar.

plan 1 *n* plan *m*. **2** *vt* (for future) planear; (economy) planificar; (intend) pensar; **to p. on doing sth** tener la intención de hacer algo.

▸**plan for** *vt* (disaster) prevenirse contra.

plane¹ avión *m*.

plane² (tool) cepillo *m*.

plane³ p. (tree) plátano *m*.

plan·et planeta *f*.

plank tabla *f*.

plant¹ 1 *n* planta *f*. **2** *vt* (flowers) plantar; (bomb) colocar.

plant² (factory) planta *f*(industrial).

plas·ter yeso *m*; (for broken limb) escayola *f*.

plas·ter cast (for broken arm) escayola *f*.

plas·tic 1 *n* plástico *m*. **2** *adj* (cup, bag) de plástico.

plas·tic sur·ger·y cirugía *f* plástica.

plate plato *m*; (sheet) placa *f*.

plat·form plataforma *f*; (at meeting) tribuna *f*; (at station) andén *m*.

plau·si·ble *adj* plausible.

play 1 *vt* (game) jugar a; (team) jugar contra; (instrument, tune) tocar; (part) hacer (el papel) de; **to p. a record** poner un disco; *fig* **to p. a part in sth** participar en algo. **2** *vi* jugar (with con). **3** *n* obra *f* de teatro.

▸**play back** *vt* (tape) volver a poner.

▸**play down** *vt* quitar importancia a.

play·er jugador, -a *mf*; (in play) (man) actor *m*; (woman) actriz *f*.

play·ground (in school) patio *m* de recreo; (recreation ground) parque *m* infantil.

play·group jardín *m* de infancia.

play·ing card carta *f*.

play·ing field campo *m* de deportes.

play·time recreo *m*.

plea (request) petición *f*, súplica *f*; (in court) alegato *m*.

plead 1 *vt* **to p. sb's cause** defender la causa de algn; **to p. ignorance** (give as excuse) alegar ignorancia. **2** *vi* (beg) rogar, suplicar; **to p. with sb** suplicar a algn que haga algo; (in court) **to p. guilty/not guilty** declararse culpable/inocente.

pleas·ant *adj* agradable.

pleas·ant·ly *adv* agradablemente.

please 1 *adv* por favor; **'p. do not smoke'** 'se ruega no fumar'. **2** *vt* (give pleasure to) complacer. **3** *vi* **do as you p.** haz lo que quieras.

pleased *adj* (happy) contento, -a; (satisfied) satisfecho, -a; **p. to meet you!** ¡encantado, -a!

pleas·ing *adj* (pleasant) agradable.

pleas·ure placer *m*; **with p.** con mucho gusto.

pleat pliegue *m*.

pleat·ed *adj* plisado, -a.

pledge 1 *n* promesa *f*. **2** *vt* prometer.

plen·ti·ful *adj* abundante.

plen·ty **p. of potatoes** muchas patatas; **p. of time** tiempo de sobra.

pli·ers *npl* alicates *mpl*, tenazas *fpl*.

plot¹ 1 *n* (conspiracy) complot *m*; (story) argumento *m*. **2** *vi* conspirar.

plot² (ground) terreno *m*; (for building) solar *m*.

plow *n* arado *m*. **2** *vt* arar.

pluck *vt* (flowers) coger; (chicken) desplumar.

plug 1 *n* (in bath etc) tapón *m*; (electric) enchufe *m*; **2/3 pin p.** clavija bipolar/tripolar. **2** *vt* (hole) tapar.

▸**plug in 1** *vt* enchufar. **2** *vi* enchufarse.

plum (fruit) ciruela *f*.

plumb·er fontanero, -a *mf*.

plumb·ing (system) fontanería *f*.

plump *adj* (person) rechoncho, -a; (baby) rellenito, -a.

plunge 1 *vt* (immerse) sumergir; (thrust) arrojar. **2** *vi* (dive) zambullirse; (fall) caer.

plu·ral *adj & n* plural (*m*); **in the p.** en plural.

plus *prep* más; **three p. four makes**

seven tres más cuatro hacen siete.

p.m. *(from midday to early evening)* de la tarde; *(at night)* de la noche.

pneu·mat·ic *adj* neumático, -a.

pneu·mat·ic drill martillo *m* neumático.

poach *vt (egg)* escalfar.

PO Box apartado *m* (de Correos).

pock·et bolsillo *m*.

pock·et·book bolso *m*.

pock·et·ful a p. of un bolsillo de.

pock·et mon·ey dinero *m* de bolsillo.

po·em poema *m*.

po·et poeta *mf*.

po·et·ic *adj* poético, -a.

po·et·ry poesía *f*.

point 1 *n (sharp end)* punta *f*, *(place)* punto *m*; *(score)* tanto *m*; *(moment)* **at that p.** en aquel momento; **to be on the p. of doing sth** estar a punto de hacer algo; **there's no p. in going** no merece la pena ir; **six p. three** seis coma tres; **up to a p.** hasta cierto punto; **power p.** toma *f* de corriente; **points** *(on railway)* agujas *fpl*. 2 *vt (way etc)* indicar; **to p. a gun at sb** apuntar a algn con una pistola. 3 *vi* **to p. to sth/sb** *(with finger)* señalar algo/a algn con el dedo.

▸ **point out** *vt* indicar; *(mention)* hacer resaltar.

point·ed *adj (sharp)* puntiagudo, -a.

point·less *adj* sin sentido.

poi·son 1 *n* veneno *m*. 2 *vt* envenenar.

poi·son·ous *adj (plant, snake)* venenoso, -a; *(gas)* tóxico, -a.

poke *vt (fire)* atizar; *(with finger)* dar con la punta del dedo a; *(with stick)* dar con la punta del bastón a; **to p. one's head out** asomar la cabeza.

▸ **poke about, poke around** *vi* fisgonear *or* hurgar en.

pok·er *(for fire)* atizador *m*.

po·lar *adj* polar.

po·lar bear oso *m* polar.

Pole polaco, -a *mf*.

pole¹ palo *m*.

pole² *(north, south)* polo *m*.

po·lice *npl* policía *f sing*.

po·lice car coche *m* patrulla.

po·lice·man policía *m*.

po·lice sta·tion comisaría *f*.

po·lice·wom·an (mujer *f*) policía *f*.

pol·i·cy política *f*, *(insurance)* póliza *f* (de seguros).

po·li·o poliomielitis *f*.

Pol·ish 1 *adj* polaco, -a. 2 *n (language)* polaco *m*.

pol·ish 1 *vt* pulir; *(furniture)* encerar; *(shoes)* limpiar. 2 *n (for furniture)* cera *f*; *(for shoes)* betún *m*; *(for nails)* esmalte *m*.

▸ **polish off** *vt (food)* zamparse.

▸ **polish up** *vt fig* perfeccionar.

po·lite *adj* educado, -a.

po·lite·ly *adv* educadamente.

po·lite·ness educación *f*.

po·lit·i·cal *adj* político, -a.

pol·i·ti·cian político, -a *mf*.

pol·i·tics política *f*.

poll votación *f*; *(survey)* encuesta *f*; **to go to the polls** acudir a las urnas.

pol·len polen *m*.

poll·ing sta·tion colegio *m* electoral.

pol·lute *vt* contaminar.

pol·lu·tion contaminación *f*.

po·lo p. neck sweater jersey *m* de cuello vuelto.

pol·y·es·ter poliéster *m*.

pol·y·tech·nic politécnico *m*.

pol·y·thene polietileno *m*.

pom·e·gran·ate granada *f*.

pond estanque *m*.

po·ny poney *m*.

po·ny·tail cola *f* de caballo.

poo·dle caniche *m*.

pool *(of water, oil etc)* charco *m*; **swimming p.** piscina *f*.

pooped *adj fam* hecho, -a polvo.

poor 1 *adj* pobre; *(quality)* malo, -a. 2 *npl* **the p.** los pobres.

poor·ly 1 *adv (badly)* mal. 2 *adj (ill)* enfermo, -a.

pop 1 *vt (burst)* hacer reventar. 2 *vi*

(burst) reventar; *fam* **I'm just popping over to Ian's** voy un momento a casa de Ian. **3** *n (drink)* gaseosa *f;* *fam (father)* papá *m; (music)* música *f* pop.

▸**pop in** *vi fam* entrar un momento.

pop·corn palomitas *fpl.*

Pope the P. el Papa.

pop·py amapola *f.*

Pop·si·cle® polo *m.*

pop sing·er cantante *mf* pop.

pop·u·lar *adj* popular; *(fashionable)* de moda.

pop·u·lar·i·ty popularidad *f.*

pop·u·lat·ed *adj* **thinly p.** poco poblado.

pop·u·la·tion población *f.*

porch *(of house)* porche *m; (veranda)* terraza *f.*

pork carne *f* de cerdo.

por·ridge gachas *fpl* de avena.

port *(harbor, of computer)* puerto *m.*

por·ta·ble *adj & n* portátil *(m).*

por·ter *(in hotel etc)* portero, -a *mf.*

port·fo·li·o *(for papers, of artist, politician)* cartera *f.*

port·hole portilla *f.*

por·tion *(part, piece)* parte *f; (of food)* ración *f.*

por·trait retrato *m.*

Por·tu·guese 1 *adj* portugués, -esa. **2** *n (person)* portugués, -esa *mf; (language)* portugués *m.*

pose 1 *vt (problem)* plantear; *(threat)* representar. **2** *vi (for painting)* posar; **to p. as** hacerse pasar por.

posh *adj* elegante; *(person)* presumido, -a; *(accent)* de clase alta.

po·si·tion posición *f; (location)* situación *f; (rank)* rango *m;* **to be in a p. to do sth** estar en condiciones de hacer algo.

pos·i·tive *adj* positivo, -a; *(sign)* favorable; *(sure)* seguro, -a.

pos·i·tive·ly *adv (constructively)* positivamente; *(to answer)* afirmativamente; *(for emphasis)* verdaderamente, realmente.

pos·sess *vt* poseer.

pos·ses·sions *npl* bienes *mpl.*

pos·ses·sive *adj* posesivo, -a.

pos·si·bil·i·ty posibilidad *f.*

pos·si·ble *adj* posible; **as much as p.** todo lo posible; **as often as p.** cuanto más mejor; **as soon as p.** cuanto antes.

pos·si·bly *adv* posiblemente; *(perhaps)* quizás; **I can't p. come** no puedo venir de ninguna manera.

post¹ *(wooden)* poste *m.*

post² *(job)* puesto *m.*

▸**post up** *vt (notice)* fijar.

post·age franqueo *m.*

post·age stamp sello *m* (de correos).

post·al *adj* postal.

post·al or·der giro *m* postal.

post·card *(tarjeta f)* postal *f.*

post·er póster *m; (advertising)* cartel *m.*

post·grad·u·ate posgraduado, -a *mf.*

post·man cartero *m.*

post·mark matasellos *m inv.*

post of·fice oficina *f* de correos; **where is the p.?** ¿dónde está correos?

post·pone *vt* aplazar.

post·pone·ment aplazamiento *m.*

pot *(for cooking)* olla *f; (for flowers)* maceta *f.*

po·ta·to *(pl potatoes)* patata *f, Am* papa *f.*

po·tent *adj* potente.

po·ten·tial 1 *adj* potencial. **2** *n* potencial *m.*

pot·ter alfarero, -a *mf.*

pot·ter·y *(craft, place)* alfarería *f; (objects)* cerámica *f.*

pot·ty orinal *m.*

pouch bolsa *f* pequeña; *(of animal)* bolsa *f* abdominal.

poul·try *(live)* aves *fpl* de corral; *(food)* pollos *mpl.*

pounce *vi* **to p. on** abalanzarse encima de.

pound¹ *(weight)* libra *f.*

pound² *(for dogs)* perrera *f*; *(for cars)* depósito *m* de coches.

pour 1 *vt* verter; **to p. sb a drink** servirle una copa a algn. **2** *vi* **it's pouring with rain** está lloviendo a cántaros.

▸**pour away** *vt (liquid)* vaciar.

▸**pour in** *vi (water)* entrar a raudales; *(applications)* llegar sin parar.

▸**pour out 1** *vt* verter. **2** *vi (liquid, people)* salir a raudales.

pov·er·ty pobreza *f*.

pow·der 1 *n* polvo *m*. **2** *vt* **to p. one's nose** empolvarse la cara.

pow·dered *adj (milk)* en polvo.

pow·er fuerza *f*, *(energy)* energía *f*, *(ability, authority)* poder *m*; *(nation)* potencia *f*; **to be in p.** estar en el poder.

pow·er·ful *adj (influential)* poderoso, -a; *(engine, machine)* potente.

pow·er point enchufe *m*.

pow·er sta·tion central *f* eléctrica.

prac·ti·cal *adj* práctico, -a.

prac·ti·cal joke broma *f* pesada.

prac·ti·cal·ly *(almost)* casi.

prac·tice 1 *n (exercise)* práctica *f*; *(in sport)* entrenamiento *m*; *(rehearsal)* ensayo *m*; *(habit)* costumbre *f*; *(way of doing sth)* práctica *f*; **to be out of p.** no estar en forma; **in p.** en la práctica. **2** *vt* practicar; *(principle)* poner en práctica; *(profession)* ejercer. **3** *vi* practicar; *(in sport)* entrenar; *(rehearse)* ensayar; *(doctor)* practicar; *(lawyer)* ejercer.

praise 1 *n* alabanza *f*. **2** *vt* alabar.

prank travesura *f*, *(joke)* broma *f*.

prawn gamba *f*.

pray *vi* rezar.

prayer oración *f*.

preach *vi* predicar.

pre·cau·tion precaución *f*.

pre·cede *vt* preceder.

prec·e·dent precedente *m*.

pre·ced·ing *adj* precedente.

pre·cinct *(administrative, police division)* distrito *m*.

pre·cious *adj* precioso, -a.

pre·cise *adj* preciso, -a; *(meticulous)* meticuloso, -a.

pre·co·cious *adj* precoz.

pred·a·tor depredador *m*.

pre·de·ces·sor antecesor, -a *mf*.

pre·dic·a·ment apuro *m*, aprieto *m*.

pre·dict *vt* predecir.

pre·dict·a·ble *adj* previsible.

pre·dic·tion pronóstico *m*.

pref·ace prefacio *m*.

pre·fer *vt* preferir; **I p. coffee to tea** prefiero el café al té.

pref·er·a·ble *adj* preferible (**to** a).

pref·er·a·bly *adv* preferentemente.

pref·er·ence preferencia *f*.

pre·fix prefijo *m*.

preg·nan·cy embarazo *m*.

preg·nant *adj* embarazada.

pre·his·tor·i(·)c(al) *adj* prehistórico, -a.

prej·u·dice *(bias)* prejuicio *m*.

pre·lim·i·nar·y *adj* preliminar.

pre·ma·ture *adj* prematuro, -a.

prem·is·es *npl* local *m*; **on the p.** en el local.

pre·mi·um prima *f*.

prep·a·ra·tion preparación *f*; *(plan)* preparativo *m*.

pre·pare 1 *vt* preparar; **to p. to do sth** prepararse para hacer algo. **2** *vi* prepararse (**for** para).

pre·pared *adj (ready)* preparado, -a; **to be p. to do sth** *(willing)* estar dispuesto, -a a hacer algo.

prep·o·si·tion preposición *f*.

pre·school *adj* preescolar.

pre·scribe *vt (medicine)* recetar.

pre·scrip·tion *(medical)* receta *f*.

pres·ence presencia *f*; *(attendance)* asistencia *f*.

pres·ent¹ 1 *adj (in attendance)* presente; *(current)* actual; **p. tense** (tiempo *m*) presente *m*. **2** *n (time)* presente *m*; **at p.** actualmente.

pre·sent² 1 *vt (opportunity)* ofrecer; *(problems)* plantear; *(prize)* entregar;

(introduce) (person, program) presentar; **to p. sb with sth** obsequiar a algn con algo. **2** *n (gift)* regalo *m*.

pres·en·ta·tion presentación *f*, **p. ceremony** ceremonia *f* de entrega.

pres·ent·er animador, -a *mf*.

pres·ent·ly *adv (soon)* dentro de poco; *(now)* ahora.

pres·er·va·tion conservación *f*.

pres·er·va·tive conservante *m*.

pre·serve 1 *vt (keep)* mantener. **2** *n* conserva *f*.

pre·side *vi* presidir; **to p. over** *or* **at sth** presidir algo.

pres·i·den·cy presidencia *f*.

pres·i·dent presidente, -a *mf*.

pres·i·den·tial *adj* presidencial.

press 1 *vt* apretar; *(button)* pulsar; *(iron)* planchar; *(urge)* presionar; **to p. sb to do sth** presionar a algn para que haga algo. **2** *vi (push)* apretar; **to p. (down) on sth** hacer presión sobre algo. **3** *n (newspapers)* prensa *f*.

▸**press on** *vi* seguir adelante.

press con·fer·ence rueda *f* de prensa.

pres·sure presión *f*; **to bring p. (to bear) on sb** ejercer presión sobre algn.

pres·sure cook·er olla *f* a presión.

pres·sure gauge manómetro *m*.

pre·sume *vt* suponer.

pre·tend *vti* fingir.

pre·text pretexto *m*; **on the p. of** so pretexto de.

pret·ty 1 *adj (thing)* bonito, -a; *(person)* guapo, -a. **2** *adv* bastante; **p. much the same** más o menos lo mismo.

pre·vail *vi* predominar; **to p. upon** *or* **on sb to do sth** *(persuade)* persuadir *or* convencer a algn para que haga algo.

pre·vent *vt* impedir; *(accident)* evitar; **to p. sb from doing sth** impedir a algn hacer algo.

pre·ven·tion prevención *f*.

pre·vi·ous *adj* anterior.

pre·vi·ous·ly *adv* previamente.

prey presa *f*, *fig* víctima *f*.

price precio *m*.

price list lista *f* de precios.

pric·ey *adj fam* carillo(a).

prick *vt* picar; **to p. one's finger** pincharse el dedo.

prick·ly *adj* espinoso, -a; *(touchy)* enojadizo, -a.

pride 1 *n* orgullo *m*; *(arrogance)* soberbia *f*; **to take p. in sth** enorgullecerse de algo. **2** *vt* **to p. oneself on** enorgullecerse de.

priest sacerdote *m*, cura *m*.

pri·mar·i·ly *adv* ante todo.

pri·mar·y 1 *adj* principal; **p. education/school** enseñanza *f*/escuela *f* primaria. **2** *n (election)* (elección *f*) primaria *f*.

Prime Min·is·ter primer, -a ministro, -a *mf*.

prime num·ber número *m* primo.

prim·i·tive *adj* primitivo, -a.

prim·rose primavera *f*.

prince príncipe *m*; **P. Charming** Príncipe Azul.

prin·cess princesa *f*.

prin·ci·pal 1 *adj* principal. **2** *(of college etc)* director, -a *mf*.

prin·ci·ple principio *m*; **on p.** por principio.

print 1 *vt (publish)* publicar; *(write)* escribir con letra de imprenta. **2** *n* letra *f*; *(of hand, foot)* huella *f*; *(of photo)* copia *f*; **out of p.** agotado, -a.

▸**print out** *vt* imprimir.

print·ed *adj* impreso(a); **printed matter** impresos *mpl*.

print·er *(person)* impresor, -a *mf*; *(machine)* impresora *f*.

print·ing *(industry)* imprenta *f*; *(process)* impresión *f*.

print-out impresión *f*.

pri·or *adj* anterior; **without p. warning** sin previo aviso.

pri·or·i·ty prioridad *f*.

pris·on prisión *f*.

pris·on·er preso, -a *mf*; **to hold sb p.** detener a algn.

pri·va·cy intimidad *f*.

pri·vate 1 adj privado, -a; (individual) particular; (personal) personal; (letter) confidencial. **2** n (soldier) soldado m raso.

pri·vate·ly adv en privado; (personally) personalmente.

prize premio m.

prize-giv·ing distribución f de premios.

prize-win·ner premiado, -a mf.

pro¹ pro m; **the pros and cons** los pros y los contras.

pro² abbr of **professional** fam profesional mf.

pro³ prefix (in favour of) pro-.

prob·a·ble adj probable.

prob·a·bly adv probablemente.

probe 1 n (medical instrument, spacecraft) sonda f; (investigation) sondeo m. **2** vt (with medical instrument) sondar; (investigate) investigar.

▸**probe into** vt investigar.

prob·lem problema m.

prob·lem·at·i(·)c(al) adj problemático, -a.

pro·ceed vi proceder, seguir; **to p. to do sth** ponerse a hacer algo.

pro·ceeds npl ganancias fpl.

proc·ess 1 n proceso m; **in the p. of** en vías de. **2** vt procesar.

proc·essed cheese queso m fundido.

pro·ces·sion desfile m; (religious) procesión f.

proc·es·sor procesador m.

pro·duce 1 vt producir, (manufacture) fabricar; (give birth to) dar a luz a; (show) enseñar; (bring out) sacar. **2** n productos mpl.

pro·duc·er productor, -a mf. (manufacturer) fabricante mf.

pro·duc·tion producción f; (manufacture) fabricación f; **p. line** cadena f de montaje.

pro·duc·tive adj productivo, -a.

pro·duc·tiv·i·ty productividad f.

pro·fes·sion profesión f.

pro·fes·sion·al 1 adj profesional;

(polished) de gran calidad. **2** n profesional mf.

pro·fes·sor catedrático, -a mf.

prof·it 1 n beneficio m; **to make a p. on** sacar beneficios de. **2** vi **to p. from** aprovecharse de.

prof·it·a·ble adj rentable; (worthwhile) provechoso, -a.

pro·found adj profundo, -a.

pro·gram 1 n programa m; (plan) plan m. **2** vti programar.

pro·gram·ming programación f.

prog·ress 1 n progreso m; **to make p.** hacer progresos; **in p.** en curso. **2** vi avanzar; (develop) desarrollarse; (medically) mejorar.

pro·gres·sive adj (increasing) progresivo, -a; (in politics) progresista.

pro·hib·it vt prohibir; **to p. sb from doing sth** prohibir a algn hacer algo.

proj·ect proyecto m; (at school) trabajo m.

pro·jec·tor proyector m.

pro·long vt prolongar.

prom·e·nade (at seaside) paseo m marítimo.

prom·i·nent adj (important) importante; (famous) eminente.

prom·ise 1 n promesa f; **to show p.** ser prometedor, -a. **2** vti prometer.

prom·is·ing adj prometedor, -a.

pro·mote vt ascender; (product) promocionar.

pro·mo·tion (in rank) ascenso m; (of product) promoción f.

prompt adj (quick) rápido, -a; (punctual) puntual. **2** adv **at 2 o'clock p.** a las 2 en punto.

prone adj **to be p. to do sth** ser propenso, -a a hacer algo.

pro·noun pronombre m.

pro·nounce vt pronunciar.

pro·nun·ci·a·tion pronunciación f.

proof prueba f.

prop¹ 1 n (physical support) puntal m; (psychological support) sostén m. **2** vt (lean) apoyar.

▸**prop up** vt apoyar.

prop² *(in theatre) fam* accesorio *m.*

prop·a·gan·da propaganda *f.*

pro·pel·ler hélice *f.*

prop·er *adj* adecuado, -a; *(real)* auténtico, -a; **p. noun** nombre propio.

prop·er·ly *(suitably, correctly, decently)* correctamente.

prop·er·ty *(possession)* propiedad *f;* **personal p.** bienes *mpl.*

pro·por·tion proporción *f, (part, quantity)* parte *f.*

pro·por·tion·al *adj* proporcional (to a).

pro·pos·al propuesta *f;* **p. of marriage** propuesta de matrimonio.

pro·pose 1 *vt* proponer; *(suggest)* sugerir. **2** *vi (ask to marry)* declararse.

prop·o·si·tion propuesta *f.*

props *npl (in theater)* accesorios *mpl.*

prose prosa *f, (translation)* traducción *f* inversa.

pros·e·cute *vt* procesar.

pros·e·cu·tion *(action)* proceso *m,* juicio *m;* **the p.** *(in court)* la acusación.

pros·pect *(outlook)* perspectiva *f, (hope)* esperanza *f.*

pros·per·i·ty prosperidad *f.*

pros·per·ous *adj* próspero, -a.

pro·tect *vt* **to p. sb from sth** proteger a algn de algo.

pro·tec·tion protección *f.*

pro·tec·tive *adj* protector, -a.

pro·test 1 *n* protesta *f.* **2** *vi* protestar.

Prot·es·tant *adj & n* protestante *(mf).*

pro·test·er manifestante *mf.*

proud *adj* orgulloso, -a; *(arrogant)* soberbio, -a.

proud·ly *adv* con orgullo; *(arrogantly)* con soberbia.

prove *vt* demostrar; **it proved to be disastrous** resultó desastroso, -a.

prov·erb refrán *m,* proverbio *m.*

pro·vide *vt* proporcionar; *(supplies)* suministrar.

pro·vid·ed *conj* **p. (that)** con tal de que.

prov·ince provincia *f.*

pro·vin·cial *adj* provincial; *pej* provinciano, -a.

pro·vi·sion·al *adj* provisional.

pro·voke *vt* provocar.

prowl *vi* merodear; **to p. about** *or* **around** rondar.

prowl·er merodeador *m.*

prune¹ ciruela *f* pasa.

prune² *vt (roses etc)* podar.

psy·chi·at·ric *adj* psiquiátrico, -a.

psy·chi·a·trist psiquiatra *mf.*

psy·cho·log·i·cal *adj* psicológico, -a.

psy·chol·o·gist psicólogo, -a *mf.*

psy·chol·o·gy psicología *f.*

pub bar *m.*

pub·lic 1 *adj* público, -a; **p. holiday** fiesta *f* nacional. **2** *n* **the p.** el público; **in p.** en público.

pub·li·ca·tion publicación *f.*

pub·lic·i·ty publicidad *f.*

pub·lic·ly *adv* públicamente.

pub·lish *vt* publicar, editar.

pub·lish·er editor, -a *mf.*

pub·lish·ing *(business)* industria *f* editorial.

pud·ding pudín *m; (dessert)* postre *m.*

pud·dle charco *m.*

puff 1 *n (of smoke)* bocanada *f.* **2** *vi (person)* jadear; **to p. on one's pipe** chupar la pipa.

pull 1 *n* **to give sth a p.** *(tug)* dar un tirón a algo. **2** *vt (tug)* dar un tirón a; *(drag)* tirar de; **to p. a muscle** sufrir un tirón en un músculo; **to p. the trigger** apretar el gatillo; **to p. sth to pieces** hacer pedazos algo.

▸ **pull apart** *vt* desmontar.

▸ **pull down** *vt (building)* derribar.

▸ **pull in 1** *vt (crowds)* atraer. **2** *vi* **to p. in(to the station)** llegar a la estación.

▸ **pull out 1** *vt (withdraw)* retirar. **2** *vi (car)* **to p. out to overtake** salirse para adelantar.

▸ **pull over** *vi* hacerse a un lado.

▸ **pull through** *vi* reponerse.

▸ **pull up 1** *vt (uproot)* desarraigar; *(draw close)* acercar. **2** *vi (stop)* pararse.

pull·o·ver jersey *m*.

pulse *(in body)* pulso *m*.

pump 1 *n* bomba *f*. **2** *vt* bombear.

▸ **pump up** *vt (tire)* inflar.

pump·kin calabaza *f*.

punch[1] **1** *n (for making holes)* perforadora *f*. **2** *vt (ticket)* picar.

punch[2] **1** *n (blow)* puñetazo *m*. **2** *vt (with fist)* dar un puñetazo a.

punc·tu·al *adj* puntual.

punc·tu·a·tion puntuación *f*.

punc·ture 1 *n* pinchazo *m*. **2** *vt (tire)* pinchar.

pun·ish *vt* castigar.

pun·ish·ment castigo *m*.

pu·pil[1] *(at school)* alumno, -a *mf*.

pu·pil[2] *(in eye)* pupila *f*.

pup·pet títere *m*.

pup·py cachorro, -a *mf* (de perro).

pur·chase 1 *n* compra *f*. **2** *vt* comprar.

pur·chas·er comprador, -a *mf*.

pur·chas·ing pow·er poder *m* adquisitivo.

pure *adj* puro, -a.

pure·ly *adv* simplemente.

pur·ple *adj* morado, -a.

pur·pose propósito *m*; **on p.** a propósito.

pur·pose·ly *adv* adrede.

purse *(bag)* bolso *m*.

pur·sue *vt (criminal)* perseguir; *(person)* seguir.

pur·suit *(of criminal)* persecución *f*, *(of animal)* caza *f*, *(of pleasure)* búsqueda *f*, *(pastime)* pasatiempo *m*.

push 1 *n* empujón *m*; **to give sb a p.** dar un empujón a algn. **2** *vt* empujar; *(button)* pulsar; **to p. one's finger into a hole** meter el dedo en un agujero. **3** *vi* empujar.

▸ **push aside** *vt (object)* apartar.

▸ **push in** *vi* colarse.

▸ **push off** *vi fam* **p. off!** ¡lárgate!

▸ **push on** *vi (continue)* seguir adelante.

▸ **push through** *vt (crowd)* abrirse paso entre; *(law)* hacer aceptar (a la fuerza).

pushed *adj* **to be p. for time/money** estar justo, -a de tiempo/dinero.

push·y *adj* (pushier, pushiest) *fam* agresivo, -a.

puss, puss·y minino *m*.

put* *vt* poner; *(place)* colocar; *(insert)* meter; *(express)* expresar; *(invest) (money)* invertir; **to p. a stop to sth** poner término a algo; **to p. a question to sb** hacer una pregunta a algn.

▸ **put across** *vt (idea etc)* comunicar.

▸ **put aside** *vt (money)* ahorrar; *(time)* reservar.

▸ **put away** *vt (tidy up)* recoger; *(save money)* ahorrar.

▸ **put back** *vt (postpone)* aplazar.

▸ **put by** *vt (money)* ahorrar.

▸ **put down** *vt (set down)* dejar; *(criticize)* criticar; *(write down)* apuntar.

▸ **put forward** *vt (theory)* exponer; *(proposal)* hacer.

▸ **put in** *vt (install)* instalar; *(complaint, request)* presentar; *(time)* pasar.

▸ **put off** *vt (postpone)* aplazar; *(switch off) (radio, light)* apagar; **to p. sb off (doing) sth** *(dissuade)* disuadir a algn de (hacer) algo.

▸ **put on** *vt (clothes)* poner(se); *(switch on) (radio)* poner; *(light)* encender; **to p. on weight** engordar.

▸ **put out** *vt (switch off, extinguish)* apagar; *(place outside)* sacar; *(extend) (arm)* extender; *(hand)* tender; *(annoy)* molestar; *(inconvenience)* incordiar.

▸ **put through** *vt (on telephone)* **p. me through to Pat, please** póngame con Pat, por favor.

▸ **put together** *vt (assemble)* montar.

▸ **put up** *vt (raise)* levantar; *(picture)* colocar; *(curtains)* colgar; *(tent)* armar; *(prices)* subir; *(accommodate)* alojar; **to p. up a fight** ofrecer resistencia.

▸**put up with** vt aguantar.

put·ty masilla f.

puz·zle 1 n rompecabezas m inv; (mystery) misterio m. **2** vt dejar perplejo, -a.

puz·zling adj extraño, -a.

py·lon torre f (de conducción eléctrica).

pyr·a·mid pirámide f.

Q

qual·i·fi·ca·tion (diploma etc) título m.

qual·i·fied adj capacitado, -a; **q. teacher** profesor m titulado.

qual·i·fy vi (in competition) quedar clasificado, -a; **to q. as** (doctor etc) sacar el título de.

qual·i·ty (excellence) calidad f, (attribute) cualidad f.

quan·ti·ty cantidad f.

quar·rel 1 n (argument) riña f, pelea f. **2** vi (argue) reñir.

quar·rel·ing disputas fpl.

quar·ry cantera f.

quart cuarto m de galón (0,94 litros).

quar·ter cuarto m; (coin) cuarto m (de dólar); (district) barrio m; **it's a q. to three, it's a q. of three** son las tres menos cuarto.

quar·ter·back quarterback m, Méx mariscal m de campo

quartz cuarzo m; **q. watch** reloj m de cuarzo.

queen reina f.

queer adj (strange) extraño, -a.

quench vt apagar.

que·ry (question) pregunta f.

ques·tion 1 n pregunta f, (problem, issue) asunto m; **to ask sb a q.** hacer una pregunta a algn; **out of the q.**

imposible; **that's out of the q.** ¡ni hablar! **2** vt (interrogate) interrogar; (query) poner en duda.

ques·tion·a·ble adj (doubtful) dudoso, -a; (debatable) discutible.

ques·tion · mark signo m de interrogación.

ques·tion·naire cuestionario m.

quib·ble vi poner pegas (with a).

quiche quiche f.

quick adj (fast) rápido, -a; **be q.!** ¡date prisa!

quick·ly adv deprisa.

qui·et adj (silent) silencioso, -a; (calm, not crowded) tranquilo, -a.

qui·et·ly adv (silently) silenciosamente; (calmly) tranquilamente; **he spoke q.** habló en voz baja.

quit* **1** vt (leave) dejar; **q. making that noise!** ¡deja de hacer ese ruido! **2** vi (go) irse; (resign) dimitir.

quite adv (entirely) totalmente; (rather) bastante; **q. a few** bastantes; **q. often** con bastante frecuencia; **q. (so)!** ¡exacto!

quiz **q. show** concurso m.

quo·ta (proportional share) cuota f, parte f, (prescribed amount, number) cupo m.

quo·ta·tion cita f, (commercial) cotización f.

quo·ta·tion marks npl comillas fpl.

quote 1 vt (cite) citar; **to q. a price** dar un presupuesto. **2** n cita f, (commercial) presupuesto m.

R

rab·bi rabino m.

rab·bit conejo, -a mf.

ra·bies rabia f.

race¹ 1 n (in sport) carrera f. **2** vt (car, horse) hacer correr; **I'll r. you!** ¡te echo una carrera! **3** *vi (go quickly)* correr.

race² *(people)* raza *f.*

race·horse caballo *m* de carreras.

ra·cial *adj* racial.

rac·ing carreras *fpl.*

rac·ing bike *(motorbike)* moto *f* de carreras; *(bicycle)* bicicleta *f* de carreras.

rac·ing car coche *m* de carreras.

rac·ing driv·er piloto *mf* de carreras.

rac·ism racismo *m.*

ra·cist *adj & n* racista *(mf).*

rack *(shelf)* estante *m; (for clothes)* percha *f,* **luggage r.** portaequipajes *m inv;* **roof r.** baca *f.*

rack·et¹ *(din)* jaleo *m.*

rack·et² *(for tennis etc)* raqueta *f.*

ra·dar radar *m.*

ra·di·a·tion radiación *f.*

ra·di·a·tor radiador *m.*

rad·i·cal *adj* radical.

ra·di·o radio *f;* **on the r.** en *or* por la radio; **r. station** emisora *f* (de radio).

ra·di·o·ac·tive *adj* radiactivo, -a.

rad·ish rábano *m.*

ra·di·us radio *m.*

raf·fle rifa *f.*

raft balsa *f.*

rag *(torn piece)* harapo *m; (for cleaning)* trapo *m,* **rags** *(clothes)* trapos *mpl.*

rage 1 *n (fury)* cólera *f.* **2** *vi (person)* estar furioso, -a.

rag·ged *adj (clothes)* hecho, -a jirones; *(person)* harapiento, -a.

raid 1 *n (by police)* redada *f; (robbery etc)* atraco *m.* **2** *vt (police)* hacer una redada (en); *(rob)* asaltar.

rail barra *f, (railing)* barandilla *f, (on railroad)* carril *m;* **by r.** *(send sth)* por ferrocarril; *(travel)* en tren.

rail·ings *npl* verja *f sing.*

rail·road ferrocarril *m.*

rail·road sta·tion estación *f* de ferrocarril.

rail·road track vía *f* férrea.

rail·way line vía *f* férrea.

rain 1 *n* lluvia *f;* **in the r.** bajo la lluvia. **2** *vi* llover; **it's raining** llueve.

rain·bow arco *m* iris.

rain·coat impermeable *m.*

rain·y *adj* lluvioso, -a.

raise 1 *n* aumento *m* (de sueldo). **2** *vt* levantar; *(voice)* subir; *(increase)* aumentar; *(money, help)* reunir; *(issue, question)* plantear; *(crops, children)* criar.

rai·sin pasa *f.*

rake 1 *n (garden tool)* rastrillo *m.* **2** *vt (leaves)* rastrillar.

ral·ly *(political)* mitin *m.*

► **rally around** *vi (help out)* echar una mano.

ram 1 *n (sheep)* carnero *m.* **2** *vt (drive into place)* hincar; *(crash into)* chocar con.

ram·ble *(walk)* caminata *f.*

ramp rampa *f.*

ran *pt of* **run.**

ranch rancho *m.*

ran·dom 1 *n* at r. al azar. **2** *adj* fortuito, -a; **r. selection** selección *f* hecha al azar.

range 1 *n (of mountains)* cordillera *f, (of products)* gama *f, (of missile)* alcance *m; (stove)* cocina *f* de carbón. **2** *vi (extend)* extenderse (*to* hasta); **prices r. from five to twenty dollars** los precios oscilan entre cinco y veinte dólares.

rank *(position in army)* graduación *f, (in society)* rango *m;* **(taxi) r.** parada *f* de taxis.

ran·som rescate *m.*

rape 1 *n* violación *f.* **2** *vt* violar.

rap·id *adj* rápido, -a.

rap·id·ly *adv* rápidamente.

rap·ist violador, -a *mf.*

rare *adj* poco común; *(steak)* poco hecho, -a.

rare·ly *adv* raras veces.

ras·cal granuja *mf.*

rash¹ *(on skin)* sarpullido *m.*

rash² *adj (reckless)* impetuoso, -a; *(words, actions)* precipitado, -a.

rash·ly *adv* a la ligera.

rasp·ber·ry frambuesa f.

rat rata f.

rate 1 n tasa f; **at any r.** (anyway) en cualquier caso; (of interest, exchange) tipo m; **at the r. of** (speed) a la velocidad de; (quantity) a razón de. **2** vt (estimate) estimar; (evaluate) tasar; (consider) considerar.

rath·er adv (quite) más bien, bastante; (more accurately) mejor dicho; **r. than** (instead of) en vez de; (more than) más que; **she would r. stay here** prefiere quedarse aquí.

rat·ing (score) valoración f.

ra·tio razón f.

ra·tion 1 n (allowance) ración f, **rations** víveres mpl. **2** vt racionar.

ra·tion·al adj racional.

ra·tion·ing racionamiento m.

rat·tle 1 n (toy) sonajero m; (instrument) carraca f. **2** vt (keys etc) hacer sonar. **3** vi sonar; (metal) repiquetear; (glass) tintinear; (window, shelves) vibrar.

rav·en·ous adj I'm r. tengo un hambre que no veo.

raw adj (uncooked) crudo, -a; **r. material** materia f prima; **r. flesh** carne f viva.

ray rayo m.

ra·zor (for shaving) maquinilla f de afeitar.

ra·zor blade hoja f de afeitar.

reach 1 vt (arrive at) llegar a; (contact) localizar. **2** vi alcanzar. **3** n (range) alcance m; **out of r.** fuera del alcance; **within r.** al alcance.

▶**reach out** vi (with hand) extender la mano.

re·act vi reaccionar.

re·ac·tion reacción f.

re·ac·tor reactor m.

read* vt leer; (decipher) descifrar.

▶**read about** vt leer.

▶**read out** vt leer en voz alta.

▶**read up on** vt estudiar.

read·er lector, -a mf; (book) libro m de lectura.

read·i·ly adv (easily) fácilmente;

(willingly) de buena gana.

read·ing lectura f; fig interpretación f.

read·y adj (prepared) listo, -a; (willing) dispuesto, -a; **r. to** (about to) a punto de; **r. cash** dinero m en efectivo.

read·y-cooked adj precocinado, -a.

read·y-made adj confeccionado, -a; (food) preparado, -a.

re·al adj verdadero, -a; (genuine) auténtico, -a.

re·al es·tate bienes mpl inmuebles.

re·al es·tate a·gent agente mf inmobiliario, -a.

re·al·is·tic adj realista.

re·al·i·ty realidad f.

re·al·ize vt (become aware of) darse cuenta de; **don't you r. that ...?** ¿no te das cuenta de que ...?

re·al·ly adv (truly) verdaderamente; **r.?** ¿de veras?

re·al·tor agente mf inmobiliario, -a.

rear¹ 1 n (back part) parte f de atrás. **2** adj trasero, -a; **r. entrance** puerta f de atrás.

rear² 1 vt (breed, raise) criar. **2** vi **to r. up** (horse) encabritarse.

re·ar·range vt (furniture) colocar de otra manera; (set new date) fijar otra fecha para.

rea·son 1 n motivo m; **for no r.** sin razón. **2** vi (argue, work out) razonar.

rea·son·a·ble adj (fair) razonable; (sensible) sensato, -a.

rea·son·a·bly adv (fairly, quite) bastante.

rea·son·ing razonamiento m.

re·as·sure vt (comfort) tranquilizar; (restore confidence in) dar confianza a.

re·as·sur·ing adj consolador, -a.

re·bel 1 adj & n rebelde (mf). **2** vi rebelarse (**against** contra).

re·bel·lion rebelión f.

re·bound 1 n (of ball) rebote m. **2** vi (ball) rebotar.

re·build vt reconstruir.

re·call *vt (remember)* recordar.

re·ceipt *(paper)* recibo *m*; **receipts** *(takings)* recaudación *f sing.*

re·ceive *vt* recibir.

re·ceiv·er *(of phone)* auricular *m*; *(radio)* receptor *m*.

re·cent *adj* reciente; **in r. years** en los últimos años.

re·cent·ly *adv* recientemente.

re·cep·tion *(party, of TV pictures etc)* recepción *f*; *(welcome)* acogida *f*, **r. (desk)** recepción *f*.

re·cep·tion·ist recepcionista *mf*.

re·charge *vt (battery)* recargar.

rec·i·pe receta *f*.

re·cip·i·ent receptor, -a *mf*, *(of letter)* destinatario, -a *mf*.

re·cite *vti* recitar.

reck·less *adj (unwise)* imprudente.

reck·on *vt (calculate)* calcular; *fam (think)* creer.

▸ **reckon on** *vt* contar con.

▸ **reckon with** *vt (take into account)* contar con.

re·claim *vt (recover)* recuperar; *(demand back)* reclamar; *(marshland etc)* convertir.

rec·og·nize *vt* reconocer.

rec·ol·lect *vt* recordar.

rec·ol·lec·tion recuerdo *m*.

rec·om·mend *vt* recomendar.

rec·om·men·da·tion recomendación *f*.

re·cord 1 *n (of music etc)* disco *m*; *(in sport etc)* récord *m*; *(document)* documento *m*; *(case history)* historial *m* médico; **public records** archivos *mpl.* **2** *vt (relate)* hacer constar; *(note down)* apuntar; *(music, voice)* grabar.

re·cord·ed *adj* grabado, -a.

re·cord·er *(musical instrument)* flauta *f*, **(tape) r.** magnetófono *m*; *(video)* **r.** vídeo *m*.

re·cord·ing grabación *f*.

re·cord play·er tocadiscos *m inv*.

re·cov·er 1 *vt (items, time)* recuperar; *(consciousness)* recobrar. **2** *vi (from illness etc)* reponerse; *(economy)* recuperarse.

rec·re·a·tion *(entertainment)* diversión *f*; *(school playtime)* recreo *m*.

re·cruit recluta *m*.

rec·tan·gle rectángulo *m*.

rec·tan·gu·lar *adj* rectangular.

re·cy·cle *vt* reciclar.

red 1 *adj* rojo, -a; **r. light** semáforo *m* en rojo; **r. wine** vino *m* tinto; **to go r.** ponerse colorado, -a; **to have r. hair** ser pelirrojo, -a. **2** *n (color)* rojo *m*; **to be in the r.** estar en números rojos.

red-hand·ed *adj* **to catch sb r.** coger a algn con las manos en la masa.

red·head pelirrojo, -a *mf*.

red-hot *adj* al rojo vivo.

re·di·rect *vt (forward)* remitir a la nueva dirección.

re·do* *vt (exercise, house)* rehacer.

re·duce *vt* reducir.

re·duc·tion *(decrease)* reducción *f*, *(cut in price)* descuento *m*.

re·dun·dan·cy despido *m*.

re·dun·dant *adj* **to be made r.** perder el empleo; **to make sb r.** despedir a algn.

reed *(plant)* caña *f*.

reef arrecife *m*.

reel *(spool)* bobina *f*, carrete *m*.

re·fec·to·ry refectorio *m*.

re·fer 1 *vt* **to r. a matter to a tribunal** remitir un asunto a un tribunal. **2** *vi (allude)* referirse (**to** a).

ref·e·ree 1 *n* árbitro, -a *mf*. **2** *vt* arbitrar.

ref·er·ence referencia *f*, *(character report)* informe *m*; **with r. to** referente a, con referencia a.

ref·er·en·dum referéndum *m*.

re·fill 1 *n (replacement)* recambio *m*; *(another drink)* otra copa *f*. **2** *vt* rellenar.

re·flect 1 *vt (light, attitude)* reflejar; **to be reflected** reflejarse. **2** *vi (think)* reflexionar.

re·flec·tion *(indication, mirror image)* reflejo *m*.

re·flex reflejo *m*.

re·form 1 *n* reforma *f*. **2** *vt* reformar.

re·frain *vi* abstenerse (**from** de).

re·fresh vt refrescar.

re·fresh·er course cursillo m de reciclaje.

re·fresh·ing adj refrescante.

re·fresh·ment refresco m.

re·frig·er·a·tor nevera f.

ref·uge refugio m; **to take r.** refugiarse.

ref·u·gee refugiado, -a mf.

re·fund 1 n reembolso m. **2** vt reembolsar.

re·fus·al negativa f.

re·fuse 1 vt (reject) rechazar; **to r. sb sth** negar algo a algn; **to r. to do sth** negarse a hacer algo. **2** vi negarse.

re·gain vt recuperar.

re·gard 1 n (concern) consideración f; **with r. to, as regards** (con) respecto a; **give him my regards** dale recuerdos de mi parte. **2** vt (consider) considerar.

re·gard·ing prep (con) respecto a.

re·gard·less 1 prep r. of a pesar de; **r. of the outcome** pase lo que pase. **2** adv a toda costa.

reg·i·ment regimiento m.

re·gion región f, zona f; **in the r. of** aproximadamente.

re·gion·al adj regional.

reg·is·ter 1 n registro m. **2** vt (record) registrar; (letter) certificar. **3** vi (enter one's name) inscribirse; (at university) matricularse.

reg·is·tra·tion inscripción f; (at university) matrícula f.

re·gret 1 n (remorse) remordimiento m; (sadness) pesar m. **2** vt arrepentirse de, lamentar.

reg·u·lar 1 adj regular; (usual) normal; (frequent) frecuente.

reg·u·lar·ly adv con regularidad.

reg·u·late vt regular.

reg·u·la·tion 1 n (control) regulación f; (rule) regla f. **2** adj reglamentario, -a.

re·hears·al ensayo m.

re·hearse vti ensayar.

reign 1 n reinado m. **2** vi reinar.

rein·deer reno m.

re·in·force vt (strengthen) reforzar.

re·in·force·ments npl refuerzos mpl.

reins (for horse) riendas fpl.

re·in·state vt (to job) reincorporar.

re·ject vt rechazar.

re·jec·tion rechazo m.

re·joice vi regocijarse (**at, over** de).

re·late 1 vt (connect) relacionar; (tell) contar. **2** vi relacionarse (**to** con).

re·lat·ed adj (linked) relacionado, -a (**to** con); **to be r. to sb** ser pariente de algn.

re·la·tion (link) relación f; (family) pariente, -a mf; **in** or **with r. to** (con) respecto a.

re·la·tion·ship (link) relación f; (between people) relaciones fpl.

rel·a·tive 1 n pariente, -a mf. **2** adj relativo, -a.

rel·a·tive·ly adv relativamente.

re·lax 1 vi relajarse; **r.!** ¡cálmate! **2** vt (calm) relajar; (loosen) aflojar.

re·lax·a·tion (rest) relajación f.

re·laxed adj relajado, -a.

re·lease 1 n (setting free) liberación f; (of product) puesta f en venta; (film) estreno m; (press release) comunicado m. **2** vt (set free) poner en libertad; (let go) soltar; (product, record) poner a la venta; (film) estrenar.

rel·e·vance pertinencia f.

rel·e·vant adj pertinente (**to** a); **it is not r.** no viene al caso.

re·li·a·bil·i·ty (of person) formalidad f; (of thing) fiabilidad f.

re·li·a·ble adj (person) de fiar; (thing) fiable.

re·lief alivio m; (aid) auxilio m; (in art, geography) relieve m.

re·lieve vt aliviar; (substitute) relevar.

re·li·gion religión f.

re·li·gious adj religioso, -a.

rel·ish (seasoning) condimento m.

re·load vt (gun, camera) recargar.

re·luc·tance desgana f.

re·luc·tant *adj* reacio, -a; **to be r. to do sth** estar poco dispuesto, -a a hacer algo.

re·luc·tant·ly *adv* de mala gana.

▸**re·ly on** *vt (count on)* contar con; *(be dependent on)* depender de.

re·main *vi (stay)* permanecer, quedarse; *(be left)* quedar.

re·main·ing *adj* restante.

re·mark 1 *n* comentario *m*. **2** *vt* comentar.

re·mark·a·ble *adj (extraordinary)* extraordinario, -a.

re·mark·a·bly *adv* extraordinariamente.

re·me·di·al *adj* **r. classes** clases *fpl* para niños atrasados en los estudios.

rem·e·dy 1 *n* remedio *m*. **2** *vt* remediar.

re·mem·ber 1 *vt (recall)* acordarse de. **2** *vi* acordarse.

re·mind *vt* recordar; **r. me to do it** recuérdame que lo haga.

re·mind·er aviso *m*.

re·morse remordimiento *m*.

re·mote *adj (far away)* remoto, -a; *(isolated)* aislado, -a.

re·mote con·trol mando *m* a distancia.

re·mov·al *(moving house)* mudanza *f*; *(getting rid of)* eliminación *f*; **r. man** hombre *m* de la mudanza; **r. van** camión *m* de mudanzas.

re·move *vt* quitar.

re·new *vt (contract etc)* renovar; *(talks etc)* reanudar.

rent 1 *n (of building, car, TV)* alquiler *m*. **2** *vt* alquilar.

▸**rent out** *vt* alquilar.

rent·al *(of house etc)* alquiler *m*.

rent·al car coche *m* de alquiler.

re·or·gan·ize *vt* reorganizar.

re·pair 1 *n* reparación *f*; **in good/bad r.** en buen/mal estado. **2** *vt* arreglar; *(car)* reparar; *(clothes)* remendar.

re·pair·man técnico *m*.

re·pay *vt* devolver; *(debt)* liquidar.

re·pay·ment pago *m*.

re·peat 1 *vt* repetir. **2** *n (repetition)* repetición *f*; *(on TV)* reposición *f*.

re·peat·ed *adj* repetido, -a.

re·peat·ed·ly *adv* repetidas veces.

re·pel *vt (fight off)* repeler.

rep·e·ti·tion repetición *f*.

re·pet·i·tive *adj* repetitivo, -a.

re·place *vt (put back)* volver a poner en su sitio; *(substitute)* sustituir.

re·place·ment *(person)* sustituto, -a *mf*; *(part)* pieza *f* de recambio.

re·play repetición *f*.

rep·li·ca réplica *f*.

re·ply 1 *n* respuesta *f*. **2** *vi* responder.

re·port 1 *n* informe *m*; *(piece of news)* noticia *f*; *(in newspaper, on TV etc)* reportaje *m*; *(rumor)* rumor *m*; **school r.** informe *m* escolar. **2** *vt (tell police, authorities about)* denunciar; *(journalist)* hacer un reportaje sobre; **it is reported that …** se dice que … **3** *vi (committee etc)* hacer un informe; *(journalist)* hacer un reportaje; *(to work etc)* presentarse.

re·port·ed *adj* **r. speech** estilo *m* indirecto.

re·port·ed·ly *adv* según se dice.

re·port·er periodista *mf*.

rep·re·sent *vt* representar.

rep·re·sen·ta·tive representante *mf*.

re·pro·duce 1 *vt* reproducir. **2** *vi* reproducirse.

re·pro·duc·tion reproducción *f*.

rep·tile reptil *m*.

re·pub·lic república *f*.

re·pub·li·can *adj & n* republicano, -a *(mf)*; **R. Party** Partido *m* Republicano.

rep·u·ta·ble *adj (company etc)* acreditado, -a; *(person, products)* de toda confianza.

rep·u·ta·tion reputación *f*.

re·quest 1 *n* petición *f*. **2** *vt* pedir.

re·quire *vt (need)* necesitar; *(demand)* exigir.

re·quired *adj* necesario, -a.

res·cue 1 *n* rescate *m*. **2** *vt* rescatar.

re·search 1 *n* investigación *f*. **2** *vti* investigar.

re·search·er investigador, -a *mf.*

re·sem·blance semejanza *f.*

re·sem·ble *vt* parecerse a.

re·sent *vt* ofenderse por.

re·sent·ment resentimiento *m.*

res·er·va·tion reserva *f.*

re·serve 1 *n* reserva *f; (in sport)* suplente *mf;* **to keep sth in r.** guardar algo de reserva. **2** *vt* reservar.

re·served *adj* reservado, -a.

res·er·voir embalse *m,* pantano *m.*

res·i·dence *(home)* residencia *f; (address)* domicilio *m.*

res·i·dent *adj & n* residente *(mf).*

res·i·den·tial *adj* residencial.

re·sign 1 *vt* to r. oneself to sth resignarse a algo. **2** *vi* dimitir.

res·ig·na·tion *(from a job)* dimisión *f.*

re·sist *vt (not yield)* resistir; *(oppose)* oponerse a; **I couldn't r. telling her** no pude resistir a la tentación de decírselo.

re·sis·tance resistencia *f.*

re·sit *vt (exam)* volver a presentarse a.

re·sort *(recourse)* recurso *m; (place)* lugar *m* de vacaciones; **as a last r.** como último recurso; **tourist r.** centro *m* turístico.

▶ **resort to** *vt* recurrir a.

re·source recurso *m.*

re·spect 1 *n (reference)* respeto *m;* **in that r.** a ese respecto; **with r. to** con referencia a. **2** *vt* respetar.

re·spect·a·ble *adj* respetable; *(clothes)* decente.

re·spec·tive *adj* respectivo, -a.

re·spond *vi* responder (**to** a).

re·sponse *(reply)* respuesta *f; (reaction)* reacción *f.*

re·spon·si·bil·i·ty responsabilidad *f.*

re·spon·si·ble *adj* responsable (**for** de).

rest¹ 1 *n (break)* descanso *m; (peace)* tranquilidad *f.* **2** *vt (lean)* apoyar. **3** *vi* descansar.

rest² the r. *(remainder)* el resto; the

r. of the day el resto del día; **the r. of the girls** las demás chicas.

res·tau·rant restaurante *m.*

rest·ful *adj* relajante.

rest·less *adj* inquieto, -a.

re·store *vt (give back)* devolver; *(repair)* restaurar.

re·strain *vt* contener; **to r. one's anger** reprimir la cólera; **to r. oneself** contenerse.

re·straint *(restriction)* restricción *f; (moderation)* moderación *f.*

re·strict *vt* restringir.

re·strict·ed *adj* restringido, -a; **r. area** zona *f* restringida.

re·stric·tion restricción *f.*

rest·room aseos *mpl.*

re·sult resultado *m;* **as a r. of** como consecuencia de.

re·sume 1 *vt (journey, work, conversation)* reanudar; *(control)* reasumir. **2** *vi* recomenzar.

ré·su·mé resumen *m.*

re·tail 1 *n* r. price precio *m* de venta al público. **2** *vt* vender al por menor. **3** *adv* al por menor.

re·tail·er detallista *mf.*

re·tain *vt* conservar.

re·tire *vi (stop working)* jubilarse; *(withdraw)* retirarse; **to r. for the night** irse a la cama.

re·tired *adj* jubilado, -a.

re·tire·ment jubilación *f.*

re·treat 1 *n (of troops)* retirada *f; (shelter)* refugio *m.* **2** *vi* retirarse *(from de).*

re·trieve *vt (recover)* recuperar; *(of dog)* cobrar.

re·turn 1 *n (coming or going back)* regreso *m; (giving back)* devolución *f; (profit)* beneficio *m;* r. ticket billete *m* de ida y vuelta. **2** *vt (give back)* devolver. **3** *vi (come or go back)* regresar.

re·turn·a·ble *adj (bottle)* retornable.

re·veal *vt (make known)* revelar; *(show)* dejar ver.

rev·e·la·tion revelación *f.*

re·venge venganza *f*; **to take r. on sb for sth** vengarse de algo en algn.

re·verse 1 *adj* inverso, -a. **2** *n* quite the **r.** todo lo contrario; **r. (gear)** marcha fatrás. **3** *vt* **to r. the charges** poner una conferencia a cobro revertido. **4** *vi (in car)* dar marcha atrás; **to r. in/out** entrar/salir marcha atrás.

re·vert *vi* volver (**to** a).

re·view 1 *n (in press)* crítica *f*. **2** *vt (book etc)* hacer una crítica de.

re·vise *vt (look over)* revisar; *(at school)* repasar.

re·vi·sion revisión *f*; *(at school)* repaso *m*.

re·viv·al *(of interest, custom, country)* resurgimiento *m*; *(of play)* reposición *f*.

re·vive *vt (unconscious person)* reanimar.

re·volt rebelión *f*.

re·volt·ing *adj* repugnante.

rev·o·lu·tion revolución *f*.

rev·o·lu·tion·ar·y *adj & n* revolucionario, -a *(mf)*.

re·volve *vi* girar; *fig* **to r. around** girar en torno a.

re·volv·er revólver *m*.

re·volv·ing *adj* giratorio, -a; **r. door** puerta *f* giratoria.

re·ward 1 *n* recompensa *f*. **2** *vt* recompensar.

re·wind* 1 *vt (tape)* rebobinar. **2** *vi* rebobinarse.

rhet·o·ric retórica *f*.

rheu·ma·tism reúma *m*.

rhi·noc·er·os rinoceronte *m*.

rhu·barb ruibarbo *m*.

rhyme 1 *n* rima *f*; *(poem)* poema *m*. **2** *vi* rimar.

rhythm ritmo *m*.

rib costilla *f*.

rib·bon cinta *f*; *(in hair etc)* lazo *m*.

rice arroz *m*.

rich 1 *adj* rico, -a. **2** *npl* the **r.** los ricos.

rich·es *npl* riquezas *fpl*.

rid *vt* **to get r. of sth** deshacerse de algo.

rid·dle *(puzzle)* adivinanza *f*; *(mystery)* enigma *m*.

ride 1 *n* paseo *m*; **a short bus r.** un corto trayecto en autobús; **horse r.** paseo a caballo. **2** *vt* (bicycle, horse)* montar en; **can you r. a bike?** ¿sabes montar en bici? **3** *vi* (on horse)* montar a caballo; *(travel) (on bus, train etc)* viajar.

rid·er *(of horse) (man)* jinete *m*, *(woman)* amazona *f*; *(of bicycle)* ciclista *mf*, *(of motorbike)* motociclista *mf*.

ridge *(of mountain)* cresta *f*.

ri·dic·u·lous *adj* ridículo, -a.

rid·ing equitación *f*.

ri·fle rifle *m*.

rig (oil) **r.** *(onshore)* torre *f* de perforación; *(offshore)* plataforma *f* petrolífera.

right 1 *adj (not left)* derecho, -a; *(correct)* correcto, -a; *(suitable)* adecuado, -a; *(proper)* apropiado, -a; *(exact) (time)* exacto, -a; **all r.** de acuerdo; **r.?** ¿vale?; **that's r.** eso es; **isn't that r.?** ¿no es verdad?; **the r. word** la palabra justa; **to be r.** tener razón; **the r. time** *(appropriate time)* el momento oportuno; **r. angle** ángulo *m* recto. **2** *n (right side)* derecha *f*, *(right hand)* mano *f* derecha; *(in politics)* **the R.** la derecha; *(lawful claim)* derecho *m*; **r. and wrong** el bien y el mal. **3** *adv (correctly)* bien; *(to the right)* a la derecha; **r. away** en seguida; **to turn r.** girar a la derecha; **go r. on** sigue recto; **r. at the top** en todo lo alto; **r. in the middle** justo en medio; **r. to the end** hasta el final.

right-hand *adj* derecho, -a.

right-hand·ed *adj (person)* que usa la mano derecha, diestro, -a.

right·ly *adv* debidamente; **and r. so** y con razón.

right-wing *adj* de derechas, derechista.

rig·id *adj* rígido, -a.

rim *(edge)* borde *m*.

rind (of fruit, cheese) corteza f.

ring¹ 1 n (of doorbell, alarm clock) timbre m; (of phone) llamada f. **2** vt* (bell) tocar; (on phone) llamar por teléfono. **3** vi* (bell, phone etc) sonar.

ring² 1 n sortija f; (wedding ring) anillo m; (metal hoop) aro m; (circle) círculo m; (group of people) corro m; (in boxing) cuadrilátero m; (for bullfights) ruedo m. **2** vt (surround) rodear.

▸**ring out** vi (bell etc) resonar.

ring·lead·er cabecilla mf.

rinse vt aclarar; (dishes) enjuagar.

▸**rinse out** vt enjuagar.

ri·ot 1 n disturbio m; **r. police** policía f antidisturbios. **2** vi amotinarse.

rip 1 n (tear) rasgón m. **2** vt rasgar. **3** vi rasgarse.

▸**rip off** vt fam **to r. sb off** timar a algn.

▸**rip up** vt hacer pedacitos.

ripe adj maduro, -a.

rip·en vti madurar.

rip-off fam timo m.

rise 1 n (of slope, hill) cuesta f; (in prices, temperature) subida f; (of wages) aumento m; **to give r. to** ocasionar. **2** vi* (prices, temperature) subir; (wages) aumentar; (from bed) levantarse; (stand up) levantarse; (city, building) erguirse.

ris·ing 1 adj (sun) naciente; (tide) creciente; (prices) en aumento. **2** n (rebellion) levantamiento m.

risk 1 n riesgo m; **at r.** en peligro; **to take risks** arriesgarse. **2** vt arriesgar; **I'll r. it** correré el riesgo.

risk·y adj arriesgado, -a.

rit·u·al adj & n ritual (m).

ri·val 1 adj & n rival (mf). **2** vt rivalizar con.

riv·er río m.

road carretera f; (street) calle f; (way) camino m; **r. accident** accidente m de tráfico; **r. safety** seguridad f vial.

road·side borde m de la carretera.

road·way calzada f.

road·works npl obras fpl.

roam 1 vt vagar por. **2** vi vagar.

roar 1 n (of lion) rugido m; (of bull, sea, wind) bramido m. **2** vi (lion, crowd) rugir; (bull, sea, wind) bramar.

roast 1 adj (meat) asado, -a; **r. beef** rosbif m. **2** n asado m. **3** vt (meat) asar; (coffee, nuts) tostar. **4** vi asarse.

rob vt robar; (bank) atracar.

rob·ber ladrón, -a mf; **bank r.** atracador, -a mf.

rob·ber·y robo m.

robe (ceremonial) toga f; bata f.

rob·in petirrojo m.

ro·bot robot m.

rock 1 n roca f; (stone) piedra f; (music) música f rock. **2** vt (chair) mecer; (baby) acunar; (shake) sacudir. **3** vi (move back and forth) mecerse; (shake) vibrar.

rock·et 1 n cohete m. **2** vi (prices) dispararse.

rock·ing chair mecedora f.

rod (of metal) barra f; (stick) vara f; **fishing r.** caña f de pescar.

rogue granuja m.

role, rôle papel m; **to play a r.** desempeñar un papel.

roll 1 n rollo m; (bread) **r.** bollo m; (of drum) redoble m. **2** vt hacer rodar. **3** vi (ball) rodar; (animal) revolcarse.

▸**roll by** vi (years) pasar.

▸**roll down** vt (blinds) bajar; (sleeves) bajarse; (hill) bajar rodando.

▸**roll over** vi dar una vuelta.

▸**roll up** vt (paper etc) enrollar; (blinds) subir; **to r. up one's sleeves** (ar)remangarse.

roll·er rodillo m; **rollers** (for hair) rulos mpl.

roll·er skate patín m de ruedas.

roll·ing pin rodillo m (de cocina).

roll·ing stock material m rodante.

Ro·man adj & n romano, -a (mf).

Ro·man Cath·o·lic adj & n católico, -a (mf) (romano, -a).

ro·mance (love affair) aventura f amorosa.

ro·man·tic adj & n romántico, -a (mf).

roof tejado *m*; *(of car)* techo *m*.

roof rack baca *f*.

room habitación *f*; *(space)* espacio *m*; **single r.** habitación individual; **make r. for me** hazme sitio.

room·mate compañero, -a *mf* de habitación.

room·y *adj* amplio, -a.

root raíz *f*; **to take r.** echar raíces.

▸**root for** *vt* **to r. for a team** animar a un equipo.

▸**root out, root up** *vt* arrancar de raíz.

rope *(small)* cuerda *f*, *(big)* soga *f*.

▸**rope off** *vt* acordonar.

rose rosa *f*; **r. bush** rosal *m*.

rot *vi* pudrirse.

ro·ta·tion rotación *f*.

rot·ten *adj (decayed)* podrido, -a; *fam (very bad)* malísimo, -a; *(health)* enfermo, -a; **I feel r.** me encuentro fatal.

rough *adj (surface, skin)* áspero, -a; *(terrain)* accidentado, -a; *(road)* desigual; *(sea)* agitado, -a; *(rude)* grosero, -a; *(violent)* violento, -a; *(approximate)* aproximado, -a; *(plan etc)* preliminar; **r. draft** borrador *m*; **r. sketch** esbozo *m*.

rough·ly *adv (crudely)* toscamente; *(not gently)* bruscamente; *(approximately)* aproximadamente.

round 1 *adj* redondo, -a. **2** *n (of drinks)* ronda *f*, *(at golf)* partido *m*; *(at cards)* partida *f*, *(in boxing)* round *m*; *(in a competition)* eliminatoria *f*; **rounds** *(doctor's)* visita *f sing*. **3** *adv* **all year r.** durante todo el año; **to invite sb r.** invitar a algn a casa. **4** *prep (place etc)* alrededor de; **r. here** por aquí; **r. the corner** a la vuelta de la esquina.

▸**round up** *vt (cattle)* acorralar; *(people)* reunir.

round·a·bout 1 *n (merry-go-round)* tiovivo *m*; *(on road)* glorieta *f*. **2** *adj* indirecto, -a.

round trip viaje *m* de ida y vuelta.

route ruta *f*, *(of bus)* línea *f*.

rou·tine rutina *f*.

row¹ fila *f*; **three times in a r.** tres veces seguidas.

row² *vi (in a boat)* remar.

row³ 1 *n (quarrel)* bronca *f*, *(noise)* jaleo *m*. **2** *vi* pelearse.

row·boat bote *m* de remos.

row house casa *f* adosada.

roy·al 1 *adj* real. **2** *npl* **the Royals** los miembros de la Familia Real.

roy·al·ty *(royal person(s))* miembro(s) *m(pl)* de la Familia Real; **royalties** derechos *mpl* de autor.

rub 1 *vt* frotar; *(hard)* restregar; *(massage)* friccionar. **2** *vi* rozar *(against* contra).

▸**rub down** *vt* frotar; *(horse)* almohazar; *(surface)* raspar.

▸**rub in** *vt (cream etc)* frotar con.

▸**rub off** *vt (erase)* borrar.

▸**rub out** *vt* borrar.

rub·ber *(substance)* caucho *m*; *(eraser)* goma *f* (de borrar).

rub·ble escombros *mpl*.

ru·by rubí *m*.

ruck·sack mochila *f*.

rud·der timón *m*.

rude *adj (impolite)* maleducado, -a; *(foul-mouthed)* grosero, -a.

rude·ness *(impoliteness)* falta *f* de educación; *(offensiveness)* grosería *f*.

rug alfombra *f*.

rug·by rugby *m*.

ru·in 1 *n* ruina *f*; **in ruins** en ruinas. **2** *vt* arruinar; *(spoil)* estropear.

rule 1 *n* regla *f*; *(of monarch)* reinado *m*; **as a r.** por regla general. **2** *vti (govern)* gobernar; *(monarch)* reinar.

▸**rule out** *vt* descartar.

rul·er *(monarch)* soberano, -a *mf*; *(for measuring)* regla *f*.

rul·ing 1 *adj (in charge)* dirigente; **the r. party** el partido en el poder. **2** *n (of judge)* fallo *m*.

rum ron *m*.

Ru·ma·ni·an 1 *adj* rumano, -a. **2** *n (person)* rumano, -a *mf*, *(language)* rumano *m*.

rum·mage sale mercadillo *m* de caridad.

ru·mor 1 *n* rumor *m*. **2** *vt* **it is rumored that** se rumorea que.

run 1 *n* (*act of running, in stocking*) carrera *f*; (*trip*) vuelta *f*; **on the r.** fugado, -a; **to go for a r.** hacer footing; (*in car*) dar un paseo; **in the long r.** a largo plazo; **ski r.** pista *f* de esquí. **2** *vt** correr; (*business*) llevar; (*company*) dirigir; (*organize*) organizar; **to r. errands** hacer recados; **to r. a program** pasar un programa. **3** *vi** (*person, river*) correr; (*color*) desteñirse; (*operate*) funcionar; (*film, play*) estar en cartel; **your nose is running** tienes catarro; **trains r. every two hours** hay trenes cada dos horas; **we're running low on milk** nos queda poca leche.

▸ **run across** *vt* (*meet*) tropezar con.

▸ **run away** *vi* fugarse.

▸ **run down** *vt* (*stairs*) bajar corriendo; (*knock down*) atropellar.

▸ **run in** *vi* entrar corriendo.

▸ **run into** *vt* (*room etc*) entrar corriendo en; (*people, problems*) tropezar con; (*crash into*) chocar contra.

▸ **run off** *vi* escaparse.

▸ **run out** *vi* (*exit*) salir corriendo; (*finish*) agotarse; (*contract*) vencer; **to r. out of** quedarse sin.

▸ **run over** *vt* (*knock down*) atropellar.

run·a·way *adj* (*vehicle*) incontrolado, -a; (*inflation*) galopante; (*success*) clamoroso, -a.

rung (*of ladder*) peldaño *m*.

run·ner-up subcampeón, -ona *mf*.

run·ning 1 *n* atletismo *m*; (*management*) dirección *f*. **2** *adj* **r. water** agua *f* corriente; **three weeks r.** tres semanas seguidas.

run·ny *adj* (*nose*) que moquea.

run·way pista *f* (de aterrizaje y despegue).

rush 1 *n* (*hurry*) prisa *f*; (*hustle and bustle*) ajetreo *m*; **there's no r.** no corre prisa. **2** *vt* (*do hastily*) hacer de prisa; **to r. sb to hospital** llevar a algn urgentemente al hospital. **3** *vi* (*go quickly*) precipitarse.

▸ **rush around** *vi* correr de un lado a otro.

▸ **rush off** *vi* irse corriendo.

rush hour hora *f* punta.

Rus·sian 1 *adj* ruso, -a. **2** *n* (*person*) ruso, -a *mf*; (*language*) ruso *m*.

rust 1 *n* herrumbre *f*. **2** *vi* oxidarse.

rust·y *adj* oxidado, -a.

RV *abbr of* recreational vehicle autocaravana *f*.

rye centeno *m*; **r. bread** pan *m* de centeno.

S

sack 1 *n* (*bag*) saco *m*. **2** *vt* (*employee*) despedir a.

sa·cred *adj* sagrado, -a.

sac·ri·fice 1 *n* sacrificio *m*. **2** *vt* sacrificar.

sad *adj* triste.

sad·den *vt* entristecer.

sad·dle *n* (*for horse*) silla *f* (de montar).

sad·ly *adv* tristemente.

sad·ness tristeza *f*.

safe 1 *adj* (*unharmed*) ileso, -a; (*out of danger*) a salvo; (*not dangerous*) inocuo, -a; (*secure, sure*) seguro, -a; **s. and sound** sano, -a y salvo, -a. **2** *n* (*for money etc*) caja *f* fuerte.

safe·guard 1 *n* (*protection*) salvaguarda *f*; (*guarantee*) garantía *f*. **2** *vt* proteger, salvaguardar.

safe·ly *adv* con toda seguridad; **to arrive s.** llegar sin accidentes.

safe·ty seguridad *f*.

safe·ty belt cinturón *m* de seguridad.

safe·ty pin imperdible *m*.

sag *vi* (*roof*) hundirse.

said 1 *pt & pp of* say. **2** *adj* dicho, -a.

sail 1 n (canvas) vela f; (trip) paseo m
en barco; **to set s.** zarpar. **2** vt (ship)
gobernar. **3** vi ir en barco; (set sail)
zarpar.

sail·board tabla f de windsurf.

sail·boat barco m de vela.

sail·ing navegación f; (yachting) vela f.

sail·or marinero m.

saint n santo, -a mf; (before all masculine names except those beginning
Do or To) San; (before feminine
names) Santa.

sake n for the s. of por (el bien de);
for your own s. por tu propio bien.

sal·ad ensalada f.

sal·ad bowl ensaladera f.

sal·ad dress·ing aliño m.

sal·a·ry salario m.

sale n venta f; (at low prices) rebajas
fpl; **for** or **on s.** en venta.

sale price adj (article) a precio
rebajado.

sales·clerk dependiente, -a mf.

sales·man vendedor m; (in shop)
dependiente m; (commercial representative) representante m.

sales tax impuesto m de venta.

sales·wom·an vendedora f; (in
shop) dependienta f; (commercial representative) representante f.

sa·li·va saliva f.

salm·on salmón m.

sa·lon salón m.

salt 1 n sal f; **bath salts** sales de baño. **2** vt (add salt to) echar sal a.

salt cel·lar salero m.

salt·y adj salado, -a.

sal·va·tion salvación f; **S. Army**
Ejército m de Salvación.

same 1 adj mismo, -a; **at the s. time**
al mismo tiempo; **the two cars are ▶ the s.** los dos coches son iguales. **2**
pron el mismo, la misma, lo mismo;
all the s., just the s. aun así; **it's all
the s. to me** (a mí) me da igual.

sam·ple 1 n muestra f. **2** vt (wines)
catar; (dish) probar.

sand arena f.

san·dal sandalia f.

sand cas·tle castillo m de arena.

sand·pa·per papel m de lija.

sand·wich (roll) bocadillo m;
(sliced bread) sandwich m.

sand·y adj (earth, beach) arenoso, -a; (hair) rubio, -a, rojizo, -a.

san·i·tar·y s. napkin compresa f.

San·ta Claus Papá Noel m.

sar·dine sardina f.

sat pt & pp of **sit**.

satch·el cartera f (de colegial).

sat·el·lite satélite m; **s. dish** antena
f parabólica.

sat·in satén m.

sat·is·fac·tion satisfacción f.

sat·is·fac·to·ry adj satisfactorio, -a.

sat·is·fy vt satisfacer; (fulfill) cumplir con.

sat·is·fy·ing adj satisfactorio, -a.

sat·u·rate vt saturar; (with de).

Sat·ur·day sábado m.

sauce salsa f.

sauce·pan cacerola f; (large) olla f.

sau·cer platillo m.

Sau·di A·ra·bi·an adj & n saudita
(mf), saudí (m).

sau·na sauna f.

sau·sage (frankfurter) salchicha f;
(cured) salchichón m; (spicy) chorizo
m.

save 1 vt (rescue) rescatar; (put by,
computer file) guardar; (money)
ahorrar; (food) almacenar; **it saved
him a lot of trouble** le evitó muchos
problemas. **2** n (in soccer) parada f.

sav·ings npl ahorros mpl.

sav·ings ac·count cuenta f de
ahorros.

sav·ings bank caja f de ahorros.

saw[1] n (tool) sierra f. **2** vti* serrar.

saw off vt serrar.

saw[2] pt of **see**.

sax·o·phone saxofón m.

say* vt decir; **it is said that ...** se
dice que ...; **that is to s.** es decir;
what does the sign s.? ¿qué pone
en el letrero?; **shall we s. Friday
then?** ¿quedamos el viernes, pues?

say·ing refrán *m*.

scab *(on cut)* costra *f*.

scaf·fold·ing andamio *m*.

scald *vt* escaldar.

scale[1] *(of fish, on skin)* escama *f*; *(in boiler)* incrustaciones *fpl*.

scale[2] escala *f*; *(extent)* alcance *m*.

scales *npl* **(pair of) s.** *(shop, kitchen)* balanza *f sing*; *(bathroom)* báscula *f sing*.

scan 1 *vt (text, graphics)* escanear; *(scrutinize)* escrutar; *(glance at)* ojear. **2** *n (by ultrasound)* exploración *f* ultrasónica; *(in gynaecology etc)* ecografía *f*.

scan·dal escándalo *m*; *(gossip)* chismes *mpl*.

Scan·di·na·vi·an *adj & n* escandinavo, -a *(mf)*.

scan·ner escáner *m*.

scar cicatriz *f*.

scarce *adj* escaso, -a.

scarce·ly *adv* apenas.

scar·ci·ty escasez *f*.

scare *vt* asustar.

▸**scare away, scare off** *vt* ahuyentar.

scare·crow espantapájaros *m inv*.

scarf *(pl* **scarves** *or* **scarfs)** *(long, woolen)* bufanda *f*; *(square)* pañuelo *m*.

scar·let *adj* **s. fever** escarlatina *f*.

scar·y *adj* espantoso, -a; *(film)* de terror.

scat·ter 1 *vt (papers etc)* esparcir; *(disperse)* dispersar. **2** *vi* dispersarse.

sce·nar·i·o *(of film)* guión *m*; *(situation)* situación *f* hipotética.

scene *(in theater etc)* escena *f*; *(place)* lugar *m*; **to make a s.** *(fuss)* montar un espectáculo.

scen·er·y *(landscape)* paisaje *m*; *(in theater)* decorado *m*.

scent *(smell)* olor *m*; *(perfume)* perfume *m*.

sched·ule 1 *n (plan, agenda)* programa *m*; *(timetable)* horario *m*; **on s.** a la hora (prevista); **to be behind**

s. llevar retraso. **2** *vt (plan)* programar.

sched·uled *adj* previsto, -a; **s. flight** vuelo *m* regular.

scheme *(plan)* plan *m*; *(project)* proyecto *m*; *(trick)* ardid *m*.

schmuck *fam* lelo, -a *mf*.

schol·ar *(learned person)* erudito, -a *mf*; *(pupil)* alumno, -a *mf*.

schol·ar·ship *(grant)* beca *f*.

school *(primary)* escuela *f*; *(secondary)* colegio *m*; *(university)* universidad *f*; **s. year** año *m* escolar.

school·boy alumno *m*.

school·girl alumna *f*.

school·mate compañero, -a *mf* de clase.

school·teach·er profesor, -a *mf*; *(primary school)* maestro, -a *mf*.

sci·ence ciencia *f*; *(school subject)* ciencias *fpl*.

sci·ence fic·tion ciencia-ficción *f*.

sci·en·tif·ic *adj* científico, -a.

scis·sors *npl* tijeras *fpl*.

scold *vt* regañar, reñir.

scone bollo *m*.

scoop *(in press)* exclusiva *f*.

scoot·er *(child's)* patinete *m*; *(adult's)* Vespa® *f*.

scope *(range)* alcance *m*; *(freedom)* libertad *f*.

scorch *vt (burn)* quemar; *(singe)* chamuscar.

score 1 *n (in sport)* tanteo *m*; *(cards, golf)* puntuación *f*; *(result)* resultado *m*; *(twenty)* veintena *f*; *(music)* partitura *f*. **2** *vt (goal)* marcar; *(points)* conseguir. **3** *vi (in sport)* marcar un tanto; *(soccer)* marcar un gol; *(keep the score)* llevar el marcador.

scorn desprecio *m*.

Scot escocés, -esa *mf*.

Scotch 1 *adj* **S. tape®** cinta *f* adhesiva, celo® *m*. **2** *n (whiskey)* whisky *m* escocés.

Scots *adj* escocés, -esa.

Scots·man escocés *m*.

Scots·wom·an escocesa *f*.

scoun·drel canalla *m*.

scout boy s. boy *m* scout; **(talent)** s. cazatalentos *m inv.*

scram·ble 1 *vi* trepar; **to s. up a tree** trepar a un árbol. **2** *vt* **scrambled eggs** huevos *mpl* revueltos. **3** *n (climb)* subida *f*, *fig* **it's going to be a s.** *(rush)* va a ser muy apresurado.

scrap¹ 1 *n (small piece)* pedazo *m*; **scraps** *(of food)* sobras *fpl.* **2** *vt (discard)* desechar; *(idea)* descartar.

scrap² 1 *n (fight)* pelea *f*. **2** *vi* pelearse **(with** con).

scrap·book álbum *m* de recortes.

scrape 1 *vt (paint, wood)* raspar; *(graze)* arañarse. **2** *vi (rub)* rozar. **3** *n (trouble)* lío *m.*

▸**scrape through** *vti (exam)* aprobar por los pelos.

scrap met·al chatarra *f.*

scrap pa·per papel *m* de borrador.

scratch 1 *n (on skin, paintwork)* arañazo *m*; **to be up to s.** dar la talla; **to start from s.** partir de cero. **2** *vt (with nail, claw)* arañar; *(paintwork)* rayar; *(to relieve itching)* rascarse.

scream 1 *n* chillido *m*. **2** *vt (insults etc)* gritar. **3** *vi* **to s. at sb** chillar a algn.

screen *(movable partition)* biombo *m*; *(cinema, TV, computer)* pantalla *f.*

screw 1 *n* tornillo *m*. **2** *vt* atornillar; **to s. sth down** *or* **in** *or* **on** fijar algo con tornillos.

screw·driv·er destornillador *m.*

scrib·ble *vt (message etc)* garabatear.

script *(of film)* guión *m*; *(in exam)* examen *m.*

scrub *vt* frotar.

scrub brush estregadera *f.*

scrum *(in rugby)* melée *f*; **s. half** medio *m* melée.

scu·ba div·ing submarinismo *m.*

sculp·ture escultura *f.*

scum *(on liquid)* espuma *f*, *fig* escoria *f.*

sea mar *m or f*; **by the s.** a orillas del mar; **out at s.** en alta mar; **to go by s.** ir en barco.

sea·food mariscos *mpl.*

sea·front paseo *m* marítimo.

sea·gull gaviota *f.*

seal¹ *(animal)* foca *f.*

seal² *n (official stamp)* sello *m*; *(airtight closure)* cierre *m* hermético. **2** *vt (with official stamp)* sellar; *(with wax)* lacrar; *(close)* cerrar.

▸**seal off** *vt (area)* acordonar.

seam *(in cloth)* costura *f.*

search 1 *vt (files etc)* buscar en; *(building, suitcase)* registrar; *(person)* cachear. **2** *vi* buscar; **to s. through** registrar. **3** *n* búsqueda *f*; *(of person)* cacheo *m*; **in s. of** en busca de.

sea·shell concha *f* marina.

sea·shore *(beach)* playa *f.*

sea·sick *adj* **to get s.** marearse.

sea·sick·ness mareo *m.*

sea·side playa *f.*

sea·son¹ *(of year)* estación *f*; *(for sport etc)* temporada *f*, **high/low s.** temporada *f* alta/baja.

sea·son² *vt (food)* sazonar.

sea·son·al *adj* estacional.

sea·son·ing condimento *m.*

sea·son tick·et abono *m.*

seat 1 *n* asiento *m*; *(place)* plaza *f*; *(in cinema, theater)* localidad *f*; *(in government)* escaño *m*; **to take a s.** sentarse. **2** *vt (guests etc)* sentar; *(accommodate)* tener cabida para.

seat·ing asientos *mpl.*

sea·weed alga *f* (marina).

sec·ond¹ *adj* segundo, -a; **every s. day** cada dos días. **2** *n (in series)* segundo, -a *mf*; *(gear)* segunda *f*; **the s. of October** el dos de octubre. **3** *adv* **to come s.** terminar en segundo lugar.

sec·ond² *(time)* segundo *m.*

sec·ond·ar·y *adj* secundario, -a.

sec·ond-class 1 *adj* de segunda clase. **2** *adv* **to travel s.** viajar en segunda.

sec·ond-hand *adj & adv* de segunda mano.

sec·ond·ly *adv* en segundo lugar.

se·cret adj secreto, -a; **in s.** en secreto.

sec·re·tar·y secretario, -a mf.

se·cret·ly adv en secreto.

sec·tion sección f.

sec·u·lar adj (music, art) profano, -a.

se·cure 1 adj seguro, -a; (window, door) bien cerrado, -a; (ladder etc) firme. **2** vt (fix) sujetar; (window, door) cerrar bien; (obtain) obtener.

se·cure·ly adv (firmly) firmemente.

se·cu·ri·ty seguridad f, (financial guarantee) fianza f.

se·dan (automobile) turismo m.

se·da·tion sedación f.

sed·a·tive adj & n sedante (m).

see* vti ver; **let's s.** a ver; **s. you (later)/soon!** ¡hasta luego/pronto!; **to s. sb home** acompañar a algn a casa.

▸**see about** vt (deal with) ocuparse de.

▸**see off** vt (say goodbye to) despedirse de.

▸**see out** vt (show out) acompañar hasta la puerta.

▸**see through** vt fam **to s. through sb** verle el plumero a algn; **to s. sth through** (carry out) llevar algo a cabo.

▸**see to** vt (deal with) ocuparse de.

seed semilla f, (of fruit) pepita f.

see·ing conj **s. that** dado que.

seek* 1 vt (look for) buscar; (ask for) solicitar. **2** vi buscar; **to s. to do sth** procurar hacer algo.

seem vi parecer; **I s. to remember his name was Colin** creo recordar que su nombre era Colin; **it seems to me that** me parece que; **so it seems** eso parece.

seem·ing·ly adv aparentemente, según parece.

see·saw balancín m.

seg·ment segmento m; (of orange) gajo m.

seize vt (grab) agarrar; **to s. an opportunity** aprovechar una ocasión; **to s. power** hacerse con el poder.

sel·dom adv rara vez, raramente.

se·lect vt (thing) escoger; (team) seleccionar.

se·lec·tion (people or things chosen) selección f, (range) surtido m.

se·lec·tive adj selectivo, -a.

self-as·sur·ance confianza f en uno mismo.

self-as·sured adj seguro, -a de uno mismo, -a.

self-con·fi·dence confianza f en uno mismo, -a.

self-con·fi·dent adj seguro, -a de uno mismo, -a.

self-con·scious adj cohibido, -a.

self-con·trol autocontrol m.

self-de·fense autodefensa f.

self-em·ployed adj (worker) autónomo, -a.

self-ev·i·dent adj evidente, patente.

self·ish adj egoísta.

self-re·spect amor m propio.

self-righ·teous adj santurrón, -ona.

self-serv·ice 1 n (in shop etc) autoservicio m. **2** adj de autoservicio.

sell* 1 vt vender. **2** vi venderse.

▸**sell out** vt **we're sold out of sugar** se nos ha agotado el azúcar; **sold out** (sign at theater) agotadas las localidades.

sell·er vendedor, -a mf.

se·mes·ter semester m.

semi- prefix semi-.

sem·i·cir·cle semicírculo m.

sem·i·co·lon punto y coma m.

sem·i·con·duc·tor semiconductor m.

sem·i·de·tached casa f adosada.

sem·i·fi·nal semifinal f.

sem·i·nar seminario m.

sem·o·li·na sémola f.

sen·ate senado m.

sen·a·tor senador, -a mf.

send* 1 vt enviar; (cause to become) volver. **2** vi **to s. for sb** mandar llamar a algn.

▸**send away** 1 vt (dismiss) despedir. **2**

vi **to s. away for sth** escribir pidiendo algo.

▸**send back** *vt (goods etc)* devolver.

▸**send in** *vt (application etc)* mandar; *(troops)* enviar.

▸**send off** *vt (letter etc)* enviar; *(player)* expulsar.

▸**send on** *vt (luggage) (ahead)* facturar.

▸**send out** *vt (person)* echar; *(invitations)* enviar.

▸**send up** *vt* hacer subir; *(make fun of)* burlarse de.

send·er remitente *mf.*

sen·ior 1 *adj (in age)* mayor; *(in rank)* superior; *(with longer service)* más antiguo, -a; **William Armstrong S.** William Armstrong padre. **2** *n (at school)* estudiante *mf* del último curso; **she's three years my s.** *(in age)* me lleva tres años.

sen·sa·tion sensación *f.*

sen·sa·tion·al *adj (marvelous)* sensacional.

sense 1 *n (faculty)* sentido *m; (of word)* significado *m; (meaning)* sentido *m;* **s. of direction/humor** sentido *m* de la orientación/del humor; **common s.** sentido *m* común; **it doesn't make s.** no tiene sentido; **to come to one's senses** recobrar el juicio. **2** *vt* sentir.

sense·less *adj (absurd)* absurdo, -a.

sen·si·ble *adj (wise)* sensato, -a; *(choice)* acertado, -a; *(clothes, shoes)* práctico, -a.

sen·si·tive *adj* sensible; *(touchy)* susceptible; *(skin)* delicado, -a.

sen·si·tiv·i·ty sensibilidad *f, (touchiness)* susceptibilidad *f.*

sen·tence 1 *n* frase *f, (legal)* sentencia *f,* **life s.** cadena *f* perpetua. **2** *vt (judge)* condenar.

sen·ti·ment *(sentimentality)* sensiblería *f, (feeling)* sentimiento *m; (opinion)* opinión *f.*

sep·a·rate 1 *vt* separar **(from** de). **2** *vi* separarse. **3** *adj* separado, -a; *(different)* distinto, -a.

sep·a·rate·ly *adv* por separado.

sep·a·ra·tion separación *f.*

Sep·tem·ber se(p)tiembre *m.*

se·quence *(order)* orden *m; (series)* sucesión *f.*

ser·geant sargento *m; (of police)* cabo *m.*

se·ri·al *(on TV etc)* serial *m; (soap opera)* telenovela *f.*

se·ries *inv* serie *f.*

se·ri·ous *adj* serio, -a; *(causing concern)* grave; **I am s.** hablo en serio.

se·ri·ous·ly *adv (in earnest)* en serio; *(dangerously, severely)* gravemente.

ser·vant *(domestic)* criado, -a *mf.*

serve *vt* servir; *(customer)* atender; **it serves him right** bien merecido lo tiene.

▸**serve out, serve up** *vt* servir.

serv·er *(for computers)* servidor *m.*

serv·ice 1 *n* servicio *m; (maintenance)* mantenimiento *m;* **s. (charge) included** servicio incluido. **2** *vt (car, machine)* revisar.

serv·ice ar·e·a área *f* de servicio.

serv·ice sta·tion estación *f* de servicio.

ses·sion sesión *f.*

set¹ *vt* (*put, place)* poner, colocar; *(time, price)* fijar; *(record)* establecer; *(mechanism etc)* ajustar; **to s. one's watch** poner el reloj en hora; **to s. the table** poner la mesa; **to s. sb free** poner en libertad a algn. **2** *vi* (*sun, moon)* ponerse; *(jelly, jam)* cuajar; **to s. to** *(begin)* ponerse a. **3** *n (stage) (for film)* plató *m; (in theater)* escenario *m; (scenery)* decorado *m;* **shampoo and s.** lavado y marcado *m.* **4** *adj (task, idea)* fijo, -a; *(date, time)* señalado, -a; *(ready)* listo, -a; **s. phrase** frase *f* hecha; **to be s. on doing sth** estar empeñado, -a en hacer algo.

▸**set about** *vt (begin)* empezar.

▸**set aside** *vt (time, money)* reservar.

▸**set back** *vt (delay)* retrasar.

▸**set down** vt (luggage etc) dejar (en el suelo).

▸**set off 1** vi (depart) salir. **2** vt (bomb) hacer estallar; (burglar alarm) hacer sonar.

▸**set out 1** vi (depart) salir; **to s. out for ...** partir hacia ...; **to s. out to do sth** proponerse hacer algo. **2** vt (arrange) disponer; (present) presentar.

▸**set up 1** vt (tent, stall) montar; (business etc) establecer. **2** vi establecerse.

set² (series) serie f, (of golf clubs, keys etc) juego m; (of tools) estuche m; (of people) grupo m; (in math) conjunto m; (tennis) set m; **TV s.** televisor m; **chess s.** juego m de ajedrez.

set·back revés m, contratiempo m.

set·tee sofá m.

set·ting (background) marco m.

set·tle 1 vt (decide on) acordar; (date, price) fijar; (debt) pagar; (account) saldar. **2** vi (bird, insect) posarse; (put down roots) afincarse; **to s. into an armchair** acomodarse en un sillón.

▸**settle down** vi (put down roots) instalarse; (marry) casarse; (child) calmarse; (situation) normalizarse.

▸**settle with** vt (pay debt to) ajustar cuentas con.

set·tle·ment (agreement) acuerdo m; (colony) asentamiento m.

set·tler colono, -a mf.

sev·en adj & n siete (m) inv.

sev·en·teen adj & n diecisiete (m) inv.

sev·enth adj & n séptimo, -a (mf).

sev·en·ti·eth adj & n septuagésimo, -a (mf).

sev·en·ty adj & n setenta (m) inv; **in the seventies** en los (años) setenta.

sev·er·al adj varios, -as. **2** pron algunos, -as.

se·vere adj severo, -a; (climate, blow) duro, -a; (illness, loss) grave.

se·ver·i·ty severidad f.

sew* vti coser.

▸**sew on** vt coser.

▸**sew up** vt (mend) remendar.

sew·er alcantarilla f.

sew·ing costura f.

sew·ing ma·chine máquina f de coser.

sex sexo m; **s. education** educación f sexual; **to have s. with sb** tener relaciones sexuales con algn.

sex·u·al adj sexual.

sex·y adj sexy.

sh! interj ¡chitón!, ¡chh!

shab·by adj (garment) raído, -a; (unkempt) desaseado, -a.

shade (shadow) sombra f, (lampshade) pantalla f, (of color) matiz m; **in the s.** a la sombra.

shad·ow sombra f.

shad·y adj (place) a la sombra.

shaft (of tool) mango m; (of mine) pozo m; (of elevator) hueco m; (beam of light) rayo m.

shake* **1** vt sacudir; (bottle) agitar; **the news shook him** la noticia le conmocionó; **to s. hands with sb** estrechar la mano a algn; **to s. one's head** negar con la cabeza. **2** vi (person, building) temblar.

shall v aux (used to form future tense) (first person only) **I s.** (or **I'll**) **buy it** lo compraré; **I s. not** (or **I shan't**) **say anything** no diré nada.
▪ (used to form questions) (usually first person) **s. I close the door?** ¿cierro la puerta?; **s. we go?** ¿nos vamos?

shal·low adj poco profundo, -a.

shame vergüenza f, (pity) pena f, **what a s.!** ¡qué lástima!

shame·ful adj vergonzoso, -a.

sham·poo 1 n champú m. **2** vt (one's hair) lavarse.

shape forma f, **to take s.** tomar forma; **in good/bad s.** (condition) en buen/mal estado; **to be in good s.** (health) estar en forma.

share.1 n (portion) parte f, (financial) acción f. **2** vt (divide) dividir; (have in common) compartir.

▸**share in** *vt* participar en.

▸**share out** *vt* repartir.

share·hold·er accionista *mf*.

shark (*fish*) tiburón *m*.

sharp 1 *adj* (*razor, pencil, knife*) afilado, -a; (*needle*) puntiagudo, -a; (*bend*) cerrado, -a; (*pain, cry*) agudo, -a. **2** *adv* **at 2 o'clock s.** a las dos en punto.

sharp·en *vt* (*knife*) afilar; (*pencil*) sacar punta a.

sharp·en·er sacapuntas *m*.

sharp·ly *adv* (*abruptly*) bruscamente.

shat·ter 1 *vt* hacer añicos. **2** *vi* hacerse añicos.

shave 1 *n* afeitado *m*; **to have a s.** afeitarse. **2** *vt* (*person*) afeitar. **3** *vi* afeitarse.

shav·er (**electric**) **s.** máquina *f* de afeitar.

shav·ing brush brocha *f* de afeitar.

shav·ing cream crema *f* de afeitar.

shawl chal *m*.

she *pers pron* ella.

shed¹ (*in garden*) cobertizo *m*; (*workmen's storage*) barraca *f*.

shed² *vt* (*blood, tears*) derramar.

sheep *inv* oveja *f*.

sheep·skin piel *f* de carnero.

sheer *adj* (*utter*) total, puro, -a; (*cliff*) escarpado, -a; (*drop*) vertical; (*stockings*) fino, -a.

sheet (*on bed*) sábana *f*; (*of paper*) hoja *f*, (*of tin, glass, plastic*) lámina *f*, (*of ice*) capa *f*.

shelf (*pl* **shelves**) (*on bookcase*) estante *m*; **shelves** estantería *f*.

shell 1 *n* (*of egg, nut*) cáscara *f*, (*of tortoise etc*) caparazón *m*; (*of snail etc*) concha *f*, (*from gun*) obús *m*. **2** *vt* (*peas*) desvainar; (*with guns*) bombardear.

shell·fish *inv* marisco *m*; mariscos *mpl*.

shel·ter 1 *n* (*protection*) abrigo *m*; **to take s.** refugiarse (**from** de); **bus s.** marquesina *f*. **2** *vt* proteger. **3** *vi* refugiarse.

shelv·ing estanterías *fpl*.

shep·herd pastor *m*.

sher·iff sheriff *m*.

sher·ry jerez *m*.

shield *n* escudo *m*; (*of policeman*) placa *f*. **2** *vt* proteger (**from** de).

shift 1 *n* (*change*) cambio *m*; (*period of work, group of workers*) turno *m*; (**gear**) **s.** cambio *m* de velocidades. **2** *vt* (*change*) cambiar; (*move*) cambiar de sitio. **3** *vi* (*move*) mover; (*change place*) cambiar de sitio.

shin espinilla *f*.

shine 1 *vi** brillar. **2** *vt* (*lamp*)* dirigir; (*pt & pp* **shined**) (*polish*) sacar brillo a; (*shoes*) limpiar. **3** *n* brillo *m*.

shin·y *adj* brillante.

ship barco *m*.

ship·ping barcos *mpl*.

ship·wreck 1 *n* naufragio *m*. **2** *vt* **to be shipwrecked** naufragar.

ship·yard astillero *m*.

shirt camisa *f*.

shiv·er 1 *vi* (*with cold*) tiritar; (*with fear*) temblar. **2** *n* escalofrío *m*.

shock 1 *n* (*jolt*) choque *m*; (*scare*) susto *m*; (*in medical sense*) shock *m*. **2** *vt* (*scandalize*) escandalizar.

shock ab·sorb·er amortiguador *m*.

shock·ing *adj* (*causing horror*) espantoso, -a; (*disgraceful*) escandaloso, -a.

shoe zapato *m*; **shoes** calzado *m sing*.

shoe·lace cordón *m* (de zapatos).

shoe pol·ish betún *m*.

shoot 1 *n* (*on plant*) brote *m*; (*of vine*) sarmiento *m*. **2** *vt** (*fire on*) pegar un tiro a; (*wound*) herir (de bala); (*kill*) matar; (*execute*) fusilar; (*film*) rodar, filmar; (*with still camera*) fotografiar. **2** *vi** (*with gun*) disparar (**at** sb sobre, a algn).

▸**shoot down** *vt* (*aircraft*) derribar.

▸**shoot off** *vi* (*leave quickly*) salir a escape.

▸**shoot up** *vi* (*prices*) dispararse.

shoot·ing 1 *n* (*shots*) tiros *mpl*;

(murder) asesinato *m; (hunting)* caza *f; (of film)* rodaje *m.* **2** *adj (pain)* punzante.

shoot·ing star estrella *f* fugaz.

shop 1 *n* tienda *f; (large store)* almacén *m.* **2** *vi* hacer compras; **to go shopping** ir de compras.

shop as·sis·tant dependiente, -a *mf.*

shop·keep·er tendero, -a *mf.*

shop·ping *(purchases)* compras *fpl.*

shop·ping bag bolsa *f* de la compra.

shop·ping bas·ket cesta *f* de la compra.

shop·ping cen·ter centro *m* comercial.

shop win·dow escaparate *m.*

shore *(of sea, lake)* orilla *f; (coast)* costa *f.*

short 1 *adj* corto, -a; *(not tall)* bajo, -a; **in a s. while** dentro de un rato; **in the s. term** a corto plazo; **'Bob' is s. for 'Robert'** 'Bob's es el diminutivo de 'Robert'; **to be s. of food** andar escaso, -a de comida. **2** *adv* **to cut s.** *(vacation)* interrumpir; *(meeting)* suspender; **we're running s. of coffee** se nos está acabando el café.

short·age escasez *f.*

short·cut atajo *m.*

short·en *vt (skirt, visit)* acortar.

short·hand typ·ist taquimecanógrafo, -a *mf.*

short·ly *adv (soon)* dentro de poco; **s. after** poco después.

shorts *npl* **a pair of s.** un pantalón corto; *(underpants)* unos calzoncillos.

short·sight·ed *adj (person)* miope.

short-term *adj* a corto plazo.

shot¹ *(act, sound)* disparo *m; (sport)* tiro *m* (a puerta); *(photography)* foto *f; (in film)* toma *f.*

shot² *pt & pp of* **shoot.**

shot·gun escopeta *f.*

should *v aux (duty)* deber; **all**

employees **s. wear helmets** todos los empleados deben llevar casco; **he s. have been an architect** debería haber sido arquitecto. ▪ *(probability)* deber de; **he s. have finished by now** ya debe de haber acabado. ▪ *(conditional use)* **if anything strange s. happen** si pasara algo raro; **I s. like to ask a question** quisiera hacer una pregunta.

shoul·der hombro *m; (beside road)* arcén *m.*

shoul·der bag bolso *m* (de bandolera).

shout 1 *n* grito *m.* **2** *vti* gritar; **to s. at sb** gritar a algn.

shout·ing gritos *mpl.*

shove 1 *n* empujón *m.* **2** *vt* empujar. **3** *vi* empujar; *(jostle)* dar empellones.

shov·el 1 *n* pala *f.* **2** *vt* mover con pala.

show 1 *vt* (ticket etc)* mostrar; *(painting etc)* exponer; *(film)* poner; *(latest plans etc)* presentar; *(teach)* enseñar; *(temperature, way etc)* indicar; **to s. sb to the door** acompañar a algn hasta la puerta. **2** *vi* (be visible)* notarse; **what's showing?** *(at cinema)* ¿qué ponen? **3** *n (entertainment)* espectáculo *m;* **on s.** expuesto, -a; **boat s.** salón *m* náutico; **motor s.** salón *m* del automóvil.

▶ **show off 1** *vt (flaunt)* hacer alarde de. **2** *vi* farolear.

▶ **show up 1** *vt (embarrass)* dejar en evidencia. **2** *vi (arrive)* aparecer.

show·er *(rain)* chaparrón *m; (bath)* ducha *f;* **to have a s.** ducharse.

show·ing *(cinema performance)* sesión *f.*

show-off farolero, -a *mf.*

shrimp camarón *m.*

shrink* 1 *vt* encoger. **2** *vi* encoger(se).

shrub arbusto *m.*

shrug *vt* **to s. one's shoulders** encogerse de hombros.

shud·der *vi (person)* estremecerse.

shuf·fle vt (cards) barajar.

shut 1 vt* cerrar. **2** vi* cerrarse. **3** adj cerrado, -a.

▸**shut down 1** vt (factory) cerrar. **2** vi (factory) cerrar.

▸**shut off** vti (gas, water etc) cortar.

▸**shut out** vt (lock out) dejar fuera a.

▸**shut up 1** vt (close) cerrar; (imprison) encerrar. **2** vi (keep quiet) callarse.

shut·ter (on window) postigo m.

shut·tle (plane) puente m aéreo; (space) s. transbordador m espacial.

shy adj (timid) tímido, -a; (reserved) reservado, -a.

shy·ness timidez f.

sick adj (ill) enfermo, -a; fam (fed up) harto, -a; **s. leave** baja f por enfermedad; **to feel s.** (about to vomit) tener ganas de devolver; **to be s.** devolver.

sick·ness (illness) enfermedad f; (nausea) náuseas fpl.

side n lado m; (of coin etc) cara f; (of hill) ladera f; (edge) borde m; (of lake, river) orilla f; (team) equipo m; (in politics) partido m; **by s.** junto a; **by my s.** a mi lado; **s. by s.** juntos; **she's on our s.** está de nuestro lado; **to take sides with sb** ponerse de parte de algn.

side·board aparador m.

side·burns npl patillas fpl.

side·light piloto m.

side·walk acera f.

side·ways adv de lado.

sid·ing (on railroad) apartadero m, vía f muerta.

siege sitio m, cerco m; **to lay s. to** sitiar.

sieve colador m; (coarse) criba f.

sift vt tamizar.

sigh 1 vi suspirar. **2** n suspiro m.

sight (faculty) vista f; (spectacle) espectáculo m; **at first s.** a primera vista; **to catch s. of** divisar; **to lose s. of** sth/sb perder algo/a algn de vista; **within s.** a la vista.

sight·see·ing to go s. hacer turismo.

sign 1 n (signal) señal f; (trace) rastro m; (notice) anuncio m; (board) letrero m. **2** vti (letter etc) firmar.

▸**sign on** vi (worker) firmar un contrato; (unemployed person) apuntarse al paro.

▸**sign up** vi (soldier) alistarse; (worker) firmar un contrato.

sig·nal 1 n señal f. **2** vt (direction etc) indicar.

sig·na·ture firma f.

sig·nif·i·cant adj (important) importante.

sig·nif·i·cant·ly adv (markedly) sensiblemente.

sig·ni·fy vt (mean) significar; (show, make known) indicar.

sign·post poste m indicador.

si·lence 1 n silencio m. **2** vt acallar.

si·lent adj silencioso, -a; (film) mudo, -a; **to remain s.** guardar silencio.

si·lent·ly adv silenciosamente.

silk seda f.

sill (of window) alféizar m.

sil·ly adj (stupid) tonto, -a; (ridiculous) ridículo, -a.

sil·ver 1 n (metal) plata f; (tableware) vajilla f de plata. **2** adj de plata; **s. paper** papel m de plata.

sil·ver·plat·ed adj plateado, -a.

sil·ver·ware vajilla f de plata.

sim·i·lar adj semejante (to a); **to be s.** parecerse.

sim·i·lar·i·ty semejanza f.

sim·ple adj sencillo, -a.

sim·pli·fy vt simplificar.

sim·ply adv (only) simplemente; (just, merely) meramente.

si·mul·ta·ne·ous adj simultáneo, -a.

si·mul·ta·ne·ous·ly adv simultáneamente.

sin pecado m.

since 1 adv (ever) s. desde entonces. **2** prep desde; **she has been living here s. 1975** vive aquí desde 1975. **3** conj (time) desde que; **how long is it s. you last saw him?** ¿cuánto tiempo hace (desde) que lo viste por

última vez? ▪ *(because, as)* ya que.
sin·cere *adj* sincero, -a.
sin·cere·ly *adv* sinceramente;
Yours s. *(in letter)* (le saluda) atentamente.
sin·cer·i·ty sinceridad *f.*
sing* *vti* cantar.
sing·er cantante *mf.*
sin·gle 1 *adj* solo, -a; *(unmarried)* soltero, -a; **s. bed/room** cama *f*/habitación *f* individual. **2** *n (record)* single *m.*
▸**single out** *vt (choose)* escoger.
sin·gle-mind·ed *adj* resuelto, -a.
sin·gu·lar 1 *adj (noun form etc)* singular. **2** *n* singular *m.*
sin·gu·lar·ly *adv* excepcionalmente.
sin·is·ter *adj* siniestro, -a.
sink¹ *(in kitchen)* fregadero *m.*
sink²* *vi (ship)* hundirse.
▸**sink in** *vi (penetrate)* penetrar; *fig* causar impresión.
sip *vt* beber a sorbos.
sir señor *m*; *(title)* sir.
si·ren sirena *f.*
sis·ter hermana *f.*
sis·ter-in-law cuñada *f.*
sit* 1 *vt (child etc)* sentar (**in, on** en); *(exam)* presentarse a. **2** *vi (action)* sentarse; *(be seated)* estar sentado, -a.
▸**sit around** *vi* holgazanear.
▸**sit down** *vi* sentarse.
▸**sit up** *vi* incorporarse.
site *(area)* lugar *m*; **building s.** solar *m*; *(under construction)* obra *f.*
sit·ting room sala *f* de estar.
sit·u·at·ed *adj* to be s. estar situado, -a.
sit·u·a·tion situación *f.*
six *adj & n* seis *(m) inv.*
six·teen *adj & n* dieciséis *(m) inv.*
sixth 1 *adj* sexto, -a. **2** *n (in series)* sexto, -a *mf*; *(fraction)* sexto *m.*
six·ti·eth *adj & n* sexagésimo, -a *(mf).*
six·ty *adj & n* sesenta *(m) inv.*
size tamaño *m*; *(of garment)* talla *f*;

(of shoes) número *m*; *(of person)* estatura *f.*
skate 1 *n* patín *m.* **2** *vi* patinar.
skate·board monopatín *m.*
skat·er patinador, -a *mf.*
skat·ing patinaje *m.*
skat·ing rink pista *f* de patinaje.
skel·e·ton esqueleto *m.*
sketch *n (preliminary drawing)* bosquejo *m*; *(on TV etc)* sketch *m.* **2** *vt (preliminary drawing)* bosquejar.
skew·er pincho *m*, broqueta *f.*
ski 1 *n* esquí *m.* **2** *vi* esquiar; **to go skiing** ir a esquiar.
skid 1 *n* patinazo *m.* **2** *vi* patinar.
ski·er esquiador, -a *mf.*
ski·ing esquí *m.*
skilled *adj (dextrous)* hábil, diestro, -a; *(expert)* experto, -a; *(worker)* cualificado, -a.
skill·ful *adj* hábil.
ski lift telesquí *m*; *(with seats)* telesilla *f.*
skill *(ability)* habilidad *f*, *(technique)* técnica *f.*
skilled *adj (worker)* cualificado, -a.
skim milk leche *f* desnatada.
skin piel *f*; *(of face)* cutis *m*; *(complexion)* tez *f*, *(of fruit)* piel *f.*
skin-div·ing submarinismo *m.*
skin·ny *adj* flaco, -a.
skip¹ 1 *vi (jump)* saltar, brincar; *(with rope)* saltar a la comba. **2** *vt (omit)* saltarse.
skip² *(container)* contenedor *m.*
skirt falda *f.*
skull calavera *f*, *(cranium)* cráneo *m.*
sky cielo *m*; **s. blue** azul *m* celeste.
sky·scrap·er rascacielos *m inv.*
slack *adj (not taut)* flojo, -a; **business is s.** hay poco negocio.
slack·en *vt (rope)* aflojar; *(speed)* reducir.
slacks *npl* pantalones *mpl.*
slam 1 *n (of door)* portazo *m.* **2** *vt (bang)* cerrar de golpe; **to s. the door** dar un portazo. **3** *vi* cerrarse de golpe.
slang jerga *f* popular.

slant 1 *n* inclinación *f.* **2** *vi* inclinarse.

slap 1 *n* palmada *f;* *(in face)* bofetada *f.* **2** *vt* pegar con la mano; *(hit in face)* dar una bofetada a; **to s. sb on the back** dar a algn una palmada en la espalda.

slate pizarra *f.*

slaugh·ter 1 *n (of animals)* matanza *f, (of people)* carnicería *f.* **2** *vt (animals)* matar; *(people)* masacrar.

slave esclavo, -a *mf.*

slav·er·y esclavitud *f.*

sleep 1 *n* sueño *m.* **2** *vi** dormir; **to go to s.** dormirse.

▸**sleep in** *vi (oversleep)* quedarse dormido, -a.

sleep·er *(on train) (coach)* coche-cama *m; (berth)* litera *f.*

sleep·ing bag saco *m* de dormir.

sleep·ing car coche-cama *m.*

sleep·ing pill somnífero *m.*

sleep·y *adj* **to be** *or* **feel s.** tener sueño.

sleet 1 *n* aguanieve *f.* **2** *vi* **it's sleeting** cae aguanieve.

sleeve *(of garment)* manga *f, (of record)* funda *f.*

sleigh trineo *m.*

slen·der *adj (thin)* delgado, -a; *fig (hope, chance)* remoto, -a.

slept *pt & pp* of **sleep.**

slice 1 *n (of bread)* rebanada *f, (of cake)* trozo *m; (of meat)* loncha *f.* **2** *vt (food)* cortar en rodajas.

slide 1 *n (in playground)* tobogán *m; (photographic)* diapositiva *f;* **s. pro·jector** proyector *m* de diapositivas. **2** *vt* deslizar; *(furniture)* correr. **3** *vi** deslizarse; *(slip)* resbalar.

slid·ing *adj (door, window)* corredizo, -a.

slight *adj (small)* pequeño, -a; *(trivial)* leve; **not in the slightest** en absoluto.

slight·ly *adv (a little)* ligeramente.

slim 1 *adj (person)* delgado, -a; *(slender)* esbelto, -a. **2** *vi* adelgazar.

slim·y *adj* (**slimier, slimiest**) *(mud-*

dy) lodoso, -a; *(snail)* baboso, -a; *fig (person)* zalamero, -a.

sling 1 *n (for arm)* cabestrillo *m.* **2** *vt** (throw)* tirar.

slip 1 *n (mistake)* error *m; (moral)* desliz *m; (under skirt)* combinación *f, (of paper)* papelito *m.* **2** *vi (slide)* resbalar. **3** *vt* **to s. sth into sth** meter algo en algo; **to s. sth to sb** dar algo a algn con disimulo.

▸**slip away** *vi (person)* escabullirse.

▸**slip off** *vt (clothes)* quitarse rápidamente.

▸**slip on** *vt (clothes)* ponerse rápidamente.

▸**slip out** *vi (leave)* salir.

▸**slip up** *vi (make a mistake)* equivocarse.

slip·per zapatilla *f.*

slip·per·y *adj* resbaladizo, -a.

slit *(opening)* hendidura *f, (cut)* raja *f.*

slo·gan (e)slogan *m*, lema *m.*

slope 1 *n (incline)* cuesta *f, (of mountain)* ladera *f, (of roof)* vertiente *f.* **2** *vi* inclinarse.

slop·ing *adj* inclinado, -a.

slot *(for coin)* ranura *f, (opening)* rendija *f.*

slot ma·chine *(for gambling)* (máquina *f*) tragaperras *f inv* ; *(vending machine)* distribuidor *m* automático.

slow 1 *adj* lento, -a; *(clock)* atrasado, -a; *(stupid)* torpe; **in s. motion** a cámara lenta; **to be s. to do sth** tardar en hacer algo. **2** *adv* despacio.

▸**slow down, slow up** *vi* ir más despacio; *(in car)* reducir la velocidad.

slow·ly *adv* despacio.

slug *(animal)* babosa *f.*

slump 1 *n (drop in sales etc)* bajón *m; (economic depression)* crisis *f* económica. **2** *vi (sales etc)* caer de repente; *(prices)* desplomarse; *(the economy)* hundirse.

slums barrios bajos *mpl.*

sly *adj (cunning)* astuto, -a.

smack 1 *n (slap)* bofetada *f.* **2** *vt*

(slap) dar una bofetada a; *(hit)* golpear.

small *adj (elegant)* pequeño, -a; *(in height)* bajo, -a; **s. change** cambio *m.*

small·pox viruela *f.*

smart *adj (elegant)* elegante; *(clever)* listo, -a.

smash 1 *vt (break)* romper; *(shatter)* hacer pedazos. **2** *vi (break)* romperse; *(shatter)* hacerse pedazos.

▸**smash into** *vt (vehicle)* estrellarse contra.

smash·ing *adj fam* estupendo, -a.

smell 1 *n (sense)* olfato *m; (odor)* olor *m.* **2** *vt** oler. **3** *vi** oler *(of* a); *(stink)* apestar; **it smells good/like lavender** huele bien/a lavanda.

smell·y *adj* (**smellier, smelliest**) *fam* maloliente, apestoso, -a.

smile 1 *n* sonrisa *f.* **2** *vi* sonreír.

smock *(blouse)* blusón *m.*

smoke 1 *n* humo *m.* **2** *vi* fumar; *(chimney etc)* echar humo. **3** *vt (tobacco)* fumar; **to s. a pipe** fumar en pipa.

smok·er *(person)* fumador, -a *mf; (compartment)* vagón *m* de fumadores.

smooth *adj (surface)* liso, -a; *(skin)* suave; *(beer, wine)* suave; *(flight)* tranquilo, -a.

▸**smooth out** *vt (creases)* alisar.

▸**smooth over** *vt* **to s. things over** limar asperezas.

smooth·ly *adv* sobre ruedas.

smug·gle *vt* pasar de contrabando.

smug·gler contrabandista *mf.*

smug·gling contrabando *m.*

snack bocado *m.*

snack bar cafetería *f.*

snail caracol *m.*

snake *(big)* serpiente *f; (small)* culebra *f.*

snap 1 *n (photo)* (foto *f*) instantánea *f.* **2** *vt (branch etc)* partir (en dos). **3** *vi (break)* romperse.

▸**snap off** *vt (branch etc)* arrancar.

snap·shot (foto *f*) instantánea *f.*

snatch 1 *vt (grab)* arrebatar. **2** *vi* **to**

s. at intentar agarrar.

sneak·ers *npl* zapatillas *fpl* de deporte.

sneer *vi* **to s. at** hacer un gesto de desprecio a.

sneeze 1 *n* estornudo *m.* **2** *vi* estornudar.

sniff *vt (flower etc)* oler.

snip *vt* cortar a tijeretazos.

snook·er billar *m* ruso.

snore 1 *n* ronquido *m.* **2** *vi* roncar.

snor·ing ronquidos *mpl.*

snow 1 *n* nieve *f.* **2** *vi* nevar; **it's snowing** está nevando.

snow·ball bola *f* de nieve.

snow·drift ventisquero *m.*

snow·flake copo *m* de nieve.

snow·man hombre *m* de nieve.

snow·plow quitanieves *m inv.*

snow·storm nevada *f.*

so 1 *adv (to such an extent)* tanto; **he was so tired that …** estaba tan cansado que …; **so long!** ¡hasta luego! ▪ *(degree)* tanto; **we loved her so (much)** la queríamos tanto; **so many books** tantos libros. ▪ *(thus, in this way)* así; **and so on, and so forth** y así sucesivamente; **if so** en este caso; **I think/hope so** creo/espero que sí. ▪ *(also)* **I'm going to Spain — so am I** voy a España — yo también. **2** *conj (expresses result)* así que; **so you like England, do you?** así que te gusta Inglaterra, ¿no? ▪ *(expresses purpose)* para que; **I'll put the key here so (that) everyone can see it** pongo la llave aquí para que todos la vean.

soak 1 *vt (washing, food)* remojar. **2** *vi (washing, food)* estar en remojo.

▸**soak up** *vt* absorber.

soaked through *adj (person)* empapado, -a.

soak·ing *adj (object)* empapado, -a; *(person)* calado, -a hasta los huesos.

soap jabón *m.*

soap flakes jabón *m* en escamas.

soap pow·der jabón *m* en polvo.

soap·y *adj* jabonoso, -a.

sob 1 n sollozo m. **2** vi sollozar.

so·ber adj (not drunk, moderate) sobrio, -a.

soc·cer fútbol m.

soc·cer play·er futbolista mf.

so·cial adj social; **s. climber** arribista mf; **s. security** seguridad f social; **s. welfare** seguro m social; **s. work** asistencia f social; **s. worker** asistente, -a mf social.

so·cial·ist adj & n socialista (mf).

so·ci·e·ty sociedad f.

sock calcetín m.

sock·et (for electricity) enchufe m.

so·da s. water soda f; (fizzy drink) gaseosa f.

so·fa sofá m; **s. bed** sofá m cama.

soft adj (not hard) blando, -a; (skin, color, hair, light, music) suave; (drink) no alcohólico, -a; **s. drinks** refrescos mpl.

soft·ball = juego parecido al béisbol jugado en un campo más pequeño y con una pelota más blanda.

soft·en 1 vt (leather, heart) ablandar; (skin) suavizar. **2** vi (leather, heart) ablandarse; (skin) suavizarse.

soft·ly adv (gently) suavemente; (quietly) silenciosamente.

soft·ware software m; **s. package** paquete m.

soil (earth) tierra f.

so·lar adj solar.

sol·dier soldado mf.

sole¹ (of foot) planta f; (of shoe, sock) suela f.

sole² (fish) lenguado m.

sole·ly adv (only) únicamente; (entirely) exclusivamente.

sol·emn adj solemne.

so·lic·i·tor abogado, -a mf.

sol·id 1 adj (not liquid) sólido, -a; (firm) firme; (not hollow, pure) (metal) macizo, -a; (reliable) formal. **2** n sólido m.

sol·i·dar·i·ty solidaridad f.

so·lo solo m.

so·lu·tion solución f.

solve vt resolver.

sol·vent adj & n solvente (m).

some 1 adj (with plural nouns) unos, -as, algunos, -as; (several) varios, -as; (a few) unos, -as cuantos, -as; **there were s. roses** había unas rosas. ▪ (with singular nouns) algún, alguna; (a little) un poco de; **there's s. wine left** queda un poco de vino. ▪ (certain) cierto, -a; **to s. extent** hasta cierto punto. ▪ (unspecified) algún, alguna; **s. day** algún día; **s. other time** otro día. ▪ (quite a lot of) bastante; **it's s. distance away** queda bastante lejos. **2** pron algunos, -as, unos, -as. ▪ (a few) unos, -as cuantos, -as. ▪ (a little) un poco.

some·bod·y pron alguien; **s. else** otro, -a.

some·how adv (in some way) de alguna forma; (for some reason) por alguna razón.

some·one pron = **somebody**.

some·place adv = **somewhere**.

som·er·sault (by acrobat etc) voltereta f.

some·thing pron & n algo; **is s. the matter?** ¿le pasa algo?; **s. else** otra cosa; **s. of the kind** algo por el estilo.

some·time adv algún día.

some·times adv a veces.

some·what adv un tanto.

some·where adv (in some place) en alguna parte; (to some place) a alguna parte.

son hijo m.

song canción f; (of bird) canto m.

son-in-law yerno m.

soon adv (within a short time) dentro de poco; (quickly) rápidamente; (early) pronto; **s. afterwards** poco después; **as s. as** en cuanto; **as s. as possible** cuanto antes; **I would just as s. stay at home** prefiero quedarme en casa; **I would (just) as s. read as watch TV** tanto me da leer como ver la tele.

soot hollín m.

soothe vt (calm) tranquilizar; (pain) aliviar.

so·phis·ti·cat·ed *adj* sofisticado, -a.

sore 1 *adj (aching)* dolorido, -a; *(painful)* doloroso, -a; *fam (angry)* enfadado, -a; **to have a s. throat** tener dolor de garganta. **2** *n* llaga *f*.

sor·row pena *f*.

sor·ry 1 *adj* **I feel very s. for her** me da mucha pena; **to be s. (about sth)** sentir (algo); **I'm s. I'm late** siento llegar tarde. **2** *interj (apology)* ¡perdón!; *(for repetition)* ¿cómo?

sort 1 *n (kind)* clase *f*, tipo *m*; *(brand)* marca *f*; **it's a s. of teapot** es una especie de tetera. **2** *vt (classify)* clasificar.

▸ **sort out** *vt (classify)* clasificar; *(put in order)* ordenar; *(problem)* solucionar.

soul alma *f*.

sound¹ 1 *n* sonido *m*; *(noise)* ruido *m*; **I don't like the s. of it** no me gusta nada la idea. **2** *vt (bell, trumpet)* tocar. **3** *vi (trumpet, bell, alarm)* sonar; *(give an impression)* parecer; **it sounds interesting** parece interesante.

sound² 1 *adj (healthy)* sano, -a; *(in good condition)* en buen estado; *(safe, dependable)* seguro, -a. **2** *adv* **to be s. asleep** estar profundamente dormido, -a.

sound·proof *adj* insonorizado, -a.

soup sopa *f*; *(thin, clear)* caldo *m*.

sour *adj (fruit, wine)* agrio, -a; *(milk)* cortado, -a.

source fuente *f*.

south 1 *n* sur *m*; **in the s. of England** en el sur de Inglaterra. **2** *adj* del sur. **3** *adv (location)* al sur; *(direction)* hacia el sur.

south·bound *adj (con)* dirección sur.

south·east *n & adj* sudeste *(m)*.

south·ern *adj* del sur.

south·ern·er sureño, -a *mf*.

south·ward *adj & adv* hacia el sur.

south·west *n & adj* suroeste *(m)*.

sou·ve·nir recuerdo *m*.

sov·er·eign·ty soberanía *f*.

sow* *vt* sembrar.

space 1 *n* espacio *m*; *(room)* sitio *m*. **2** *vt (also* **s. out***)* espaciar.

space age era *f* espacial.

space·ship nave *f* espacial.

space shut·tle transbordador *m* espacial.

spa·cious *adj* espacioso, -a.

spade¹ *(for digging)* pala *f*.

spade² *(in cards) (international pack)* pica *f*, *(Spanish pack)* espada *f*.

spa·ghet·ti espaguetis *mpl*.

span *vt (river etc)* extenderse sobre, atravesar; *(period of time etc)* abarcar.

Span·iard español, -a *mf*.

Span·ish 1 *adj* español, -a. **2** *n (language)* español *m*, castellano *m*; **the S.** los españoles.

spank *vt* zurrar.

spank·ing cachete *m*.

spare 1 *vt (do without)* prescindir de; **can you s. me 10?** ¿me puedes dejar 10?; **I can't s. the time** no tengo tiempo; **there's none to s.** no sobra nada; **s. me the details** ahórrate los detalles. **2** *adj (left over)* sobrante; *(surplus)* de sobra; **a s. moment** un momento libre; **s. part** *(pieza f de)* recambio *m*; **s. room** cuarto *m* de los invitados; **s. wheel** rueda *f* de recambio. **3** *n (for car etc) (pieza f de)* recambio *m*.

spark chispa *f*.

spar·kle *vi (diamond, glass)* destellar; *(eyes)* brillar.

spar·kling *adj* **s. wine** vino *m* espumoso.

spark·plug bujía *f*.

spar·row gorrión *m*.

speak* **1** *vt (utter)* decir; *(language)* hablar. **2** *vi* hablar; **to s. to sb** hablar con algn; **speaking!** ¡al habla!; **who's speaking, please?** ¿de parte de quién?

▸ **speak up** *vi* hablar más fuerte.

speak·er *(in dialog)* interlocutor, -a *mf*, *(lecturer)* conferenciante *mf*; *(of* *language)* hablante *mf;* (*loudspeaker)* altavoz *m;* **(public) s.** orador, -a *mf.*

spear lanza *f.*

spe·cial *adj* especial.

spe·cial·ist especialista *mf.*

spe·ci·al·i·ty especialidad *f.*

spe·cial·ize *vi* especializarse (**in** en).

spe·cial·ly *adv (specifically)* especialmente; *(on purpose)* a propósito.

spe·ci·al·ty especialidad *f.*

spe·cies *inv* especie *f.*

spe·cif·ic *adj* específico, -a; *(precise)* preciso, -a; **to be s.** concretar.

spec·i·fi·ca·tion specifications datos *mpl* específicos.

spec·i·men *(sample)* muestra *f; (example)* ejemplar *m.*

spec·ta·cle *(display)* espectáculo *m;* **spectacles** *(glasses)* gafas *fpl, Am* lentes *mpl, Am* anteojos *mpl.*

spec·tac·u·lar *adj* espectacular.

spec·ta·tor espectador, -a *mf.*

spec·trum espectro *m.*

spec·u·late *vi* especular.

spec·u·la·tion especulación *f.*

speech *(faculty)* habla *f; (address)* discurso *m;* **to give a s.** pronunciar un discurso.

speed *n* velocidad *f; (rapidity)* rapidez *f.* **2** *vi** *(exceed speed limit)* conducir con exceso de velocidad.

▸**speed up 1** *vt* acelerar. **2** *vi (person)* darse prisa.

speed·boat lancha *f* rápida.

speed lim·it velocidad *f* máxima.

speed·om·e·ter velocímetro *m.*

spell[1]* *vt (write)* escribir; *(letter by letter)* deletrear; **how is that spelled?** ¿cómo se escribe eso?

spell[2] *(magical)* hechizo *m.*

spell[3] *(period)* período *m; (short period)* rato *m;* **cold s.** ola *f* de frío.

spell·ing ortografía *f.*

spend* *vt (money)* gastar (**on** en); *(time)* pasar.

sphere esfera *f.*

spice 1 *n* especia *f.* **2** *vt (food)* sazonar.

spic·y *adj* sazonado, -a; *(hot)* picante.

spi·der araña *f;* **s.'s web** telaraña *f.*

spike *(sharp point)* punta *f.*

spill* **1** *vt (liquid)* derramar. **2** *vi (liquid)* derramarse.

▸**spill over** *vi* desbordarse.

spin* *vt (wheel etc)* hacer girar; *(washing)* centrifugar.

spin·ach espinacas *fpl.*

spine *(of back)* columna *f* vertebral.

spi·ral espiral *f.*

spire aguja *f.*

spir·its *npl (alcoholic drinks)* licores *mpl.*

spir·i·tu·al *adj* espiritual.

spit[1]* *vti* escupir.

spit[2] *(for cooking)* asador *m.*

spite in s. of a pesar de; **in s. of the fact that** a pesar de que.

spite·ful *adj (remark)* malévolo, -a.

splash 1 *vt (spray)* salpicar. **2** *vi* **to s. (about)** *(in water)* chapotear.

splen·did *adj* espléndido, -a.

splin·ter *(wood)* astilla *f.*

split 1 *n (crack)* grieta *f; (tear)* desgarrón *m.* **2** *vt** *(crack)* hender; *(cut)* partir; *(tear)* rajar; *(divide)* dividir.

▸**split up 1** *vt (break up)* partir; *(divide up)* dividir; *(share out)* repartir. **2** *vi (couple)* separarse.

spoil* *vt (ruin)* estropear; *(child)* mimar.

spoke[1] *pt of* **speak.**

spoke[2] *(of wheel)* radio *m.*

spo·ken *pp of* **speak.**

spokes·man portavoz *mf.*

sponge 1 *n* esponja *f.* **2** *vt (wash)* lavar con esponja.

▸**sponge down** *vt* lavar con esponja.

sponge cake bizcocho *m.*

spon·sor 1 *vt* patrocinar. **2** *n* patrocinador, -a *mf.*

spon·ta·ne·ous *adj* espontáneo, -a.

spool bobina *f.*

spoon cuchara *f; (small)* cucharita *f.*

spoon·ful cucharada *f.*

sport deporte *m*.

sports·man deportista *m*.

sports·wom·an deportista *f*.

spot 1 *n* (*dot*) punto *m*; (*on fabric*) lunar *m*; (*stain*) mancha *f*; (*pimple*) grano *m*; (*place*) sitio *m*; **to decide sth on the s.** decidir algo en el acto. **2** *vt* (*notice*) notar; (*see*) ver.

spot·less *adj* (*very clean*) impecable.

spot·light foco *m*.

spot·ted *adj* (*speckled*) moteado, -a.

spouse cónyuge *mf*.

spout (*of jug*) pico *m*; (*of teapot*) pitorro *m*.

sprain 1 *n* esguince *m*. **2** *vt* **to s. one's ankle** torcerse el tobillo.

spray 1 *n* (*aerosol*) spray *m*. **2** *vt* (*insecticide, perfume*) pulverizar.

spray can aerosol *m*.

spread 1 *n* (*for bread*) pasta *f*; **cheese s.** queso *m* para untar. **2** *vt** (*unfold*) desplegar; (*lay out*) extender; (*butter etc*) untar; (*news*) difundir; (*rumor*) hacer correr; (*panic*) sembrar. **3** *vi** (*stretch out*) extenderse; (*news*) difundirse; (*rumor*) correr; (*disease, fire*) propagarse.

spread·sheet hoja *f* de cálculo.

spring[1] (*season*) primavera *f*.

spring[2] **1** *n* (*of water*) fuente *f*; (*of watch etc*) resorte *m*. **2** *vi** (*jump*) saltar.

spring·board trampolín *m*.

spring on·ion cebolleta *f*.

spring·time primavera *f*.

sprin·kle *vt* (*with water*) rociar (**with** de); (*with sugar*) espolvorear (**with** de).

sprin·kler (*for water*) aspersor *m*.

sprout (*Brussels*) **sprouts** coles *fpl* de Bruselas.

spur espuela *f*.

spurt *vi* (*liquid*) chorrear.

spy 1 *n* espía *mf*. **2** *vi* espiar (**on** a).

spy·ing espionaje *m*.

square 1 *n* cuadrado *m*; (*in town*) plaza *f*. **2** *adj* cuadrado, -a; **a s. meal** una buena comida.

squash[1] *vt* (*crush*) aplastar.

squash[2] (*sport*) squash *m*.

squat *vi* (*crouch*) agacharse.

squeak *vi* (*hinge, wheel*) chirriar; (*shoes*) crujir.

squeal 1 *n* chillido *m*. **2** *vi* (*animal, person*) chillar.

squeeze 1 *vt* apretar; (*lemon etc*) exprimir; (*sponge*) estrujar. **2** *vi* **to s. in** apretujarse. **3** *n* (*pressure*) estrujón *m*; (*of hand*) apretón *m*; (*hug*) abrazo *m*; (*crush*) apiñamiento *m*.

▸**squeeze up** *vi* (*on bench etc*) correrse.

squint 1 *n* bizquera *f*; **to have a s.** ser bizco, -a. **2** *vi* ser bizco, -a; **to s. at sth** (*with eyes half-closed*) mirar algo con los ojos entrecerrados.

squir·rel ardilla *f*.

squirt 1 *vt* lanzar a chorro. **2** *vi* **to s. out** salir a chorros.

St. *abbr of Saint* San, Sto., Sta; *abbr of Street* C/.

stab *vt* apuñalar.

sta·bil·i·ty estabilidad *f*.

sta·ble[1] *adj* estable.

sta·ble[2] (*for horses*) cuadra *f*.

stack 1 *n* (*pile*) montón *m*; *fam* **stacks of …** un montón de … **2** *vt* (*pile up*) amontonar.

sta·di·um estadio *m*.

staff (*personnel*) personal *m*; (*of army*) estado *m* mayor.

staff·room sala *f* de profesores.

stag venado *m*.

stage 1 *n* (*platform*) plataforma *f*; (*in theater*) escenario *m*; (*of development, journey*) etapa *f*; **in stages** por etapas. **2** *vt* (*play*) poner en escena.

stag·ger 1 *vi* tambalearse. **2** *vt* (*hours, work*) escalonar.

stain 1 *n* mancha *f*. **2** *vt* manchar.

stained glass win·dow vidriera *f* de colores.

stain·less *adj* (*steel*) inoxidable.

stair peldaño *m*; **stairs** escalera *f* *sing*.

stair·case escalera *f*.

stake *(stick)* estaca *f.*

stale *adj (food)* pasado, -a; *(bread)* duro, -a.

stalk *(of plant)* tallo *m; (of fruit)* rabo *m.*

stall 1 *n (in market)* puesto *m; (in theater)* **stalls** platea *f sing.* **2** *vi (of engine)* calarse.

stam·mer 1 *n* tartamudeo *m.* **2** *vi* tartamudear.

stamp 1 *n (postage stamp)* sello *m,* *Am* estampilla *f; (with foot)* patada *f.* **2** *vt (with postage stamp)* poner el sello a; **self-addressed stamped envelope** sobre *m* franqueado; **to s. one's feet** patear.

▸**stamp out** *vt (racism etc)* acabar con.

stamp col·lect·ing filatelia *f.*

stance postura *f.*

stand 1 *n (of lamp, sculpture)* pie *m; (market stall)* puesto *m; (at exhibition)* stand *m; (in stadium)* tribuna *f;* **newspaper s.** quiosco *m* de prensa. **2** *vt* (place) poner, colocar; *(tolerate)* aguantar. **3** *vi* (place) estar de pie; *(get up)* levantarse; *(be situated)* encontrarse; *(remain unchanged)* permanecer.

▸**stand around** *vi* estar sin hacer nada; *(wait)* esperar.

▸**stand aside** *vi* apartarse.

▸**stand back** *vi (allow sb to pass)* abrir paso.

▸**stand by 1** *vi (do nothing)* quedarse sin hacer nada; *(be ready)* estar listo, -a. **2** *vt (person)* apoyar.

▸**stand down** *vi fig* retirarse.

▸**stand for** *vt (mean)* significar; *(tolerate)* aguantar.

▸**stand in** *vi* sustituir (**for** -).

▸**stand out** *vi (mountain etc, fig person)* destacar(se).

▸**stand up** *vi (get up)* ponerse de pie; *fig* **to s. up for sb** defender a algn; *fig* **to s. up to sb** hacer frente a algn.

stan·dard 1 *n (level)* nivel *m; (criterion)* criterio *m; (norm)* estándar *m* *inv;* **s. of living** nivel de vida. **2** *adj* normal.

stand·by *adj* **s. ticket** billete *m* sin reserva.

stand·ing *adj (not sitting)* de pie.

stand·point punto *m* de vista.

stand·still **at a s.** *(car, traffic)* parado, -a; *(industry)* paralizado, -a; **to come to a s.** *(car, traffic)* pararse; *(industry)* paralizarse.

stank *pt* of **stink**.

sta·ple 1 *n (fastener)* grapa *f.* **2** *vt* grapar.

sta·pler grapadora *f.*

star 1 *n* estrella *f.* **2** *vt (film)* tener como protagonista. **3** *vi (in film)* protagonizar.

stare 1 *n* mirada *f* fija. **2** *vi* mirar fijamente; **to s. at sb** mirar fijamente a algn.

start 1 *n (beginning)* principio *m; (of race)* salida *f; (advantage)* ventaja *f.* **2** *vt (begin)* empezar, comenzar; **to s. doing sth** empezar a hacer algo. **3** *vi (begin)* empezar, comenzar; *(engine)* arrancar; *(take fright)* asustarse; **starting from Monday** a partir del lunes.

▸**start off** *vi (leave)* salir.

▸**start on** *vt* empezar.

▸**start up 1** *vt (engine)* arrancar. **2** *vi (car)* arrancar.

start·er *(in car)* motor *m* de arranque; *(food)* entrada *f.*

star·tle *vt* asustar.

star·va·tion hambre *m.*

starve *vi* pasar hambre; **to s. to death** morirse de hambre.

starv·ing *adj* **I'm s.!** estoy muerto,·-a de hambre.

state 1 *n* estado *m;* **The States** (los) Estados Unidos. **2** *vt* declarar.

state·ment declaración *f; (financial)* estado *m* de cuenta; **monthly s.** balance *m* mensual.

states·man estadista *m.*

stat·ic *adj* estático, -a.

sta·tion estación *f.*

sta·tion·ar·y *adj (not moving)* inmóvil.

sta·tion·er·y *(paper)* papel *m* de escribir; *(pens, ink etc)* artículos *mpl* de escritorio.

sta·tion·mas·ter jefe *m* de estación.

sta·tion wag·on camioneta *f*.

sta·tis·tic estadística *f*.

stat·ue estatua *f*.

stay 1 *n* estancia *f*. 2 *vi (remain)* quedarse; *(reside temporarily)* alojarse; **she's staying with us for a few days** ha venido a pasar unos días con nosotros.

‣ **stay away** *vi (not attend)* no asistir; **s. away from her** no te acerques a ella.

‣ **stay in** *vi* quedarse en casa.

‣ **stay out** *vi* **to s. out all night** no volver a casa en toda la noche.

‣ **stay out of** *vt (not interfere in)* no meterse en.

‣ **stay up** *vi (not go to bed)* no acostarse; *(fence etc)* mantenerse en pie.

stead·i·ly *adv (improve)* constantemente; *(walk)* con paso seguro; *(gaze)* fijamente; *(rain, work)* sin parar.

stead·y *adj* firme; *(prices)* estable; *(demand, speed)* constante.

steak bistec *m*.

steal* *vti* robar.

steam 1 *n* vapor *m*. 2 *vt (food)* cocer al vapor.

‣ **steam up** *vi (window etc)* empañarse.

steam·roll·er apisonadora *f*.

steel acero *m*; **s. industry** industria *f* siderúrgica.

steep *adj (hill etc)* empinado, -a; *(price, increase)* excesivo, -a.

stee·ple aguja *f*.

steer *vt* dirigir; *(car)* conducir; *(ship)* gobernar.

steer·ing wheel volante *m*.

stem *(of plant)* tallo *m*; *(of glass)* pie *m*.

ste·nog·ra·pher taquígrafo *m*.

‣ **step** 1 *n* paso *m*; *(measure)* medida *f*; *(stair)* peldaño *m*; **s. by s.** poco a poco; **steps** *(outdoor)* escalinata *f sing*; *(indoor)* escalera *f sing*. 2 *vi* dar un paso.

‣ **step aside** *vi* apartarse.

‣ **step back** *vi* retroceder.

‣ **step down** *vi* renunciar; *(resign)* dimitir.

‣ **step forward** *vi (volunteer)* ofrecerse.

‣ **step in** *vi* intervenir.

‣ **step into/out of** *vt (car etc)* entrar en/salir de.

‣ **step up** *vt* aumentar.

step·broth·er hermanastro *m*.

step·daugh·ter hijastra *f*.

step·fa·ther padrastro *m*.

step·lad·der escalera *f* de tijera.

step·moth·er madrastra *f*.

step·sis·ter hermanastra *f*.

step·son hijastro *m*.

ster·e·o 1 *n* estéreo *m*. 2 *adj* estereo(fónico, -a).

ster·il·ize *vt* esterilizar.

ster·ling *n* libras *fpl* esterlinas

stew estofado *m*, cocido *m*.

stew·ard *(on plane)* auxiliar *m* de vuelo.

stew·ard·ess *(on plane)* azafata *f*.

stick¹ palo *m*; *(walking stick)* bastón *m*.

stick² 1 *vt* meter; *(with glue etc)* pegar; **he stuck his head out of the window** asomó la cabeza por la ventana. 2 *vi (become attached)* pegarse; *(window, drawer)* atrancarse.

‣ **stick down** *vt (stamp)* pegar.

‣ **stick on** *vt (stamp)* pegar.

‣ **stick out** 1 *vi (project)* sobresalir; *(be noticeable)* resaltar. 2 *vt (tongue)* sacar.

‣ **stick to** *vt (principles)* atenerse a.

‣ **stick up** *vt (poster)* fijar.

‣ **stick up for** *vt* defender.

stick·er *(label)* etiqueta *f* adhesiva; *(with slogan)* pegatina *f*.

stick·ing plas·ter tirita *f*, curita *f*.

stick·y adj pegajoso, -a; (label) engomado, -a.

stiff adj rígido, -a; (joint) entumecido, -a; **to have a s. neck** tener tortícolis.

sti·fle 1 vt sofocar. **2** vi sofocarse.

sti·fling adj sofocante.

still 1 adv (up to this time) todavía, aún; (nonetheless) no obstante; (however) sin embargo; (with comparative) (even) aún; **s. colder** aún más frío. **2** adj (calm) tranquilo, -a; (motionless) inmóvil.

stim·u·late vt estimular.

sting 1 n picadura f. **2** vt* picar.

stink* vi apestar (**of** a).

▸**stink out** vt (room) apestar.

stir vt (liquid) remover.

▸**stir up** vt (memories, curiosity) despertar.

stir·rup estribo m.

stitch puntada f; (in knitting) punto m; (for surgery etc) punto m (de sutura).

stock 1 n (goods) existencias fpl; (selection) surtido m; (broth) caldo m; **out of s.** agotado, -a; **to have sth in s.** tener existencias de algo; **stocks and shares** acciones fpl. **2** vt (have in stock) tener existencias de.

▸**stock up** vi abastecerse (**on, with** de).

Stock Ex·change Bolsa f (de valores).

stock·ing media f; **a pair of stockings** unas medias.

Stock Mar·ket Bolsa f.

stock·pile vt almacenar; (accumulate) acumular.

stock·y adj (stockier, stockiest) (squat) rechoncho, -a; (heavily built) fornido, -a.

sto·len pp of **steal**.

stom·ach estómago m; **s. upset** trastorno m gástrico.

stone piedra f.

stool taburete m.

stop 1 n parada f; (break) pausa f; **to come to a s.** pararse; **to put a s. to sth** poner fin a algo. **2** vt parar; (gas, water supply) cortar; (prevent) evitar; **to s. sb from doing sth** impedir a algn hacer algo; **to s. doing sth** dejar de hacer algo. **3** vi (person, moving vehicle) pararse; (cease) terminar; (stay) pararse.

▸**stop by** vi pasarse; **I'll s. by at the office** me pasaré por la oficina.

▸**stop off** vi pararse un rato.

▸**stop up** vt (hole) tapar.

stop-off parada f; (flying) escala f.

stop·o·ver parada f.

stop·watch cronómetro m.

store 1 n (stock) provisión f; (warehouse) almacén m; (shop) tienda f; **department s.** gran almacén m. **2** vt (furniture, computer data) almacenar; (keep) guardar; **to s. (up)** acumular.

store·room despensa f.

stork cigüeña f.

storm tormenta f; (with wind) vendaval m.

storm·y adj (weather) tormentoso, -a.

sto·ry¹ (tale) historia f; (account) relato m; (article) artículo m; (plot) trama f; **tall s.** cuento m chino.

sto·ry² piso m.

stove (for heating) estufa f; (cooker) cocina f; (oven) horno m.

straight 1 adj (not bent) recto, -a; (hair) liso, -a; (honest) honrado, -a; (answer) sincero, -a; (drink) solo, -a. **2** adv (in a straight line) en línea recta; (directly) directamente; (frankly) francamente; **keep s. ahead** sigue todo recto; **s. away** en seguida.

straight·en vt (sth bent) enderezar, poner derecho, -a; (tie, picture) poner bien; (hair) alisar.

▸**straighten out** vt (problem) resolver.

straight·for·ward adj (easy) sencillo, -a.

strain 1 vt (eyes, voice) forzar;

(heart) cansar; *(liquid)* filtrar; *(vegetables, tea)* colar. **2** n tensión f; *(effort)* esfuerzo m; *(exhaustion)* agotamiento m.

strain·er colador m.

strand *(of thread)* hebra f; *(of hair)* pelo m.

strand·ed adj **to leave stranded** dejar plantado, -a.

strange adj *(unknown)* desconocido, -a; *(unfamiliar)* nuevo, -a; *(odd)* extraño, -a.

strang·er *(unknown person)* desconocido, -a mf; *(outsider)* forastero, -a mf.

stran·gle vt estrangular.

strap *(on bag)* correa f; *(on dress)* tirante m.

straw paja f; *(for drinking)* pajita f.

straw·ber·ry fresa f; *(large)* fresón m.

streak *(line)* raya f; *(in hair)* reflejo m; **s. of lightning** rayo m.

stream *(brook)* arroyo m; *(current)* corriente f; *(flow)* flujo m.

street calle f; **the man in the s.** el hombre de la calle.

street·car tranvía m.

street lamp farol m.

street map, street plan *(plano m)* callejero m.

strength fuerza f; *(of rope etc)* resistencia f; *(of emotion, color)* intensidad f.

strength·en vt reforzar; *(intensify)* intensificar.

stress **1** n estrés m; *(emphasis)* hincapié m; *(on word)* acento m. **2** vt *(emphasize)* subrayar; *(word)* acentuar.

stress·ful adj estresante.

stretch vt *(elastic)* estirar; *(arm, hand)* alargar. **2** vi estirarse. **3** n *(of land)* extensión f; *(of time)* intervalo m.

▸**stretch out** **1** vt *(arm, hand)* alargar; *(legs)* estirar. **2** vi *(countryside, years etc)* extenderse.

stretch·er camilla f.

strict adj estricto, -a.

strict·ly adv *(categorically)* terminantemente; *(precisely)* estrictamente; **s. speaking** en sentido estricto.

strict·ness severidad f.

stride **1** n zancada f. **2** vi* **to s.** *(along)* andar a zancadas.

strike **1** vt* *(hit)* golpear; *(collide with)* chocar contra; *(match)* encender; *(impress)* impresionar; **the clock struck three** el reloj dio las tres; **it strikes me …** me parece … **2** vi* *(workers)* declararse en huelga. **3** n *(by workers)* huelga f; **on s.** en huelga; **to go (out) on s.** declararse en huelga; **to call a s.** convocar una huelga.

▸**strike out** vi **to s. out at sb** arremeter contra algn.

▸**strike up** vt *(friendship)* trabar; *(conversation)* entablar; *(tune)* empezar a tocar.

strik·er *(worker)* huelguista mf.

strik·ing adj *(eye-catching)* llamativo, -a; *(impressive)* impresionante.

string *(cord, of guitar)* cuerda f.

strip[1] vi *(undress)* desnudarse.

strip[2] tira f; *(of metal)* cinta f, lámina f.

▸**strip off** vi *(undress)* desnudarse.

stripe raya f.

striped adj a rayas.

strive* vi **to s. to do sth** esforzarse por hacer algo.

stroke **1** n *(blow)* golpe m; *(in swimming)* brazada f; *(illness)* apoplejía f; **a s. of luck** un golpe de suerte. **2** vt acariciar.

stroll **1** vi dar un paseo; **he strolled across the square** cruzó la plaza a paso lento. **2** n paseo m.

stroll·er *(for baby)* cochecito m.

strong adj fuerte; *(durable)* sólido, -a.

struc·ture estructura f; *(building)* edificio m.

strug·gle **1** vi luchar. **2** n lucha f; *(physical fight)* pelea f.

stub *(of cigarette)* colilla f; *(of check)* matriz f.

stub·born adj testarudo, -a.

stub·born·ness testaruda f.

stuck 1 pt & pp of **stick²**. **2** adj (caught, jammed) atrancado, -a; **I'm s.** (unable to carry on) no puedo seguir.

stud (on clothing) tachón m.

stu·dent estudiante mf.

stu·di·o (TV etc) estudio m; (artist's) taller m; **s. apartment** estudio.

stud·y 1 vti estudiar; **to s. to be a doctor** estudiar para médico. **2** n estudio m.

stuff 1 vt (container) llenar (with de); (in cooking) rellenar (with con or de); (cram) atiborrar (with de). **2** n (material) material m; (things) cosas fpl, trastos mpl.

stuffed up adj (nose) tapado, -a.

stuff·ing relleno m.

stuff·y adj (room) mal ventilado, -a; (atmosphere) cargado, -a.

stum·ble vi tropezar; fig **to s. across** or **on** tropezar con or dar con.

stump (of tree) tocón m.

stun vt aturdir; (news etc) sorprender.

stunned adj (amazed) estupefacto, -a.

stun·ning adj (blow) duro, -a; (news) sorprendente; fam (woman, outfit) fenomenal.

stu·pid adj estúpido, -a.

stu·pid·i·ty estupidez f.

stur·dy adj robusto, -a.

stut·ter 1 vi tartamudear. **2** n tartamudeo m.

sty (pen) pocilga f.

style estilo m; (of dress) modelo m; (fashion) moda f.

styl·ish adj con estilo.

sub·ject 1 n (citizen) súbdito m; (topic) tema m; (at school) asignatura f; (of sentence) sujeto m. **2** vt someter.

sub·junc·tive subjuntivo m.

sub·ma·rine 1 n submarino m. **2** adj submarino, -a.

sub·scribe vi suscribirse (**to** a).

sub·scrib·er abonado, -a mf.

sub·scrip·tion (to magazine) suscripción f, abono m.

sub·side vi (land) hundirse; (floodwater) bajar.

sub·si·dy subvención f.

sub·stance sustancia f.

sub·stan·tial adj (sum, loss) importante; (meal) abundante.

sub·sti·tute 1 vt sustituir. **2** n (person) suplente mf, (thing) sucedáneo m.

sub·sti·tu·tion sustitución f.

sub·ti·tle subtítulo m.

sub·tle adj sutil.

sub·tract vt restar.

sub·trac·tion resta f.

sub·urb barrio m periférico; **the suburbs** las afueras.

sub·ur·ban adj suburbano, -a.

sub·way (underground railway) metro m.

suc·ceed vi (person) tener éxito; **to s. in doing sth** conseguir hacer algo.

suc·cess éxito m.

suc·cess·ful adj de éxito; (business) próspero, -a; **to be s. in doing sth** lograr hacer algo.

suc·cess·ful·ly adv con éxito.

suc·ces·sion sucesión f, serie f; **in s.** sucesivamente.

suc·ces·sive adj sucesivo, -a, consecutivo, -a.

suc·ces·sor sucesor, -a mf.

such 1 adj (of that sort) tal, semejante; **artists s. as Monet** artistas como Monet. ■ (so much, so great) tanto, -a; **he's always in s. a hurry** siempre anda con tanta prisa; **s. a lot of books** tantos libros. **2** adv (so very) tan; **it's s. a long time** hace tanto tiempo; **she's s. a clever woman** es una mujer tan inteligente.

suck 1 vt (liquid) sorber, chupar; (at breast) mamar. **2** vi (baby) mamar.

► **suck up** vt (with straw) aspirar.

sud·den adj (hurried) repentino, -a; (unexpected) imprevisto, -a; **all of a s.** de repente.

sud·den·ly *adv* de repente.

suds *npl* espuma *f* de jabón.

sue 1 *vt* demandar. **2** *vi* presentar una demanda.

suede ante *m*; *(for gloves)* cabritilla *f*.

suf·fer *vti* sufrir; **to s. from** sufrir de.

suf·fer·er *(from disease)* enfermo, -a *mf*.

suf·fer·ing *(affliction)* sufrimiento *m*; *(pain, torment)* dolor *m*.

suf·fi·cient *adj* suficiente, bastante.

suf·fi·cient·ly *adv* suficientemente, bastante.

suf·fix sufijo *m*.

suf·fo·cate 1 *vt* asfixiar. **2** *vi* asfixiarse.

sug·ar 1 *n* azúcar *m* or *f*. **2** *vt* azucarar.

sug·ar bowl azucarero *m*.

sug·gest *vt (propose)* sugerir; *(advise)* aconsejar; *(indicate, imply)* indicar.

sug·ges·tion *(proposal)* sugerencia *f*.

su·i·cide suicidio *m*.

suit 1 *n* traje *m* de chaqueta; *(in cards)* palo *m*. **2** *vt (be convenient for)* convenir a; *(be right, appropriate for)* ir bien a; **red really suits you** el rojo te favorece mucho; **s. yourself!** ¡como quieras!

suit·a·ble *adj (convenient)* conveniente; *(appropriate)* adecuado, -a; **the most s. woman for the job** la mujer más indicada para el puesto.

suit·case maleta *f*.

suite *(of furniture)* tresillo *m*; *(of hotel rooms, music)* suite *f*.

sulk *vi* enfurruñarse.

sul·tan·a *(raisin)* pasa *f* (de Esmirna).

sum *(arithmetic problem, amount)* suma *f*; *(total amount)* total *m*; *(of money)* importe *m*.

▸ **sum up** *vt* resumir.

sum·ma·rize *vt* resumir.

sum·ma·ry resumen *m*.

sum·mer 1 *n* verano *m*. **2** *adj (vacation etc)* de verano; *(resort)* de veraneo.

sum·mer·time verano *m*.

sum·mon *vt (meeting, person)* convocar; *(aid)* pedir.

▸ **summon up** *vt (resources)* reunir; **to s. up one's courage** armarse de valor.

sum·mons 1 *n (call)* llamada *f*, llamamiento *m*; *(to court)* citación *f* judicial. **2** *vt (to court)* citar.

sun sol *m*.

sun·bathe *vi* tomar el sol.

sun·burn quemadura *f* de sol.

sun·burnt *adj (burnt)* quemado, -a por el sol; *(tanned)* bronceado, -a.

sun·dae helado *m* de fruta y nueces.

Sun·day domingo *m*.

sun·glass·es *npl* gafas *fpl* de sol.

sun·lamp lámpara *f* solar.

sun·light *(luz f* del) sol *m*.

sun·ny *adj (day)* de sol; **it is s.** hace sol.

sun·rise salida *f* del sol.

sun·roof *(on car)* techo *m* corredizo.

sun·set puesta *f* del sol.

sun·shade sombrilla *f*.

sun·shine *(luz f* del) sol *m*.

sun·stroke insolación *f*.

sun·tan bronceado *m*; **s. oil** *(aceite m)* bronceador *m*; **s. lotion** leche *f* bronceadora.

sun·tanned *adj* bronceado, -a.

su·per *adj fam* fenomenal.

su·perb *adj* espléndido, -a.

su·per·fi·cial *adj* superficial.

su·per·in·ten·dent *(of apartment building)* portero, -a *mf*.

su·pe·ri·or *adj* superior.

su·pe·ri·or·i·ty superioridad *f*.

su·per·mar·ket supermercado *m*.

su·per·sti·tion superstición *f*.

su·per·sti·tious *adj* supersticioso, -a.

su·per·vise *vt* supervisar; *(watch over)* vigilar.

su·per·vi·sor supervisor, -a *mf*.

sup·per cena *f*; **to have s.** cenar.

sup·ple *adj* flexible.

sup·ple·ment 1 *n* suplemento *m*. **2** *vt* complementar.

sup·ply 1 *n (provision)* suministro *m*; *(delivery)* provisión *f*; **supplies** *(food)* víveres *mpl*. **2** *vt (provide)* suministrar; *(with provisions)* aprovisionar; *(information)* facilitar.

sup·port 1 *n* soporte *m*; *(moral)* apoyo *m*. **2** *vt (weight etc)* sostener; *(back)* apoyar; *(team)* ser (hincha) de; *(family)* mantener.

sup·port·er *(political)* partidario, -a *mf*; *(in sport)* hincha *mf*.

sup·por·tive *adj* **he was supportive (of)** apoyó mucho (a), fue muy comprensivo (con).

sup·pose *vt* suponer; *(presume)* creer; **I s. not/so** supongo que no/sí; **you're not supposed to smoke in here** no está permitido fumar aquí dentro; **you're supposed to be in bed** deberías estar acostado ya.

sup·press *vt* suprimir; *(feelings, laugh etc)* contener; *(news, truth)* callar; *(revolt)* sofocar.

sure *adj* seguro, -a; **I'm s. (that) …** estoy seguro, -a de que …; **make s. that it's ready** asegúrate de que esté listo.

sure·ly *adv (without a doubt)* seguramente; **s. not!** ¡no puede ser!

sur·face superficie *f*; **s. area** área *f* de la superficie; **by s. mail** por vía terrestre *or* marítima.

surf·board tabla *f* de surf.

surf·ing surf *m*, surfing *m*.

surge 1 *n (growth)* alza *f*; *(of sea, sympathy)* oleada *f*, fig *(of anger, energy)* arranque *m*. **2** *vi* **to s. forward** *(people)* avanzar en tropel.

sur·geon cirujano, -a *mf*.

sur·ger·y *(operation)* cirugía *f*; **s. hours** horas *fpl* de consulta.

sur·gi·cal *adj* quirúrgico, -a; **s. spirit** alcohol *m* de 90°.

sur·name apellido *m*.

sur·plus 1 *n (of goods)* excedente *m*;

(of budget) superávit *m*. **2** *adj* excedente.

sur·prise 1 *n* sorpresa *f*; **to take sb by s.** coger desprevenido, -a a algn. **2** *adj (visit)* inesperado, -a; **s. attack** ataque *m* sorpresa. **3** *vt* sorprender.

sur·prised *adj* sorprendido, -a; **I should not be s. if it rained** no me extrañaría que lloviera.

sur·pris·ing *adj* sorprendente.

sur·pris·ing·ly *adv* de modo sorprendente.

sur·ren·der *vi (give in)* rendirse.

sur·round *vt* rodear.

sur·round·ing *adj* circundante.

sur·round·ings *npl* alrededores *mpl*.

sur·veil·lance vigilancia *f*.

sur·vey *(of trends etc)* encuesta *f*.

sur·vey·or agrimensor, -a *mf*.

sur·vive 1 *vi* sobrevivir. **2** *vt* sobrevivir a.

sur·vi·vor superviviente *mf*.

sus·pect 1 *n* sospechoso, -a *mf*. **2** *vt (person)* sospechar (**of** de); *(think likely)* imaginar.

sus·pend *vt* suspender; *(pupil)* expulsar por un tiempo.

sus·pend·ers *npl* tirantes *mpl*.

sus·pense suspense *m*.

sus·pen·sion suspensión *f*.

sus·pi·cion sospecha *f*; *(mistrust)* recelo *m*; *(doubt)* duda *f*; *(trace)* pizca *f*.

sus·pi·cious *adj (arousing suspicion)* sospechoso, -a; *(distrustful)* receloso, -a; **to be s. of sb** desconfiar de algn.

swal·low¹ *vt (drink, food)* tragar.

swal·low² *(bird)* golondrina *f*.

▸**swallow down** *vt* tragarse.

swamp ciénaga *f*.

swan cisne *m*.

swap 1 *n* intercambio *m*. **2** *vt* cambiar.

swarm enjambre *m*.

sway *vi (swing)* balancearse; *(totter)* tambalearse.

swear* 1 *vt (vow)* jurar. **2** *vi (curse)* decir palabrotas.

swear·word palabrota *f.*

sweat 1 *n* sudor *m.* **2** *vi* sudar.

sweat·er suéter *m.*

sweat·shirt sudadera *f.*

Swede *(person)* sueco, -a *mf.*

Swed·ish 1 *adj* sueco, -a. **2** *n (language)* sueco *m.*

sweep* *vti* barrer.

▸**sweep aside** *vt* apartar bruscamente; *(objections)* rechazar.

▸**sweep away** *vt (dust)* barrer; *(storm)* arrastrar.

▸**sweep out** *vt (room)* barrer.

▸**sweep up** *vi* barrer.

sweet 1 *adj* dulce; *(sugary)* azucarado, -a; *(pleasant)* agradable; *(person, animal)* encantador, -a. **2** *n (candy)* caramelo *m*; *(chocolate)* bombón *m*; *(dessert)* postre *m.*

sweet·corn maíz *m* dulce.

sweet·en *vt (tea etc)* azucarar.

sweet·ly *adv* dulcemente.

sweet shop confitería *f.*

swell 1 *n (of sea)* marejada *f,* oleaje *m.* **2** *adj fam* fenomenal. **3** *vi* (part of body)* hincharse; *(river)* subir.

▸**swell up** *vi* hincharse.

swell·ing hinchazón *f.*

swerve *vi (car)* dar un viraje brusco.

swift 1 *adj* rápido, -a, veloz. **2** *n (bird)* vencejo *m (común).*

swim 1 *vi** nadar; **to go swimming** ir a nadar. **2** *vt* (the Mississippi)* pasar a nado. **3** *n* baño *m*; **to go for a s.** ir a darse un baño.

swim·mer nadador, -a *mf.*

swim·ming natación *f.*

swim·ming pool piscina *f.*

swim·ming trunks bañador *m.*

swim·suit bañador *m.*

swing 1 *n (for playing)* columpio *m.* **2** *vi* (move back and forth)* balancearse; *(arms, legs)* menearse; *(in swing)* columpiarse. **3** *vt* (arms, legs)* menear.

Swiss 1 *adj* suizo, -a. **2** *n inv (person)* suizo, -a *mf*; **the S.** *pl* los suizos.

switch 1 *n (for light etc)* interruptor *m.* **2** *vt (jobs, direction)* cambiar de.

▸**switch off** *vt* apagar.

▸**switch on** *vt* encender.

▸**switch over** *vi* cambiar **(to** a).

swol·len *adj (ankle, face)* hinchado, -a.

swop *vt* = **swap**.

sword espada *f.*

syl·la·ble sílaba *f.*

syl·la·bus programa *m* de estudios.

sym·bol símbolo *m.*

sym·bol·ic *adj* simbólico, -a.

sym·me·try simetría *f.*

sym·pa·thet·ic *adj (showing pity)* compasivo, -a; *(understanding)* comprensivo, -a; *(kind)* amable.

sym·pa·thize *vi (show pity)* compadecerse **(with** de); *(understand)* comprender.

sym·pa·thy *(pity)* compasión *f,* *(condolences)* pésame *m*; *(understanding)* comprensión *f*; **to express one's s.** dar el pésame.

sym·pho·ny sinfonía *f.*

symp·tom síntoma *m.*

syn·a·gogue sinagoga *f.*

syn·o·nym sinónimo *m.*

sy·ringe jeringuilla *f.*

syr·up jarabe *m*, almíbar *m.*

sys·tem sistema *m.*

T

ta *interj fam* gracias.

tab *(flap)* lengüeta *f.*

ta·ble mesa *f*; **to lay** *or* **set the t.** poner la mesa.

ta·ble·cloth mantel *m.*

ta·ble·mat salvamanteles *m inv.*

ta·ble·spoon cuchara *f* de servir.

ta·ble·spoon·ful cucharada *f.*

tab·let *(pill)* pastilla *f.*

tack *(small nail)* tachuela *f.*

tack·le vt (task) emprender; (problem) abordar; (grapple with) agarrar; (in sport) placar; (in soccer) entrar a.

tack·y adj fam (shoddy) cutre.

tact tacto m.

tact·ful adj diplomático, -a.

tac·tic táctica f; **tactics** táctica f sing.

taf·fy caramelo m duro.

tag (label) etiqueta f.

tail cola f.

tai·lor sastre m.

take* vt tomar; (bus etc) coger; (accept) aceptar; (win) ganar; (prize) llevarse; (eat, drink) tomar; (accompany) llevar; (endure) aguantar; (consider) considerar; (require) requerir; **she's taking (a degree) in law** estudia derecho; **to t. an exam (in …)** examinarse (de …); **it takes an hour to get there** se tarda una hora en ir hasta allí; **it takes courage** se necesita valor.

▶ **take after** vt parecerse a.

▶ **take along** vt llevar (consigo).

▶ **take apart** vt (machine) desmontar.

▶ **take away** vt (carry off) llevarse; (in math) restar (**from** de); **to t. sth away from sb** quitarle algo a algn.

▶ **take back** vt (give back) devolver; (receive back) recuperar; (withdraw) retirar.

▶ **take down** vt (lower) bajar; (write) apuntar.

▶ **take in** vt (include) abarcar; (understand) entender; (deceive) engañar.

▶ **take off 1** vt quitar; (lead or carry away) llevarse; (deduct) descontar; **he took off his jacket** se quitó la chaqueta. **2** vi (plane) despegar.

▶ **take on** vt (undertake) encargarse de; (acquire) tomar; (employ) contratar.

▶ **take out** vt sacar; **he's taking me out to dinner** me ha invitado a cenar fuera; (insurance) sacarse; (stain, tooth) quitar.

▶ **take over 1** vt (office, post) tomar

posesión de. **2** vi **to t. over from sb** relevar a algn.

▶ **take up** vt (occupy) ocupar; **I've taken up the guitar** he empezado a tocar la guitarra.

take·off (of plane) despegue m.

take·o·ver (of company) absorción f.

tak·ings npl (of shop, business) recaudación f sing.

takeout 1 n (food) comida f para llevar; (restaurant) restaurante m de comida para llevar. **2** adj (food) para llevar.

tale cuento m; **to tell tales** contar chismes.

tal·ent talento m.

tal·ent·ed adj dotado, -a.

talk 1 vi hablar; (chat) charlar; (gossip) chismorrear. **2** vt hablar; **to t. nonsense** decir tonterías. **3** n (conversation) conversación f; (words) palabras fpl; (gossip) chismes mpl; (lecture) charla f; **there's t. of …** se habla de …

▶ **talk into** vt **to t. sb into sth** convencer a algn para que haga algo.

▶ **talk out of** vt **to t. sb out of sth** disuadir a algn de que haga algo.

▶ **talk over** vt discutir.

talk·a·tive adj hablador, -a.

tall adj alto, -a; **a tree ten meters t.** un árbol de diez metros (de alto); **how t. are you?** ¿cuánto mides?

tam·bou·rine pandereta f.

tame 1 adj (animal) domado, -a; (by nature) manso, -a. **2** vt domar.

tam·pon tampón m.

tan 1 n (of skin) bronceado m. **2** vt (skin) broncear. **3** vi ponerse moreno, -a.

tan·ger·ine clementina f.

tan·gled adj enredado, -a.

tank (container) depósito m; (with gun) tanque m.

tank·er (ship) tanque m; (for oil) petrolero m.

tap¹ vt (knock) golpear sauvemente; (with hand) dar una palmadita a. **2**

vi **to t. at the door** llamar suavemente a la puerta. **3** *n* golpecito *m*.
tap² *(for water)* grifo *m*.
tape 1 *n* cinta *f*; **sticky t.** cinta *f* adhesiva. **2** *vt* pegar (con cinta adhesiva); *(record)* grabar (en cinta).
tape meas·ure cinta *f* métrica.
tape re·cord·er magnetófono *m*, casete *m*.
tar alquitrán *m*.
tar·get *(object aimed at)* blanco *m*; *(purpose)* meta *f*.
tar·iff tarifa *f*, arancel *m*.
tar·pau·lin lona *f*.
tart *(to eat)* tarta *f*.
tar·tan tartán *m*.
task tarea *f*.
taste 1 *n* *(sense)* gusto *m*; *(flavor)* sabor *m*; *(liking)* afición *f*; **it has a burnt t.** sabe a quemado; **in bad t.** de mal gusto; **to have (good) t.** tener (buen) gusto. **2** *vt* *(sample)* probar. **3** *vi* **to t. of sth** saber a algo.
tast·y *adj* sabroso, -a.
tat·tered *adj* hecho, -a jirones.
tat·too 1 *vt* tatuar. **2** *n* *(mark)* tatuaje *m*.
tax 1 *n* impuesto *m*; **t. free** exento, -a de impuestos; **t. collector** recaudador, -a *mf* (de impuestos). **2** *vt* gravar; *(patience etc)* poner a prueba.
tax·a·ble *adj* imponible.
tax·i taxi *m*.
tax·i driv·er taxista *mf*.
tax·i rank parada *f* de taxis.
tax·pay·er contribuyente *mf*.
tea té *m*; *(meal)* merienda *f*.
tea·bag bolsita *f* de té.
tea break descanso *m*.
teach* 1 *vt* enseñar; *(subject)* dar clases de; **to t. sb (how) to do sth** enseñar a algn a hacer algo. **2** *vi* ser profesor, -a.
teach·er profesor, -a *mf*.
teach·ing enseñanza *f*.
tea·cup taza *f* de té.
team equipo *m*.
▸**team up** *vi* **to t. up with sb** juntarse con algn.

tea·pot tetera *f*.
tear¹ lágrima *f*; **to be in tears** estar llorando.
tear² 1 *vt** rasgar; **to t. sth out of sb's hands** arrancarle algo de las manos a algn. **2** *vi** *(cloth)* rasgarse. **3** *n* desgarrón *m*.
▸**tear off** *vt* arrancar.
▸**tear out** *vt* arrancar.
▸**tear up** *vt* hacer pedazos.
tease *vt* tomar el pelo a.
tea ser·vice *or* **set** juego *m* de té.
tea·spoon cucharilla *f*.
tea·spoon·ful cucharadita *f*.
teat *(of bottle)* tetina *f*.
tea·time hora *f* del té.
tea tow·el paño *m* (de cocina).
tech·ni·cal *adj* técnico, -a.
tech·ni·cian técnico, -a *mf*.
tech·nique técnica *f*.
tech·no·log·i·cal *adj* tecnológico, -a.
tech·nol·o·gy tecnología *f*.
ted·dy bear oso *m* de felpa.
teen·age *adj* adolescente.
teen·ag·er adolescente *mf*.
tee-shirt camiseta *f*.
teeth *npl see* **tooth**.
tee·to·tal·ler abstemio, -a *mf*.
tel·e·com·mu·ni·ca·tions *npl* telecomunicaciones *fpl*.
tel·e·gram telegrama *m*.
tel·e·phone 1 *n* teléfono *m*; **to speak to sb on the t.** hablar por teléfono con algn. **2** *vt* telefonear a, llamar por teléfono a.
tel·e·phone booth cabina *f* (telefónica).
tel·e·phone call llamada *f* telefónica.
tel·e·phone di·rec·to·ry guía *f* telefónica.
tel·e·phone num·ber número *m* de teléfono.
tel·e·scope telescopio *m*.
tel·e·vise *vt* televisar.
tel·e·vi·sion televisión *f*; **t. (set)** televisor *m*; **on t.** en la televisión.
tell* 1 *vt* decir; *(relate)* contar;

(inform) comunicar; *(order)* mandar; *(distinguish)* distinguir; **to t. sb about sth** contarle algo a algn; **to t. sb to do sth** decir a algn que haga algo. **2** *vi* **who can t.?** *(know)* ¿quién sabe?

▶ **tell off** *vt* reñir.

tell·er *(cashier)* cajero, -a *mf.*

tell·tale chivato, -a *mf.*

tem·per *(mood)* humor *m*; **to keep one's t.** no perder la calma; **to lose one's t.** perder los estribos.

tem·per·a·ture temperatura *f*; **to have a t.** tener fiebre.

tem·ple *(building)* templo *m.*

tem·po·rar·i·ly *adj* temporalmente, *Am* temporariamente.

tem·po·rar·y *adj* provisional; *(setback, improvement)* momentáneo, -a; *(teacher)* sustituto, -a.

tempt *vt* tentar; **to t. sb to do sth** incitar a algn a hacer algo.

temp·ta·tion tentación *f.*

tempt·ing *adj* tentador, -a.

ten *adj & n* diez *(m) inv.*

ten·an·cy *(of house)* alquiler *m*; *(of land)* arrendamiento *m.*

ten·ant *(of house)* inquilino, -a *mf.*

tend *vi* *(be inclined)* tender, tener tendencia **(to** a).

ten·den·cy tendencia *f.*

ten·der *adj* *(affectionate)* cariñoso, -a; *(meat)* tierno, -a.

ten·nis tenis *m.*

ten·nis court pista *f* de tenis.

tense² *adj* tenso, -a.

tense² *(of verb)* tiempo *m.*

ten·sion tensión *f.*

tent tienda *f* de campaña.

tenth *adj & n* décimo, -a *(mf).*

term *(period)* período *m*; *(of study)* trimestre *m*; *(word)* término *m*; **terms** *(conditions)* condiciones *fpl*; **to be on good/bad terms with sb** tener buenas/malas relaciones con algn.

ter·mi·nal 1 terminal *f*; *(for computer)* terminal *m.* **2** *adj* *(patient, illness)* terminal.

ter·mi·nate 1 *vt* terminar; **to t. a**

pregnancy abortar. **2** *vi* terminarse.

ter·race *(of houses)* hilera *f* de casas; *(patio)* terraza *f.*

ter·raced hous·es casas *fpl* (de estilo uniforme) en hilera.

ter·ri·ble *adj* terrible; **I feel t.** me encuentro fatal.

ter·ri·bly *adv* terriblemente.

ter·ri·fic *adj* fenomenal.

ter·ri·fy *vt* aterrorizar.

ter·ri·fy·ing *adj* aterrador, -a.

ter·ri·to·ry territorio *m.*

ter·ror terror *m.*

ter·ror·ist *adj & n* terrorista *(mf).*

ter·ror·ize *vt* aterrorizar.

test 1 *vt* probar; *(analyze)* analizar. **2** *n* *(of product)* prueba *f*; *(in school)* examen *m*; *(of blood)* análisis *m.*

tes·ta·ment testamento *m*; **Old/New T.** Antiguo/Nuevo Testamento.

tes·ti·mo·ny testimonio *m*, declaración *f.*

test tube probeta *f.*

text 1 *n* texto *m*; **t. (message)** mensaje *m* de texto. **2** *vt* *(send text message to)* enviar un mensaje de texto a.

text·book libro *m* de texto.

tex·tile 1 *n* tejido *m.* **2** *adj* textil.

tex·ture textura *f.*

Thai *adj & n* tailandés, -esa *(mf).*

than *conj* que; *(with numbers)* de; **he's older t. me** es mayor que yo; **more interesting t. we thought** más interesante de lo que creíamos; **more t. once** más de una vez; **more t. ten people** más de diez personas.

thank *vt* agradecer; **t. you** gracias.

thank·ful *adj* agradecido, -a.

thanks *npl* gracias *fpl*; **no, t.** no, gracias; **t. to** gracias a.

thanks·giv·ing T. Day Día *m* de Acción de Gracias.

that 1 *dem adj* *(pl* **those)** *(masculine)* ese; *(feminine)* esa; *(further away)* *(masculine)* aquel; *(feminine)* aquella; **at t. time** en aquella época; **t. book** ese/aquel libro; **t. one** ése/aquél. **2** *dem pron* *(pl* **those)** ése *m*, ésa f, (further away) aquél m, aquélla f, (indefinite) eso; (remote) aquello; **after t.** después de eso; **like t.** así; **don't talk like t.** no hables así; **t.'s right** eso es; **t.'s where I live** allí vivo yo; **what's t.?** ¿qué es eso?; **who's t.?** ¿quién es?; **all those I saw** todos los que vi; **there are those who say that ...** hay quien dice que .... **3** rel pron que; **all t. you said** todo lo que dijiste; **the letter t. I sent you** la carta que te envié; **the car t. they came in** el coche en el que vinieron; **the moment t. you arrived** el momento en que llegaste. **4** conj que; **come here so t. I can see you** ven aquí para que te vea; **he said (t.) he would come** dijo que vendría. **5** adv así de, tan; **that much** tanto, -a; **cut off t. much** córteme un trozo así de grande; **t. old** tan viejo; **we haven't got t. much money** no tenemos tanto dinero.

thaw 1 vt (snow) derretir; (food, freezer) descongelar. **2** vi descongelarse; (snow) derretirse. **3** n deshielo m.

the def art el, la; pl los, las; **at** or **to t.** al, a la; pl a los, a las; **of** or **from t.** del, de la; pl de los, de las; **the voice of the people** la voz del pueblo; **George t. Sixth** Jorge Sexto.

the·a·ter teatro m.

theft robo m.

their poss adj su; (pl) sus.

theirs poss pron (el) suyo, (la) suya; (pl) (los) suyos, (las) suyas.

them pers pron pl (direct object) los, las; (indirect object) les; **I know t.** los or las conozco; **I shall tell t. so** se lo diré (a ellos or ellas); **it's t.!** ¡son ellos!; **speak to t.** hábleles. ▪ (with preposition) ellos, ellas; **walk in front of t.** camine delante de ellos; **with t.** con ellos.

them·selves pers pron pl (as subject) ellos mismos, ellas mismas; (as direct or indirect object) se; (after a preposition) sí mismos, sí mismas;

they did it by t. lo hicieron ellos solos.

then 1 adv (at that time, in that case) entonces; (next, afterwards) luego; **since t.** desde entonces; **till t.** hasta entonces; **go t.** pues vete. **2** conj entonces.

the·o·ry teoría f.

there adv (indicating place) allí, allá; (nearer speaker) ahí; **is Peter t.?** ¿está Peter?; **that man t.** aquel hombre; **t. is, t. are** hay; **t. were six of us** éramos seis.

there·fore adv por lo tanto.

ther·mom·e·ter termómetro m.

Ther·mos® T. (flask) termo m.

these 1 dem adj pl estos, -as. **2** dem pron pl éstos, -as; see **this**.

the·sis tesis f inv.

they pron ellos, ellas; **t. are dancing** están bailando; **t. alone** ellos solos. ▪ (indefinite) **t. say that ...** se dice que ....

thick adj (book, slice, material) grueso, -a; (wood, vegetation) espeso, -a; **a wall two meters t.** un muro de dos metros de espesor.

thick·en 1 vt espesar. **2** vi espesarse.

thick·ness (of wall etc) espesor m; (of wire, lips) grueso m; (of liquid, forest) espesura f.

thief (pl thieves) ladrón, -ona mf.

thigh muslo m.

thim·ble dedal m.

thin 1 adj delgado, -a; (hair, vegetation) ralo, -a; (liquid) claro, -a; **a t. slice** una loncha fina. **2** vt to **t. (down)** (paint) diluir.

thing cosa f; **my things** (clothing) mi ropa f sing; (possessions) mis cosas.

think* 1 vt pensar, creer; **I t. so/not** creo que sí/no; **I thought as much** ya me lo imaginaba. **2** vi pensar (of, about en); **what do you t.?** ¿a ti qué te parece?

▶**think over** vt reflexionar; **we'll have to t. it over** lo tendremos que pensar.

▶ **think up** vt idear.

thin·ly adv ligeramente.

third 1 adj tercero, -a; (before masculine singular noun) tercer; **(on) the t. of March** el tres de marzo. **2** n (in series) tercero, -a mf, (fraction) tercera parte f.

third·ly adv en tercer lugar.

thirst sed f.

thirst·y adj **to be t.** tener sed.

thir·teen adj & n trece (m).

thir·ty adj & n treinta (m).

this 1 dem adj (pl these) (masculine) este; (feminine) esta; **t. book/these books** este libro/estos libros; **t. one** éste, ésta. **2** (pl these) dem pron (indefinite) esto; **t. is different** esto es distinto; **it was like t.** fue así; **t. is where we met** fue aquí donde nos conocimos; **it should have come before t.** debería haber llegado ya; (introduction) **t. is Mr Álvarez** le presento al Sr. Álvarez; (on the phone) **t. is Julia (speaking)** soy Julia. ■ (specific person or thing) éste m, ésta f, **I prefer these to those** me gustan más éstos que aquéllos. **3** adv **he got t. far** llegó hasta aquí; **t. small/big** así de pequeño/grande.

thorn espina f.

thor·ough adj (careful) minucioso, -a; (work) concienzudo, -a; (knowledge) profundo, -a; **to carry out a t. inquiry into a matter** investigar a fondo un asunto.

thor·ough·ly adv (carefully) a fondo; (wholly) completamente.

those 1 dem adj esos, -as; (remote) aquellos, -as. **2** dem pron ésos, -as; (remote) aquéllos, -as; (with rel) los, las; see that **1 & 2**.

though 1 conj aunque; **as t.** como si; **it looks as t. he's gone** parece que se ha ido. **2** adv sin embargo.

thought 1 pt & pp of **think**. **2** (act of thinking) pensamiento m; (reflection) reflexión f.

thought·ful adj (considerate) atento, -a.

thought·less adj (person) desconsiderado, -a; (action) irreflexivo, -a.

thou·sand adj & n mil (m) inv; **thousands of people** miles de personas.

thread 1 n hilo m. **2** vt (needle) enhebrar.

threat amenaza f.

threat·en vt amenazar; **to t. to do sth** amenazar con hacer algo.

threat·en·ing adj amenazador, -a.

three adj & n tres (m) inv.

thresh·old umbral m.

threw pt of **throw**.

thrill (excitement) emoción f.

thrilled adj emocionado, -a; **I'm t. about the trip** estoy muy ilusionado, -a con el viaje.

thrill·er (book) novela f de suspense; (film) película f de suspense.

thrill·ing adj emocionante.

thrive* vi (person) rebosar de salud; (business) prosperar; **he thrives on it** le viene de maravilla.

thriv·ing adj próspero, -a.

throat garganta f.

throne trono m.

through 1 prep (place) a través de, por; **to look t. the window** mirar por la ventana. ■ (time) a lo largo de; **all t. his life** durante toda su vida. ■ (by means of) por, mediante. ■ (because of) a or por causa de; **t. ignorance** por ignorancia. **2** adj **t. train** un tren directo. **3** adv (from one side to the other) de un lado a otro; **to let sb t.** dejar pasar a algn; **to get t. to sb** comunicar con algn; **I'm t. with him** he terminado con él.

through·out 1 prep por todo, -a; **t. the year** durante todo el año. **2** adv (place) en todas partes; (time) todo el tiempo.

throw* vt tirar; (to the ground) derribar; (party) dar.

▶ **throw away** vt (trash, money) tirar; (money) malgastar; (opportunity) perder.

▸**throw out** vt (trash) tirar; (person) echar.

▸**throw up** vti devolver.

thrust* 1 vt empujar con fuerza; **he t. a letter into my hand** me puso una carta violentamente en la mano. **2** n (push) empujón m; (of aircraft) empuje m.

thud ruido m sordo.

thug (lout) gamberro m; (criminal) criminal m.

thumb pulgar m.

thumb·tack chincheta f.

thun·der 1 n trueno m. 2 vi tronar.

thun·der·storm tormenta f.

Thurs·day jueves m.

thus adv así, de esta manera; **and t. ...** así que ....

tick¹ 1 n (sound) tic-tac m; (mark) marca f de visto bueno. **2** vi hacer tic-tac. **3** vt marcar.

▸**tick off** vt (mark) marcar.

▸**tick over** vi (engine) funcionar al ralentí.

tick² (insect) garrapata f.

tick·et (for bus etc) billete m; (for theater) entrada f; (for lottery) décimo m; (receipt) recibo m.

tick·et col·lec·tor revisor, -a mf.

tick·et of·fice taquilla f.

tick·le vt hacer cosquillas a.

tick·lish adj **to be t.** (person) tener cosquillas.

tic-tac-toe tres en raya m.

tide marea f.

ti·di·ly adv (to put away) ordenadamente.

ti·dy 1 adj (room, habits) ordenado, -a; (appearance) arreglado, -a. **2** vt arreglar. **3** vi **to t. (up)** ordenar las cosas.

tie 1 vt (shoelaces etc) atar; **to t. a knot** hacer un nudo. **2** n (around neck) corbata f; (match) partido m; (draw) empate m.

▸**tie up** vt (parcel, dog) atar.

ti·ger tigre m.

tight 1 adj apretado, -a; (clothing) ajustado, -a; (seal) hermético, -a; **my shoes are too t.** me aprietan los zapatos. **2** adv estrechamente; (seal) herméticamente; **hold t.** agárrate fuerte; **shut t.** bien cerrado, -a.

tight·en 1 vt (screw) apretar; (rope) tensar; fig **to t. (up) restrictions** intensificar las restricciones. **2** vi apretarse; (cable) tensarse.

tights npl (thin) panties mpl; (thick) leotardos mpl.

tile 1 n (of roof) teja f; (glazed) azulejo m; (for floor) baldosa f. **2** vt (roof) tejar; (wall) alicatar; (floor) embaldosar.

till¹ (for cash) caja f.

till² 1 prep hasta; **from morning t. night** de la mañana a la noche; **t. then** hasta entonces. **2** conj hasta que.

tilt 1 vi **to t. over** volcarse; **to t. (up)** inclinarse. **2** vt inclinar.

tim·ber madera f (de construcción).

time 1 n tiempo m; (era) época f; (point in time) momento m; (time of day) hora f; (occasion) vez f; **all the t.** todo el tiempo; **for some t.** (past) desde hace algún tiempo; **I haven't seen him for a long t.** hace mucho (tiempo) que no lo veo; **in a short t.** en poco tiempo; **in t.** a tiempo; **in three weeks' t.** dentro de tres semanas; **(at) any t. (you like)** cuando quiera; **at that t.** (en aquel) entonces; **at the same t.** al mismo tiempo; **at times** a veces; **from t. to t.** de vez en cuando; **he may turn up at any t.** puede llegar en cualquier momento; **on t.** puntualmente; **what's the t.?** ¿qué hora es?; **t. of the year** época f del año; **to have a good/bad t.** pasarlo bien/mal; **four at a t.** cuatro a la vez; **next t.** la próxima vez; **three times four** tres (multiplicado) por cuatro; **four times as big** cuatro veces más grande. **2** vt (speech) calcular la duración de; (race) cronometrar; (choose the time of) escoger el momento oportuno para.

tim·er (device) temporizador m.

time·ta·ble horario *m*.

tim·id *adj* tímido, -a.

tim·ing *(timeliness)* oportunidad *f*; *(coordination)* coordinación *f*; *(in race)* cronometraje *m*.

tin *(metal)* estaño *m*; *(container)* lata *f*.

tin·foil papel *m* de estaño.

tinned *adj* enlatado, -a; **t. food** conservas *fpl*.

tin·o·pen·er abrelatas *m inv*.

ti·ny *adj* diminuto, -a.

tip[1] *(end)* punta *f*; *(of cigarette)* colilla *f*.

tip[2] **1** *n (gratuity)* propina *f*; *(advice)* consejo *m*. **2** *vt* dar una propina a.

tip[3] **1** *vt* inclinar. **2** *vi* to **t. (up)** ladearse; *(cart)* bascular.

▸**tip over 1** *vt* volcar. **2** *vi* volcarse.

tipped cig·a·rette cigarrillo *m* con filtro.

tip·toe on t. de puntillas.

tire[1] *(of vehicle)* neumático *m*.

tire[2] **1** *vt* cansar. **2** *vi* cansarse.

▸**tire out** *vt* agotar.

tired *adj* cansado, -a; **t. out** rendido, -a; **to be t.** estar cansado, -a; **to be t. of sth** estar harto, -a de algo.

tired·ness cansancio *m*.

tir·ing *adj* agotador, -a.

tis·sue *(handkerchief)* Kleenex® *m*.

ti·tle título *m*.

to 1 *prep (with place)* a; *(towards)* hacia; **he went to France/Japan** fue a Francia/al Japón; **I'm going to Mary's** voy a casa de Mary; **it is thirty miles to New York** Nueva York está a treinta millas; **the train to Madrid** el tren de Madrid; **to the east** hacia el este; **to the right** a la derecha. ▪ *(time)* **ten (minutes) to six** las seis menos diez. ▪ *(with indirect object)* a; **he gave it to his cousin** se lo dio a su primo. ▪ *(towards)* **he was very kind to me** se portó muy bien conmigo. ▪ *(with infinitive)* **to buy/ to come** comprar/venir; *(in order to)* para; *(with verbs of motion)* a; **he did it to help me** lo hizo para ayudarme;

he stopped to talk se detuvo a hablar; **difficult to do** difícil de hacer; **ready to listen** dispuesto, -a a escuchar; **the first to complain** el primero en quejarse; **this is the time to do it** éste es el momento de hacerlo; **to have a great deal to do** tener mucho que hacer.

toad sapo *m*.

toad·stool hongo *m* (venenoso).

toast 1 *n* slice of **t.** tostada *f*. **2** *vt* tostar.

toast·er tostador *m* (de pan).

to·bac·co tabaco *m*.

to·bac·co·nist t.'s (shop) estanco *m*.

to·bog·gan tobogán *m*.

to·day *adv* hoy.

tod·dler niño, -a *mf* pequeño, -a.

toe dedo *m* del pie.

toe·nail uña *f* del dedo del pie.

tof·fee caramelo *m*.

to·geth·er *adv* junto, -a, juntos, -as; **all t.** todos juntos; **t. with** junto con.

toi·let wáter *m*; *(public)* servicios *mpl*.

toi·let pa·per or **tissue** papel *m* higiénico.

toi·let·ries *npl* artículos *mpl* de aseo.

toi·let roll rollo *m* de papel higiénico.

toi·let wa·ter *(perfume)* agua *f* de colonia.

to·ken *(for telephone)* ficha *f*; **book t.** vale *m* para comprar libros.

told *pt & pp of* **tell**.

tol·er·ance tolerancia *f*.

tol·er·ant *adj* tolerante.

tol·er·ate *vt* tolerar.

toll *(for road)* peaje *m*.

toll-free num·ber teléfono *m* gratuito.

to·ma·to *(pl* tomatoes*)* tomate *m*.

tomb tumba *f*.

to·mor·row *adv* mañana; **the day after t.** pasado mañana; **t. night** mañana por la noche.

ton tonelada f; fam **tons of** montones de.

tone tono m.

tongs npl (for sugar, hair) tenacillas fpl; (fire) t. tenazas fpl.

tongue lengua f.

ton·ic (drink) tónica f.

to·night adv esta noche.

tonne = ton.

ton·sil amígdala f.

ton·sil·li·tis amigdalitis f.

too adv (also) también; (excessively) demasiado; **t. much/many** demasiado, -a, demasiados, -as; **ten dollars t. much** diez dólares de más; **t. much money** demasiado dinero; **t. old** demasiado viejo.

took pt of **take**.

tool (utensil) herramienta f.

tooth (pl **teeth**) diente m.

tooth·ache dolor m de muelas.

tooth·brush cepillo m de dientes.

tooth·paste pasta f dentífrica. .

tooth·pick mondadientes m inv.

top¹ 1 n (upper part) parte f de arriba; (of hill) cumbre f; (of tree) copa f; (surface) superficie f; (of list etc) cabeza f; (of bottle etc) tapón m; (best) lo mejor; **on t. of** encima de. **2** adj (part) superior, de arriba; (best) mejor; **the t. floor** el último piso.

▸**top up** vt llenar hasta el tope.

top² (toy) peonza f.

top·ic tema m.

torch (burning) antorcha f.

tor·ment vt atormentar.

tor·na·do tornado m.

tor·toise tortuga f de tierra.

tor·toise·shell 1 adj de carey. **2** n carey m.

tor·ture 1 vt torturar; (cause anguish) atormentar. **2** n tortura f; (anguish) tormento m.

toss 1 vt (ball) tirar; (throw about) sacudir; **to t. a coin** echar a caro o cruz. **2** vi **to t. about** agitarse; (in sport) **to (up)** sortear.

total m; (in check) importe m.

t adv totalmente.

touch 1 vt tocar; (lightly) rozar; (emotionally) conmover. **2** vi tocarse; (lightly) rozarse. **3** n toque m; (light contact) roce m; (sense of touch) tacto m; **in t. with sb** en contacto con algn.

▸**touch down** vi (plane) aterrizar.

touch·down (of plane) aterrizaje m; (in football) ensayo m.

touch·y adj (person) susceptible.

tough adj (material, competitor etc) fuerte; (test, criminal, meat) duro, -a; (punishment) severo, -a; (problem) difícil.

tour 1 n (journey) viaje m; (of palace etc) visita f; (of city) recorrido m turístico; (of theatrical company, team) gira f; **on t.** de gira. **2** vt (country) viajar por; (building) visitar. **3** vi estar de viaje.

tour·ism turismo m.

tour·ist turista mf; **t. class** clase f turista.

tour·ist of·fice oficina f de información turística.

tour·na·ment torneo m.

tow vt remolcar.

to·wards prep hacia; **our duty t. others** nuestro deber para con los demás.

tow·el toalla f.

tow·er torre f.

tow·er block torre f.

town ciudad f; (small) pueblo m; **to go into t.** ir al centro.

town coun·cil ayuntamiento m.

town hall ayuntamiento m.

town·house casa f de la ciudad.

town·ship municipio m.

tow truck grúa f.

tox·ic adj tóxico, -a.

toy juguete m.

toy·shop juguetería f.

trace 1 n (sign) indicio m, vestigio m. **2** vt (drawing) calcar; (locate) seguir la pista de.

trac·ing pa·per papel m de calco.

track (mark) huellas fpl; (pathway) camino m; (for running) pista f; (of

railroad) vía f; *(on record)* canción f.
to be on the right t. ir por buen camino; **to be on the wrong t.** haberse equivocado.
track·suit chandal m.
trac·tor tractor m.
trade 1 n *(job)* oficio m; *(sector)* industria f; *(commerce)* comercio m. **2** vi comerciar (**in** en). **3** vt **to t. sth for sth** trocar algo por algo.
trade·mark marca f *(de fábrica)*; **registered t.** marca registrada.
trad·er comerciante mf.
trade un·ion sindicato m.
trad·ing comercio m.
tra·di·tion tradición f.
tra·di·tion·al adj tradicional.
traf·fic n tráfico m.
traf·fic jam atasco m.
traf·fic lights npl semáforo m sing.
traf·fic sign señal f de tráfico.
trag·e·dy tragedia f.
trag·ic adj trágico, -a.
trail 1 vt **to t. sth** (along) *(drag)* arrastrar algo. **2** vi *(drag)* arrastrarse; **to t.** (along) *(linger)* rezagarse. **3** n senda f; *(bigger)* pista f; *(of smoke)* estela f.
trail·er *(behind vehicle)* remolque m; *(caravan)* caravana f.
train¹ n tren m; **to go by t.** ir en tren.
train² **1** vt *(in sport)* entrenar; *(animal)* amaestrar; *(teach)* formar. **2** vi entrenarse; *(be taught)* prepararse.
trained adj *(skilled)* cualificado, -a.
train·ee aprendiz, -a mf.
train·er *(in sport)* entrenador, -a mf; *(of dogs)* amaestrador, -a mf; *(of lions)* domador, -a mf.
train·ing entrenamiento m; *(instruction)* formación f.
trai·tor traidor, -a mf.
tram tranvía m.
tramp *(person)* vagabundo, -a mf.
tran·quil·iz·er tranquilizante m.
trans·fer 1 vt trasladar; *(funds)* transferir; **a transferred charge call** una conferencia a cobro revertido. **2** n traslado m; *(of funds)* transferencia

f; *(picture, design)* calcomanía f.
trans·fu·sion transfusión f *(de sangre)*.
tran·sis·tor transistor m.
tran·sit in t. de tránsito.
tran·si·tive adj transitivo, -a.
trans·late vt traducir.
trans·la·tion traducción f.
trans·la·tor traductor, -a mf.
trans·mis·sion transmisión f.
trans·mit vt transmitir.
trans·par·ent adj transparente.
trans·plant trasplante m.
trans·port 1 vt transportar. **2** n transporte m.
trap 1 n trampa f. **2** vt *(animal, fugitive)* atrapar; **to t. sb into doing sth** lograr con ardides que algn haga algo.
trap door trampilla f.
trash *(inferior goods)* bazofia f; *(household waste)* basura f; fam *(worthless thing)* birria f; fam *(nonsense)* tonterías fpl.
trash can cubo m de la basura.
trash dump vertedero m.
trash·y adj fam *(book, film)* sin valor.
trav·el 1 vi viajar; *(vehicle, electric current)* ir; **to t. through** recorrer. **2** vt recorrer. **3** n viajes mpl; **t. agency** agencia f de viajes; **t. sickness** mareo m.
trav·el·er viajero, -a mf; **t.'s check** cheque m de viaje.
trav·el·ing 1 adj *(salesman)* ambulante. **2** n los viajes mpl; **I'm fond of t.** me gusta viajar.
tray *(for food)* bandeja f.
treach·er·ous adj *(dangerous)* peligroso, -a.
tread* vi pisar.
▸ **tread on** vt pisar.
treas·ure tesoro m.
treas·ur·er tesorero, -a mf.
treat 1 n *(present)* regalo m. **2** vt tratar; *(regard)* considerar; **he treated them to dinner** les invitó a cenar.
treat·ment *(of person)* trato m; *(of*

subject, patient) tratamiento *m.*

treb·le 1 *vt* triplicar. **2** *vi* triplicarse.

tree árbol *m.*

trem·ble *vi* temblar.

tre·men·dous *adj (huge)* enorme; *(success)* arrollador, -a; *(shock etc)* tremendo, -a; *fam (marvellous)* estupendo, -a.

trench *(ditch)* zanja *f, (for troops)* trinchera *f.*

trend·y *adj* (**trendier, trendiest**) *fam (person)* moderno, -a; *(clothes)* a la última.

tri·al *(in court)* juicio *m.*

tri·an·gle triángulo *m.*

tri·an·gu·lar *adj* triangular.

tribe tribu *f.*

trib·ute *(mark of respect)* homenaje *m;* **to pay t. to** rendir homenaje a.

trick 1 *n (ruse)* ardid *m; (dishonest)* engaño *m; (practical joke)* broma *f, (of magic, knack)* truco *m;* **to play a t. on sb** gastarle una broma a algn. **2** *vt* engañar.

trick·le 1 *vi (water)* gotear. **2** *n* hilo *m.*

trick·y *adj (situation)* delicado, -a; *(problem)* difícil.

tri·cy·cle triciclo *m.*

trig·ger *(of gun)* gatillo *m.*

trim *vt (cut)* recortar; *(expenses)* disminuir.

trip 1 *n (journey)* viaje *m; (excursion)* excursión *f.* **2** *vi* **to t. (up)** *(stumble)* tropezar (**over** con).

tri·ple 1 *vt* triplicar. **2** *vi* triplicarse.

tri·umph 1 *n* triunfo *m.* **2** *vi* triunfar.

triv·i·al *adj* trivial.

trol·ley carro *m.*

trom·bone trombón *m.*

troop·er *(soldier)* soldado *m* de caballería; *(policeman)* policía *mf.*

troops tropas *fpl.*

tro·phy trofeo *m.*

trop·i·cal *adj* tropical.

trot 1 *vi* trotar. **2** *n* trote *m.*

trou·ble 1 *n (misfortune)* desgracia *f, (problems)* problemas *mpl; (effort)* esfuerzo *m;* **to be in t.** estar en un

apuro; **it's not worth the t.** no merece la pena; **to take the t. to do sth** molestarse en hacer algo; **to have liver t.** tener problemas de hígado. **2** *vt (distress)* afligir; *(worry)* preocupar; *(bother)* molestar.

trou·sers *npl* pantalón *m sing.*

trout trucha *f.*

tru·ant **to play t.** hacer novillos.

truck camión *m.*

true *adj* verdadero, -a; *(faithful)* fiel; **to come t.** cumplirse; **it's not t.** no es verdad; **it's t. that** ... es verdad que ....

trump *(in card game)* triunfo *m.*

trum·pet trompeta *f.*

trunk *(of tree, body)* tronco *m; (of elephant)* trompa *f, (case)* baúl *m; (of car)* maletero *m.*

trunks *npl* (**swimming**) **t.** bañador *m sing.*

trust 1 *n* confianza *f.* **2** *vt (rely upon)* fiarse de; **to t. sb with sth** confiar algo a algn.

truth verdad *f.*

try 1 *vt (attempt)* intentar; *(test)* probar. **2** *vi* intentar; **to t. to do sth** tratar de *or* intentar hacer algo. **3** *n (attempt)* tentativa *f, (in rugby)* ensayo *m.*

▸ **try on** *vt (dress)* probarse.

▸ **try out** *vt* probar.

try·ing *adj (person)* molesto, -a, pesado, -a.

T-shirt camiseta *f.*

tub *(container)* tina *f, (bath)* bañera *f.*

tube tubo *m; (in body)* conducto *m.*

tuck *vt* **to t. in the bedclothes** remeter la ropa de la cama; **to t. sb in** arropar a algn; **to t. one's shirt into one's trousers** meterse la camisa por dentro (de los pantalones).

Tues·day martes *m.*

tuft *(of hair)* mechón *m; (of wool etc)* copo *m.*

tug 1 *vt (pull at)* tirar de; *(haul along)* arrastrar; *(boat)* remolcar. **2** *n (boat)* remolcador *m.*

tug·boat remolcador *m.*

tu·i·tion instrucción *f*; **private t.** clases *fpl* particulares; **t. fees** tasas *fpl*.

tu·lip tulipán *m*.

tum·ble 1 *vi* (*person*) caerse. **2** *n* caída *f*.

tum·ble dry·er secadora *f*.

tum·bler (*glass*) vaso *m*.

tum·my *fam* estómago *m*; (*belly*) barriga *f*.

tu·mor tumor *m*.

tu·na atún *m*.

tune 1 *n* (*melody*) melodía *f*; **in/out of t.** afinado/desafinado; **to sing out of t.** desafinar. **2** *vt* (*instrument*) afinar; (*engine*) poner a punto.

▸**tune in to** *vt* (*on radio etc*) sintonizar.

tun·ing (*of instrument*) afinación *f*.

Tu·ni·sian *adj & n* tunecino, -a (*mf*).

tun·nel túnel *m*.

tur·ban turbante *m*.

tur·key pavo *m*.

Turk turco, -a *mf*.

Turk·ish 1 *adj* turco, -a. **2** *n* (*language*) turco *m*.

turn 1 *vt* (*revolve*) girar; (*page, head, gaze*) volver; (*change*) transformar (**into** en); **he's turned forty** ha cumplido los cuarenta. **2** *vi* (*revolve*) girar; (*change direction*) torcer; (*turn round*) volverse; (*become*) volverse; **to t. to sb** (*for help*) acudir a algn. **3** *n* (*of wheel*) vuelta *f*; (*in road*) curva *f*; (*in game, line*) turno *m*; **it's your t.** te toca a ti; **to take turns (at doing sth)** turnarse (para hacer algo).

▸**turn around** *vi* (*of person*) volverse.

▸**turn away 1** *vt* (*person*) rechazar. **2** *vi* volver la cabeza; (*move away*) alejarse.

▸**turn back 1** *vt* (*person*) hacer retroceder. **2** *vi* volverse.

▸**turn down** *vt* (*gas, radio etc*) bajar; (*reject*) rechazar.

▸**turn into 1** *vt* convertir en. **2** *vi* convertirse en.

▸**turn off** *vt* (*light, TV, radio, engine*)

apagar; (*water, gas*) cortar; (*faucet*) cerrar.

▸**turn on** *vt* (*light, TV, radio, engine*) encender; (*water, gas*) abrir la llave de; (*faucet*) abrir.

▸**turn out 1** *vt* (*extinguish*) apagar. **2** *vi* **it turns out that ...** resulta que ...; **things have turned out well** las cosas han salido bien.

▸**turn over 1** *vt* (*turn upside down*) poner al revés; (*page*) dar la vuelta a. **2** *vi* volverse.

▸**turn round 1** *vt* volver. **2** *vi* (*rotate*) girar.

▸**turn up 1** *vt* (*collar*) levantar; (*TV, volume*) subir; (*light*) aumentar la intensidad de. **2** *vi* (*arrive*) presentarse.

turn·ing (*in road*) salida *f*.

tur·nip nabo *m*.

turn·pike autopista *f* de peaje.

turn·up (*of trousers*) vuelta *f*.

tur·tle tortuga *f*.

tur·tle·neck **a t. sweater** un jersey de cuello alto.

tusk colmillo *m*.

tu·tor (*at university*) tutor, -a *mf*; **private t.** profesor, -a *mf* particular.

TV TV.

tweez·ers *npl* pinzas *fpl*.

twelfth *adj & n* duodécimo, -a (*mf*).

twelve *adj & n* doce (*m*) *inv*; **t. o'clock** las doce.

twen·ti·eth *adj & n* vigésimo, -a (*mf*).

twen·ty *adj & n* veinte (*m*) *inv*.

twice *adv* dos veces; **he's t. as old as I am** tiene el doble de años que yo; **t. as big** el doble de grande.

twig ramita *f*.

twi·light crepúsculo *m*.

twin *n* mellizo, -a *mf*; **identical twins** gemelos *mpl* (idénticos); **t. beds** camas *fpl* gemelas.

twine bramante *m*.

twirl 1 *vt* girar rápidamente. **2** *vi* (*spin*) girar rápidamente; (*dancer*) piruetear.

twist 1 *vt* torcer; **to t. one's ankle**

torcerse el tobillo. **2** *n (movement)* torsión *f*; *(in road)* vuelta *f*.

▸ **twist off** *(lid)* desenroscar.

two *adj & n* dos *(m) inv*.

two-way *adj (street)* de dos direcciones.

type 1 *n (kind)* tipo *m*; *(print)* caracteres *mpl*. **2** *vti* escribir a máquina.

type·writ·er máquina *f* de escribir.

type·writ·ten *adj* escrito, -a a máquina.

typ·i·cal *adj* típico, -a.

typ·ing mecanografía *f*.

typ·ist mecanógrafo, -a *mf*.

U

UFO *abbr of* **unidentified flying object** OVNI *m*.

ug·li·ness fealdad *f*.

ug·ly *adj* feo, -a; *(situation)* desagradable.

ul·cer *(sore)* llaga *f*; *(internal)* úlcera *f*.

ul·ti·mate *adj (final)* último, -a; *(aim)* final; *(basic)* esencial.

um·brel·la paraguas *m inv*.

um·pire árbitro *m*.

ump·teen *adj fam* muchísimos, -as, la tira de.

un·a·ble *adj* to be u. to do sth no poder hacer algo.

un·ac·cept·a·ble *adj* inaceptable.

un·ac·cus·tomed *adj* he's u. to this climate no está acostumbrado a este clima.

u·nan·i·mous *adj* unánime.

u·nan·i·mous·ly *adv* unánimemente.

un·at·trac·tive *adj (idea, appearance)* poco atractivo, -a.

un·a·vail·a·ble *adj* no disponible; Mr Smith is u. today Mr Smith no le puede atender hoy.

un·a·void·a·ble *adj* inevitable; *(accident)* imprevisible.

un·a·void·a·bly *adv* inevitablemente.

un·a·ware 1 *adj* to be u. of sth ignorar algo. **2** *adv (without knowing)* inconscientemente; it caught me u. me cogió desprevenido.

un·bear·a·ble *adj* insoportable.

un·be·liev·a·ble *adj* increíble.

un·break·a·ble *adj* irrompible.

un·but·ton *vt* desabrochar.

un·cer·tain *adj (not certain)* incierto, -a; *(doubtful)* dudoso, -a; *(hesitant)* indeciso, -a.

un·cer·tain·ty incertidumbre *f*.

un·changed *adj* igual.

un·cle tío *m*.

un·clear *adj* poco claro, -a.

un·com·fort·a·ble *adj* incómodo, -a.

un·com·mon *adj (rare)* poco común.

un·con·nect·ed *adj* no relacionado, -a.

un·con·scious *adj* inconsciente (of de).

un·con·sti·tu·tion·al *adj* inconstitueional, anticonstitucional.

un·con·vinc·ing *adj* poco convincente.

un·co·op·er·a·tive *adj* poco cooperativo, -a.

un·cork *vt (bottle)* descorchar.

un·cov·er *vt* destapar; *(discover)* descubrir.

un·dam·aged *adj (article etc)* sin desperfectos.

un·de·cid·ed *adj (person)* indeciso, -a.

un·de·ni·a·ble *adj* innegable.

un·der 1 *prep* debajo de; *(less than)* menos de; u. the circumstances dadas las circunstancias; u. there allí debajo. **2** *adv* debajo.

un·der- *prefix (below)* sub-, infra-; *(insufficiently)* insuficientemente.

un·der·charge *vt* cobrar menos de lo debido.

un·der·clothes *npl* ropa *f sing* interior.

un·der·done *adj* poco hecho, -a.

un·der·es·ti·mate *vt* subestimar.

un·der·go* *vt* experimentar; *(change)* sufrir; *(test etc)* pasar por.

un·der·grad·u·ate estudiante *mf* universitario, -a.

un·der·ground *adj* subterráneo, -a.

un·der·line *vt* subrayar.

un·der·mine *vt* socavar, minar.

un·der·neath 1 *prep* debajo de. **2** *adv* debajo. **3** *n* parte *f* inferior.

un·der·pants *npl* calzoncillos *mpl.*

un·der·pass paso *n* subterráneo.

un·der·shirt camiseta *f.*

un·der·stand* *vti* entender.

un·der·stand·a·ble *adj* comprensible.

un·der·stand·ing 1 *n (intellectual grasp)* comprensión *f*; *(agreement)* acuerdo *m.* **2** *adj* comprensivo, -a.

un·der·stood 1 *pt & pp of* **understand**. **2** *adj (agreed on)* convenido, -a.

un·der·take* *vt (responsibility)* asumir; *(task, job)* encargarse de; *(promise)* comprometerse a.

un·der·tak·er empresario, -a *mf* de pompas fúnebres; **undertaker's** funeraria *f.*

un·der·tak·ing *(task)* empresa *f.*

un·der·wa·ter 1 *adj* submarino, -a. **2** *adv* bajo el agua.

un·der·wear *inv* ropa *f* interior.

un·do* *vt* deshacer; *(button)* desabrochar.

un·done *adj (knot etc)* deshecho, -a; **to come u.** *(shoelace)* desatarse; *(button, blouse)* desabrocharse; *(necklace etc)* soltarse.

un·doubt·ed·ly *adv* indudablemente.

un·dress 1 *vt* desnudar. **2** *vi* desnudarse.

un·eas·y *adj (worried)* preocupado, -a; *(disturbing)* inquietante; *(uncomfortable)* incómodo, -a.

un·em·ployed 1 *adj* **to be u.** estar en paro. **2** *npl* **the u.** los parados.

un·em·ploy·ment paro *m.*

un·e·ven *adj (not level)* desigual; *(bumpy)* accidentado, -a; *(variable)* irregular.

un·e·vent·ful *adj* sin acontecimientos.

un·ex·pect·ed *adj (unhoped for)* inesperado, -a; *(event)* imprevisto, -a.

un·ex·pect·ed·ly *adv* inesperadamente.

un·fair *adj* injusto, -a.

un·fair·ly *adv* injustamente.

un·fair·ness injusticia *f.*

un·faith·ful *adj (friend)* desleal; *(husband, wife)* infiel.

un·fa·mil·iar *adj (unknown)* desconocido, -a; **to be u. with sth** no conocer bien algo.

un·fash·ion·a·ble *adj* pasado, -a de moda; *(ideas etc)* poco popular.

un·fas·ten *vt (knot)* desatar; *(clothing, belt)* desabrochar.

un·fa·vor·a·ble *adj* desfavorable.

un·fin·ished *adj* inacabado, -a.

un·fit *adj (food, building)* inadecuado, -a; *(person)* no apto, -a **(for** para); *(incompetent)* incompetente; *(physically)* incapacitado, -a; **to be u.** no estar en forma.

un·fold *vt (sheet)* desdoblar; *(newspaper)* abrir.

un·for·get·ta·ble *adj* inolvidable.

un·for·giv·a·ble *adj* imperdonable.

un·for·tu·nate *adj (person, event)* desgraciado, -a; **how u.!** ¡qué mala suerte!

un·for·tu·nate·ly *adv* desgraciadamente.

un·friend·ly *adj* antipático, -a.

un·fur·nished *adj* sin amueblar.

un·grate·ful *adj (unthankful)* desagradecido, -a.

un·hap·pi·ness tristeza *f.*

un·hap·py *adj* triste.

un·harmed *adj* ileso, -a, indemne.

un·health·y adj (ill) enfermizo, -a; (unwholesome) malsano, -a.

un·help·ful adj (advice) inútil; (person) poco servicial.

un·hook vt (from hook) descolgar; (clothing) desabrochar.

un·hurt adj ileso, -a.

un·hy·gi·en·ic adj antihigiénico, -a.

u·ni·form adj & n uniforme (m).

un·im·por·tant adj poco importante.

un·in·hab·it·ed adj despoblado, -a.

un·in·jured adj ileso, -a.

un·in·ten·tion·al adj involuntario, -a.

un·in·ter·est·ing adj poco interesante.

un·ion 1 n unión f; (organization) sindicato m. 2 adj sindical.

u·nique adj único, -a.

u·nit unidad f; (piece of furniture) módulo m. 2 (team) equipo m; kitchen u. mueble m de cocina.

u·nite 1 vt unir. 2 vi unirse.

u·ni·ver·sal adj universal.

u·ni·verse universo m.

u·ni·ver·si·ty 1 n universidad f. 2 adj universitario, -a.

un·just adj injusto, -a.

un·kind adj (not nice) poco amable; (cruel) despiadado, -a.

un·know·ing·ly inconscientemente, inadvertidamente.

un·known adj desconocido, -a.

un·lead·ed adj (gasoline) sin plomo.

un·less conj a menos que (+ subjunctive), a no ser que (+ subjunctive).

un·like prep a diferencia de.

un·like·ly adj (improbable) poco probable.

un·lim·it·ed adj ilimitado, -a.

un·load vti descargar.

un·lock vt abrir (con llave).

un·luck·y adj (unfortunate) desgraciado, -a; to be u. (person) tener mala

suerte; (thing) traer mala suerte.

un·made adj (bed) deshecho, -a.

un·mar·ried adj soltero, -a.

un·nec·es·sar·y adj innecesario, -a.

un·no·ticed adj desapercibido, -a; to let sth pass u. pasar algo por alto.

un·oc·cu·pied adj (house) desocupado, -a; (seat) libre.

un·pack 1 vt (boxes) desembalar; (suitcase) deshacer. 2 vi deshacer la(s) maleta(s).

un·paid adj (bill, debt) impagado, -a; (work) no retribuido, -a.

un·pleas·ant adj (not nice) desagradable; (unfriendly) antipático, -a (to con).

un·plug vt desenchufar.

un·pop·u·lar adj impopular; to make oneself u. ganarse la antipatía de algn.

un·pre·dict·a·ble adj imprevisible.

un·pre·pared adj (speech etc) improvisado, -a; (person) desprevenido, -a.

un·rea·son·a·ble adj poco razonable; (demands) desmedido, -a.

un·rec·og·niz·a·ble adj irreconocible.

un·re·lat·ed adj (not connected) no relacionado, -a.

un·re·li·a·ble adj (person) de poca confianza; (information) que no es de fiar; (machine) poco fiable.

un·rest (social etc) malestar m.

un·roll vt desenrollar.

un·safe adj (activity, journey) peligroso, -a; (building, car, machine) inseguro, -a; to feel u. sentirse expuesto, -a.

un·sat·is·fac·to·ry adj insatisfactorio, -a.

un·screw vt destornillar.

un·skilled adj (worker) no cualificado, -a.

un·sta·ble adj inestable.

un·stead·i·ly adv (to walk) con paso inseguro.

un·stead·y *adj (not firm)* inestable; *(table, chair)* cojo, -a; *(hand, voice)* tembloroso, -a.

un·suc·cess·ful *adj (person, negotiation)* fracasado, -a; *(attempt, effort)* vano, -a; *(candidate)* derrotado, -a; **to be u. at sth** no tener éxito con algo.

un·suc·cess·ful·ly *adv* sin éxito.

un·suit·a·ble *adj (person)* no apto, -a; *(thing)* inadecuado, -a.

un·suit·ed *adj (person)* no apto, -a; *(thing)* impropio, -a (**to** para).

un·sure *adj* poco seguro, -a; **to be u. of sth** no estar seguro, -a de algo.

un·tan·gle *vt* desenmarañar.

un·ti·dy *adj (room, person)* desordenado, -a; *(hair)* despeinado, -a; *(appearance)* desaseado, -a.

un·tie *vt* desatar.

un·til 1 *conj* hasta que; **u. she gets back** hasta que vuelva. **2** *prep* hasta; **u. now** hasta ahora; **not u. Monday** hasta el lunes no.

un·true *adj (false)* falso, -a.

un·used *adj (car)* sin usar; *(stamp)* sin matar.

un·u·su·al *adj (rare)* poco común; *(exceptional)* excepcional.

un·u·su·al·ly *adv* excepcionalmente.

un·veil *vt* descubrir.

un·want·ed *adj* no deseado, -a.

un·well *adj* to be u. estar malo, -a.

un·will·ing *adj* to be u. to do sth no estar dispuesto, -a a hacer algo.

un·will·ing·ly *adv* de mala gana.

un·wor·thy *adj* indigno, -a.

un·wrap *vt (gift)* desenvolver; *(package)* deshacer.

un·zip *vt* bajar la cremallera de.

up 1 *prep (movement)* **to climb up the mountain** escalar la montaña; **to walk up the street** ir calle arriba. ▪ *(position)* en lo alto de; **further up the street** más adelante (en la misma calle). **2** *adv (upwards)* arriba; **further up** hacia arriba; **from ten dollars up** de diez dólares para arriba; **right up (to the top)** hasta arriba (del todo); **to go** *or* **come up** subir; **to walk up and down** ir de un lado a otro. ▪ *(towards)* hacia; **to come** *or* **go up to sb** acercarse a algn. ▪ *(increased)* **bread is up** el pan ha subido. ▪ *(wrong)* **what's up (with you)?** ¿qué pasa (contigo)?; **something must be up** debe pasar algo. ▪ **up to** *(as far as, until)* hasta; **I can spend up to five dollars** puedo gastar un máximo de cinco dólares; **up to here** hasta aquí; **up to now** hasta ahora. ▪ **to be up to** *(depend on)* depender de; *(be capable of)* estar a la altura de; **he's up to something** está tramando algo. **3** *adj (out of bed)* levantado, -a; *(finished)* terminado, -a; **time's up** (ya) es la hora. **4** *vt (increase)* aumentar. **5** *n* **ups and downs** altibajos *mpl*.

up·date *vt* actualizar, poner al día.

up·grade 1 *vt (promote)* ascender; *(improve)* mejorar la calidad de; *(software, hardware)* actualizar. **2** *n (of software, hardware)* actualización *f*.

up·hill *adv* cuesta arriba.

up·hold* *vt* sostener.

up·on *prep* sobre.

up·per *adj* superior.

up·right 1 *adj (vertical)* vertical; *(honest)* honrado, -a. **2** *adv* derecho.

up·roar tumulto *m*.

up·scale *adj (newspaper, program)* dirigido, -a a un público selecto.

up·set 1 *vt* (shock)* trastornar; *(worry)* preocupar; *(displease)* disgustar; *(spoil)* desbaratar; *(make, ill)* sentar mal a. **2** *adj (shocked)* alterado, -a; *(displeased)* disgustado, -a; **to have an u. stomach** sentirse mal del estómago.

up·side-down al revés.

up·stairs 1 *adv* arriba. **2** *n* piso *m* de arriba.

up-to-date *adj (current)* al día; *(modern)* moderno, -a; **to be u. with sth** estar al tanto de algo.

up·town zona *f*residencial.

up·ward(s) *adv* hacia arriba; **from ten (years) u.** a partir de los diez años; *fam* **u. of** algo más de.

urge *vt (incite)* incitar; *(press)* instar; *(plead)* exhortar; *(advocate)* preconizar; **to u. that sth should be done** insistir en que se haga algo.

ur·gen·cy urgencia *f*.

ur·gent *adj* urgente; *(need, tone)* apremiante.

ur·gent·ly *adv* urgentemente.

u·rine orina *f*.

U·ru·guay·an *adj & n* uruguayo, -a *(mf)*.

us *pers pron (as object)* nos; *(after prep, 'to be')* nosotros, -as; **she wouldn't believe it was us** no creía que fuéramos nosotros; **let's forget it** olvidémoslo.

us·age *(habit, custom)* costumbre *f*, *(linguistic)* uso *m*.

use 1 *vt*utilizar; *(consume)* consumir; **what is it used for?** ¿para qué sirve? **2** *n* uso *m*; **'not in u.'** 'no funciona'; **to be of u.** servir; **to make (good) u. of sth** aprovechar algo; **it's no u.** es inútil; **it's no u. crying** no sirve de nada llorar.

▸**use up** *vt* acabar; *(food)* consumir; *(gas)* agotar; *(money)* gastar.

used[1] *adj (second-hand)* usado, -a.

used[2] 1 *v aux* **where did you u. to live?** ¿dónde vivías (antes)?; **I u. to play the piano** solía tocar el piano; **I u. not to like it** antes no me gustaba. **2** *adj* **to be u. to sth** estar acostumbrado, -a a algo.

use·ful *adj* útil; *(practical)* práctico, -a; **to come in u.** venir bien.

use·ful·ness utilidad *f*.

use·less *adj* inútil.

us·er usuario, -a *mf*.

us·er-friend·ly *adj* de fácil manejo.

u·su·al *adj* corriente; **as u.** como siempre.

u·su·al·ly *adv* normalmente.

u·ten·sil utensilio *m*; **kitchen utensils** batería *f sing* de cocina.

u·til·i·ty (public) u. empresa *f* de servicio público.

ut·ter[1] *vt (words)* pronunciar; *(cry, threat)* lanzar.

ut·ter[2] *adj* total.

ut·ter·ly *adv* completamente.

U-turn cambio *m* de sentido.

V

va·can·cy *(job)* vacante *f*, *(room)* habitación *f* libre.

va·cant *adj (empty)* vacío, -a; *(room, seat)* libre.

va·ca·tion vacaciones *fpl*; **on v.** de vacaciones.

va·ca·tion·er summer v. veraneante *mf*.

vac·ci·nate *vt* vacunar.

vac·ci·na·tion vacuna *f*.

vac·cine vacuna *f*.

vac·uum 1 *vt* limpiar con aspiradora. **2** *n* vacío *m*.

vac·uum clean·er aspiradora *f*.

vague *adj (imprecise)* vago, -a; *(indistinct)* borroso, -a.

vague·ly *adv* vagamente.

vain *adj* **in v.** en vano.

val·id *adj* válido, -a.

val·ley valle *m*.

val·u·a·ble 1 *adj* valioso, -a. **2** *npl* **valuables** objetos *mpl* de valor.

val·ue valor *m*; **to get good v. for money** sacarle jugo al dinero.

valve *(of machine, heart)* válvula *f*.

van furgoneta *f*.

van·dal gamberro, -a *mf*.

van·dal·ize *vt* destrozar.

va·nil·la vainilla *f*.

van·ish *vi* desaparecer.

var·i·a·ble *adj & n* variable *(f)*.

var·i·ant variante *f*.

var·ied *adj* variado, -a.

va·ri·e·ty *(diversity)* variedad *f*,

(assortment) surtido m; **for a v. of reasons** por razones diversas.

va·ri·e·ty show espectáculo m de variedades.

var·i·ous adj diversos, -as.

var·nish 1 n barniz m. **2** vt barnizar.

var·y vti variar.

vase florero m.

Vas·e·line® vaselina f.

vast adj vasto, -a.

VAT abbr of **value added tax** IVA m.

VCR abbr of **video cassette recorder** (grabador m de) vídeo m.

veal ternera f.

veg·e·ta·ble verdura f.

veg·e·tar·i·an adj & n vegetariano, -a (mf).

veg·e·ta·tion vegetación f.

ve·hi·cle vehículo m.

veil velo m.

vein vena f.

vel·vet terciopelo m.

vend·ing ma·chine máquina f expendedora.

ven·dor vendedor, -a mf.

Ve·ne·tian blind persiana f graduable.

Ven·e·zue·lan adj & n venezolano, -a (mf).

ven·ti·la·tion ventilación f.

ven·ture 1 vt arriesgar, aventurar; **he didn't v. to ask** no se atrevió a preguntarlo. **2** vi arriesgarse; **to v. out of doors** atreverse a salir. **3** n empresa f arriesgada, aventura f.

ven·ue *(meeting place)* lugar m de reunión; *(for concert etc)* local m.

verb verbo m.

ver·bal adj verbal.

ver·dict veredicto m; *(opinion)* opinión f.

verge *(of road)* arcén m.

verse *(stanza)* estrofa f; *(poetry)* versos mpl; *(of song)* copla f.

ver·sion versión f.

ver·sus prep contra.

ver·ti·cal adj vertical.

ver·y adv muy; **v. much** muchísimo; **at the v. latest** como máximo; **the v.**

first/last el primero/último de todos; **at this v. moment** en este mismo momento.

vest *(undershirt)* camiseta f; chaleco m.

vet veterinario, -a mf.

vet·er·an veterano, -a mf; **(war) v.** ex combatiente mf.

vi·a prep por.

vi·brate vi vibrar **(with** de).

vi·bra·tion vibración f.

vic·ar párroco m.

vice¹ vicio m.

vice² *(tool)* torno m de banco.

vi·cious adj *(violent)* violento, -a; *(malicious)* malintencionado, -a; *(cruel)* cruel.

vic·tim víctima f.

vic·to·ry victoria f.

vid·e·o vídeo m; **v. (cassette)** videocasete m; **v. (cassette recorder)** vídeo m.

vid·e·o cam·er·a videocámara f.

vid·e·o game videojuego m.

vid·e·o·tape cinta f de vídeo.

view *(sight)* vista f; *(opinion)* opinión f; **to come into v.** aparecer; **in v. of the fact that ...** dado que ....

view·er *(of TV)* televidente mf.

view·find·er visor m.

view·point punto m de vista.

vil·la *(country house)* casa f de campo.

vil·lage *(small)* aldea f; *(larger)* pueblo m.

vil·lag·er aldeano, -a mf.

vil·lain villano, -a mf; *(in movie, play)* malo, -a mf.

vin·e·gar vinagre m.

vine·yard viñedo m.

vi·o·lence violencia f.

vi·o·lent adj violento, -a.

vi·o·lent·ly adv violentamente.

vi·o·lin violín m.

VIP abbr of **very important person** fam vip mf.

vir·gin n virgen f.

vir·tu·al adj virtual; **v. reality** realidad f virtual.

vir·tu·al·ly *adv (almost)* prácticamente.

vir·tue virtud *f*; **by v. of** en virtud de.

vi·rus virus *m inv.*

vi·sa visado *m*, *Am* visa *f.*

vis·i·ble *adj* visible.

vis·it 1 *vt* visitar. **2** *n* visita *f*; **to pay sb a v.** hacerle una visita a algn.

vis·it·ing hours *npl* horas *fpl* de visita.

vis·i·tor *(guest)* invitado, -a *mf*; *(tourist)* turista *mf.*

vi·tal *adj (essential)* fundamental.

vi·tal·ly *adv* **it's v. important** es de vital importancia.

vi·ta·min vitamina *f.*

viv·id *adj (color)* vivo, -a; *(description)* gráfico, -a.

vo·cab·u·lar·y vocabulario *m.*

vo·ca·tion·al *adj* profesional

vod·ka vodka *m or f.*

voice voz *f*; **at the top of one's v.** a voz en grito.

vol·ca·no *(pl volcanoes)* volcán *m.*

volt·age voltaje *m.*

vol·ume volumen *m.*

vol·un·tar·y *adj* voluntario, -a.

vol·un·teer 1 *n* voluntario, -a *mf.* **2** *vi* ofrecerse (**for** para).

vom·it *vti* vomitar.

vote 1 *n* voto *m*; *(voting)* votación *f.* **2** *vti* votar.

vot·er votante *mf.*

vouch·er vale *m.*

vow·el vocal *f.*

voy·age viaje *m*; *(crossing)* travesía *f.*

vul·gar *adj (coarse)* ordinario, -a; *(in poor taste)* de mal gusto.

W

wad *(of paper)* taco *m*; *(of cotton wool)* bolita *f*; *(of money)* fajo *m.*

wad·dle *vi* andar como los patos.

wade *vi* caminar por el agua.

wad·ing pool piscina *f* para niños.

wa·fer barquillo *m.*

wag 1 *vt* menear. **2** *vi (tail)* menearse.

wage earn·er asalariado, -a *mf.*

wages *npl* salario *m sing.*

wag·on camión *m*; *(of train)* vagón *m.*

waist cintura *f.*

wait 1 *n* espera *f*; *(delay)* demora *f.* **2** *vi* esperar; **to keep sb waiting** hacer esperar a algn.

▶ **wait behind** *vi* quedarse.

▶ **wait up** *vi* **to w. up for sb** esperar a algn levantado, -a.

wait·er camarero *m.*

wait·ing 'no w.' 'prohibido aparcar'.

wait·ing room sala *f* de espera.

wait·ress camarera *f.*

wait·staff camareros *mpl.*

wake* 1 *vt* **to w. sb (up)** despertar a algn. **2** *vi* **to w. (up)** despertar(se).

walk 1 *n (long)* caminata *m*; *(short)* paseo *m*; **it's an hour's w.** está a una hora de camino; **to go for a w.** dar un paseo. **2** *vt (dog)* pasear. **3** *vi* andar; *(to a specific place)* ir andando.

▶ **walk away** *vi* alejarse.

▶ **walk in** *vi* entrar.

▶ **walk off** *vi* marcharse; **to walk off with sth** *(steal, win easily)* llevarse algo.

▶ **walk out** *vi* salir.

walk·er paseante *mf*; *(in sport)* marchador, -a *mf.*

walk·ing *(hiking)* excursionismo *m.*

walk·ing stick bastón *m.*

Walk·man® *(pl Walkmans)* Walkman® *m.*

wall *(exterior)* muro *m*; *(interior)* pared *f.*

wal·let cartera *f.*

wall·pa·per 1 *n* papel *m* pintado. **2** *vt* empapelar.

wal·nut nuez *f.*

wal·rus morsa f.

wan·der 1 vt **to w. the streets** vagar por las calles. **2** vi (aimlessly) vagar; (stray) desviarse; (mind) divagar; **his glance wandered round the room** recorrió el cuarto con la mirada.

▸ **wander about** vi deambular.

want vt querer; (desire) desear; (need) necesitar; **to w. to do sth** querer hacer algo; **you're wanted on the phone** te llaman al teléfono.

war guerra f; **to be at w.** estar en guerra (with con).

ward (of hospital) sala f.

war·den (of residence) guardián, -ana mf; **game w.** guarda m de coto.

ward·robe armario m (ropero).

ware·house almacén m.

warm 1 adj caliente; (water) tibio, -a; **a w. day** un día de calor; **I am w.** tengo calor; **it is (very) w. today** hoy hace (mucho) calor. **2** vt calentar.

▸ **warm up 1** vt calentar; (soup) (re)calentar. **2** vi calentarse; (food) (re)calentarse; (person) entrar en calor.

warmth calor m.

warn vt advertir (**about** sobre; **against** contra); **he warned me not to go** me advirtió que no fuera; **to w. sb that ...** advertir a algn que ...

warn·ing (of danger) advertencia f; (notice) aviso m.

warn·ing light piloto m.

war·rant 1 n (legal order) orden f judicial. **2** vt (justify) justificar; (guarantee) garantizar.

war·ran·ty n (for goods) garantía f.

war·ri·or guerrero, -a mf.

war·ship buque m de guerra.

wart verruga f.

war·time tiempos mpl de guerra.

war·y adj (warier, wariest) cauteloso, -a; **to be w. of doing sth** dudar en hacer algo; **to be w. of sb/sth** recelar de algn/algo.

was pt of **be**.

wash 1 n **to have a w.** lavarse. **2** vt lavar; (dishes) fregar; **to w. one's hair** lavarse el pelo. **3** vi (have a wash) lavarse.

▸ **wash away** vt (of sea) llevarse; (traces) borrar.

▸ **wash off** vi quitarse lavando.

▸ **wash out 1** vt (stain) quitar lavando. **2** vi quitarse lavando.

▸ **wash up** vi lavarse rápidamente.

wash·a·ble adj lavable.

wash·ba·sin lavabo m.

wash·cloth manopla f.

wash·ing (action) lavado m; (of clothes) colada f; (dirty) ropa f sucia; **to do the w.** hacer la colada.

wash·ing ma·chine lavadora f.

wash·room servicios mpl.

wasp avispa f.

waste 1 n (unnecessary use) desperdicio m; (of resources, effort, money) derroche m; (of time) pérdida f; (trash) basura f; **radioactive w.** desechos mpl radiactivos. **2** vt (squander) desperdiciar; (resources) derrochar; (time, chance) perder.

waste·bin cubo m de la basura.

waste ground (in town) descampado m.

waste·pa·per papeles mpl usados.

waste·pa·per bas·ket papelera f.

watch 1 n reloj m. **2** vt (observe) observar; (keep an eye on) vigilar; (be careful of) tener cuidado con. **3** vi (look) mirar.

▸ **watch out** vi **w. out!** ¡cuidado!

▸ **watch out for** vt tener cuidado con; (wait for) esperar.

watch·strap correa f (de reloj).

wa·ter 1 n agua f. **2** vt (plants) regar.

▸ **water down** vt (drink) aguar.

wa·ter·col·or acuarela f.

wa·ter·cress berro m.

wa·ter·fall cascada f; (very big) catarata f.

wa·ter·ing can regadera f.

wa·ter·mel·on sandía f.

wa·ter·proof adj (material) impermeable; (watch) sumergible.

wa·ter·ski·ing esquí m acuático.

wa·ter·tight adj hermético, -a.
wave 1 n (at sea) ola f; (in hair, radio) onda f. **2** vt agitar; (brandish) blandir. **3** vi agitar el brazo; **she waved (to me)** (greeting) me saludó con la mano; (goodbye) se despidió (de mí) con la mano.
wave·length longitud f de onda.
wav·y adj ondulado, -a.
wax 1 n cera m. **2** vt encerar.
way n (route, road) camino m; (distance) distancia f; (means, manner) manera f; **on the w.** en el camino; **on the w.** here de camino para aquí; **which is the w. to the station?** ¿por dónde se va a la estación?; **w. in** entrada f; **w. out** salida f; **on the w. back** en el viaje de regreso; **on the w. up/down** en la subida/bajada; **(get) out of the w.!** ¡quítate de en medio!; **you're in the w.** estás estorbando; **come this w.** venga por aquí; **which w. did he go?** ¿por dónde se fue?; **that w.** por allá; **a long w. off** lejos; **do it this w.** hazlo así; **which w. did you do it?** ¿cómo lo hiciste?; **no w.!** ¡ni hablar!
we pers pron nosotros, -as.
weak adj débil; (team, piece of work, tea) flojo, -a.
weak·en 1 vt debilitar; (argument) quitar fuerza a. **2** vi debilitarse; (concede ground) ceder.
weak·ness debilidad f; (character flaw) punto m flaco.
wealth riqueza f.
wealth·y adj rico, -a.
weap·on arma f.
wear 1 vt* (clothes) llevar (puesto, -a); (shoes) calzar; **he wears glasses** lleva gafas; **he was wearing a jacket** llevaba chaqueta. **2** n (deterioration) desgaste m; **normal w. and tear** desgaste m natural.
▸ **wear off** vi (effect, pain) pasar.
▸ **wear out 1** vt gastar; fig (exhaust) agotar. **2** vi gastarse.
wea·ry adj (tired) cansado, -a.
wea·sel comadreja f.

weath·er tiempo m; **the w. is fine** hace buen tiempo; **to feel under the w.** no encontrarse bien.
weath·er fore·cast parte m meteorológico.
weave* vt tejer; (intertwine) entretejer.
web (of spider) telaraña f.
wed·ding boda f.
wed·ding ring alianza f.
wedge 1 n cuña f; (for table leg) calce m. **2** vt calzar.
Wednes·day miércoles m.
wee adj esp Scot pequeñito, -a.
weed mala hierba f.
week semana f; **a w. (ago) today/ yesterday** hoy hace/ayer hizo una semana; **a w. today** de aquí a ocho días.
week·day día m laborable.
week·end fin m de semana; **at or on the w.** el fin de semana.
week·ly 1 adj semanal. **2** adv semanalmente. **3** n (magazine) semanario m.
weep* vi llorar.
weigh vti pesar.
weight peso m; **to lose w.** adelgazar; **to put on w.** engordar.
weird adj raro, -a.
wel·come 1 adj (person) bienvenido, -a; (news) grato, -a; (change) oportuno, -a; **to make sb w.** acoger a algn calurosamente; **you're w.!** ¡no hay de qué! **2** n (greeting) bienvenida f. **3** vt acoger; (more formally) darle la bienvenida a; (news) acoger con agrado; (decision) aplaudir.
weld vt soldar.
wel·fare (social security) seguridad f social.
well¹ (for water) pozo m.
well² 1 adj (healthy) bien; **he's w. está bien** (de salud); **to get w.** reponerse; **all is w.** todo va bien. **2** adv (properly) bien; **w. done!** ¡muy bien!; **as w.** también; **as w. as** así como; **children as w. as adults** tanto niños como adultos. **3** interj

(surprise) ¡vaya!; **w., as I was saying** pues *(bien)*, como iba diciendo.
well·be·haved *adj (child)* formal; *(dog)* manso.
well·be·ing bienestar *m.*
well·in·formed *adj* bien informado, -a.
wel·ling·tons *npl* botas *fpl* de goma.
well-known *adj* (bien) conocido, -a.
well-man·nered *adj* educado, -a.
well-off *adj* acomodado, -a.
well-to-do *adj* acomodado, -a.
Welsh 1 *adj* galés, -esa. **2** *n (language)* galés *m;* **the W.** *pl* los galeses.
Welsh·man galés *m.*
Welsh·wom·an galesa *f.*
went *pt of* **go.**
were *pt of* **be.**
west 1 *n* oeste *m;* **in** *or* **to the w.** al oeste. **2** *adj* occidental. **3** *adv* al oeste.
west·bound *adj* (con) dirección oeste.
west·ern 1 *adj* del oeste, occidental. **2** *n (film)* western *m.*
west·ward *adj* hacia el oeste.
west·wards *adv* hacia el oeste.
wet 1 *adj* mojado, -a; *(slightly)* húmedo, -a; *(rainy)* lluvioso, -a; **'w. paint'** 'recién pintado'. **2** *vt** mojar.
whale ballena *f.*
wharf *(pl* wharves) muelle *m.*
what 1 *adj (in questions)* qué; **ask her w. color she likes** pregúntale qué color le gusta. **2** *pron (in questions)* qué; **w. are you talking about?** ¿de qué estás hablando?; **he asked me w. I thought** me preguntó lo que pensaba; **I didn't know w. to say** no sabía qué decir; **w. about your father?** ¿y tu padre (qué)?; **w. about going tomorrow?** ¿qué te parece si vamos mañana?; **w. did you do that for?** ¿por qué hiciste eso?; **w. (did you say)?** ¿cómo?; **w. is it?** *(definition)* ¿qué es?; **what's the matter?** ¿qué pasa?; **w.'s it called?** ¿cómo se llama?; **w.'s this

for?** ¿para qué sirve esto? **3** *interj* **w. a goal!** ¡qué golazo!
what·ev·er 1 *adj* **w. day you want** cualquier día que quieras; **of w. color** no importa de qué color; **nothing w.** nada en absoluto; **with no interest w.** sin interés alguno. **2** *pron (anything, all that)* (todo) lo que; **do w. you like** haz lo que quieras; **don't tell him w. you do** no se te ocurra decírselo; **w. (else) you find** cualquier (otra) cosa que encuentres.
wheat trigo *m.*
wheel 1 *n* rueda *f.* **2** *vt (bicycle)* empujar.
wheel·bar·row carretilla *f.*
wheel·chair silla *f* de ruedas.
when 1 *adv* cuando; *(in questions)* cuándo; **w. did he arrive?** ¿cuándo llegó?; **tell me w. to go** dime cuándo he de irme; **the days w. I work** los días en que trabajo. **2** *conj* cuando; **I'll tell you w. she comes** te lo diré cuando llegue.
when·ev·er *conj (when)* cuando; *(every time)* siempre que.
where *adv (in questions)* dónde; *(direction)* adónde; *(at, in which)* donde; *(direction)* adonde; **w. are you going?** ¿adónde vas?; **w. do you come from?** ¿de dónde es usted?; **tell me w. you went** dime adónde fuiste.
where·a·bouts 1 *adv* **w. do you live?** ¿por dónde vives? **2** *n* paradero *m.*
where·as *conj (but, while)* mientras que.
where·by *adv* por el *or* la *or* lo cual.
wher·ev·er *conj* dondequiera que; **I'll find him w. he is** le encontraré dondequiera que esté; **sit w. you like** siéntate donde quieras.
wheth·er *conj (if)* si; **I don't know w. it is true** no sé si es verdad; **I doubt w. he'll win** dudo que gane.
which 1 *adj* qué; **w. color do you prefer?** ¿qué color prefieres?; **w. one?** ¿cuál?; **w. way?** ¿por dónde?; **tell me w. dress you like** dime qué

vestido te gusta. **2** *pron (in questions)* cuál, cuáles; **w. of you did it?** ¿quién de vosotros lo hizo? ▪ *(relative)* que; *(after preposition)* que, el/la que, los/las que; **here are the books (w.) I have read** aquí están los libros que he leído; **the accident (w.) I told you about** el accidente de que te hablé; **the car in w. he was traveling** el coche en (el) que viajaba; **this is the one (w.) I like** éste es el que me gusta; **I played three sets, all of w. I lost** jugué tres sets, todos los cuales perdí. ▪ *(referring to a clause)* lo cual; **he won, w. made me very happy** ganó, lo cual me alegró mucho.

which·ev·er 1 *adj* el/la que, cualquiera que; **I'll take w. books you don't want** tomaré los libros que no quieras; **w. system you choose** cualquiera que sea el sistema que elijas. **2** *pron* el que, la que.

while 1 *conj (time)* mientras; *(although)* aunque; *(whereas)* mientras que; **he fell asleep w. driving** se durmió mientras conducía. **2** *n (length of time)* rato *m*; **in a little w.** dentro de poco.

whim capricho *m*.

whine *vi (child)* lloriquear; *(complain)* quejarse.

whip 1 *n (for punishment)* látigo *m*. **2** *vt (as punishment)* azotar; *(cream etc)* batir.

▶**whip out** *vt* sacar rápidamente.

whirl *vi* to **w. (round)** girar con rapidez; *(leaves etc)* arremolinarse.

whisk 1 *n (for cream)* batidor *m*; *(electric)* batidora *f*. **2** *vt (cream etc)* batir.

whisk·ers *(of cat)* bigotes *mpl*.

whis·key whisky *m*.

whis·per 1 *n* susurro *m*. **2** *vt* decir en voz baja. **3** *vi* susurrar.

whis·tle 1 *n (instrument)* pito *m*; *(sound)* silbido *m*. **2** *vt (tune)* silbar. **3** *vi (person, kettle, wind)* silbar; *(train)* pitar.

white 1 *adj* blanco, -a; **to go w.** *(face)* palidecer; *(hair)* encanecer; **w. coffee** café *m* con leche. **2** *n (color, of eye)* blanco *m*; *(of egg)* clara *f*.

white-wash *vt (wall)* blanquear.

whiz(z) *vi (sound)* silbar; **to w. past** pasar volando.

who *pron (in questions) sing* quién; *pl* quiénes; **w. are they?** ¿quiénes son?; **w. is it?** ¿quién es?; **I don't know w. did it** no sé quién lo hizo. ▪ *rel (defining)* que; *(nondefining)* quien, quienes, el/la cual, los/las cuales; **those w. don't know** los que no saben; **Elena's mother, w. is very rich ...** la madre de Elena, la cual es muy rica ...

who·ev·er *pron* quienquiera que; **give it to w. you like** dáselo a quien quieras; **w. you are** quienquiera que seas.

whole 1 *adj (entire)* entero, -a; *(in one piece)* intacto, -a; **a w. week** una semana entera; **he took the w. lot** se los llevó todos. **2** *n* **the w. of New York** todo Nueva York; **on the w.** en general.

whole·meal *adj* integral.

whole·sale *adv* al por mayor.

whole·sal·er mayorista *mf*.

whol·ly *adv* enteramente, completamente.

whom *pron (question)* a quién. ▪ *(after preposition)* **of** or **from w.?** ¿de quién? ▪ *rel* a quien, a quienes; **those w. I have seen** aquéllos a quienes he visto. ▪ *rel (after preposition)* quien, quienes, el/la cual, los/las cuales; **my brothers, both of w. are miners** mis hermanos, que son mineros los dos.

whoop·ing cough tos *f* ferina.

whose 1 *pron* de quién, de quiénes; **w. are these gloves?** ¿de quién son estos guantes? ▪ *rel* cuyo(s)/cuya(s); **the man w. children we saw** el hombre a cuyos hijos vimos. **2** *pron* **w. car/house is this?** ¿de quién es este coche/esta casa?

why adv por qué; (for what purpose) para qué; **w. did you do that?** ¿por qué hiciste eso?; **w. not go to bed?** ¿por qué no te acuestas?; **I don't know w. he did it** no sé por qué lo hizo; **there's no reason w. you shouldn't go** no hay motivo para que no vayas.

wick mecha f.

wick·ed adj malvado, -a; (awful) malísimo, -a.

wick·er 1 n mimbre f. **2** adj de mimbre.

wide 1 adj (road, trousers) ancho, -a; (area, knowledge, support, range) amplio, -a; **it is ten meters w.** tiene diez metros de ancho. **2** adv **w. awake** totalmente despierto, -a; **w. open** abierto, -a de par en par.

wide·ly adv (to travel etc) extensamente.

wid·en 1 vt. ensanchar; (interests) ampliar. **2** vi ensancharse.

wide·spread adj (unrest, belief) general; (damage) extenso, -a.

wid·ow viuda f.

wid·ow·er viudo m.

width anchura f.

wife (pl wives) esposa f.

wig peluca f.

wild adj (animal, tribe) salvaje; (plant) silvestre; (temperament, behavior) alocado, -a; (appearance) desordenado, -a; (passions etc) desenfrenado, -a.

wil·der·ness desierto m.

wild·life fauna f.

wild·ly adv (rush round etc) como un, -a loco, -a; (hit out) a tontas y a locas.

will¹ 1 n voluntad f; (testament) testamento m; **good/ill w.** buena/mala voluntad; **of my own free w.** por mi propia voluntad; **to make one's w.** hacer testamento. **2** vt fate willed that … el destino quiso que …

will² v aux they **w. come** vendrán; **w. he be there? — yes, he w.** ¿estará allí? — sí (, estará); **you w. or**

you'll tell him, won't you? se lo dirás, ¿verdad?; **you w. be here at eleven!** ¡debes estar aquí a las once!; **be quiet, w. you! — no, I won't!** ¿quiere callarse? — no quiero; **will you have a drink? — yes, I w.** ¿quiere tomar algo? — sí, por favor.

will·ing adj (obliging) complaciente; **to be w. to do sth** estar dispuesto, -a a hacer algo.

will·ing·ly adv de buena gana.

will·ing·ness buena voluntad f.

wil·low **w. (tree)** sauce m.

win 1 n victoria f. **2** vt* ganar; (prize) llevarse; (victory) conseguir. **3** vi* ganar.

wind¹ viento m; (in stomach) gases mpl.

wind²·* 1 vt (onto a reel) enrollar; (clock) dar cuerda a. **2** vi (road, river) serpentear.

▸**wind back** vt (film, tape) rebobinar.

▸**wind on** vt (film, tape) avanzar.

wind·mill molino m (de viento).

win·dow ventana f; (of vehicle, of ticket office etc) ventanilla f; **(shop)** **w.** escaparate m.

win·dow box jardinera f.

win·dow clean·er limpiacristales mf inv.

win·dow·pane cristal m.

win·dow·sill alféizar m.

wind·shield parabrisas m inv; **w. wiper** limpiaparabrisas m inv.

wind·surf·ing windsurfing m.

wind·y adj **it is very w. today** hoy hace mucho viento.

wine vino m; **w. list** lista f de vinos.

wine·glass copa f (para vino).

wing ala f.

wink 1 n guiño m. **2** vi (person) guiñar el ojo.

win·ner ganador, -a mf.

win·ning adj (person, team) ganador, -a; (number) premiado, -a.

win·nings npl ganancias fpl.

win·ter 1 n invierno m. **2** adj de invierno.

wipe vt limpiar; **to w. one's feet /**

nose limpiarse los pies/la nariz.

▶ **wipe away** vt (tear) enjugar.

▶ **wipe off** vt quitar frotando.

▶ **wipe out** vt (erase) borrar.

▶ **wipe up** vi secar los platos.

wip·er (in vehicle) limpiaparabrisas m.

wire alambre m; (electric) cable m.

wire mesh/net·ting tela f metálica.

wir·ing (of house) instalación f eléctrica.

wis·dom (good sense) (of person) cordura f; (of action) sensatez f; (learning) sabiduría f.

wise adj sabio, -a; a w. man un sabio; **it would be w. to keep quiet** sería prudente callarse.

wish 1 n (desire) deseo m (for de); **give your mother my best wishes** salude a su madre de mi parte; **with best wishes, Peter** (at end of letter) saludos de Peter. **2** vt (want) desear; **I w. I could stay longer** me gustaría poder quedarme más tiempo; **I w. you had told me!** ¡ojalá me lo hubieras dicho!; **to w. for sth** desear algo.

wit (humour) ingenio m; (person) ingenioso, -a mf; **wits** (intelligence) inteligencia f; fig **to be at one's wits' end** estar para volverse loco, -a.

witch bruja f.

with prep con; **the man w. the glasses** el hombre de las gafas; **w. no hat** sin sombrero; **he went w. me/you** fue conmigo/contigo; **he's w. Ford** trabaja para Ford; **to fill a vase w. water** llenar un jarrón de agua; **it is made w. butter** está hecho con mantequilla.

with·draw* 1 vt retirar; (statement) retractarse de; **to w. money from the bank** sacar dinero del banco. **2** vi retirarse; (drop out) renunciar.

with·draw·al retirada f.

with·er vi marchitarse.

with·hold* vt (money) retener; (decision) aplazar; (consent) negar;

(information) ocultar.

with·in prep (inside) dentro de; **w. five kilometers of the town** a menos de cinco kilómetros de la ciudad; **w. the hour** dentro de una hora; **w. the next five years** durante los cinco próximos años.

with·out prep sin; **w. a coat** sin abrigo; **he did it w. my knowing** lo hizo sin que lo supiera yo.

wit·ness 1 n (person) testigo mf. **2** vt (see) presenciar.

wob·bly adj poco firme; (table, chair) cojo, -a.

wolf (pl wolves) lobo m.

wom·an (pl women) mujer f; **old w.** vieja f.

won·der 1 n no **w. he hasn't come** con razón no ha venido. **2** vt (ask oneself) preguntarse; **I w. why** ¿por qué será? **3** vi **it makes you w.** te da qué pensar.

won·der·ful adj maravilloso, -a.

won't = will not.

wood (forest) bosque m; (material) madera f; (for fire) leña f.

wood·en adj de madera.

wood·work (craft) carpintería f.

wool lana f.

wool·en 1 adj de lana. **2** npl woolens géneros mpl de lana.

word palabra f; **in other words ...** es decir ...; **I'd like a w. with you** quiero hablar contigo un momento; **words** (of song) letra f.

word·ing expresión f; **I changed the w. slightly** cambié algunas palabras.

word proc·ess·ing procesamiento m de textos.

word proc·es·sor procesador m de textos.

wore pt of **wear**.

work 1 n trabajo m; **his w. in the field of physics** su labor en el campo de la física; **out of w.** parado, -a; **a piece of w.** un trabajo; **a w. of art** una obra de arte; **works** (factory) fábrica f. **2** vt (drive) hacer trabajar;

(machine) manejar; *(mechanism)* accionar. **3** *vi* trabajar (**on, at** en); *(machine)* funcionar; *(drug)* surtir efecto; *(system)* funcionar.

▶**work out 1** *vt (plan)* idear; *(problem)* solucionar; *(solution)* encontrar; *(amount)* calcular. **2** *vi (train)* hacer ejercicio; **it works out to 5 each** sale a 5 cada uno.

worked up *adj* **to get worked up** excitarse.

work·er trabajador, -a *mf*; *(manual)* obrero, -a *mf*.

work·force mano *f* de obra.

work·ing *adj (population, capital)* activo, -a; **w. class** clase *f* obrera; **it is in w. order** funciona.

work·man *(manual)* obrero *m*.

work·out entrenamiento *m*.

work·shop taller *m*.

work·sta·tion estación *f* de trabajo.

world 1 *n* mundo *m*; **all over the w.** en todo el mundo. **2** *adj (record, war)* mundial; **w. champion** campeón, -ona *mf* mundial; **The W. Cup** el Mundial *m*.

world·wide *adj* mundial.

worm lombriz *f*.

worn *adj* gastado, -a.

worn-out *adj (thing)* gastado, -a; *(person)* agotado, -a.

wor·ry 1 *vt* preocupar. **2** *vi* preocuparse (**about** por); **don't w.** no te preocupes. **3** *n* inquietud *f*; **my main w.** mi principal preocupación.

wor·ry·ing *adj* preocupante.

worse *adj & adv* peor; **to get w.** empeorar; **w. than ever** peor que nunca.

wors·en *vti* empeorar.

wor·ship *vt* adorar.

worst 1 *adj & adv* peor; **the w. part about it is that …** lo peor es que … **2** *n (person)* el/la peor, los/las peores.

worth 1 *adj* a house w. **$50,000** una casa que vale 50,000 dólares; **a book w. reading** un libro que merece la

pena leer; **how much is it w.?** ¿cuánto vale?; **it's w. your while, it's w. it** vale la pena. **2** *n* valor *m*; **five dollars' w. of gas** gasolina por valor de 5 dólares.

worth·while *adj* valioso, -a, que vale la pena.

wor·thy *adj (deserving)* digno, -a *(of* de).

would *v aux (conditional)* **I w. go if I had time** iría si tuviera tiempo; **he w. have won but for that** habría ganado si no hubiera sido por eso. ■ *(willingness)* **w. you do me a favor?** ¿quiere hacerme un favor?; **w. you like a cigarette?** ¿quiere un cigarrillo?; **the car wouldn't start** el coche no arrancaba. ■ *(custom)* **we w. go for walks** solíamos dar paseos.

wound 1 *n* herida *f*. **2** *vt* herir.

wrap *vt* envolver.

▶**wrap up 1** *vt* envolver. **2** *vi* **w. up well!** ¡abrígate!

wrap·per *(of sweet)* envoltorio *m*.

wrap·ping pa·per papel *m* de envolver.

wreath *(pl* **wreaths)** *(of flowers)* corona *f*.

wreck 1 *n (sinking)* naufragio *m*; *(ship)* barco *m* naufragado; *(of car, plane)* restos *mpl*. **2** *vt (car, machine)* destrozar; *(holiday)* estropear.

wrench *(tool)* llave *f*.

wres·tle *vi* luchar.

wres·tler luchador, -a *mf*.

wres·tling lucha *f*.

wring* *vt (clothes)* escurrir.

wrin·kle arruga *f*.

wrist muñeca *f*.

wrist·watch reloj *m* de pulsera.

write* *vti* escribir (**about** sobre); **to w. sb** escribir a.

▶**write back** *vi* contestar.

▶**write down** *vt* poner por escrito; *(note)* apuntar.

▶**write off** *vt sep (debt)* condonar.

▶**write off for** *vt* pedir por escrito.

▶**write out** *vt (check)* extender; *(recipe)* escribir.

write·pro·tect·ed *adj* protegido, -a contra escritura.

writ·er *(by profession)* escritor, -a *mf; (of book, letter)* autor, -a *mf.*

writ·ing *(script)* escritura *f; (handwriting)* letra *f;* **in w.** por escrito.

writ·ing pa·per papel *m* de escribir.

wrong 1 *adj (erroneous)* incorrecto, -a; *(unsuitable)* inadecuado, -a; *(time)* inoportuno, -a; *(not right) (person)* equivocado, -a; *(immoral etc)* malo, -a; **my watch is w.** mi reloj anda mal; **to go the w. way** equivocarse de camino; **I was w. about that boy** me equivoqué con ese chico; **to be w.** no tener razón; **what's w. with smoking?** ¿qué tiene de malo fumar?; **what's w. with you?** ¿qué te pasa? **2** *adv* mal; **to get it w.** equivocarse; **to go w.** *(plan)* salir mal. **3** *n (evil, bad action)* mal *m;* **you were w. to hit him** hiciste mal en pegarle; **to be in the w.** tener la culpa.

wrong·ly *adv (incorrectly)* incorrectamente.

X

X·mas *abbr of* **Christmas** Navidad *f.*

X-ray 1 *n (picture)* radiografía *f;* **to have an X.** hacerse una radiografía. **2** *vt* radiografiar.

Y

yacht yate *m.*

yard[1] *(measure)* yarda *f (aprox 0,914 metros).*

yard[2] patio *m;* jardín *m; (of school)* patio *m* (de recreo).

yarn hilo *m.*

yawn 1 *vi* bostezar. **2** *n* bostezo *m.*

year año *m; (at school)* curso *m;* **I'm ten years old** tengo diez años.

year·ly *adj* anual.

yeast levadura *f.*

yell 1 *vi* gritar **(at** a). **2** *n* grito *m.*

yel·low *adj & n* amarillo, -a *(m).*

yes *adv* sí.

yes·ter·day *adv* ayer; **the day before y.** anteayer; **y. morning** ayer por la mañana.

yet 1 *adv* not y. todavía no; **as y.** hasta ahora; **I haven't eaten y.** no he comido todavía. ▪ *(in questions)* ya; **has he arrived y.?** ¿ha venido ya? **2** *conj (nevertheless)* sin embargo.

yo·gurt yogur *m.*

yolk yema *f.*

you *pers pron (subject) (familiar use) (sing)* tú; *(pl)* vosotros, -as; *(polite use) (sing)* usted; *(pl)* ustedes; **how are y.?** ¿cómo estás?, ¿cómo estáis? ▪ *(object) (familiar use) (sing) (before verb)* te; *(after preposition)* ti; *(pl) (before verb)* os; *(after preposition)* vosotros, -as; **I saw y.** te vi, os vi; **with y.** contigo, con vosotros, -as. ▪ *(object) (polite use) (sing) (before verb)* le; *(after preposition)* usted; *(pl) (before verb)* les; *(after preposition)* ustedes; **I saw y.** le vi, les vi; **with y.** con usted, con ustedes. ▪ *(subject) (impers use)* **y.** never know nunca se sabe.

young 1 *adj* joven; *(brother etc)* pequeño, -a. **2** *n* **the y.** los jóvenes *mpl; (animals)* las crías.

young·ster muchacho, -a *mf.*

your *poss adj (familiar use) (referring to one person)* tu, tus; *(referring to more than one person)* vuestro, -a, vuestros, -as. ▪ *(polite use)* su, sus. *(impers use)* **the house is on y.** right la casa queda a la derecha; **they clean y. shoes for you** te limpian los zapatos.

yours *poss pron (familiar use) (refer-ring to one person)* el tuyo, la tuya, los tuyos, las tuyas; *(referring to more than one person)* el vuestro, la vuestra, los vuestros, las vuestras; **the house is y.** la casa es tuya. ▪ *(polite use)* el suyo, la suya; *(pl)* los suyos, las suyas; **the house is y.** la casa es suya.

your·self *(pl* **yourselves)** **1** *pers pron (familiar use) sing* tú mismo, -a; *pl* vosotros, -as mismos, -as; **by y.** (tú) solo; **by yourselves** vosotros, -as so-los, -as. ▪ *(polite use) sing* usted mis-mo, -a; *pl* ustedes mismos, -as; **by y.** (usted) solo, -a; **by yourselves** (uste-des) solos, -as. **2** *reflexive pron* **did you wash y.?** *(familiar use) sing* ¿te lavaste?; *pl* ¿os lavasteis?; *(polite use) sing* ¿se lavó?, *pl* ¿se lavaron?

youth juventud *f*; *(young man)* joven *m*.

youth club club *m* juvenil.

Yu·go·slav *adj & n* yugoslavo, -a *(mf)*.

Z

ze·bra cebra *f*.

ze·ro cero *m*.

zig·zag **1** *n* zigzag *m*. **2** *vi* zigza-guear.

zip *n* **z. (fastener)** cremallera *f*.

▶**zip up** *vt* subir la cremallera de.

ZIP code código *m* postal.

Zip® drive unidad *f* Zip®.

zip·per cremallera *f*.

zit *fam (pimple)* espinilla *f*.

zone zona *f*.

zoo zoo *m*.

zuc·chi·ni calabacín *m* .